Simulation, Optimization, and Machine Learning for Finance

Simulation, Optimization, and Machine Learning for Finance

second edition

Dessislava A. Pachamanova, Frank J. Fabozzi, and Francesco A. Fabozzi

The MIT Press
Cambridge, Massachusetts
London, England

The MIT Press
Massachusetts Institute of Technology
77 Massachusetts Avenue, Cambridge, MA 02139
mitpress.mit.edu

The MIT Press would like to thank the anonymous peer reviewers who provided comments on drafts of this book. The generous work of academic experts is essential for establishing the authority and quality of our publications. We acknowledge with gratitude the contributions of these otherwise uncredited readers.

This book was set in Times New Roman by Westchester Publishing Services. Printed and bound in the United States of America.

Library of Congress Cataloging-in-Publication Data

Names: Pachamanova, Dessislava A., author.
Title: Simulation, optimization, and machine learning for finance / Dessislava A. Pachamanova, Frank J. Fabozzi, Francesco A. Fabozzi.
Description: Second edition. | Cambridge, Massachusetts : The MIT Press, [2025] | Includes bibliographical references and index.
Identifiers: LCCN 2024042690 (print) | LCCN 2024042691 (ebook) | ISBN 9780262049801 (hardcover) | ISBN 9780262383769 (pdf) | ISBN 9780262383776 (epub)
Subjects: LCSH: Finance—Mathematical models—Computer programs.
Classification: LCC HG106 .P33 2025 (print) | LCC HG106 (ebook) | DDC 332.0285/53—dc23/eng/20250218
LC record available at https://lccn.loc.gov/2024042690
LC ebook record available at https://lccn.loc.gov/2024042691

10 9 8 7 6 5 4 3 2 1

EU Authorised Representative: Easy Access System Europe, Mustamäe tee 50, 10621 Tallinn, Estonia | Email: gpsr.requests@easproject.com

Dessislava A. Pachamanova
To my children, Anna and Coleman, my husband, Christian, my father, Angel, and in memory of my mother, Rossitsa

Frank J. Fabozzi
To the memory of my sister, Lucy Fabozzi

Francesco A. Fabozzi
To my mother, Donna

Contents

Preface

Simulation, Optimization, and Machine Learning for Finance, second edition, is a comprehensive guide to three essential quantitative tools used in asset management and corporate finance. The book begins with a solid theoretical foundation and complements it with practical implications and relevant financial background needed to appreciate the applications of these tools. This approach ensures a thorough understanding of simulation, optimization, and machine learning (ML), making the content valuable to both industry practitioners and academic audiences. This book is an extensively updated edition of *Simulation and Optimization in Finance*, which was originally published in 2010.

Appendices and additional instructor materials for this book can be found on MIT Press's website. They are stored under the Resources tab on the book's landing page.

Book Structure and Content Overview

The book is organized into the following six parts, spanning 23 chapters:

- Part I, "Background Topics," covers important finance concepts (chapter 2), and reviews probability distributions (chapter 3) and inferential statistics (chapter 4), laying the groundwork for the subsequent topics in the book. The important finance concepts covered are the time value of money, the various asset classes, basic trading terminology, calculation of rate of return, valuation, and advanced concepts in fixed income. Probability distributions are essential in finance for modeling and describing the behavior of random variables, which represent a wide range of uncertainties, such as asset returns, interest rates, asset cash flow, and market movements. By understanding different types of distributions, decision makers can better predict and model the behavior of financial markets. This knowledge helps in assessing risk, pricing assets, managing portfolios effectively, and selecting capital projects. Inferential statistics, another cornerstone of financial analysis, provides decision makers with the tools to make predictions and draw meaningful conclusions based on data samples.
- Part II, "Fundamentals of Simulation, Optimization, and Machine Learning," provides the fundamentals of the three quantitative tools that are the focus of the book. Because of the inherent complexity and uncertainty associated with outcomes in financial

markets, *simulation* (chapter 5) offers a powerful tool for modeling financial markets, evaluating investment strategies, and managing risk. *Optimization*, which uses mathematical models that select the most favorable alternative that either maximizes or minimizes a particular objective from a set of available alternatives under a given set of constraints (depending on what is wanted), is covered in chapters 6 and 7. Optimization under uncertainty techniques (chapter 7) is particularly important in finance because it allows the decision maker to incorporate randomness. Decision making in finance relies heavily on the insights from data and their analysis, so the remaining chapters in part III cover data types and measurements (chapter 8), regression (chapter 9), ML (chapter 10), and natural language processing (NLP; chapter 11).

- Part III, "Applications to Asset Management," begins with foundational asset allocation models like mean-variance analysis (chapter 12) and progresses through advanced risk measurement concepts (chapter 13) and practical portfolio management for both equity (chapter 14) and fixed income (chapter 15), which use the quantitative tools described in the earlier parts of the book.
- Part IV, "Asset Pricing Models," explains the intricacies of asset pricing models, incorporating both classical and dynamic frameworks. Factor models (chapter 16) are essential for understanding how different risks are priced in financial markets and are pivotal in the construction of portfolios and in strategic investment decisions. Stochastic processes (chapter 17) are crucial for modeling the randomness inherent in financial markets and provide the framework necessary to describe the evolution of asset prices over time under uncertainty. Together, the two chapters in this part offer a comprehensive view of how assets are valued in the context of both theoretical and practical market scenarios, emphasizing the role of stochastic processes in dynamic asset pricing. This blend of factor models and stochastic methods provides a robust tool kit for predicting asset prices and making informed investment decisions in uncertain conditions.
- Part V, "Financial Derivatives and Mortgage-Backed Securities," explains the fundamentals of derivatives (chapter 18), their valuation through simulation (chapter 19), and their role in risk management and return enhancement (chapter 20). It also covers mortgage-backed securities (MBSs), the second-largest sector of the bond market (chapter 21). Financial derivatives and residential mortgage-backed securities (RMBSs) are covered together in this part due to their shared characteristics and underlying financial principles. Both financial instruments derive their value from underlying assets. In the case of derivatives, the value might be linked to a stock or stock index, an interest rate, or a foreign-exchange rate. MBS are valued based on the performance of a pool of residential mortgage loans that are the collateral for the security. Understanding the valuation process for these instruments is challenging for valuation and assessing risks. Moreover, financial engineers use derivatives to create synthetic financial instruments and to tailor specific risk-return profiles for clients. Similarly, MBSs are structured by pooling residential mortgage loans and tranching the cash flows to cater to different investor preferences regarding interest-rate risk and yield. Covering both financial derivatives and MBSs in the same part provides a holistic understanding of complex financial instruments, shows the interconnectedness of different financial products, and offers an appreciation of the sophisticated techniques used for managing risk.

- Part VI, "Capital Budgeting and Real Options," focuses on capital budgeting, a critical process through which company management evaluates and makes decisions about potential significant investments or expenditures. This process, which typically involves a substantial sum of money, is integral to strategic financial management. Within this context, decision making often occurs under conditions of uncertainty, requiring the application of sophisticated financial models and methodologies, including simulation, optimization, and statistical modeling (chapter 22). Applying real options in capital budgeting (chapter 23) further enhances these decision-making frameworks. A real option provides the right, but not the obligation, to undertake certain business initiatives, such as deferring, abandoning, expanding, or contracting a project based on future market conditions or project performance. This approach borrows from financial options theory, which is used to price options in the financial markets. Real options theory is particularly valuable in capital budgeting since it promotes managerial flexibility to adapt and revise decisions in response to unexpected market developments, allows management to delay a decision until more information is available, and provides a systematic way to quantify risk and incorporate it into capital budgeting.

Target Audience and Educational Use

This book is designed for practitioners and students with a basic understanding of calculus and statistics. It is ideal for self-study or as a textbook in finance and quantitative methods courses. The theoretical rigor combined with practical examples makes it accessible to a broad audience, bridging the gap typically present for those without advanced mathematical training. The accompanying website offers additional resources, including downloadable materials for several chapters and software guidelines, enhancing the learning experience, and providing practical insights into complex topics.

The book can be used as a textbook for upper-level undergraduate or graduate (such as master's of business administration or master's) courses in applied quantitative methods, operations research, decision sciences, or financial engineering; finance courses in derivatives, investments, or corporate finance with an emphasis on modeling; or as a supplement in a special topics course in quantitative methods or finance. In addition, the book can be used as a student self-study aid or as a reference for student projects.

The book assumes that the reader has no background in finance or advanced quantitative methods except for basic calculus and statistics. Most quantitative concepts necessary for understanding the notation or applications are introduced and explained in end notes, online chapter appendices, and online software appendices. This makes the book suitable for readers with a wide range of backgrounds, and particularly as a textbook for classes with mixed audiences (such as engineering and business students). In fact, the idea for this book project matured after years of searching by two of the authors for an appropriate textbook for a course with a mixed audience that needed a good reference for both finance and quantitative methods topics.

Every chapter follows the same basic outline. The concepts are introduced in the main body of the chapter, and illustrations are provided as exhibits. At the end of each chapter, there is a summary that contains the most important discussion points. A "Software Hints" section (in the online appendices; see the next section of this preface) provides instructions and code for implementing the examples in each chapter.

Before proceeding with the main body of this book, we recommend browsing through the five online appendices with tutorials—namely, appendix A, "Basic Linear Algebra Concepts"; appendix B, "Introduction to @RISK"; appendix C, "Introduction to MATLAB"; appendix D, "Introduction to Visual Basic for Applications"; and appendix E, "Introduction to Python." They provide background on basic mathematical and programming concepts that enable readers to understand the implementation and the code provided in the "Software Hints" sections.

The chapters that introduce fundamental concepts all reference code that can be found on the companion website. Some more advanced chapters do not; the idea is that at that point, students are sufficiently familiar with the applications and models to put together examples on their own based on the code provided in previous chapters. The material in the advanced chapters can also be used as templates for student course projects.

We recognize that this book is extensive and covers a broad range of topics, which may not all be suited for a single semester's syllabus. Instructors are encouraged to customize the content to meet the specific needs and interests of their courses. Depending on the focus of your curriculum, you may choose to concentrate on chapters that align closely with your teaching objectives and the learning outcomes desired for your students. This approach allows for flexibility and ensures that the material remains manageable and relevant. Detailed chapter summaries and key concepts can help in deciding which sections might best serve your course's structure and pacing.

A typical course may start with the material in chapters 2 through 11. It can then cover the material in chapters 12 through 14, which focus on applications of optimization for single-period optimal portfolio allocation and risk management. The course then proceeds with chapters 16 through 19, which introduce static and dynamic asset pricing models through simulation, as well as derivative pricing by simulation, and ends with chapters 22 and 23, which discuss applications of simulation and optimization in capital budgeting. The remaining chapters represent good assignments for final projects because they use concepts similar to other chapters, but in a different context and without as much implementation detail. Depending on the nature of the course, only some of chapters 2 through 11 will need to be covered explicitly; but the information in these chapters is useful in case the instructor would like to assign the chapters as reading for students who lack some of the necessary background for the course.

Online Appendices

In the first edition of this book, most of the chapters had a "Software Hints" section at the end that explained how to use the applications discussed in the chapter with Microsoft Excel, Palisades Decision Tools, Microsoft Visual Basic for Applications (VBA), and MATLAB. We elected not to include "Software Hints" at the end of the chapters in this edition; instead, we include them online and have provided updated tutorials in an additional, open-source language: Python. As in the first edition, we assume basic familiarity with spreadsheets and Excel. Readers do not need to learn all these software tools to use the book; they can choose a particular tool depending on their level of familiarity and comfort with spreadsheet programs (Excel) and their add-ins (Palisades Decision Tools, Excel Solver) versus programming environments such as MATLAB and Python. Specifically, users with finance and social science backgrounds typically prefer an Excel-based implementation, whereas users with engineering and quantitative backgrounds prefer MATLAB and Python. Some tasks and implementations are easier in one environment than in the other, and students who have used this book in the form of lecture notes in the past have felt they benefited from learning about multiple platforms.

Although Excel and other programs are used extensively in this book, we were wary of turning it into a software tutorial. Our goal was to combine concepts and tools for implementing them in an effective manner without necessarily covering every aspect of working in a specific software environment.

We have attempted to implement all examples correctly, of course. That said, the code and models are provided "as is" and are intended only to illustrate the concepts in this book. Readers who use the code for financial decision making are doing so at their own risk. For full information on the terms of use of the code, please see the licensing information in each file on the companion website.

The following websites provide useful information about Palisade Decision Tools Suite, MATLAB, and Python. Readers can download trial versions or purchase the software:

- Palisade Decision Tools Suite, https://palisade.lumivero.com/
- MATLAB, http://www.mathworks.com
- Python, https://www.python.org/

How Content of the Second Edition Compares to the First Edition

The following table summarizes the contents of the book and explains the relationship between the first and second editions:

Part No.	Chapter No.	Chapter Title	Comment
	1	Introduction	Modified from chapter 1 in first edition
I	2	Important Finance Concepts	Modified from chapter 2 in first edition
	3	Random Variables and Probability Distributions	New chapter based on chapter 3 in first edition
	4	Inferential Statistics	New chapter based on chapter 3 in first edition
II	5	Simulation Modeling	Updated version of chapter 4 in first edition
	6	Optimization Modeling	Updated version of chapter 5 in first edition
	7	Optimization under Uncertainty	Updated version of chapter 6 in first edition
	8	Data and Data Science	New chapter
	9	Regression Models	New chapter
	10	Machine Learning	New chapter
	11	Natural Language Processing	New chapter
III	12	Asset Allocation Models	Expanded version of chapter 7 in first edition
	13	Advanced Portfolio Risk Measures	Revised version of chapter 8 in first edition

(continued)

Part No.	Chapter No.	Chapter Title	Comment
	14	Equity Portfolio Selection in Practice	Expanded version of chapter 9 in first edition
	15	Fixed-Income Portfolio Management in Practice	Expanded version of chapter 10 in first edition
IV	16	Factor Models	Expanded version of chapter 11 in first edition
	17	Modeling Asset Price Dynamics	Revised version of chapter 12 in first edition
V	18	Introduction to Derivatives	Revised version of chapter 13 in first edition
	19	Pricing Derivatives with Simulation	Revised version of chapter 14 in first edition
	20	Using Derivatives in Portfolio Management	Revised version of chapter 16 in first edition
	21	Structuring and Pricing Residential Mortgage-Backed Securities	Chapter 15 in first edition
VI	22	Capital Budgeting under Uncertainty	Chapter 17 in first edition
	23	Applications of Real Options to Capital Budgeting	Chapter 18 in first edition
Appendices		Appendix A: Basic Linear Algebra Concepts	Appendix A in first edition
		Online Appendix B: Introduction to @RISK	Updated appendix B in first edition
		Online Appendix C: Introduction to MATLAB	Updated appendix C in first edition
		Online Appendix D: Introduction to Visual Basic for Applications	Updated appendix D in first edition
		Online Appendix E: Introduction to Python	New appendix
		Online Appendices: Software Hints	Updated and extended software hints from the end of various chapters in first edition

Acknowledgments

In writing a book that covers such a wide range of topics in simulation, optimization, machine learning (ML), and finance, we were fortunate to have received valuable help from a number of individuals. In first edition of the book, the following people commented on chapters or sections of chapters or provided helpful references and introductions:

- Anthony Corr, BrettMcElwee, and Max Capetta of Continuum Capital Management
- Nalan Gulpinar of the University of Warwick Business School
- Craig Stephenson of Babson College
- Hugh Crowther of Crowther Investment, LLC
- Pamela Drake of James Madison University

Zack Coburn implemented most of the Microsoft Visual Basic for Applications (VBA) code for the online appendices in chapters 12 and 19. Christian Hicks helped with writing and testing some of the VBA code in the book, such as the VBA implementation of the American option pricing model with least squares in chapter 19. Professor Mark Potter of Babson College allowed us to modify his case, "Reebok International: Strategic Asset Allocation," for use as an example in chapter 23, and some of the ideas are based on case spreadsheet models further developed by Professors Kathy Hevert and Richard Bliss of Babson College. The real estate valuation project example in section 22.6.3 is based on ideas by Matt Bujnicki, Matt Enright, and Alec Kyprianou.

We would also like to thank Wendy Gudgeon and Stan Brown from Palisade Software, and Steve Wilcockson, Naomi Fernandes, Meg Vulliez, Chris Watson, and Srikanth Krishnamurthy of Mathworks for their help with obtaining most recent versions of the software used in the book and for additional materials useful for implementing some of the examples.

In the current edition, we received feedback, particularly for the chapters on ML, from the following individuals:

- Nolan Alexander of Haidar Capital
- Marcos López de Prado of Cornell University and Abu Dhabi Investment Authority
- Sergio M. Focardi of the University of Genoa's Department of Engineering (DIME)
- Michael Imerman of the University of California, Irvine

- Linus Kaiser
- Ahmet Karagozoglu of Hofstra University and New York University
- Jang Ho Kim of Graduate School of Management of Technology, Korea University
- Woo Chang Kim of Korea Advanced Institute of Science and Technology (KAIST)
- Petter N. Kolm of New York University's Courant Institute of Mathematical Sciences
- Yongjae Lee of Ulsan National Institute of Science and Technology (UNIST)
- Mengxin Li, Teaching & Research Assistant for the Master of Finance program at Johns Hopkins University
- Jim Kyung-Soo Liew of Johns Hopkins Carey Business School
- Slavi Marinov of Man AHL
- Abdolreza Nazemi of Karlsruhe Institute of Technology (KIT)
- Joseph Simonian of Autonomous Investment Technologies LLC and Scientific Beta
- Radu S. Tunaru of University of Sussex
- Justin Wang, graduate student at Johns Hopkins University

About the Authors

DESSISLAVA A. PACHAMANOVA is Professor and Zwerling Family Endowed Term Chair at Babson College and Research Affiliate at the Massachusetts Institute of Technology. Her research and consulting span multiple fields, including robust optimization, risk management, simulation, predictive analytics and machine learning, natural language processing, and operations. She has authored and coauthored dozens of articles in operations research, finance, accounting, engineering, marketing and management journals. She also has coauthored numerous book chapters, as well as two other books in computational finance and risk management: *Robust Portfolio Optimization and Management* and *Portfolio Construction and Analytics*. Professor Pachamanova serves on several journal editorial boards, has held leadership positions in finance and operations research interest groups in professional societies, and is the recipient of numerous research, teaching, and case writing awards. She holds an AB from Princeton University and a PhD from the Sloan School of Management at the Massachusetts Institute of Technology.

FRANK J. FABOZZI is a professor of practice at Carey Business School at Johns Hopkins University. He serves as the editor of the *Journal of Portfolio Management*, the *Journal of Financial Data Science*, and an editor of *Annals of Operations Research*. The author of many finance and applied mathematics books, he received the CFA Institute Research Foundation's James R. Vertin Award and the C. Stewart Sheppard Award and was inducted into the Fixed Income Society's Hall of Fame. From 1988–2023, he served on the board of directors of the BlackRock fixed-income complex. He earned an MA and a BA in economics from the City College of New York where he was elected to Phi Beta Kappa. Professor Fabozzi earned a PhD in economics from the Graduate Center of the City University of New York and was awarded an honorary doctorate of humane letters from Nova Southeastern University. He holds the professional designations of Chartered Financial Analyst and Certified Public Accountant.

FRANCESCO A. FABOZZI is the research director at the Yale School of Management International Center for Finance. He serves as the managing editor of the *Journal of Financial Data Science* and the director of data science at the CFA Institute Research Foundation. He is a Curriculum Committee Member of the Financial Data Professional (FDP) Institute.

He has coauthored several books in investment management and quantitative methods, as well as several articles in peer-review journals including the *Journal of Financial Econometrics, Annals of Operations Research, Journal of International Money and Finance. The Journal of Derivatives, and The Journal of Fixed Income*. His primary research interests include machine learning, natural language processing, and factor investing. He holds a BA in economics from Princeton University, an MS in financial analytics, and a PhD in data science from the Stevens Institute of Technology.

1

Introduction

"Finance" is a broad term that is used to describe activities associated with making financial decisions that investors and businesses face under conditions of uncertainty. Investors allocate their funds among financial assets to accomplish their investment objectives. Business entities raise funds by issuing claims in the form of debt (e.g., loans and bonds) or equity (e.g., common stock) and, in turn, invest those funds in capital projects with various degrees of risk as to a project's potential outcome. Drawing on fundamental economic principles and tools in statistics and management science, finance provides the framework for making decisions as to how investors and businesses should accomplish their financial goals.

The field of finance has three specialty areas: (1) capital markets and capital market theory, (2) financial management, and (3) portfolio management. The specialty field of *capital markets and capital market theory* focuses on the study of the financial system, the structure of interest rates, and the pricing of risky assets. *Financial management*, sometimes called *business finance*, is the specialty area of finance concerned with financial decision making within a business entity. Although we often refer to financial management as *corporate finance*, the principles of financial management also apply to other forms of business, as well as to government entities. Moreover, not all nongovernment business enterprises are corporations. Financial managers are primarily concerned with investment and financing decisions within the business. Making investment decisions that involve long-term capital expenditures is referred to as *capital budgeting*. *Portfolio management* deals with the management of individual or institutional funds. This specialty area of finance—also commonly referred to as *investment management, asset management, money management,* and *wealth management*—involves selecting an investment strategy and then selecting the specific assets to be included in a portfolio.

A critical element common to all three specialty areas in finance is the concept of risk. Measuring and quantifying risk are critical for the fair valuation of an asset, the selection of capital budgeting projects in financial management, the selection of individual asset holdings, and portfolio construction in portfolio management. The field of *risk management* includes the identification, measurement, and control of risk in a business entity or a portfolio.

Tools from the fields of statistics, management science, data science, and machine learning (ML) have been employed to deal with the risks associated with individual assets, capital budgeting projects, and selecting assets in portfolio construction. The use of such tools is now commonplace in the financial industry. For example, in portfolio management, practitioners run statistical routines to identify risk factors that drive asset returns, scenario analyses to evaluate the risk of their positions, and algorithms to find the optimal way to allocate assets or execute a trade.

This book focuses on three categories of quantitative tools—optimization, simulation, and ML algorithms—and discusses their applications in finance. Although different conceptually, these three groups of tools interface with each other. For example, simulation and ML are often used to enhance optimization algorithms, and optimization is a critical tool for estimating statistical models and building successful ML algorithms. Learning about all three categories enables a financial modeler to identify the appropriate context for application of combinations of these tools and employ more sophisticated analysis to obtain richer insights. In this chapter, we briefly introduce the three groups of techniques and provide an overview of the structure of the book.

1.1 Optimization

Optimization is an area in applied mathematics that, most generally, deals with efficient algorithms for finding an optimal solution among a set of solutions that satisfy given constraints. The first application of optimization in finance was suggested by Harry Markowitz (1952), in a seminal paper that outlined his mean-variance optimization framework for optimal asset allocation. Some other classical problems in finance that can be solved by optimization algorithms include:

- Is there a possibility of making a riskless profit, given the market prices of related securities? (This opportunity is called an *arbitrage opportunity*.)
- How should trades be executed to reach a target allocation with minimum transaction costs?
- Given a limited capital budget, which capital budgeting projects should be selected?
- Given estimates for the costs and benefits of a multistage capital budgeting project, at what stage should the project be expanded/abandoned?

Traditional optimization modeling assumes that the inputs to the algorithms are certain, but there is also a branch of optimization that studies the optimal decision under uncertainty about the problem parameters. Fast and reliable algorithms exist for many classes of optimization problems, and advances in computing power have made optimization techniques a viable and useful part of the financial modeler's standard tool set.

1.2 Simulation

Simulation is a technique for replicating uncertain processes and evaluating decisions under uncertain conditions. Perhaps the earliest application of simulation in finance was in financial management. Hertz (1964) argued that traditional valuation methods for investments omitted from consideration an important component: the fact that many of the inputs were inaccurate. He suggested modeling the uncertainty through probability-weighted scenarios, which would allow for obtaining a range of outcomes for the value of the investments and associated probabilities for each outcome. These ideas were forgotten for a while, but they have experienced tremendous growth in the last two decades. Simulation is now used not only in financial management but also in risk management and the pricing of various financial instruments. In portfolio management, for example, the correlated behavior of different factors over time is simulated to estimate portfolio risk measures. In pricing financial options or complex securities, such as mortgage-backed securities (MBSs), paths for the underlying risk factors are simulated; and the fair price of the securities is estimated as the average of the discounted payoffs over those paths. We will see numerous examples of such simulation applications in this book.

Simulation bears some resemblance to an intuitive tool for modifying original assumptions in financial models—what-if analysis—that has been used for a long time in financial applications. In *what-if analysis*, each uncertain input in a model is assigned a range of possible values—typically the best, worst, and most likely values—and the modeler analyzes what happens to the decision under these scenarios. The important additional component in simulation modeling, however, is that there are probabilities associated with the various outcomes. This allows for obtaining an additional piece of information compared to what-if analysis: the probabilities that specific final outcomes will happen. Probability theory is so fundamental to understanding the nature of simulation analysis, that we include chapter 3, on the most important aspects of probability theory that are relevant for simulation modeling.

1.3 Machine Learning

Machine learning (ML), a subfield of *artificial intelligence* (AI), is a collection of tools for analyzing data that automate the building of analytical models for decision making. Familiarity with ML and programming concepts has become a necessity for financial modelers in today's data-driven world.

The term "artificial intelligence" was first defined in a research proposal in 1955 as "that of making a machine behave in ways that would be called intelligent if a human were so behaving."[1] AI is based on the idea that machines (i.e., computers) can learn from data, identify patterns in the data, and then make decisions requiring only minimal human intervention. It is employed to perform tasks that are complex in much the same manner that humans solve problems.

The definition of AI basically means making a machine look smart. It is a general term. One way of achieving AI is via ML. Arthur Samuel, pioneer in computer gaming and AI, coined the term "machine learning" in 1959, defining it as the "ability to learn without being explicitly programmed."

Basically, ML is a modeling framework that does not depend on any specific theory. When applied to problems in finance, it is a purely statistical analysis of financial phenomena. Although ML has been applied to many areas of business, its applications to finance have been primarily in the investment management area.

1. "A Proposal for the Dartmouth Summer Research Project on Artificial Intelligence," prepared by J. McCarthy of Dartmouth College, M. L. Minsky, of Harvard University, N. Rochester of IBM Corporation, and C. E. Shannon of Bell Telephone Laboratories (http://www-formal.stanford.edu/jmc/history/dartmouth/dartmouth.html).

1.4 Organization of the Book

The book is divided into six parts. Part I provides a review of foundational financial concepts (chapter 2), as well as of the probability and statistics concepts used throughout this book: probability distributions (chapter 3) and inferential statistics (chapter 4). Part II covers the three main groups of tools: simulation modeling (chapter 5), optimization (chapters 6 and 7), and ML (chapter 10), together with important related concepts: data and data science (chapter 8), regression, a tool of ML (chapter 9), and natural language processing (NLP; chapter 11).

The remaining four parts of the book apply these tools. Applications to asset management are covered in part III, in chapters 12–15. Chapters 16 and 17 in part IV describe important models for asset pricing and provide an accessible introduction to models of asset price dynamics using simulation. Understanding how to implement these models is a prerequisite for the material in part V (chapters 18–21), which deals with the pricing and use of financial derivatives and MBSs. The last part of the book, part VI, includes two chapters dealing with capital budgeting. In those chapters, we discuss applications of simulation and optimization in capital budgeting (chapter 22) and real option valuation (chapter 23).

There are five online appendices that accompany this book, which review linear algebra concepts, @RISK, MATLAB, Microsoft Visual Basic for Applications (VBA) in Microsoft Excel, and Python.

1.5 A Closer Look at Each Chapter

We begin by listing important finance terminology in chapter 2. This includes basic theory of interest rates; terminology associated with equities, fixed-income securities, and trading; calculation of rate of return; and useful concepts in fixed income, such as spot rates, forward rates, yield, duration, and convexity.

Chapter 3 presents an introduction to probability theory. We review probability distributions such as the normal distribution and the binomial distribution and measures of central tendency and variability and strength of codependence between random variables. Understanding these concepts is paramount to understanding the simulation and ML models discussed in the book. Chapter 4 explains inferential statistics covering estimating statistics and hypothesis testing.

Chapter 5 introduces simulation as a methodology. We discuss the process of determining inputs for and interpreting output from simulation models and explain the methodology behind generating random numbers from different probability distributions. We also touch upon developments in efficient random number generation, which provides the foundation for the advanced simulation methods for financial derivative pricing, discussed in part V of the book.

In chapter 6, we provide a practical introduction to optimization. We discuss the most encountered types of optimization problems in finance and elaborate on the concept of "difficult" versus "easy" optimization problems. We introduce optimization duality and describe intuitively how optimization algorithms work. Illustrations of simple finance problems that can be handled with optimization techniques are provided, including examples of optimal portfolio allocation and cash-flow matching from the field of portfolio management and capital budgeting from the field of financial management. We also discuss dynamic programming—a technique for solving optimization problems over multiple stages. Finally, we review available software for different types of optimization problems and portfolio optimization in particular.

Classical optimization methods often assume that the parameters in optimization problems are deterministic and precise. However, these parameters are typically estimated using error-prone statistical procedures or subjective evaluations, leading to estimates that may contain significant errors. When optimization routines rely on poorly estimated inputs, their outputs can range from being at best unhelpful to, at worst, seriously misleading. Therefore, it is critical to understand how to handle uncertainty in the estimates of input parameters within optimization problems. Chapter 7 provides a comprehensive overview of various methods for optimization under uncertainty and delves into the fundamental concepts of dynamic programming under uncertainty, stochastic programming, and robust optimization. To enhance understanding, we also include practical examples that illustrate the application of these methods. You will find that these techniques reappear in several real-world applications discussed throughout the book.

Building models in finance often requires using data. Understanding the terminology associated with different types of financial datasets, as well as common traps that can lead to erroneous conclusions is very important, especially for the application of ML techniques covered in later chapters of the book. Chapter 8 covers concepts such as quantitative and qualitative data, structured versus unstructured data, alternative data, labeled versus unlabeled data, data measurement scales, and big data. It also describes data issues such as inaccurate, missing, or sparse data, outliers, and unbalanced datasets.

In chapter 9, we delve into the topic of regression—a versatile tool that holds significance for both economists, who often regard it as an econometrics tool for inference, and data scientists, who recognize it as a valuable ML tool. Our coverage encompasses various aspects of regression, beginning with the standard regression model, commonly referred to as ordinary least squares (OLS) regression. This model is primarily employed for predicting quantitative dependent variables. In addition, we explore specialized regression techniques, such as linear probability models, logistic regression, probit regression, and discriminant analysis. These methods are particularly useful when the dependent or response variable is binary or categorical, allowing us to determine whether an observation belongs to a specific group or category.

Chapter 10 explains the field of ML, providing in-depth insights into the concept of computer learning. In this chapter, we delve into various aspects of ML, including its different categories, the diverse applications of ML models, a survey of the most widely used ML algorithms, and essential techniques for validating these models.

The subject of chapter 11 is NLP. Like ML, NLP is a subfield of AI that focuses on the interaction between computers and human language. It deals with tasks such as language understanding, language generation, sentiment analysis, machine translation, and text summarization. ML methods are instrumental in solving a wide range of NLP tasks.

In chapter 12, we delve into the critical aspect of portfolio management known as the "asset allocation decision." This strategic decision revolves around the allocation of a portfolio's funds across various asset classes. We use the concept of optimization to explore one of the most widely used approaches to asset allocation: the mean-variance framework, which serves as the cornerstone of modern portfolio theory. Furthermore, we provide insights into alternative approaches to asset allocation.

Chapter 13 extends the classical mean-variance portfolio optimization theory to a more general mean-risk setting. We cover the most used alternative risk measures that are generally better suited than variance for describing investor preferences when asset return distributions are skewed, or fat-tailed. We focus on two popular portfolio risk measures—value-at-risk (VaR) and conditional value-at-risk (CVaR)—and show how to estimate them using simulation. We also formulate the problems of optimal asset allocation under these risk measures using optimization.

Chapter 14 describes how the three tools described in this book are applied in practice in constructing an equity (common stock) portfolio. We review constraints that are typically faced by portfolio managers and show how to formulate them as optimization problems. We also show how the classical framework for portfolio allocation can be extended to include transaction costs, and discuss index tracking, optimization of trades across multiple client accounts, and robust portfolio optimization techniques to minimize estimation error.

While chapter 14 focuses mostly on equity portfolio management, chapter 15 discusses the specificities of fixed-income (bond) portfolio management. Many of the same concepts are used in equity and fixed-income portfolio management (which are defined in chapter 2); however, fixed-income securities have some fundamental differences from equities, so the concepts cannot always be applied in the same way in which they would be applied for equity portfolios. We review classical measures of bond portfolio risk, such as duration, key rate duration, and spread duration. We discuss bond portfolio optimization relative to a benchmark index. We also give examples of how optimization can be used in liability-driven bond portfolio strategies such as immunization and cash-flow matching.

Chapter 16 transitions from the topic of portfolio management to the topic of asset pricing and introduces standard financial models for explaining asset returns—the capital asset pricing model (CAPM), which is based on the mean-variance framework described in chapter 12, the arbitrage pricing theory (APT), and factor models. Factor models are widely used in portfolio management—they not only help to model the processes that drive asset prices, but also substantially reduce the computational burden for statistical estimation and asset allocation optimization algorithms.

Chapter 17 focuses on dynamic asset pricing models, which are based on random processes. We examine the most used types of random walks and illustrate their behavior through simulation. The models discussed include arithmetic, geometric, different types of mean-reverting random walks, and more advanced hybrid models. In our presentation in the chapter, we assume that changes in asset prices happen at discrete time intervals. At the end, we extend the concept of a random walk to a random process in continuous time. The concepts introduced in chapter 17 are reused multiple times when we discuss the valuation of complex securities and multistage investments in part V of the book.

Chapter 18 introduces the topic of financial derivatives. It describes the main classes of financial derivative contracts (futures and forwards, options, and swaps), explains the important concepts of arbitrage and hedging, and reviews classical methods for pricing derivatives, such as the Black-Scholes formula and binomial trees.

Chapter 19 builds on the material in chapter 18, but it focuses on the use of simulation and ML for pricing complex securities. Some of the closed-form formulas provided in chapter 17 and the assumptions behind them become more intuitive when illustrated through simulation of the random processes followed by the underlying securities. Much of the chapter is dedicated to variance-reduction techniques, such as antithetic variables, stratified sampling, importance sampling, and control variates, as well as quasi–Monte Carlo methods. Such techniques are widely used today for efficient implementation of simulations for pricing securities and estimating sensitivity to different market factors.

Chapter 20 builds on chapters 12, 13, 14, 18, and 19 and discusses how derivatives can be used for portfolio risk management and return enhancement strategies. Simulation is essential for estimating the risk of a portfolio that contains complex financial instruments, but the process can be very slow in the case of large portfolios. We highlight some numerical issues, standard simulation algorithms, and review methods that have been suggested for reducing the computational burden.

The numerical pricing methods in chapter 21 are based on similar techniques as the ones discussed in chapter 19, but the context is different. We introduce a complex type of fixed-income security—MBS—and discuss in detail a part of the simulation that is specific to fixed-income securities, generating scenarios for future interest rates and the entire yield curve.

Chapters 22 and 23 cover a different area of finance—financial management. Chapter 22 begins by examining discounted cash flow (DCF) methodologies used in the assessment of corporate investment projects. It then explores, through a case study, the application of simulation techniques to estimate stand-alone risk and augment the analysis of these projects.

Chapter 23 introduces the real options framework, emphasizing the importance of considering existing options in project valuation. Unlike DCF analysis, which assumes no project flexibility once a decision is made, the real options framework acknowledges the potential for changes and adaptations. While it is acknowledged that determining the inputs for valuing real options can be quite challenging, the actual techniques for pricing these real options are rooted in the methodologies introduced in chapters 18 and 19 for pricing financial options. In this new context, techniques such as simulation, multistage optimization, and ML models can again prove valuable.

I

Background Topics

2

Important Finance Concepts

This chapter reviews important finance concepts that are used throughout this book. We discuss the concepts of the time value of money, different asset classes, basic trading terminology, calculation of rate of return, valuation, and advanced concepts in fixed income, such as duration, convexity, key rate duration, and total return.

2.1 Basic Theory of Interest

One of the most fundamental concepts in finance is that of the time value of money. A specific amount of money received today does not have the same nominal value in the future because of the possibility of investing the money today and earning interest. This section explains the rules for computing interest and outlines the basic elements of dealing with cash flows obtained today and in the future. These concepts will reappear many times throughout the book—they are critical for pricing financial instruments and making investment decisions.

2.1.1 Compound Interest

Most bank accounts, loans, and investment interest calculations use some form of compounding. Simply put, *compound interest* involves interest on interest. Let us explain the concept with an example. If you deposit \$100 in a bank deposit that pays 3% per year, you will have \$103 at the end of the year. Suppose that you keep the money in the bank for a second year, again at 3% interest. Compound interest means that the interest during the second year will be accrued on the entire amount that you had in the bank at the end of the first year—not only on your original deposit of \$100, but also on the interest accrued during the first year. Therefore, at the end of the second year, you will have

$$\$103 + 0.03 \cdot \$103 = \$106.09$$

If there were no compounding, you would have an additional \$3 at the end of the first year, and again at the end of the second year. That is, the total amount in your account at the end of the second year would be \$106. In general, the formula for computing the future value of an initial capital C invested for n years at interest rate r per year (compounded annually) is

$$C \cdot (1+r)^n \tag{2.1}$$

In our example, computing the interest with and without compounding made a difference of only 9 cents. The effect of compounding on the investment can be substantial, however, especially over a long time horizon. For example, you can verify that if you invest $C at an interest rate of 7% per year with annual compounding, your investment will double in size in approximately 10 years. This increase is significantly larger than if interest is not compounded—that is, if you simply add up the interest on the original investment over the 10 years. (The latter would be $10 \cdot 0.07 = 0.70$, or a 70% increase in the original investment.)

Interest does not necessarily need to be compounded once per year—it can be compounded daily, monthly, quarterly, or continuously. Usually, however, the interest rate r is still quoted as an annual rate. For example, with quarterly compounding, an interest of $r/4$ is accrued each quarter on the amount at the beginning of the quarter. At the end of the first quarter, the original amount C grows to $C \cdot (1+r/4)$. At the end of the second quarter, the amount becomes $(C \cdot (1+r/4) \cdot (1+r/4))$. At the end of the first year, the total amount in the account is $C \cdot (1+r/4)^4$. After n years, $C of initial capital grows to

$$C \cdot (1+r/4)^{4 \cdot n}.$$

In general, if the frequency of compounding is m times per year at an annual rate r (called the *nominal rate*), the amount at the end of n years will be

$$C \cdot (1+r/m)^{m \cdot n}. \tag{2.2}$$

The *effective* annual rate is the actual interest rate that is paid over the year—that is, the rate r_{eff} such that

$$C \cdot (1+r/m)^{\text{m}} = C \cdot (1+r_{\text{eff}}). \tag{2.3}$$

So, for example, if there is quarterly compounding and the nominal annual rate is 3%, the effective interest rate is

$$r_{\text{eff}} = (1+0.03/4)^4 - 1 = 0.0303 = 3.03\%.$$

Again, the difference between the nominal and the effective annual rate does not seem that large (only 0.03%); however, the difference increases with the compounding frequency.

Suppose we divide the year into very, very small time intervals. You can think of compounding interest every millisecond. So the number m in the expression for computing the compound interest rate becomes so large it can be considered infinite. It turns out that when m tends to infinity, the expression $(1+r/m)^m$ tends to a very specific number, e^r, where the number e has the value 2.7182 . . . (it has infinitely many digits after the decimal point).[1]

Therefore, with continuous compounding, $C of initial capital becomes $C \cdot e^{r \cdot 1}$ at the end of the first year, $C \cdot e^{r \cdot 2}$ at the end of the second year, and $C \cdot e^{r \cdot n}$ after n years. If we are interested in the amount of capital after, say, five months, and we are given the nominal

1. The value for the number e is so often used in applications that it can be computed with almost any software package. For example, in Microsoft Excel, the expression = `exp(1)` returns the value of e^1, which is 2.7183, rounded to four digits after the decimal point. In Python or MATLAB, `exp(1)` gives the same answer.

interest rate r as an annual rate, we first convert five months to years (5 months = 5/12 year), and then compute the future amount of capital as $C \cdot e^{r \cdot (5/12)}$.

Let us provide a concrete example. If the nominal interest rate is 3% per year and we invest \$100, then with continuous compounding, the amount at the end of the first year is $100 \cdot e^{0.03 \cdot 1} = \$103.05$. Therefore, the effective annual rate is 3.05%—higher than the effective annual rate of 3.03% with quarterly compounding that we computed earlier. After five months, the amount in the account will be $100 \cdot e^{0.03 \cdot (5/12)} = \$101.26$.

2.1.2 Present Value and Future Value

In the previous section, we explained the concept of interest. Suppose that you have \$100 today and you put it in a savings account paying 3% interest per year. At the end of the year, your \$100 will become \$103. Now suppose that somebody gives you a choice between receiving \$100 today or \$100 one year from now. The two options would not be equivalent to you. Given the opportunity to invest the money at 3% interest, you would demand \$103 one year from now to make you indifferent between the two options. In this example, the \$103 received at the end of the year can be considered the future value of \$100 received today, whereas \$100 is the present value of \$103 received one year from now. This is the important concept of the time value of money—money to be received in the future is less valuable than the same nominal amount of money received immediately.

Formally, the *present value* (sometimes also called the *discounted value*) of a single cash flow CF is the amount of money that must be invested today to generate the future cash flow. The present value of a cash flow depends on (1) the length of time until the cash flow will be received and (2) the interest rate, which is called the *discount rate* in this context.

The present value (PV) of a cash flow CF received n years from now when the interest rate r is compounded annually is computed as

$$PV(CF) = \frac{CF}{(1+r)^n}. \tag{2.4}$$

The expression

$$\frac{1}{(1+r)^n}$$

is called the *discount factor*. The discount factor (let us call it d_n) is the number by which we need to multiply the future cash flow to obtain its present value. Note that the discount factor is a number less than 1—the present value of the cash flow is less than the future value in nominal terms because it is assumed that the interest accrued between the present and the future date will be a nonnegative amount.

The conversion between present and future value follows the interest calculation rules that we introduced in the previous section. For example, if the annual interest rate r is continuously compounded, the present value of a cash flow CF received n years from now is

$$PV(CF) = \frac{CF}{e^{r \cdot n}} = CF \cdot e^{-r \cdot n}. \tag{2.5}$$

In this case, the discount factor is $d_n = e^{-r \cdot n}$.

It is easy to see how the concepts of present and future value extend when the present is not today's date. For example, suppose that we have invested \$100 today for three years in an account paying an annual rate of 3% compounded continuously. At the end of year 1, we will have $\$100 \cdot e^{0.03 \cdot 1} = \$103.05$ in the account. At the end of year 2, we will have $\$100 \cdot e^{0.03 \cdot 2} = \$106.18$ in the account. The amounts \$103.05 and \$106.18 are the future values of \$100 on hand today, in year 1 and year 2 dollars.

The present values of \$103.05 received at the end of year 1 and \$106.18 received at the end of year 2 are both \$100 ($\$103.05 \cdot e^{-0.03 \cdot 1}$ and $\$106.18 \cdot e^{-0.03 \cdot 2}$, respectively). Note that we can compute the present value of \$106.18 received at the end of year 2 in two ways. The first is to discount directly to the present, $\$106.18 \cdot e^{-0.03 \cdot 2}$. The second is to discount \$106.18 first to its present value in year 1 dollars ($\$106.18 \cdot e^{-0.03 \cdot 1} = \$103.05$), and then discount the year 1 dollars to today's dollars ($\$103.05 \cdot e^{-0.03 \cdot 1} = \$100.00$). The latter technique will be useful when pricing financial derivatives and real options in chapters 18, 19, and 23.

2.2 Asset Classes

An *asset* is any possession that has value in an exchange. Assets can be classified as tangible or intangible. A tangible asset's value depends on particular physical properties of the asset. Buildings, land, and machinery are examples of tangible assets. Intangible assets, by contrast, represent legal claims to some future benefit and their value bears no relation to the form, physical or otherwise, in which the claims are recorded. Financial assets, financial instruments, or securities are intangible assets. For these instruments, the typical future benefit comes in the form of a claim to future cash.

In most developed countries, the four major asset classes are (1) common stocks, (2) bonds, (3) cash equivalents, and (4) real estate. An asset class is defined in terms of the investment attributes that the members of an asset class have in common. These investment characteristics include (1) the major economic factors that influence the value of the asset class and, as a result, correlate highly with the returns of each member included in the asset class; (2) have a similar risk and return characteristic; and (3) have a common legal or regulatory structure. Based on this way of defining an asset class, the correlation between the returns of different asset classes would be low.

The preceding four major asset classes can be extended to create other asset classes. From the perspective of a U.S. investor, for example, the four major asset classes listed earlier have been expanded as follows by separating foreign securities from U.S. securities: (1) U.S. common stocks, (2) non-U.S. (or foreign) common stocks, (3) U.S. bonds, (4) non-U.S. bonds, (5) cash equivalents, and (6) real estate.

Common stocks and bonds are further partitioned into more asset classes. For example, U.S. common stocks (also referred to as U.S. *equities*) are differentiated based on market capitalization. *Market capitalization* (*market cap*) is computed as the number of shares outstanding times the market price per share. The term is often used as a proxy for the size of a company. Companies are usually classified as *large cap, medium cap (mid-cap), small cap*, or *micro cap*, depending on their market capitalization. The division is somewhat arbitrary, but generally, micro-cap companies have a market capitalization of less than \$250 million, small-cap companies have a market capitalization between \$250 million and \$1 billion, mid-cap companies have market capitalization between \$1 billion and \$5 billion, and large-cap companies have market capitalization of more than \$5 billion. Companies with a market capitalization of more than \$250 billion are sometimes called *mega-caps*.

In addition to equity asset classes based on market capitalization, the equity area has asset classes based on what is known as *value* and *growth*. Although a company's market is easy to determine given the market price per share and the number of shares outstanding, defining "value" and "growth" stocks is not. Basically, a *value stock* is the common stock of a company that an investor believes is currently selling in the market below what it is truly worth and thereby offers the potential to generate a superior return. There are various measures such as the market price relative to earnings per share (price-earnings ratio), market price relative to book value per share, and market price relative to earnings growth that are commonly used to assess whether a company's stock is a value stock. Any stock not classified as a value stock is treated as a growth stock.

The asset classes in the bond market can be categorized in several ways. One way is by the credit rating. In this categorization of bond asset classes, it is based on investment-grade and noninvestment bonds. Later in this chapter, we describe what is meant by investment-grade bonds and noninvestment-grade bonds. A second way of categorizing asset classes in the bond market is by the maturity of the bonds: short term, intermediate term, and long term. Finally, sectors of the bond market can be used to categorize asset classes. For example, there is the U.S. Treasury and government agency sector, corporate bond sector, mortgage-backed security (MBS) sector, and asset-backed securities (ABS) sector.

Publicly traded stocks and bonds, along with cash, are asset classes that are referred to as *traditional asset classes*. All other asset classes are referred to as *nontraditional asset classes* or *alternative asset classes*. They include real estate, commodities, private equity and debt, and hedge funds.

Along with the designation of asset classes comes a barometer to be able to quantify the performance of the asset class—the risk, return, and the correlation of the return of the asset class with that of another asset class. The barometer is called a *benchmark index*, a *market index*, or simply an *index*. There are service providers (third-party vendors) that provide these indices for all asset classes. Some popular stock market indices used by professional money managers are

- Standard & Poor's 500 (S&P 500) index, which includes 505 stocks[2] that make up about 75% of the U.S. stock market. It is a common benchmark for the large market cap asset class.
- Standard & Poor's 400 index (S&P Midcap 400), which is made up of 400 midmarket cap stocks.
- Russell 3000 index, which has 3,000 stocks that make up almost 98% of the U.S. stock market. It is often used as a benchmark to represent the equity market asset class overall.
- Russell 2000 index, which has 2,000 stocks that represents the small market cap asset class.

For bonds, several Wall Street banks and third-party vendors have developed bond indices to represent the different bond asset classes. The most popular broad-based U.S. bond market index is the Bloomberg Barclays U.S. Aggregate Bond Index.

2. The S&P 500 includes 505 stocks rather than 500 because some companies in the index (such as Alphabet and Meta) have multiple share classes, each of which is listed as a separate stock within the index.

Investors use indices in two ways. First, they evaluate the performance of professional managers whom they hire to manage their assets. Second, they use optimization and simulation modeling to determine how an investor's funds should be allocated to the various asset classes. We'll see examples of this in later chapters.

In practice, one cannot invest in an index. Consequently, in more realistic modeling to determine how funds should be allocated among the asset classes, an *exchange-traded fund (ETF)* that invests in an asset class is used. An ETF is a collective investment vehicle that we will describe later in this chapter. For example, in modeling to determine asset allocation, rather than using the S&P 500 index, some ETFs that can be used are the SPDR S&P 500 ETF Trust (ticker symbol SPY), the iShares Core S&P 500 ETF (ticker symbol IVV), or the Vanguard S&P 500 ETF (ticker symbol VOO). The iShares Core Aggregate Bond ETF (ticker symbol AGG) can be used to represent the aggregate bond market. If an allocation is sought for intermediate-term corporate bonds, the Vanguard Intermediate-Term Corporate Bond ETF (ticker symbol VCIT) can be used. The point is that an index has no expenses associated with investing in any of the securities in the index and no management fee as well. Yet, in the real world, investors face such expenses. An ETF is a low-cost vehicle for investing in an asset class, and it offers a more realistic vehicle to represent the risk and return of an asset class than an index does.

2.2.1 Equities

Most generally, *equity* means ownership in a corporation in the form of common stock. *Common stock* is securities that entitle the holder to a share of a company's success through dividends and/or capital appreciation and provide voting rights in a company. The terms "equities" and "stocks" are often used interchangeably.

A *dividend* is a payment (usually quarterly) disbursed by a company to its shareholders out of the company's current or retained earnings. Dividends can be given as cash (*cash dividends*), additional stock (*stock dividends*), or other property. Dividends are usually paid by companies that have reached their growth potential, so they cannot benefit by reinvesting their earnings into further expansion.

Capital appreciation refers to growth in the stock price. Because of capital appreciation, investors can make money by investing in a company still in its growth phase, even if it does not pay dividends.

2.2.2 Fixed-Income Securities

In its simplest form, a *fixed-income security* is a financial obligation of an entity that promises to pay a specified sum of money at specified future dates. The entity that promises to make the payment is called the *issuer* of the security. Some examples of issuers are central governments such as the U.S. government and the French government; government-related agencies of a central government, such as Fannie Mae and Freddie Mac in the United States; a municipal government such as those of the state of New York in the United States and the city of Rio de Janeiro in Brazil; a corporation such as Coca Cola in the United States and Yorkshire Water in the United Kingdom; and supranational governments such as the World Bank.

Fixed-income securities fall into two general categories: debt obligations and preferred stock. In the case of a debt obligation, the issuer is called the *borrower*. The investor that purchases such a fixed-income security is said to be the *lender* or *creditor*. Debt obligations are virtually loans with interest, where the interest is paid over time in the form of coupons. The promised payments that the issuer agrees to make at the specified dates have two components: interest and principal payments. (The principal represents repayment of the funds borrowed at the end—that is, at the *maturity date* for the debt obligation.) Fixed-income securities that are debt obligations include *bonds*, *asset-backed securities (ABSs)*, and *bank loans*. Bonds are loans taken out by corporations, government entities, or municipalities. Bank loans are loans by banks to companies or individuals. ABSs are securities backed by pools of loans—mortgages or assets (e.g., cars). The assets in ABS pools are typically too small or illiquid to be sold individually. Pooling the assets allows them to be sold in pieces to investors, a process known as *securitization*. The largest number of ABSs are backed by pools of mortgages and are referred to as *mortgage-backed securities (MBSs)*. We will discuss MBSs, ABSs, and securitization in more detail in chapter 21.

In contrast to a fixed-income security that represents a debt obligation, *preferred stock* represents an ownership interest in a corporation. Dividend payments are made to the preferred stockholder and represent a distribution of the corporation's profits. Unlike investors that own a corporation's common stock, investors that own the preferred stock can realize only a contractually fixed dividend payment. Moreover, the payments that must be made to preferred stockholders have priority over the payments that a corporation pays to common stockholders. In the case of the bankruptcy of a corporation, preferred stockholders are given preference over common stockholders. Consequently, preferred stock is a form of equity that has characteristics like bonds.

Prior to the 1980s, fixed-income securities were simple investment products. Holding aside default by the issuer, the investor knew how long interest would be received and when the amount borrowed would be repaid. Moreover, most investors purchased these securities to hold them to their maturity date. Beginning in the 1980s, the fixed-income world changed. First, fixed-income securities became more complex. There are features in many of these securities that make it difficult to determine when the amount borrowed will be repaid and for how long interest will be received. For some securities, it is difficult to determine the amount of interest that will be received. Second, the hold-to-maturity investor was replaced by institutional investors that actively trade fixed-income securities.

In this book, we will often use the terms "fixed-income securities" and "bonds" interchangeably. Next, we introduce various features of fixed-income securities and explain how these features affect the risks associated with investing in fixed-income securities. This introduction is only cursory. For an in-depth overview of fixed-income products, we refer the reader to Fabozzi (2007).

The *term to maturity* of a bond is the number of years that the debt is outstanding or the number of years remaining prior to the final principal payment. The *maturity date* of a bond refers to the date that the debt will cease to exist, at which time the issuer will redeem the bond by paying the outstanding balance.

The *par value* of a bond is the amount that the issuer agrees to repay the bondholder at or by the maturity date. This amount is also referred to as the *principal value*, *face value*, *redemption value*, and *maturity value*.

Because bonds can have different par values, the practice is to quote the price of a bond as a percentage of its par value. A value of 100 means "100% of par value." For example, if a bond has a par value of $1,000 and the issue is selling for $900, this bond would be said to be selling at 90. If a bond is quoted at 103 19/32 and has a par value of $1 million, then the dollar price is $(103.59375/100) \cdot \$1{,}000{,}000 = \$1{,}035{,}937.50$.

A bond may trade above or below its par value. When a bond trades below its par value, it is said to be *trading at a discount*. When a bond trades above its par value, it is said to be *trading at a premium*.

The *coupon rate*, also called the *nominal rate*, is the interest rate that the issuer agrees to pay each year. The annual amount of the interest payment made to bondholders during the term of the bond is called the *coupon*. The coupon is calculated by multiplying the coupon rate by the par value of the bond. In other words,

$$\text{Coupon} = (\text{Coupon rate}) \cdot (\text{Par value})$$

For example, a bond with a 5% coupon rate and a par value of $1,000 will pay annual interest of $50 (= 0.05 · $1,000).

In the United States, the usual practice is for the issuer to pay the coupon in two semi-annual installments. MBSs and ABSs typically pay interest monthly. For bonds issued in some markets outside the United States, coupon payments are made only once per year.

Not all bonds make periodic coupon payments. For example, *zero-coupon bonds* do not pay out coupons during the life of the bond. The holder of a zero-coupon bond realizes interest by buying the bond substantially below its par value (i.e., buying the bond at a discount). Interest is then paid at the maturity date, where the interest is the difference between the par value and the price paid for the bond.

In addition, the coupon rate on a bond need not be fixed over the bond's life. *Floating-rate securities*, sometimes also called *floaters* or *variable-rate securities*, have coupon payments that reset periodically according to a reference rate. The typical formula (called the *coupon formula*) on certain determination dates when the coupon rate is reset is as follows:

$$\text{Coupon rate} = (\text{Reference rate}) + (\text{Quoted margin})$$

An example of a floating rate security is an *inflation-linked* (or *inflation-indexed*) bond. The U.S. Department of the Treasury issues inflation-adjusted securities referred to as *Treasury Inflation Protection Securities (TIPS)*. The coupon formula's reference rate is the inflation rate as measured by the Consumer Price Index for All Urban Consumers (CPI-U). Corporations and agencies in the United States also issue inflation-linked bonds.

A floater may have a restriction on the maximum or minimum coupon rate that will be paid at any reset date. The maximum (minimum) coupon rate is called a *cap* (a *floor*).

Typically, the coupon formula for a floater is such that the coupon rate increases when the reference rate increases and decreases when the reference rate decreases. However, there are issues whose coupon rate moves in the opposite direction from the change in the reference rate. Such issues are called *inverse floaters* or *reverse floaters*. Such securities give an investor who believes that interest rates will decline the opportunity to obtain a higher coupon interest rate.[3]

3. Inverse floaters were behind the Orange County bankruptcy of 1994; at the time, the largest municipality bankruptcy had repercussions across the entire municipalities bond market and raised the cost of capital for municipalities across the U.S.

Accrued Interest Bond issuers do not disburse coupon interest payments every day. Instead, payments are made on prespecified dates. (As we mentioned earlier, in the United States, coupon interest is typically paid every six months.) Thus, if an investor sells a bond between coupon payments and the buyer holds it until the next coupon payment, then the entire coupon interest earned for the period will be paid to the buyer of the bond since the buyer will be the holder of record. The seller of the bond gives up the interest from the time of the last coupon payment until the time when the bond is sold. The amount of interest over this period that will be received by the buyer even though it was earned by the seller is called *accrued interest.*

In the United States and many other countries, the bond buyer must pay the bond seller the accrued interest. The amount that the buyer pays the seller is the agreed-upon price for the bond plus accrued interest. This amount is called the *full price.* (Some market participants refer to this as the *dirty price.*) The agreed-upon bond price without accrued interest is simply referred to as the *price.* (Some refer to it as the *clean price.*)

There are exceptions to the rule that the bond buyer must pay the bond seller accrued interest. The most important exception is when the issuer has not fulfilled their promise to make periodic interest payments. In this case, the issuer is said to be *in default.* In such instances, the bond is sold without accrued interest and is said to be *traded flat.*

Provisions for Paying off Bonds The most common structure in the United States and Europe for paying the principal for both corporate and government bonds is to pay the entire amount in one lump sum at the maturity date. Such bonds are said to have a *bullet maturity.*

Fixed-income securities backed by pools of loans, such as MBSs and ABSs, often have a schedule of partial principal payments. Such fixed-income securities are said to be *amortizing securities.* For many loans, the payments are structured such that when the last loan payment is made, the entire amount owed is fully paid.

An issue may have a *call provision* granting the issuer the option to retire (i.e., pay off) all or part of the issue prior to the stated maturity date. Some issues specify that the issuer must retire a predetermined amount of the issue periodically.

Conversion Privilege A *convertible bond* is an issue that grants the bondholder the right to convert the bond for a specified number of shares of common stock. Such a feature allows the bondholder to take advantage of favorable movements in the price of the issuer's common stock. An *exchangeable bond* allows the bondholder to exchange the issue for a specified number of shares of common stock of a corporation different from the issuer of the bond.

Currency Denomination The payments that the issuer makes to the bondholder can be in any currency. For example, an issue in which payments to bondholders are in U.S. dollars is called a *dollar-denominated issue.* However, nothing prevents the issuer from making payments in different currencies. In fact, there can be issues whose coupon payments are in one currency and whose principal payment is in another. Issues with this characteristic are called *dual-currency issues.*

Embedded Options Some bonds have embedded options granted to the issuers or the bondholders. Options granted to issuers, for example, may include the right to call the issue (i.e., to pay the issue in full before the maturity date). As we mentioned earlier in this section, such bonds are referred to as *callable bonds*. Options granted to bondholders may include a conversion privilege, or a right to put the issue (i.e., demand immediate payment of the remaining principal). The latter option has value when interest rates rise above the issue's coupon rate because the bondholders are better off investing their money elsewhere. We will discuss financial options in more detail in chapters 18 through 20.

It is important to note whether a bond has embedded options because those options change a bond's characteristics and value. As we will see in section 2.5, estimating the fair price of a bond requires projecting its cash flows between now and its maturity. These cash flows and their timing are influenced by the existence of options.

Credit Risk Investing in fixed-income securities exposes investors to *credit risk*. While investors commonly refer to credit risk as if it were one-dimensional, it actually takes three forms: default risk, credit spread risk, and downgrade risk.

Default risk is the risk that the issuer will fail to satisfy the terms of the obligation with respect to the timely payment of interest and repayment of the amount borrowed. To gauge credit default risk, investors rely on analysis performed by nationally recognized statistical rating organizations (more popularly known as *rating agencies*) that perform credit analyses of bond issues and issuers and express their conclusions in the form of a *credit rating*. The three major rating agencies are Moody's Investors Service, Standard & Poor's (S&P), and Fitch, and their bond rating systems are summarized in exhibit 2.1. Bond issues that are assigned a rating in the top four categories in the exhibit are referred to as *investment-grade bonds*. Bond issues that carry a rating below the top four categories are referred to as *noninvestment-grade bonds*, or more popularly as *high-yield bonds* or *junk bonds*. Thus, the bond market can be divided into two sectors: the *investment-grade sector* and the *noninvestment-grade sector*. *Distressed debt* is a subcategory of noninvestment-grade bonds. These bonds may be in bankruptcy proceedings, may be in default of coupon payments, or may be in some other form of distress. Historically, U.S. Treasuries are not rated because they are viewed as default-free.

Credit spread is the premium over the government or risk-free rate required by the market for taking on a certain assumed credit exposure. The benchmark is often a U.S. Treasury issue for the given maturity. Typically, if all other factors are held constant, the higher the credit rating, the smaller the credit spread to the benchmark rate. *Credit spread risk*, the second type of credit risk, is the risk of financial loss resulting from changes in the level of credit spreads used in the marking-to-market of a debt instrument. Changes in market credit spreads affect the portfolio's value and can lead to losses for traders or underperformance relative to a benchmark for portfolio managers.

As just explained, investors gauge the credit default risk of an issue by looking at the credit ratings assigned to issues by the rating agencies. Once a credit rating is assigned to a debt obligation, a rating agency monitors the issuer's credit quality and can reassign a different credit rating. An improvement in the credit quality of an issue or issuer is rewarded with a better credit rating, referred to as an *upgrade*; a deterioration in the credit rating of an issue or issuer is penalized by assigning an inferior credit rating, referred to as a *downgrade*. The actual or anticipated downgrading of an issue or issuer increases the

Moody's	S&P	Fitch	Summary Description
	Investment Grade—High-Credit Worthiness		
Aaa	AAA	AAA	Prime, maximum safety
Aa1	AA+	AA+	
Aa2	AA	AA	High-grade, high-credit quality
Aa3	AA–	AA–	
A1	A+	A+	
A2	A	A	Upper-medium grade
A3	A–	A–	
Baa1	BBB+	BBB+	
Baa2	BBB	BBB	Lower-medium grade
Baa3	BBB–	BBB–	
	Speculative—Lower-Credit Worthiness		
Ba1	BB+	BB+	
Ba2	BB	BB	Low-grade, speculative
Ba3	BB–	BB–	
B1		B+	
B2	B	B	Highly speculative
B3		B–	
	Predominantly Speculative, Substantial Risk, or in Default		
Caa	CCC+	CCC+	Substantial risk, in poor standing
	CCC	CCC	
Ca	CC	CC	May be in default, very speculative
C	C	C	Extremely speculative
	CI		Income bonds, no interest being paid
		DDD	
	D	DD	Default
		D	

Exhibit 2.1
Bond ratings systems of Moody's, Standard & Poor's, and Fitch credit rating agencies.

credit spread and results in a decline in the price of the issue or the issuer's bonds. This type of risk is called *downgrade risk* and is closely related to credit spread risk. A rating agency may announce in advance that it is reviewing a particular credit rating and then go further and state that the review is a precursor to a possible downgrade or upgrade. This announcement is referred to as *putting the issue under credit watch.* The rating agencies periodically publish, in the form of a table, information about how issues that they have rated have changed over time. This table, called a *rating migration table* or *rating transition table*, is useful for investors to assess potential downgrades and upgrades.

2.2.3 Collective Investment Vehicles

Collective investment vehicles are products managed by asset management firms. These investment vehicles involve investors pooling funds and investing those funds in certain financial assets. The investors then have an equity interest in the net assets (i.e., assets minus liabilities) of the fund's portfolio. In general, the advantages associated with investing by means of a collective investment vehicle rather than directly in financial assets are obtaining superior portfolio diversification, achieving better liquidity, and acquiring the expertise of professional asset management.

Each share of a collective investment vehicle represents a proportional interest in the net assets in which the funds are invested, called the *net asset value (NAV)*. The NAV equals the market value of the portfolio minus the liabilities divided by the number of shares owned by the fund's investors:

$$\text{NAV} = \frac{\text{Market value of portfolio} - \text{Liabilities}}{\text{Number of shares outstanding}}$$

The major collective investment vehicles are open-end funds, closed-end funds, ETFs, hedge funds, and real estate investment trusts.

Open-end funds, commonly referred to simply as *mutual funds*, are portfolios of securities. A mutual fund's NAV is determined only once each trading day, at the close of the trading day. All new investments in the mutual fund and withdrawals from the fund during the day are priced at the closing NAV. The total number of shares in a mutual fund increases if more investments than withdrawals are made during the day.

The shares of a *closed-end fund* are like those of the common stock of a corporation. The new shares of a closed-end fund are initially issued by an underwriter, and after their issuance, the number of shares remains constant. That is, after the initial issuance, no sales or purchases of closed-end fund shares are made by the fund's portfolio manager as with mutual funds. Instead, the shares are traded on a secondary market. The price of a share of a closed-end fund is determined by supply and demand for the shares in the market in which the fund shares are traded. The share price is related to the NAV. The price may be above, equal to, or below the NAV.

An ETF is a collective investment vehicle with many of the same features as open-end funds, but it trades like stocks on an exchange. In a sense, ETFs are like closed-end funds, in that they may sell at a premium or discount to their NAVs. Every ETF is based on a benchmark index, and the ETF portfolio manager seeks to match the performance of that index. That is, the portfolio manager seeks the same total return for the ETF as that of the index. The ETF's performance will always deviate from the benchmark index because the fund will incur management fees (lower than for open-end and closed-end funds) and transaction costs. For this reason, in asset allocation models, ETFs are used as a proxy for an asset class since they better reflect the return that can be realized from investing in an asset class.

It would be nice to be able to define what a *hedge fund* is by, say, pointing to its definition in federal securities law. However, no such legal definition exists, nor is there any universally accepted definition. Hedge funds use a wide range of trading strategies and techniques in an attempt to earn superior returns. The strategies used by a hedge fund can include one or more of the following:

- Leverage, or the use of borrowed funds
- Short selling, or the sale of a financial instrument that the investor does not own in anticipation of a decline in that financial instrument's price

- Arbitrage, or the simultaneous buying and selling of related financial instruments to realize a profit from the temporary misalignment of their prices
- Risk control, or the use of financial instruments (such as derivatives) to reduce the risk of loss

Note that risk control is more general than hedging. In a hedge, one often thinks about eliminating risk. Risk control means that risk is mitigated to the degree the investor desires. Very few hedge funds employ hedging in the sense of eliminating all risks.

Real estate investment trusts (REITs) are stocks that represent an interest in an underlying pool of real estate properties. A REIT is like a closed-end fund because the stock is publicly traded and the market price can differ from that of the REIT's NAV. In the case of REITs, the investments in the portfolio are real estate properties. The principal advantage of REITs is that they allow investors access to an illiquid asset class that would be difficult for an individual investor to invest in directly. Moreover, because a REIT has a large number of properties in its portfolio, individual investors obtain better diversification than by investing directly in real estate properties. REIT ETFs are traded based on various REIT indices.

2.3 Basic Trading Terminology

In this book, we use basic terminology associated with buying and selling securities. This section briefly explains some important trading terms.

2.3.1 Borrowing Funds to Purchase Securities

Often, investors borrow funds to purchase securities. Such investment strategies are known as *leveraged strategies*. The expectation is that the money earned by investing in the securities purchased with the borrowed funds will exceed the borrowing cost. Several sources of funds are available to an investor when borrowing funds. When securities are purchased with borrowed funds, the most common practice is to use the securities as collateral for the loan. In such instances, the transaction is referred to as a *collateralized loan*. Two collateralized borrowing arrangements are used by investors: margin buying and repurchase agreements.

Margin Buying In a margin buying arrangement, the funds borrowed to buy the securities are provided by the broker, and the broker gets the money from a bank. The interest rate that banks charge brokers for these transactions is called the *call money rate* (or *broker loan rate*). The broker charges the investor the call money rate plus a service charge. In the United States, the Securities and Exchange Act of 1934 prohibits brokers from lending more than a specified percentage of the market value of the securities.

Margin buying is the most common collateralized borrowing arrangement for common stock investors—both individual (retail) investors and institutional investors—and retail bond investors. It is less common for bond institutional investors.

Repurchase Agreement The collateralized borrowing arrangement used by institutional investors in the bond market is the repurchase agreement. A *repurchase agreement* is the sale of a security with a commitment by the seller to repurchase the same security from the purchaser at a specified price at a designated future date. The *repurchase price* is the price at which the seller and the buyer agree that the seller will repurchase the security on a specified future date, called the *repurchase date*. The difference between the repurchase price and the sale price is the dollar interest cost of the loan. Based on the dollar interest cost, the sales price, and the length of the repurchase agreement, an implied interest rate can be computed. This implied interest rate is called the *repo rate*. The advantage to the investor of using this borrowing arrangement is that the interest rate is less than the cost of bank financing. When the loan term is one day, it is called an *overnight repo* (or *overnight RP*); a loan for more than one day is called a *term repo* (or *term RP*). The repo rate varies from transaction to transaction depending on various factors.

2.3.2 Long and Short Positions

When an investor takes a position in the market by buying a security, the investor is said to be taking a *long position* in the security. Obviously, the investor gains from a long position if the security's price increases after the purchase.

When an investor borrows a security from a broker and sells it, understanding that the security must be returned later, the investor is said to be taking a *short position* in the security (or *selling it short*). Short-selling strategies are useful if the investor believes the security price will fall. After borrowing the security from the broker today, the investor can sell the security in the market at today's price, repurchase the security later at a (hopefully) lower price, and return the security to the broker while realizing a profit.

2.4 Calculating the Rate of Return

Section 2.2 discussed two asset classes in detail. In this section, we explain an important concept associated with assets—the rate of return, which, in some ways, resembles an interest rate.

The *simple rate of return* (usually called just *return*) on an asset is the percentage difference between the amount received from investing in the asset and the amount originally invested in the asset:

$$\text{Return} = (\text{Amount received} - \text{Amount invested})/(\text{Amount invested})$$

To compute the return, of course, we need to specify the investment horizon in advance.

Suppose that we invest $\$C_t$ in an asset at time t, and the value of our investment is $\$C_T$ at time T. The return on the asset between times t and T, which we denote as $r_{(t,T)}$,[4] is

$$r_{(t,T)} = \frac{C_T - C_t}{C_t}. \tag{2.6}$$

4. In general, we use the notation $r_{(t_1,t_2)}$ to denote the return between times t_1 and t_2.

If we are given the return and the initial amount invested, and we would like to compute the amount received from our investment, we would use the following equality:

$$C_T = C_t \cdot (1 + r_{(t,T)}). \tag{2.7}$$

In this sense, the rate of return acts similarly to the rate of interest.

When the asset is a stock, the return can be calculated as

$$r_{(t,T)} = \frac{P_T - P_t + D_t}{P_t}, \tag{2.8}$$

where P_t and P_T are the market prices of the stock at times t and T, respectively, and D_t is the dividends paid between times t and T.

Returns are compounded much in the way that compound interest is. Let us explain this with an example. Suppose that an initial capital of $C_0 = \$1{,}000$ in some investment has value $C_1 = \$1{,}300$ at the end of year 1, and value $C_2 = \$1{,}000$ at the end of year 2. What is the return on the investment over the two years?

We know, of course, that the return should be 0 since the initial capital is identical to the capital at the end of two years:

$$r_{(0,2)} = (C_2 - C_0)/C_0 = (1{,}000 - 1{,}000)/1{,}000 = 0$$

If we compute the returns over the two years separately, we get a return of 30% ($r_{(0,1)} = (1{,}300 - 1{,}000)/1{,}000 = 0.30$) over year 1 and a return of approximately –23% ($r_{(1,2)} = (1{,}000 - 1{,}300)/1{,}300 = -0.23$) over year 2. If we add these two returns, we would obtain a return of 30% – 23% = 7%, which is intuitively wrong.

Instead, we compound the returns over the two time periods and obtain the following for the return at the end of two years:

$$r_{(0,2)} = (1 + 0.30) \cdot (1 - 0.23) - 1 = 0.001$$

This number is 0 (there is some rounding error), which agrees with our intuition.[5]

In general, an investment of \$1 at time 0 will grow to $(1 + r_{(0,1)})(1 + r_{(1,2)}) \ldots (1 + r_{(t-1,t)})$ dollars at the end of year t, and the return $r_{(0,t)}$ from time 0 to time t equals

$$r_{(0,t)} = (1 + r_{(0,1)})(1 + r_{(1,2)}) \cdots (1 + r_{(t-1,t)}) - 1 \tag{2.9}$$

The expression $(1 + r_{(t,T)})$ is called the *gross return*. In the previous two-year example, the gross return over the two years is $(1 + r_{(0,2)}) = 1.00$. The gross return over year 1 is $(1 + r_{(0,1)}) = 1.30$, and the gross return over year 2 is $(1 + r_{(1,2)}) = 0.77$.

5. To see this, note that the capital at the end of the second year is

$$C_2 = (1 + r_{(1,2)})C_1 = (1 + r_{(1,2)})[(1 + r_{(0,1)})C_0] = (1 + r_{(1,2)})(1 + r_{(0,1)})C_0.$$

Therefore, the return over the two years is

$$r_{(0,2)} = \frac{C_2 - C_0}{C_0} = \frac{(1 + r_{(1,2)})(1 + r_{(0,1)})C_0 - C_0}{C_0} = (1 + r_{(1,2)})(1 + r_{(0,1)}) - 1.$$

Returns can also be expressed in geometric (log) form. The *log return* between times t and T is defined as

$$\log(1+r_{(t,T)}) \tag{2.10}$$

where *log* is the natural logarithm—that is, the function such that $e^{\log(x)}=x$.[6,7] Note that when using log returns, the implicit assumption is that returns are accumulated continuously (think of the analogy with continuously compounded interest).

It is easy to see that

$$\log(1+r_{(t,T)}) = \log\left(1+\frac{C_T - C_t}{C_t}\right) = \log\left(\frac{C_T}{C_t}\right). \tag{2.11}$$

If the time interval (t,T) is small, the numerical value of the return $r_{(t,T)}$ will also be small. Therefore, $\log(1+r_{(t,T)})$ will be approximately $r_{(t,T)}$ for short time periods.[8]

If we are dealing with a stock, then

$$\log(1+r_{(t,T)}) = \log\left(1+\frac{P_T - P_t + D_t}{P_t}\right) = \log\left(\frac{P_T + D_t}{P_t}\right). \tag{2.12}$$

There are several advantages to using log returns in financial modeling, whose applications will become clearer when financial derivative pricing models are discussed in chapters 18 and 19. On an intuitive level, log returns are more economically meaningful because the asset price can never become negative, regardless of how negative the returns may be. (This is not the case with the definition of return introduced at the beginning of this section.) Furthermore, the log return over multiple time periods is the sum of the one-period log returns. Namely,

$$\begin{aligned}\log(1+r_{(0,t)}) &= \log((1+r_{(0,1)})(1+r_{(1,2)})\cdots(1+r_{(t-1,t)}))\\ &= \log(1+r_{(0,1)}) + \log(1+r_{(1,2)}) + \cdots + \log(1+r_{(t-1,t)})\end{aligned}$$

Finally, a widely used concept in bond portfolio management is *total return*. The total return is computed as

$$\text{Total return} = (\text{Amount received})/(\text{Amount invested})$$

where the amount received is comprised of three sources:

- The coupon payments
- The change in the value of the bond

6. We introduced the number e in section 2.1.

7. In Excel, the natural logarithm function is ln. For example, =ln(5) returns 1.6094. The result 1.6094 is the number such that e raised to the power of that number equals 5; that is, $e^{1.6094}=5$. In Python, the natural logarithm function is also ln, whereas in some languages like MATLAB, it is log.

8. It is a mathematical property of the natural logarithm function that $\log(1+x)$ when x is small is approximately equal to x. To see this, write the Taylor expansion of $\log(1+x)$ as

$$\log(1+x) = x - \frac{1}{2}x^2 + \frac{1}{3}x^3 - \cdots$$

When x is "small," the terms involving squares, cubes, and higher powers of x are even smaller and can be ignored, so x remains the only significant term.

- Income from the reinvestment of coupon payments and principal repayment (in the case of amortizing securities) from the time of receipt to the end of the investment horizon

For example, suppose that an investor purchases a fixed-income security for \$90 and expects a return over a one-year investment horizon from the three sources equal to \$5. Then the expected total return is 5.56% (=\$5/\$90). Total return is discussed in more detail in section 2.6.8.

2.5 Valuation

Valuation is the process of determining the fair value of a financial asset. This process is also referred to as *valuing* or *pricing* a financial asset. The fundamental principle of financial asset valuation is that the value of an asset is equal to the present value of its expected cash flows. This principle applies regardless of the financial asset. Thus, the valuation of a financial asset involves the following three steps:

1. Estimate the expected cash flows.
2. Determine the appropriate interest rate or rates that should be used to discount the cash flows.
3. Calculate the present value of the expected cash flows found in step 1 using the interest rate or interest rates determined in step 2.

In this book, we introduce many different valuation models. Here, we discuss classic valuation models for stocks and bonds.

2.5.1 Valuation Models for Equities

Common stock can be considered a perpetual security—the owner of the shares has the right to receive a portion of cash flows from the company paid out as dividends. The value of one share should equal the present value of all the future cash flows (dividends) that the owner of the stock expects to receive from that share. Hence, to value one share, the investor must forecast future dividends. This approach to the common stock valuation is referred to as the *discounted cash flow (DCF) approach*, and the first dividend discount model dates back to Williams (1938).

The *theoretical* (also called *fair*) *value* of the stock price is

$$\frac{D_1}{(1+r)}+\frac{D_2}{(1+r)^2}+\frac{D_3}{(1+r)^3}+\cdots \tag{2.13}$$

where r is an appropriate discount rate. Note that this is an infinite sum.

Future dividends are uncertain, and whether a corporation pays dividends is decided by its board of directors. If a company does not pay dividends (e.g., it retains earnings), however, the same principle applies, as the retained earnings should eventually be paid as dividends. In that case, the fair value of the stock is defined as the present value of the DCF stream.

Later in this book, we will discuss optimal portfolio allocation. One of the inputs to such models is the expected return of a security. It is intuitive how an estimate of this return can be produced from cash flow discount models for the stock price—the expected return on a stock would be the value of r in the previous formula, which makes the value calculated with the formula equal to the observed market price of the stock. Since the formula for the price contains an infinite sum, additional assumptions must be made to compute the expected return. For example, one can attempt to forecast the price P_T of the stock at some future date T, in which case the formula becomes

$$P_0 = \frac{D_1}{(1+r)} + \frac{D_2}{(1+r)^2} + \frac{D_3}{(1+r)^3} + \cdots + \frac{P_T}{(1+r)^T}. \tag{2.14}$$

From here, the value of the expected return can be found by trial and error.

Alternatively, one can assume that future dividends will grow at a constant rate g. This model was developed by Gordon (1962) and is therefore often referred to as the *Gordon model*. We have

$$D_{t+1} = D_t \cdot (1+g) = D_1 \cdot (1+g)^{t-1}. \tag{2.15}$$

Therefore, the infinite sum in the dividend discount model becomes

$$D_1 \cdot \frac{1}{(1+r)} \cdot \left(1 + \frac{(1+g)^1}{(1+r)^1} + \frac{(1+g)^2}{(1+r)^2} + \cdots\right). \tag{2.16}$$

The infinite sum inside the parentheses can now be computed in closed form because it is a sum of an infinite geometric series of the kind

$$1 + q + q^2 + q^3 + \cdots$$

where q in this case is $(1+g)/(1+r)$, which equals

$$\frac{1}{1-q}$$

Therefore, the Gordon model results in a stock price of

$$\frac{D_1}{r-g} \tag{2.17}$$

Given the current market price of the stock and using the preceding formula, a value for the expected return r can be derived.

There are numerous other valuation models, and a complete review is beyond the scope of this book. It is important to keep in mind, however, that all the parameters that go into these models need to be estimated, and if the various quantities are defined by different accounting practices or forecasting models, they can lead to significantly different valuations.

2.5.2 Valuation Models for Fixed-Income Securities

The value of a bond is the discounted sum of its payments. In other words,

$$B_0 = \frac{C_1}{(1+r)} + \frac{C_2}{(1+r)^2} + \frac{C_3}{(1+r)^3} + \cdots + \frac{C_T}{(1+r)^T} \tag{2.18}$$

where C_t denotes the cash flow (coupons or coupon plus principal) paid at date t. While the concept is simple, the details of its implementation, including how to determine an

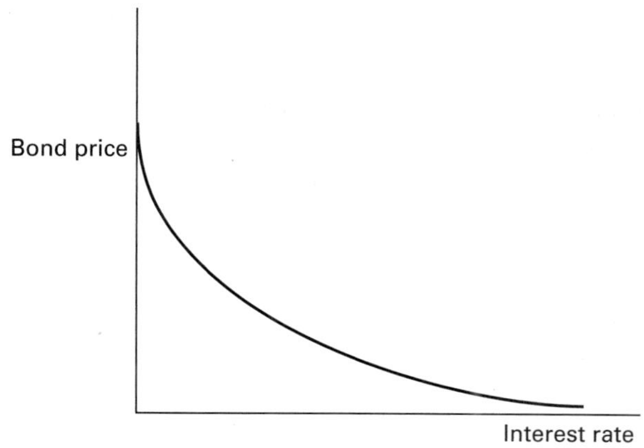

Exhibit 2.2
Relationship between the bond price and the discount rate.

appropriate discount rate, can lead to different valuations. The minimum interest rate r that the investor should require is the prevalent discount rate in the marketplace on a default-free cash flow. In the United States, U.S. Treasuries are considered the norm for default-free securities. This is one of the reasons why the Treasury market is closely watched.

Consider a bond with a \$100 principal, a coupon rate of 10% paid annually, and a term to maturity of three years. Assume a discount rate of 6%. Today's value of the bond is

$$\frac{10}{(1+0.06)}+\frac{10}{(1+0.06)^2}+\frac{110}{(1+0.06)^3}=\$110.69.$$ [9]

If a 12% annual discount rate was used, the bond value today would have been

$$\frac{10}{(1+0.12)}+\frac{10}{(1+0.12)^2}+\frac{110}{(1+0.12)^3}=\$95.20.$$

Note that the value of the bond is lower when the interest rate is higher. This is an important property of bond prices: when interest rates go up, bond prices generally decline. The opposite is true as well—when interest rates go down, bond prices generally increase. (See exhibit 2.2.) The relationship between bond prices and interest rates is nonlinear: the bond price is a *convex* function of interest rates.[10] You can observe this by

9. Most bonds traded in the United States.S. pay coupons semiannually. To value them, one uses the same formula but divides the annual coupon rate and the applicable discount rate by 2. For example, if the bond in this example paid a \$10 coupon semiannually with a term to maturity of three years, we would divide the interest rate of 6% by 2 (so it becomes 3%) and find the present value of six cash flows of \$5 (= \$10/2). The value of the bond would be

$$\frac{5}{(1+0.03)}+\frac{5}{(1+0.03)^2}+\frac{5}{(1+0.03)^3}+\frac{5}{(1+0.03)^4}+\frac{5}{(1+0.03)^5}+\frac{105}{(1+0.03)^6}=\$110.80.$$

Note that a semiannual interest rate of 3% is not equivalent to an annual rate of 6% because of the effects of compounding. However, the convention in the bond market is to quote annual interest rates that are double the semiannual interest rates, so this bond value calculation is technically correct.

10. Convex functions are discussed in more detail in chapter 6. See exhibit 6.3 in chapter 6 for a picture of a convex function.

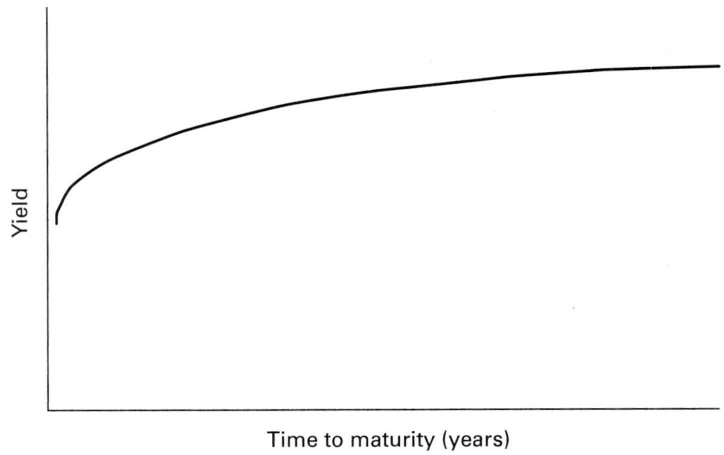

Exhibit 2.3
Upward-sloping yield curve.

computing the bond values for several values of the discount rate. The shape of the relationship between bond prices and interest rates is important for risk management purposes. We will discuss it in more detail in the context of bond portfolio management in chapter 14.

When one observes bond prices in the market, one can use the information about the bond and its market price to determine the interest rate that makes the present value of the stream of cash flows equal to the bond price. This implied interest rate is called *yield to maturity* (YTM), or simply *yield.* It is quoted on an annual basis. To find it, one would use an iterative trial-and-error procedure. In other words, different values for the yield will be tried until the computed present value of the bond cash flows equals the observed value.

Since the cash flows are every six months, the YTM found by solving the equation for the bond price is a semiannual YTM. This yield can be annualized by either doubling the semiannual yield or compounding the yield. The market convention is to annualize the semiannual yield by simply doubling its value. The YTM computed on the basis of this market convention is called the *bond-equivalent yield.* It is also referred to as a *yield on a bond-equivalent basis.*

Observed bond yields tend to be different depending on the time to maturity. The plot of bond yields in relation to the time to maturity is referred to as the *yield curve.* An example of a yield curve is given in exhibit 2.3. The usual shape of the yield curve is upward sloping; however, the curve can have different shapes depending on market conditions. The reason why an upward-sloping curve is considered normal is that investors are assumed to demand more yield for long-term investments than for short-term investments. Long-term investments are subject to more uncertainty. However, sometimes long-term bonds have lower yields than short-term bonds. In the latter case, we refer to the yield curve as an *inverted yield curve.* If the yields for all maturities were the same, of course, the curve would simply be a flat, horizontal line.

Knowledge of the yield curve is helpful because it allows us to position a particular bond with regard to other bonds in its class and compute the required yield for a bond. The *required yield* reflects the yield for financial instruments with comparable risk to a bond we are trying to price. Given the required yield, we can determine the bond's price by using the required yield as the interest rate r in the pricing formula shown earlier in this section.

In the previous bond value calculation examples, we assumed that the discount rate is the same for all cash flows. The discount rates are typically different depending on the length of time until the cash flow will be received. The U.S. Treasury rates, the relevant reference rates for default-free cash flows, are closely followed. To see how the value of the bond would be computed when the discount rates for the cash flows are different, consider again the example of the bond with \$100 principal, a coupon rate of 10% paid annually, and a term to maturity of three years. Assume that the discount rates for years 1, 2, and 3 are 6.00%, 6.80%, and 7.20%, respectively. Today's value of the bond is

$$\frac{10}{(1+0.06)}+\frac{10}{(1+0.0680)^2}+\frac{110}{(1+0.0720)^3}=\$108.55.$$

2.6 Important Concepts in Fixed Income

This section reviews important concepts in fixed income.

2.6.1 Spot Rates

The spot rate is the interest rate charged for money held from the present time until a prespecified time t. The convention is to quote spot rates as yearly rates, but the specific characteristics of the compounding (whether yearly, m time periods per year, or continuous) vary. The interest rates used in the section on valuation were all spot rates.

Sometimes spot rates are referred to as *zero rates* (short for *zero-coupon rates*) because they are in fact the return on a zero-coupon bond that is bought today and paid out a certain number of years in the future. Suppose that the 5-year Treasury spot (zero) rate with continuous compounding is quoted as 6% per annum. This means that if the price of a 5-year zero-coupon bond today is B_0 and the payout after five years is B_5, then the following holds:

$$B_5=B_0\cdot e^{0.06\cdot 5}.$$

In general, let s_t denote the spot rate for time period t.[11] Then, if B_t denotes the price of a zero-coupon bond with maturity t, we have

$$B_t=B_0\cdot e^{S_t\cdot t}.$$

2.6.2 The Term Structure of Interest Rates

The *term structure of interest rates* defines the relationship between time and interest rates, with spot rates as the underlying interest rates. It is usually presented as a graph like the yield curve in exhibit 2.3. The term structure in interest rates is in fact a yield curve, but its meaning is a bit more academic, as it focuses on pure interest rates for default-free securities rather than yields. Knowledge of the term structure is crucial for pricing and trading purposes.

11. As mentioned earlier, we assume that s_t is quoted as a yearly rate.

The obvious way to find the term structure of interest rates is to compute the interest rates implied in the prices of a series of zero-coupon default-free bonds. However, it is difficult to find zero-coupon bonds that span all maturities, especially long maturities.[12] This does not diminish the importance or usefulness of constructing the term structure. The term structure can be constructed from coupon-bearing bonds via a procedure called *bootstrapping*.[13] The idea is to use several coupon-bearing bonds, determine the spot rates implied by the bonds with the shortest maturity, use that knowledge to compute the spot rate implied by the bond with the next-shortest maturity, and proceed in this manner until the whole term structure is constructed. The same method is used to construct other spot rate curves.[14] There will obviously be gaps in the term structure because we cannot necessarily determine every point on the curve from market prices. Interpolation and polynomial approximations are used to complete the term structure, given a few points.

Given a term structure of interest rates, discount factors for securities of different maturities can be determined. For example, if a coupon bond pays coupons six months from now and a year from now, we can read the interest rates corresponding to six months and one year from the term structure and use those rates to discount the cash flows from the bond's coupons when valuing the bond.

2.6.3 Forward Rates

Forward rates can be thought of as the current market consensus of future spot rates: they are interest rates for money to be invested between two dates in the future but under terms agreed upon today. The concept of forward rates is very useful for pricing and investment purposes. Similar to spot rates, forward rates are quoted as yearly rates.

Forward rates can be derived from the term structure of interest rates. Examples of forward rates that can be extrapolated from the Treasury yield curve include

- 6-month forward rate six months from now
- 6-month forward rate three years from now
- 1-year forward rate one year from now
- 3-year forward rate two years from now
- 5-year forward rate three years from now

We will use the following notation to denote forward rates: ${}_tf_m$, where the subscript t indicates a t-year interest rate and the subscript m indicates that the t years begin m years from now. For example, ${}_{0.5}f_3$ is the 6-month forward rate three years from now, and ${}_3f_2$ is the 3-year forward rate two years from now. When $m=0$, the forward rate is the same as the spot rate—that is, ${}_tf_0 = s_t$.

12. The 6-month and 1-year Treasury securities (called *Treasury bills*) are issued as zero-coupon instruments. The longest maturity for Treasury bonds is 30 years.

13. "Bootstrapping" can be a confusing term because it has completely different meanings in finance and simulation. We will discuss the statistical concept of bootstrapping in section 3.11.3.

14. See chapter 6 in Fabozzi (2007) for an illustration of the bootstrapping procedure.

How do we compute forward rates? Consider, for example, an investor with a 1-year investment horizon that is faced with the following two choices:

- Buy a 2-year Treasury note.
- Buy a 1-year Treasury bill and, when it matures in one year, buy another 1-year Treasury bill.

The investor would be indifferent between the two choices only if the return on the two is the same. If one of them offers a better return than the other, all investors would prefer that option, which will drive up its price and hence reduce its return until it equals the return on the option that was less desirable at the beginning.[15] The value of an investment of $\$C$ with the first option after two years will be

$$C \cdot (1+s_2)^2,$$

where s_2 is the 2-year spot rate. The return on a 2-year investment with the second option will be

$$C \cdot (1+s_1) \cdot (1+{}_1f_1),$$

where s_1 is the 1-year spot rate, and ${}_1f_1$ is the implied rate in a 1-year Treasury bill purchased one year from now—that is, the 1-year forward 1 year from now. Since the returns on the two investments must be equal, we get

$$(1+s_2)^2 = (1+s_1) \cdot (1+{}_1f_1),$$

which allows us to compute the forward rate ${}_1f_1$ as

$${}_1f_1 = \frac{(1+s_2)^2}{(1+s_1)} - 1.$$

For m time periods ahead, we have

$${}_1f_m = \frac{(1+s_{m+1})^{m+1}}{(1+s_m)^m} - 1.$$

In general, if we are given the term structure, and hence have information about spot rates s_t and s_T for two times t and T, then we can estimate the forward rate between t and T, ${}_{(T-t)}f_t$, as

$${}_{(T-t)}f_t = \frac{(1+s_T)}{(1+s_t)} - 1.$$

2.6.4 Credit Spreads

When cash flows are not default-free, the Treasury rates cannot be used to discount them for valuation purposes. This is because, technically, to compensate for the risk they are

15. This is an example of a *no-arbitrage argument*: if two investments have the same cash flows and the same risk, they should have the same return; otherwise, there would be an arbitrage opportunity. We will discuss the concept of arbitrage in chapter 17.

taking, investors should require a higher yield from default-risky than from default-free securities. For pricing default-risky securities, a *term structure of credit spreads* is often used, where a credit spread is defined as the difference between the yield on a default-free bond and a default-risky bond with the same cash flow characteristics. Dealer firms typically estimate a term structure for credit spreads for each credit rating and market sector. Generally, the credit spread increases with time to maturity. In addition, the shape of the term structure is not the same for all credit ratings. Typically, the lower the credit rating, the steeper the term structure of credit spreads. This is because the risk of default is higher when the default-risky security is a longer-term investment.

2.6.5 Duration

The value of a bond investment is sensitive to changes in interest rates. This is because if the discount rates used to evaluate the different cash flows from the bond change, so will its price. All other things being equal, bonds with long maturities are more sensitive to changes in interest rates than bonds with short maturities. However, maturity alone is not sufficient for measuring the degree of interest rate sensitivity. Intuitively, the higher the bond's coupon rate, the more dependent the bond's total dollar return will be on reinvesting the coupon payments to produce the YTM at the time of purchase. Hence, a change in interest rates during the bond's life can substantially impact the total return.

Duration is a measure of the sensitivity of a bond's price with respect to changes in interest rates, which takes into consideration the issues previously discussed. In mathematical terms, it is the derivative of the bond price with respect to interest rates; that is, it measures *first-order sensitivity*. As exhibit 2.2 showed, the relationship between the bond price and interest rates is in fact nonlinear, so the duration would not explain the exact change in bond prices for a given change in interest rates. Convexity, which we will describe in section 2.6.6, complements duration to provide a more accurate description of the sensitivity. It is important to note, however, that both duration and convexity describe the sensitivity of bond prices to interest rates when there is a *parallel shift in the yield curve*; that is, when the rates for all maturities move up or down simultaneously and by the same number of basis points. This clearly places a limitation on the usefulness of duration and convexity as measures of bond interest rate risk. Nevertheless, duration and convexity are very popular, fundamental tools in fixed-income analysis.

Even though defining duration as the first derivative of the price/yield function is mathematically correct, it is not really used in practice because it is difficult to explain to clients what the relevance of such a mathematical concept is to measuring actual investment risk. Instead, duration is typically explained as the approximate price sensitivity of a bond to a 100-basis-point change in rates. Thus, a bond with a duration of 5 will change by approximately 5% for a 100-basis-point change in interest rates (i.e., if the yield required for this bond changes by approximately 100 basis points). For a 50-basis-point change in interest rates, the bond's price will change by approximately 2.5%; for a 25-basis point change in interest rates, the price change would be 1.25%, and so on.

Let us now define duration more rigorously. The exact formulation is

$$\frac{\text{Price if yields decline} - \text{Price if yields rise}}{2 \cdot (\text{Initial price}) \cdot (\text{Change in yield in decimal})}. \tag{2.19}$$

Let D denote duration, B_0 denote the initial price, Δy denote the change in yield, B_- denote the price if yields decrease by Δy, and B_+ denote the price if yields increase by Δy. We have

$$D = \frac{B_- - B_+}{2 \cdot B_0 \cdot \Delta y}. \tag{2.20}$$

It is important to understand that the two values in the numerator of equation (2.20) B_- and B_+, are the estimated values obtained from a valuation model if interest rates change. Consequently, the duration measure is only as good as the valuation model employed to obtain these estimated values. The more difficult it is to estimate the value of a bond, the less confidence a portfolio manager may have in the estimated duration. We will see in chapter 15 that the duration of a portfolio is nothing more than a market-weighted average of the duration of the bonds comprising the portfolio. Hence, a portfolio's duration is sensitive to the estimated duration of the individual bonds.

To illustrate the duration calculation, consider the following bond: a 6% coupon 5-year bond trading at par value to yield 6%. The current price is \$100. Suppose that the yield is changed by 50 basis points. Thus, $\Delta y = 0.005$ and $B_0 = \$100$. This is a simple bond to value if interest rates or yield is changed. If the yield is decreased to 5.5%, the value of this bond would be \$102.1600. If the yield is increased to 6.5%, the value of this bond would be \$97.8944. Therefore, $B_- = \$102.1600$ and $B_+ = \$97.8944$. Substituting these values into equation (2.20), we obtain

$$D = \frac{102.1600 - 97.8944}{2 \cdot (100) \cdot (0.005)} = 4.27.$$

Dollar Duration In estimating the sensitivity of the price of a bond to changes in interest rates, we looked at the percentage price change. However, for two bonds with the same duration but trading at different prices, the dollar price change will not be the same. To see this, suppose that we have two bonds, A and B, that both have durations of 5. Suppose further that the current prices of A and B are \$100 and \$90, respectively. A 100-basis-point change for both bonds will change the price by approximately 5%. This means a price change of \$5 (5% times \$100) for A, and a price change of \$4.5 (5% times \$90) for B.

The dollar price change of a bond can be measured by multiplying duration by the full dollar price and the number of basis points (in decimal form) and is called the *dollar duration*. That is,

$$\text{Dollar duration} = (\text{Duration}) \cdot (\text{Dollar price}) \cdot (\text{Change in rates in decimal}).$$

The dollar duration for a 100-basis-point change in rates is

$$\text{Dollar duration} = (\text{Duration}) \cdot (\text{Dollar price}) \cdot 0.1.$$

So, for bonds A and B, the dollar duration for a 100-basis-point change in rates is as follows:

$$\text{For bond A: Dollar duration} = 5 \cdot \$100 \cdot 0.01 = \$5.0$$
$$\text{For bond B: Dollar duration} = 5 \cdot \$90 \cdot 0.01 = \$4.5$$

Knowing the dollar duration allows a portfolio manager to neutralize the risk of the bond position. For example, consider a position in bond B. If a trader wants to eliminate the interest rate risk exposure of this bond,[16] the trader will look for a position in one or more other financial instruments, such as an interest rate derivative,[17] whose value will change in the opposite direction to bond B's price by an amount equal to $4.50. So if the trader has a long position in B, the position will decline in value by $4.50 for a 100-basis-point increase in interest rates. To eliminate this risk exposure, the trader can take a position in another financial instrument whose value increases by $4.50 if interest rates increase by 100 basis points.

The dollar duration can also be computed without knowing a bond's duration. This is done by simply looking at the average price change for a bond when interest rates are increased and decreased by the same number of basis points.

Modified Duration, Macaulay Duration, and Effective Duration A popular form of duration that is used by practitioners is *modified duration,* the approximate percentage change in a bond's price for a 100-basis-point change in interest rates if the bond's cash flows do not change when interest rates change. What this means is that in calculating the values used in the numerator of equation (2.20), the cash flows used to calculate the current price are assumed. Therefore, the change in the bond's value when interest rates change by a small number of basis points is due solely to discounting at the new yield level.

Modified duration is related to another measure commonly cited in the bond market: *Macaulay duration*. The formula for this measure, first used by Frederick Macaulay in 1938, is rarely used in practice, so it will not be produced here. For a bond that pays coupon interest semiannually, modified duration is related to Macaulay duration as follows:

$$\text{Modified duration} = \text{Macaulay duration}/(1 + \text{yield}/2), \tag{2.21}$$

where yield is the bond's YTM in decimal form. Practically, there is very little difference in the computed values for modified duration and Macaulay duration.

The assumption that the cash flows will not change when interest rates change makes sense for bonds because the issuer's payments are not altered when interest rates change. This is not the case for bonds with embedded options, MBSs, and certain types of ABSs. A change in interest rates may alter the expected cash flows for these securities.[18]

For such bonds, specific valuation models consider how changes in interest rates will affect cash flows. When the values used in the numerator of the equation for duration are obtained from a valuation model that considers both the discounting at different interest rates and how the cash flows can change, the resulting duration is referred to as *effective duration* or *option-adjusted duration.*

Spread Duration for Fixed-Rate Bonds Duration is a measure of the change in the value of a bond when rates change. The interest rate that is assumed to shift is the Treasury rate. However, for non-Treasury securities, the yield equals the Treasury yield plus a

16. A strategy that reduces or eliminates risk is called *hedging.* We will discuss hedging in more detail in section 17.2.2.

17. Interest rate derivatives are discussed in chapters 17, 18, and 20.

18. Such securities are discussed in chapter 18.

spread to the Treasury yield curve. The price of a bond exposed to credit risk can change, even though Treasury yields are unchanged because the spread required by the market changes. A measure of how a non-Treasury issue's price will change if the spread sought by the market changes is called *spread duration* and is a measure of credit spread risk, described earlier in this chapter. For example, a spread duration of 2.2 for a security means that if the Treasury rate is unchanged but spreads change by 100 basis points, the security's price will change by approximately 2.2%.

2.6.6 Convexity

The duration measure indicates that regardless of whether interest rates increase or decrease, the approximate percentage price change is the same. However, while for small changes in yield the percentage price change will be the same for an increase or decrease in yield, this is not true for large changes in yield. This suggests that duration is only a good approximation of the percentage price change for a small change in yield.

The reason for this is that duration is in fact a first approximation for a small change in yield. The approximation can be improved by using a *second-order approximation*. This approximation is referred to as *convexity*. The use of this term in the industry is unfortunate since the term "convexity" is also used to describe the shape or curvature of the price/yield relationship. The convexity measure of a security can be used to approximate the change in price that is not explained by duration.

Convexity Measure The convexity measure of a bond can be approximated using the following formula:

$$\text{Convexity measure} = \frac{B_+ + B_- - 2 \cdot B_0}{2 \cdot B_0 \cdot (\Delta y)^2} \tag{2.21}$$

where the notation is the same as used earlier to define duration.

For a hypothetical 6%, 25-year bond selling to yield 9%, we can compute that for a 10-basis-point change in yield ($\Delta y = 0.001$), we have $B_0 = 70.3570$, $B_- = 71.1105$, and $B_+ = 69.6164$. Substituting these values into the convexity measure given by equation (2.21), we obtain

$$\text{Convexity measure} = \frac{69.6164 + 71.1105 - 2 \cdot 70.3570}{2 \cdot 70.3570 \cdot (0.001)^2} = 91.67$$

We will see how to use this convexity measure shortly. Before doing so, however, there are three points that should be noted. First, there is no simple interpretation of the convexity measure, as there is for duration.[19] Second, it is more common for market participants to refer to the value computed in equation (2.21) as the "convexity of a bond" rather than the "convexity measure of a bond." Finally, the convexity measures reported by dealers and vendors will differ. The reason is that the convexity value obtained from equation (2.21) will be scaled for the reason explained later in this chapter.

19. This intuition is mostly mathematical—convexity represents a quadratic approximation to the relative curvature at a given point of the price-yield curve, whereas duration represents a linear approximation. In effect, we are constructing the Taylor series of the bond price around a specific point of the price-yield curve and considering the first two terms in the approximation.

Convexity Adjustment to Percentage Price Change Given the convexity measure, the approximate percentage price change adjustment due to the bond's convexity (i.e., the percentage price change not explained by duration) is

$$\text{Convexity adjustment to percentage price change} = \text{Convexity measure} \cdot (\Delta y)^2 \cdot 100. \quad (2.22)$$

For example, for the 6%, 25-year bond selling to yield 9%, the convexity adjustment to the percentage price change based on duration if the yield increases from 9% to 11% is

$$91.67 \cdot (0.02)^2 \cdot 100 = 3.67.$$

If the yield decreased from 9% to 7%, the convexity adjustment to the approximate percentage price change based on duration would also be 3.67%.

The approximate percentage price change based on duration and the convexity adjustment is found by adding the two estimates. So, for example, if yields changed from 9% to 11%, the estimated percentage price change would be as follows:

$$\begin{aligned} \text{Estimated change approximated by duration} &= -21.20\% \\ \text{Convexity adjustment} &= +\ 3.66\% \\ \text{Total estimated percentage price change} &= -17.54\% \end{aligned}$$

The actual percentage price change can be computed to be –18.03%. Hence, the approximation has improved compared to using only duration.

For a decrease of 200 basis points, from 9% to 7%, the approximate percentage price change would be as follows:

$$\begin{aligned} \text{Estimated change approximated by duration} &= +21.20\% \\ \text{Convexity adjustment} &= +\ 3.66\% \\ \text{Total estimated percentage price change} &= +24.86\% \end{aligned}$$

The actual percentage price change can be computed to be 25.46%. Once again, we see that duration combined with the convexity adjustment does a good job of estimating the sensitivity of a bond's price change to large changes in yield.

The bond prices used to calculate the convexity measure can be obtained by assuming either that when the yield changes, the expected cash flows do not change, or that they do change. In the former case, the resulting convexity is referred to as *standard convexity*. (Actually, in the industry, convexity is not qualified by the adjective "standard.") *Effective convexity*, in contrast, assumes that the cash flows do change when yields change. The distinction is the same as the one made for duration.

As with duration, for bonds with embedded options, there can be a large difference between the calculated standard convexity and effective convexity. In fact, for all option-free bonds, either convexity measure will have a positive value. For bonds with embedded options, the calculated effective convexity can be negative when the calculated modified convexity is positive.

2.6.7 Key Rate Duration

As explained earlier, duration assumes that when interest rates change, all the yields on the yield curve change by the same amount. This is a problem when using duration for a portfolio that will typically have bonds with different maturities. Consequently, it is necessary to be able to measure the exposure of a bond or bond portfolio to shifts in the yield curve. There have been several approaches to measuring yield curve risk. The most used measure is *key rate duration,* introduced by Thomas Ho.[20]

The basic principle of key rate duration is to change the yield for a particular maturity of the yield curve and determine the sensitivity of either an individual bond or a portfolio to that change holding all other yields constant. The sensitivity of the change in the bond's value or portfolio's value to a particular change in yield is called *rate duration.* There is a rate duration for every point on the yield curve. Consequently, there is not just one rate duration. Rather, there is a set of durations representing each maturity on the yield curve. Note that the total change in the value of a bond or a portfolio if all rates change by the same number of basis points is in fact the standard duration of a bond or portfolio.

Ho's approach focuses on 11 key maturities of the Treasury yield curve. These rate durations are called *key rate durations.* The specific maturities on the spot rate curve for which a key rate duration is measured are 3 months, 1 year, 2 years, 3 years, 5 years, 7 years, 10 years, 15 years, 20 years, 25 years, and 30 years. Changes in rates between any two key rates are calculated using a linear approximation.

A key rate duration for a particular portfolio maturity should be interpreted as follows: Holding the yield for all other maturities constant, the key rate duration is the approximate percentage change in the value of a portfolio (or bond) for a 100-basis-point change in the yield for the maturity whose rate has been changed. Thus, a key rate duration is quantified by changing the yield of the maturity of interest and determining how the value or price changes. In fact, the duration formula given by equation (2.20) is used. The prices denoted by B_- and B_+ in the equation are the prices in the case of a bond, and the portfolio values in the case of a bond portfolio found by holding all other interest rates constant and changing the yield for the maturity whose key rate duration is sought.

The concept of key rate durations is very important when evaluating portfolio risk. We will discuss this concept again in chapter 15.

2.6.8 Total Return

An investor who purchases a bond can expect to receive a dollar return from one or more of these three sources:

- The periodic coupon interest payments made by the issuer
- Income from reinvestment of the periodic interest payments (the *interest-on-interest component*)
- Any capital gain (or capital loss—negative dollar return) when the bond matures or is sold

Any measure of a bond's potential yield should take into consideration each of these three potential sources of return. The YTM takes into account coupon interest and any capital gain (or loss). It also considers the interest-on-interest component. Implicit in the YTM computation, however, is the assumption that the coupon payments can be reinvested at the computed YTM. Reinvesting the coupon interest payments at a rate of interest less than the

20. See, for example, Ho (1999).

YTM, for example, will produce a lower yield than the YTM. This risk is called *reinvestment risk*.

Rather than assuming that the coupon interest payments are reinvested at the YTM, an investor can make an explicit assumption about the reinvestment rate based on expectations. The *total return* is a measure of yield that incorporates an explicit assumption about the reinvestment rate.

The total return measure allows a portfolio manager to project the performance of a bond based on the planned investment horizon and expectations concerning reinvestment rates and future market yields. This permits the portfolio manager to evaluate which of several potential bonds considered for acquisition will perform the best over the planned investment horizon. As we have emphasized, this cannot be done using the YTM. Using total return to assess performance over some investment horizon is called *horizon analysis*. When a total return is calculated over an investment horizon, it is referred to as a *horizon return*. The terms "horizon return" and "total return" are typically used interchangeably.

An often-cited objection to the total return measure is that it requires the portfolio manager to formulate assumptions about reinvestment rates and future yields, as well as to think in terms of an investment horizon. Unfortunately, some portfolio managers find comfort in measures such as the YTM simply because they do not require incorporating any particular expectations. The horizon analysis framework, however, enables the portfolio manager to analyze the performance of a bond under different interest rate scenarios for reinvestment rates and future market yields. This procedure is referred to as *scenario analysis*. Only by investigating multiple scenarios can the portfolio manager see how sensitive the bond's performance will be to each scenario.[21]

To illustrate scenario analysis, consider a portfolio manager who is deciding on whether to purchase a 20-year, 9% option-free bond selling at $109.896 per $100 of par value. The YTM for this bond is 8%. Assume also that the portfolio manager's investment horizon is three years. The portfolio manager believes that the reinvestment rate can vary from 3% to 6.5% and the projected yield at the end of the investment horizon can vary from 5% to 12%. Exhibit 2.4(A) shows different projected yields at the end of the three-year investment horizon, and exhibit 2.4(B) gives the corresponding price for the bond at the end of the investment horizon. For example, consider the 10% projected yield at the end of the investment horizon. The price of a 17-year option-free bond with a coupon rate of 9% would be $91.9035. Exhibit 2.4(C) shows the total future dollars at the end of three years under various scenarios for the reinvestment rate and the projected yield at the end of the investment horizon. For example, with a reinvestment rate of 4% and a projected yield at the end of the investment horizon of 10%, the total future dollars would be $120.290. Exhibit 2.4(D) shows the total return on an effective rate basis for each scenario.

Exhibit 2.4 is useful for a portfolio manager for assessing the potential outcome of a bond (or portfolio) over the investment horizon. For example, the portfolio manager knows that the maximum and minimum total returns for the scenarios shown in the table will be 16.72% and –1.05%, respectively, and also knows the scenarios under which each will be realized.

21. As we will see later, a more advanced form of scenario analysis is simulation, which will be the focus of this book.

Bond A: 9% coupon, 20-year option-free bond
Price: $109.896
Yield to maturity: 8%
Investment horizon: Three years

A. Projected Yield at End of Investment Horizon

5.00%	6.00%	7.00%	8.00%	9.00%	10.00%	11.00%	12.00%

B. Projected Sale Price at End of Investment Horizon

145.448	131.698	119.701	109.206	100.000	91.9035	84.763	78.4478

C. Total Future Dollars

Reinv. Rate	**5.00%**	**6.00%**	**7.00%**	**8.00%**	**9.00%**	**10.00%**	**11.00%**	**12.00%**
3.0%	173.481	159.731	147.734	137.239	128.033	119.937	112.796	106.481
3.5%	173.657	159.907	147.910	137.415	128.209	120.113	112.972	106.657
4.0%	173.834	160.084	148.087	137.592	128.387	120.290	113.150	106.834
4.5%	174.013	160.263	148.266	137.771	128.565	120.469	113.328	107.013
5.0%	174.192	160.443	148.445	137.950	128.745	120.648	113.508	107.193
5.5%	174.373	160.623	148.626	138.131	128.926	120.829	113.689	107.374
6.0%	174.555	160.806	148.809	138.313	129.108	121.011	113.871	107.556
6.5%	174.739	160.989	148.992	138.497	129.291	121.195	114.054	107.739

D. Total Return (Effective Rate)

Reinv. Rate	**5.00%**	**6.00%**	**7.00%**	**8.00%**	**9.00%**	**10.00%**	**11.00%**	**12.00%**
3.0%	16.44	13.28	10.37	7.69	5.22	2.96	0.87	−1.05
3.5%	16.48	13.32	10.41	7.73	5.27	3.01	0.92	−0.99
4.0%	16.52	13.36	10.45	7.78	5.32	3.06	0.98	−0.94
4.5%	16.56	13.40	10.50	7.83	5.37	3.11	1.03	−0.88
5.0%	16.60	13.44	10.54	7.87	5.42	3.16	1.08	−0.83
5.5%	16.64	13.49	10.59	7.92	5.47	3.21	1.14	−0.77
6.0%	16.68	13.53	10.63	7.97	5.52	3.26	1.19	−0.72
6.5%	16.72	13.57	10.68	8.02	5.57	3.32	1.25	−0.66

Exhibit 2.4
Scenario analysis.

Another way to use scenario analysis is to assess the likelihood that an investment objective will not be realized. For example, suppose that a life insurance company has issued a three-year guaranteed investment contract in which it has guaranteed an effective annual interest rate of 7.02%. Suppose that the premiums are invested in the bond analyzed in exhibit 2.4, and that the portfolio manager's investment objective is a minimum return of 7.02% plus a spread of 100 basis points. The spread represents the profit that the life insurance company seeks to earn. Thus, the minimum return is 8.02%. From exhibit 2.4, the portfolio manager can see that if the yield at the end of the investment horizon is 8% or greater, and if the reinvestment rate over the three-year investment horizon is less than 6.5%, a total return on an effective rate basis will be less than the investment objective of a minimum return of 8.02%.

Summary

- Compound interest involves earning interest on the interest from an investment.
- The present value of a future cash flow is the amount of money that must be invested today to generate the future cash flow.
- The discount factor is the number by which we need to multiply the future cash flow to obtain its present value.
- In portfolio management, the most important decision made is the allocation of funds among asset classes.
- Asset classes are classified as traditional and alternative asset classes.
- Traditional asset classes include publicly traded stocks and bonds, along with cash.
- All other asset classes are referred to as "nontraditional asset classes" or "alternative asset classes."
- Alternative asset classes include real estate, commodities, private equity and debt, and hedge funds.
- A benchmark index is available for all asset classes, but in practice, exchange-traded funds (ETFs), if available for an asset class, are used as a proxy for investing in asset classes.
- Collective investment vehicles are pooled funds from investors, which are then invested in financial instruments.
- The value of collective investment vehicles is the net asset value (NAV), which is equal to the market value of the portfolio minus the liabilities divided by the number of shares outstanding.
- Collective investment vehicles include open-end funds (also called "mutual funds"), closed-end funds, ETFs, hedge funds, and real estate investment trusts.
- Borrowing funds to purchase securities is known as a "leveraged strategy." Two borrowing arrangements used by investors are margin buying and repurchase agreements.
- When an investor takes a position in the market by buying a security, the investor is said to be in a "long position" in the security. When an investor borrows a security from a broker and sells it, with the understanding that the security must be returned later, the investor is said to be taking a "short position" in the security (or "selling it short").
- The simple rate of return (usually called just "return") on an asset is the percentage difference between the amount received from investing in the asset and the amount originally invested in the asset.
- The log return is computed as the natural logarithm of 1 plus the return (called the "gross return"). When using log returns, the implicit assumption is that returns are accumulated continuously.

- Investors in fixed-income securities are exposed to credit risk, which includes default risk, credit spread risk, and downgrade risk.
- Default risk is gauged by credit ratings assigned by rating agencies.
- Valuation is the process of determining the fair value of a financial asset. The fundamental principle of financial asset valuation is that its value is equal to the present value of its expected cash flows.
- The implied interest rate that makes the present value of a stream of cash flows from a bond equal to the bond's market price is the yield to maturity (YTM), or simply the yield.
- The spot rate (also called the "zero rate") is the interest rate charged for money held from the present time until a prespecified time t.
- The term structure defines the relationship between time and interest rates, with spot rates as the underlying interest rates.
- Forward rates are the current market consensus of future spot rates; they are interest rates for money to be invested between two dates in the future, but under terms agreed upon today.
- For pricing default-risky securities, a term structure of credit spreads is often used, where a credit spread is defined as the difference between the yield on a default-free bond and a default-risky bond with the same cash flow characteristics.
- Duration is a measure of the sensitivity of a bond's price with respect to changes in interest rates. It is a first-order approximation to the change in bond price when interest rates change by a fixed amount.
- Convexity is a second-order approximation to the change in bond price when interest rates change by a fixed amount. It allows for estimating the curvature of the relationship between changes in bond price and changes in interest rates more accurately.
- Spread duration is a measure of the exposure of a fixed-income security or portfolio to credit spread risk.
- Total return is a more complete measure of a bond's potential return than YTM. It takes into consideration the periodic coupon interest payments made by the issuer, the income from reinvestment of the periodic interest payments (the interest-on-interest component) without assuming that they will be reinvested at the same rate, and any capital gain (or capital loss—negative dollar return) when the bond matures or is sold.

3

Random Variables and Probability Distributions

To deal with risk, we need a way to model the uncertainty in the world around us. Mathematically, information about uncertainty can be summarized in probability distributions. This chapter reviews the concepts of random variables and probability distributions. We focus on probability distributions and summary measures for the most widely used probability distributions in financial applications.

3.1 What Is a Probability Distribution?

A natural way to think of uncertainty is in terms of scenarios. *Scenarios* represent the possible events that could happen. For example, the value of a stock that you own but are contemplating selling may go up (one scenario) or down (another scenario) one year from now. To these scenarios, you could assign *probabilities*, which reflect your estimate of the likelihood that the scenarios will occur. For example, you estimate that the probability that the stock's value will go up is 0.30 (30%), and the probability that it will go down is 0.70 (70%).

The information contained in the scenarios and the probabilities can be summarized in probability distributions. Basically, *probability distributions* are listings of the possible uncertain values and their probabilities. This information is often presented in graphs—we will see examples of this later in this chapter. We will also see that to analyze and summarize insights from probability distributions, we need to have numbers (not categories) on the horizontal axis of the graph, popularly referred to as the "x-axis." Thus, it is not a good idea to create a probability distribution for which the random event mentioned in the previous paragraph—that the stock's value will go up or down—is plotted because "up" and "down" are not numerical quantities.

To create a probability distribution, we need to assign numerical values to the uncertain outcomes. Let us think of the outcome "up" as 1, and of the outcome "down" as 0. Such *mapping* of events to numerical values is called a *random variable.* The term is a misnomer, though, because random variables are neither random nor variables. They are numerical representations, or, equivalently, function assignments, of the outcomes of uncertain events to numbers. Probability distributions are plots of distributions of random variables and do not necessarily map one-to-one to a list of outcomes.

Note that the two probabilities of the two scenarios for the movement of the value of the stock add up to 1 (100%). This is because we assume that only one of the two events can happen (so, for example, the stock's value cannot stay the same), which means that the two scenarios exhaust the possible states of the world and thus should add up to 100%. This is a general feature of probability distributions—the probabilities of all the values of the random variable in the probability distribution must add up to 1, or 100%. We should not specify a probability distribution in which they do not add up to 1. For example, if we wanted to add a third scenario—say, that the value of the stock stays the same—then we would need to reassign probabilities to the three scenarios in such a way that the total sum of the probabilities remains 1.

3.2 Bernoulli Probability Distribution and Probability Mass Functions

Exhibit 3.1 shows the probability distribution described in the previous section, in which there are two scenarios. It is in fact a special kind of distribution, and it is used so often that it has a name—the *Bernoulli distribution.* The random variable that follows this distribution (the random variable takes values 0 and 1) is called the *Bernoulli random variable.* Let us call this random variable $\tilde{X}$. Notice that a tilde sign (~) is placed over the X, which is used to denote uncertainty and randomness.

We can describe one possible distribution of the Bernoulli type as

$$P(\tilde{X}=0)=0.70,$$

$$P(\tilde{X}=1)=0.30.$$

We read a mathematical statement of this kind as "the probability that the random variable $\tilde{X}$ takes a value of 0 is 0.70, or 70%." This listing of values of the random variable and the associated probabilities is called the *probability mass function* (PMF). It only exists for random variables that take *discrete* (countably many) values; that is, that have discrete probability distributions. More generally, given a probability p, the PMF for a Bernoulli distribution is

$$p(\tilde{X}=x)=\begin{cases} 1-p, & x=0 \\ p, & x=1 \end{cases}.$$

We used x inside the parentheses to signal that this is the *realization* of the random variable $\tilde{X}$, not the random variable $\tilde{X}$ itself (which is a function); and x is a specific value that $\tilde{X}$ takes.

The graph in exhibit 3.1 corresponds to the preceding probability listing as follows: there is a bar at each of the values that the random variable can take (0 and 1), and the height of the bar equals the probability that the specific value for the random variable occurs. The heights of all bars in the graph add up to 1.

3.3 Binomial Probability Distribution and Discrete Distributions

Now suppose that you would like to model whether the value of the stock will be up or down in three years. Every year, it can go up with probability 0.30 and down with probability 0.70. Let the specific realizations of this Bernoulli random variable for each of the

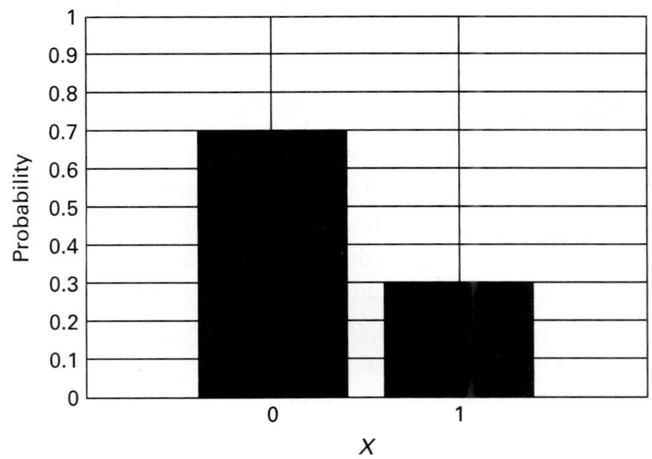

Exhibit 3.1
Bernoulli distribution with $p = 0.3$.

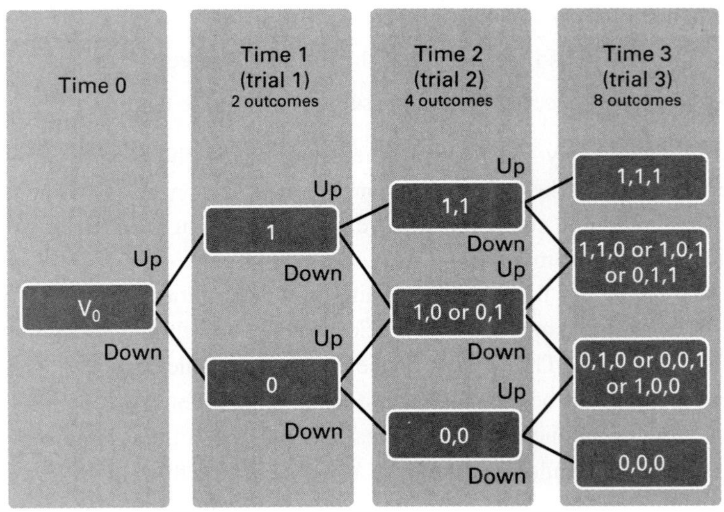

Exhibit 3.2
Movement of stock's value over three years: 1 = "success" (stock's value goes up). At the end of three years, we can have three successes in a row, two successes out of three, one success out of three, or no successes. The (0,1) combinations in the tree show the order of the successes or the failures up to that point in time.

three years be X_1, X_2, and X_3.[1] We can visualize the movement of the stock value from the tree drawn in exhibit 3.2. (Keep this picture in mind, as variations of it will appear again and again in financial instrument pricing applications.) For example, when $X_1 = 1$, $X_2 = 1$, and $X_3 = 1$, the movement in all three years is up and the stock's value will be at its highest.

1. The notation X_i, a capital letter corresponding to the name of the random variable and followed by an index, is a standard statistics notation to denote the ith observation in a sample of observations drawn from the distribution of the random variable $\tilde{X}$.

Since you would like to sell the stock for as much money as you can, let us call the event of the value of the stock going up in any particular year a "success." Assume that the success in one year is independent of the success in another year and let us count the number of successes out of the three possible times. This is going to be an uncertain quantity. The probability distribution of the number of successes in a prefixed number of trials is called the *binomial* distribution. In our example, the number of trials is 3 because, in each of the three years, there is a chance that the trial will be a success (the stock's value will go up) or a failure (the stock's value will go down). Note that the Bernoulli distribution is, in fact, a special case of the binomial distribution in which the number of trials is 1. The binomial distribution is very important and widely used in various applications—from statistical analysis of polling results to modeling prices of financial securities and evaluating the economic prospects of a capital budgeting project.

To be mathematically specific, the binomial distribution can be used when the following four conditions are satisfied:

1. The number of trials is fixed in advance.
2. There can be only two outcomes (success and failure).
3. Success in each trial is independent of the result of the previous trial.
4. The probability of success remains the same from trial to trial.

Perhaps the easiest way to envision whether applying the binomial distribution is appropriate is to think of whether the situation under evaluation is equivalent to a sequence of coin flips with the same coin, in which we are interested in the probability that we get a given number (x) of tails in n flips.

Suppose that we would like to plot the binomial distribution of the random variable describing the price movements of the stock over the next three years. What would be the values on the x-axis? The values for the random variable can be 0, 1, 2, or 3—the number of successes can be either 0 (the stock's value went down every year), 1 (the stock's value went up in one of the three years, but down in the remaining two), and so on. We will denote the random variable by $\tilde{X}$, but note that this is not the same random variable as the random variable in section 3.2. To create the listing of probabilities, we compute

$$
\begin{aligned}
P(\tilde{X}=0) &= (0.70)\cdot(0.70)\cdot(0.70) = 0.343 = 34.3\% \\
P(\tilde{X}=1) &= (0.30)\cdot(0.70)\cdot(0.70) + (0.70)\cdot(0.30)\cdot(0.70) \\
&\quad + (0.70)\cdot(0.70)\cdot(0.30) = 0.441 = 44.1\% \\
P(\tilde{X}=2) &= (0.30)\cdot(0.30)\cdot(0.70) + (0.70)\cdot(0.30)\cdot(0.30) \\
&\quad + (0.30)\cdot(0.70)\cdot(0.30) = 0.189 = 18.9\% \\
P(\tilde{X}=3) &= (0.30)\cdot(0.30)\cdot(0.30) = 0.027 = 2.70\%
\end{aligned}
$$

Therefore, the distribution can be represented as the graph in exhibit 3.3.

To clarify why the probabilities were computed in the way just illustrated, note that there is only one way to have three successes in three trials ($\tilde{X}=3$): when every trial is a success. The probability of this event is the product of the probabilities that each of the

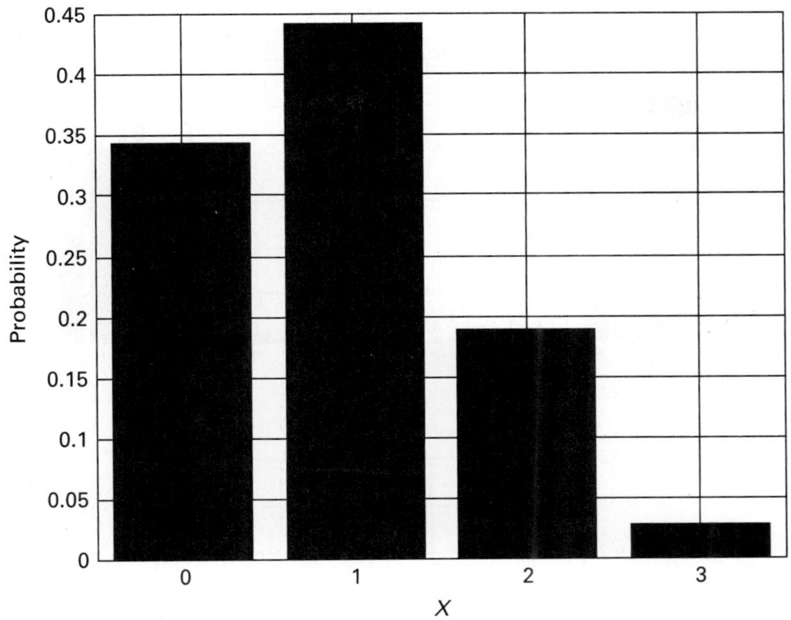

Exhibit 3.3
Binomial distribution with $n = 3$ trials and $p = 0.30$ probability of success.

three trials is a success. (The multiplication of probabilities to obtain the total probability is permitted because the trials are assumed to be independent.) However, there are three ways to have one success in three trials: The success can be in the first, second, or third trial. To account for these different combinations, we can use the following well-known formula from the branch of mathematics called *combinatorics* (sometimes called the "science of counting"):

$$\frac{n!}{x!(n-x)!}.$$

The preceding formula computes the number of ways in which one can select x out of n objects. The symbol "$n!$" (pronounced "n factorial") stands for the expression $1 \cdot 2 \cdot \ldots \cdot n$. The exact formula for computing the probability of obtaining x successes in n trials when the probability of success is p (in our example, $p = 0.30$) is

$$P(\tilde{X} = x) = \frac{n!}{x!(n-x)!} p^x (1-p)^{n-x}, x = 0, \ldots, n$$

This is the PMF of the binomial distribution and is the formula that software packages use to compute the binomial distribution probabilities. Note that depending on the magnitude of the probability of success, the binomial distribution can be shaped differently. Exhibit 3.4 illustrates the binomial distribution for three different values of the probability of success.

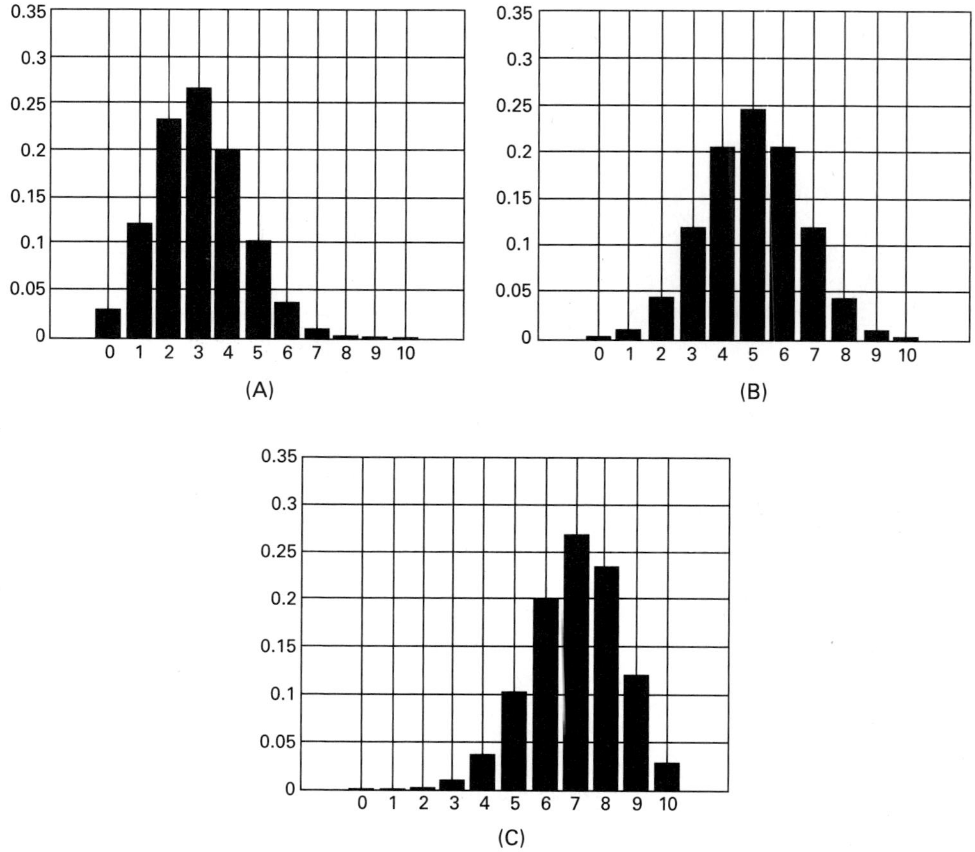

Exhibit 3.4
Shape of binomial distributions with the same number of trials ($n = 10$) and different values for the probability of success p: (A) $p = 0.3$; (B) $p = 0.5$; (C) $p = 0.7$.

3.4 Normal Distribution and Probability Density Functions

The binomial distribution is a *discrete* probability distribution because the values that the random variable can take are countable (0, 1, 2, etc.). Let us see what happens if we try to model the movements of the stock in 100 years. Exhibit 3.5 shows the binomial distribution for the probability of success of 0.30 and number of trials $n = 3$, 20, and 100.

Note that the binomial distribution begins to look symmetric as the number of trials increases. Also, the range of values begins to look like a *continuum*. When the random variable takes values on a range, as opposed to discrete points, the random variable is called *continuous*, and its probability distribution is called *continuous* as well. Continuous distributions are defined by their *probability density functions* (PDFs)—functions that describe the shape of the curve on the graph. They are often denoted by the standard mathematical notation for functions, $f(x)$, where x represents the possible values the random variable can take.

A common mistake is to think of $f(x)$ as the probability that the random variable will take the value x, analogous to how we defined the PMF $p(x)$. This is incorrect. The value

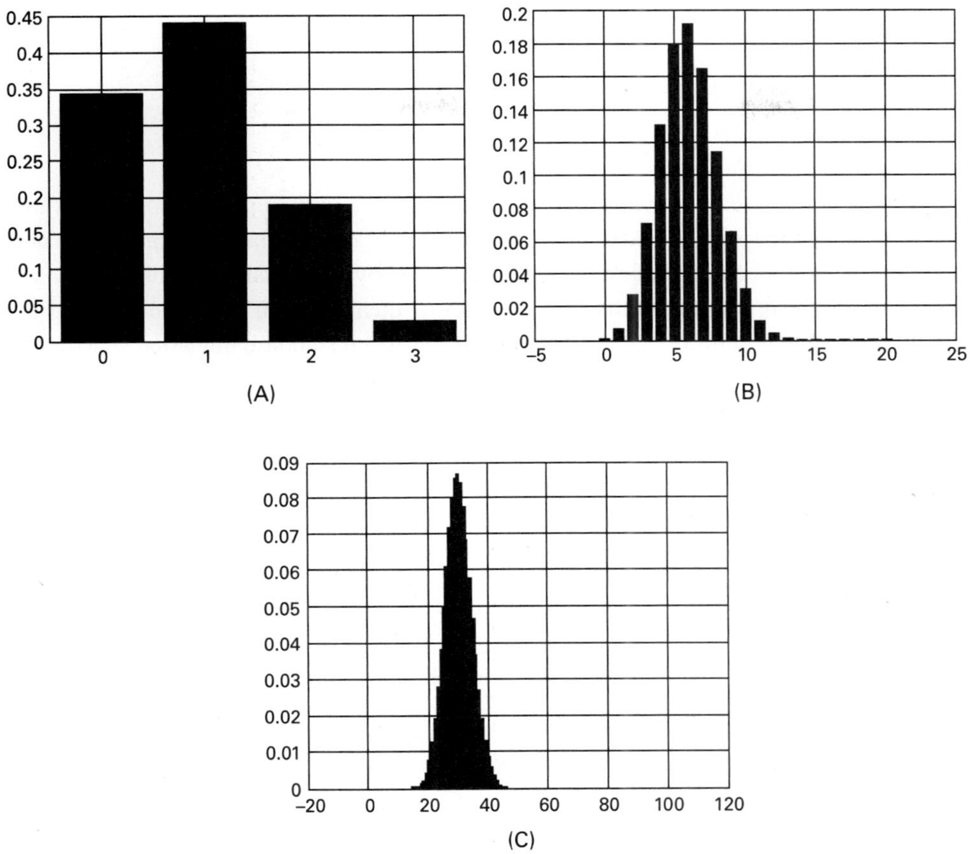

Exhibit 3.5
Shape of binomial distributions with the same probability of success $p=0.3$ and an increasing number of trials n: (A) $n=3$; (B) $n=20$; (C) $n=100$.

of $f(x)$ may be greater than 1, which a probability cannot be. Instead, we need to think about probabilities for continuous distributions in terms of an *area* under a curve that describes the probability distribution. Intuitively, continuous distributions are associated with areas under the PDF $f(x)$ because a continuum represents an infinite number of values that the random variable can take. If we try to assign a bar whose height equals a nonzero probability to each value that the random variable can take, as we did in the case of the binomial distribution, the total sum of all bars (and, hence the total probability for that distribution) will be infinity. However, the total probability, added up over all possible values for the random variable, cannot be more than 1.

Consequently, a better way to think of the probability of each particular value of the random variable is as infinitely small (virtually, 0), but then realize that when many of these values are added together, they have a significant probability mass. This is the concept of *integration* in calculus. The area under a given curve can be computed by adding up an infinite number of tiny areas above intervals of length dx on the x-axis. The probability that a continuous random variable takes values between two constants a and b can be expressed as the integral

$$\int_a^b f(x)\,dx$$

and the total probability (the area under the entire curve) should be 1:

$$\int_{-\infty}^{\infty} f(x)\,dx = 1.$$

It turns out that the binomial distribution approaches a very important continuous distribution, called the *normal distribution*, as the number of trials becomes large. The normal distribution is bell-shaped and is entirely defined by two parameters: its mean μ and standard deviation σ. This means that if we know them, we can draw the shape of the distribution. (We will introduce the concepts of mean and standard deviation shortly. For now, just think of μ and σ as inputs to the formula for the normal distribution PDF.) This is because the formula gives the normal PDF:

$$f(x) = \frac{1}{\sigma\sqrt{2\pi}} e^{-\frac{(x-\mu)^2}{2\sigma^2}}.$$

The standard normal distribution has $\mu=0$ and $\sigma=1$ (see exhibit 3.6).

You may also encounter the notation $f(x|\mu, \sigma)$; that is,

$$f(x|\mu, \sigma) = \frac{1}{\sigma\sqrt{2\pi}} e^{-\frac{(x-\mu)^2}{2\sigma^2}}.$$

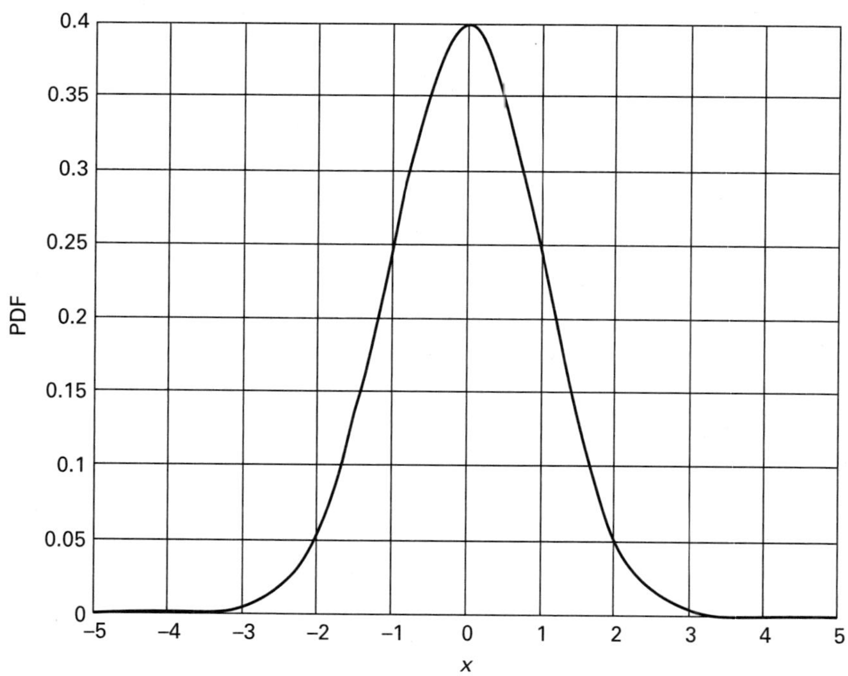

Exhibit 3.6
Standard normal distribution.

The symbol | stands for "conditional on" or "given." In other words, given specific values of μ or σ, the preceding formula gives the PDF for the normal distribution. The symbol "|" also will be useful in other circumstances, such as stating the PDF of a random variable as being conditional on the realization of another random variable. For example, the probability distribution of asset returns in one time period may depend on ("be conditional on") the realization of asset returns in the previous time period. We will provide a more formal definition of conditioning in section 3.10.

The normal distribution appears surprisingly often in nature and was studied in detail well before its prominent use in finance. Modern-day random process modeling in finance has borrowed a lot of findings from natural sciences such as physics and biology. For example, a classical assumption in modeling asset returns is that the changes in asset prices over small periods of time are normally distributed (even though the empirical evidence from real-world markets does not support the position that changes in asset returns follow a normal distribution). We will use the normal distribution extensively in this book.

The binomial and the normal distributions are famous representatives of the two classes of probability distributions: discrete and continuous. However, numerous other useful probability distributions appear in practice. We will review some of these distributions later in this chapter. But first, let us introduce a couple of important concepts for describing probability distributions.

3.5 Concept of Cumulative Probability

Cumulative probability is the probability that a random variable takes a value that is less than or equal to a given value. Cumulative probability is an important concept and is available as a function from several software packages, including Microsoft Excel, Python, and MATLAB. The *cumulative distribution function* (CDF) can be thought of as a listing of the cumulative probabilities up to every possible value that the random variable can take. Examples of CDFs for a continuous and a discrete distribution are shown in exhibit 3.7. The CDFs always start at 0 and end at 1, but the PDF or PMF of the

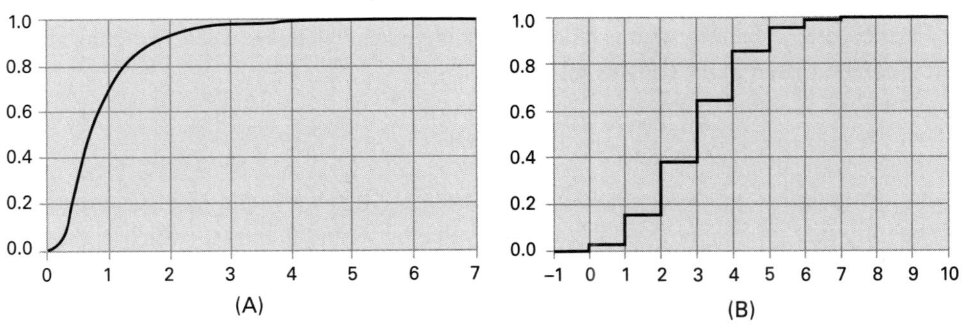

Exhibit 3.7
The CDFs of (A) a continuous random variable (lognormal) and (B) a discrete random variable (binomial with 10 trials and probability of success 0.30). The values on the horizontal axes are the values that the random variables take.

underlying random variable determines the shape of the curve on the graph. (The CDF for a discrete random variable has a characteristic staircase-like shape—i.e., "step function" in mathematical jargon.)

To show how one would compute cumulative probability for a discrete distribution, let us consider the binomial distribution example from section 3.3, which is also the CDF plotted in exhibit 3.7(B).

Suppose that the probability of success is 0.30, and we would like to compute the probability that the number of successes in 10 trials will be at most six. Intuitively, we are trying to estimate the total height of the first seven bars in the picture in exhibit 3.4(B). We can write this expression as

$$\begin{aligned} P(\tilde{X} \leq 6) &= P(\tilde{X} = 0) + \cdots + P(\tilde{X} = 6) \\ &= \frac{10!}{0!(10-0)!} 0.30^0 (1-0.30)^{10-0} + \cdots \\ &+ \frac{10!}{6!(10-6)!} 0.30^6 (1-0.30)^{10-6} \\ &= \sum_{k=0}^{6} \frac{10!}{k!(10-k)!} 0.30^k (1-0.30)^{10-k} \end{aligned}$$

where we have used the classical symbol $\sum$ for sum.

To construct the entire CDF, we would perform the same calculation for all possible values of $\tilde{X}$; that is, compute $P(\tilde{X} \leq 0)$, $P(\tilde{X} \leq 1), \ldots, P(\tilde{X} \leq 10)$. We would then plot $\tilde{X}$ on the x-axis and the corresponding $P(\tilde{X} \leq x)$ on the vertical axis (which by convention is referred to as the "y-axis").

For continuous distributions, we would replace the sum with an integral and find the area under the PDF that is less than or equal to a given constant. For example, if $f(x)$ is the PDF of a continuous probability distribution (such as the normal distribution and other distributions such as t, chi-square, and exponential distributions that we describe later in this chapter), then the CDF (usually denoted by $F(x)$) can be computed as

$$F(x) = P(\tilde{X} \leq x) = \int_{-\infty}^{x} f(x)\,dx.$$

Further, the probability that a random variable takes values between two constants a and b can be linked to the CDF as follows:

$$P(a \leq \tilde{X} \leq b) = \int_{a}^{b} f(x)\,dx = F(b) - F(a).$$

To illustrate this, let us look at exhibit 3.8. Suppose that we would like to compute the probability that the random variable takes a value between 20 and 60 (which is the area under the PDF between 20 and 60 and is 45.7% according to the graph). To compute that probability, we can equivalently compute the cumulative probability (the area) up to 20 (which is 39.9% according to the graph) and subtract it from the cumulative probability (the area) up to 60 (which is 100% – 14.4% = 85.6%). We obtain $F(60) - F(20) = 85.6\% - 39.9\% = 45.7\%$, which is the same value.

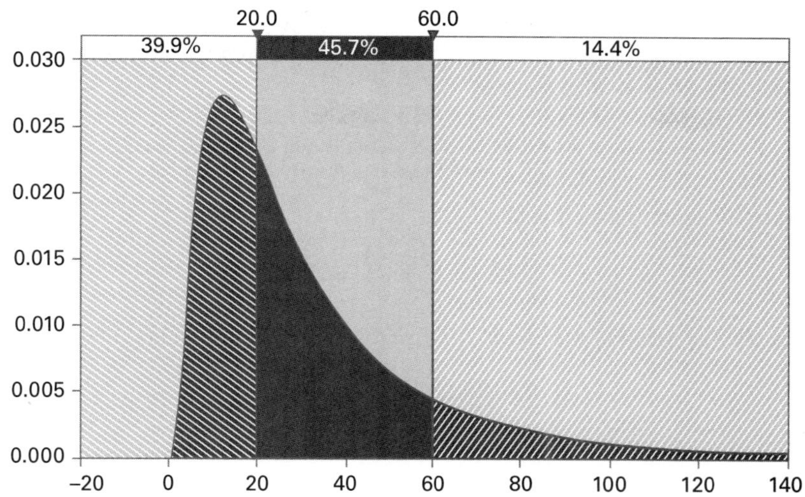

Exhibit 3.8
Calculation of the probability that the random variable falls between 20 and 60 as a difference of the cumulative probabilities up to 20 and 60.

3.6 Describing Distributions

A probability distribution can be used to represent the uncertain outcomes of a project or the possible future value of an investment in an asset. But what does the picture of this probability distributions tell us, and how can we convey the most important insights to others? This section introduces mathematical terminology for describing probability distributions. Specifically, the graph of a probability distribution gives us information about

- Where the most likely or most representative outcomes are (central tendency)
- Whether we can be optimistic or pessimistic about the future (skew)
- What the risk is (spread and tails of the distribution)

Finance practitioners are also often concerned with how "fat" the tails of the distribution are, which tells us how likely it is that "extreme" events; that is, events that are very far from the "representative" outcomes in the middle of the distribution, will occur. We will discuss a measure of this distribution characteristic (*kurtosis*) in section 3.6.4.

3.6.1 Measures of Central Tendency

Measures of central tendency include the mean, median, and mode. For theoretical reasons, the mean is by far the most utilized measure in financial applications, even though it has some serious drawbacks, most notably its sensitivity to extreme values. So we discuss the mean in the most detail here and briefly review the other two measures.

Mean On an intuitive level, the *mean* (also called the "expected value" or the "average") is the weighted average of all possible outcomes in the distribution, where the weights equal the probabilities that these values are taken. This is easier to imagine in the case of discrete distributions than in the case of continuous distributions, but the main idea is the same.

In mathematical jargon, the mean is called the *first moment* of a probability distribution.[2] It is denoted as $E[\tilde{X}]$ (for "expected value of the random variable $\tilde{X}$").

In the case of a discrete distribution,

$$E[\tilde{X}] = \sum_{\text{All values } x \text{ of the random variable}} x \cdot P(\tilde{X} = x) \quad .$$

In the case of a continuous distribution,

$$E[\tilde{X}] = \int_{-\infty}^{\infty} x \cdot f(x)\,dx.$$

For example, the mean of the Bernoulli distribution in section 3.2 is

$$0 \cdot 0.70 + 1 \cdot 0.30 = 0.30.$$

The mean of a normal distribution can be computed as

$$E[\tilde{X}] = \int_{-\infty}^{\infty} x \cdot \frac{1}{\sigma\sqrt{2\pi}} e^{-\frac{(x-\mu)^2}{2\sigma^2}}\,dx.$$

In the case of the normal distribution, of course, this calculation is redundant since the parameter μ in the expression inside the integral is actually the mean. However, the mean is not a parameter in the PDF formulas for most probability distributions, and this is the calculation that would be used to compute it. To practice, you can compute the preceding integral and verify that the calculation indeed gives μ as the answer.

As a final remark, we note that the mean is not always the "middle point" of the range of the distribution. (We will see ample examples in this book.) One outlier (i.e., one value

2. A complete review of probability theory is beyond the scope of this book, but the concept of moments of probability distributions is often mentioned in quantitative finance, so let us explain briefly what a *moment-generating function* (MGF) is. The kth moment of a random variable is defined as

$$m_k(\tilde{X}) = E[\tilde{X}^k] = \begin{cases} \displaystyle\sum_{\text{All values x of the random variable}} x^k \cdot \mathrm{P}(X = x) \\ \displaystyle\int_{-\infty}^{\infty} x^k \cdot f(x)\,dx \end{cases} .$$

For many useful cases (albeit not for all because for some distributions, some moments may not exist), knowing these moments allows us to identify uniquely the actual probability distribution. The MGF lets us generate these moments. It is defined as

$$M_t(\tilde{X}) = E[e^{t\tilde{X}}] = \begin{cases} \displaystyle\sum_{\text{All values x of the random variable}} e^{tx} \cdot \mathrm{P}(X = x) \\ \displaystyle\int_{-\infty}^{\infty} e^{tx} \cdot f(x)\,dx \end{cases}$$

By setting the value of the parameter t to different values (that., 1, 2, 3, etc.), we can recover the first, second, and third moments, and so on. Although this construction looks rather awkward, it is very useful for proving theoretical results such as "The sum of two independent normal random variables is also a normal random variable." (The sum of two random variables does not necessarily have the same distribution as the random variables in the general case.) This is done by computing the MGF of the sum of two normal variables, and then checking if the resulting MGF is of the same type as the MGF of a normal random variable, which is computationally more convenient than computing the actual probability distribution of the sum of two random variables.

for the random variable that is very far from the others) can shift the mean significantly. Note also that the mean does not have to be one of the values of the probability distribution, as the previous Bernoulli example illustrated. (The mean for the Bernoulli distribution was 0.30, which is not 0 or 1.) The mean is merely the "center of gravity" of the probability distribution.

Median The *median* is a more robust measure of the "middle" of the distribution. It is the value on the horizontal axis so that 50% of the distribution lies on each side of it. Since the median does not take into consideration where the values on each side of it lie (as opposed to the mean, which considers the actual values and their probabilities of occurrence), the median is not as influenced by the presence of extreme values (values that are very far from the center of the distribution) as the mean.

Mode The *mode* of a distribution is the most likely outcome. One can think of it as the value at which the PDF/PMF of the distribution is at its highest. For example, in exhibit 3.4, the mode of the first binomial distribution is 3, the mode of the second distribution is 5, and the mode of the third distribution is 7.

You may have heard about "unimodal" or "bimodal" distributions. These terms just refer to how many "peaks" the distribution has. Almost all theoretical distributions used in financial modeling are unimodal, as their properties are easier to model mathematically. The distributions that we have introduced so far, for example, are unimodal. Of course, real-world data do not always follow neat mathematical rules and may present you with distributions that have more than one mode.

3.6.2 Measures of Risk

Variance and Standard Deviation When thinking of risk, one usually thinks of how far the actual realization of an uncertain variable will fall from what one *expects*. Therefore, a natural way to define a measure of uncertainty is the *spread*, or *dispersion* of a distribution. Two measures that describe the spread of the distribution are *variance* and *standard deviation*. The two are strongly related: the standard deviation is the square root of the variance, and we usually need to compute the variance before computing the standard deviation. Exhibit 3.9 illustrates the relationship between variance/standard deviation and the spread of the distribution. Suppose that we are considering investing in two assets, A and B. The probability distribution for B has a wider spread and higher variance/standard deviation than the probability distribution for A.

Mathematically, the variance of a random variable is related to the *second moment* of a probability distribution and is computed as follows.

For discrete distributions:

$$\mathrm{Var}(\tilde{X}) = \sum_{\text{All values x of the random variable}} (\mathrm{x} - \mu)^2 \cdot \mathrm{P}(X = x)$$

For continuous distributions:

$$Var(\tilde{X}) = \int_{-\infty}^{\infty} (x - \mu)^2 \cdot f(x)\,dx$$

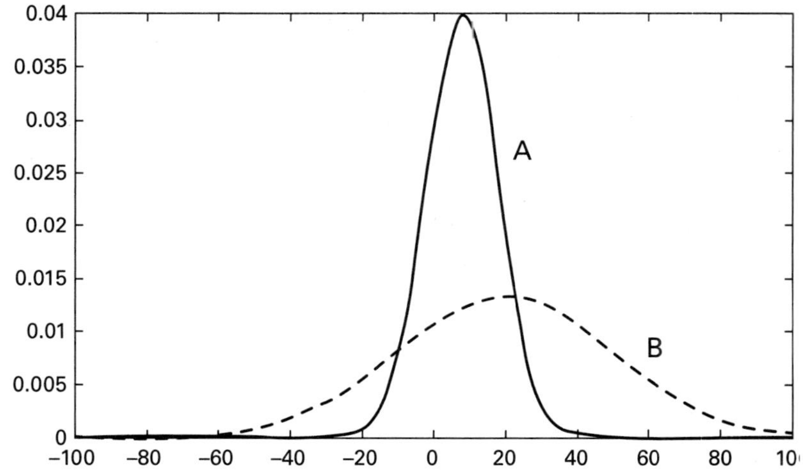

Exhibit 3.9
Comparison of two probability distributions in terms of risk and central tendency.

In the preceding equations, μ denotes the mean of the distribution.

Stated in words, the variance is the sum of the squared deviations of all values in the probability distribution from the mean (used as a measure for the center) of the distribution. The reason why squared deviations are used is so deviations to the left of the mean do not cancel deviations to the right of the mean when added together.[3] Otherwise, a distribution that has many observations far from the center, and therefore has a large "spread," may end up with the same variance as a distribution with values very close to the mean and a small spread. In fact, a distribution that has a very wide spread may end up with a variance of zero if all large positive deviations from the mean have corresponding large negative deviations. This would make variance useless as a measure of spread.

Sometimes a more convenient (and equivalent) way of expressing the variance is through the equation

$$Var(\tilde{X}) = E[\tilde{X}^2] - (E[\tilde{X}])^2$$
$$= \sum_{\text{All values } x} x^2 \cdot \mathrm{P}(\tilde{X} = x) - \left(\sum_{\text{All values } x} x \cdot \mathrm{P}(\tilde{X} = x) \right)^2 \quad \text{(in the discrete case)}$$
$$= \int^{\infty} x^2 \cdot f(x)dx - \left(\int^{\infty} x \cdot f(x)dx\right)^2 \quad \text{(in the continuous case).}$$

These expressions link the variance explicitly to the first and the second moments of the distribution.

The variance of a distribution measures the spread in square units of the random variable, and the number is difficult to interpret. The *standard deviation* is widely used instead. The standard deviation simply takes the square root of the variance ($\sigma_X = \sqrt{Var(\tilde{X})}$) and presents a measure of the average deviation of the values in the distribution from the mean that has the same units as the random variable, hence making it easier to interpret.

3. Recall that squaring a number always results in a nonnegative number, so the sum of squared terms is also nonnegative.

In the financial context, "standard deviation" is often used interchangeably with the term "volatility."

Coefficient of Variation Let us consider again the graph in exhibit 3.9. We mentioned that the probability distribution for A has a smaller standard deviation than the probability distribution for B, but we also noticed that the mean of the distribution for A is lower than the mean for the distribution for B. If you had to invest in one of them, which one would you choose? This situation brings up the idea of measuring spread (the "risk" of the distribution) relative to the mean (the "representative" value of the distribution). This is the statistical concept of *coefficient of variation* (CV), which is reported in percentages and is mathematically expressed as

$$CV = \frac{\sigma}{\mu} \times 100,$$

where μ is the mean and σ is the standard deviation of the distribution. The CV gives us a unit-free ratio that can be used to compare random variables. Suppose the CV for investment A is 70% and the CV for investment B is 50%. In that case, we may decide that investment A is riskier than B relative to the average return that we can expect, even though investment A has a smaller standard deviation.

CV represents the trade-off between expectation and risk from the statistical point of view. In finance, the inverse ratio is often used (i.e., instead of the amount of risk per unit of expected reward, one looks at the expected reward per unit of risk). The financial measure became popular based on work by Sharpe (see, e.g., Sharpe 1994). We will talk about the Sharpe ratio in the context of portfolio optimization in chapter 12. The main idea behind using both measures, however, is the same.

Range The *range* of a random variable is the difference between the maximum and the minimum value that a random variable can take. It can sometimes be used as a measure of riskiness; however, be aware that it is not applicable in many situations. For example, some important probability distributions, such as the normal distribution, have an infinite range, as the random variables can take values from negative infinity to positive infinity. You should also be extremely careful when using range in the context of simulation. We will discuss this issue further in chapter 5.

Percentiles Another useful term for describing distributions is the *percentile.* The α-percentile of a distribution is the number on the x-axis such that a percentage α of the total probability lies to the left of that number. Probability distributions can be compared by their percentiles: for example, if the fifth percentile of the distribution for investment B in exhibit 3.9 is less than the fifth percentile of the distribution for investment A, we may argue that investment B is riskier than investment A because there is a 5% probability that it will result in a lower outcome than investment A. We will use percentiles extensively later in this book, in the context of analyzing simulation results (chapter 5) and portfolio risk management (chapter 13).

3.6.3 Skew

Distributions can be symmetric or asymmetric (skewed), depending on whether the tails at the two ends of the distribution are the same or different. Whether distributions are further classified as *left-skewed* (*negatively skewed*) or *right-skewed* (*positively skewed*) basically depends on where the mean is relative to the median. Symmetric distributions have the same mean and median, whereas left-skewed distributions have a longer left tail (which implies that the mean is to the left of the median, as it has been skewed by extreme values). There are several rather involved definitions that are used to represent skew mathematically, and it is beyond the scope of the book to present them here. The important thing to note is that all the formulas for skew use the *third moment* of a probability distribution and agree on the intuitive definition of skew: that left skew means a longer left tail, whereas right skew means a longer right tail. The normal distribution, which is symmetric, has a skew of 0.

3.6.4 Kurtosis

In finance, we are frequently interested in the behavior in the "tails" of a distribution. If the tails are "fat," this means that extreme observations are more likely to happen, and expected values are not as useful. *Kurtosis* measures the "fatness" of the tails of a distribution. The normal distribution, which is used as the standard for comparison, has a kurtosis of 3. A kurtosis of more than 3 (in general, high value for kurtosis) means that the probability distribution has fatter tails and a sharper peak than the normal distribution, whereas a low value for kurtosis means that the tails are "leaner" than the tails of the normal distribution.[4] The mathematical formula for kurtosis, just like the formula for skew, is rather involved, but the important thing to note is that kurtosis is related to the *fourth moment* of a probability distribution.

3.7 Brief Overview of Some Important Probability Distributions

This section lists some additional important probability distributions, their PMFs/PDFs, and summary measures. For an overview of these and other probability distributions and how they arise in practice, see, for example, Evans, Hastings, and Peacock (2000).

3.7.1 Discrete Distributions

We have already discussed two discrete distributions, the binomial distribution and the Bernoulli distribution. Next, we discuss two other discrete distributions: the discrete uniform distribution and the Poisson distribution. Other interesting discrete distributions that will not be covered here are geometric distribution, hypergeometric distribution, and negative binomial distribution.

Discrete Uniform Distribution The *discrete uniform distribution* represents a situation in which a random variable can take a prespecified number of discrete values and each value has an equal chance of occurring. A simple example of such distribution is a

4. Some software and simulation software packages report *excess kurtosis*, rather than kurtosis, as the default. The excess kurtosis is computed as the value for kurtosis minus 3 (the kurtosis of the normal distribution), so the normal distribution has kurtosis of 0. Make sure that you check the help file for the software package that you are using before you interpret the value for kurtosis in statistical output.

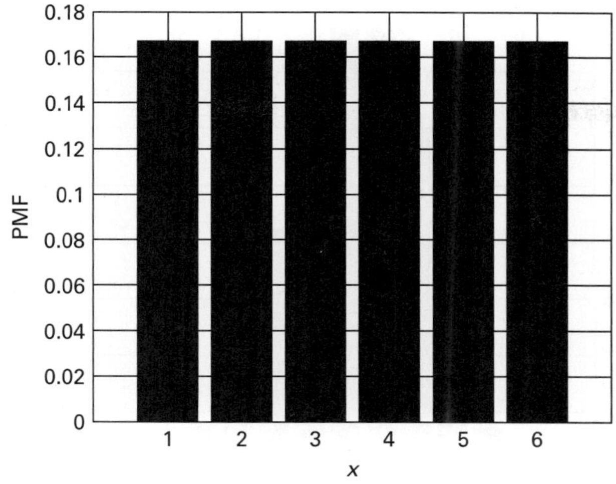

Exhibit 3.10
Discrete uniform distribution.

roll of a fair die: there are six possible outcomes, 1, 2, 3, 4, 5, 6, and each of them happens with the same probability (see exhibit 3.10).

It can be easily seen that if the random variable can take N values and if the total probability needs to be 1, then the probability of each individual value should be $1/N$. Therefore, the PMF of the discrete uniform distribution is

$$P(\tilde{X} = x) = \frac{1}{N}.$$

The discrete uniform distribution is very useful in a variety of applications, and we will encounter it again, for example, when learning about sampling by bootstrapping in chapter 13.

Poisson Distribution The *Poisson distribution* applies in situations in which one is concerned about the probability of having a given number of arrivals in a prespecified time interval, where these arrivals are assumed to be independent of one another. It is widely used for modeling jumps in electricity prices (referred to as "spikes" because prices typically return to their original levels), and in credit risk modeling because defaults or other credit-related events can be modeled as "arrivals" in a random process.[5] We will look at applications in chapter 17.

The Poisson PMF is given by

$$f(x) = \frac{\lambda^x}{x!} e^{-\lambda}.$$

It requires an input parameter, λ, that corresponds to the average number of arrivals during the time period.

5. The Poisson distribution is also widely used in operations management applications, such as queue management, revenue management, and call center staffing.

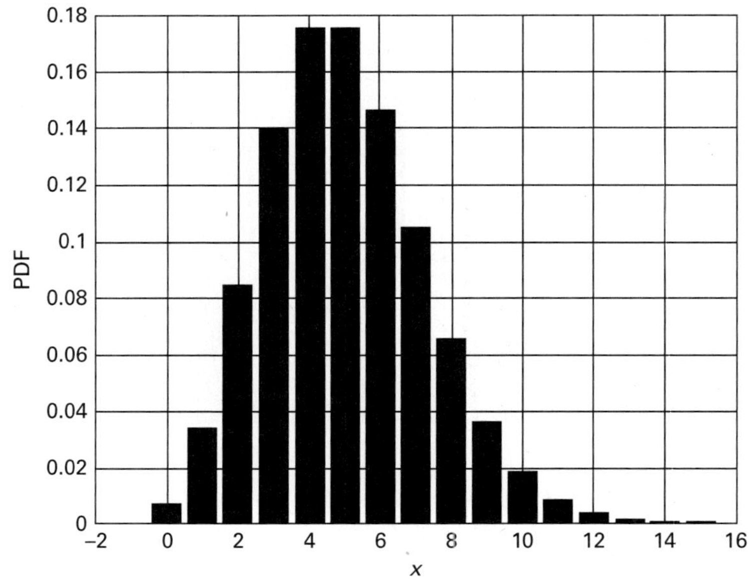

Exhibit 3.11
Poisson distribution with $\lambda = 5$.

A picture of a Poisson distribution with $\lambda = 5$ is shown in exhibit 3.11. You can imagine incorporating the distribution into a model for the process followed by the price of electricity, in which the price spikes on average five times per day because of transmission constraints or unexpected outages. The Poisson distribution in the picture is slightly skewed, which means that the probability that fewer than five spikes occur in a day is slightly more than the probability that more than five spikes occur in a day.

The Poisson distribution has several interesting properties. Notably, it looks very much like a binomial distribution if the number of trials in the binomial distribution is large, and the probability of success at every trial is adjusted so the probability of success remains constant as the number of trials grows large. More precisely, a binomial random variable with a number of trials n and probability of success λ / n at every trial approaches a Poisson distribution with parameter λ as n grows large.

Furthermore, the Poisson distribution looks like the normal distribution if the parameter λ (mean arrivals per unit time) grows large. In fact, the effect is noticeable for λ as small as 20 arrivals. (Plot the distribution with @RISK or MATLAB to see its shape.) As λ increases, the Poisson distribution approaches a normal distribution with mean λ and standard deviation $\sqrt{\lambda}$.

3.7.2 Continuous Distributions

In addition to the normal distribution that we described earlier, the continuous distributions that we review are the

- Continuous uniform distribution
- Triangular distribution
- Student's t-distribution

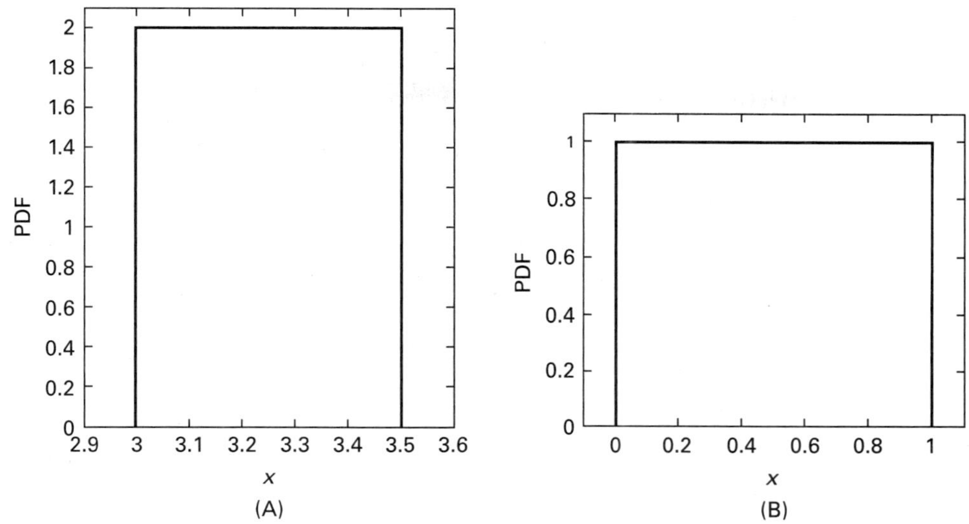

Exhibit 3.12
Examples of continuous uniform distributions: (A) on the interval [3, 3.5]; (B) on the interval [0, 1].

- Lognormal distribution
- Exponential distribution
- Chi-square distribution
- Beta distribution

Other interesting continuous distributions that are not discussed here are gamma (Erlang) distribution, Cauchy distribution, and Gumbel (extreme value) distribution.

Continuous Uniform Distribution The *continuous uniform distribution* represents a situation in which a random variable can take a continuum of values on a *range* (say, between two numbers a and b) with equal probability. This distribution presents a simple example of why the value of the PDF $f(x)$ at point x should not be treated as the probability of x. Since the total probability mass under the PDF needs to be 1, the height of the line on the graph of the uniform distribution (i.e., the value of the PDF at each point on the range $[a,b]$) is $1/(b-a)$. This number can be greater than 1, depending on the values of a and b, which is not allowed for a probability. For example, if a is 3 and b is 3.5, then $(b-a)=0.5$, and the PDF $f(x)$ at any point x between 3 and 3.5 is $1/0.5=2$ (see exhibit 3.12(A)).

To summarize, the PDF of the continuous uniform distribution is

$$f(x)=\frac{1}{b-a}, \quad a \leq x \leq b.$$

The "standard" continuous uniform distribution on the interval [0,1] (i.e., when $a=0$ and $b=1$) plays a very important role in simulation. We will return to this topic in chapters 5 and 19.

Triangular Distribution A *triangular distribution* is a simple distribution with wide applications in capital budgeting, marketing, and decision analysis. It is often used when

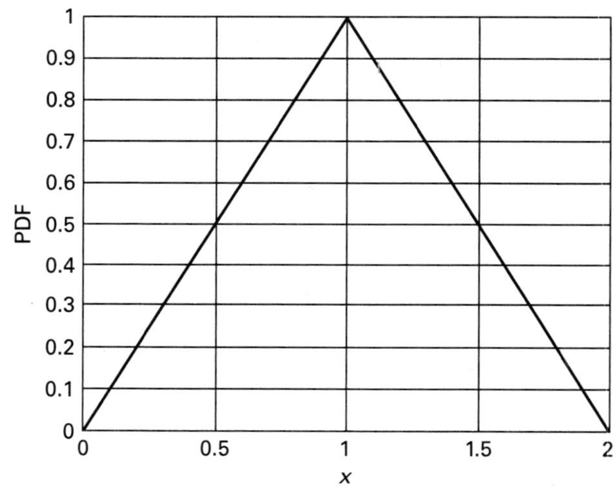

Exhibit 3.13
Triangular distribution.

we do not have very much information about the underlying distribution, but we can specify a worst-case scenario (1), a best-case scenario (2), and a most likely scenario (3). Exhibit 3.13 shows an example of a triangular distribution. Its PDF draws a triangle, and the triangle does not need to be symmetric. The PDF is given by

$$f(x) = \begin{cases} \dfrac{2(x-a)}{(b-a)(c-a)} & \text{for } a \leq x \leq c \\ \dfrac{2(b-x)}{(b-a)(b-c)} & \text{for } c \leq x \leq b \\ 0 & \text{otherwise} \end{cases}$$

Student's *t*-Distribution The *Student's t-distribution* (or simply *t*-distribution) looks very much like the normal distribution in shape, but the weight in the tails is determined by parameter ν (associated with degrees of freedom in statistics).[6] Examples of *t*-distributions for different values are given in exhibit 3.14. The PDF for the *t*-distribution is

$$f(x) = \frac{\Gamma\left(\dfrac{\nu+1}{2}\right)}{\Gamma\left(\dfrac{\nu}{2}\right)} \frac{1}{\sqrt{\nu\pi}} \frac{1}{\left(1+\dfrac{x^2}{\nu}\right)^{\frac{\nu+1}{2}}},$$

where $\Gamma(y)$ is the so-called *gamma function* ($\Gamma(y) = \int_0^\infty t^{y-1} e^{-t}\, dt$).

The *t*-distribution arises in some very important applications in statistics in calculating confidence interval (CI) estimates for the true mean of a distribution and hypothesis testing

6. W. S. Gossett stumbled across this distribution while working for the Guinness brewery in Dublin. At the time, he was not allowed to publish his discovery under his own name, so he used the pseudonym *Student*, and this is how the distribution is known today.

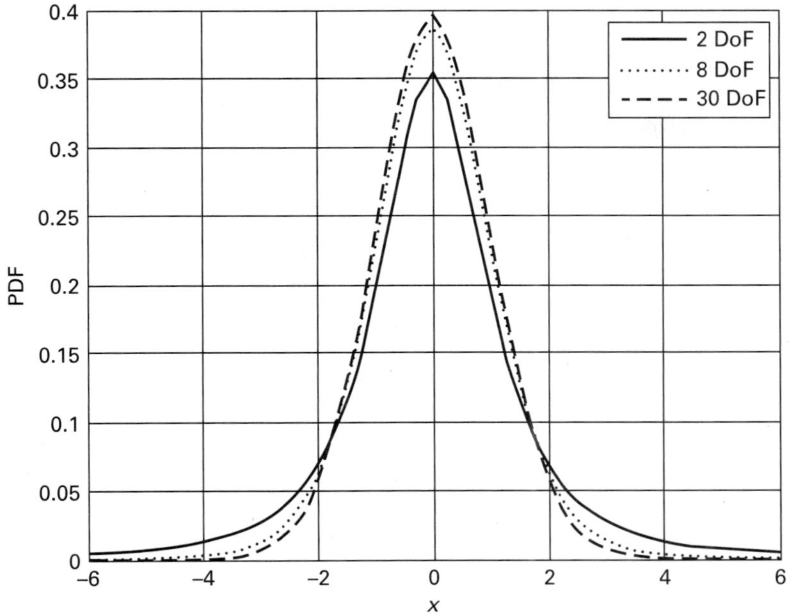

Exhibit 3.14
Examples of t-distributions for different degrees of freedom. DoF = degrees of freedom.

(see sections 3.11.2 and 3.11.4). Since simulation bears strong resemblance to statistical sampling, we will encounter the t-distribution when we discuss simulation in chapter 5.

Lognormal Distribution The *lognormal distribution* has one of the most prominent uses in modern finance. It arises when values for the random variable cannot be negative, and it tends to be asymmetrically distributed, which has been observed for stock prices and real estate prices (see exhibit 3.15). The PDF of the lognormal distribution is

$$f(x) = \frac{1}{x\sigma\sqrt{2\pi}} e^{-\frac{(\ln(x)-\mu)^2}{2\sigma^2}}, \quad x > 0$$

Note the resemblance to the PDF for the normal distribution from 3.4. In fact, there is a very direct relationship between a lognormal and a normal random variable. Specifically, if $\tilde{Y}$ is a normal random variable with mean μ and standard deviation σ, then the random variable $\tilde{X} = e^{\tilde{Y}}$ is lognormal with the previous PDF.

Exponential Distribution The *exponential distribution* is related to the Poisson distribution. While the Poisson distribution measures the number of arrivals in each time period (assuming that arrivals are independent), the exponential distribution measures the time between independent arrivals. The PDF of the exponential distribution is

$$f(x) = \lambda e^{-\lambda x}, \quad x \geq 0.$$

In fact, parameter λ is the same parameter in the definition of the Poisson distribution.

If we expect an average of λ arrivals during a unit of time, then the average time that we would expect between arrivals is $1/\lambda$ (which happens to be the mean of the exponential

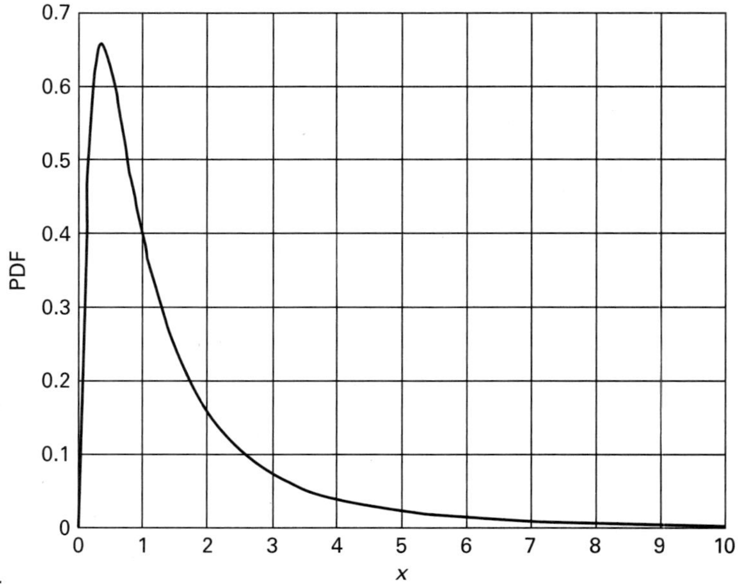

Exhibit 3.15
Lognormal distribution.

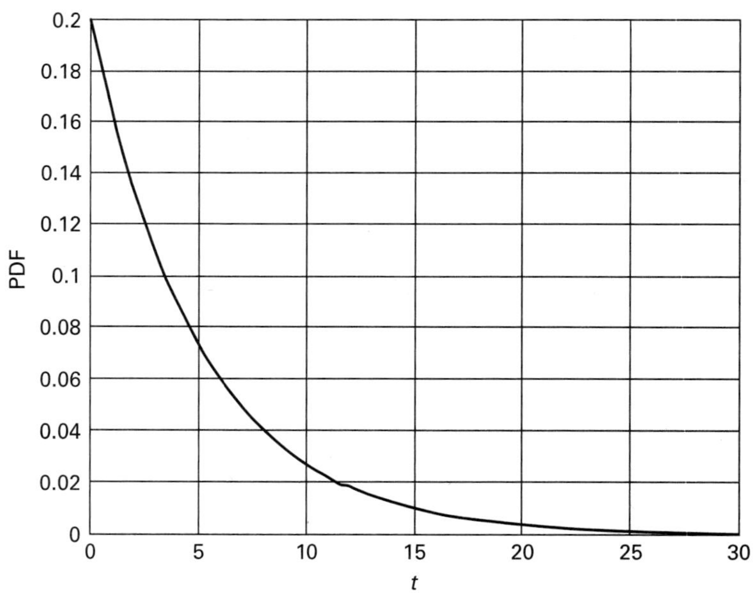

Exhibit 3.16
Exponential distribution with $\lambda = 0.02$.

distribution). A graph of the exponential distribution is shown in exhibit 3.16. Note that if we "slice" the distribution vertically and consider the piece of the curve to the right of the value at which we sliced, that piece has the same shape as the original distribution. This is the so-called memoryless property of the exponential distribution, which counterintuitively means that the distribution of the time until the next arrival does not depend on how long you have waited. Specifically, if 30 minutes have already elapsed, the probability that you will see an arrival after 10 minutes is the same as the probability that you would have seen an arrival after 10 minutes at the beginning of the first time period of 30 minutes.

Like the Poisson distribution, the exponential distribution is widely used in credit risk modeling and in high-frequency modeling of the arrival time between orders in financial markets (referred to as *trade duration*).

Chi-Square Distribution The *chi-square distribution* (often denoted as χ^2 *distribution*) is used predominantly in hypothesis testing in statistics. The reason why we list it here, given our focus on financial applications, is because it is the basis for goodness-of-fit tests that decide whether a particular distribution is appropriate for modeling an observed set of data. The sum of k independent squared normal random variables follows a chi-square distribution with k degrees of freedom.[7]

The PDF of the chi-square distribution is given by

$$f(x) = \frac{2^{\frac{-k}{2}}}{\Gamma\left(\frac{k}{2}\right)} x^{\frac{k}{2}-1} e^{\frac{-x}{2}}, \quad x > 0,$$

where Γ is the gamma function, as defined earlier in this section, and k is the degrees of freedom. A picture of the distribution is shown in exhibit 3.17.

Beta Distribution The *beta distribution* is very flexible in terms of shape and is useful for representing a variety of models of uncertainty. In contrast to other distributions, which have a distinctive skew, the beta distribution is defined by two parameters, α and β, which define its shape and skew. The precise formula for the PDF is

$$f(x) = \frac{x^{\alpha-1}(1-x)^{\beta-1}}{\frac{\Gamma(\alpha)\Gamma(\beta)}{\Gamma(\alpha+\beta)}}, \quad x > 0, \ \alpha > 0, \beta > 0.$$

Exhibit 3.18 illustrates the shape with parameter values equal to 4 and 6, and 6 and 4, respectively. You can observe that the skew of the beta distribution changes depending on the relative magnitudes of α and β.

7. The squared random variables arise when computing squared differences between observed values (which vary because the sample is random) and expected values. Chi-square goodness-of-fit tests consider the sum of the total squared differences between the observed frequencies of values in a sample and the expected frequencies if the sample came from a particular distribution. Whether the difference between what was observed and what was expected is statistically large depends on the value of the difference relative to the critical value of the chi-square test statistic, which is computed from the chi-square distribution. See the brief introduction to hypothesis testing in chapter 4.

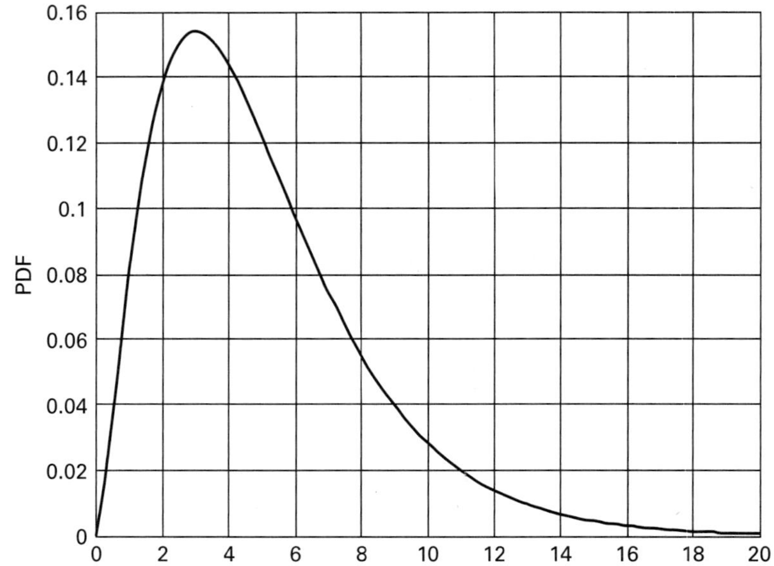

Exhibit 3.17
Chi-square distribution with 5 degrees of freedom.

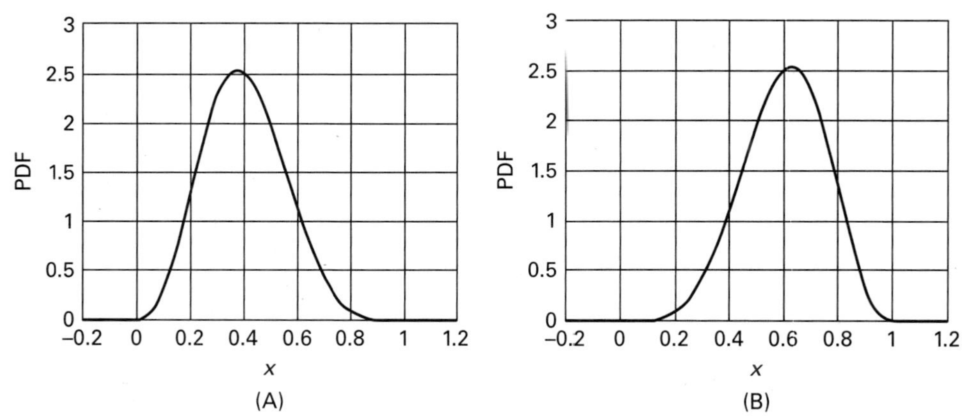

Exhibit 3.18
Examples of beta distributions: (A) a beta distribution with parameter values equal to 4 and 6; (B) a beta distribution with parameter values equal to 6 and 4.

3.8 Dependence between Two Random Variables: Covariance and Correlation

So far, we have shown how one can describe a single random variable. In finance, we often need to worry about the relationships between two or more variables. For example, in the context of investments, if the return on investment A in exhibit 3.9 goes up on average, does the return on investment B go up as well? In capital budgeting, if the value of one project that we are considering goes down, will the value of other projects in the company's portfolio go up or down? If we can measure these kinds of relationships, we can, for example, protect ourselves against extreme situations in which all our investments crash simultaneously.

Two commonly used measures of codependence between random variables are *covariance,* often denoted by *Cov*, and *correlation,* often denoted by the Greek letter rho (ρ). The two are strongly related.

The idea behind covariance is to measure simultaneous deviations from the means for two random variables, X and Y. If $\tilde{X}$ takes a value above its mean μ_X, does $\tilde{Y}$ take a value above its mean μ_Y as well? If it does, then we would like to increase our measure of covariation to reflect a higher degree of codependence. If the two random variables move in opposite directions (i.e., when one of them takes a value above its mean, the other one takes a value below its mean), then we would like to subtract from our measure of covariation. Mathematically, this idea is expressed as

$$Cov(\tilde{X},\tilde{Y}) = E[(\tilde{X}-\mu_X)(\tilde{Y}-\mu_y)].$$

Recall that E stands for "expectation," or "average." Thus, the covariance measures whether the two random variables move together on average. If the covariance is 0, the two variables are independent.

The concept of covariance appears very often in modern portfolio theory, and we will come back to it in chapter 13. However, sometimes it is more convenient to use a normalized form of the expression for covariance—the *correlation coefficient.* The problem with covariance is that its units are products of the original units of the two random variables, so the number for covariance is difficult to interpret. The correlation coefficient divides the covariance by the product of the standard deviations of the two random variables:

$$\rho = Corr(\tilde{X},\tilde{Y}) = \frac{Cov(\tilde{X},\tilde{Y})}{\sigma_X \sigma_Y}$$

The result is a value that is always between–1 and 1. If the correlation between two random variables is close to 1, they are strongly positively correlated; that is, if one of them takes a value above its mean, the other one is very likely to take a value above its mean as well. If the correlation is close to–1, they are strongly negatively correlated; that is, if one of them takes a value above its mean, the other one is very likely to take a value below its mean. If the correlation is 0, then the two variables are independent—meaning that knowing whether one of them is above or below its mean value does not tell you anything about where the value of the other variable may be.

An important observation here is that covariance and correlation exist only for pairs of random variables. They are not computed for more than two variables at a time. Thus, if the situation calls for analysis of dependence between more than two random variables, the covariances and correlations are reported in a table (referred to as a "covariance matrix" and "correlation matrix," respectively). If there are N variables to analyze, the covariance and the correlation tables have N rows and N columns apiece. The entry in the ith row and jth column is the covariance/correlation of the ith variable and the jth variable. The values in the diagonal of these matrices (i.e., entries in the ith row and ith column) are equal to the variance of the ith variable (in the case of covariance matrix) and 1 (in the case of the correlation matrix). Appendix A, "Basic Linear Algebra Concepts," available online, briefly introduces matrix arrays. We will discuss covariance and correlation matrices in more detail in chapter 13.

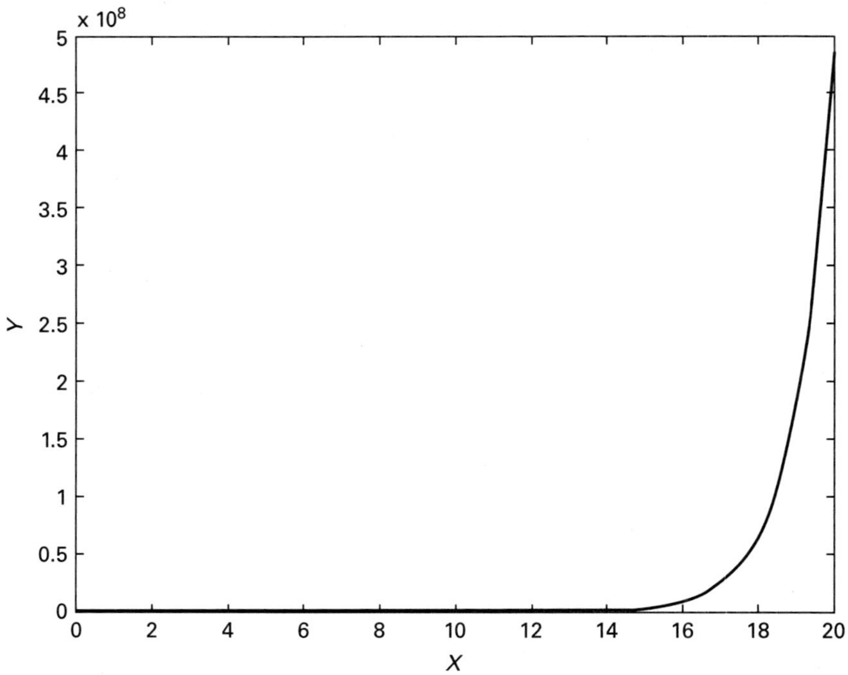

Exhibit 3.19
A connected graph of the realizations of $\tilde{X}$ versus the realizations of $\tilde{Y} = e^{\tilde{X}}$.

When dealing with financial data, we often need to be concerned with autocorrelation. *Autocorrelation* exists when the realizations of a random process over time (such as the movement of a stock price) depend on the history of the process; that is, when a random variable (such as the stock return) in one time period is correlated with itself (the return) during previous time periods. We will see examples of this in chapters 17, 19, and 21.

It is worth noting that while covariance and correlation are very useful measures of dependence and are widely used in financial applications, they do not paint a complete picture of how random variables are codependent and can sometimes be misleading. This is particularly true in cases in which two variables are nonlinearly related.[8] Exhibit 3.19 contains one such illustration. Consider two random variables, $\tilde{X}$ and $\tilde{Y}$, where $\tilde{X}$ follows a continuous uniform distribution on the interval [0,20], and $\tilde{Y} = e^{\tilde{X}}$ Here, 100 observations from the probability distribution of $\tilde{X}$ are drawn, the corresponding values for $\tilde{Y}$ are computed, and the points are plotted in exhibit 3.19. Note that $\tilde{X}$ and $\tilde{Y}$ are perfectly dependent—knowing the value of $\tilde{X}$, we can predict the exact value for $\tilde{Y}$. Yet, when we compute the correlation coefficient between $\tilde{X}$ and $\tilde{Y}$, we get a value of about 0.5. The latter shows relatively strong positive dependence, but is not 1; that is, it does not reflect the fact that $\tilde{X}$ and $\tilde{Y}$ are actually perfectly dependent. The correlation coefficient would measure the dependence correctly, however, if $\tilde{X}$ and $\tilde{Y}$ had a linear

8. In other words, their relationship cannot be portrayed as a straight line.

relationship; that is, if $\tilde{Y}$ were a linear function of $\tilde{X}$ of the kind $a\tilde{X} + b$ for some constants a and b.

3.9 Sums of Random Variables

As mentioned in section 3.4, we often need to consider more than one uncertainty at a time, and thus we need tools to deal with sums of random variables, such as the behavior of our total investments or overall return on multiple projects. Summarizing the joint probability distributions for sums of two or more random variables is not as easy as summing the two distributions. In this section, we review a few important facts about analyzing sums of random variables.

Suppose that the return on investment A in exhibit 3.9 is the random variable $\tilde{X}$ and the return on investment B is the random variable $\tilde{Y}$. Let $E[\tilde{Y}]$ and $E[\tilde{Y}]$ be the expected returns of the two investments, and σ_X and σ_Y be their standard deviations. Suppose now that we invest 0.40 (40%) of our funds in A and 0.60 (60%) of our funds in B. Therefore, the return on the portfolio is $0.40 \cdot \tilde{X} + 0.60 \cdot \tilde{Y}$. What is the expected return on the portfolio, and what is the portfolio's standard deviation?

First, we need to ask what the expected values are of $0.40 \cdot \tilde{X}$ and $0.60 \cdot \tilde{Y}$. Note that even though 0.40 and 0.60 are numbers (constants), the products $0.40 \cdot \tilde{X}$ and $0.60 \cdot \tilde{Y}$ are random variables because they depend on random variables.

It turns out that for any random variable $\tilde{X}$,

$$E[a \cdot \tilde{X}] = a \cdot E[\tilde{X}]$$

if a is a constant.

Furthermore, it is always true that the expectation of the sum of two random variables is equal to the sum of the expectations:

$$E[\tilde{X} + \tilde{Y}] = E[\tilde{X}] + E[\tilde{Y}].$$

Therefore,

$$E[a \cdot \tilde{X} + b \cdot \tilde{Y}] = a \cdot E[\tilde{X}] + b \cdot E[\tilde{Y}].$$

This allows us to compute the expected value of our portfolio:

$$E[0.40 \cdot \tilde{X} + 0.60 \cdot \tilde{Y}] = 0.40 \cdot E[\tilde{X}] + 0.60 \cdot E[\tilde{Y}].$$

What about the risk of the portfolio? Most people would be tempted to extend the preceding reasoning to portfolio variance and standard deviation as well. However, variance and standard deviation are not nearly as convenient as the expectation operator. It turns out that

$$Var[a \cdot \tilde{X}] = a^2 \cdot Var[\tilde{X}]$$
$$Var(\tilde{X} + \tilde{Y}) = Var(\tilde{X}) + Var(\tilde{Y}) + 2 \cdot Cov(\tilde{X}, \tilde{Y}),$$

and

$$Var(a \cdot \tilde{X} + b \cdot \tilde{Y}) = a^2 \cdot Var(\tilde{X}) + b^2 \cdot Var(\tilde{Y}) + 2 \cdot a \cdot b \cdot Cov(\tilde{X}, \tilde{Y}).$$

There are no "nice" formulas for the standard deviation of a sum of random variables. We basically need to compute the variance of the sum (as we just did) and take the square root of the resulting expression to compute the standard deviation.[9]

There are two things to note. First, the constants a and b are squared once they are taken out of the expression inside the parentheses for the variance. Second, there is an additional term in the sum of the variances, which involves the covariance of the two random variables. Why does this hold at an intuitive level? We will provide some examples of this effect in chapter 10, but the main idea is that if the random variables move in opposite directions on average (meaning that their covariance is negative), the variance of their sum (i.e., the variance of the portfolio) is reduced. We are more likely to get extreme values for the combination of investments if they move in the same direction; that is, if they are strongly positively correlated. This was one of the great insights that came out of Harry Markowitz's theory on optimal portfolio allocation, which won him the 1990 Nobel Memorial Prize in Economic Sciences. It led to the proliferation of *diversification* as a strategy in managing assets.

So far, we have reviewed what happens to the mean and the variance of a sum of two random variables. What about the actual probability distribution of a random variable that equals the sum of two random variables, such as $\tilde{Z} = \tilde{X} + \tilde{Y}$?

It turns out that computing the distribution of $\tilde{Z}$ is not as easy as adding up the PMFs or PDFs of $\tilde{X}$ and $\tilde{Y}$. If it was, a total sum of probabilities for the distribution of $\tilde{Z}$ would be more than 1. Moreover, the distribution of the sum of the two random variables may look nothing like the distributions of the individual variables. For example, exhibit 3.20 illustrates the distribution of the sum of two uniform random variables on [0,1]. The resulting distribution is the triangular distribution. Intuitively, this makes sense. For example, the mean values for both uniform distributions are in the middle—at 0.5. So it appears logical that most of the mass for the sum of the probability distributions would be in the middle too—at the sum of the expected values, $0.5 + 0.5 = 1$. Also, the range for the new variable $\tilde{Z}$ should be [0,2]. This is because the ranges for $\tilde{X}$ and $\tilde{Y}$ are both [0,1], so the minimum value for their sum is $0 + 0 = 0$ and the maximum value for their sum is $1 + 1 = 2$.

Unfortunately, most sums of probability distributions are not as easy to visualize. The actual formula for computing the distribution of the sum of two random variables involves nontrivial integration and is referred to as *convolution*. Let $f_X(x)$, $f_Y(y)$, and $f_Z(z)$ be the PDFs of the random variables $\tilde{X}$, $\tilde{Y}$ and $\tilde{Z}$ at points x, y, and z, respectively. Then the PDF for the sum $\tilde{Z}$ is

9. Note that this also eliminates the possibility that the standard deviation of the sum of two random variables is the sum of the standard deviations of the two variables. This is *never* true if the two random variables have different variances. If the two variables are independent (and the covariance is 0), we get

$$\sigma_{a \cdot \tilde{X} + b \cdot \tilde{Y}} = \sqrt{Var(a \cdot \tilde{X} + b \cdot \tilde{Y})} = \sqrt{a^2 \cdot Var(\tilde{X}) + b^2 \cdot Var(\tilde{Y})}$$
$$\neq a \cdot \sqrt{Var(\tilde{X})} + b \cdot \sqrt{Var(\tilde{Y})} = a \cdot \sigma_{\tilde{X}} + b \cdot \sigma_{\tilde{Y}}$$

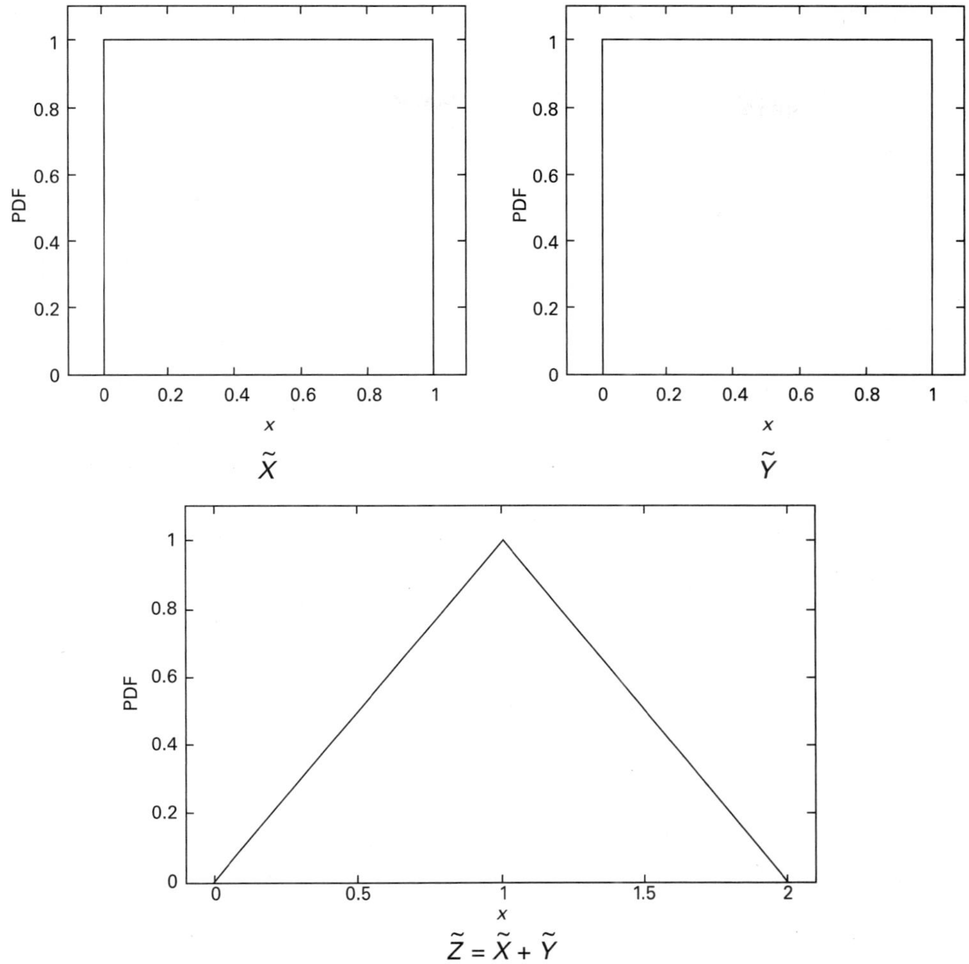

Exhibit 3.20
Sum (convolution) of two uniform random variables. The resulting probability distribution is triangular.

$$f_Z(z) = \int_{-\infty}^{\infty} f_Y(z-x) f_X(x)\, dx.$$

As we learn more about simulation techniques in chapter 5, the advantages of using simulation to evaluate such complex integrals will become evident.

3.10 Joint Probability Distributions and Conditional Probability

The previous section reviewed a number of important facts about sums of random variables. In this section, we introduce the concepts of joint probability distribution and conditional probability, which are also useful in situations in which we are dealing with more than one random variable.

Joint probability is simply the probability that two random variables take two values at the same time. The joint PMF of two discrete random variables $\tilde{X}$ and $\tilde{Y}$ is denoted as $p(\tilde{X}, \tilde{Y})$ or $p(\tilde{X} = x, \tilde{Y} = y)$. The joint PDF of two continuous random variables $\tilde{X}$ and $\tilde{Y}$

is denoted as $f(\tilde{X}, \tilde{Y})$. When $\tilde{X}$ and $\tilde{Y}$ both follow a specific probability distribution, their joint probability distribution is typically called a *multivariate distribution*. For example, if $\tilde{X}$ and $\tilde{Y}$ both follow normal distributions, their joint distribution is called *multivariate normal distribution*. If $\tilde{X}$ and $\tilde{Y}$ both follow binomial distributions, their joint distribution is called *multinomial distribution*.

In section 3.4, we briefly introduced the notation |, which means "conditional on." Conditioning on information has important applications in financial modeling, and we will see examples of it later in this book, such as when we introduce variance reduction techniques in chapter 19.

When two random variables are dependent, then knowing something about the realization of one of them should give us information about the likely realizations of the other one. (If it did not, then the two variables would be independent by definition.) The *conditional probability* that a random variable $\tilde{X}$ will take a value x given that a random variable $\tilde{Y}$ has taken value y is

$$P(\tilde{X} = x \middle| \tilde{Y} = y) = \frac{P(\tilde{X} = x \text{ and } \tilde{Y} = y)}{P(\tilde{Y} = y)}.$$

Intuitively, the fact that $\tilde{Y}$ has taken the value y eliminates some of the possible outcomes for $\tilde{X}$, and the revised probability that $\tilde{X}$ will take a value x is computed as a percentage of all those instances in which $\tilde{X} = x$, given $\tilde{Y} = y$.

The *conditional PDF* of a continuous random variable $\tilde{X}$ given $\tilde{Y}$ is

$$f_{\tilde{X}|\tilde{Y}}(x|y) = \frac{f_{\tilde{X},\tilde{Y}}(x, y)}{f_{\tilde{Y}}(y)}.$$

This concept and notation extend to the summary measures for probability distributions as well. The *conditional expectation* of the random variable $\tilde{X}$, given that $\tilde{Y}$ has taken value y, is simply the weighted average for the values of $\tilde{X}$ that are possible given the realization y of $\tilde{Y}$. The conditional expectation is denoted as $E[\tilde{X}|\tilde{Y} = y]$, and the notation carries over to variance, covariance, and so on. The following facts hold:

$$E[\tilde{X}] = E_Y[E_X[\tilde{X} \mid \tilde{Y}]]$$
$$Var(\tilde{X}) = E_X[Var(\tilde{X} \mid \tilde{Y})] + Var(E_X[\tilde{X} \mid \tilde{Y}])$$
$$\text{cov}(\tilde{X}, \tilde{Z}) = E_Y[\text{cov}(\tilde{X}, \tilde{Z}) \mid \tilde{Y}] + \text{cov}(E_X[\tilde{X} \mid \tilde{Y}], E_Z[\tilde{Z} \mid \tilde{Y}]).$$

For example, the first statement says that if we compute the mean of the possible values of a random variable $\tilde{X}$ when a specific realization of a random variable $\tilde{Y}$ has occurred, and then compute the sum (integral) of the means of the possible value of $\tilde{X}$ for all possible realizations of $\tilde{Y}$ (weighted by the probability of obtaining these realizations for $\tilde{Y}$), we should obtain the actual mean of $\tilde{X}$.

3.11 Risk Versus Uncertainty

Throughout this book, and in fact often in conversation and writings, the terms "risk" and "uncertainty" are used interchangeably. But is risk equivalent to uncertainty? Economists have argued this question of "risk as uncertainty" or "risk versus uncertainty." The distinction between risk and uncertainty was first made in 1921 by two leading economists, Frank Knight and John Maynard Keynes.

The distinction that Knight (1921) made between risk and uncertainty is as follows. He argued that risk applies to decision making when the outcome of the decision is unknown, but the decision maker can fairly accurately quantify the probability associated with each outcome that may arise from that decision. Knight referred to this risk as "measurable risk" or "risk proper." In contrast, he viewed uncertainty as applying to decisions in which the decision maker cannot know all the information needed to obtain all the probabilities associated with the outcomes. This situation gives rise to what is referred to as *Knightian uncertainty* and what Knight called "unmeasurable uncertainty" or "true uncertainty."

John Maynard Keynes (1921) made a similar distinction, arguing that there is risk that can be calculated and another sort of risk, which he labeled "irreducible uncertainty." Keynes recognized that in some decisions, the risks cannot be calculated because attempting to do so would require relying on assumptions about the future that have no basis in probability theory.

Here is a simple example. Suppose that you are presented with a game of chance that involves betting on the color of a ball that you select from an urn containing 100 balls. The urn holds black balls and yellow balls. To play this game of chance, you must pay $100. If you select a black ball, then you lose the $100. However, if you select a yellow ball, you receive $300. In determining to play this game of chance, do you face risk or uncertainty? Since you do not know how many black balls and yellow balls are in the urn, no probability distribution for the potential outcome of this game of chance can be determined. Thus, according to Knight and Keynes, you face uncertainty. However, if you are told the composition of the urn in terms of the number of black balls and yellow balls, you can determine the probability of the outcome that a ball selected may be black or yellow. Consequently, you would face risk in this game of chance, according to Knight and Keynes.

In practice, is the distinction between risk and uncertainty made by Knight and Keynes important in decision making? This is a long-running debate among economists: some have argued that the two concepts are the same, while others argue that the distinction is crucial. The worldwide financial crisis of 2008–2009, however, supported the importance of the Knight-Keynes view of the distinction between risk and uncertainty. One of the major factors that contributed to the 2008–2009 global financial crisis was the failure of risk management models to provide a warning about the financial problems that led to the financial crisis. It appears that the management of financial entities thought that they had adequate risk models to prevent a major collapse in the financial system. That is, management of financial entities failed to recognize that they were dealing with situations that involved Knightian uncertainty or Keynes's irreducible uncertainty.

Summary

- Uncertainty can be represented by random variables with associated probability distributions.

- Probability distributions can be viewed as listings of all the possible values that can happen and the corresponding probability of occurrence, and they are conveniently represented in graphs (histograms and bar charts).
- Probability distributions can be discrete or continuous. Discrete distributions are defined over a countable number of values, whereas continuous distributions are defined over a range. Discrete distributions are described by probability mass functions (PMFs), whereas continuous distributions are described by probability density functions (PDFs).
- A continuous random variable can take an infinite number of values, and the probability of each individual value is 0. In the context of continuous distributions, we replace the concept of probability of a value with the concept of probability of an interval of values, and the probability is the area under the PDF.
- Probability distributions can be summarized in terms of central tendency (mean, median, and mode), variability (standard deviation, variance, coefficient of variance (CV), range, percentile, etc.), skewness, and kurtosis.
- The mean, variance, skew, and kurtosis of a probability distribution are related to the first, second, third, and fourth moments of the distribution. The moments of a probability distribution can be computed from its moment-generating function. Inversely, if the moments of a probability distribution are known, most generally, the distribution can be uniquely identified. However, sometimes the moments do not exist.
- Important discrete probability distributions include the binomial distribution, Bernoulli distribution, discrete uniform distribution, and Poisson distribution.
- Important continuous probability distributions include the normal distribution, the continuous uniform distribution, the triangular distribution, the Student's t-distribution, the lognormal distribution, the exponential distribution, the chi-square distribution, and the beta distribution.
- Covariance and correlation are measures of the average codependence of two random variables.

4

Inferential Statistics

Probability distributions, reviewed in chapter 3, can be used to model and evaluate risk. Finance practitioners, however, do not necessarily know the true (also referred to as "population") probability distributions or underlying uncertainty. Instead, they usually have access to *data* that have been collected or "sampled." To translate observations from empirical probability distributions created from sampled data into generalizable insights about the real population probability distribution, one needs to use tools from *inferential statistics*, which is the subject of this chapter. Simulation modeling, described in chapter 5, can be viewed as a data generator because it involves sampling scenarios, and the inferential statistics concepts covered in this chapter are critical for understanding both simulation as a tool and the output from simulation modeling.

First, let us explain the difference between population and sample in more detail. Suppose that an equity portfolio manager is interested in performing some analysis on the stocks in the Russell 2000 index, a stock market index that is used as a benchmark for small capitalization companies in the U.S. stock market. There are 2,000 stocks in this index, which by definition make up the universe of stocks and therefore represent the *entire population*. Now suppose that in conducting the analysis, the portfolio manager randomly selects only 200 stocks from the index and uses them as representatives of all stocks in the index. Then the portfolio manager is only dealing with a *sample* from the population since not all U.S. small capitalization stocks are included in the analysis. Similarly, historical data on the monthly returns of a particular stock can be considered a sample from the true (population) distribution of possible stock returns. Note that we cannot assume that we know the population distribution unless one could prove that all possible values for returns are restricted only to that set of historical values.

Measures used to describe the real population probability distribution such as mean, variance, and skewness (covered in section 3.6) are referred to as *population parameters*. The same measures (mean, variance, skewness, etc.) estimated from a sample of the population are referred to as *sample statistics*. We note that sample statistics vary from sample to sample. The measurement of the population parameters is therefore inherently subject to *sampling error*.

Summarizing the properties of the population or the sample is known as *descriptive statistics*. In contrast, *inferential statistics*, or *inductive statistics*, is a field where statistical and mathematical methodologies are used to allow a decision maker to make inferences about characteristics of a population based on sample data from that population, while trying to control for the extent to which errors of inference may occur.

This chapter covers two main areas of inferential statistics: estimating population parameters from sample statistics and hypothesis testing. Estimating population parameters from sample statistics involves calculating a statistical measure from a sample drawn from a population and then making inferences about the corresponding population parameter. An estimate for the population parameter can be a single number (called a *point estimate*) or a range of values in which the parameter is likely to be found with some associated probability called a *confidence interval* (CI). A very important result in this area is the Central Limit Theorem (CLT), covered in section 4.1.1. Hypothesis testing is used to investigate whether a relationship among variables observed in a sample is significant enough to reject a hypothesis about the relationship in the population.

4.1 Estimating Population Parameters from Sample Statistics

Suppose that you have collected a sample of n independent observations $X_1, \ldots, X_n$. You can imagine grouping similar observations together into "bins" (which can be as small as a single number) and creating a histogram of observed values. This histogram will be an *empirical probability distribution.* An *estimator* is then used to calculate a sample statistic of interest, such as the mean. The estimator can be thought of as instructions for processing the sample data to obtain a valid representative of the population parameter. The exact structure of the estimator is predetermined before the sample is realized. After defining the estimator, one simply needs to enter the sample values accordingly. Due to the estimator's dependence on the random sample, the estimator is itself random. A particular value of the estimator based on the realization of some sample is called an *estimate.*

As we mentioned earlier, all the concepts for describing central tendency, spread, skew, covariability, and so on (explained in section 3.6) are valid for empirical distributions derived from samples of data, but their values are referred to as *sample statistics.* When dealing with sampled data, we need to consider the fact that there is inevitably some noise due to the limited number of observations in the sample. With financial data in particular, we can never observe or anticipate everything that can happen. We are not only limited in our ability to reconstruct a probability distribution from a fixed number of observations and forecasts but also need to worry about rare events, which are difficult to observe and thus are not necessarily a part of our sample. Hence, our estimates of the population parameters of the "underlying" probability distribution for the empirical data are inherently inaccurate.

There are commonly used notations to differentiate between summary measures for the population and sample distribution. Population parameters are usually denoted by Greek letters such as μ (for mean), σ (for standard deviation), σ^2 (for variance), and ρ (for correlation). Sample statistics are usually denoted by Latin letters, such as $\overline{X}$ (for sample mean), s (for sample standard deviation), s^2 (for sample variance), and r (for sample correlation). To compute these sample statistics, we use formulas for the corresponding parameters, as shown in exhibit 4.1.

- Sample mean:

$$\bar{X}=\frac{1}{n}\cdot\sum_{i=1}^{n}X_n$$

- Sample variance:

$$s^2=\frac{1}{n-1}\cdot\sum_{i=1}^{n}(X_n-\bar{X})^2$$

- Sample standard deviation:

$$s=\sqrt{\frac{1}{n-1}\cdot\sum_{i=1}^{n}(X_n-\bar{X})^2}$$

- Sample covariance:

$$\mathrm{SCov}(\tilde{X},\tilde{Y})=\frac{1}{n-1}\cdot\sum_{i=1}^{n}(X_n-\bar{X})(Y_n-\bar{Y})$$

- Sample correlation:

$$r(\tilde{X},\tilde{Y})=\frac{\mathrm{SCoV}(\tilde{X},\tilde{Y})}{s_X s_Y}$$

Exhibit 4.1
Sample statistics.

Note that the principle behind computing the sample mean is very similar to that of computing the mean of a general probability distribution. The mean is still a weighted average of the possible values of the random variable. Our sample contains n independent observations, so the probability of each of them must be $1/n$ (otherwise, the total probability would not add up to 1). Therefore, to compute the mean, we are weighing each observation by its probability of occurrence ($1/n$) and adding up the observations.

A substantial amount of research in statistics has been dedicated to finding ways to accurately estimate the population parameters through sampling. For example, covariance and correlation estimates are widely used in forecasting the return on assets for portfolio management purposes, and they are notoriously inaccurate because, as surprising as it seems, there are not enough data to estimate them reliably. (This is complicated by the fact that they vary over time.) The correlation coefficient described in section 3.8 is the classical Pearson correlation coefficient. Another kind of correlation coefficient that is particularly useful in the case of noisy sampled data is the Spearman correlation. It does not incorporate as much information about the data as the Pearson correlation coefficient, but it tends to be more stable than the Pearson correlation when there is noise in the data. The Spearman correlation is a rank correlation. In other words, instead of considering the *values* of the random variables, it computes the correlation between the ranks of the observations in a sample. The mean of the rank replaces the mean of the random variable.

4.1.1 Central Limit Theorem

Suppose that we have a sample of n independent observations $X_1, \ldots, X_n$ *drawn from the same underlying distribution*. The shorthand for this statement is that $X_1, \ldots, X_n$ are i.i.d. (i.e., independent and identically distributed). Let us assume that the mean of the underlying distribution is μ_X and its standard deviation is σ_X. Let S_n denote the sum of the n observations; that is,

$$S_N = \sum_{n=1}^{N} X_n .$$

Then, so long as the sample size n is moderately large (the rule of thumb is greater than 30), and under some relatively mild technical conditions on the underlying probability distribution, the distribution of the sum S_n is normal with mean equal to $\mu_S = n \cdot \mu_X$ and standard deviation $\sigma_S = \sigma_X \cdot \sqrt{n}$. This means that if we are to take many samples (always of size n) from this distribution, compute the sums of the n observations for each of these samples, and plot these sums, we would obtain a graph that looks very much like the normal distribution.

The expressions for the mean and the standard deviation of the sum of i.i.d. random variables in the CLT follow easily from the rules in section 3.9. However, the fact that the distribution of the sum approaches normal is not at all obvious. It is one of the greatest theoretical results linking probability theory and applied statistics and is, to a large extent, the reason for the popularity of the normal distribution in practice. The power of the CLT is the conclusion that many real-world phenomena should be well described by the normal distribution, even if the underlying random process that generates them is unknown.

The CLT result serves as the justification for many practitioners to use the normal distribution as an approximation when they analyze the risk of their investments. The argument is that as returns accumulate over time, things become normal. The problem arises, however, if the assumptions behind the CLT are not satisfied in practice. For example, the underlying distributions from which samples are drawn change over time depending on market conditions, and there can be correlations across returns from different time periods, so the i.i.d. assumption does not necessarily hold. The nonnormality of returns is especially pronounced in high-frequency trading, as the time intervals between trades are too short to allow "things to approach" the normal distribution. As we will see in parts II and III of this book, this kind of reasoning can lead to a gross underestimation of investment risk.

Note that CLT requires that certain conditions on the population distribution are met, such as finiteness of the variance. If the variance or even the mean do not exist, another theorem, the *Generalized Central Limit Theorem*, can be applied under certain conditions. These conditions are beyond the scope of this book.

4.1.2 Quality Criteria of Estimators

There is more than one estimator that can be used to obtain an estimate for a parameter. Given a choice of estimators, a natural question is whether one estimator is superior to the others that can be used. In fact, depending on the probability distribution of the population, estimators suitable for the very same parameters can vary quite remarkably when it comes to the quality of their estimation. Here, we will explain some of the most employed *quality criteria*: bias, precision, and consistency.

4.1.2.1 Bias An important consideration in the selection of an estimator is the average behavior of that estimator over all possible samples. The estimator may not equal the value of the population parameter and, in fact, could be considerably different from it. This is to be expected because of the variability of the underlying sample. However, the average value of the estimator can typically be controlled.

To understand this, first consider the *sampling error* measured by the difference between the estimate and the population parameter. Due to the uncertainty of each sample, the difference between the two values is random. The expected value of the sample error is referred to as the *bias*. Estimators for which the expected value of the bias is zero are preferable, and in such cases, the estimator is said to be *unbiased.* If the expected value of the sampling error (i.e., the bias) is not zero, then the estimator is said to be *unbiased.*

Let's look at two estimators, the mean and the variance for a sample used to estimate the population mean and variance as shown in exhibit 4.1. It can be seen that the sample mean is an unbiased estimator of the population mean, which provides support for its widespread use regardless of the probability distribution.

Now, consider the case of the sample variance as an estimator for the population variance. The formula for the variance of the population of size N, σ^2, with a mean μ for the random variable x is

$$\sigma^2 = \frac{1}{N} \cdot \Sigma(x - \mu)^2 \tag{4.1}$$

If equation (4.1) is applied to a sample of size n ($n < N$) and the mean of the sample, $\bar{X}$, is used, then the sample variance (s^2) would be

$$s^2 = \frac{1}{n-1} \cdot \sum_{i=1}^{n} (X_n - \bar{X})^2 \tag{4.2}$$

If this estimator of the sample variance is used, it can be shown that the bias (i.e., the expected value of the sampling error) is $-\frac{1}{n}\sigma^2$. That is, the formula for the sample variance as given by equation (4.2) is a biased estimator of the population variance. More specifically, it is a downward bias. Note that when the sample size (n) is large, then the bias becomes negligible.

What is an unbiased estimator for the variance? Look at exhibit 4.1 for the formula of the sample variance. It differs from formula (4.2) in that the term $1/n$ is replaced by $1/(n—1)$. It can be shown that the formula for the variance in exhibit 4.1 is an unbiased estimator of the population variance.

4.1.2.2 Precision Although bias as a quality criterion tells us about the expected deviation of the estimator from the population parameter, it does not tell us about the variability or spread of the estimator. For a reliable inference for the parameter value, an estimator with small variability would be preferred. This criterion for an estimator is referred to as the *precision* of an estimator, and an estimator with high precision is preferred.

To understand the precision criterion, assume that we repeatedly (say, m times) draw samples of given size n. Using an estimator for each of these m samples, we then compute the respective population parameter estimate. From these m population parameter estimates, we obtain an empirical distribution of the estimates, including an empirical spread given by the sample distribution of the estimates.

Drawing on the CLT, we know that with increasing sample size n, the empirical distribution will eventually look like the normal distribution for most estimators. However, regardless of any empirical distribution of estimates, an estimator has a theoretical sampling distribution for each sample size n. So the random estimator is a random variable distributed by the law of the sampling distribution. The larger the sample size n, the more the empirical and the sampling distributions will look alike. The sampling distribution provides a theoretical measure of the spread of the estimator (namely, its variance). The square root of the variance is called the *standard error* or *estimator variance*.

Suppose that an estimator has a bias of zero. Although this is desirable, this criterion may be too restrictive if an estimator has only a slight bias but has a favorably small variance (high precision) compared to all other estimators, biased or unbiased. A quality criterion accounting for both bias and precision of an estimator is the *mean-squared error* (MSE), which is defined as the expected squared sampling error and is composed of two parts. The first part is the estimator variance, and the second part is the square of the bias. When selecting an estimator, the objective can be to identify the MSE-minimal estimator from among the possible estimators.

MSE-minimal estimators are not available for all population parameters. In such cases, it is necessary to assess the trade-off between reducing either the bias or the estimator variance over a set of possible estimators. Therefore, we simply try to find a minimum-variance estimator of all unbiased estimators, which is called the *minimum-variance unbiased estimator*. This is done because in many applications, unbiasedness takes priority over precision.

4.1.2.3 Consistency Another important aspect of estimation is the potential change in the behavior of the estimator as the sample size n varies. For example, suppose that some estimator is biased for any given sample size n, but it gradually loses its bias as n increases. Here, we will analyze an estimator as the sample size approaches infinity. That is, what are the large sample properties (also referred to as *asymptotic* properties) of an estimator? This property is referred to as *consistency*.

An estimator is consistent if more data provide more information. Generally, an estimator is inconsistent if an arbitrarily large amount of data does not allow one to obtain an estimate that is near or close to the population parameter. If an estimator is inconsistent, there is little reason to look into what other properties an estimator may have. Hence, consistency is one of the most fundamental properties that an estimator should exhibit.

An estimator is said to be *weakly consistent* if the estimator converges in probability to some constant as the sample size approaches infinity. Basically, weakly consistent means that as the sample size becomes arbitrarily large, the probability that an estimator will assume a value that is a specified small amount away from that constant will become increasingly negligible.

It is important to emphasize that the reason why the consistency of an estimator is an important property is because an estimator with this property can be relied upon to systematically give sound results with respect to the true population parameter. By increasing the sample size n, estimates will deviate from the population parameter only in rare cases.

4.1.3 Confidence Intervals

One of the consequences of the CLT is that it allows us to make statements about the accuracy of our estimate of the sample mean. The sample mean $\bar{X}$ shown in exhibit 4.1 can be expressed as a sum of n i.i.d. variables, $X_1/n, \ldots, X_n/n$. Therefore, the CLT applies. Using the rules in section 3.9, it can be shown that the sample mean $\bar{X}$ follows an approximately normal distribution with mean $\mu_{\bar{X}} = \mu_X$ and standard deviation $\sigma_{\bar{X}} = \sigma_X/\sqrt{n}$.

Therefore, we know the variability of our sample mean estimate. The standard deviation of $\bar{X}$, also called the *standard error of the estimate*, is inversely proportional to the square root of the number of observations in the sample. Not surprisingly, the more observations that we have, the more accurate our estimate of the true value of the distribution will be. In practice, of course, we do not know the true standard deviation σ_X (if we knew that, we would know the mean as well, so we would not be trying to estimate the mean). So, we need to make some adjustments—use the standard deviation s from the sample to approximate σ_X—and modify the estimation slightly to account for the additional inaccuracy that using a sample statistic in the formula brings.[1]

The concept of CI estimates is to present not only a point estimate for the population parameter of interest (in this case, one value calculated as the sample mean $\bar{X}$), but also to state how far this estimate will be from the true parameter (the true mean of the underlying distribution). This is achieved by stating an interval centered at $\bar{X}$ whose length depends on

1. The variability of the estimate (the larger the standard error of $\bar{X}$, the less likely it is that we will get the correct estimate for the true mean from the sample)
2. The degree of confidence that we would like to have that this interval will cover the true mean (represented by $(100-\alpha)\%$, where α is a selected *level of significance*)

Typical values for the confidence level include 90%, 95%, and 99%. The exact formula for a two-sided $(100-\alpha)\%$ CI for the sample mean $\bar{X}$ is

$$\left[\bar{X} - t_{(100-\alpha/2),n-1}\frac{s}{\sqrt{n}}, \bar{X} + t_{(100-\alpha/2),n-1}\frac{s}{\sqrt{n}}\right], \tag{4.3}$$

where $t_{(100-\alpha/2),\,n-1}$ is the $(100-\alpha)$th percentile (the value on the horizontal axis) of a t-distribution with $n-1$ degrees of freedom.[2] Stated in words, the $(100-\alpha)\%$ CI for the sample mean $\bar{X}$ states that the probability that the interval computed from formula (4.3) covers the true mean μ is $(100-\alpha)\%$.

As we saw in exhibit 3.17, the t-distribution becomes very close to the normal distribution as the parameter for degrees of freedom v (which here equals $n-1$) becomes large. In the context of simulation, where sample sizes would generally be large, replacing the

1. This is where the discovery of Student's t-distribution made a substantial contribution to modern statistics.

2. Several software packages have commands for computing the value of t, including Microsoft Excel, Python, and MATLAB. In most statistical packages, one would use a command of the kind tinv($100-\alpha/2$, degrees of freedom). Excel has a similar command (=TINV(α, degrees of freedom)), but it is a bit inconsistent. It takes in as an argument α, not $100-\alpha/2$, to compute the $(100-\alpha/2)$th percentile of the t-distribution.

value of the percentile from the t-distribution with the value of the percentile from the normal distribution will make no difference for all practical purposes.

4.1.4 Bootstrapping

The CI estimate for the mean is the CI most widely used in practice. However, sometimes, we need to evaluate the accuracy of other parameter estimates for one or more distributions. For example, we may be concerned about how accurate our estimates of the distribution percentile or skewness are. (This kind of application is relevant in portfolio risk management.) Alternatively, suppose that a financial manager analyzing two investment projects computed the correlation between historical returns and two projects from exhibit 3.9 and has discovered that it is 0.6. Is this a strong correlation in the statistical sense; that is, does it appear to be strong just by chance (because the financial manager picked a good sample), or can the financial manager expect that it will remain strong in other samples, given the overall variability in this sample's data?

The procedure of computing the CI estimate of the mean is representative of classical methods in statistics, which relied on mathematical formulas to describe the accuracy of a sample statistic estimate. There are some theoretical results on CI estimates for distribution parameters other than the mean, but in general, the results are not as easy to summarize as the closed-form expression for the CI estimate for the mean from section 4.1.2.

Bootstrapping[3] is a statistical technique that is useful in such situations. It involves drawing multiple samples of the same size (say, k samples) at random from the observations in the original sample of n observations. Each of the k samples is drawn with replacement—that is, every time an observation is drawn, it is placed back in the original sample and is eligible to be drawn again, whether in the same sample or in future samples.

After drawing k samples from the original sample, the statistic corresponding to the parameter that we are interested in estimating (whether it is percentile, skewness, correlation, or a general function of the random variable) is computed for each of the k samples. The so-obtained k values for the sample statistic are used to form an approximation of the estimator's *sampling distribution*. This sampling distribution can be used, for example, to determine what values of the sample statistic are most likely to occur, what the variability of the estimate is, and what the 5th and the 95th percentiles of the approximate sampling distribution are. These percentiles provide an approximation for the CI for the true parameter that we are trying to estimate.

At first glance, this technique appears pointless. Why don't we collect k more samples instead of reusing the same dataset k times? The reason is that it is expensive to collect data, and sometimes additional data collection is not an option, especially with financial data.

Bootstrapping is used not only for evaluating the accuracy in the estimate of a probability distribution parameter, but also as a simple method for generating forecasts for

3. As explained in chapter 2, there is a methodology commonly used in bond analysis to derive the term structure of interest rates that is referred to as *bootstrapping*. The statistical concept of bootstrapping described in this chapter has nothing to do with that methodology.

uncertain quantities based on a set of historical observations for risk management purposes. The concept of simulation is necessary to understand how the bootstrap method is actually applied, as the random draws from the original sample need to be generated with a random number generator.[4]

4.2 Hypothesis Testing

Hypothesis testing is a fundamental concept in statistics. The procedure is as follows: We start by stating a hypothesis about a parameter for the distribution corresponding to a variable of interest. This hypothesis is referred to as the *null hypothesis and typically denoted by* H_0. The alternative hypothesis is the statement that the null hypothesis is not true and has a value different from what is asserted by the null hypothesis.

Commonly denoted by H_1, the alternative hypothesis can be that the value that is being tested is not equal to the value assumed by the null hypothesis, or that the value is either greater than or less than the value claimed by the null hypothesis.

Suppose that the null hypothesis is that the value of some population parameter μ is zero, expressed as follows:

$$H_0\text{: } \mu = 0$$

The alternative hypothesis is the opposite of H_0 and can be written as $H_1\text{: } \mu \neq 0$.

Two other possible pairs of null and alternative hypotheses are

$$H_0\text{: } \mu \geq 0;\ H_1\text{: } \mu < 0$$

$$H_0\text{: } \mu \leq 0;\ H_1\text{: } \mu > 0$$

When the alternative hypothesis is $H_1\text{: } \mu \neq 0$, then we have a *two-tail test of the null hypothesis,* or simply a *two-tail test*; when the alternative hypothesis is either $H_1\text{: } \mu < 0$ or $H_1\text{: } \mu > 0$, then we have a *one-tail test of the null hypothesis,* or simply a *one-tail test.*

Here are two examples. Suppose that a portfolio manager claims that the skew of the distribution for the returns of the S&P 500 index is 0.[5] That is, H_0: skewness = 0. To test that claim, a sample of S&P 500 returns over some reasonable time period is obtained and the skew for that sample of returns is computed as –0.11. The statistical hypothesis testing methodology allows the portfolio manager to test whether the value obtained from the sample is sufficiently close to the hypothesized value of 0 to conclude that in fact, the real skew could indeed be 0, and the difference is only a consequence of sampling error. Depending on what portfolio managers are trying to test for, they could use a one-tail or two-tail test. For example, if the managers are only concerned about substantially lower values of skewness than 0 (and not both lower and higher values of skewness), they could use a one-sided test.

In our second example, let's use a common hypothesis test performed in asset management: backtesting an investment strategy. In backtesting an investment strategy, the objective

4. See chapter 5 for a discussion of the simulation technique.

5. As we will see later in this book, although often unjustified, making assumptions like these substantially simplifies risk measurement and derivative pricing.

might be to outperform a benchmark by, say, at least 40 basis points after considering transaction costs and management fees. The null hypothesis in this case would be H_0: Strategy return $\geq$ 40 basis points. The alternative hypothesis is H_1: Strategy return < 40 basis points (a one-tail test). Suppose that via backtesting, it is determined that the strategy produced an average return of 36 basis points. While 36 basis points is clearly below the minimum target of 40 basis points, there is variation in the backtested returns (i.e., a probability distribution is generated from the investment strategy return). That variation must be considered in hypothesis testing to determine if the average of 36 basis points is below 40 basis points or if it is close enough to 40 to support the null hypothesis that the strategy is effective.

4.2.1 The Test Statistic for Accepting or Rejecting the Null Hypothesis

What do we mean when we say that we must test whether the average of 36 basis points is less than 40 basis points? It is whether the average of 36 basis points is less than 40 basis points from a statistical perspective.

To test whether the difference between the hypothesized and the observed values is statistically significant (i.e., large enough to be considered a reason to reject the original hypothesis), a quantity called a *test statistic* is computed, which is a function of the observed and hypothesized parameters. In some cases, this test statistic follows a known probability distribution. For example, if we are testing a hypothesis about the sample mean, then the test statistic is the *t*-statistic (introduced in section 4.1.2) because the sample means follows a *t*-distribution with degrees of freedom equal to the sample size minus 1. Knowing that the test statistic follows a specific distribution, we can check whether the test statistic obtained from the sample is very far from the center of the distribution, which tells us whether the sample estimate that was obtained would be a rare occurrence if the hypothesized value were true.

There are different ways to measure the rarity of the observed sample statistic. Statistical software packages typically report a *p*-value, which is the probability that, if our null hypothesis were true, we would get a more extreme sample statistic than the one we observed. If the *p*-value is small (the actual cutoff is arbitrary, but the values typically used are 1%, 5% or 10%), then we would reject the null hypothesis. This is because a small *p*-value means that there is a very low probability that we would have obtained a sample statistic as extreme as the one that we obtained if the hypothesis were true; that is, that the current test statistic is in the tails of the distribution.

The type of hypothesis test that we have described so far is called the *one-sample hypothesis test* because it interprets the information for only one sample. There are *two-sample hypothesis tests* that compare observed statistics from two samples with the goal of testing whether two populations are statistically different. They could be used, for example, to compare whether the returns of one investment strategy have been statistically better on average than the returns from another investment strategy.

Finally, more sophisticated hypothesis tests are used in the background for several important applications in financial modeling. Multivariate regression analysis, which we will discuss in chapter 5, uses hypothesis testing to determine whether a forecasting model is statistically significant. Goodness-of-fit tests, which are used in the context of fitting probability distributions to observed data, use statistical hypothesis testing to determine whether the observed data are statistically significantly close to a hypothesized probability distribution. Chi-square tests are a very popular type of goodness-of-fit test. (See also the discussion on selecting probability distributions as inputs for simulation models in section 5.1.1 in chapter 5.)

4.2.2 Parametric Versus Nonparametric Tests

In hypothesis testing, an assumption about the probability distribution of the population from the sample is drawn and may or may not be made. When assumptions are made about the parameters of the population distribution from which the sample is drawn, the test is said to be a *parametric test*. For example, if it is assumed in a hypothesis test that the population distribution is normal (a typical assumption made in finance), then the test is a parametric test. In contrast, when testing a hypothesis that makes no assumption about the population distribution, the test is said to be a *nonparametric test* or a *distribution-free test*.

4.2.3 Types of Errors in Hypothesis Testing

In hypothesis testing, the decisions that can be made fall into the following matrix:

Decision about Null Hypothesis	**Null Hypothesis Is True**	**Null Hypothesis Is False** (i.e., alternative hypothesis is true)
Accept	Correct	Error (Type II error)
Reject	Error (Type I error)	Correct

Notice that in two cases, the decision is correct. In the two other cases, there is an error. These errors are commonly referred to as a *Type I error* and *Type II error*:

Type I error: The error resulting by rejecting the null hypothesis, even though it is actually true. Type I error is also referred to as an *α error*.

Type II error: The error resulting from not rejecting the null hypothesis, even though the alternative hypothesis is true. Type II error is also referred to as a *β error*.

Let's explain these errors in the context of backtesting investment strategies. In evaluating an investment strategy, the null hypothesis is usually that the strategy is not profitable. The errors made in hypothesis testing as they apply to evaluating investment strategies can be referred to as a *false discovery error* and a *missed discovery error*. A *false discovery error* is made when an investment strategy is found to be profitable when in fact it is not. This is the Type I error (the null hypothesis is rejected when it is in fact true). A *missed discovery error* results when an investment strategy is found to be unprofitable when in fact it is profitable (the null hypothesis is not rejected when it is actually false). This is a Type II error.

Summary

- Summarizing the properties of the population or the sample through measures like mean, variance, and skewness is referred to as *descriptive statistics*. Methodologies that allow a decision maker to make inferences about characteristics of a population based on sample data from that population fall into the field of *inferential statistics*.

- A population parameter refers to a *summary measure* of a population, whereas a measure estimated from a sample of the population is referred to as a sample statistic.
- Two main areas of inferential statistics are estimating sample statistics and hypothesis testing.
- An estimator is rule or a method for arriving at an estimate of the value of a population parameter from sample data. Due to the estimator's dependence on the random sample, the value of the estimator is itself random. An estimate is a particular value of the estimator based on the realization of some sample.
- Empirical distributions are derived from sample data. All summary measures for probability distributions apply to empirical distributions.
- The Central Limit Theorem (CLT) states that as the sample size n increases, the sampling distribution of the sum of n observations that independent and identically distributed (i.i.d.) approaches a normal distribution, regardless of what the underlying population distribution is. This is especially true for large sample sizes and well-behaved underlying distributions.
- Since there is more than one estimator that can be used to obtain an estimate for a population parameter, there are quality criteria that can be used to select the estimator, including bias, precision, and consistency.
- A confidence interval (CI) allows a decision maker to state both an estimate of a parameter of an unknown probability distribution and the decision maker's confidence in that estimate.
- Bootstrapping is a statistical technique for evaluating the accuracy of sample statistics based on one sample of observations. It involves drawing multiple samples from the original sample, calculating the sample statistic in each of them, and analyzing the resulting distribution of the sample statistic. Bootstrapping can also be used as a simple way to generate future forecasts for uncertain quantities based on a sample of past observations.
- Hypothesis testing is a statistical methodology for evaluating whether the value of a sample statistic is significantly different from the expected value of a parameter of interest. It is used in many applications, including goodness-of-fit tests, multivariate regression analysis, and comparisons of two populations.
- The two errors in hypothesis testing are Type I error (rejecting the null hypothesis, even though it is actually true) and Type II error (not rejecting the null hypothesis even though the alternative hypothesis is true). Type I error is also referred to as α *error* and Type II error is also referred to as β *error*.

II

Fundamentals of Simulation, Optimization, and Machine Learning

5

Simulation Modeling

This chapter reviews the main idea behind Monte Carlo (MC) simulation and discusses important issues in its application to problems in finance, such as the number of scenarios to generate, interpretation of output, and efficient ways to simulate random numbers.

5.1 Monte Carlo Simulation: A Simple Example

As explained in chapter 3, risk analysis is based on modeling uncertainty, and uncertainty can be represented mathematically by probability distributions. These probability distributions are the building blocks for simulation models. Namely, simulation models take probability distribution assumptions on the uncertainties as inputs and generate scenarios (often referred to as *trials*) that happen with probabilities described by the probability distributions. They then record what happens to variables of interest (called *output variables*) over these scenarios and let us analyze the characteristics of the output probability distributions (see exhibit 5.1).

Let us start with a simple example. Suppose that you want to invest \$1,000 in the U.S. stock market for one year. To do so, you decide that you want to invest in a stock index representing the performance of the stock market. Specifically, you invest in a mutual fund whose investment objective is to reproduce the return performance on the S&P 500. A mutual fund with such an objective is called an *index fund*. We will denote the initial investment, or capital, invested in the index fund as C_0 (i.e., $C_0 = \$1,000$). How much money do you expect to have at the end of the year? Let us label the amount of capital at the end of the year as $\tilde{C}_1$.[1] Note that $\tilde{C}_1$ will be a random variable because it will depend on how the market (i.e., S&P 500) performs during the year. If we let $\tilde{r}_{0,1}$ denote the market return over the time period $[0,1)$, then $\tilde{C}_1$ will equal

$$C_0 + \tilde{r}_{0,1}C_0$$

or, equivalently,

$$(1 + \tilde{r}_{0,1})C_0$$

1. Recall from chapter 3 that we use a tilde (~) to denote uncertain quantities and random variables.

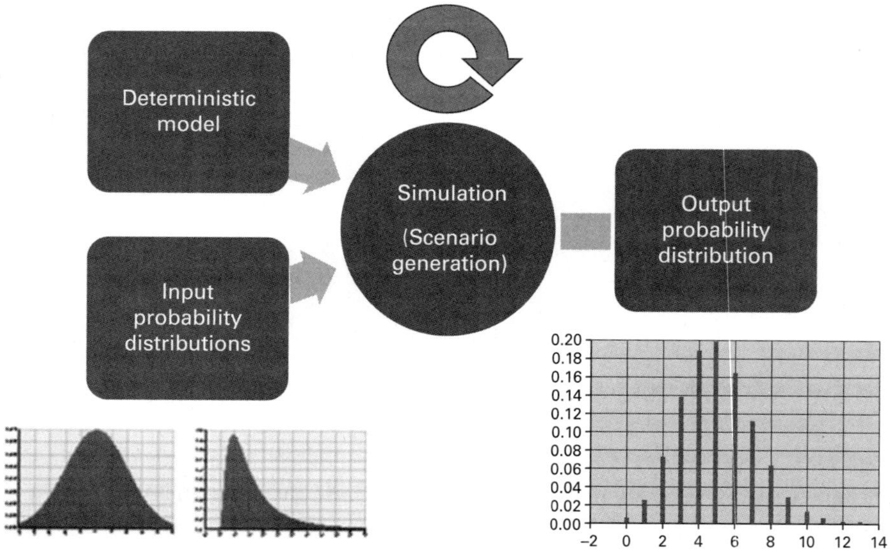

Exhibit 5.1
Typical MC simulation system.

As explained in chapter 2, the return $r_{t,t+1}$ over a time period $[t, t+1)$ can be computed as

$$\frac{P_{t+1} - P_t + D_t}{P_t}$$

where P_t and P_{t+1} are the values of the S&P 500 at times t and $t+1$, respectively, and D_t is the amount of dividends paid over that time period. In this example, we can think of P_t and P_{t+1} as the S&P 500 index levels at the beginning ($t=0$) and the end of the year ($t=1$), respectively, and assume that D_t is 0.

To estimate the end-of-year capital that you would have, you can guess the return on the market and compute the resulting value for $\tilde{C}_1$. However, this would give you only a point estimate of the possible values for your investment. A more sophisticated approach is to generate scenarios for the market return over the year and compute $\tilde{C}_1$ in each of these scenarios. In other words, you can represent future returns by a probability distribution,[2] generate scenarios that are representative of this probability distribution, and then analyze the resulting distribution of your end-of-year capital. The resulting probability distribution of $\tilde{C}_1$ will be a set of scenarios itself. You can create a percentage histogram of the outcomes; that is, collect the outcomes of the scenarios into nonoverlapping bins and draw bars above all the bins with heights corresponding to the percentage of times that outcomes in each bin were obtained in the simulation. This will allow you to visualize the *approximate* probability distribution of $\tilde{C}_1$ and analyze it with the statistical measures described in section 4.1 in chapter 4 (central

2. Note that there are an infinite number of values that a return can take because a return is expressed as a percentage. So, while you can certainly input a discrete set of possible scenarios for return, it is not unnatural to assume that the actual realization of the return is drawn from a *continuous* probability distribution.

tendency, skew, variability, etc.). The distribution for $\tilde{C}_1$ from the simulation will be only an approximation because it will depend both on the *number* of scenarios and on the *set* of scenarios that you generated for $\tilde{r}_{0,1}$. Intuitively, if you generate 1,000 scenarios that cover the possible values for $\tilde{r}_{0,1}$ well, you can expect to obtain a better representation of the distribution of $\tilde{C}_1$ than if you had generated only two scenarios.

5.1.1 Selecting Probability Distributions for the Inputs

The first question that you need to ask yourself when creating the simulation model about the future values of your funds is what distribution is appropriate for modeling the future market returns. One possible starting point is to look at a historical distribution of past returns and assume that the future will behave in the same way. When creating scenarios for future realizations, then, you can draw randomly from historical scenarios. This is a very simple approach, which is based on the *bootstrapping* technique described in chapter 4.

Another possibility is to assume a particular probability distribution for future returns, and use historical data to estimate the *parameters* of this distribution; that is, the parameters that determine the specific shape of the distribution, such as the expected value (μ) and standard deviation (σ) for a normal distribution (see section 3.4), λ for a Poisson distribution (see section 3.7.1), or α and β for a beta distribution (see section 3.7.2). For example, if you assume a normal distribution for returns, you can use the historical variability of returns as a measure of the standard deviation σ of this normal distribution and the historical average (mean) as the expected return μ of the normal distribution.

A third approach is not to start with a particular distribution, but rather to use historical data to find a distribution for returns that provides the best *fit* to the data. As mentioned in chapters 3 and 4, the chi-square hypothesis test is one possible goodness-of-fit test. Other goodness-of-fit tests include the Kolmogorov-Smirnov (K-S) test, the Anderson-Darling (A-D) test, and root-mean-squared-error (RMSE).[3] Most simulation software packages have commands that can test the goodness of fit for different probability distributions.[4]

Yet a fourth way is to ignore the past and look forward, constructing a probability distribution based on your subjective guess about how the uncertain variable in your model will behave. For example, using the beta distribution from exhibit 3.18(A) to model the

3. There is no rule for which goodness-of-fit test is determined "best." Each of them has advantages and disadvantages. The chi-square test is the most general one, and it can be used for data that come from both continuous and discrete distributions; however, to calculate the chi-square test statistic, one needs to divide the data into bins, and the results depend strongly on how the bins are determined. The K-S and the A-D tests apply only to continuous distributions. They do not depend on dividing the data into bins, so their results are less arbitrary. The K-S statistic is concerned primarily with whether the *centers* of the empirical and the expected distribution are close. In contrast, A-D focuses on the discrepancy between the *tails* of the observed and the expected distribution. For all three tests, the smaller the value of the test statistic, the closer the fit is. Most statistical software packages also report a *p*-value; that is, a probability, in addition to a test statistic. The larger the *p*-value, the closer the fit is. Finally, the RMSE measures the squared error of the differences between observed and the expected values. The smaller the number, the better, but the actual magnitude of the RMSE depends on the distribution and data at hand.

4. @RISK has a **Distribution Fitting** button in its ribbon in Microsoft Excel, which allows the user to (1) specify whether the distribution to be fitted is continuous or discrete (which narrows down the type of goodness-of-fit tests); (2) check a list of distributions that need to be checked for goodness of fit; and (3) tweak options in the computation of the chi-square goodness-of-fit statistic. @RISK then lists, in order of goodness of fit, the possible probability distributions and their parameters.

MATLAB's Statistics Toolbox contains a **Distribution Fitting** tool as well, as does the SciPy library in Python.

future market return will express a more pessimistic view of the market compared to the beta distribution in exhibit 3.18(B) or a normal distribution because most of the probability mass in the distribution in exhibit 3.18(A) is to the left, so low values for return will happen more often when scenarios are generated.

It is important to realize that none of these approaches will provide *the answer*. Simulation is a great tool for modeling uncertainty, but the outcome is only as good as the inputs provided to our models. We discuss ways for defining input distributions in specific applications in the book. The art of simulation modeling is in providing good inputs and interpreting the results carefully.

5.1.2 Interpreting Monte Carlo Simulation Output

For the purposes of our example, let us assume that the return on the market over the next year will follow a normal distribution. (This is a widely used assumption in practice, even though few empirical studies find evidence to support it.) Suppose that over the past 10 years, a stock market index returned 8.79% per annum on average, with a standard deviation of 14.65%. We will use these numbers as approximations for the average return and the standard deviation of the return on your investment in the stock market over the next year. Relying on historical data is flawed, but a reasonable starting point.

This chapter's online Software Hints appendix goes step by step through the implementation of our simple example. Here, we discuss the output that one would obtain after generating 100 scenarios for the market return over the next year. Note that to generate these scenarios, we simply need to draw 100 numbers from a normal distribution with mean 8.79% and standard deviation 14.65%. The input to the simulation, then, would be a sequence of 100 numbers such as

0.0245
−0.1561
0.1063
0.1300
−0.0801
0.2624
0.2621
0.0824
0.1358
0.1135
0.0605

and so on.

The output graph would look like exhibit 5.2. Summary statistics obtained based on the 100 values of the distribution are provided to the right of the graph.[5]

5. Note that, depending on the specific set of 100 scenarios that we have generated, the graph will look different. Therefore, the descriptive statistics and the look of the graph presented here will only be close to what you would obtain if you try to repeat this experiment.

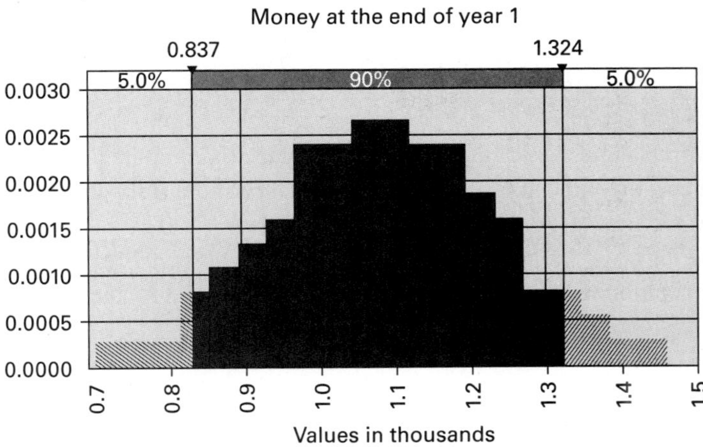

Number of values	100
Mean	$ 1,087.90
Std deviation	$ 146.15
Skewness	0.0034442
Kurtosis	2.871695
Mode	$ 1,118.96
5% Perc	$ 837.40
95% Perc	$ 1,324.00
Minimum	$ 708.81
Maximum	$ 1,458.52

Exhibit 5.2
Histogram and summary statistics for the end-of-year distribution of 100 simulated values for $1,000 invested at the beginning of the year.

If historical trends hold, you would expect to have $1,087.90 on average at the end of the first year. The standard deviation of the end-of-year capital that you would expect is $146.15; that is, on average, you would expect to be $146.15 off the mean value. With 5% probability, you will not be able to make more than $837.00 (the 5th percentile of the distribution), and with 95% probability, you will make less than $1,324.00 (the 95th percentile of the distribution). The skewness is close to 0 and the kurtosis is close to 3, which means that the simulated distribution is close to normal. (In fact, the output distribution is normal because the input distribution provided for the simulation of this simple relationship was normal, but the estimate from the simulation will never be perfectly accurate.)

Be careful when interpreting minima and maxima in a simulation. Theoretically, the minimum and maximum that we could have obtained in this simulation are negative and positive infinity because the probability distribution for the return (the normal distribution) has an infinite range. We did not obtain a particularly small minimum or a particularly large maximum because we simulated only 100 values. An event in the tail of the distribution with a probability of occurring of less than 1 / 100 would be unlikely to appear in this set of simulated values. The minimum and the maximum are highly sensitive to the number of simulated values and whether the simulated values in the tails of the distribution provide good representation for the tails of the distribution. There are smart ways to simulate scenarios so the tails are well represented (we will talk about such methods later in this chapter), but nevertheless the minimum and the maximum values obtained in a simulation should be interpreted with care.

In chapter 4, we explained the statistical concept of confidence interval (CI) estimates. The main idea was the following: In statistics when we want to estimate a specific parameter of a distribution, such as the mean, we take a sample and observe what the value of the parameter is in the sample (in technical terms, we record the value of the *sample statistic* for the mean). Instead of reporting a single value for our estimate for the mean, we could report an interval whose length is related to the probability that the true distribution parameter indeed lies in that interval.

Simulation is very similar to statistical sampling, as it represents uncertainty by generating scenarios and sampling values for the output parameter of interest from an underlying probability distribution. When we estimate the average (or any other parameter of interest) of the sample of scenarios, we run into the same issue statisticians do—we need to worry about the accuracy of our estimate. To compute a 95% CI estimate for the average end-of-year capital, we use the 95% CI formula from chapter 4, and substitute the values obtained from the simulation statistics: $N = 100$, $\bar{X} = 1{,}087.90$, and $s = 146.15$. The value for $t_{(100-\alpha/2)\%,\ N-1}$ for 95% CI is the value of the 97.5th percentile of the standard t-distribution with 99 degrees of freedom, which is 1.98. The 95% CI is therefore

$$\left(1{,}087.90 - 1.98 \cdot \frac{146.15}{\sqrt{100}},\ 1{,}087.90 + 1.98 \cdot \frac{146.15}{\sqrt{100}}\right) = (\$1{,}058.90,\ \$1{,}116.90).$$

Therefore, if the 100 scenarios were *independent* when generated, we can be 95% confident that the true average end-of-year capital will be between \$1,058.90 and \$1,116.90. It just happens that because of the simplicity of the example, we know exactly what the true mean is. It is $(1 + 0.0879) \cdot 1{,}000 = \$1{,}087.90$ because 8.79% was assumed to be the true mean of the distribution of returns (see section 3.9 for calculating the means of functions of random variables), and it is indeed contained inside the 95% CI. In 5% of all possible collections of 100 scenarios, however, we will be unlucky to draw a very extreme sample of scenarios, and the true mean will not be contained in the CI that we obtain. Note that if we had calculated a 99% CI, then this would happen in only 1% of the cases. If we generated $4N$ (instead of N) scenarios, the 95% CI's length would be half the current length. (This is because the square root of the number of scenarios is contained in the denominator of the expression that determines the length of the CI.) We will revisit the issue of CI estimation and the implications for accuracy again later in this chapter, when we talk about the number of scenarios needed in a simulation.

Also, later in this chapter, we will explain how random numbers are generated. We will see that drawing "independent" samples from distributions is not the most efficient way to simulate random numbers that provide good representations of the underlying probability distributions. Most simulation engines nowadays use a sophisticated methodology that estimates parameters from the distribution of output variables of interest more accurately. The previous CI formula we used is a conservative bound rather than an exact estimate for the actual accuracy in estimating the mean. Still, it is a useful benchmark to have.

5.2 Why Use Simulation?

The example in the previous section illustrated a very basic MC simulation system. We started with a deterministic model that involved a relationship between an input variable (market return $\tilde{r}_{0,1}$) and an output variable of interest (capital at the end of 1 year, $\tilde{C}_1$). We modeled the input variable as a realization of a probability distribution (we assumed a normal distribution), generated scenarios for that input variable, and tracked what the value of the output variable was in every scenario by computing it through the formula that defines the relationship between $\tilde{C}_1$ and $\tilde{r}_{0,1}$. This is the general form of simulation models illustrated in exhibit 5.1.

Despite its simplicity, this example allows us to point out one of the advantages of simulation modeling over pure mathematical modeling. Simulation enables us to evaluate (approximately) a *function* of a random variable. In this case, the function is very simple—the end-of-year capital, $\tilde{C}_1$, depends on the realization of the returns through the equation $(1+\tilde{r}_{0,1})C_0$. If we are given a probability distribution for $\tilde{r}_{0,1}$, in some cases we can compute the probability distribution for $\tilde{C}_1$ in closed form. For example, if $\tilde{r}_{0,1}$ followed a normal distribution with mean $\mu_{0,1}=E[\tilde{r}_{0,1}]$ and standard deviation $\sigma_{0,1}$, then $\tilde{C}_1$ would follow a normal distribution too, with mean $(1+\mu_{0,1})C_0$ and standard deviation $\sigma_{0,1}C_0$.

However, if $\tilde{r}_{0,1}$ did not follow a normal distribution, or if the output variable $\tilde{C}_1$ were a more complex function of the input variable $\tilde{r}_{0,1}$, it would be difficult (indeed practically impossible) to derive the probability distribution of $\tilde{C}_1$ from the probability distribution of $\tilde{r}_{0,1}$. Using simulation simplifies matters substantially.

Three other important advantages of simulation can be appreciated only in more complex situations. The first is that simulation enables us to visualize the probability distribution resulting from compounding probability distributions for multiple input variables. The second is that it allows us to incorporate correlations between input variables. The third is that simulation is a low-cost tool for checking the effect of changing a strategy on an output variable of interest. Next, we extend the investment example to provide illustrations of such situations.

5.2.1 Multiple Input Variables and Compounding Distributions

Suppose now that you are planning for retirement and decide to invest in the market for the next 30 years (instead of only the next year). Suppose that your initial capital is still \$1,000. You are interested in the return (and, ultimately, in the end-of-year capital, $\tilde{C}_{30}$) that you will have after 30 years.

Let us assume that every year, your investment returns from investing in the S&P 500 will follow a normal distribution with the mean and standard deviation from the example in section 5.1.2. The final capital that you have will depend on the realizations of 30 random variables—one for each year you are invested in the market.[6] Through simulation in section 5.1.2, we found that the probability distribution of the capital at the end of the first year will be normal. What will the probability distributions for the total return and the capital at the end of the 30th year look like? Will they be normal?

As explained in chapter 2, an investment of \$1 at time 0 will grow to $(1+\tilde{r}_{0,1})(1+\tilde{r}_{1,2})\cdots(1+\tilde{r}_{t-1,t})$ dollars at the end of year t, and the total return $\tilde{r}_{0,t}$ from time 0 to time t equals

$$\tilde{r}_{0,t}=(1+\tilde{r}_{0,t})(1+\tilde{r}_{1,2})\cdots(1+\tilde{r}_{t-1,t})-1.$$

Interestingly, the probability distribution of $\tilde{r}_{0,t}$ is not normal, and neither is the distribution of the capital at the end of 30 years. (The latter is basically a scaled version of the

6. We do not discuss the possibility that returns in different years may be correlated here. We will learn how to create more sophisticated models for asset returns in chapter 12.

distribution of total return since it can be obtained as $\tilde{C}_{0,t} = (1+\tilde{r}_{0,t}) \cdot C_0$, and the initial capital C_0 is a constant [nonrandom] number). In general, here are some useful facts to keep in mind when dealing with multiple input probability distributions:

- When a constant is added to a random variable, as with 1 added to the random variable $\tilde{r}_{0,1}$, the distribution of $(1+\tilde{r}_{0,1})$ has the same shape as the distribution of $\tilde{r}_{0,1}$; however, it is shifted to the right by 1.
- As we saw in section 3.9, when a random variable is added to another random variable (e.g., $\tilde{r}_{0,1}+\tilde{r}_{1,2}$), we cannot simply add the two probability distributions. In fact, even in cases when the two distributions have the same shape, the probability distribution of the sum of the random variables does not necessarily have the same shape. There are some exceptions—for instance, if we add two independent normal random variables, the probability distribution of the sum is normal. However, holding aside this case, this is not true in general.
- In our example, we are *multiplying* two random variables, $(1+\tilde{r}_{0,1})$ and $(1+\tilde{r}_{1,2})$ to obtain the total return. Products of random variables are even more difficult to visualize than sums of random variables. Again, it virtually never happens that a product of several random variables results in a random variable with that same probability distribution, even if the random variables all follow the same probability distributions. The lognormal distribution, which we introduced in section 3.7.2, is a rare exception, and this is one of the reasons why the lognormal distribution is used so often in financial modeling. (Specific applications of the lognormal distribution are discussed in chapter 17.)

Fortunately, simulation makes visualizing the probability distribution of the product easy. Exhibit 5.3 presents the output distributions for total return and capital at the end of 30 years. We can observe (both from the graph and from the statistics for skewness and kurtosis) that the distribution is very skewed, even though the distributions for individual returns in each of the 30 years were symmetric.

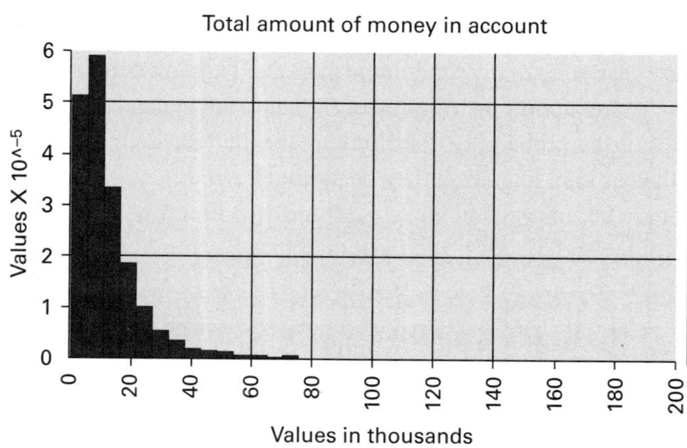

Number of values	5000
Mean	$ 12,587.62
Std deviation	$ 10,948.39
Skewness	3.349066
Kurtosis	28.24214
Mode	$ 4,458.97
5% Perc	$ 2,655.55
95% Perc	$ 32,481.38
Minimum	$ 609.75
Maximum	$194,355.00

Exhibit 5.3
Output distribution for the amount of capital after 30 years.

5.2.2 Incorporating Correlations

Let us now complicate the situation more. Suppose that you have the opportunity to invest in stocks and Treasury bonds over the next 30 years, and today you allocate 50% of your capital to the stock market by investing in the index fund, and put 50% in bonds. Furthermore, suppose that, over the 30 years, you never rebalance your portfolio (i.e., you do not change the allocation between stocks and bonds). What will the portfolio return after 30 years?

Historically, stock market and Treasury bond market returns have exhibited extremely low, but often statistically significant, negative correlation. This is because these two asset classes tend to move in opposite directions. When the stock market is performing poorly, investors tend to move their money to what they perceive to be safer investments such as bonds; conversely, when the stock market is performing well, investors tend to reallocate their portfolio, increasing their allocation to the stock market and reducing their allocation to bonds.

Visualizing the impact of multiple input variables at the same time and incorporating correlations between these variables are very difficult to do in an analytical way. Simulation eliminates the need for complex mathematics but preserves the benefits of creating richer and more accurate models. Correlations can be incorporated implicitly (by generating joint scenarios for realizations of input variables, such as by sampling from observed past data) or explicitly (by specifying a correlations matrix as an input to the simulation). Here, we give an example in which the correlations are specified as an input.

Let us assume that the correlation between the stock market and the Treasury bond market returns will be about –0.2. Let us also assume for the purposes of this exercise that the annualized return on the Treasury bonds in your portfolio will be normally distributed with mean 4% and standard deviation 7%. Therefore, the returns on the stock market and the bond market follow a multivariate normal distribution with a correlation coefficient of –0.2.

Exhibit 5.4 shows the output distribution after generating 5,000 scenarios for stock market (as measured by the S&P 500) returns and Treasury bond returns over 30 years. The shape of the distribution of the capital available after 30 years is like the shape of the distribution from exhibit 5.3, but the variability is smaller. This issue is discussed further in the next section.

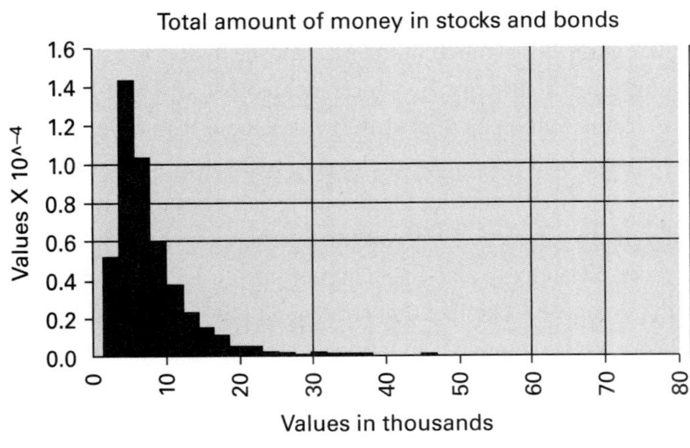

Number of values	5000
Mean	$ 7,892.80
Std Deviation	$ 5,233.10
Skewness	2.921482
Kurtosis	20.48869
Mode	$ 5,050.96
5% Perc	$ 2,951.82
95% Perc	$ 17,457.43
Minimum	$ 1,408.63
Maximum	$ 79,729.34

Exhibit 5.4
Histogram and summary statistics of the capital after 30 years from investing in the S&P 500 and Treasury bonds, considering the correlation between the returns on stocks and bonds.

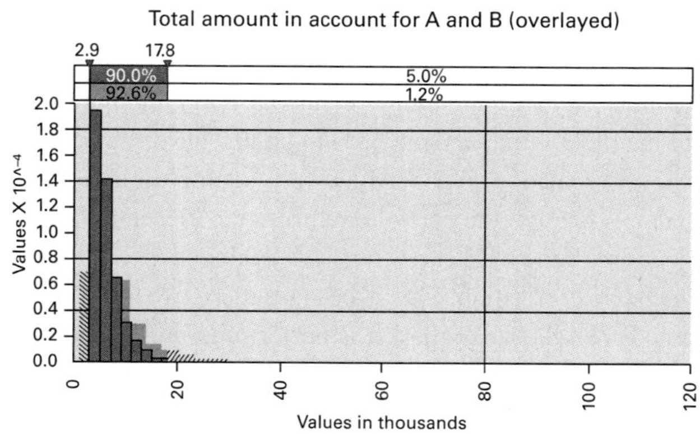

	Strategy A	Strategy B
Number of values	5000	5000
Mean	$ 7,905.30	$ 6,040.17
Std Deviation	$ 5,341.57	$ 3,219.06
Skewness	3.698306	3.514493
Kurtosis	43.44567	41.09948
Mode	$ 4,856.33	$ 4,389.39
5% Perc	$ 2,930.51	$ 2,809.56
95% Perc	$ 17,834.32	$ 11,940.22
Minimum	$ 1,131.24	$ 1,287.31
Maximum	$ 116,550.20	$ 70,578.09

Exhibit 5.5
Comparison of strategy A (equal allocation to stocks and bonds) and strategy B (allocation of 30% to stocks and 70% to bonds).

5.2.3 Evaluating Decisions

In the end, the goal of using simulation is to help us make decisions. Is a 50–50 portfolio allocation in stocks and bonds better than a 30–70 allocation? We will refer to the former allocation as strategy A, and to the latter as strategy B. Let us evaluate the distribution of the capital at the end of 30 years for each allocation strategy and use that knowledge to decide on the better allocation. Notice that it is unclear what "better" means in the context of uncertainty. We need to think about whether "better" for us means higher return on average, lower risk, acceptable trade-off between the two, or something else. Exhibit 5.5 contains the summary statistics of the simulated capital at the end of 30 years with each allocation over 5,000 scenarios.

We can observe that although strategy A performs better than strategy B as evaluated based on the mean capital at the end of 30 years, strategy A's standard deviation is higher. In terms of risk–return trade-off, as measured by the coefficient of variation (CV), strategy A's CV is 67.57% ($5,341.57/$7,905.30), whereas strategy B's CV is 53.29% ($3,219.06/ $6,040.17), which makes strategy A appear riskier than strategy B. This is apparent also from the overlay chart shown in exhibit 5.5—much of the mass of the histogram for strategy B is contained within the histogram for strategy A, which means that strategy B has less variability and results in less extreme outcomes than strategy A. One lesson here, however, is that the standard deviation may not be a good measure of risk when the underlying distributions are asymmetric. Strategy A's 5th percentile, for example, is higher than strategy B's 5th percentile, meaning that if you are concerned with events that happen with 5% probability, strategy A would be less risky. Strategy A also has a higher upside—its 95th percentile is higher than strategy B's 95th percentile.[7] The fact that strategy A has a high upside penalizes its standard deviation relative to the standard deviation of strategy B because it results in more outcomes that are far from the mean. A high standard deviation is not necessarily a bad thing if the largest deviations from the mean happen on the upside.

7. We could be looking at the minimum and maximum realized outcomes as measures of the riskiness of strategy A and strategy B as well but recall that those are very sensitive to the number of trials in the simulation and should be interpreted with care.

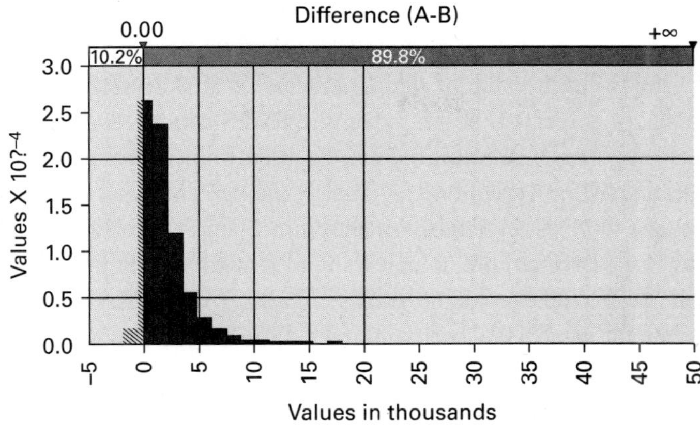

Number of values	5000
Mean	$ 1,865.13
Std deviation	$ 2,214.87
Skewness	3.506451
Kurtosis	40.18968
Mode	$ 687.75
5% Perc	$ (254.41)
95% Perc	$ 6,027.23
Minimum	$ (1,829.78)
Maximum	$ 45,972.08

Exhibit 5.6
Histogram and summary statistics for the difference between the capital at the end of 30 years with strategy A and strategy B.

It should be clear from the discussion so far that the summary statistics do not tell the whole story. It is important to look at the entire distribution of outcomes. Suppose now that we would like to compare strategy A to strategy B on a scenario-by-scenario basis. In what percentage of scenarios does strategy B perform better than strategy A? One efficient way to answer this question is to create an additional variable, Difference (A – B), that keeps track of the difference between the capital at the end of 30 years from strategy A and strategy B during the simulation. Exhibit 5.6 shows a histogram of Difference (A – B) and presents its summary statistics.

It is interesting to observe that even though Strategy A appeared riskier than strategy B based on the summary statistics in exhibit 5.5 (strategy A's standard deviation was almost twice the standard deviation of strategy B), strategy A results in lower realized outcomes than strategy B in only 10.2% of the 5,000 generated scenarios. (As the graph in exhibit 5.6 illustrates, 10.2% of the 5,000 scenarios for Difference (A – B) have values less than 0.) This perspective on the risk of one strategy versus the risk of another is valuable because it can substantially affect the final decision on which strategy to choose. For example, problematic scenarios can be specifically identified, and in some situations, such as capital budgeting, managerial action can be taken to avoid them. Therefore, a strategy that appears riskier may be selected if it is desirable for other qualitative reasons.

When comparing two alternative decisions under uncertainty, it is technically correct (and fair) to evaluate them under the same set of scenarios. For example, when obtaining the summary statistics for strategy A and strategy B earlier, we should have used the same set of 5,000 scenarios for both. This would eliminate circumstances in which we happened to generate more favorable scenarios when evaluating one of the strategies than the other, which would have led us to conclude (erroneously) that the strategy evaluated over the more favorable set of scenarios is better.

In principle, if we generate a huge number of scenarios for the two strategies, even if the scenarios are not the same, the estimates will be quite accurate. However, generating a large number of scenarios is time consuming. Moreover, even a difference of a few digits after the decimal point may be significant in some financial applications.

The **RiskSimtable** command in @RISK does what we want by default—it generates the number of scenarios that we specify, and then evaluates the values of the output variable over the same set of scenarios for each value of the parameters in **RiskSimtable**. Thus, comparing summary statistics of several strategies when the **RiskSimtable** command is used is technically correct. However, **RiskSimtable** can be used only if one parameter changes at a time. (In our example, we varied one parameter: the percentage of capital to invest in stocks. The percentage to invest in bonds was determined automatically based on how much capital was left.) If we have a more complex situation with several parameters that can be tweaked, we will need to run every simulation separately. In that case, we would need to tell @RISK to simulate the same 5,000 scenarios even if we run the simulation with two separate calls. The way to do this is to specify the *seed* of the simulation under the **Sampling** tab of the dialog box that pops up after clicking on the **Settings Commands** button. We will explain what exactly the seed of the simulation is in section 5.4. For now, it is only important to understand that it determines how the random numbers are generated. By default, @RISK changes the seed every time it runs a simulation (as do other simulation packages). If we enter a particular number for the seed (depending on the software, different ranges for possible seed values are available), we will be fixing the scenarios that will be generated, which would enable @RISK to generate the same sequence of scenarios again the next time that it runs the simulation. MATLAB and Python have similar options for setting the seed in a simulation.

If the program is not too long, the relationships are not overly complicated, and the intended number of scenarios is not too large, then there is an easier alternative way to ensure that decisions are evaluated over the same set of scenarios. If we are evaluating the portfolio allocation example from this section in a spreadsheet, we can dedicate specific cells to the input variables (returns) that are common to all strategies that we need to evaluate. We can then reference the same cells during a simultaneous simulation for the capital at the end of the 30 years with each strategy, as is done in worksheet **Stock+Bond (2)** of the file **Ch5-ReturnSim.xlsx**. This will ensure that the same realizations of the input random variables in those cells are used for computing the output values for all strategies. In programming languages like MATLAB and Python, we can dedicate variables in our program that store the generated scenarios, and then evaluate all the different strategies over that same set of scenarios. Storing 5,000 scenarios is not a problem, but if there are multiple variables and the number of scenarios increases substantially, we could run into memory problems.

5.3 Important Questions in Simulation Modeling

5.3.1 How Many Scenarios Are Necessary?

A simulation may not be able to capture all possible realizations of uncertainties in the model. For instance, think about the distribution of the end-of-year capital in section 5.1.1. As we explained in section 5.1.2., the possible number of values for the simulation output variable—the end-of-year capital—is technically infinite. Thus, we could never obtain the exact distribution of $\tilde{C}_1$ or the exact expected value $\tilde{C}_1$ by simulation. We can, however, get close. The accuracy of the estimation will depend on the number of generated scenarios. As discussed in section 5.1.2, if the scenario generation is truly random, then the variability (the standard error) of the estimate of the true expected value will be $s/\sqrt{N}$, where s is the standard deviation of the simulated values for the output variable, and n is the number of scenarios.

Hence, to double the accuracy of estimating the mean of the output distribution, we would need to quadruple (roughly) the number of scenarios. For instance, in the example in section 5.2, we generated 100 scenarios and calculated that the average capital after 1 year is $1,087.90, and that the 95% CI for the estimate of the average capital is ($1,058.90, $1,116.90). We concluded that we can be 95% confident that the true expected capital will be between $1,058.90 and $1,116.90; that is, that the true mean will not be further than $29 from the mean estimated from the simulation ($1,087.90). Now suppose that we had obtained the same numbers for sample mean ($1,087.90) and sample standard deviation ($146.15), but we generated four times as many (400) scenarios. The 95% CI would have been[8]

$$\left(1{,}087.90 - 1.97 \cdot \frac{146.15}{\sqrt{400}}, 1{,}087.90 + 1.97 \cdot \frac{146.15}{\sqrt{400}}\right) = (\$1{,}073.53, \$1{,}102.27).$$

This means that we could be 95% confident that the true mean would not be more than $14.37 from the simulated mean of $1,087.90, which is about half of the amount by which we could be off ($29) when we generate 100 scenarios. Therefore, our accuracy has increased about twofold after quadrupling the number of generated scenarios.

Increasing the number of scenarios to improve accuracy can get expensive computationally, especially in more complicated multiperiod situations, such as the simulation of a 30-year investment in section 5.2.1. Fortunately, there are modern methods for the generation of random numbers and scenarios that can help reduce the computational burden.

While the average output from a simulation is important, it is often not the only quantity of interest, something that practitioners tend to forget when using simulations to value complex financial instruments. As we will see from the applications in this book, for example, in assessing the risk of a portfolio, a portfolio manager may be interested in the percentiles of the distribution of outputs, or the worst-case and best-case scenarios. Unfortunately, it is not as straightforward to determine the accuracy of estimates of percentiles and other sample statistics from a simulation. There are some useful results from probability theory that apply (see, e.g., chapter 9 in Glasserman 2004), and we can use bootstrapping, as described in chapter 4. However, in general, the question of how many scenarios we should generate to get a good representation of the output distribution does not have an easy answer. This issue is complicated further by the fact that results from probability theory do not necessarily apply to many of the scenario-generating methods used in practice, which do not simulate purely random samples of observations, but instead use smarter simulation methods that reduce the number of scenarios needed to achieve good estimate accuracy. Some of these methods are discussed later in this chapter and in chapter 19.

8. Note that the value for $t_{(100-\alpha/2)\%,n-1}$ has decreased slightly as well—this is because we now have more observations (i.e., more degrees of freedom), so the t-distribution is less spread out and is closer to the normal distribution.

5.3.2 Estimator Bias

In chapter 4, we described the statistical concept of *estimator bias*. Estimator bias is important in simulation applications because it shows whether an estimator estimates the right thing on average (i.e., whether it approaches the true parameter that one needs to estimate given a sufficient number of replications). For example, the average obtained from a sample of scenarios is an unbiased estimator of the true mean of a distribution because if we generate many samples and compute the sample averages, the average of these averages will approach the true mean. Depending on the way that scenarios are generated, however, one may introduce a bias in the estimate of the parameter of interest. (This parameter does not need to be the mean of the distribution.) The magnitude of the bias is determined by the difference between the average value of the estimator that would be obtained if we generated many samples, and the true value of the parameter that we are trying to estimate.

Let us go back to the multiperiod retirement planning example in section 5.2.1. We compounded the returns of the original capital of $1,000 every year to obtain the return distribution of over 30 years. Intuitively, though, returns should be compounded a lot more frequently to obtain a fair representation of a continuously compounded total return. The fact that we discretized the sample space by considering specific points of evaluation of the returns introduced an error, a bias, in our estimate of the total return.

This issue is important in the evaluation of financial derivatives, which we will see in part V. The prices of financial instruments are typically assumed to follow continuous random processes, but time is often discretized when constructing simulation models. The average of the outcomes (the expected present value) is considered to be the fair price of the financial instrument; however, simulating asset prices in this manner generates a bias in the estimate of the expected present value because the simulated changes in the asset price along the way are not continuous or instantaneous, but rather happen over a fixed-length time interval. This kind of bias is referred to as *discretization error bias*. In some cases, such as the case of geometric Brownian motion with fixed drift and volatility (which is discussed in chapter 17), we can obtain an unbiased estimator of the average financial derivative payoff by simulating future asset prices with a continuous-time formula. However, in many instances, it is not possible to find such a closed-form expression for the future asset price. For example, such a formula does not exist when the volatilities for asset prices are time-dependent, or when one uses a mean-reversion process to describe the evolution of the underlying price. (Such random processes are discussed in chapter 17.) In such cases, we can reduce the time interval length to reduce the bias, but it is important to keep in mind that reducing the time interval length increases the number of steps necessary to generate a random path for the future asset price, and the process then becomes computationally expensive.

5.3.3 Estimator Efficiency

If there are two ways to obtain an estimate of a quantity of interest and the estimators are otherwise equivalent in terms of bias, which estimator should be preferred; that is, which estimator is more "efficient"? For example, consider two unbiased estimators of the mean, both of which are obtained as averages from a sample of independent replications. Their standard errors will be given by

$$\frac{s_1}{\sqrt{N_1}} \text{ and } \frac{s_2}{\sqrt{N_2}}$$

where s_1 and s_2 are the standard deviations from the samples of scenarios and N_1 and N_2 are the number of scenarios for each of the estimators. Statistical theory states that one should prefer the estimator with the smaller standard deviation because it is more accurate.

In the case of simulation, however, such statistical concepts need to be extended to include numerical and computational considerations. For example, suppose that it takes longer to generate the scenarios for the estimator with the smaller standard deviation. Is that estimator still preferable, given that one can use the extra time to generate additional scenarios for the other estimator, thus reducing the latter estimator's standard error? It is natural (and, theoretically, justified) to modify the statistical measure of variability and efficiency so it includes a concept of time. If τ_1 and τ_2 are the times that it takes to generate one scenario for each of the two estimators, then one should select the estimator with the smaller of the time-adjusted standard errors $s_1\sqrt{\tau_1}, s_2\sqrt{\tau_2}$.

5.4 Random Number Generation

At the core of MC simulation is the generation of random numbers. In fact, however, generating random numbers from a wide variety of distributions reduces to generating random numbers from the continuous uniform distribution on the unit interval [0,1]; that is, to generating random numbers on the interval [0,1] in such a way that each value between 0 and 1 is equally likely to occur.[9] Many computer languages and software packages have a command for generating a random number between 0 and 1: =RAND() in Excel, rand(1) in MATLAB, random() in Python, and rand() in C++.

5.4.1 Inverse Transform Method

A common method for converting a random number between 0 and 1 to a number from an arbitrary probability distribution is to evaluate the so-called inverse of the cumulative probability distribution function at the random number u generated from a continuous uniform distribution (denoted by $F^{-1}(u)$). The idea works because the total mass for a probability distribution is always 1, and the cumulative probability for any value of the distribution (defined as the probability that this particular value or any value below it will occur) is always between 0 and 1. In effect, you can imagine that by generating a random number between 0 and 1, you are picking a number on the horizontal axis of the cumulative distribution function (CDF) plots in exhibit 3.7. As mentioned in chapter 3, the shape of the CDF depends on the specific probability distribution. To generate a random number from a probability distribution with a specific CDF, we can track the x-coordinate for the point on the CDF that has the random number between 0 and 1 as a y-coordinate. Note

9. Recall that the continuous uniform distribution looks like a simple rectangle (exhibit 3.12), and it is very easy to compute probabilities and cumulative probabilities for the values for the continuous uniform random variable. Because the length of the interval is 1 and the total area under the PDF must be 1, the height of the curve should be 1 as well. Therefore, the probability that the continuous uniform random variable takes a value between two numbers a and b (the area under the PDF between a and b) is simply $(b-a)\cdot 1$; that is, $b-a$.

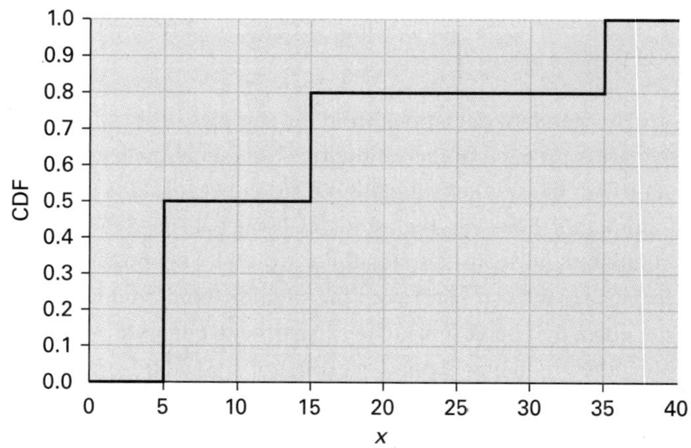

Exhibit 5.7
Graph of the CDF of a discrete distribution.

that if a particular value from the distribution of the random variable happens with high probability, the CDF evaluated at that point on the horizontal axis will contain a long vertical segment. A uniform random number generated on [0,1] will have a larger chance of falling in a segment that is long, so the value from the distribution that we would like to simulate will indeed happen with higher probability.

The Inverse Transform for Discrete Distributions To give a concrete example, let us see how inverting the cumulative probability distribution works for discrete distributions. Suppose that given a random number generator for numbers between 0 and 1, we would like to simulate values for a random variable that takes the value 5 with probability 50%, the value 15 with probability 30%, and the value 35 with probability 20%. Exhibit 5.7 illustrates the CDF of this probability distribution. Let us split the unit interval [0,1] on the vertical axis into three intervals based on the cumulative probabilities 50%, 80%, and 100% for obtaining the values 5, 15, and 35: [0,0.5], (0.5,0.8], and (0.8,1], respectively. If the random number that is drawn from the uniform distribution falls in the interval [0,0.5] (which happens 50% of the time if the number generator is truly random), then we trace the value on the horizontal axis that corresponds to the point on the CDF with a y-coordinate equal to the generated random number, and record that value (which is 5) for that trial. If the random number is in the interval (0.05, 0.8] (which happens with probability 30%), then we record a value of 15 for that trial. Finally, if the random number is in the third interval (which happens with probability 20%), we record a value of 35. Thus, if many trials are run, the values 5, 15, and 35 are generated with the desired probabilities.[10]

10. To understand better how this works, you can practice generating values from a general discrete probability distribution in Excel. For example, we can simulate these values with the corresponding probabilities by creating a table with the interval ranges in the first two columns and the corresponding values (5, 15, and 35) in the third column, and using the Excel function VLOOKUP(lookup_value,table_array,col_index_num).

The Inverse Transform for Continuous Distributions Some probability distributions have closed-form expressions for their inverse cumulative distributions. The exponential distribution is one such example. In section 3.7.2, we introduced the probability density function (PDF) of the exponential distribution:

$$f(x) = \lambda e^{-\lambda x}, \quad x \geq 0$$

The CDF of the exponential distribution can be computed as[11]

$$\begin{aligned} F(x) = P(X \leq x) &= \int_0^x \lambda e^{-\lambda t}\, dt \\ &= \left(-\frac{1}{\lambda} \lambda e^{-\lambda t} \right)\Bigg|_{t=x} - \left(-\frac{1}{\lambda} \lambda e^{-\lambda t} \right)\Bigg|_{t=0} \\ &= -e^{-\lambda x} - (-e^{-\lambda \cdot 0}) \\ &= 1 - e^{-\lambda x}. \end{aligned}$$

To compute the inverse function, we express x in terms of the CDF $F(x)$. We have

$$e^{-\lambda x} = 1 - F(x),$$

and therefore

$$x = -\frac{1}{\lambda} \ln(1 - f(x)).$$

If we generate a random number between 0 and 1 for $F(x)$, we can use this expression to find the corresponding random number x that comes from an exponential distribution.

The inverse transform method can be viewed as a method of picking *random percentiles* from a particular distribution. To build further intuition, let us generate a random number from a normal distribution with mean μ and standard deviation σ. Suppose that we request a random number between 0 and 1, and the random number generator returns 0.975. To find the uniquely corresponding random number from a normal distribution with mean μ and standard deviation σ, we find the value on the horizontal axis for a normal distribution with mean μ and standard deviation σ so 97.5% of the probability mass (the area under the PDF) is to the left of that value.[12] In contrast to the exponential distribution, however, the percentiles of the normal distribution cannot be calculated in closed form. A random number generator would *approximate* the inverse of the cumulative normal distribution function at a particular point.

11. We present the calculation here because the exponential distribution is often used in modeling the arrival time of credit-risky events when pricing credit derivatives and managing bond portfolio risk (see chapter 16).

12. In Excel, the function =`NORMINV(RAND(), mean, standard deviation)` can be used to find that random number on the x-axis (the x-percentile) of a normal distribution with the specified mean and standard deviation. Specialized simulation software packages use such algorithms to generate a random variable from any distribution. @RISK does it behind the scenes when the user specifies directly the probability distribution to be generated by clicking on the **Define Distribution** button. In MATLAB, one can use both the direct and the indirect approaches. For example, to generate a single number from a normal distribution, one can enter `norminv(rand(1), mean, standard deviation)`. More recent versions of MATLAB's Statistics Toolbox contain direct commands for generating random numbers from a variety of distributions, such as, `normrnd` for normal random variables and `poissrnd` for Poisson random variables. Type `lookfor rnd` at the MATLAB prompt for a listing of available distributions, and see the online appendices for how such commands are used.

While using the inverse transform method is common, alternative methods exist for generating random numbers from distributions for which the inverse of the CDF is not easy to compute. Such methods include

- The acceptance-rejection method
- The composition method
- The ratio of uniforms method

Most of these methods, however, still rely on generating random numbers from the uniform distribution on [0,1]. For more details, see Fishman (2006) and Glasserman (2004).

Because the normal distribution is so widely used in practice, a number of methods have been developed specifically for efficient simulation of univariate and multivariate normal random variables. Such methods include the Box-Muller algorithm (Box and Muller 1958), and the BeasleySpringer-Moro methodology for approximating the inverse normal distribution (Beasley and Springer 1977; Moro 1995).

5.4.2 What Defines a "Good" Random Number Generator?

Given the discussion in the previous section, generating good uniform random numbers on [0,1] is critical for the performance of simulation algorithms. Interestingly, defining "good" random number generation is not as straightforward as it appears. Early random number generators tried to use truly random events for random number generation, such as the amount of background cosmic radiation. In practice, however, this kind of random number generation is time consuming and difficult. Moreover, it was realized that the ability to reproduce the random number sequence and to analyze the random number characteristics is a desirable property for random number generators. In particular, the ability to reproduce a sequence of random numbers allows for reducing the variance of estimates and debugging computer code by rerunning experiments in the same conditions in which they were run in previous iterations of code development.

Most simulation software employs random number generation algorithms that produce streams of numbers that appear to be random but in fact are a result of a clearly defined series of calculation steps in which the next random number x_n in the sequence is a function of the previous random number x_{n-1}; that is, $x_n = g(x_{n-1})$. The sequence starts with a number called the *seed*, and if the same seed is used in several simulations, each simulation sequence will contain exactly the same numbers, which is helpful for running fair comparisons between different strategies evaluated under uncertainty. It is quite an amazing statistic that some of these recursion formulas (named *pseudorandom number generators*) define sequences of numbers that imitate random behavior well and appear to (roughly) obey some major laws of probability, such as the Central Limit Theorem (CLT; chapter 4) and the Glivenko-Cantelli Theorem.[13]

13. The Glivenko-Cantelli Theorem is a statement about the behavior of an empirical CDF as the number of independent and identically distributed (i.i.d.) observations recorded from the underlying distribution grows. Glivenko (1933) and Cantelli (1933) showed that as the number of observations grows, the empirical CDF approaches true CDF uniformly.

In general, a pseudorandom number generator is considered good if it satisfies the following conditions:

- The numbers in the generated sequence are uniformly distributed between 0 and 1. This can be tested by running a chi-square or a Kolmogorov-Smirnov test.
- The sequence has a long cycle (i.e., it takes many iterations before the sequence begins repeating itself).[14]
- The numbers in the sequence are not autocorrelated.[15] This can be verified by running a Durbin-Watson test on the sequence of numbers. The Durbin-Watson test is widely used in statistics for identifying autocorrelation in time series of observations.

Next, some important types of pseudorandom number generators are surveyed. The goal is not to provide comprehensive coverage of random number generators, but rather to give you a flavor of the main ideas behind the method of producing apparently random numbers with deterministic algorithms.

5.4.3 Pseudorandom Number Generators

One of the earliest pseudorandom number generators is called the *midsquare technique*. It takes a number (the seed), squares it, and uses the set of middle digits as the next random number. For example, suppose that the seed is 5381. (It can be any number.) The members of the sequence of random numbers between 0 and 1 are then generated as

$$5381^2 = 28\underline{9551}61;\ \text{middle four digits} = 9551;\ \text{random number} = \mathbf{0.9551},$$

$$95512 = 91\underline{2216}01;\ \text{middle four digits} = 2216;\ \text{random number} = \mathbf{0.2216},$$

and so forth.

It is easy to predict when such an approach may run into difficulties. As soon as the middle digits become a small number such as 1 or 0, the sequence ends with the same numbers generated over and over again; that is, the sequence converges to a constant value such as 0, or to a very short cycle of values.

A better, commonly used type of pseudorandom number generator is a *congruential* pseudorandom number generator. It generates a sequence of numbers of the form

$$x_n = g(x_{n-1}) \mod m,$$

where mod m stands for "*modulus m*," and $g(x_{n-1})$ mod m is the remainder after dividing $g(x_{n-1})$ by m. For example, 5 mod 3 = 2, 15 mod 5 = 0, and so on. The remainder is then scaled by another number (e.g., divided by m), and the resulting number is used as the uniform random number on the interval [0, 1]. Note that $g(x_{n-1})$ mod m will always be an integer between 0 and $m-1$. Thus, to create a good representation of randomness, one would

14. A long cycle is desirable because if the random number generator converges to only a small set of values for the random number, we cannot obtain a good representation of the probability distribution that we are trying to sample.

15. See section 3.8 for a definition of autocorrelation.

want to make the range for the modulus as large as possible. For a 32-bit computer, for example, the maximum integer that can be stored is $2^{31}-1$, which is large enough for practical purposes.

As an example, consider a simple *linear congruential pseudorandom generator* of the form

$$x_n = Ax_{n-1} \mod m.$$

(It is called "linear" because Ax_{n-1} is a linear function of x_{n-1}.) The first number in the sequence, x_0, is the seed. Algebraically, the expression for generating x_n can be written as[16]

$$x_n = Ax_{n-1} - m\left\lfloor \frac{Ax_{n-1}}{m} \right\rfloor.$$

(The lower brackets notation is standard for "the largest integer less than or equal to Ax_{n-1}/m.") Then the sequence of fractions x_n/m is used as a sequence of pseudorandom numbers on the interval $[0,1]$.

Suppose that $A=3$, $m=10$, and the seed $x_0=1052$. We have the following sequence of random numbers:

$$x_1 = 3\cdot 1052 - 10\cdot\left\lfloor \frac{3\cdot 1052}{10} \right\rfloor = 3\cdot 1052 - 10\cdot\lfloor 315.6 \rfloor = 3\cdot 1052 - 10\cdot 315 = 6$$

Therefore, the random number is $6/10$, or **0.6**.

$$x_2 = 3\cdot 6 - 10\cdot\left\lfloor \frac{3\cdot 6}{10} \right\rfloor = 3\cdot 6 - 10\cdot\lfloor 1.8 \rfloor = 3\cdot 6 - 10\cdot 1 = 8.$$

Therefore, the next random number is $8/10$, or **0.8**, and so on.

More generally, advanced random number generators include

- Linear congruential generators (LCGs)
- Multiplicative recursive generators (MRGs)
- Feedback shift registers (FSRs)
- Generalized feedback shift registers (GFSRs)
- Combined multiplicative recursive generators (CMRGs)
- Twisted generalized feedback shift registers (TGFSRs)
- Add-with-carry (AWC) and subtract-with-borrow (SWB) generators
- Inversive generators (IGs)

FSRs, GFSRs, and TGFSRs generate new numbers by operating recursively on *bits* of previously generated random numbers. LCGs, MRGs, CMRGs, AWC/SWB generators, and IGs operate recursively on previously generated random numbers. For more details, see, for example, McLeish (2005) and Fishman (2006). Most pseudorandom number generators

16. The intuition is that the remainder after division with m is the difference between the number Ax_{n-1} and the largest number that is divisible by m but is still less than Ax_{n-1}.

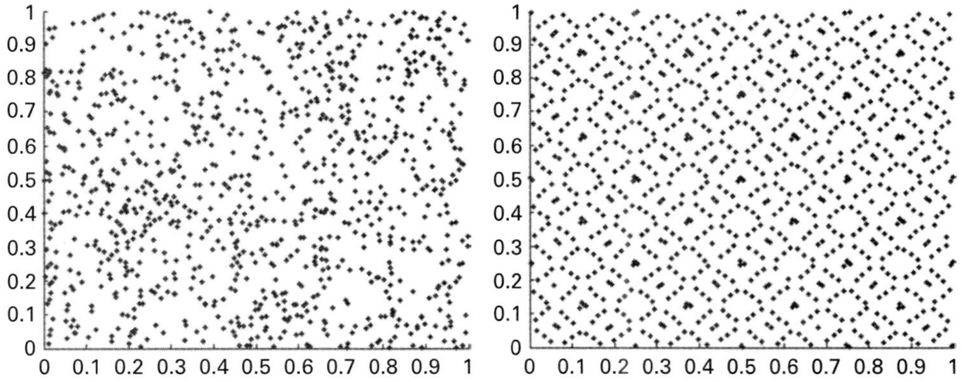

Exhibit 5.8
A total of 1,000 simulated number values for two uniform random variables on the interval [0,1]: (A) pseudo-random number generator; (B) Sobol quasirandom sequence.

used in popular software products nowadays have been thoroughly tested and are quite good, but it is important to keep in mind that pseudorandom number generators in software packages that are not explicitly built for simulation purposes (such as Excel) are usually not as good as random number generators in specialized simulation/mathematical software.

5.4.4 Quasirandom (Low-Discrepancy) Sequences

A truly random number generator may produce clustered observations (see exhibit 5.8(A)), which necessitates generating many scenarios to obtain a good representation of the output distribution of interest. Quasirandom sequences instead ensure a smooth representation of the range by continuously filling in gaps on the unit interval [0,1] left by previously generated random numbers (see an example of 1,000 generated values of a quasirandom sequence in exhibit 5.8(B)). The term "quasirandom" is actually a misnomer because, unlike pseudorandom number sequences, quasirandom number sequences do not pretend to be random. They are deterministic on purpose, and their roots can be found in real analysis and abstract algebra rather than in simulation or probability theory. The term *low-discrepancy sequences* is often used interchangeably with the term *quasirandom sequences*, and it is more accurate.

Famous quasirandom sequences include Sobol (1967), Faure (1982), Halton (1960), and Hammersley (1960). These sequences build on a family of Van der Corput sequences.[17] For example, the Van der Corput sequence of base 2 is

$$\frac{1}{2}, \frac{1}{4}, \frac{3}{4}, \frac{1}{8}, \frac{5}{8}, \frac{3}{8}, \frac{7}{8}, \ldots$$

The actual generation of Van der Corput sequences is somewhat technical, but the outcome is intuitive. Note that as new points are added to the sequence, they appear on alternate sides of $\frac{1}{2}$ in a balanced way. The main idea is that as the number of generated values increases, the sequence covers uniformly the unit interval.

17. Such sequences are discussed in detail in chapter 19.

The values generated with quasirandom sequences are treated as random numbers for the purposes of simulation modeling. In particular, instead of generating random numbers between 0 and 1 and inverting them to obtain an arbitrary probability distribution, we would invert the numbers in the quasirandom sequence. Different sequences have different advantages for specific financial applications, but the Faure and Sobol sequences in particular have been proven to generate very accurate estimates for derivative pricing in tests.[18] We will see applications of quasirandom sequences when the pricing of mortgage-backed securities (MBSs) and other financial derivatives are discussed in chapters 19 and 21.

5.4.5 Stratified Sampling

A variety of *variance reduction techniques* are used to speed up execution and improve accuracy in simulations. We discuss some of them in the context of financial derivative pricing in chapter 19. Here, we will introduce one kind of random number generation—stratified sampling—that is now the default method of sampling in some simulation software packages such as @RISK. The term *stratified sampling* is used because of the analogy with the statistical methodology of collecting a representative sample by dividing the population into groups, or *strata*, of similar characteristics and collecting information about each strata. This technique ensures that all important groups are represented in the final sample.

Like quasirandom number generation, stratified sampling tries to address the problem of "clustering observations" mentioned in section 5.4.4. In contrast to quasirandom number generator techniques, however, which are deliberately nonrandom, stratified sampling preserves some degree of randomness. It just tries to distribute the randomness along the entire range of the probability distribution by dividing the ranges of possible values for every input random variable into a fixed number of strata and simulating values over these ranges.

Stratified sampling is valuable not only because it improves accuracy, but also because it helps include extreme observations into the simulation. Observations in the tails of input distributions that are typically less likely to be generated may never occur in a simulation because the probability of their occurrence is small. Such observations, however, contain important information about extreme events that are of particular interest in financial applications. To ensure that they appear in the simulation, one would have to generate a huge number of scenarios.

A simple example of stratifying the numbers in the [0,1] interval is to divide the [0,1] interval into k smaller intervals of equal length:

$$\left(0,\frac{1}{k}\right],\left(\frac{1}{k},\frac{2}{k}\right],\ldots,\left(\frac{k-1}{k},1\right].$$

Random numbers can then be drawn sequentially from each small interval. Therefore, values from the tails of the distribution of interest (which will be generated when uniform random numbers from the intervals $\left(0,\frac{1}{k}\right]$ and $\left(\frac{k-1}{k},1\right]$ are drawn) obtain better representation.

18. See the survey in Boyle, Broadie, and Glasserman (1997).

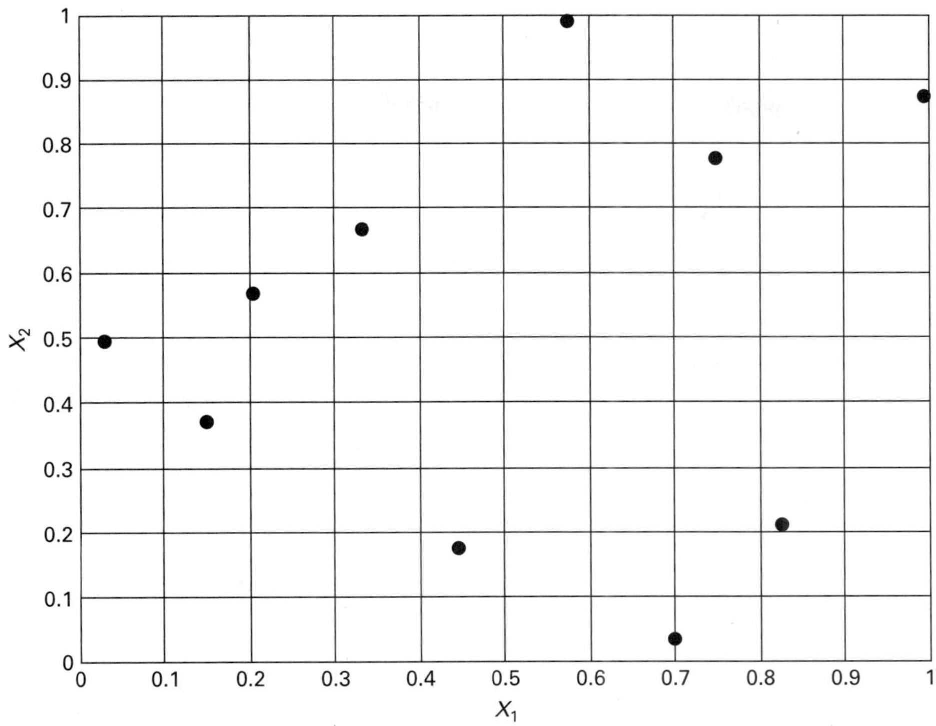

Exhibit 5.9
A Latin hypercube sample for two random variables ($p = 2$) and 10 strata along each dimension ($k = 10$).

In multiple dimensions (i.e., when simulating several random variables), this method extends to dividing a hypercube (as opposed to an interval) into smaller hypercubes and drawing an observation along each dimension of these hypercubes. The sample size required to cover all strata, however, may become prohibitive. Suppose, for example, that you have k intervals (strata) for each of p dimensions (i.e., each of p random variables). This means that there are k^p hypercubes; that is, we need to simulate at least k^p random numbers to have a number in each stratum. Generating random numbers, however, is computationally expensive. An enhanced extension to the basic stratified sampling method is *Latin hypercube sampling* (an option in many advanced simulation software products), which permutes the coordinates of an initially generated random vector of observations—one observation within each small hypercube—to reduce the number of times that an actual random number is generated while ensuring that all strata are sufficiently well represented (see exhibit 5.9).

The method works as follows. First, we generate a random number within each small interval along each dimension. In the example in exhibit 5.9, where we have two random variables (i.e., two dimensions), we would generate random numbers

$$x_1^{(1)}, \ldots, x_1^{(k)}$$

along the first dimension, and numbers

$$x_2^{(1)}, \ldots, x_2^{(k)}$$

along the second dimension. If we consider points with coordinates

$$(x_1^{(1)}, x_2^{(1)}), \ldots, (x_1^{(k)}, x_2^{(k)})$$

we would have random points in all the little squares along the diagonal of the large [0,1] square. The first point is a point in the little square $\left[0, \frac{1}{k}\right]^2$, the second point is a point in the little square $\left(\frac{1}{k}, \frac{2}{k}\right]^2$, and so on. (In multiple dimensions, combining the random numbers for the corresponding small intervals to create random points with p coordinates would create random points in the little hypercubes along the main diagonal of the [0,1] hypercube.)

Now permute the coordinates of the points along each dimension.[19] For example, consider the points

$$(x_1^{(10)}, x_2^{(3)}), (x_1^{(2)}, x_2^{(1)}) \ldots, (x_1^{(k-3)}, x_2^{(2)}).$$

In other words, the first coordinates are still the random numbers generated along the first dimension, and the second coordinates are still the random numbers generated along the second dimension, but the order of the random numbers within each dimension has changed. The new points are not all in the hypercubes around the diagonal, and as exhibit 5.9 illustrates, exactly one random point falls in each of the k small intervals into which each axis is partitioned. If we consider all possible permutations of these coordinates, we will fill all the small hypercubes. Thus, we would perform stratified sampling by generating only $k \cdot p$ random numbers (and permuting them), rather than generating k^p random numbers.[20]

Summary

- Monte Carlo (MC) simulation is a valuable tool for evaluating functional relationships between variables, visualizing the effect of multiple correlated variables, and testing strategies.
- MC simulation involves creating scenarios for output variables of interest by generating scenarios for input variables for which we have more information. The art of MC simulation modeling is in selecting input probability distributions wisely and interpreting output distributions carefully.
- The distributions of output variables can be analyzed by statistical techniques. Statistics of interest include measures of central tendency (average, mode), measures of volatility (standard deviation, percentiles), skewness, and kurtosis. Minima and maxima

19. To permute, you can first draw one of the coordinates at random, then draw one coordinate from the remaining ones, and continue doing so until only one is left.

20. The Latin hypercube sampling method works well for generating independent random variables. Still, complications occur when we need to generate correlated random variables. See chapter 4 in Glasserman (2004) for further discussions and examples.

from simulations should be interpreted with care because they often depend on the input assumptions and are very sensitive to the number of trials in the simulation.

- The accuracy of estimation through simulation is related to the number of generated scenarios. Unfortunately, the relationship is nonlinear—to double the accuracy, we need to more than quadruple the number of scenarios.
- Generating a random number from an arbitrary probability distribution in many cases reduces to generating a random number from the uniform distribution on the interval [0,1].
- Random number generation is not trivial, and simulation software packages do not produce truly random numbers. There is value, however, in generating random number sequences that are replicable, and thus not completely random.
- Pseudorandom number generators attempt to imitate random behavior by creating sequences of random numbers that obey statistical laws.
- Quasirandom number generators do not pretend to generate random numbers—they try to address the clustering problem observed in truly random number generation and ensure a smooth representation of the range of the distribution by continuously filling in gaps on the unit interval [0,1] left by previously generated random numbers. Quasirandom sequences that have been particularly successful in financial applications include the Faure and Sobol sequences.
- Stratified sampling, of which Latin hypercube sampling is an advanced example, aims to provide good representation of a probability distribution by dividing the range of the random variable into smaller ranges, or "strata," and generating random numbers within each stratum. This method disperses simulated values more evenly over the range of the distribution, addresses the clustering problem of random number generation, and provides better representation for the tails of the distribution.

6

Optimization Modeling

This chapter introduces optimization, a methodology for selecting an optimal strategy, given an objective and a set of constraints. Optimization appears in a variety of financial applications, including portfolio allocation, portfolio rebalancing, trading strategies, identifying arbitrage opportunities, and pricing financial derivatives. We will encounter it again in chapters 12, 13, 14, 15, and 23, among others. In this chapter, we motivate the discussion by a simple example and describe how optimization problems are formulated and solved.

Let us recall the retirement example from section 5.2.2 in chapter 5. We showed how to compute the realized return on the portfolio of stocks and bonds if we allocate 50% of our capital in each of the two investments. Can we obtain a better portfolio return with a different allocation? (As discussed in section 5.2.3, a "better" return is not well defined in the context of uncertainty, so for the sake of argument, let us assume that "better" means higher *expected* return.) We found that if the allocation is (100%, 0%) instead of (50%, 50%), we end up with a higher portfolio expected return but also a higher portfolio standard deviation. What about an allocation of (30%, 70%)? It turned out that the portfolio expected return is lower, and so is the standard deviation. What about an allocation of (20%, 80%)?

In this example, we are dealing with only two investments and have no additional requirements regarding the portfolio structure. It is, however, still difficult to enumerate all the possibilities and find those that provide the optimal trade-off of return and risk. In practice, portfolio managers are handling thousands of investments and need to worry about transaction costs, requirements on the portfolio composition, and trading constraints, which makes it impossible to find the best portfolio allocation by trial-and-error. The optimization methodology provides a disciplined way to approach the problem of optimal asset allocation.

6.1 Optimization Formulations

The increase in computational power and the tremendous pace of developments in the operations research field in the past 25 to 30 years has led to highly efficient algorithms and user-friendly software for solving optimization problems of many different kinds. The art of optimization modeling is therefore in framing a situation so the formulation fits within recognized frameworks for problem specifications and can be passed to optimization solvers. It is important to understand the main building blocks of optimization formulations, as well as the limitations of the software and the insights that can be gained from the output of optimization solvers.

An optimization problem formulation consists of three parts:[1]

- A set of *decision variables* (usually represented as an $N \times 1$–dimensional vector array[2] $\mathbf{x}$)
- An *objective function*, which is a function of the decision variables ($f(\mathbf{x})$)
- A set of *constraints* defined by functions ($g_i(\mathbf{x})$, $h_j(\mathbf{x})$), $i = 1, \ldots, I, j = 1, \ldots, J$ of the general form $g_i(\mathbf{x}) \leq 0$ (inequality constraints) and $h_j(\mathbf{x}) = 0$ (equality constraints)

The decision variables are numerical quantities that represent the decisions to be made. In the portfolio example, the decision variables could be the portfolio weights (or alternatively, they could be the amounts to allocate to each asset class). The objective function is a mathematical expression of the goal, and the constraints are mathematical expressions of the limitations in the business situation. In our example, the objective function could be an expression to compute the expected portfolio return, and the constraints could include an expression that computes total portfolio risk. We can then maximize the expression of the objective function subject to an upper limit on the risk we are willing to tolerate. (We will derive actual formulations in chapters 12 through 15.)

Optimization software expects users to specify all three components of an optimization problem, although it is sometimes possible to have optimization problems with no constraints. The latter kind of optimization problems is referred to as *unconstrained optimization*. Unconstrained optimization problems are typically solved with standard techniques from calculus,[3] and the optimal solution is selected from all possible points in the N-dimensional space of the decision variables $\mathbf{x}$. When there are constraints, only some points in that space will be *feasible* (i.e., will satisfy the constraints). The values of the decision variables that are feasible and result in the best value for the objective function are called the *optimal solution*. Optimization solvers typically return only one optimal solution. However, it is possible to have multiple optimal solutions; that is, multiple feasible solutions $\mathbf{x}$ that produce the same optimal value for the objective function.[4]

When formulating optimization problems, it is important to realize that the decision variables need to participate in the mathematical expressions for the objective function and the constraints that are passed to an optimization solver because the whole idea of optimization algorithms is that they can tweak the values of the decision variables in these expressions in a smart, computationally efficient way to produce the best value for the objective function with values for the decision variables that satisfy all the constraints. In other words, we cannot simply pass the expression

1. See online appendix A for a review of the matrix-vector notation.

2. Optimization formulations can handle decision variables that are matrix arrays as well, but these types of problems are too advanced for the purposes of this book. This area of optimization is called *semidefinite programming*. See Fabozzi et al. (2007) for a discussion of its applications in finance.

3. In other words, set the derivative of the objective function to zero.

4. Unfortunately, there is no straightforward way to request that all optimal solutions be listed in optimization software output. If we are interested in checking whether there is another optimal solution, we need to modify the optimization problem formulation to exclude the current optimal solution and rerun the optimization solver again. If a second optimal solution exists, the solver will find it when the first optimal solution is no longer a feasible option.

$$\text{Maximize} \quad \text{Portfolio expected return}$$

to an optimization solver unless the portfolio expected return is expressed as a function of the decision variables (the portfolio weights). As we will derive in chapter 12, the expected portfolio return can be expressed in terms of the portfolio weights as $\mathbf{w}'\boldsymbol{\mu}$, where $\mathbf{w} = (w_1, \ldots, w_N)'$ and $\boldsymbol{\mu} = (\mu_1, \ldots, \mu_N)'$ are N-dimensional arrays containing the weights and the expected returns of the N assets in the portfolio, respectively. So the objective function would be written as

$$\max_{\mathbf{w}} \quad \mathbf{w}'\boldsymbol{\mu}$$

which is interpreted as "maximize the value of $\mathbf{w}'\boldsymbol{\mu}$ over the possible values for $\mathbf{w}$."

In addition, the input data in a classical optimization problem formulation need to be fixed numbers, not random variables. For example, the objective function of an optimization problem cannot be passed to a solver as

$$\text{Maximize} \quad \text{Portfolio return}$$

where portfolio return $= \mathbf{w}'\tilde{\mathbf{r}}$, and $\tilde{\mathbf{r}} = (\tilde{r}_1, \ldots, \tilde{r}_N)'$ is the N-dimensional array with uncertain asset returns with some probability distributions. Some areas in optimization, such as robust optimization and stochastic programming, study methodologies for solving optimization problems in which the input data are subject to uncertainty and follow theoretical or empirical probability distributions. However, in the end, the methods for solving such problems reduce to specifying the coefficients in the optimization problem as *fixed* numbers that are representative of the underlying probability distributions in a particular way.

6.1.1 Minimization versus Maximization

Most generally, optimization solvers require an optimization problem formulation to be of the following kind:

$$\begin{aligned} \min_{\mathbf{x}} \quad & f(\mathbf{x}) \\ \text{subject to} \quad & g_i(\mathbf{x}) \leq 0 \quad i = 1, \ldots, I \\ & h_j(\mathbf{x}) = 0 \quad j = 1, \ldots, J \end{aligned}$$

There are variations on this formulation, some of which have to do with whether the optimization problem falls in a specific class. (Different categories of optimization problems based on the form of their objective function and the shape of their feasible set are discussed in section 6.2.) Some optimization software syntax allows for specifying only minimization problems, while other optimization software packages are more flexible and accept both minimization and maximization problems.

Standard formulation requirements, however, are not as restrictive as they appear at first sight. For example, an optimization problem that involves finding the maximum of a function $f(\mathbf{x})$ can be recast as a minimization problem by minimizing the expression $-f(\mathbf{x})$, and vice versa—an optimization problem that involves finding the minimum of function $f(\mathbf{x})$ can be recast as a maximization problem by maximizing the expression $-f(\mathbf{x})$. To obtain the actual value of the objective function, one then flips the sign of the optimal value. Exhibit 6.1 illustrates the situation for a quadratic function of one variable x. The optimal value for

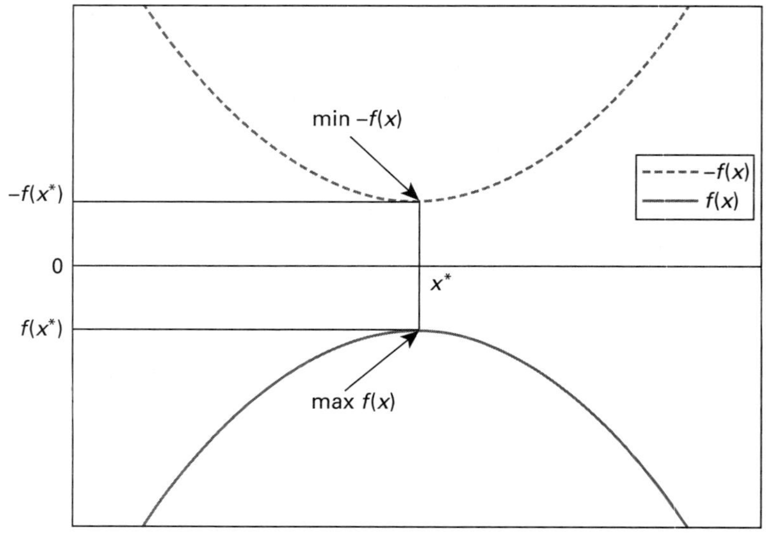

Exhibit 6.1
Example of the optimal objective function values for a quadratic objective function $f(x)$ of a single decision variable x.

max $f(x)$ is obtained at the optimal solution x^*. The optimal value for min $-f(x)$ is obtained at x^* as well. Notice also that

$$\max_x f(x) = -\min_x - f(x)$$

For the previous portfolio expected return maximization example, stating the objective function as

$$\max_{\mathbf{w}} \mathbf{w}'\boldsymbol{\mu}$$

or

$$\min_{\mathbf{w}} - \mathbf{w}'\boldsymbol{\mu}$$

will produce the same optimal values for the decision variables **w**. To get the actual optimal objective function value for $\max_{\mathbf{w}} \mathbf{w}'\boldsymbol{\mu}$, we would flip the sign of the optimal objective function value obtained after minimizing $-\mathbf{w}'\boldsymbol{\mu}$.

6.1.2 Local versus Global Optima

In optimization, we distinguish between two types of optimal solutions: global and local. A *global optimal solution* is the best solution for any value of the decision variables vector **x** in the set of *all* feasible solutions. A *local optimal solution* is the best solution in a *neighborhood* of feasible solutions. In other words, the objective function value at any point close to a local optimal solution is worse than the objective function value at the local optimal solution. Exhibit 6.2 illustrates the global (point A) and local (point B) optimal solutions for the unconstrained minimization of a function of two variables.

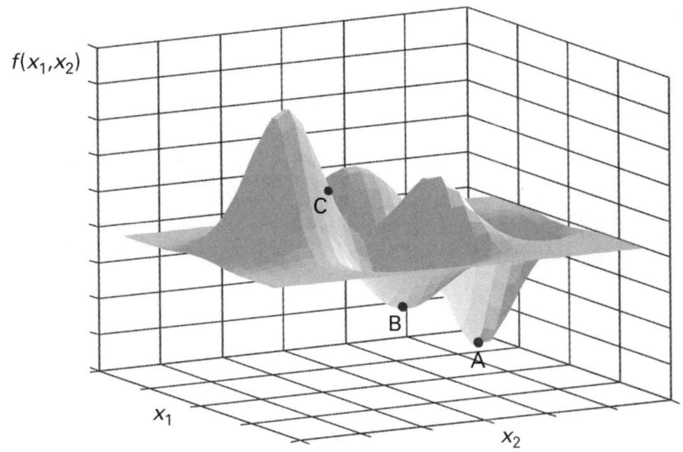

Exhibit 6.2
Global (point A) versus local (point B) minimum for a function of two variables, x_1 and x_2.

Most classical optimization algorithms can only find local optima. They start at a point and go through solutions in a direction in which the objective function value improves. Their performance has an element of luck that has to do with picking a good starting point for the algorithm. For example, if a nonlinear optimization algorithm starts at point C in exhibit 6.2, it may find the local minimum B first and never get to the global minimum A. In the general case, finding the global optimal solution can be difficult and time consuming and involve finding all local optimal solutions first and then picking the best one among them.

The good news is that in some cases, optimization algorithms can explore the special structure of the objective function and the constraints to deliver stronger results. In addition, for some categories of optimization problems, a local optimal solution is, in fact, guaranteed to be the global optimal solution, and many optimization problems in finance have that property. (We review the most important kinds of such "nice" optimization problems in section 6.2.) This makes recognizing the type of optimization problem in a given situation and formulating the optimization problem in a way that enables optimization algorithms to take advantage of the special problem structure even more critical.

6.1.3 Multiple Objectives

In practice, we often encounter situations in which we would like to optimize several objectives at the same time. For example, a portfolio manager may want to maximize the portfolio expected return and skew while minimizing the variance and the kurtosis. There is no straightforward way to pass several objectives to an optimization solver. A multiple-objective optimization problem needs to be reformulated as an optimization problem with a single objective. There are a couple of commonly used methods to do this. We can assign weights to the various objectives and optimize the weighted sum of objectives as a single-objective function. Alternatively, we can optimize the most important objective and include the other objectives as constraints after assigning to each of them a bound on the value that we are willing to tolerate.

6.2 Important Types of Optimization Problems

Optimization problems can be categorized based on the form of their objective function and constraints, as well as the kind of decision variables. The type of optimization problem with which we are faced a particular situation determines what software is appropriate, the efficiency of the algorithm for solving the problem, and the degree to which the optimal solution returned by the optimization solver is trustworthy and useful. Awareness of this fact is particularly helpful in situations in which there are multiple ways to formulate the optimization problem. The way in which we state the formulation will determine whether the optimization solver will be able to exploit any special structure in the problem, as well as whether it can achieve stronger results.

6.2.1 Convex Programming

As mentioned in section 6.1.2, some general optimization problems have a nice structure in the sense that a local optimal solution is guaranteed to be the global optimal solution. *Convex optimization problems* have that property. A general convex optimization problem takes the form

$$\begin{aligned} \min_{x} \quad & f(\mathbf{x}) \\ \text{subject to} \quad & g_i(\mathbf{x}) \leq 0 \quad i = 1, \ldots, I \\ & \mathbf{Ax} = \mathbf{b} \end{aligned}$$

where both $f(\mathbf{x})$ and $g_i(\mathbf{x})$ are convex functions, and $\mathbf{Ax} = \mathbf{b}$ is a system of linear equalities. A *convex function* of a single variable x has the shape shown in exhibit 6.3(A). For a convex function, a line that connects any two points on the curve is always above the curve. The opposite of a convex function is a *concave function* (see exhibit 6.3(B)), which looks like a "cave." For a concave function, a line that connects any two points on the curve is always below the curve.

Convex programming problems encompass several classes of problems with special structure, including *linear programming* (LP), some *quadratic programming* (QP), *second-order cone programming* (SOCP), and *semidefinite programming* (SDP). Algorithms for solving convex optimization problems are more efficient than algorithms for solving general nonlinear problems, but it is important to keep in mind that even within the class of convex problems, some convex problems are computationally more challenging than others. LP

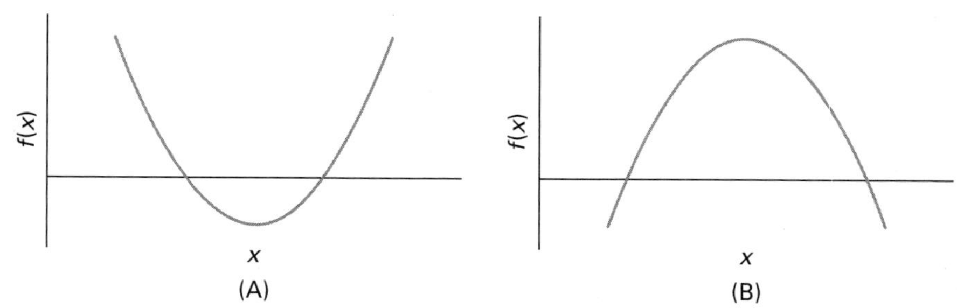

Exhibit 6.3
Examples of (A) a convex function and (B) a concave function.

problems are best studied and easiest to solve with commercial solvers, followed by convex QP problems, SOCP problems, and SDP problems.

We introduce LP, QP, and SOCP in more detail next. Many classical problems in finance involve LP and QP, including asset-liability problems, portfolio allocation problems, and some financial derivative pricing applications. SDP problems are advanced formulations that have become more widely used in financial applications with recent advances in the field of robust optimization. They are beyond the scope of this book, but we refer interested readers to Fabozzi et al. (2007) for a detailed overview of robust optimization formulations.

6.2.2 Linear Programming

Linear programming (LP) refers to optimization problems in which both the objective function and the constraints are linear expressions in the decision variables.[5] The standard formulation statement for linear optimization problems is

$$\begin{aligned} \min_{\mathbf{x}} \quad & \mathbf{c'x} \\ \text{subject to} \quad & \mathbf{Ax} = \mathbf{b} \\ & \mathbf{x} \geq \mathbf{0} \end{aligned}$$

All optimization problems involving linear expressions for the objective function and the decision variables can be converted to this standard form. Section 6.3.1 will present an example.

Linear optimization problems are the easiest kind of problems to solve. Modern specialized optimization software can handle LP formulations with hundreds of thousands of decision variables and constraints in seconds. In addition, linear optimization problems belong to the class of convex problems for which a local optimal solution is guaranteed to be the global optimal solution. (This is discussed in more detail in section 6.4.2.) LPs arise in several finance applications, such as asset allocation and identification of arbitrage opportunities. The sample optimization problem formulations in sections 6.3.1 and 6.3.2 are linear optimization problems.

6.2.3 Quadratic Programming

QP problems have an objective function that is a quadratic expression in the decision variables, as well as constraints that are linear expressions in the decision variables. The standard form of a quadratic optimization problem is

$$\begin{aligned} \min_{\mathbf{x}} \quad & \frac{1}{2}\mathbf{x'Qx} + \mathbf{c'x} \\ \text{subject to} \quad & \mathbf{Ax} = \mathbf{b} \\ & \mathbf{x} \geq \mathbf{0} \end{aligned}$$

5. Linear expressions involve sums and differences of terms of the *constant decision variable* and exclude expressions like *constant* · *decision variable*^{2}, *decision variable 1* · *decision variable 2*, *decision variable 1*/*decision variable 2*, log(*decision variable*), and so on. Note that an expression of *constant*^{2} · *decision variable* is still a linear expression in the decision variable, even if it is not a linear expression in the constant. Linear optimization formulations are concerned only with whether the expressions in the objective function and constraints are linear expressions in the decision variables.

where $\mathbf{x}$ is an N-dimensional vector of decision vectors, as before, and the other arrays are input data:

$\mathbf{Q}$ is an $N \times N$ matrix

$\mathbf{c}$ is an N-dimensional vector

$\mathbf{A}$ is a $J \times N$ matrix

$\mathbf{b}$ is a J-dimensional vector

When matrix $\mathbf{Q}$ is positive semidefinite,[6] then the objective function is convex. (It is the sum of a convex quadratic term and a linear function, and a linear function is both convex and concave.) Since the objective function is convex and the constraints are linear expressions, we have a convex optimization problem. This problem can be solved by efficient algorithms, and we can trust that any local optimum they find is in fact the global optimum. When $\mathbf{Q}$ is not positive semidefinite, however, the quadratic problem can have several local optimal solutions and stationary points and is therefore more difficult to solve.

The most prominent use of QP in finance is for asset allocation and trading models. We will see examples in chapters 12 through 15.

6.2.4 Second-Order Cone Programming

Second-order cone programs take the general form

$$\begin{aligned} \min_{\mathbf{x}} \quad & \mathbf{c}'\mathbf{x} \\ \text{subject to} \quad & \mathbf{A}\mathbf{x} = \mathbf{b} \\ & \left\| \mathbf{C}_i \mathbf{x} + \mathbf{d}_i \right\| \leq \mathbf{c}_i'\mathbf{x} + e_i, \quad i = 1, \ldots, I \end{aligned}$$

where $\mathbf{x}$ is an N-dimensional vector of decision vectors, as before, and the other arrays are input data:

$\mathbf{c}$ is an N-dimensional vector

$\mathbf{A}$ is a $J \times N$ matrix

$\mathbf{b}$ is a J-dimensional vector

$\mathbf{C}_i$ are an $I_i \times N$ matrix

$\mathbf{d}_i$ are I_i-dimensional vectors

e_i are scalars

The notation $\|.\|$ stands for second norm, or Euclidean norm. (It is sometimes denoted as $\|.\|_2$ to differentiate it from other types of norms.) The Euclidean norm of an N-dimensional vector $\mathbf{x}$ is defined as

$$\left\| \mathbf{x} \right\| = \sqrt{x_1^2 + \cdots + x_N^2}$$

The SOCP class of problems is more general than the classes covered in sections 6.2.2 and 6.2.3. LPs, convex QPs, and convex problems with quadratic objective functions and quadratic constraints can be reformulated as SOCPs with some algebra.

6. See appendix A for a definition of positive semidefinite matrix.

It turns out that SOCP problems share many nice properties with linear programs, so algorithms for their optimization are very efficient. SOCP formulations arise often in robust optimization applications. Such formulations are discussed in section 6.3.

6.2.5 Integer and Mixed-Integer Programming

So far, we have classified optimization problems according to the form of the objective function and the constraints. Optimization problems can be classified also according to the type of decision variables $\mathbf{x}$. Namely, when the decision variables are restricted to be integer (or, more generally, discrete) values, we refer to the corresponding optimization problem as an *integer programming* (IP) or a *discrete problem*. When some decision variables are discrete and some are continuous, we refer to the optimization problem as a *mixed-integer programming* (MIP) problem. In special cases of integer problems in which the decision variables can only take values 0 or 1, we refer to the optimization problem as a *binary optimization problem*.

Integer and mixed-integer optimization formulations are useful for formulating extensions to classical portfolio allocation problems. Index-tracking formulations and many constraints on portfolio structure faced by managers in practice require modeling with discrete decision variables. Examples of constraints include maximum number of assets to be held in the portfolio (so-called *cardinality constraints*), maximum number of trades, round lot constraints (constraints on the size of the orders in which assets can be traded in the market),[7] and fixed transaction costs. Simple illustrations of integer modeling are provided in the next section and are further discussed in chapter 14.

6.3 Optimization Problem Formulation Examples

To provide better intuition for how optimization problems are formulated, we give a few simplified examples of financial problem formulations. We will see more advanced nonlinear problems formulations in the context of portfolio applications in chapters 12 through 14.

The first example in this section is explained in detail so the process of optimization problem formulation can be explicitly outlined. The problem formulation is the crucial step—once we can define a business situation as one of the optimization problem types reviewed in section 6.2, we can find the optimal solution with optimization software. Later in this chapter, we explain how optimization formulations can be input into solvers and how the output can be retrieved and interpreted.

6.3.1 Portfolio Allocation

The manager of the endowment funds at a large university is tasked with investing a \$10 million donation to the university endowment. The portfolio manager has decided to invest these funds only in mutual funds[8] and is considering the following four: an aggressive

7. In the stock market, a round lot is 100 shares. In the bond market, the size of a round lot varies with the type of bond.

8. A mutual fund, more specifically an open-end investment company, uses proceeds from the sale of shares to the public to invest in various securities. The value of one share of a mutual fund is computed by dividing the difference between the mutual fund's asset and liabilities by the number of shares outstanding. This value is called the *net asset value* (NAV). Mutual funds have different investment objectives. In the case of a money market fund, the

Fund Type	Growth	Index	Bond	Money Market
Fund number	1	2	3	4
Expected return	20.69%	5.87%	10.52%	2.43%
Risk level	4	2	2	1
Max. investment	40%	40%	40%	40%

Exhibit 6.4
Data for the portfolio manager problem.

growth fund (fund 1), an index fund (fund 2), a corporate bond fund (fund 3), and a money market fund (fund 4), each with a different expected annual return and risk level.[9] The investment guidelines established by the board of trustees limit the percentage of the money that can be allocated to any single type of investment to 40% of the total amount. The data for the portfolio manager's task are provided in exhibit 6.4. In addition, to contain the risk of the investment to an acceptable level, the amount of money allocated to the aggressive growth and the corporate bond funds cannot exceed 60% of the portfolio and the aggregate average risk level of the portfolio cannot exceed 2. (The risk level is an internally assigned risk level of 1–5 based on criteria developed with the approval of the board of trustees.) What is the optimal portfolio allocation for achieving the maximum expected return at the end of the year, if no short selling is allowed?[10]

To formulate the optimization problem, the first thing that we need to ask ourselves is what the objective is. In this case, the logical objective is to maximize the expected portfolio return. The second step is to think of how to define the decision variables. The decision variables need to be specified in such a way as to allow for expressing the objective as a mathematical expression of the quantities that the manager can control to achieve his objective. The latter point is obvious but sometimes missed when formulating optimization problems for the first time. For example, while the market return on the assets is a variable and increasing market returns will increase the portfolio's return, changing the behavior of the market is not under the manager's control. The manager, however, can change the amounts that he invests in different assets to achieve his objective.[11] Thus, the vector of **decision variables** can be defined as

$$\mathbf{x} = (x_1, x_2, x_3, x_4)\text{: amounts(in \$) invested in Fund 1, 2, 3, and 4, respectively.}$$

Let the vector of expected returns be $\boldsymbol{\mu} = (20.69\%, 5.87\%, 10.52\%, 2.43\%)$. Then, the objective function can be written as

fund manager can only invest in short-term, high-quality investments (i.e., money market instruments). This type of mutual fund has the lowest risk and therefore the lowest expected return (see exhibit 6.4).

9. This is just a simplified example of portfolio allocation with risk considerations. Definitions of risk and more sophisticated portfolio allocation schemes are discussed in detail in chapters 12 through 14.

10. See chapter 2 for a definition and discussion of short selling.

11. As we mentioned earlier, there are often different ways to formulate an optimization problem for the same business situation. For example, the decision variables for this example can be defined as the percentages invested (rather than the dollar amounts invested) in each fund. The problem formulation will be very similar, and the optimal solution will be the same qualitatively.

$$f(\mathbf{x}) = \boldsymbol{\mu}'\mathbf{x} = (20.69\%) \cdot x_1 + (5.87\%) \cdot x_2 + (10.52\%) \cdot x_3 + (2.43\%) \cdot x_4.$$

It is always a good idea to write down the actual description and the units for the decision variables, the objective function, and the constraints. For example, the units of the objective function value in this example are dollars.

Finally, we have several constraints:

- The total amount invested should be \$10 million. This can be formulated as $x_1 + x_2 + x_3 + x_4 = 10{,}000{,}000$.
- The total amount invested in funds 1 and 3 cannot be more than 60% of the total investment (\$6 million). This can be written as $x_1 + x_3 \leq 6{,}000{,}000$.
- The average risk level of the portfolio cannot be more than 2. This constraint can be expressed as $4 \cdot$ (proportion of investment with risk level 4) $+ 2 \cdot$ (proportion of investment with risk level 2) $+ 1 \cdot$ (proportion of investment with risk level 1) ≤ 2 or, mathematically,

$$\frac{4 \cdot x_1 + 2 \cdot x_2 + 2 \cdot x_3 + 1 \cdot x_4}{x_1 + x_2 + x_3 + x_4} \leq 2.$$

Note that this is not a linear constraint. (We are dividing decision variables by decision variables.) Based on the discussion in section 6.2.2, from a computational perspective it is better to have linear constraints whenever we can. There are a couple of ways to convert this particular constraint into a linear constraint. For example, we can multiply both sides of the inequality by $x_1 + x_2 + x_3 + x_4$, which is a nonnegative number, and will preserve the sign of the inequality as is. In addition, in this example we know that the total amount $x_1 + x_2 + x_3 + x_4 = 10{,}000{,}000$, so the constraint can be formulated as

$$4 \cdot x_1 + 2 \cdot x_2 + 2 \cdot x_3 + 1 \cdot x_4 \leq 2 \cdot 10{,}000{,}000.$$

The maximum investment in each fund cannot be more than 40% of the total amount (\$4,000,000). These constraints can be written as

$$x_1 \leq 4{,}000{,}000,\ x_2 \leq 4{,}000{,}000,\ x_3 \leq 4{,}000{,}000,\ x_4 \leq 4{,}000{,}000.$$

Finally, given the no short-selling requirement, the amounts invested in each fund cannot be negative. (Note that we are assuming that the portfolio manager can invest only the \$10,000,000 and cannot borrow more.) Mathematically, the *nonnegativity constraints* are expressed as

$$x_1 \geq 0,\ x_2 \geq 0,\ x_3 \geq 0,\ x_4 \geq 0.$$

Even though they seem obvious in this example, they still need to be specified explicitly for the optimization solver.

The final optimization formulation can be written in matrix form. The objective function is

$$\max_{x_1, x_2, x_3, x_4} \begin{bmatrix} 0.2069 & 0.0587 & 0.1052 & 0.0243 \end{bmatrix} \cdot \begin{bmatrix} x_1 \\ x_2 \\ x_3 \\ x_4 \end{bmatrix}.$$

Let us organize the constraints into groups according to their signs (which will be useful when solving the problem with optimization software):

$$\text{Equality}(=): [1 \quad 1 \quad 1 \quad 1] \cdot \begin{bmatrix} x_1 \\ x_2 \\ x_3 \\ x_4 \end{bmatrix} = 10{,}000{,}000$$

$$\text{Inequality}(\leq): \begin{bmatrix} 1 & 0 & 1 & 0 \\ 4 & 2 & 2 & 1 \\ 1 & 0 & 0 & 0 \\ 0 & 1 & 0 & 0 \\ 0 & 0 & 1 & 0 \\ 0 & 0 & 0 & 1 \end{bmatrix} \cdot \begin{bmatrix} x_1 \\ x_2 \\ x_3 \\ x_4 \end{bmatrix} \leq \begin{bmatrix} 6{,}000{,}000 \\ 20{,}000{,}000 \\ 4{,}000{,}000 \\ 4{,}000{,}000 \\ 4{,}000{,}000 \\ 4{,}000{,}000 \end{bmatrix}.$$

$$\text{Nonnegativity}(\geq): \begin{bmatrix} x_1 \\ x_2 \\ x_3 \\ x_4 \end{bmatrix} \geq \begin{bmatrix} 0 \\ 0 \\ 0 \\ 0 \end{bmatrix}.$$

This is an LP problem. It would look like the standard form in section 6.2.2 except for the inequality (≤) constraints. We can rewrite the LP in standard form by converting them to equality constraints. We introduce six additional nonnegative variables $\mathbf{s} = (s_1, \ldots, s_6)$ (called *slack variables*), one for each constraint in the group Inequality (≤):

$$\left[\begin{array}{cccc|cccccc} 1 & 0 & 1 & 0 & 1 & 0 & 0 & 0 & 0 & 0 \\ 4 & 2 & 2 & 1 & 0 & 1 & 0 & 0 & 0 & 0 \\ 1 & 0 & 0 & 0 & 0 & 0 & 1 & 0 & 0 & 0 \\ 0 & 1 & 0 & 0 & 0 & 0 & 0 & 1 & 0 & 0 \\ 0 & 0 & 1 & 0 & 0 & 0 & 0 & 0 & 1 & 0 \\ 0 & 0 & 0 & 1 & 0 & 0 & 0 & 0 & 0 & 1 \end{array}\right] \cdot \begin{bmatrix} x_1 \\ x_2 \\ x_3 \\ x_4 \\ s_1 \\ s_2 \\ s_3 \\ s_4 \\ s_5 \\ s_6 \end{bmatrix} = \begin{bmatrix} 6{,}000{,}000 \\ 20{,}000{,}000 \\ 4{,}000{,}000 \\ 4{,}000{,}000 \\ 4{,}000{,}000 \\ 4{,}000{,}000 \end{bmatrix}.$$

Then we add the nonnegativity constraints on the slack variables to the problem formulation:

$$[x_1, x_2, x_3, x_4, s_1, s_2, s_3, s_4, s_5, s_6,]' \geq 0.$$

Current Bond Price (p_i)	\$102.36	\$110.83	\$96.94	\$114.65	\$96.63	
Cash Flows (c_{it})						Obligations (m_t)
$t=1$	\$ 2.50	\$ 5.00	\$ 3.00	\$ 4.00	\$ 3.50	\$ 100,000.00
$t=2$	\$ 2.50	\$ 5.00	\$ 3.00	\$ 4.00	\$ 3.50	\$ 200,000.00
$t=3$	\$ 2.50	\$ 5.00	\$ 3.00	\$ 4.00	\$ 3.50	\$ 100,000.00
$t=4$	\$ 2.50	\$ 5.00	\$ 3.00	\$ 4.00	\$ 3.50	\$ 200,000.00
$t=5$	\$102.50	\$ 5.00	\$ 3.00	\$ 4.00	\$ 3.50	\$ 800,000.00
$t=6$		\$105.00	\$ 3.00	\$ 4.00	\$ 3.50	\$1,200,000.00
$t=7$			\$103.00	\$ 4.00	\$ 3.50	\$ 400,000.00
$t=8$				\$104.00	\$103.50	\$1,000,000.00

Exhibit 6.5
Cash flow matching the example data.

Optimization solvers in the past required that the problem be passed in standard form; however, solvers and optimization languages are much more flexible today, and they do their own conversion to standard form. As this example illustrates, it is easy to go from a general linear problem formulation to the standard form. Different optimization software packages—Microsoft Excel's Solver, Palisade's Evolver, MATLAB's Optimization Toolbox, and Python libraries such as Pyomo and PuLP—have their own problem input specifications, but these specifications are straightforward to handle.

6.3.2 Cash-Flow Matching

Consider an asset manager who is managing funds for the corporate sponsor of a defined benefit pension plan that needs to ensure a particular stream of semiannual cash payments over the next four years for retiring plan participants.[12] For example, the pension plan may have semiannual obligations representing annuity payments. Let the cash obligations for the eight payment dates of the next four years be represented by vector $\mathbf{m}=(m_1, \ldots, m_8)$.

The asset manager is considering investing in five high-quality investment-grade bonds on behalf of its client, the pension plan. Over the next eight payment dates (i.e., semiannually), bond i pays out coupons $\mathbf{c}_i=(c_{i1}, \ldots, c_{i8})$. If the bond matures at date t, the corresponding c_{it} equals the coupon rate plus the principal. The bonds currently trade at ask prices $\mathbf{p}=(p_1, \ldots, p_5)$. The relevant data are provided in exhibit 6.5. The asset manager would like to ensure that the bond coupon payments cover the pension plan's obligations.[13]

To formulate this problem, we must again ask ourselves what the fund's objective is. Although it is not stated explicitly in the problem, it makes sense for the objective to be to minimize the cost of acquiring the bonds today while still meeting all expected future obligations.

12. In a defined benefit pension plan, the sponsor of the plan, such as a corporation or a municipality, has contractually agreed to make payments to the plan participants of a specified amount after the participant retires. In contrast, in a defined contribution retirement plan, the employer agrees to set aside prior to the employee's retirement only a certain amount of money each year, but it is the responsibility of the employee to invest those funds.

13. In our illustration, we are assuming high-quality investment-grade bonds. This means that the issuers of these bonds have a low probability of failing to meet their obligation to make the coupon payments.

The decision variables can be defined as the amounts $\mathbf{x} = (x_1, x_2, x_3, x_4, x_5)$ to invest in each of the five bonds. The cost of acquiring the bonds today is

$$\sum_{i=1}^{5} p_i \cdot x_i = \mathbf{p}'\mathbf{x}.$$

The constraints are that at each payment date, the cash flows from the coupons of all the bonds are at least as large as the liabilities. Therefore, the optimization problem can be stated as

$$\begin{aligned} \min_{x_1,\ldots,x_5} \quad & \sum_{i=1}^{5} p_i \cdot x_i \\ \text{subject to} \quad & \sum_{i=1}^{5} c_{it} \cdot x_i \geq m_t \quad t = 1,\ldots,8 \\ & x_i \geq 0, \quad i = 1,\ldots,5. \end{aligned}$$

Again, this formulation is an LP because both the objective function and the constraints are linear functions of the decision variables x_1, x_2, x_3, x_4, and x_5.

In practice, the amounts for the bond investments may need to be presented as *round lots*. This can be achieved by using integer variables. We can introduce new integer variables $\mathbf{z} = (z_1, z_2, z_3, z_4, z_5)$ that correspond to the number of lots of each bond to buy. Suppose that a lot for bond i is l_i. To obtain the optimal number of lots of each bond to purchase, we rewrite the problem formulation here as

$$\begin{aligned} \min_{x_1,\ldots,x_5,z_1,\ldots,z_5} \quad & \sum_{i=1}^{5} p_i \cdot x_i \\ \text{subject to} \quad & \sum_{i=1}^{5} c_{it} \cdot x_i \geq m_t, \quad t = 1,\ldots,8 \\ & x_i \geq 0, \quad i = 1,\ldots,5 \\ & x_i = z_i \cdot l_i, \quad i = 1,\ldots,5 \\ & z_i \text{ integer}, \quad i = 1,\ldots,5. \end{aligned}$$

Since some of the variables are continuous (x_1, x_2, x_3, x_4, x_5) and some are discrete (z_1, z_2, z_3, z_4, z_5), the LP formulation becomes MIP, which is computationally harder to solve.

For implementation of this example of cash-flow matching, see this chapter's online section "Software Hints." Note, however, that although the LP formulation can be solved with any solver, some solvers may have trouble solving the MIP, or they may return an incorrect solution.[14]

6.3.3 Capital Budgeting

The operating manager at a pharmaceutical company is considering funding proposals for eight research and development (R&D) projects, but she has limited funds C (C = \$1,000,000). The cost of investing in project i is c_i, and the present value of project i's estimated benefit is b_i. Specific numbers c_i and b_i are shown in exhibit 6.6. (We will explain how projects are valued in chapters 22 and 23.) Each project is on a "take it or leave it" basis; that is, it is not

14. We will discuss optimization solvers and software later in this chapter.

Project	1	2	3	4	5	6	7	8
Project cost	$400.00	$350.00	$200.00	$100.00	$300.00	$250.00	$300.00	$350.00
Project benefits (PV)	$950.00	$780.00	$440.00	$215.00	$630.00	$490.00	$560.00	$600.00
Benefit/cost ratio	2.38	2.23	2.20	2.15	2.10	1.96	1.87	1.71

Exhibit 6.6
Costs, present value (PV) of project benefits, and benefit-to-cost ratios for each of the eight R&D projects. All numbers are in thousands of dollars.

possible to fund a project partially. Which projects should the operating manager fund to maximize the present value of the expected total benefit?

If we did not know about optimization problem formulations, a logical approach would be to rank the projects according to their benefit-to-cost ratios, and to pick as many (in order of decreasing benefit-to-cost ratios) as can be funded with the \$1 million budget.

Going from left to right in the table in exhibit 6.6, we select projects 1, 2, and 3. The total cost is

$$\$400{,}000 + \$350{,}000 + \$200{,}000 = \$950{,}000,$$

so we stop after selecting project 3. The present value of the total benefits is

$$\$950{,}000 + \$780{,}000 + \$440{,}000 = \$2{,}170{,}000.$$

Is this the best we can do? Notice that we were left with a budget of about \$50,000 that we could have invested. No project can be had for \$50,000, but suppose that we replaced project 3 with project 6, which had an outlay of \$250,000 and would have exhausted the budget of \$1 million. The total benefit from investing in projects 1, 2, and 6 is

$$\$950{,}000 + \$780{,}000 + \$490{,}000 = \$2{,}200{,}000,$$

which is higher than the number we got with the first approach. In fact, there is a combination of projects that results in an even higher expected benefit: projects 1, 3, 4, and 5. The total benefit is

$$\$950{,}000 + \$440{,}000 + \$215{,}000 + \$630{,}000 + \$2{,}235{,}000,$$

and it turns out that this is the maximum benefit that we can get for an investment budget of \$1 million.

It is not easy to see immediately that the combination of projects 1, 3, 4, and 5 gave the optimal solution, and this was a simple problem in which the manager was faced with no additional constraints. It is even harder to identify the optimal solution once further conditions on the projects are imposed.

This situation is a good example of how binary optimization can be useful for financial applications. Let us introduce decision variables $x_1, \ldots, x_8$ (one corresponding to each project) that equal 1 if the project is selected, and 0 otherwise. The total benefit then can be computed as

$$\begin{aligned} &\$950{,}000 \cdot x_1 + \$780{,}000 \cdot x_2 + \$440{,}000 \cdot x_3 + \$215{,}000 \cdot x_4 \\ &+ \$630{,}000 \cdot x_5 + \$490{,}000 \cdot x_6 + \$560{,}000 \cdot x_7 + \$600{,}000 \cdot x_8 \end{aligned}$$

Note that if the decision is not to invest in project i, then the benefit of that project is not counted toward the total benefit. The total cost of funding the selected projects can be computed in a similar manner.

We can now formulate the optimization problem as follows:

$$\begin{aligned} \min_{x_1,\ldots,x_8} \quad & \sum_{i=1}^{8} b_i \cdot x_i \\ \text{subject to} \quad & \sum_{i=1}^{8} c_i \cdot x_i \leq C \\ & x_i \text{ binary}, \quad i = 1, \ldots, 8. \end{aligned}$$

Solving this problem will produce the optimal solution that was previously mentioned:

$$(x_1, x_2, x_3, x_4, x_5, x_6, x_7, x_8) = (1, 0, 1, 1, 1, 0, 0, 0).$$

Now suppose that the manager is facing additional constraints:

(a) If she funds project 1, she must fund project 8 as well.

(b) Projects 4 and 5 are mutually exclusive since their goals are virtually the same; that is, if the manager funds project 4, she will not fund project 5, and vice versa.

Let us first formulate the problem with constraint (a). The condition needs to be formulated mathematically; that is, classical optimization solvers do not understand "if–then" statements.[15] We can express the condition as an additional constraint

$$x_1 \geq x_8$$

or, equivalently, as

$$x_1 - x_8 \leq 0.$$

To gain some intuition, note that if the manager finds that it is optimal to invest in project 1 (i.e., $x_1 = 1$), then the constraint given here will force x_8 to be 1 as well; that is, the optimal solution will contain investments in both projects 1 and 8. However, if the manager does not invest in project 1 (i.e., $x_1 = 0$), then x_8 is free to be 0 or 1; that is, the manager may or may not invest in project 8.

The optimal solution with the additional constraint (a) turns out to be to invest in projects 2, 4, 5, and 6, for a total estimated benefit of $2,115,000.

Now let us formulate constraint (b). Again, we need to express it mathematically. We can state the condition as

$$x_4 + x_5 \leq 1.$$

This will work because for the constraint to be satisfied, only one of the variables x_4 and x_5 can be 1. (They may both be 0, of course.) Therefore, the manager would be able to invest in at most either project 4 or project 5. The optimal solution when both constraints (a) and (b) are added to the original optimization problem is

$$(x_1, x_2, x_3, x_4, x_5, x_6, x_7, x_8) = (0, 1, 0, 1, 0, 1, 1, 0)$$

for a total benefit of $2,045,000 and a total cost of $1,000,000. In other words, the manager should invest in projects 2, 4, 6, and 7.

6.4 Optimization Algorithms

How do optimization solvers find the optimal solution for a problem? As a general rule, optimization algorithms have an iterative nature. They start with an initial solution and generate a sequence of intermediate solutions until they get close to the optimal solution.

15. Some randomized search solvers accept such conditions (see sections 6.4.4 and 6.7). However, such algorithms do not guarantee that they will find the optimal solution.

The degree of closeness is determined by a parameter called *tolerance*, which usually has some default value but can often be modified by the user. The tolerance parameter is usually linked to a measure of the distance between the current and the subsequent solution or to the incremental progress made by subsequent iterations of the algorithm in improving the objective function value. If subsequent iterations of the algorithm bring very little change relative to the status quo, the algorithm terminates.

The optimization algorithms in today's optimization software are rather sophisticated, and an extensive introduction to these algorithms is beyond the scope of this book. However, many optimization solvers let the user select which optimization algorithm to apply to a specific problem, and some basic knowledge of what algorithms are used for different classes of optimization solvers is helpful for deciding what optimization software to use and what options to select for the problem at hand.

6.4.1 Linear Optimization: The Simplex Algorithm and Interior Point Methods

The first optimization algorithm, called the *simplex algorithm*, was developed by George Dantzig in 1947. It solves linear optimization problems by iteratively solving systems of linear equations to find intermediate feasible solutions in a way that continually improves the value of the objective function. The name of the algorithm refers to the geometric term *simplex*. A two-dimensional simplex is a triangle—a set of points that lie between the lines that can be drawn between $2+1$ points in the two-dimensional space.

In N-dimensional space, a simplex is a collection of all the points that can be enclosed by hyperplanes connecting the outermost points in the set.[16] (See exhibit 6.7.) It turns out that the feasible sets for the decision variables in linear optimization problems are simplexes, and an amazing fact about linear optimization problems is that at least one possible optimal solution must lie at the corner of the simplex. (It is possible that other optimal solutions lie on the edge of the set, however.) The simplex algorithm takes advantage of this fact. It visits the corners of the simplex that contains the feasible solutions to the linear optimization problem iteratively to find the corner solution that results in the best possible value for the objective function, which it then reports as the optimal solution. Despite its age, the simplex algorithm is still widely used for linear optimization and is remarkably efficient in practice.

In the 1980s, another class of efficient algorithms called *interior point methods* was developed, inspired by a new algorithm that Narendra Karmakar created for LP problems. In contrast to the simplex method, which traverses the simplex of feasible points along the edges and only considers the corners, interior point methods reach the optimal solution from the inside of the feasible set. If multiple optimal solutions exist, interior point algorithms may not find the corner one. Thus, if a linear optimization problem has multiple optimal solutions, solving the problem with a solver that uses the simplex algorithm versus a solver that uses an interior point algorithm may result in different optimal solutions. The advantage of interior point methods is that they can be applied not only to linear optimization problems but also to a broader class of convex optimization problems.

16. In mathematical terms, a simplex is the convex hull of a set of $N+1$ points in N-dimensional space (i.e., the minimum set that contains all the points), and any line drawn between points in the set stays within the set.

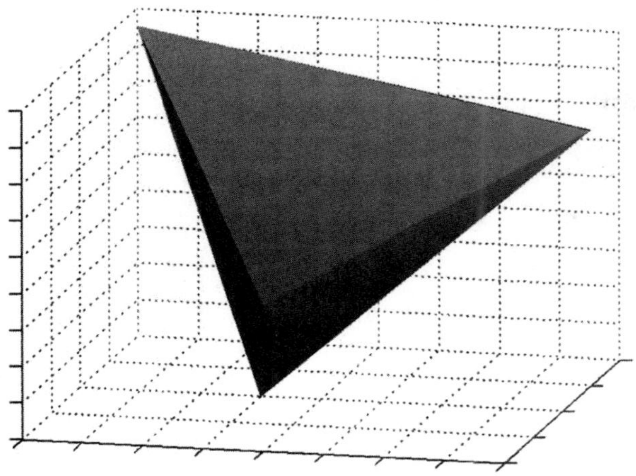

Exhibit 6.7
Simplex in three-dimensional space.

6.4.2 Constrained Nonlinear Optimization: The KKT Conditions and Lagrange Multipliers

Many nonlinear optimization algorithms are based on using information from a special set of equations that represent necessary conditions that solution $\mathbf{x}$ is optimal. These conditions are the Karush-Kuhn-Tucker (KKT) conditions for optimality. We explain the intuition behind them next.

When an optimization problem is unconstrained and the objective function is differentiable, the optimum can be found using standard techniques from calculus. If we are minimizing a function $f(x)$ of a single variable x, then the derivative of $f(x)$, $f'(x)$, must be 0 at the optimal point x^* (see exhibit 6.7). To see this, recall that the derivative represents the amount that the function will change when x changes by a small amount. If $f'(x^*)$ is less than 0, then we can move a small distance from x^* in the positive direction and achieve a smaller value for $f(x)$, so $f(x^*)$ is not in fact the minimum. Similarly, if $f'(x^*)$ is greater than 0, then we can move a small distance from x^* in the negative direction and achieve a smaller value for $f(x)$.

When there are constraints $g_i(\mathbf{x})$ and $h_j(\mathbf{x})$, a parallel condition for $\mathbf{x}^*$ to be the minimum holds, but it also involves the derivatives of the constraint functions. Namely, at the optimum $\mathbf{x}^*$, the following equality must hold:

$$f'(\mathbf{x}^*) + \sum_{i=1}^{I} u_i \cdot g_i'(\mathbf{x}^*) + \sum_{j=1}^{J} v_j \cdot h_j'(\mathbf{x}^*) = 0.$$

Here, u_i and v_j are special numbers called *Lagrange multipliers*, and u_i needs to be nonnegative. In addition, of course, for a point $\mathbf{x}^*$ to be the optimum, it needs to be feasible as well; that is, it must satisfy all constraints in the optimization problem. The Lagrange multipliers are not known in advance, but in some cases, they can be computed from the equality here and the conditions on feasibility.

The KKT conditions are a generalization of the statements given here when there are multiple decision variables. If f, $g_i(\mathbf{x})$ and $h_j(\mathbf{x})$ are functions of an N-dimensional vector of variable $\mathbf{x}$, then we need to consider the *gradients* of the objective function and the

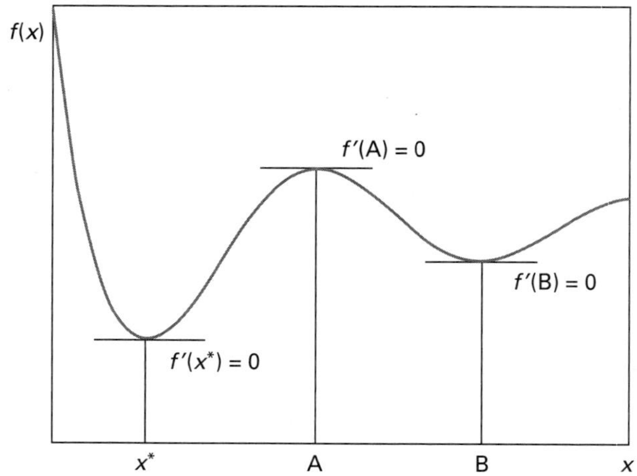

Exhibit 6.8
The condition that the derivative of function $f(x)$ is equal to 0 is satisfied at (A) the global minimum x^*, (B) a local maximum (point A), and (c) a local minimum (point B).

constraint functions.[17] Then, the KKT necessary conditions for point $\mathbf{x}^*$ to be a minimum can be expressed as

$$\nabla f(\mathbf{x}^*) + \sum_{i=1}^{I} u_i \cdot \nabla g_i(\mathbf{x}^*) + \sum_{j=1}^{J} v_j \cdot \nabla h_j(\mathbf{x}^*) = 0$$

$$u_i \geq 0, i = 1, \ldots, I$$

$$u_i \cdot g_i(\mathbf{x}^*) = 0,\ i = 1, \ldots, I$$

$$h_j(\mathbf{x}^*) = 0, j = 1, \ldots, J$$

$$g_i(\mathbf{x}^*) = 0,\ i = 1, \ldots, I$$

The last two conditions simply require that point $\mathbf{x}^*$ must satisfy all the constraints; that is, be a feasible solution and be considered a candidate for the global minimum.

Note that it is not easy to find a point $\mathbf{x}$ that satisfies the KKT conditions because, depending on the expressions for the objective function and the constraint functions, some of the equations in the system may be nonlinear. Even if a point that satisfies the KKT conditions is found, it may not be the global optimum, since the KKT conditions are necessary, but not sufficient for optimality. In other words, if point $\mathbf{x}^*$ is the global optimal solution, it must satisfy these conditions, but if point $\mathbf{x}$ satisfies these conditions, it is not necessarily the global optimal solution. This reasoning is easiest to visualize in the simple case in which we have the unconstrained minimization problem in exhibit 6.8. The derivative of $f(x)$ is 0 not only at the global minimum (x^*), but also at point A (local maximum) and point B (local

17. Recall that the gradient of a function f of N variables $x_1, x_2, \ldots, x_N$ is defined as the partial derivative with respect to each individual variable:

$$\nabla f(\mathbf{x}) = \left(\frac{\partial}{\partial x_1} f(\mathbf{x}), \ldots, \frac{\partial}{\partial x_N} f(\mathbf{x}) \right)$$

minimum). The derivative can also be 0 at so-called *inflection* points (or *saddle* points), which are neither minima nor maxima, but points at which the function changes curvature. Fortunately, the KKT conditions are necessary and sufficient for optimality in the case of convex optimization problems. They take a special form in the case of linear optimization problems and some other classes of convex problems, which are exploited in interior point algorithms for finding the optimal solution.

The importance of the KKT conditions for general nonlinear optimization is that they enable a nonlinear optimization problem to be reduced to a system of nonlinear equations, whose solution can be attained by using successive approximations. Widely used algorithms for nonlinear optimization include barrier methods, primal–dual interior point methods, and sequential QP methods. The latter tries to solve the KKT conditions for the original nonlinear problem by optimizing a quadratic approximation to a function derived from the objective function and the constraints of the original problem. For more details, see Bazaraa, Sharali, and Shetty (1993) and Freund (2004).

6.4.3 Integer Programming Algorithms

At first glance, integer and mixed-integer optimization problems appear to be easier than standard optimization problems because the number of feasible values for the decision variables to be explored appears smaller than the feasible values for optimization problems with continuous variables. In fact, however, IP problems as a general rule are more difficult and take longer to solve. Enumeration of all possible solutions for problems of realistic size is prohibitively expensive computationally, so we still need to resort to algorithms that search for the optimal solution in a smart way. Such algorithms are easier to create for problems with continuous variables than for problems with integer variables.

IP optimization problems are typically solved by branch-and-bound algorithms, branch-and-cut routines, and heuristics[18] that exploit the special structure of the problem.[19] The main idea behind many of these algorithms is to start by solving a *relaxation* of the optimization problem in which the decision variables are not restricted to be integer numbers. The algorithms then begin with the solution found in the initial stage and narrow the choices of integer solutions. In practice, a simple rounding of the initial fractional optimal solution is sometimes good enough. However, it is important to understand that simple rounding of the initial solution can lead to an integer solution that is very far from the actual optimal solution, and this problem is even more pronounced when the number of integer decision variables is large.

There are some good commercial optimization solvers that can handle linear and convex quadratic mixed-integer optimization problems. Still, there are virtually no solvers that can handle more general nonlinear mixed-integer problems easily. However, new promising methodologies at the intersection of optimization and machine learning (ML) can speed up

18. A heuristic is a logical, approximate way to solve an optimization problem which, however, is not necessarily guaranteed to produce the optimal result. The initial selection of projects based on the ranking of their benefit-to-cost ratios in the capital budgeting example in section 6.3.3 was an example of a greedy heuristic—our simple investment algorithm selected each subsequent project as the project with the highest-ranking among the projects not already selected. As we saw, this algorithm did not give us the optimal solution, although it did produce a good solution.

19. For an intuitive overview of some of these algorithms, see chapter 9 in Fabozzi et al. (2007). For a complete mathematical treatment of the subject, see, for example, Bertsimas and Tsitsiklis (1997).

the search for good solutions and address much more complex optimization problems than previously were possible to solve efficiently.

6.4.4 Randomized Search Algorithms

In this chapter, we have referred several times to the difficulty of finding the global optimal solution when there are multiple local optima. Classical nonlinear optimization algorithms typically stop when they have found a solution that is the best in its "neighborhood," and if they come across a local optimum first, they may never reach the global optimum. Some algorithms try to avoid these pitfalls by incorporating an element of randomness in their search. In other words, they allow moves to feasible solutions with the worse value of the objective function to happen with some probability rather than always seeking a direction in which the objective function improves. The hope is that this will avoid getting stuck in a local optimum.

Randomized search algorithms fall into several classes, including *simulated annealing*, *tabu search*, and *genetic algorithms*. Genetic algorithms have become an option in several popular software packages for optimization, such as Premium Solver and Palisade's Evolver, which is discussed shortly. MATLAB also has a Genetic Algorithms and Direct Search Toolbox containing simulated annealing and genetic algorithms. We explain simulated annealing and genetic algorithms in more detail so the available options in these software packages will become more intuitive.

At every step, the simulated annealing algorithm generates a new feasible solution to the optimization problem, and it generally accepts that as the next solution if the value of the objective function improves. However, even if the solution does not improve the value of the objective function, the simulated annealing algorithm accepts it with some probability. The magnitude of the probability of accepting a seemingly inferior solution as the next point in the search is determined by a positive parameter T (called the *temperature*), which is an input to the algorithm. If the temperature is low, the simulated annealing algorithm is less likely to deviate substantially from a path in which the objective function value is improving; if the temperature is high, the simulated annealing is more adventurous in picking solutions that can be very different. At an intuitive level, when the algorithm is close to the optimum, we want the temperature to be low so the algorithm stays in that neighborhood and eventually finds the optimal solution. However, at the initial stages of the algorithm, we may be better off if the temperature is high because the algorithm will scout more areas with solutions faster and will not spend time in a particular neighborhood. In advanced solvers, the default value of parameter T is usually set to a value that works reasonably well for a wide variety of difficult, highly nonlinear problems.

Like simulate annealing, genetic algorithms are useful in cases in which the objective function or the constraints are highly nonlinear or have discontinuities. However, genetic algorithms tend to be slower than classical optimization algorithms and simulated annealing because they tend to require more objective function evaluations. Despite this drawback, genetic algorithms can be more efficient than other randomized algorithms in cases in which some of the decision variables are integers or in which the optimization problem has a special structure.

Before a genetic algorithm starts, a way must be found for any potential solution to the optimization problem to be encoded as a string of integers, or binary bits. This string is referred to as a *chromosome*. It looks something like

1101 0000 1111 0010

The chromosome may be composed of *genes*, such as individual bits or groups of bits. In the preceding example, we may treat groups of four bits as genes.

At the beginning of the algorithm, a fixed number of such chromosomes are generated. (This is the initial *population*.) Each of them is assigned a *fitness score*, which evaluates how good the solution represented by that chromosome is. (The fitness score is related to the objective function value evaluated at that solution.) Then, two members from the population are selected at random. (The probability of being selected is typically related to the fitness score of a particular chromosome.) You can think of them as the "parents." The *crossover rate*, specified by the user, determines how the genes of the parents are swapped. It is often specified to be about 0.7. The *mutation rate*, also specified by the user, determines what percentage of the bits on average flip from 1 to 0 and from 0 to 1 randomly. It is usually small (e.g., 0.001). After going through a number of iterations specified by the user, the algorithm stops and returns the best solution found so far.

To summarize, randomized search algorithms for optimization have their drawbacks—they can be slow and provide no guarantee that they will find the global optimum. However, they are appropriate for handling difficult integer problems, nonlinear problems, and problems with discontinuities when traditional optimization solvers fail.

6.4.5 Algorithm Efficiency

Thus far, we have been using the word "efficient" to describe an optimization algorithm. While the term is intuitive and generally means "fast," in some cases, it is important to differentiate between different ways to measure the efficiency of an algorithm. Established conventions estimate the efficiency of an algorithm by the number of steps or the elementary operations that it takes to solve a problem of a given size. (The size of a problem is determined by the number of operations needed to solve the problem, which is related to the number of decision variables and the number of constraints.)[20] However, such bounds typically estimate the worst-case performance. Having a large number of steps does not necessarily mean worse performance in practice. For most practical purposes, we care only whether a given algorithm performs well on typical instances of the problems, not whether the algorithm is slow for some pathological examples. For example, the simplex method for linear optimization provides no guarantees on how many steps it may take to come up with the optimal solution. Yet the algorithm works remarkably well in practice.

Still, the theoretical superiority of one algorithm over another often leads to better performance in practice as well. Thus, algorithms that run in *polynomial time* in the problem size are generally preferable to algorithms that take *exponential time*. An algorithm is said to run in polynomial time if it requires $O(n^k)$ operations to solve, where n is the problem size and k is a positive integer.[21] An algorithm is said to run in exponential time if it requires $O(k^n)$ operations to solve the problem. As an example, if $k = 10$ and $n = 80$ (the problem size

20. For a more rigorous discussion, see Bertsimas and Tsitsiklis (1997).

21. Order notation (O(.)) allows us to represent the idea that an expression or a quantity is "about the same size as" another expression or quantity. A function $f(x)$ is "of the order of" a function $g(x)$ if $f(x)$ does not exceed $g(x)$ in magnitude (up to a scaling factor c) around any specific point of interest. If the specification of the point is omitted, it is usually assumed that the statement is valid for all points on the real line.

can easily be 80 for real-life problems), we will arguably need more operations to solve the optimization problem than there are atoms in the universe. No matter how much technology has improved, algorithms that run in exponential time are very hard to handle for large problems.

6.5 Optimization Duality

The Lagrange multipliers **u** and **v** from the KKT conditions discussed in section 6.4.2 have a special role in optimization theory and practice. They are in fact variables in a certain *dual* optimization problem that is related to the original, or *primal*, optimization problem in very specific ways. If the primal problem is a minimization problem, then the dual problem is a maximization problem, and vice versa. The number of variables in the dual problem is equal to the number of constraints in the primal problem, and vice versa. Moreover, there is a relationship between the optimal objective function values of the primal and the dual problem that can often be exploited. *Optimization duality theory* has numerous critical applications, including but not restricted to the following:

- A good dual-problem solution can be used to compute a bound for the value of the objective function of the primal problem, so it can be used to identify when a primal solution is near-optimal.
- For some types of convex optimization problems, it can be verified that an optimal solution to the primal problem has been found by constructing a dual-problem solution with the same objective function value.
- Sometimes the dual problem has better mathematical or computational structure than the primal problem. This fact can be used to compute optimal solutions for both the primal and the dual optimization problems. In addition, the computation of dual variables is part of a number of efficient optimization algorithms. The primal-dual interior point method (mentioned in section 6.4.2) is one such algorithm.
- We can use dual variables to perform sensitivity analysis on the primal optimization problem. The dual variable corresponding to a particular constraint in the primal problem represents the incremental change in the optimal solution value per unit increase in the value on the right side of the constraint equality or inequality.

Duality theory is not as widely used in specific financial applications as some other aspects of optimization. Still, it has been used in the context of finding arbitrage opportunities, and it plays a major part in the methodology for deriving robust optimization problem formulations for portfolio optimization problems (see section 7.3 in chapter 7). It is therefore helpful to explain how dual problems are constructed and interpreted for some important classes of optimization problems.

Consider again the general optimization problem P (the primal problem):

$$\begin{aligned} \text{P:}\quad \min_{\mathbf{x}} \quad & f(\mathbf{x}) \\ \text{s.t.} \quad & g_i(\mathbf{x}) \le 0, \quad i = 1, \ldots, I \\ & h_j(\mathbf{x}) = 0, \quad j = 1, \ldots, J. \end{aligned}$$

The dual problem D is constructed in three steps:

1. Place the constraints in the objective function by using I nonnegative multipliers u_i and J multipliers v_j to form the so-called *Lagrangian function*:

$$L(\mathbf{x},\mathbf{u}) := f(\mathbf{x}) + \mathbf{u}'g(\mathbf{x}) + \mathbf{v}'h(\mathbf{x}) = f(\mathbf{x}) + \sum_{i=1}^{I} u_i g_i(\mathbf{x}) + \sum_{j=1}^{J} v_i h_j(\mathbf{x}).$$

2. Create the dual function:

$$L^*(\mathbf{u}) := \min_{\mathbf{x}}\{f(\mathbf{x}) + \mathbf{u}'g(\mathbf{x}) + \mathbf{v}'h(\mathbf{x})\}.$$

3. Write the dual problem:

$$\begin{aligned} \text{D:}\ \max_{\mathbf{u}} \quad & L^*(\mathbf{u}) \\ \text{s.t.} \quad & \mathbf{u} \geq 0 \end{aligned}$$

Usually, we construct the dual problem in the hope that computing the optimal solution will be an easy task.

Examples of primal and dual problems for linear and quadratic problems are summarized in exhibit 6.9. The dual of the dual problem is the primal problem. That is, if you start with an optimization problem (i.e., the primal problem), formulate its dual problem, and then take the dual of that dual problem, you end up back at the original primal problem.

Note that the type of problem (LP, QP, SOCP) in the primal problem is preserved in the dual problem for all examples of convex problems. (This is not the case in general nonlinear optimization.) Moreover, it can be shown that for all these types of convex problems, the objective function value of the primal problem for a feasible primal problem solution is at

	Primal Problem	Dual Problem
LPs	$\min_{\mathbf{x}} \ \mathbf{c}'\mathbf{x}$ s.t. $\mathbf{A}\mathbf{x} = \mathbf{b}$ $\mathbf{x} \geq \mathbf{0}$	$\max_{\mathbf{x}} \ \mathbf{u}'\mathbf{b}$ s.t. $\mathbf{A}'\mathbf{u} \leq \mathbf{c}'$
	$\min_{\mathbf{x}} \ \mathbf{c}'\mathbf{x}$ s.t. $\mathbf{A}\mathbf{x} \geq \mathbf{b}$	$\max_{\mathbf{u}} \ \mathbf{u}'\mathbf{b}$ s.t. $\mathbf{A}'\mathbf{u} = \mathbf{c}$ $\mathbf{u} \geq 0$
QPs	$\min_{\mathbf{x}} \ \frac{1}{2}\mathbf{x}'\mathbf{Q}\mathbf{x} + \mathbf{c}'\mathbf{x}$ s.t. $\mathbf{A}\mathbf{x} \geq \mathbf{b}$	$\max_{\mathbf{u}} \ \mathbf{u}'\mathbf{b} - \frac{1}{2}(\mathbf{c} - \mathbf{A}'\mathbf{u})'\mathbf{Q}^{-1}(\mathbf{c} - \mathbf{A}'\mathbf{u})$ s.t. $\mathbf{u} \geq 0$
SOCPs	$\min_{\mathbf{x}} \ \mathbf{c}'\mathbf{x}$ s.t. $\lVert \mathbf{C}_i\mathbf{x} + \mathbf{d}_i \rVert \leq \mathbf{c}_i'\mathbf{x} + e_i,$ $i = 1, \ldots, I$	$\max_{\mathbf{u},\mathbf{v}} \ -\sum_{i=1}^{I} \mathbf{u}_i'\mathbf{d}_i + v_i e_i$ s.t. $\sum_{i=1}^{I} \mathbf{u}_i\mathbf{C}_i + \mathbf{v}_i\mathbf{c}_i = \mathbf{c}$ $\lVert \mathbf{u}_i \rVert \leq v_i,\ i = 1, \ldots, I$

Exhibit 6.9
Primal and dual formulations for important types of convex optimization problems.

least as large as the objective function value of the dual problem for a feasible dual problem. In fact, for these types of convex optimization problems, it is guaranteed that if the primal problem has an optimal solution, then so does the dual problem, and the respective objective function values are the same. This has important implications for optimization algorithm applications.

6.6 Multistage Optimization

Financial planning and pricing decisions often involve finding optimal strategies over multiple time periods ahead. For example, a firm may be considering a sequence of operational choices over the next few years. It is often possible to capture this multistage framework through standard optimization formulations. Still, it can be difficult and does not always allow for employing the most efficient algorithms to solve the problem. Models of dynamic choice in finance typically involve the representation of future cash flow streams and are perhaps best portrayed by a graph. On the horizontal axis, one denotes the time periods at which the cash flows occur. At each time period, nodes are used to represent different possible *states* or conditions of the dynamic system at that point in time. The collection of all states is called the *state space*. Our actions influence which state is reached at the next point in time. States that are reachable from a particular state are linked to that state.

6.6.1 Finite State Space

Examples of two simple dynamical systems are illustrated in exhibits 6.10(A) and 6.10(B). Each node in the graphs represents a state. The graphs are called *binomial trees*, or *binomial lattices*, because exactly two branches emanate from each node. The number of branches corresponds to the number of options available to the decision maker at each particular state. If there were three available choices, the number of branches emanating from each node would be three. There can also be dynamical systems with an infinite

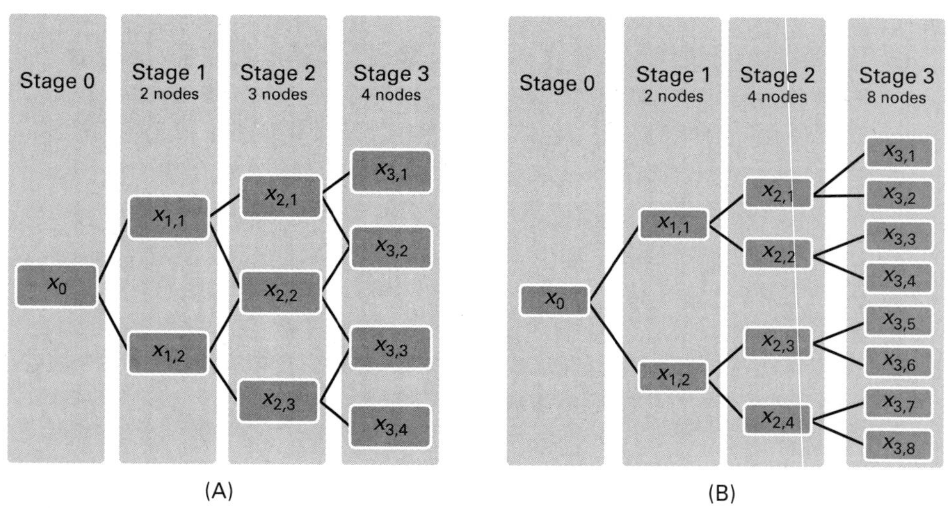

Exhibit 6.10
(A) Recombining binomial tree; (B) nonrecombining binomial tree.

number of branches emanating from each node. We will see an example later in this section. Note that the branches in exhibit 6.10(A) recombine, whereas the branches in exhibit 6.10(B) do not. Graphs with recombining branches are referred to as *recombining trees* or *recombining lattices*.

Let us consider a very simple example. Suppose that you have purchased a 3-year lease for an oil well. The estimated reserves of the well are 600,000 barrels. Every year, you can either pump oil normally (strategy 1), in which case you pump 100,000 barrels; or use an enhanced pumping method that allows you to pump 200,000 barrels (strategy 2). The increased production capacity through the enhanced pumping method comes at a price: to extract u_t barrels at time t with the enhanced method costs you $20 \cdot \frac{u_t^2}{x_t}$ dollars, where x_t is the amount of available reserves at time t. In contrast, the cost of extracting u_t barrels with the normal pumping method is $\frac{u_t^2}{x_t}$ dollars. Note that in both cases, as the amount of available oil x_t decreases, the cost of pumping increases. This expression incorporates the implicit assumption that it becomes harder to pump the oil as the reserves are depleted.

The expected price of a barrel of oil over the first, second, and third year of your lease is \$45, \$30, and \$40, respectively, and the discount factor per year is 0.9. Assuming that you can pump either 100,000 barrels or 200,000 barrels each year, what is the optimal strategy to maximize the present value (PV) of your profit from the lease?

One approach to finding the optimal solution would be to look at the price of oil in each of the three years, compute the revenue and cost from each strategy each year, and then pick the strategy that results in the best profit during that year. Unfortunately, however, the profit every year depends on the level of current oil reserves. To see this, suppose that the current reserves are expressed as x_t and the current price is p_t. The profit of strategy 1 is $pt \cdot 100{,}000 - \frac{u_t^2}{x_t}$, and the profit of strategy 2 is $p_t \cdot 200{,}000 - 20 \cdot \frac{u_t^2}{x_t}$. Therefore, optimal decisions across years are interdependent, and we cannot treat every year separately.

To describe the dynamics of the cash flows and the decisions, we first ask what would be an appropriate definition of *state* in this dynamical system. The state must incorporate all information about the system at a particular point in time. In our example, the amount of current reserves at time t, x_t, is an appropriate choice for the state. The amount of current reserves determines the cost of pumping oil, and that affects the profit and our decision.

The evolution of our dynamical system can be described by the graph in exhibit 6.11. (See also the file **Ch6-OilExample.xlsx**.) We can pump oil at the beginning of years 0, 1, and 2. The lease ends in year 3. At every node, we can make the decision to pump 100,000 or 200,000 barrels of oil, which takes us to one of the nodes at the next time period. For example, at time 0 (node A), we start with $x_0 = 600{,}000$ barrels of oil. If we pump using the normal method (i.e., our decision $u_0 = 100{,}000$), the oil reserves decrease by 100,000 and the system is at node B at time 1. If we pump using the enhanced method, the oil reserves decrease by 200,000 and the system is at node C at time 1. Depending on the node at which we are in year 1 (node B or node C), we can again decide whether to use the normal or the enhanced method ($u_1 = 100{,}000$ or $u_1 = 200{,}000$, respectively). If we are at node B at time 1, our decision will

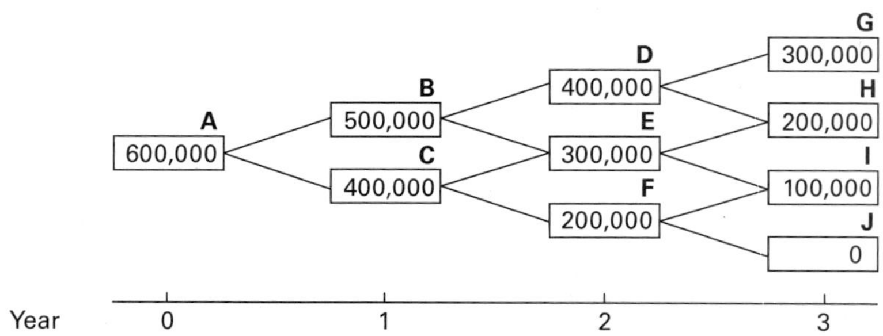

Exhibit 6.11
Binomial tree representing the state space for the oil well multistage optimization problem. (For more, see the file **Ch6-OilExample.xlsx**.)

take us either to node D (if we use the normal method) or to node E (if we use the enhanced method). If we are at node C, our decision will take us either to node E (if we use the normal method) or to node F (if we use the enhanced method). Note that this tree is recombining because, for example, we can get to node E (have reserves of 300,000 barrels) either by following the path A-B-E (pumping 100,000 in the first year and 200,000 in the second year) or the path A-C-E (pumping 200,000 in the first year and 100,000 in the second year).

Eight paths can be seen in the graph: A-B-D-G, A-B-D-H, A-B-E-H, A-B-E-I, A-C-E-H, A-C-E-I, A-C-F-I, and A-C-F-J. Each path represents a particular strategy. To find the optimal path to take, we could evaluate the present value of the profit along each path and select the path that gives us the maximum present value of profit. A calculation can be made for this example. In practice, however, we may encounter situations in which there are many more time periods, and many more possible states. The problem quickly becomes computationally intractable. For example, if we expand the number of time periods in a binomial tree to 20, the number of paths to be evaluated becomes 2^{20}, which is 1,048,576. For each of these paths, we need to store information at each time period to add it all up and obtain the present value of the profit obtained from selecting that path. Not only is the number of paths large, but it also seems superfluous to recalculate the profit at each node several times, given that some paths share nodes.

The trick of solving the problem with minimum number of calculations and minimum amount of storage required is to work backward, starting from the final nodes on the right. At each node, we can store only the information about the best path so far and forget about all the other paths. This sequential optimization method is called *dynamic programming*. Dynamic programming is based on Bellman's (1957) *Principle of Optimality*, which states that to achieve total optimality in a sequential decision process, all future decisions after reaching a particular state must be optimal with respect to that state. In other words, it is impossible to have a suboptimal decision at some intermediate state and still reach the overall optimum. Therefore, we only need to keep track of the optimal decision at each state reachable from the current state and use recursive relationships to describe the optimal decision at any particular state in terms of the optimal decisions in future states. We explain the dynamic programming algorithm as it applies to the oil well problem next.

No profit is realized at nodes G, H, I, and J because the lease has expired by then. (We assume all profit is obtained at the beginning of the year.) So we can ignore them in our calculations. At the beginning of year 2, we can be at nodes D, E or F. Suppose that we are at D; that is, the current level of oil reserves is 400,000 barrels. The profit that can be realized using the normal method is

$$40 \cdot 100{,}000 - 100{,}000^2/400{,}000 = \$3{,}975{,}000$$

The profit realized using the enhanced method is

$$40 \cdot 200{,}000 - 20 \cdot 200{,}000^2/400{,}000 = \$6{,}000{,}000.$$

Obviously, \$6,000,000 is the greater profit, so we should use the enhanced method if we are at node D.

Similarly, we can compute the highest profit at nodes E and F. If we are at E, the optimal strategy is to use the enhanced method, and the profit that we can realize is \$5,333,333.33. If we are at F, the optimal strategy is again to use the enhanced method, and the realized profit will be \$4,000,000.

Next, we consider the previous time period. At the beginning of year 1, we can be at either node B or node C.

Suppose that we are at node B; that is, the oil reserves are 500,000. If we select the normal method, we will realize a current profit of $30 \cdot 100{,}000 - 100{,}000^2/500{,}000 = \$2{,}980{,}000$, and will move to node D, which will realize an additional profit of \$5,400,000, which is the present value of \$6,000,000 in year 1 dollars ($= 0.9 \cdot \$6{,}000{,}000$). The total profit from employing the normal method in year 1, therefore, is $\$2{,}980{,}000 + \$5{,}400{,}000 = \$8{,}380{,}000$.

Suppose now that we select the enhanced method if we are at node B. This means that in the next year, we will be at node E. The current profit is \$4,400,000, and the best profit that we can realize at node E is \$5,333,333.33, so the total profit in year 1 dollars is $\$4{,}400{,}000 + 0.9 \cdot \$5{,}333{,}333.33 = \$9{,}200{,}000$. Clearly, selecting the enhanced method at node B results in a higher total profit from year 1 onward (accounting for both the profit in year 1 and the best profit that can be realized in year 2 if we are at node B in year 1).

We proceed similarly to compute the profits at nodes C and A. At each node, we record the present value of the optimal profit only from that node onward and the best strategy from that point onward. The optimal path and the profit from the best strategy at each node (from that node onward) are shown in exhibit 6.12. The optimal path—that is, the path that leads to the highest present value of total profit (\$14,664,166.67)—is A-C-E-I. This means that the optimal strategy is to use the enhanced method for the first year, the normal method for the second year, and the enhanced method again for the third year.

Note that the strategies at some nodes are not obvious. For example, if we are at node A and we look at the optimal profit realized at nodes B and C, we may be tempted to use the normal method over the first year, ending up at node B. This is because the optimal profit at node B going forward (\$9,200,000.00) is higher than the optimal profit at node C going forward (\$7,775,000.00). However, the price of oil over the first year is high enough that it turns out that, overall, it is optimal to pump more oil (using the enhanced method) during

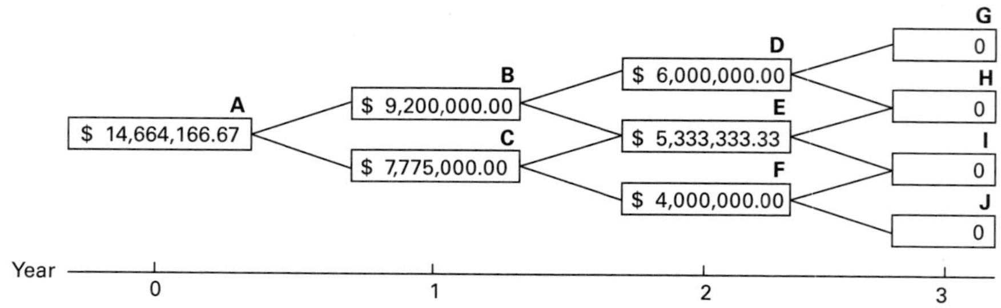

Exhibit 6.12
The optimal profit from each state onward and the optimal decision path (marked by bold line segments) for the oil well problem. The nodes in the tree match the states in exhibit 6.10.

the first year and then end up in node C, even though the optimal profit going forward from node C is less than the optimal profit going forward from B.

Standard Notation Used in Dynamic Programming Let us summarize the dynamic programming approach by introducing some standard notation. The variable that summarizes all necessary information at each state is called a *state variable*. In our example, it was x_t, the amount of oil available at time t. Our decisions (the amount of oil to pump) were represented by variable $u_t = \{100{,}000, 200{,}000\}$, which is referred to as a *control*, or *policy variable*. The state variable was a function of the control variable and the state at which we were in the previous period, and it was updated at every stage by the transition equation

$$x_{t+1} = x_t - u_t.$$

In the general case, we write $x_{t+1} = g(x_t, u_t)$.

The total number of stages in our problem was $T = 3$. Our goal was to optimize an *objective function*, the present value of the total profit, which was a sum of the present values of the profits at each stage and was a function of the state and the control variable at each stage. We can write the objective function as

$$\sum_{t=0}^{T-1} f_t(x_t, u_t).$$

To compute the optimal value of the objective function (the optimal total profit), we computed the optimal profit from that stage onward at each node of the dynamic programming algorithm. The reward (or cost, depending on the problem) *from a specific node onward* is referred to as the *value function*. It is usually denoted by V. The dynamic programming algorithm maximizes the sum of the immediate reward of the current step (say, cash flow $c(u_t)$) and the optimal reward from the following steps. The value function recursion can be written as

$$V_t(x_t) = \max_{u_t} \{c(u_t) + d \cdot V_{t+1}^*(u_t)\}$$

where $V_{t+1}^*(u_t)$ is the optimal value of the value function at stage $t+1$ over all possible values for the control u_t, and d is the discount factor over one stage. In our oil well example, we had

$$V_t(x_t) = \max \left\{ \begin{array}{l} p_t \cdot 100{,}000 - \dfrac{100{,}000^2}{x_t + 0.9} \cdot V^*_{t+1}(x_t - 100{,}000), \\ p_t \cdot 200{,}000 - \dfrac{20 \cdot 200{,}000^2}{x_t + 0.9} \cdot V^*_{t+1}(x_t - 200{,}000) \end{array} \right\}$$

where p_t was the price of oil at time t.

A dynamic programming algorithm requires a boundary condition to compute the actual values of the value function. As its name implies, a boundary condition gives information about values at the extremes. In the oil well example, we knew that the profit that could be realized at the beginning of year 3 was 0 (because the lease expires in three years). This allowed us to compute the value function at the beginning of time period 3. From there, we could compute the optimal values at the previous stages.

On the Relationship between Dynamic Programming and Classical Optimization Formulations At the beginning of this section, we mentioned that many dynamic programming formulations can be stated in a standard optimization form, although often this is not the easiest or most efficient way to approach the problem. To illustrate the relationship between dynamic programming and the classical optimization formulations discussed in sections 6.2 and 6.3, we formulate the oil well example as a standard optimization problem.

First, we introduce decision variables x_0, x_1, and x_2, which will store the optimal amount of reserves at each stage. Technically, x_0 is not a variable (we are given the initial amount of reserves), but we keep the notation for consistency.

Second, we introduce decision variables u_0, u_1, and u_2, which will store our optimal decision about the amount of oil to pump at each stage.

Next, we note that our decision choices u_0, u_1, and u_2 are discrete—we can pump only 100,000 or 200,000 barrels each year. The situation is reminiscent of the cash-flow matching problem in section 6.3.2, and more specifically of the modification of the problem, in which we restricted the bonds that are purchased to be in round lots by introducing binary variables. We can approach the oil well problem formulation in a similar way. Let z_0, z_1, and z_2 be binary variables with the following interpretation: z_t is 1 if we choose the normal method (i.e., we pump 100,000 barrels of oil), and z_t is 0 if we choose the enhanced method (i.e., we pump 200,000 barrels of oil). Then, we can link the policy decision variables u_0, u_1, and u_2 to the binary decision variables z_0, z_1, and z_2 as

$$u_t = 100{,}000 \cdot z_t + 200{,}000 \cdot (1 - z_t),\ t = 0, 1, 2.$$

This equality states the correct relationship because one of the terms in the sum is always 0. If $z_t = 1$ (i.e., we use the normal method), the second term is 0 and u_t is 100,000. If $z_t = 0$ (i.e., we use the enhanced method), the first term is 0 and u_t is 200,000.

We also need to state explicitly the relationships between the oil reserves at each stage x_0, x_1, and x_2, and the policy variables u_0, u_1, and u_2. It is easy to see that we have

$$x_t = x_{t-1} - u_{t-1},\ t = 1, 2;$$

That is, to obtain the optimal amount of reserves at each stage, we subtract the optimal amount that was pumped at the previous stage from the amount available.

The objective is to maximize the profit over all three stages, and we need to discount the profit received at future dates properly to compute the correct total present value. The optimization problem formulation, therefore, is

$$\begin{aligned}
\max_{x,u,z} \quad & p_0 \cdot u_0 - z_0 \cdot \frac{u_0^2}{x_0 - (1-z_0)\cdot 20 \cdot \frac{u_0^2}{x_0}} \\
& + 0.9 \cdot \left(p_1 \cdot u_1 - z_1 \cdot \frac{u_1^2}{x_1 - (1-z_1)\cdot 20 \cdot \frac{u_1^2}{x_1}} \right) \\
& + 0.9^2 \cdot \left(p_2 \cdot u_2 - z_2 \cdot \frac{u_2^2}{x_2 - (1-z_2)\cdot 20 \cdot \frac{u_2^2}{x_2}} \right) \\
& u_0 = 100{,}000 \cdot z_0 + 200{,}000 \cdot (1 - z_0) \\
& u_1 = 100{,}000 \cdot z_1 + 200{,}000 \cdot (1 - z_1) \\
& u_2 = 100{,}000 \cdot z_2 + 200{,}000 \cdot (1 - z_2) \\
& x_0 = 600{,}000 \\
& x_1 = x_0 - u_0 \\
& x_2 = x_1 - u_1 \\
& u_0, u_1, u_2, x_1, x_2 \geq 0 \\
& z_0, z_1, z_2 \text{ binary}.
\end{aligned}$$

Note that we used a trick in formulating the objective function because the expression for the cost is different depending on the method we use. We subtracted the cost "twice": once for the normal method and once for the enhanced method. However, we multiplied the expression for the cost of each method by an expression containing the binary variable z_t, such that only the cost for the method that is selected is subtracted from the profit; the cost for the method that is not selected is 0 in the objective function.

An implementation of the problem is presented in the worksheet **Classical Formulation** in the file **Ch6-OilExample.xlsx**. The optimal solution and optimal strategy at each stage are the same as the solution that we would obtain by using the dynamic programming algorithm as follows:

$z_0 = 0$ (use the enhanced method at stage 0)

$z_1 = 1$ (use the normal method at stage 1)

$z_2 = 0$ (use the enhanced method at stage 2)

$u_0 = 200{,}000$ (pump 200,000 barrels of oil at stage 0)

$u_1 = 100{,}000$ (pump 100,000 barrels of oil at stage 1)

$u_2 = 200{,}000$ (pump 200,000 barrels of oil at stage 2)

$x_0 = 600{,}000$ (amount of reserves at stage 0 is 600,000 barrels)

$x_1 = 400{,}000$ (amount of reserves at stage 1 is 400,000 barrels)

$x_2 = 300{,}000$ (amount of reserves at stage 2 is 300,000 barrels)

6.6.2 Infinite State Space

As we mentioned earlier in this section, in some financial applications we need to deal with dynamical systems with an infinite state space. Think, for example, of investments that are managed over multiple time periods. If the state of the system is determined by our current holdings and the percentage invested in assets represents our policy, then technically, we could have an infinite number of possible states—the possible combinations of weights of assets in the portfolio at each point in time can be infinite. In such cases, we cannot easily visualize the dynamic system, and we cannot compute the optimal strategy at every state as we did in the oil well example. The best we can do is to hope to find an expression that describes the optimal strategy in each state in terms of the information in that state. This is not always possible, and sometimes approximations are used. Next, we show an example in which the optimal strategy in each of an infinite number of states can be computed in closed form.

Let us consider modifying the oil well problem. As before, suppose you have purchased a 3-year lease for the oil well. The estimated reserves of the well are 600,000 barrels. You can use an enhanced method to pump oil that allows you to pump as much oil as you want during the year at a cost of $20 \cdot \frac{u_t^2}{x_t}$, where u_t is the amount of oil pumped and x_t is the amount of available reserves at time t. As before, the expected price of a barrel of oil over the first, second, and third year of your lease is \$45, \$30, and \$40, respectively, and the discount factor per year is 0.9. How much oil should you pump in each year to maximize your profit over the three years?

Given the similarities with the example in section 6.6.1, it is easy to see that the most appropriate choice of state for the dynamical system is the amount of oil reserves available at time t. However, we can no longer draw a binomial tree like the one in exhibit 6.10—there are an infinite number of states at each stage.

Fortunately, we can still solve the problem by using the dynamic programming recursion. Suppose we are at the beginning of year 2, with one year left on the lease. The profit at the beginning of year 2 (again, if all cash flows from the oil pumped in that year are received at that time) is $p_2 \cdot u_2 - 20 \cdot \frac{u_2^2}{x_2}$. The value function at any state at the beginning of year 2, $V_2(x_2)$, can be written as

$$V_2(x_2) = \max_{u_2} \left\{ p_2 \cdot u_2 - 20 \cdot \frac{u_2^2}{x_2} \right\}.$$

This is an unconstrained optimization problem. The expression to maximize, $p_2 \cdot u_2 - 20 \cdot \frac{u_2^2}{x_2}$, is a quadratic function in u_2, and it takes the shape in exhibit 6.3(B). It is easy to see that the maximum is given at the point where the derivative is equal to 0. The derivative with respect to u_2 is

$$p_2 - 40 \cdot \frac{u_2}{x_2}.$$

Setting the derivative to 0 yields

$$u_2^* = p_2 \cdot x_2/40.$$

Technically, there is one constraint in this optimization problem that we did not include in the calculation. We should make sure that $u_2 \leq x_2$; that is, that we do not pump more oil than we have available. It is easy to see that this will indeed be the case. Given that $p_2 = \$40$, we get $u_2^* = x_2$, that is, we should pump all oil available at time 2.

Next, we try to find the optimal amount of oil to pump one time period back (i.e., at time 1). The dynamic programming recursion tells us that u_1 will be the solution to the following optimization problem:

$$V_1(x_1) = \max_{u_1}\{\underbrace{p_1 \cdot u_1 - 20 \cdot u_1^2/x_1}_{\text{current cash flow (at time 1)}} + \underbrace{0.9}_{\text{discount factor}} \cdot \underbrace{V_2^*(u_1)}_{\text{optimal profit from next step onward}}\}$$

To solve this problem, we need to know $V_2^*(u_1)$. We can find it by plugging the optimal value u_2^* (which we already found) into the expression for profit at time 2, $V_2(x_2)$. We get

$$\begin{aligned} V_2^*(x_2) &= p_2 \cdot u_2^* - 20 \cdot (u_2^*)^2/x_2 \\ &= p_2^2 \cdot x_2/40 - 20 \cdot p_2^2 \cdot x_2^2/(40^2 \cdot x_2) \\ &= p_2^2 \cdot x_2/80 \end{aligned}$$

Therefore, the optimal value of the profit in year 1 is

$$V_1(x_1) = \max_{u_1}\left\{p_1 \cdot u_1 - 20 \cdot \frac{u_1^2}{x_1} + 0.9 \cdot p_2^2 \cdot \frac{x_2}{80}\right\}$$

As we mentioned at the end of section 6.6.1, the state variable is updated as

$$x_{t+1} = x_t - u_t$$

because the value of the available oil reserves is equal to the value of the oil reserves from the previous time period reduced by the amount we pumped over the previous time period. Therefore, we can replace x_2 in the expression for $V_1(x_1)$ with $x_1 - u_1$. We obtain

$$V_1(x_1) = \max_{u_1}\left\{-20 \cdot \frac{u_1^2}{x_1} + u_1 \cdot \left(p_1 - 0.9 \cdot \frac{p_2^2}{80}\right) + 0.9 \cdot p_2^2 \cdot \frac{x_1}{80}\right\}$$

The quadratic function to be maximized looks like the function in exhibit 6.3(B). We can find the maximum by taking the derivative with respect to u_1 and setting it to 0. The value of u_1 at which the maximum is attained is

$$u_1^* = (p_1 - 0.9 \cdot p_2^2/80) \cdot x_1/40.$$

Substituting $p_1 = \$30$ and $p_2 = \$40$, we get

$$u_1^* = (12/40) \cdot x_1 = 0.3 \cdot x_1.$$

Therefore, the optimal strategy at time 1 is to pump 30% of the available reserves. The value function is estimated as

$$V_1(x_1) = \max_{u_1} \left\{-20 \cdot u_1^2 / x_1 + u_1 \cdot (p_1 - 0.9 \cdot p_2^2/80) + 0.9 \cdot p_2^2 \cdot x_1/80\right\}$$

We proceed in a similar manner to evaluate the optimal strategy at time 0. The value function can be written as

$$V_0(x_0) = \max_{u_0}\{ \underbrace{p_0 \cdot u_0 - 20 \cdot u_0^2/x_0}_{\text{current cash flow (at time 0)}} + \underbrace{0.9}_{\text{discount factor}} \cdot \underbrace{V_1^*(u_0)}_{\text{optimal profit from next step onward}} \}.$$

Again, we have

$$x_1 = x_0 - u_0$$

and so

$$V_1^*(u_0) = 19.8 \cdot (x_0 - u_0).$$

Therefore,

$$V_0(x_0) = \max_{u_0}\left\{-20 \cdot \frac{u_0^2}{x_0} + 27.18 \cdot u_0 + 17.82 \cdot x_0\right\}.$$

(Here, we used the fact that the current price of oil is $p_0 = \$45$.) The maximum is attained at

$$u_0^* = (27.18 / 40) \cdot x_0 = 0.6795 \cdot x_0.$$

Hence, the optimal strategy at time 0 is to pump 67.95% of the available reserves. We know the reserves at time 0: $x_0 = 600{,}000$. Therefore, we can compute the actual amount to pump at time 0:

$$u_0^* = 0.6795 \cdot 600{,}000 = 407{,}700.$$

We can now trace the complete optimal strategy over the three years of the lease. At time 0, pump 67.95% of the optimal reserves, which is 407,700 barrels. At time 1, pump 30% of the remaining reserves, which is 0.30 · (600,000 − 407,700) = 57,690 barrels. At time 2, pump all remaining reserves, which is 600,000 − 407,700 − 57,690 = 134,610 barrels. The optimal profit over the three years is given by

$$V_0(x_0) = -20 \cdot 407{,}700^2/600{,}000 + 27.18 \cdot 407{,}700 + 17.82 \cdot 600{,}000 = \$16{,}232{,}643.$$

6.6.3 Steps in Formulating Multistage Optimization Problems

The dynamic programming examples in sections 6.6.1 and 6.6.2 give us some insights into the general steps that we may want to take in constructing a dynamic programming algorithm:

- Think of the solution as a sequence of decisions that occur in multiple stages and represent the total cost (alternatively, reward) as a sum of the costs (rewards) of the individual decisions.
- Define the states in the dynamical system in such a way that they summarize all relevant past information.

- Determine which state transitions are possible and then link those states. The cost/reward of moving to a state should equal the cost/reward of the decision that forces that transition.
- Write an expression that computes the optimal cost/reward recursively, starting from the last state and going backward to the state of origin.

Although this framework is helpful, in general, it is not straightforward to describe a given dynamical system in such a way as to allow for finding the solution through a dynamic programming recursion. The issue is like that of how to consider a business situation and formulate an optimization problem in such a way that it can be passed to a solver. In the case of dynamic programming, the main step to ensure a successful formulation is to find a good definition of the state space—in other words, to define the state variables in such a way that the rewards and costs of the transitions to the next state variables and the value function depend solely on the current state and decision variables. It takes practice and skill, and sometimes it is not possible to do it. However, the dynamic optimization idea in general is useful and has many variations in finance. We will see more examples of multistage optimization problems in chapters 7, 18, 19, and 23.

6.7 Optimization Software

When selecting an optimization software product, it is important to differentiate between optimization *solvers* and optimization *modeling languages.*

An optimization solver is software that implements numerical routines for finding the optimal solution of an optimization problem. Well-known commercial optimization solvers include MOSEK[22] and CPLEX[23] for linear, mixed-integer, and quadratic problems, and MINOS, SNOPT, and CONOPT for general nonlinear problems,[24] but there are a number of other commercial and free solvers available.

Optimization modeling languages are user-friendly platforms that allow the user to specify optimization problems in a more intuitive generic fashion, independent of the specific algorithmic and input requirements of optimization routines. Typically, optimization language software automates the underlying mathematical details of the optimization model formulation, but it does not actually solve the problem. It passes the formulation to a solver and retrieves the results from the solver in a convenient format. Popular optimization languages include AMPL[25] and GAMS.[26]

Optimization solvers and modeling languages are often part of *modeling environments* that handle not only the optimization, but also the input and output processing, statistical analysis, and perform other functions a user may need for a comprehensive analysis of a situation. MATLAB and Python are examples of high-level technical computing and interactive environments for model development that also enable data visualization, data analysis, and

22. See MOSEK ApS, *The MOSEK Optimization Software,* http://www.mosek.com/.
23. See https://www.ibm.com/products/ilog-cplex-optimization-studio.
24. See AIMMS, *Optimization Software for Operations Research Applications*, http://www.aimms.com.
25. See AMPL, *A Modeling Language for Mathematical Programming*, http://www.ampl.com/.
26. See GAMS, *The GAMS System*, http://www.gams.com/.

numerical simulation. The optimization solvers in MATLAB's Optimization Toolbox and Python's optimization libraries can solve a variety of constrained and unconstrained optimization problems for LP, QP, nonlinear optimization, and binary integer programming. Other examples of modeling environments include IBM ILOG CPLEX Optimization Studio, which allows users to build optimization models, which are then accessed from a subroutine library using Microsoft Visual Basic for Applications (VBA), Java, or C/C++. Thus, a user can connect optimization systems directly to data sources and make calls to optimization subroutines repeatedly. Palisade's Decision Tools Suite (https://lumivero.com/products/decision-tools/) also contains a number of software add-ins for optimization, statistical analysis, and sensitivity analysis that use a spreadsheet program—Excel—as the underlying platform.

Excel's inherent capabilities for optimization are rather limited. Excel Solver, which ships with Excel, can handle only optimization problems of small size, up to a few hundred variables and constraints. It is a perfectly acceptable solver for linear optimization problems. Still, its performance (and the output that one would obtain from it) is unreliable for more complex problems of the general nonlinear programming or IP type. FrontlineSolvers, which is sold by Frontline Systems (https://www.solver.com/), is an extended and improved version of the standard Excel Solver, and it can tackle larger optimization problems. It employs efficient interior point methods for solving classical optimization formulations and genetic algorithms for arbitrary Excel optimization models that contain spreadsheet functions such as IF, INDEX, and COUNTIF. (Such functions are not recognized in traditional optimization problem formulations.) Palisade's Evolver is another add-in for Excel that uses genetic algorithms to solve optimization problems. The Palisade Decision Tools Suite also contains RiskOptimizer, which is a tool for optimization given possible scenarios for the uncertain parameters in the problem. Finally, OpenSolver (https://opensolver.org/) is a free, Excel-based solver that can solve larger optimization problems set up in spreadsheets.

It is useful to mention that there are numerous optimization software packages that target financial applications in particular, especially portfolio management applications. Established vendors of portfolio management software include Bloomberg (https://www.bloomberg.com/professional/solutions/asset-management/portfolio-manager/), MSCI Barra (https://app2.msci.com/products/analytics/barra_portfolio_manager/), Northfield Information Services (http://www.northinfo.com/), and SimCorp/Axioma (https://www.axioma.com, https://www.simcorp.com/).

Summary

- An optimization formulation consists of three parts: (1) an objective function, (2) a set of decision variables, and (3) a set of constraints.
- A solution is feasible if it satisfies all constraints. It is optimal if it is feasible and produces the best value of the objective function among all feasible solutions.
- A solution is a local optimum if it produces the best value of the objective function among all feasible solutions in its neighborhood. There may be multiple local optima, depending on the type of optimization problem.
- Optimization problems are categorized according to (1) the form of the objective function and the constraints, and (2) the type of decision variables (discrete or continuous). Important classes of optimization problems include linear programming

(LP), quadratic programming (QP), convex programming, integer programming (IP), and mixed-integer programming (MIP).

- For convex optimization problems, a local optimal solution is also the global optimal solution.
- Using optimization duality theory, we can construct a dual problem for a given optimization problem. The dual problem may have better computational properties and help solve the primal problem or bound the optimal objective function values of the primal problem.
- The Karush-Kuhn-Tucker (KKT) conditions are necessary conditions for local optima of constrained optimization problems. Their structure is exploited by numerous algorithms for convex and general nonlinear optimization.
- Most optimization algorithms are iterative in nature. The number of iterations taken by the algorithm is determined by the stopping criteria specified by the user, such as the tolerance level.
- Important types of optimization algorithms include the simplex algorithm (for linear problems), interior point methods (for linear and convex problems), branch-and-bound or branch-and-cut algorithms (for integer programs), and randomized search algorithms (for all types of optimization problems).
- Randomized search algorithms, such as genetic algorithms, simulated annealing, and tabu search, do not guarantee the optimality of the solution that they return. Neither do general optimization algorithms when applied to nonlinear optimization problems that do not have special structure.
- Linear problems are the easiest class of optimization problems, in the sense that linear problems with hundreds of thousands of decision variables and constraints can be solved efficiently today. Convex problems (which include linear programs) have a nice structure and are typically more efficient to solve than general nonlinear programming. Integer and mixed-integer problems are challenging and require specialized optimization software.
- Dynamic programming is a method for optimization over multiple stages. It solves the problem sequentially, starting at the last stage and keeping track only of the best solution from the current stage onward.
- An optimization solver is software that implements numerical routines for finding the optimal solution of an optimization problem. Different solvers handle different kinds of optimization problems.
- An optimization modeling language automates the underlying mathematical details of the optimization model formulation, but it typically does not actually solve the problem. It passes the formulation to a solver and retrieves the results from the solver in a convenient format. The advantage of using optimization languages is that the user can formulate the problem only once and use different options for solvers.

7

Optimization under Uncertainty

The optimization formulations presented in chapter 6 have numerous applications in finance and other fields. However, that discussion omitted an important aspect of realistic optimization modeling. We assumed that the input data, such as the coefficients in front of the decision variables in the objective function and the constraints and the cash flows that happen in a multistage system, are certain. In practice, however, optimization often needs to be performed under conditions in which the input data are random or represent statistical estimates and subjective guesses. Models in which all input data are fixed or nonrandom are often referred to as *deterministic*. By contrast, models containing parameters that vary are referred to as *nondeterministic*, *probabilistic*, or *stochastic*.

Concepts from probability theory, statistics, and simulation (chapters 3, 4, and 5) can be used to extend the basic framework of deterministic optimization (chapter 6) and to deal with uncertainty. However, randomness adds a high level of complexity to optimization formulations and the output of the resulting models needs to be interpreted carefully.

There are three general approaches for incorporating considerations for uncertainty in optimization problems: dynamic programming, stochastic programming, and robust optimization. As we mentioned in section 6.6, dynamic programming methods are specifically designed to deal with stochastic uncertain systems over multiple stages. The optimization problem is solved recursively, going backward from the last state and computing the optimal solution for each possible state of the system at a particular stage. In finance, dynamic programming is used in pricing some derivative instruments, investment strategies such as statistical arbitrage, and long-term corporate financial planning.

Stochastic programming methods can be used in both single-period and multiperiod settings. They rely on representing the uncertain data by scenario and focus on finding the strategy such that, for example, the *expected* value of the objective function over all scenarios (sometimes penalized for some measure of risk) is optimal. Stochastic algorithms have been successfully applied in various financial contexts, such as management of portfolios of fixed-income securities, corporate risk management, security selection, and asset/liability management for individuals as well as for financial entities such as banks, pension funds, and insurance companies.[1] They are particularly useful in situations in which

1. See, for example, Ziemba and Mulvey (1998), Consigli and Dempster (1998), Zenios and Kang (1993), Carino and Ziemba (1998), Bogentoft, Romeijn, and Uryasev (2001) , and Hillier and Eckstein (1993).

modeling complicated dependencies in a number of uncertain parameters over multiple time periods is essential. This kind of situation often arises, for example, in managing callable bond portfolios or international asset portfolios, where the callable feature of the bonds, interest rate risk, default risk, or currency risk needs to be taken into consideration.

Robust optimization can be used to address the same type of problems as dynamic programming and stochastic programming do; however, it takes a worst-case approach to optimization formulations. In addition, in robust optimization one typically makes relatively general assumptions on the probability distributions of the uncertain parameters to work with problem formulations that are more tractable computationally.

The fields of dynamic programming, stochastic programming, and robust optimization have some overlap, but historically, they have evolved independently of each other. This chapter explains the three techniques for optimization under uncertainty in detail.

7.1 Dynamic Programming

As explained in section 6.6, dynamic programming solves a large, multistage optimization problem sequentially, starting at the last stage and proceeding backward, thus keeping track only of the optimal paths from any given time period onward.

Dynamic programming under uncertainty is sometimes also called *stochastic control.*[2] It shares the main elements of dynamic programming models considered in section 6.6: There is an underlying dynamic system and an objective function (called a *reward* or a *cost* function, depending on whether the problem is a maximization or a minimization) that is additive over time. The dynamic system at any point in time t is described by a vector of state variables $\mathbf{x}_t$ that summarizes all past information about the system. However, while the state variable in the deterministic dynamic programming problems considered in section 6.6 evolved according to the relationship:

$$\mathbf{x}_{t+1} = g_t(\mathbf{x}_t, \mathbf{u}_t)$$

where $\mathbf{u}_t$ is a vector of *control,* or *policy*, variables to be selected by the decision maker, when there is uncertainty in the system, we have

$$\mathbf{x}_{t+1} = g_t(\mathbf{x}_t, \mathbf{u}_t, \xi_t),$$

where ξ_t is a *random variable* (also called *disturbance* or *noise* depending on the context). The reward at time t, which we will denote by

$$f_t(\mathbf{x}_t, \mathbf{u}_t, \xi_t),$$

accumulates over time, as it did in the case of deterministic dynamic programming problems.

Dynamic programming problems can be defined over a *finite horizon* (e.g., over a period of time T) or an *infinite horizon*. In most financial applications, we encounter finite

2. As explained in section 7.6, this technique dates to Bellman (1957). Modern treatment of the area with applications in engineering, finance, and operations research is provided in Bertsekas (1995). Applications of dynamic programming to optimal consumption and portfolio selection are discussed, for example, in Merton (1995) and Ingersoll (1987).

horizon dynamic programming systems, so we will assume that the horizon is finite and time is discrete. The total reward/cost can then be written as

$$\sum_{t=0}^{T} f_t(\mathbf{x}_t, \mathbf{u}_t, \xi_t)$$

At the end of section 6.6.1, we presented the expression for the dynamic programming recursion. In the general case, assuming that we would like to maximize the total reward, at every state our goal was to find a policy vector $\mathbf{u}_t$ so

$$V_t(\mathbf{x}_t) = \max_{\mathbf{u}_t}\{c(\mathbf{u}_t) + d \cdot V_{t+1}^*(\mathbf{u}_t)\}.$$

In other words, we selected $\mathbf{u}_t$ so the value of the reward from this stage forward is highest. Suppose now that there is uncertainty; that is, our actions do not determine the exact outcome, but instead there is some probabilistic component in the realization of future rewards. In that case, a natural goal is to select $\mathbf{u}_t$ so the *expected* value of the reward from this stage forward is highest, where the term "expected value" is used in the sense of chapter 3; that is, it is the weighted average of possible outcomes from some probability distribution on the future values. In other words, we write

$$V_t(\mathbf{x}_t) = \max_{\mathbf{u}_t}\{c(\mathbf{u}_t) + d \cdot E[V_{t+1}^*(\mathbf{u}_t)|\mathbf{x}_t]\}$$

where $E[V_{t+1}^*(\mathbf{u}_t)|\mathbf{x}_t]$ is the expected value of the optimal reward from this stage forward, given that we are currently at state $\mathbf{x}_t$.

To build some intuition, let us go back to the oil well example from section 6.6. You have purchased a 3-year lease for an oil well. The estimated reserves of the well are 600,000 barrels. Every year, you can either pump oil normally (strategy 1), in which case you pump 100,000 barrels, or use an enhanced pumping method, which allows you to pump 200,000 barrels (strategy 2). To extract u_t barrels at time t with the enhanced method costs $20 \cdot \frac{u_t^2}{x_t}$ dollars, where x_t is the amount of available reserves at time t. To extract u_t barrels with the normal pumping method costs $\frac{u_t^2}{x_t}$ dollars. The discount factor per year is 0.9.

The implicit assumption in that example was that we knew exactly what oil prices would be in each of the three years of the lease. Suppose instead that the evolution of oil prices in each year of the lease is described by the tree in exhibit 7.1, where the numbers above the branches denote the probabilities of ending up in that node starting from the node at the previous stage. (Note that the probabilities on all branches emanating from the same node add up to 1.) In other words, every year the price can be 20% (1.2 times) higher than the price in the previous year with probability 0.40, or be 20% (0.8 times) lower than the price in the previous year with probability 0.60.

Assuming that you can pump either 100,000 barrels or 200,000 barrels each year, what is the optimal strategy to maximize the *expected* present value (PV) of your profit from the lease? Note that we can no longer know the exact value since the total profit from each node forward (except the nodes at the third stage) has an element of uncertainty. Note also that the tree in exhibit 7.1 does not represent the state space of the problem. The state space

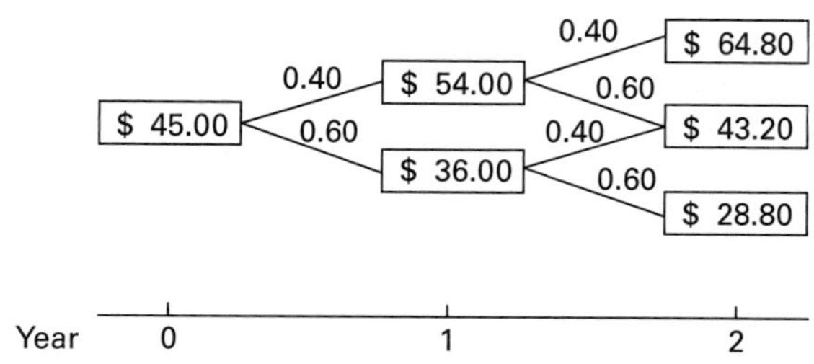

Exhibit 7.1
Price process for the oil well problem.

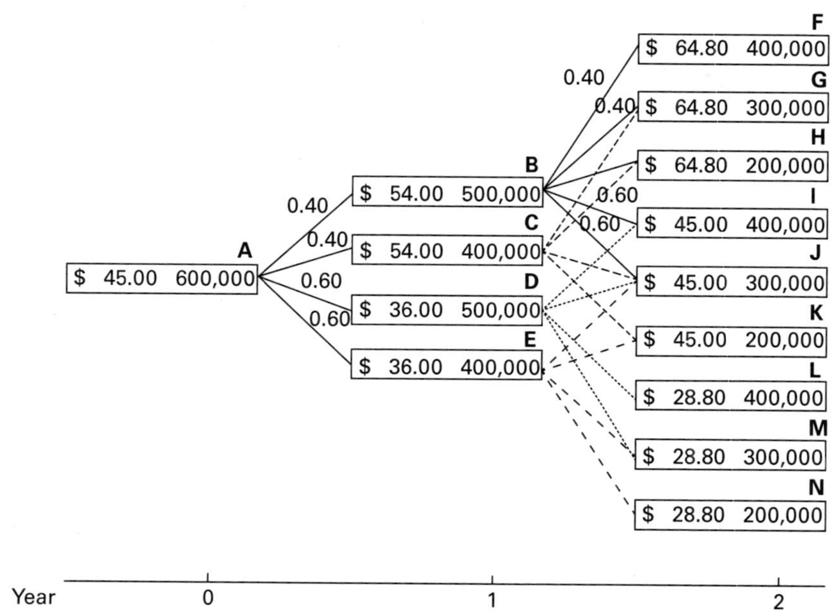

Exhibit 7.2
State space for the oil well problem.

should incorporate all information necessary to decide going forward. To decide, we need to know (1) the level of remaining reserves x_t and (2) the price p_t. (In the deterministic version of this problem in section 7.6.1, the price p_t was the same for all nodes at the same stage.) So, in a sense we have a two-dimensional tree: every state is determined by the pair (x_t, p_t). Exhibit 7.2 illustrates the state space. Note how much larger the state space is than the state space in section 7.6.1.

To solve the problem, we use a sequential optimization algorithm like the algorithm described in section 7.6.1. (See the file **Ch7-OilExample.xlsx**.) First, we compute the value function at the last-stage nodes. For example, the profit at state F is the maximum of the profits obtained using the normal or the enhanced methods at the price realized and the reserves available at node F:

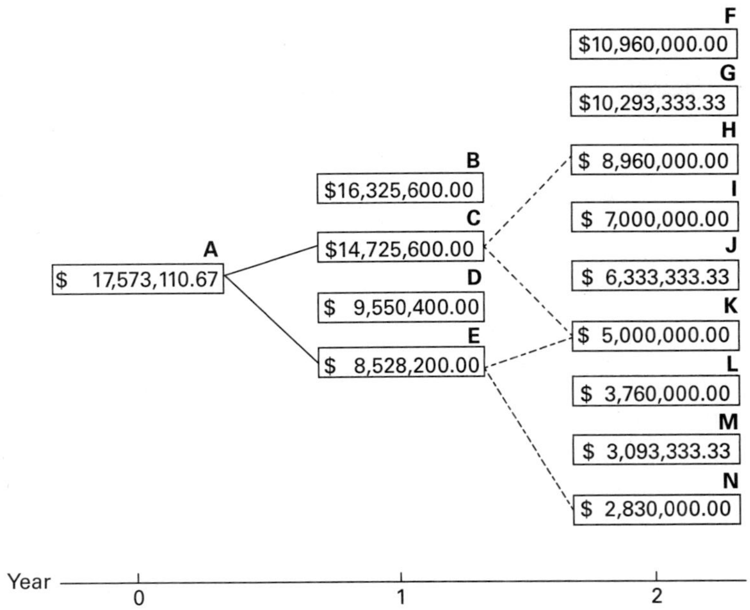

Exhibit 7.3
Optimal strategy and profit at each state.

$$V(F) = \max\left\{\begin{array}{c} 64.80 \cdot 100{,}000 - 100{,}000^2/400{,}000, \\ 64.80 \cdot 200{,}000 - 20 \cdot 200{,}000^2/400{,}000 \end{array}\right\}$$
$$= \max\{\$6{,}455{,}000, \$10{,}960{,}000\}$$
$$= \$10{,}960{,}000$$

Therefore, if we are in state F in year 3 (i.e., the price per barrel is \$64.80 and we have 400,000 barrels left), the optimal strategy is to use the enhanced method.

The values at nodes G, H, I, J, K, L, M, and N are computed similarly (exhibit 7.3). To compute the values at nodes B, C, D, and E at the previous stage, we use the recursive relation for the value function. The value function at all states at stages other than the last stage is the sum of the profit obtained at that stage and the expected (probability-weighted) discounted profit from states at the next stage that can be reached from the current state:

$$V_t(x_t, p_t) = \max\left\{\begin{array}{l} p_t \cdot 100{,}000 - \dfrac{100{,}000^2}{x_t} \\ \quad + 0.9 \cdot (0.4 \cdot V^*_{t+1}(x_t - 100{,}000, 1.2 \cdot p_t) \\ \quad + 0.6 \cdot V^*_{t+1}(x_t - 100{,}000,\ 0.8 \cdot p_t)), \\ p_t \cdot 200{,}000 - \dfrac{20 \cdot 200{,}000^2}{x_t} \\ \quad + 0.9 \cdot (0.4 \cdot V^*_{t+1}(x_t - 200{,}000,\ 1.2 \cdot p_t) \\ \quad + 0.6 \cdot V^*_{t+1}(x_t - 200{,}000, 0.8 \cdot p_t)) \end{array}\right\}.$$

For example, the profit at state B is calculated as

$$V(B) = \max \left\{ \begin{array}{l} p_B \cdot \dfrac{100{,}000.00 - 100{,}000.00^2}{x_B} \\ \quad + 0.90 \cdot (0.40 \cdot V(F) + 0.60 \cdot V(I)), \\ p_B \cdot \dfrac{200{,}000.00 - 20 \cdot 200{,}000.00^2}{x_B} \\ \quad + 0.90 \cdot (0.40 \cdot V(G) + 0.60 \cdot V(J)) \end{array} \right\}.$$

This is because if we use the normal method if we are at B, we will reduce our reserves by 100,000 to 400,000. This means that we will reach F with probability 0.40, or I with probability 0.60. By contrast, if we use the enhanced method, we will reach G with probability 0.40, or J with probability 0.60. Keeping track of the different states is quite challenging and needs to be done with care.

The optimal expected profit from state B onward is calculated to be

$$\begin{aligned} V(B) &= \max \left\{ \begin{array}{l} 54.00 \cdot 100{,}000.00 - 100{,}000.00^2 / 500{,}000.00 \\ \quad + 0.90 \cdot (0.40 \cdot 10{,}960{,}000.00 + 0.60 \cdot 7{,}000{,}000.00), \\ 54.00 \cdot 200{,}000.00 - 20 \cdot 200{,}000.00^2 / 500{,}000.00 \\ \quad + 0.90 \cdot (0.40 \cdot 10{,}293{,}333.33 + 0.60 \cdot 6{,}333{,}333.33) \end{array} \right\} \\ &= \max \{\$13{,}105{,}600.00, \$16{,}325{,}600.00) \\ &= \$16{,}325{,}600.00 \end{aligned}$$

Therefore, if we are at state B in year 2, we should choose to pump oil with the enhanced method.

We proceed in the same manner to compute the best method to use and the expected profit at nodes C, D, E, and A, in that order. We can now trace the optimal strategy over the three years (see exhibit 7.3). We start with 600,000 barrels as reserves and a price of \$45 per barrel. The optimal strategy at node A is to use the enhanced method. That takes us to either state C with probability 0.40, or state E with probability 0.60.

If we are in state C, the optimal strategy is to use the enhanced method again, which will take us to either state H or state K. In both states H and K, it is optimal to use the enhanced method again.

If we are in state E, it is optimal to use the enhanced method, which takes us to state K with probability 0.40, or N with probability 0.60. If we are at state K, it is optimal to use the enhanced method. However, if we end up at state N, it is optimal to use the normal method. The expected total profit from the oil well over the three years is the value function at node A: \$17,573,110.67.

As this example showed, the extension of dynamic programming methods to incorporate uncertainty is logical but can substantially increase the level of complexity of already computationally intensive dynamic programming algorithms. In practice, approximation algorithms are often used to reduce the size and complexity of dynamic programming problems. In particular, we would try to come up with a good estimate of the form of the optimal policy as a function of the state where we are, rather than evaluate the exact optimal policy in every state of the world.[3] We will see some examples when we discuss derivative pricing in chapters 18–19, but in general, there is no recipe for how we might select the approximation.

7.2 Stochastic Programming

Perhaps the easiest way to think of a stochastic programming formulation is to imagine writing an optimization problem formulation of the kind described in section 6.2 and searching for an optimal solution over *scenarios* for the input data.

Consider a general stochastic optimization (say, maximization) problem, in which we have an objective function $F(\mathbf{x}, \xi)$ that depends on a decision vector $\mathbf{x}$ of dimension N and a vector of uncertain parameters ξ of dimension d. Such optimization problems are not well defined since the objective depends on the unknown value of ξ. Namely, every realization of the vector of random variables ξ corresponds to a different realization of the objective function. Thus, we have a different probability distribution of objective function values for every feasible solution $\mathbf{x}$. It is wrong to say that one probability distribution is better than another unless we specify what "better" means. Hence, it is impossible to state what the optimal solution $\mathbf{x}^*$ is, since by definition the optimal solution is the one that gives the best value of the objective function.

The simplest way to make the objective well defined is to optimize it on average:

$$\max_{\mathbf{x}} f(\mathbf{x}) = E[F(\mathbf{x}, \xi)],$$

where the expectation is taken over scenarios for ξ.[4] This means that we define the optimal solution $\mathbf{x}^*$ as the solution that results in a probability distribution for the objective function value with the highest mean of all probability distributions of objective function values.

What if uncertainty is present in the constraints? In some cases, we can formulate such problems by introducing penalties for violating the constraints, thus defining a *mean-risk objective function*.[5] An alternative approach is to require that the constraints be satisfied for all possible (and in particular, the worst-case) values of the uncertain parameters. This is a stochastic programming method whose philosophy overlaps with the philosophy of *robust optimization*, which we will explain in the next section. Finally, we may impose the requirement that the constraints be satisfied with high probability. This leads to a stochastic programming formulation with *chance constraints*.

In summary, stochastic programming can be used to address the presence of uncertain input data in three types of optimization problems:

- Expected value for one-stage and multistage models
- Models involving risk measures
- Chance-constrained models

Each model type is discussed next.

3. See, for example, Chryssikou (1998) for a development of approximate dynamic programming approaches that characterize the optimal investment policy for multistage portfolio optimization problems.

4. In other words, we maximize a weighted average of objective functions, where each weight is the probability that the scenario that results in that particular objective function will occur.

5. See, for example, Mulvey, Vanderbei, and Zenios (1995) and Ruszczynski and Shapiro (2003).

7.2.1 Multistage Models

In *multistage stochastic programming models*, decision variables and constraints are divided into groups corresponding to time periods, or stages $t=1,\ldots,T$. The information structure of the model (i.e., what is known at each stage) is specified in advance. The standard form of a multistage stochastic linear program is[6]

$$\min_{\mathbf{x}} \quad \tilde{\mathbf{c}}_0'\mathbf{x}_0 + E_{\xi_1}\Big[(\tilde{\mathbf{c}}_1^{\xi_1})'\mathbf{x}_1^{\xi_1} + \cdots + E_{\xi_{T-1}|\xi_{T-2}}\Big[(\tilde{\mathbf{c}}_{T-1}^{\xi_1,\ldots,\xi_{T-1}})'\mathbf{x}_{T-1}^{\xi_1,\ldots,\xi_{T-1}}$$

$$+E_{\xi_T|\xi_{T-1}}\Big[(\tilde{\mathbf{c}}_T^{\xi_1,\ldots,\xi_T})'\mathbf{x}_T^{\xi_1,\ldots,\xi_T}\Big]\Big]\Big],$$

s.t.

$$\begin{array}{lllll}
\mathbf{A}_0\mathbf{x}_0 & & & & = \mathbf{b}_0 \\
& \mathbf{B}_0^{\xi_1}\mathbf{x}_0 + & & \mathbf{A}_1^{\xi_1}\mathbf{x}_1^{\xi_1} & = \mathbf{b}_1^{\xi_1} \\
& \ddots & & & \vdots \\
& & \mathbf{B}_{T-1}^{\xi_T}\mathbf{x}_{T-1}^{\xi_1,\ldots,\xi_{T-1}} & + \mathbf{A}_T^{\xi_T}\mathbf{x}_T^{\xi_1,\ldots,\xi_T} & = \mathbf{b}_T^{\xi_T} \\
\end{array}$$

$$\mathbf{x}_0, \mathbf{x}_1^{\xi_1}, \ldots, \mathbf{x}_{T-1}^{\xi_1,\ldots,\xi_{T-1}}, \mathbf{x}_T^{\xi_1,\ldots,\xi_T} \geq 0$$

where the array $\xi = \{\xi_1, \ldots, \xi_T\}$ represents the realizations of an underlying process that drives the uncertainty in the coefficients of the objective function, and **A** and **B** are matrices with data. Note that the vectors of solutions **x** are indexed off the vectors of uncertainty ξ_t at each stage t except at the beginning (stage 0). In stochastic programming, decision variables can be divided into two categories: anticipative and adaptive. *Anticipative decision variables* (such as $\mathbf{x}_0$ in the previous formulation) correspond to decisions that must be made at that particular stage, and all information for making the decision is available. *Adaptive decision variables* (such as $\mathbf{x}_t^{\xi_1,\ldots,\xi_t}$ in the previous formulation) depend on future realizations of the random parameters.

A large number of financial applications—such as asset-liability management, index tracking, and active investment management—can be treated as a sequence of decisions and observations and represented in this form. The "block" formulation of the stochastic optimization problem is preferable because specialized software (stochastic optimization packages in particular) can take advantage of the structure when applying decomposition algorithms for solving the problem. To complete the multistage stochastic programming model, we need to specify the structure of the random process for the uncertain coefficients, which is typically reduced to a set of scenarios. The scenarios are organized in an event tree, which at each stage describes the unfolding of the uncertainties concerning possible values of the uncertain parameters. The values of these realizations (denoted as ξ previously) are then plugged into the preceding problem formulation.

Exhibit 7.4 shows an example of such a tree if only one uncertain parameter is modeled. There are three time periods and two optimization stages. The nodes represent points in time at which the information about the realizations of the uncertain parameter is updated. They are numbered for each stage t. The numbers in bold above the nodes denote the specific realizations of the uncertain parameter. At time 0, its value is known and unique (it is 33 in this example). At that time, there is only one node (node 0), which is called the *root* of the tree. At

6. The notation $E_{\xi_t|\xi_{t-1}}[\cdot]$ means "expectation of the expression inside the brackets over realizations of the uncertain variable ξ_t at time t, conditional on the realizations of ξ_{t-1} at time $t-1$."

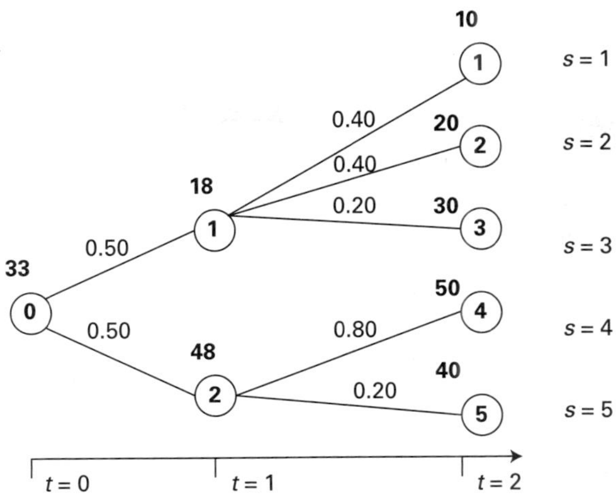

Exhibit 7.4
Simplified example of a scenario tree.

the last stage, there are S_T=5 possible scenarios, represented by the paths from the root to the *leaves* of the tree; that is, the last-stage nodes. The numbers above the arcs of the tree represent the probabilities of moving to the next node, *conditional* on having reached its ancestor node. Note that the probabilities on all branches emanating from the same node add up to 1.

Given this scenario tree, we can create the block stochastic programming formulation as follows:

- Define decision variables $\mathbf{x}_t^{(s)}$ for each possible scenario s at each time period t. There are different ways to define a set of decision variables, but one possibility is to have eight of them: $x_0^{(0)}$ for stage 0, $x_1^{(1)}$ and $x_1^{(2)}$ for stage 1, and $x_2^{(1)}$, $x_2^{(2)}$, $x_2^{(3)}$, $x_2^{(4)}$, $x_2^{(5)}$ for stage 2. In this example, the number of scenarios at each stage is equal to the number of nodes at that stage because the tree does not recombine.
- Write the objective as a function of these decision variables and the uncertain data:

$$\begin{aligned}\max_{\mathbf{x}}\,&(\mathbf{c}_0)'\mathbf{x}_0 + \pi_1^{(1)}(\mathbf{c}_1^{(1)})'\mathbf{x}_1^{(1)} + \pi_1^{(2)}(\mathbf{c}_1^{(2)})'\mathbf{x}_1^{(2)} + \pi_2^{(1)}(\mathbf{c}_2^{(1)})'\mathbf{x}_2^{(1)}\\ &+ \pi_2^{(2)}(\mathbf{c}_2^{(2)})'\mathbf{x}_2^{(2)} + \pi_2^{(3)}(\mathbf{c}_2^{(3)})'\mathbf{x}_2^{(3)} + \pi_2^{(4)}(\mathbf{c}_2^{(4)})'\mathbf{x}_2^{(4)}\\ &+ \pi_2^{(4)}(\mathbf{c}_2^{(4)})'\mathbf{x}_2^{(4)} + \pi_2^{(5)}(\mathbf{c}_2^{(5)})'\mathbf{x}_2^{(5)}\end{aligned}$$

  The objective is a sum of the reward at the initial node and the expected rewards at all remaining nodes. In the previous expression, $\pi_t^{(s)}$ denotes the probability of scenario s at time t. For example, $\pi_1^{(1)} = 0.50$ and $\pi_2^{(4)} = (0.50)(0.80) = 0.40$.

- Write a set of constraints for each stage and each scenario:

$$\begin{aligned}\text{Stage 0}: &\ \mathbf{A}_0^{(0)}\mathbf{x}_0^{(0)} = \mathbf{b}_0^{(0)}\\ \text{Stage 1}: &\ \mathbf{B}_0^{(1)}\mathbf{x}_0^{(0)} + \mathbf{A}_1^{(1)}\mathbf{x}_1^{(1)} = \mathbf{b}_1^{(1)}\\ &\ \mathbf{B}_0^{(2)}\mathbf{x}_0^{(0)} + \mathbf{A}_1^{(2)}\mathbf{x}_1^{(2)} = \mathbf{b}_1^{(2)}\\ \text{Stage 2}: &\ \mathbf{B}_1^{(1)}\mathbf{x}_1^{(1)} + \mathbf{A}_2^{(1)}\mathbf{x}_2^{(1)} = \mathbf{b}_2^{(1)}\\ &\ \mathbf{B}_1^{(2)}\mathbf{x}_1^{(1)} + \mathbf{A}_2^{(2)}\mathbf{x}_2^{(2)} = \mathbf{b}_2^{(2)}\end{aligned}$$

$$\mathbf{B}_1^{(3)}\mathbf{x}_1^{(1)} + \mathbf{A}_2^{(3)}\mathbf{x}_2^{(3)} = \mathbf{b}_2^{(3)}$$
$$\mathbf{B}_1^{(4)}\mathbf{x}_1^{(2)} + \mathbf{A}_2^{(4)}\mathbf{x}_2^{(4)} = \mathbf{b}_2^{(4)}$$
$$\mathbf{B}_1^{(5)}\mathbf{x}_1^{(2)} + \mathbf{A}_2^{(5)}\mathbf{x}_2^{(5)} = \mathbf{b}_2^{(5)}$$

Note that the constraints keep track of the ancestor of each node. For example, nodes 1, 2, and 3 at stage 2 have a common ancestor: node 1 from stage 1. So the decision variables associated with the scenarios ending at those nodes ($\mathbf{x}_2^{(1)}$, $\mathbf{x}_2^{(2)}$, and $\mathbf{x}_2^{(3)}$) are linked to the decision variable associated with node 1 from stage 1 ($\mathbf{x}_1^{(1)}$) via the first three constraints from stage 2.

- Write the so-called *nonanticipativity conditions*, if applicable. Nonanticipativity conditions make sure that scenarios with the same past have identical decisions up to the stage at which they have the same history. In this case, the nonanticipativity conditions are incorporated implicitly by our choice of decision variables and the fact that only one scenario corresponds to each node. Some formulations that involve alternative definitions of the decision variables, such as the original nonblock formulation of the portfolio problem, require stating the nonanticipativity constraints explicitly.[7]

Four common ways to create scenario trees for the uncertain parameters are[8]

- Bootstrapping historical data
- Using parametric models in which one assumes specific probability distributions and then estimates their parameters from data

7. For example, in an alternative formulation, we could associate two variables with every given node: one variable at stage t and a copy of that decision variable for each particular child of that node. This kind of representation may be convenient for formulating the problem in a modeling language, depending on how the scenario data are stored. For instance, in the scenario tree in exhibit 7.4, we could have two copies of the variable $\mathbf{x}_1^{(2)}$ (associated with node 2 at stage 1): $\mathbf{x}_1^{(2,4)}$ for its "child" node 4 at stage 2, and $\mathbf{x}_1^{(2,5)}$ fo its "child" node 5 at stage 2. Then, the constraints

$$\mathbf{B}_1^{(4)}\mathbf{x}_1^{(2)} + \mathbf{A}_2^{(4)}\mathbf{x}_2^{(4)} = \mathbf{b}_2^{(4)}$$

and

$$\mathbf{B}_1^{(5)}\mathbf{x}_1^{(2)} + \mathbf{A}_2^{(5)}\mathbf{x}_2^{(5)} = \mathbf{b}_2^{(5)}$$

should be written as

$$\mathbf{B}_1^{(4)}\mathbf{x}_1^{(2,4)} + \mathbf{A}_2^{(4)}\mathbf{x}_2^{(4)} = \mathbf{b}_2^{(4)}$$

and

$$\mathbf{B}_1^{(5)}\mathbf{x}_1^{(2,5)} + \mathbf{A}_2^{(5)}\mathbf{x}_2^{(5)} = \mathbf{b}_2^{(5)}$$

We must specify explicitly that $\mathbf{x}_1^{(2,4)} = \mathbf{x}_1^{(2,5)}$ to make sure that the nonanticipativity condition is satisfied. For further details, see, for example, Fragniere and Gondzio (2005).

8. For a survey of stochastic programming applications in financial optimization and scenario generation techniques, see Gulpinar, Rustem, and Settergren (2004). For a description of the econometric techniques used in scenario generation, see Fabozzi, Focardi, and Kolm (2006).

- Generating simple discrete distributions whose moments are then matched to moments of real data distributions
- Constructing vector autoregressive models

We need to use caution when creating the tree. Its dimension becomes unmanageable very quickly, and, as the previous simple example illustrated, the number of decision variables and constraints in the optimization problem is directly related to the number of scenarios. If, for example, you are managing a portfolio and you allow the possible returns for the N assets in the portfolio to have just two possible realizations at each stage, the total number of scenarios at the last stage is 2^{NT}. If your portfolio consists of only 10 assets and is rebalanced monthly over one year, you would need to work with 2^{120} scenarios for the possible asset returns. Optimization problems of such dimension are impossible to solve. Since the size of the problem tends to grow exponentially with the number of nodes, it is important to represent the underlying stochastic process with as few nodes as possible. However, it is also important to consider the trade-off between the dimension of the problem and the accuracy of approximating the underlying stochastic process; otherwise, little insight is gained from solving the optimization problem.

Let us now formulate a simple stochastic optimization problem. Consider again the oil well example from section 7.1. The scenario tree for the price of oil over the three years of the lease was presented in exhibit 7.1. We reproduce it in exhibit 7.5, with the scenarios explicitly labeled above or next to each node. The first number in the node labels is the time period, and the second number in the label is the scenario at that stage. Note that even though there are only three nodes at the last stage (year 2), there are four scenarios. Namely, a price of \$43.20 can be reached in two ways: the price in year 0 can go up to \$54 in year 1 and then down to \$43.20 in year 2, or go down to \$36 in year 1 and then up to \$43.20 in year 2.

We use the optimization formulation from the end of section 6.6.1 as a basis for the formulation of the multistage stochastic programming problem. Let us introduce decision variables $x_0^{(1)}$ for stage 0, $x_1^{(1)}$ and $x_1^{(2)}$ for stage 1, and $x_2^{(1)}, x_2^{(2)}, x_2^{(3)}, x_2^{(4)}$ for stage 2 in order to denote the available oil reserves in each scenario at each stage. Let us also introduce variables $u_0^{(1)}$ for stage 0, $u_1^{(1)}$ and $u_1^{(2)}$ for stage 1, and $u_2^{(1)}, u_2^{(2)}, u_2^{(3)}, u_2^{(4)}$ to denote the amounts of oil to pump in each scenario at each stage, as well as binary variables $z_0^{(1)}$ for stage 0, $z_1^{(1)}$ and $z_1^{(2)}$ for stage 1, and $z_2^{(1)}, z_2^{(2)}, z_2^{(3)}, z_2^{(4)}$ to denote the decision of whether to pump in each scenario and at each stage.

As in the original problem formulation, we have the following relationship between $u_0^{(1)}$ and $z_0^{(0)}$:

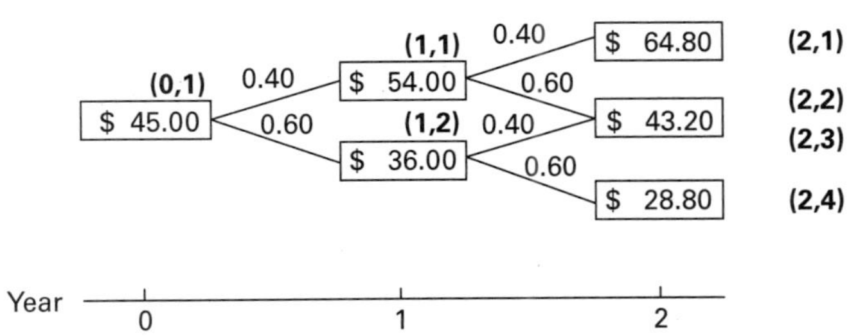

Exhibit 7.5
Scenario tree for the oil well problem, with scenario labels for each stage.

$$u_t^{(s)} = 100{,}000 \cdot z_t^{(s)} + 200{,}000 \cdot (1 - z_t^{(s)}),\ t = 0, 1, 2; s = 1, \ldots, S_t$$

We also have the relationship between the amount of oil at each stage, the amount of oil pumped at that stage, and the available reserves at the next stage. However, we need to be careful to link only variables that are associated with a specific scenario, so we need to keep track of the "ancestors" of the node at which we are; that is, we need to know how we reached a particular node. For example, let us consider the node at stage 3 in the tree that corresponds to a price of \$43.20. Since we have two ways of getting to that node, we need to write a separate equality for each scenario:

$$x_2^{(2)} = x_1^{(1)} - u_1^{(1)}$$

$$x_2^{(3)} = x_1^{(2)} - u_1^{(2)}$$

The first equality is associated with scenario 2 at stage 3: we got to the price of \$43.20 by going through node 1 at stage 1 (a price of \$54) first. The second equality is associated with scenario 3 at stage 3: we got to the price of \$43.20 by going through node 2 at stage 1 (a price of \$36) first.

The final step in the formulation is to figure out the probability of each scenario. Let us denote those by $\pi_0^{(1)}$ for stage 0, $\pi_1^{(1)}$ and $\pi_1^{(2)}$ for stage 1, and $\pi_2^{(1)}, \pi_2^{(2)}, \pi_2^{(3)}, \pi_2^{(4)}$ for stage 2. We have

$\pi_0^{(1)} = 1$ (we start at that node, so we can ignore this probability)
$\pi_1^{(1)} = 0.40$ (probability of price going up)
$\pi_1^{(2)} = 0.60$ (probability of price going down)
$\pi_2^{(1)} = 0.40 \cdot 0.40 = 0.16$ (probability of price going up twice)
$\pi_2^{(2)} = 0.40 \cdot 0.60 = 0.24$ (probability of price going up and then down)
$\pi_2^{(3)} = 0.60 \cdot 0.40 = 0.24$ (probability of price going down and then up)
$\pi_2^{(4)} = 0.60 \cdot 0.60 = 0.36$ (probability of price going down twice)

The complete stochastic programming formulation of the oil well example is as follows:

$$\begin{aligned}
\max_{x,u,z}\ & p_0^{(1)} \cdot u_0^{(1)} - z_0^1 \cdot \frac{(u_0^{(1)})^2}{x_0^{(1)}} - (1 - z_0^{(1)}) \cdot 20 \cdot \frac{(u_0^{(1)})^2}{x_0^{(1)}} \\
& + 0.9 \cdot \pi_1^{(1)} \cdot \left(p_1^{(1)} \cdot u_1^{(1)} - z_1^{(1)} \cdot \frac{(u_1^{(1)})^2}{x_1^{(1)}} - (1 - z_1^{(1)}) \cdot 20 \cdot \frac{(u_1^{(1)})^2}{x_1^{(1)}} \right) \\
& + 0.9 \cdot \pi_1^{(2)} \cdot \left(p_1^{(2)} \cdot u_1^{(2)} - z_1^{(2)} \cdot \frac{(u_1^{(2)})^2}{x_1^{(2)}} - (1 - z_1^{(2)}) \cdot 20 \cdot \frac{(u_1^{(2)})^2}{x_1^{(2)}} \right) \\
& + 0.9^2 \cdot \pi_2^{(1)} \cdot \left(p_2^{(1)} \cdot u_2^{(1)} - z_2^{(1)} \cdot \frac{(u_2^{(1)})^2}{x_2^{(1)}} - (1 - z_2^{(1)}) \cdot 20 \cdot \frac{(u_2^{(1)})^2}{x_2^{(1)}} \right) \\
& + 0.9^2 \cdot \pi_2^{(2)} \cdot \left(p_2^{(2)} \cdot u_2^{(2)} - z_2^{(2)} \cdot \frac{(u_2^{(2)})^2}{x_2^{(2)}} - (1 - z_2^{(2)}) \cdot 20 \cdot \frac{(u_2^{(2)})^2}{x_2^{(2)}} \right)
\end{aligned}$$

$$+0.9^2 \cdot \pi_2^{(3)} \cdot \left(p_2^{(3)} \cdot u_2^{(3)} - z_2^{(3)} \cdot \frac{(u_2^{(3)})^2}{x_2^{(3)}} - (1 - z_2^{(3)}) \cdot 20 \cdot \frac{(u_2^{(3)})^2}{x_2^{(3)}} \right)$$

$$+0.9^2 \cdot \pi_2^{(4)} \cdot \left(p_2^{(4)} \cdot u_2^{(4)} - z_2^{(4)} \cdot \frac{(u_2^{(4)})^2}{x_2^{(4)}} - (1 - z_2^{(4)}) \cdot 20 \cdot \frac{(u_2^{(4)})^2}{x_2^{(4)}} \right)$$

In the preceding formulation, $p_t^{(s)}$ denotes the price in scenario s at stage t. We have

$$p_0^{(1)} = \$45.00$$
$$p_1^{(1)} = \$54.00$$
$$p_1^{(2)} = \$36.00$$
$$p_2^{(1)} = \$64.80$$
$$p_2^{(2)} = \$43.20$$
$$p_2^{(3)} = \$43.20$$
$$p_2^{(4)} = \$28.80$$

The dimension of realistic multistage stochastic programming problems is typically very large, and optimization is challenging even with today's advanced technology. For certain types of stochastic problems, and linear optimization problems in particular, techniques such as nested *Benders decomposition*[9] and *importance sampling* can be used. The idea behind Benders decomposition is to split the multistage problem into a series of two-stage relations. Subproblems of much smaller size than the original problem are solved at each stage and scenario—these subproblems receive a trial solution from their ancestors and communicate a trial solution to their successors. Some stochastic programming software packages contain subroutines for decomposition of large stochastic programming problems that can be called directly. However, if we want to use standard optimization solvers, we need to implement the decomposition ourselves by calling the optimization solver repeatedly for each different subproblem.

Because the number of scenarios substantially affects the speed with which multistage stochastic optimization problems can be solved, a substantial amount of research has been dedicated to developing methodologies for effective scenario generation. The main idea is that scenario generation should not try to approximate well the probability distributions of the uncertain parameters, but rather approximate well the optimal value of the optimization problem. It has been shown that stochastic programming problems with two stages can be solved very efficiently, and with proven accuracy, by employing Monte Carlo (MC) simulation methods.[10] However, little is known about the computational complexity and the quality of approximation of MC sampling methods for multistage problems. In the financial modeling context, factor models and bundling of similar sample paths (as opposed to building entire scenario trees) have been used to reduce the dimension of such multistage problems.[11] Factor models are discussed in chapter 16.

9. See Birge (1985).

10. A good overview of recent developments in stochastic programming and importance sampling in particular is available in Ruszczynski and Shapiro (2003).

11. See Bogentoft et al. (2001) and Mulvey et al. (2000).

7.2.2 Mean-Risk Stochastic Models

Mean-risk stochastic models use an objective function that is composed of two parts: the expectation and some measure of risk.[12] As explained earlier in this section, when there is uncertainty in the coefficients in the optimization formulation, finding the optimal solution reduces to finding the solution that results in the best probability distribution of objective function values. We mentioned one definition of best probability distribution—the probability distribution with the highest mean. There are other plausible definitions, however. In particular, if we are also concerned about the degree of variability in the probability distribution of the objective function values, we can include a term in the objective function that penalizes for risk.

For example, suppose that there are N assets with random returns $\tilde{r}_1, \tilde{r}_2, \ldots, \tilde{r}_N$ in the next year. We would like to invest percentages $w_1, w_2, \ldots, w_N$ of our capital so as to maximize the portfolio expected return and penalize for the variance of the distribution of possible portfolio returns. (Portfolio risk measures are discussed in more detail in chapter 13.) Suppose that we are given a set of S possible scenarios for returns, and μ_i are the average returns for assets $i = 1, \ldots, N$ over the scenarios. Let r_i^s be the realization of the return of security i in scenario s. The return of the portfolio in scenario s is simply the sum of the individual asset returns multiplied by their weights in the portfolio; that is,

$$\sum_{i=1}^{N} r_i^s w_i$$

Let us denote the probabilities of the S scenarios by $\pi_1, \ldots, \pi_S$, where

$$\sum_{s=1}^{S} \pi_s = 1$$

The expected return on a portfolio with weights $w_1, w_2, \ldots, w_N$ over the N scenarios equals

$$\sum_{i=1}^{N} \mu_i w_i$$

and the variance of the portfolio return over the S scenarios is[13]

$$\sum_{s=1}^{S} \pi_s \left(\underbrace{\sum_{i=1}^{N} r_i^s w_i}_{\text{portfolio return in scenario } s} - \underbrace{\sum_{i=1}^{N} \mu_i w_i}_{\text{expected portfolio return}} \right)^2$$

Therefore, we can define the following objective for our portfolio optimization problem under uncertainty:

12. See section 3.6.2 in chapter 3 for an introduction to risk measures in the context of probability distributions. We will discuss risk measures in the context of portfolio allocation in part II of the book.

13. The definition of variance of a discrete probability distribution is provided in section 3.6.2.

Fund#	1	2	3	4
Scenario 1	50.39%	15.69%	23.29%	2.50%
Scenario 2	–9.02%	–3.96%	–2.25%	–2.36%
Mean return	20.69%	5.87%	10.52%	2.43%

Exhibit 7.6
Scenarios for the returns of the four funds.

$$\max_{\mathbf{w}} \sum_{i=1}^{N} \mu_i w_i - \kappa \left[\sum_{s=1}^{S} \pi_s \left(\underbrace{\sum_{i=1}^{N} r_i^s w_i}_{\text{portfolio return in scenario } s} - \underbrace{\sum_{i=1}^{N} \mu_i^s w_i}_{\text{expected portfolio return}} \right)^2 \right]$$

Here, κ is a penalty coefficient that is determined by the user—the more tolerance we have for uncertainty, the smaller the coefficient is. If we only cared about the expected portfolio return over the S scenarios, we would set κ to 0. We can specify additional constraints, as we would do in any optimization problem.

To gain some additional intuition, let us consider a simplified extension of the portfolio allocation example in section 7.3.1. Suppose that the expected returns of the four funds are the same, but we believe that their returns could end up in one of two scenarios: a "good" scenario, scenario 1, or a "bad" scenario, scenario 2 (see exhibit 7.6). Suppose also that we believe that the probability of scenario 1 is 0.30 and the probability of scenario 2 is 0.70.

The stochastic programming mean-risk formulation of this problem is

$$\begin{aligned}\max_{\mathbf{w}} \quad & 20.69 \cdot w_1 + 5.87 \cdot w_2 + 10.52 \cdot w_3 + 2.43 \cdot w_4 \\ & - \kappa \cdot 0.3 \cdot (50.39 \cdot w_1 + 15.69 \cdot w_2 + 23.29 \cdot w_3 + 2.50 \cdot w_4 \\ & - (20.69 \cdot w_1 + 5.87 \cdot w_2 + 10.52 \cdot w_3 + 2.43 \cdot w_4))^2 \\ & - \kappa \cdot 0.7 \cdot (-9.02 \cdot w_1 - 3.96 \cdot w_2 - 2.25 \cdot w_3 + 2.36 \cdot w_4 \\ & - (20.69 \cdot w_1 + 5.87 \cdot w_2 + 10.52 \cdot w_3 + 2.43 \cdot w_4))^2\end{aligned}$$

subject to the remaining constraints in the problem.

Different risk measures can be defined, of course. We will return to mean-risk models in chapters 12, 13, and 14.

7.2.3 Chance-Constrained Models

Chance-constrained stochastic optimization problems contain requirements on the probability that the solution will satisfy the constraints for all realizations of the random parameters in the problem. If the original constraint is

$$\tilde{\mathbf{a}}'\mathbf{x} \leq b$$

where $\mathbf{x}$ is the vector of decision variables and $\tilde{\mathbf{a}}$ is a vector of uncertain coefficients, then the general form of the chance constraint is

$$P(\tilde{\mathbf{a}}'\mathbf{x} > b) \leq \varepsilon$$

where P denotes *probability* and ε is some small number, such as 0.05 (5%). For the probabilistic constraint above to be satisfied, we need to find a solution $\mathbf{x}$ such that the original constraint $\tilde{\mathbf{a}}'\mathbf{x} \leq b$ is violated for at most ε% of all possible values for the uncertain coefficients. An important example of a chance-constrained stochastic programming problem in the portfolio management context is portfolio value-at-risk (VaR) optimization, which we will explore further in chapter 13.

Based on our introduction to optimization models in chapter 6, it is clear that a probabilistic constraint is not part of any of the standard optimization formulations. We need to apply different tricks to convert the constraint into a form that can be passed to an optimization solver, which involves making different assumptions. In the case in which we are given S scenarios for a vector of uncertain coefficients $\tilde{\mathbf{a}}$, we would need to replace this probabilistic constraint with an equivalent group of constraints:

$$
\begin{aligned}
&(\mathbf{a}^{(s)})'\mathbf{x} \leq b + M \cdot y_s, && s = 1, \ldots, S \\
&\sum_{s=1}^{S} y_s \leq \varepsilon \cdot S \\
&y_s \in \{0, 1\}, && s = 1, \ldots, S
\end{aligned}
$$

In the preceding formulation, M is some "large" constant relative to the size of the problem that is specified by the user. Note that we have introduced S new binary decision variables y_s, and have $S+1$ constraints instead of the original one probabilistic constraint. If $y_s = 0$, this forces the constraint

$$(\mathbf{a}^{(s)})'\mathbf{x} \leq b$$

to be satisfied; that is, for $\tilde{\mathbf{a}}'\mathbf{x} \leq b$ to be satisfied in scenario s. However, if $y_s = 1$, the term $M \cdot y_s$ is large; that is, the right side of the constraint is no longer restrictive and the constraint no longer needs to be satisfied. The additional constraint

$$\sum_{s=1}^{S} y_s \leq \varepsilon \cdot$$

limits the number of binary variables that are 1 to not more than $\varepsilon \cdot S$ (which is the integer part of $\varepsilon \cdot S$). For example, if we are given 115 scenarios for $\tilde{\mathbf{a}}$ and $\varepsilon = 5\%$, we guarantee that no more than 5 ($= 0.05 \cdot 115 = 5.75$) of the values for y are 1; that is, the constraint is not violated in more than 95% of the scenarios.

The introduction of binary variables and additional constraints significantly increases the size and complexity of the original optimization problem and can overwhelm even the best solvers when the number of scenarios (and, hence the number of binary variables) is large. Moreover, the problem type becomes nonconvex, which means that if the solver returns a solution, we cannot be confident that it is the optimal one. Therefore, probabilistic constraints need to be handled with care.

Note that a chance constraint basically requires that the $100(1-\varepsilon)$th percentile of the distribution of the random variable $\tilde{\mathbf{a}}'\mathbf{x}$ is less than the right-side limit b. Therefore, in rare cases in which we know the distribution of $\tilde{\mathbf{a}}'\mathbf{x}$ and can compute a closed-form expression for its $100(1-\varepsilon)$th percentile, we can convert a probabilistic constraint directly to a single nonprobabilistic constraint.

This is the case when all uncertain coefficients $\tilde{a}_1, \ldots, \tilde{a}_N$ in the chance constraint are assumed to come from a multivariate normal distribution. We can compute the exact $100(1-\varepsilon)$th percentile of the probability distribution $\tilde{\mathbf{a}}'\mathbf{x}$ in terms of the means of the uncertain coefficients $\tilde{\mathbf{a}}$, the standard deviations and the covariance structure of the uncertain coefficients $\tilde{\mathbf{a}}$, and the solution vector $\mathbf{x}$.

The $100(1-\varepsilon)$th percentile of the distribution of a normal random variable $\tilde{z}$ with mean μ and standard deviation σ is given by $\mu + \Phi^{-1}(1-\varepsilon) \cdot \sigma$, where $\Phi^{-1}()$ denotes the inverse of the cumulative standard normal distribution. (In other words, $\Phi^{-1}(1-\varepsilon)$ is the $100(1-\varepsilon)$th percentile of a standard normal distribution.)[14] We often encounter the notation $z_{(1-\varepsilon)}$ for the same concept. From the equations for expectation and variance of a sum of random variables, we can compute the mean of the normal random variable $\tilde{\mathbf{a}}'\mathbf{x}$ as $\hat{\mathbf{a}}'\mathbf{x}$ and its standard deviation as $\sqrt{\mathbf{x}'\Sigma\mathbf{x}}$.[15] Therefore, the deterministic constraint equivalent of the chance constraint under the assumption of normally distributed uncertain coefficients is

$$\hat{\mathbf{a}}'\mathbf{x} + z_{(1-\varepsilon)} \cdot \sqrt{\mathbf{x}'\Sigma\mathbf{x}} \leq b.$$

This is a second-order cone programming (SOCP) constraint (see section 7.2.4), which is easier to handle than a large set of constraints involving mixed-integer decision variables if you have the right solver. Recently, robust optimization techniques have been successfully applied for approximating the optimal solutions of problems with chance constraints in stochastic programming.[16] We will come back to this problem in chapter 12.

7.3 Robust Optimization

A major problem with dynamic and stochastic programming formulations is that in practice, it is often difficult to obtain detailed information on the probability distributions of the uncertainties in the model. At the same time, depending on the number of scenarios involved, dynamic and stochastic programming methods can be prohibitively costly computationally. *Robust optimization* makes optimization models robust with respect to uncertainty in the input data of optimization problems by solving so-called *robust counterparts* of these problems for appropriately defined *uncertainty sets* for the random parameters. The robust counterparts contain no uncertain coefficients; that is, they are deterministic optimization problems. In fact, the robust counterparts are worst-case formulations of the original optimization problems, where the worst case is computed over the possible values that the input parameters could take within their uncertainty sets. Typically, the uncertainty sets are defined in smart ways that do not lead to overly conservative or computationally challenging formulations. If the uncertainty sets are defined as a set of scenarios for the uncertain coefficients, robust optimization shares some features of stochastic programming. However, classical robust optimization focuses on the worst case, while classical stochastic programming focuses on the average over these scenarios.

14. See section 3.4.

15. To verify that this is the case, see online appendix A and write out the expressions for expected values and variances of sums of random variables when the random variables are given in vector/matrix form. We will discuss this in more detail in chapters 12 and 14.

16. See Chen, Sim, and Sun (2007) and Natarajan, Pachamanova, and Sim (2008).

7.3.1 Uncertainty Sets and Robust Counterparts

To provide some intuition for the robust optimization philosophy, let us consider a linear constraint of the kind $\tilde{\mathbf{a}}'\mathbf{x} \le b$. Let us assume that we use a statistical procedure to estimate some kind of "nominal," or expected, values for the elements of the vector of coefficients $\tilde{\mathbf{a}}$. We obtain estimates (let us denote them as $\hat{\mathbf{a}} = (\hat{a}_1, \ldots, \hat{a}_N)$), and 95% confidence intervals (CIs) for the true parameter values, $(\hat{a}_i - \delta_i, \hat{a}_i + \delta_i)$ for $i = 1, \ldots, N$.[17] A natural choice for an uncertainty set for $\tilde{\mathbf{a}}$ is the collection of CIs, which can be written as

$$U_\delta(\hat{\mathbf{a}}) = \{\mathbf{a} \| a_i - \hat{a}_i| \le \delta_i, i = 1,\ldots,N\}.$$

This mathematical expression states that coefficient a_i can take any value between $\hat{a}_i - \delta_i$ and $\hat{a}_i + \delta_i$, where δ_i is the nonnegative number representing the half-length of the CI formed around the estimate $\hat{a}_i$.

The robust counterpart of the preceding linear constraint is the following expression:

$$\max_{\mathbf{a} \in U_\delta(\hat{\mathbf{a}})} \{\mathbf{a}'\mathbf{x}\} \le b$$

In other words, we require that the constraint be satisfied even for the worst-case value of the expression $\mathbf{a}'\mathbf{x}$ when $\mathbf{a}$ varies in the specified uncertainty set. In this case, the worst-case value is obtained at the maximum because if the maximum value of $\mathbf{a}'\mathbf{x}$ is less than or equal to b, then the constraint is clearly satisfied for all smaller values of $\mathbf{a}'\mathbf{x}$. If the inequality were in the opposite direction (i.e.; $\tilde{\mathbf{a}}'\mathbf{x} \ge b$), then the worst case would happen at the minimum of the expression $\mathbf{a}'\mathbf{x}$. That is, the robust counterpart would be

$$\min_{\mathbf{a} \in U_\delta(\hat{\mathbf{a}})} \{\mathbf{a}'\mathbf{x}\} \ge b$$

We can easily write the robust counterpart of the constraint in a form that can be passed to an optimization solver. The maximum of the expression $\mathbf{a}'\mathbf{x}$ when $\mathbf{a}$ varies in $U_\delta(\hat{\mathbf{a}})$ is given by

$$\hat{\mathbf{a}}'\mathbf{x} + \delta' |\mathbf{x}|$$

This can be seen without any advanced mathematics. If the value of a particular decision variable x_i is nonnegative, then $|x_i| = x_i$, and the maximum value of $a_i \cdot x_i$ is obtained by multiplying the maximum possible value of a_i in the uncertainty set, $\hat{a}_i + \delta_i$, by x_i. If the value of x_i is negative, then $|x_i| = -x_i$, which is a positive number, and the maximum value of $a_i \cdot x_i$ is obtained by multiplying the maximum possible value of a_i in the uncertainty set, $\hat{a}_i + \delta_i$, by $-x_i$.

The uncertainty set considered previously, $U_\delta(\hat{\mathbf{a}})$, is extremely simple, and in fact, its applications in finance have been very limited because it is too conservative. The shape of the uncertainty set is a rectangle in two dimensions, and it looks like a box in more than two dimensions (see exhibit 7.7(A)). The robust optimization approach finds the optimal solution when $\mathbf{a}$ is at one of the corners of the box—the corner in which all elements of $\mathbf{a}$ are at their worst values in terms of constraint violation and result in the maximum value for the expression $\mathbf{a}'\mathbf{x}$.

17. See chapter 4 for a definition of CIs, and section 5.1.2 in chapter 5 for their use in simulation.

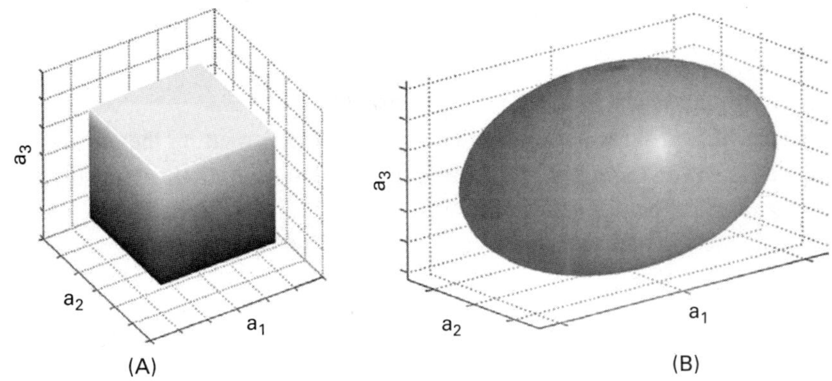

Exhibit 7.7
(A) "Box" uncertainty set in three dimensions; (B) ellipsoidal uncertainty set in three dimensions.

Instead, it may be realistic to be less conservative and assume that all uncertain coefficients will not take their worst-case values at the same time. In addition, we may have information about the standard deviations and the covariance structure of the uncertain coefficients. More advanced uncertainty sets can be specified to capture this information. A classical uncertainty set in robust optimization is the ellipsoidal uncertainty set (see exhibit 7.7(B)), which mathematically can be represented as

$$U_\delta(\hat{\mathbf{a}}) = \left\{ \mathbf{a} \,|\, (\mathbf{a} - \hat{\mathbf{a}})' \Sigma_{\mathbf{a}}^{-1} (\mathbf{a} - \hat{\mathbf{a}}) \leq \delta^2 \right\}$$

Here, $\Sigma_{\mathbf{a}}$ is the covariance matrix of the uncertain coefficients $\tilde{\mathbf{a}}$, and δ is some tolerance for robustness that is specified by the user. This uncertainty set states that the constraint should be satisfied for all values of **a** whose total squared distances from their nominal estimated values $\hat{\mathbf{a}}$ (scaled by their variability) are less than or equal to δ^2. Often, this uncertainty set is seen in the literature as

$$U_\delta(\hat{\mathbf{a}}) = \left\{ \mathbf{a} \middle| \, \| \Sigma_{\mathbf{a}}^{-1/2} (\mathbf{a} - \hat{\mathbf{a}}) \| \leq \delta \right\},$$

where $\|.\|$ stands for a second, or Euclidean norm.[18] The two expressions for the ellipsoidal uncertainty set are equivalent.

Let us now find the robust counterpart of the constraint

$$\tilde{\mathbf{a}}'\mathbf{x} \leq b$$

when the vector of uncertain coefficients $\tilde{\mathbf{a}}$ varies in the ellipsoidal uncertainty set. To obtain it, we need to find the maximum value of the expression on the left side of the constraint when $\tilde{\mathbf{a}}$ is in the uncertainty set. This reduces to solving the optimization problem

18. See section 6.2.4.

$$\max_{\mathbf{a}} \quad \mathbf{a'x}$$
$$\text{s.t.} \quad \Sigma_{\mathbf{a}}^{-1/2}(\mathbf{a}-\hat{\mathbf{a}}) \le \kappa.$$

This is an SOCP problem,[19] and for the moment, we are treating the original decision variables **x** as fixed (known). Instead, we will try to find the maximum value of the expression **a'x** when **a** is the decision variable.

Let us write the dual of the problem here (see exhibit 6.9). We obtain

$$\min_{\mathbf{u},\, \upsilon} \quad \left(-\mathbf{u'}\Sigma_{\mathbf{a}}^{-1/2}\hat{\mathbf{a}}\right) + \kappa\upsilon$$
$$\text{s.t.} \quad \Sigma_{\mathbf{a}}^{-1/2}\mathbf{u} + 0\cdot\upsilon = \mathbf{x}$$
$$\|\mathbf{u}\| \le \upsilon$$

Note that one of the constraints allows us to express **u** in terms of v and **w**:

$$\mathbf{u} = \Sigma_{\mathbf{a}}^{1/2}\|\mathbf{x}\|.$$

Therefore, the dual problem is equivalent to

$$\min_{\upsilon} \quad \mathbf{x'}\Sigma_{\mathbf{a}}^{1/2}\Sigma_{\mathbf{a}}^{-1/2}\hat{\mathbf{a}} + \kappa\upsilon$$
$$\text{s.t.} \quad \Sigma_{\mathbf{a}}^{1/2}\|\mathbf{x}\| \le \upsilon,$$

which can be rewritten as

$$\min_{\upsilon} \quad \mathbf{x'}\hat{\mathbf{a}} + \kappa\upsilon$$
$$\text{s.t.} \quad \Sigma_{\mathbf{a}}^{1/2}\|\mathbf{x}\| \le \upsilon.$$

Note that the minimum will be obtained when the constrained is satisfied with equality; that is, when

$$\upsilon = \Sigma_{\mathbf{a}}^{1/2}\|\mathbf{x}\|.$$

Therefore, the minimum will be

$$\hat{\mathbf{a}}'\mathbf{x} + \kappa\cdot\Sigma_{\mathbf{a}}^{1/2}\|\mathbf{x}\|.$$

Since this is an SOCP, duality theory states that the optimal objective function value will be the same as the value of the primal (maximization) problem. Therefore, the worst-case value for **a'x** will be given by the same expression:

$$\hat{\mathbf{a}}'\mathbf{x} + \kappa\cdot\Sigma_{\mathbf{a}}^{1/2}\|\mathbf{x}\|$$

for any fixed values of the decision variables vector **x**. Note that the preceding expression does not contain the uncertain coefficients $\tilde{\mathbf{a}}$; instead, it computes the worst-case value in

19. See section 6.2.4.

terms of parameters that are known, such as the nominal values of the uncertain coefficients $\hat{\mathbf{a}}$ and the covariance matrix of the uncertain coefficients $\Sigma_{\mathbf{a}}$. The final step is to replace the expression in the original constraint and optimize with $\mathbf{x}$ as decision variables again:

$$\hat{\mathbf{a}}'\mathbf{x} + \kappa \cdot \Sigma_{\mathbf{a}}^{1/2}\|\mathbf{x}\| \leq b.$$

This constraint formulation is equivalent to the constraint in the original problem that we wanted to solve. However, now the formulation is in a form that can be passed to an optimization solver because all the coefficients are certain.

To summarize, the methodology for creating a single optimization problem to represent the robust counterpart of a constraint is based on a trick from optimization duality. Namely, we first formulate a problem in which the original variables $\mathbf{x}$ are treated as fixed, and we try to find the worst-case value for the expression containing the vector of uncertain parameters $\tilde{\mathbf{a}}$. We then use optimization duality to convert the expression with uncertain coefficients into a constraint that does not contain uncertain parameters, and plug it into the original constraint. Finally, we solve the original optimization problem with the modified constraint and with $\mathbf{x}$ as the decision variable. While a certain amount of preprocessing is involved in formulating the robust problem, there is only one call to an optimization solver once the robust counterpart problem is formulated correctly.

The shape of the uncertainty set and the calibration of the different parameters that enter its specification play an important part in the performance of the robust counterpart in practice. The uncertainty sets that we saw in these examples were symmetric; that is, we assumed that the uncertain coefficients could deviate from their nominal values by the same amount in each direction. In theory, we could select uncertainty sets that represent better the probability distributions of the uncertain coefficients when these probability distributions are skewed.[20] "Structured" uncertainty sets can also be developed; that is, uncertainty sets that are intersections of elementary uncertainty sets or are constructed for a specific purpose.[21]

7.3.2 Multistage Robust Optimization

Robust optimization formulations can be used in multistage settings to replace dynamic programming or stochastic programming algorithms. Namely, instead of considering scenarios with realizations of the different uncertain parameters in a multistage problem, robust optimization formulations specify uncertainty sets around these parameters at each stage.

To provide an illustration, let us return to the oil well example from section 7.1. Recall that in section 7.6.1, we derived the classical optimization problem formulation for the oil problem if we knew the oil prices for each time period in advance. In a robust optimization framework, we would treat the future prices $\tilde{p}_1$ and $\tilde{p}_2$ as uncertain coefficients in the optimization problem. The robust counterpart statement of the problem would be as follows: Find the optimal strategy when oil prices in each time period take their "worst" within some prespecified uncertainty sets. The robust counterpart is then the following modification of the optimization formulation of the problem in section 7.6.1:

20. See, for example, Natarajan, Pachamanova, and Sim (2008).

21. For more details, see chapters 10 and 12 in Fabozzi et al. (2007).

$$
\begin{aligned}
\max_{x,u,z}\quad & p_0 \cdot u_0 - z_0 \cdot u_0^2 / x_0 - (1 - z_0) \cdot 20 \cdot u_0^2 / x_0 \\
& + 0.9 \cdot \min_{p_1 \in U(p_1)} \{p_1 \cdot u_1 - z_1 \cdot u_1^2 / x_1 - (1 - z_1) \cdot 20 \cdot u_1^2 / x_1\} \\
& + 0.9^2 \cdot \min_{p_2 \in U(p_2)} \{p_2 \cdot u_2 - z_2 \cdot u_2^2 / x_2 - (1 - z_2) \cdot 20 \cdot u_2^2 / x_2\} \\
\text{s.t.}\quad & u_0 = 100{,}000 \cdot z_0 + 200{,}000 \cdot (1 - z_0) \\
& u_1 = 100{,}000 \cdot z_1 + 200{,}000 \cdot (1 - z_1) \\
& u_2 = 100{,}000 \cdot z_2 + 200{,}000 \cdot (1 - z_2) \\
& x_0 = 600{,}000 \\
& x_1 = x_0 - u_0 \\
& x_2 = x_1 - u_1 \\
& u_0, u_1, u_2, x_1, x_2 \geq 0 \\
& z_0, z_1, z_2 \text{ binary}
\end{aligned}
$$

Here, $U(p_1)$ and $U(p_2)$ are some uncertainty sets for parameters $\tilde{p}_1$ and $\tilde{p}_2$. For example, if they are CIs of the kind

$$[\hat{p}_1 - \delta_1, \hat{p}_1 - \delta_2] \text{ and } [\hat{p}_2 - \delta_2, \hat{p}_2 - \delta_2]$$

then the robust counterpart is very simple—we only need to replace the expression for the objective function with

$$
\begin{aligned}
\max_{x,u,z}\quad & p_0 \cdot u_0 - z_0 \cdot u_0^2 / x_0 - (1 - z_0) \cdot 20 \cdot u_0^2 / x_0 \\
& + 0.9 \cdot \left((\hat{p}_1 - \delta_1) \cdot |u_1| - z_1 \cdot u_1^2 / x_1 - (1 - z_1) \cdot 20 \cdot u_1^2 / x_1\right) \\
& + 0.9^2 \cdot \left((\hat{p}_2 - \delta_2) \cdot |u_2| - z_2 \cdot u_2^2 / x_2 - (1 - z_2) \cdot 20 \cdot u_2^2 / x_2\right).
\end{aligned}
$$

The logic behind the derivation of the preceding expression is the same as the logic behind our derivation of the robust counterpart of a constraint at the beginning of this section, when the uncertain parameters vary in a box uncertainty set.[22] In fact, since u_1 and u_2 are restricted to be nonnegative, we can remove their absolute value signs, which will make the optimization formulation more solver-friendly.

Suppose that we consider the following intervals for the uncertainty sets for $\tilde{p}_1$ and $\tilde{p}_2$: [\$36, \$54] and [\$28.80, \$64.80], which are the minimum and the maximum values for the oil prices from the tree in exhibit 7.1. To solve the robust counterpart formulation here, we plug $\tilde{p}_1 - \delta_1 = 36$ and $\tilde{p}_2 - \delta_2 = 28.80$. We obtain the following optimal solution:

$z_0 = 0$ (use the enhanced method at stage 0)

$z_1 = 0$ (use the enhanced method at stage 1)

$z_2 = 1$ (use the normal method at stage 2)

$u_0 = 200{,}000$ (pump 200,000 barrels of oil at stage 0)

$u_1 = 200{,}000$ (pump 200,000 barrels of oil at stage 1)

22. Note that the expression in the objective function can be treated as a constraint. Namely, we can introduce a new decision variable and maximize that variable subject to an additional constraint that the new variable be less than the expression for the objective function. Therefore, if we have a method for determining the robust counterpart of a constraint, we can apply it to find the robust counterpart of the objective function as well.

$u_2 = 100{,}000$ (pump 100,000 barrels of oil at stage 2)

$x_0 = 600{,}000$ (amount of reserves at stage 0 is 600,000 barrels)

$x_1 = 400{,}000$ (amount of reserves at stage 1 is 400,000 barrels)

$x_2 = 200{,}000$ (amount of reserves at stage 2 is 300,000 barrels)

The present value of the total profit from this strategy is \$14,638,966.67. Recall that when we optimized the expected (average) total profit in section 7.1, the optimal expected profit was \$17,573,110.67. The optimal profit with the robust optimization strategy is lower because it is the profit obtained under the worst case scenario.

The optimal strategy found with the dynamic programming algorithm was to use the enhanced method in years 0 and 1, which is the same as the optimal strategy found by the robust optimization formulation for the first two years. In year 2, if the price in year 2 was \$28.80, the optimal strategy of the dynamic programming algorithm also agreed with the year 2 strategy in the robust optimization solution (to use the normal method). However, the dynamic programming solution was to use the enhanced method if the price was higher (\$43.30). The multistage robust optimization method does not give us information about strategies under scenarios other than the worst-case scenario in the uncertainty set that we specify.

Given that the dynamic programming method provided a more detailed solution than the robust optimization worst-case analysis, why would we want to use robust optimization? The answer is that in most realistic situations, dynamic programming algorithms suffer from the "curse of dimensionality"—the dimensions of the state space and the number of value function estimations and other calculations that need to be performed are so large that they can overwhelm even the most state-of-the-art software. Robust optimization keeps the dimension of the problem low, even as the number of stages and the number of states increase, but it still allows us to incorporate considerations for uncertainty when searching for the optimal strategy. Furthermore, the uncertainty sets for the uncertain parameters can be specified in clever ways, so the formulation is not overly conservative. Whether using robust optimization for a particular multistage problem is a good idea has to do with the trade-off between the amount of time or memory that it will take to solve the problem over multiple scenarios, as well as the required degree of accuracy of the solution.

The robust multistage example in which the uncertain parameters are restricted to fall within intervals is quite simplistic. However, in practice, we can specify more sophisticated uncertainty sets.

Summary

- Dynamic programming, stochastic programming, and robust optimization are all methodologies for optimization under uncertainty. Although there is overlap among the three approaches, historically they have evolved independently of each other.
- The dynamic programming approach is used for optimization over multiple stages. Its main idea is to break the large multistage problem into a sequence of smaller optimization problems, starting from the last stage and proceeding backward.

- The stochastic programming approach most generally deals with optimization problems in which scenarios are generated for the values of the uncertain parameters. The optimization may be performed so the objective function is optimized on average, or it may include penalties for constraint violation and risk considerations. Stochastic programming can be applied to both single-stage and multistage optimization problems.
- In most real-world applications, the dimensions of dynamic and stochastic programming methods are too large to handle computationally. Approximation algorithms are often used; some such algorithms employ Monte Carlo (MC) simulation and efficiently sample the state space.
- Robust optimization handles uncertainty in the coefficients of optimization problems by solving so-called robust counterparts of these problems. The robust counterparts are optimization problems formulated in terms of the worst-case realizations of the uncertain parameters within prespecified uncertainty sets.
- The robust optimization methodology can be applied in single-stage and multistage problems and can be a computationally attractive alternative to dynamic and stochastic programming methods.

8

Data and Data Science

Data[1] are a collection of facts that can be obtained from observations, experimentation, and simulation. They can take the form of numbers, text, measures, symbols, images, and recordings. There is a difference between data and information. Data are basically raw, unorganized facts. Without further processing or analysis, they are meaningless. When data are processed and analyzed, they provide *information*. According to Dykes (2016), "Information is prepared data that has been processed, aggregated and organized into a more human-friendly format that provides more context. Information is often delivered in the form of data visualizations, reports, and dashboards." The aggregating of data allows the identification of patterns. Once the information is analyzed, coupled with the decision maker's experience, *knowledge* (insight) is obtained.

Data science is an interdisciplinary field at the intersection of multiple other fields (statistics, scientific methods, computer science, and operations research), which uses data analysis and advanced computational tools and aims to extract insights from data. Data science is sometimes considered a subset of *artificial intelligence* (AI), which refers to the ability of a machine to learn how to complete tasks by thinking like a human, without explicit human instructions. *Machine learning* (ML) is a subset of AI consisting of techniques that enable computers to build applications that can learn from data and improve their accuracy over time. It provides many tools used in data science and is the subject of chapters 9 and 10.

In this chapter, we describe the various types of data, data attributes, and data issues, and explain common terminology in data science, such as *big data*.

8.1 Types of Data

Data can be classified in different ways: (1) quantitative and qualitative, (2) structured, unstructured, and semistructured, (3) labeled and unlabeled, and (4) cross-sectional and time-series.

1. According to the sixth edition of the *Publication Manual* of the Association of the American Psychological Association, the word "data" is plural, and hence the corresponding verb uses the plural form. The singular of data is "datum."

8.1.1 Quantitative Data versus Qualitative Data

The values for *quantitative data* are numerical. Generally, all real numbers are possible.[2] In some analyses, quantitative data are discrete values only, such as integers (i.e., 1, 2, 3 . . .). Time is expressed that way. Most quantitative data in finance are decimal values. The monthly return on a portfolio, fund, and investment strategy is measured using decimals, as are financial metrics such as return on assets, return on equity, leverage ratio, current ratio, debt service coverage, and turnover ratio. With quantitative data, one can perform transformations and computations.

Qualitative data are information about qualities. With this type of data, certain attributes of an item can be assigned only to categories. In some applications, quantitative data can be converted to nonquantitative data. For example, the maturity of a bond is quantitative data. However, in some analyses, the data can be transformed into qualitative data based on the amount of time remaining to maturity. A bond analyst may decide to classify holdings in a portfolio based on short, intermediate, and long maturities. The specific length of the classification is determined by the portfolio manager. For example, some portfolio managers view a short-term maturity as debt issues with a maturity of one year or less, while another may view it as less than two years. An equity analyst may classify the stocks in a portfolio based on whether they are growth or value stocks.

8.1.2 Structured Data versus Unstructured Data versus Semistructured Data

Data are also classified as structured data, unstructured data, or semistructured data. Most generally, *structured data* are information that is objectively represented and conforms to a tabular format. Microsoft Excel files and SQL databases are common examples—they rely on an underlying data relationship model to store, process, and access the data, which makes them convenient for aggregation and analysis. The data can be quantitative or nonquantitative. Data that possess the opposite attributes of those of structured data are referred to as *unstructured data.* Such data do not have a structure that is recognizable and for that reason, the information is difficult to categorize. Until it is processed for use, unstructured data are stored in their native format. Unstructured data that might be used by bond analysts would include government filings by a company, prospectuses for security offerings, and reports by other analysts about a bond issue or bond sector. These forms of unstructured data are referred to as *textual data.* Unstructured data also include photos and videos. For example, suppose an equity analyst is interested in looking at the activity of a major retailer's sales on an ongoing basis. In that case, computer satellite images of that retailer's parking lot might be used.

Semistructured data fall between structured and unstructured data. Such data do not have a strict data model structure that would allow them to be treated as structured data. Certain data within the semistructured data will have a label (discussed next), but parts of the data will be unstructured. Emails are an example of semistructured data. Although emails are similar to structured data because they will have the name of the sender, the name of the recipient, and the time that the email was sent, what makes emails unstructured is their content. Moreover, when an email has an attachment; that also qualifies as unstructured data.

2. In mathematics, a "real number" is defined as a quantity that can be expressed as an infinite decimal expansion.

There is increased use of unstructured and semistructured data in bond analysis due to the development of the field of data science. With respect to asset management, this field involves applying advanced analytical techniques to extract information from data for the purpose of making a wide range of investment decisions. The techniques, or algorithms, developed in data science can be used to extract information from unstructured and semistructured data (as well as improve the way that structured data are analyzed).

8.1.3 Labeled versus Unlabeled Data

Data that have not been tagged with a label that identifies their characteristics, classifications, or properties are referred to as *unlabeled data*. Examples of unlabeled data related to finance would be audio recordings of webcasts by security analysts or company representatives, printed articles about a company by the media or by sell-side security analysts, sharing posts (referred to as "tweets" prior to the renaming of Twitter to X), and Securities and Exchange Commission (SEC) filings by a public company.

Some unlabeled data can be enhanced by an expert assigning a meaningful or informative label to it. The task of labeling data that are currently unlabeled is sometimes referred to as *classifying* or *tagging* them, and the resulting data then are referred to as *labeled data*. For example, consider the use of tweets from social-media platforms such as X for quantifying market sentiment on a real-time basis. The objective is to provide a label representative of the overall sentiment of the tweet.

The task of labeling data can be done manually by humans, or automatically by another ML algorithm that has been trained to perform that task. This task is critical because any mistake or inaccuracy in labeling data adversely affects their informativeness. Because labeled data are required for certain types of ML algorithms, labeling errors can also adversely affect the objective and performance of such algorithms.

The importance of the labeling task also means that ML algorithms do not eliminate the need for human judgment in the investment process. For these algorithms to work effectively, experts are needed to label unlabeled data. These experts may be members of the investment management team or external consultant third-party vendors retained for this purpose.

8.1.4 Cross-Sectional Data versus Time-Series Data

Another way of classifying data is as *cross-sectional* or *time-series*. Suppose that an equity analyst is collecting data from the same quantity of interest or variable, say the daily return of stocks in the S&P 500. Each trading day, the analyst observes a return for each stock in the S&P 500. The set of data then forms what are called *time-series data*. Suppose that an equity analyst can select a particular time period of interest, such as the first quarter of the current year, and observe the returns of all stocks in the S&P 500. By doing so, the equity analyst would obtain *cross-sectional data* of the universe of stocks in that index at that particular time.

To summarize, time-series data are data related to a variable successively observed at a sequence of points in time. Cross-sectional data are values of a particular variable across some universe of items observed at a unique point in time.

8.2 Data Issues

In this section, we describe several issues with data and data collection. These include inaccurate data, missing data, sparse and dense data, outliers, and imbalanced data.

Before a dataset can be used, it must be analyzed to see if it has inaccurate data. This is referred to as *data cleansing*, which is the time-consuming process of replacing and changing data that are incorrect and dealing with missing data.

8.2.1 Inaccurate Data

A major reason for inaccurate data is manual errors that are made during the data entry process. When using multiple sources, there is also the issue of asymmetrical data, which is when information in one dataset does not reflect changes made in another dataset.

8.2.2 Missing Data

Missing data occur when the values are unknown for some of the observations of one or more variables. This is particularly common in bond price/return databases. The database may have missing data for some variables. When those variables are not the ones included in an analysis, there is no issue. However, when there are missing data for the variables to be included in a study, it can potentially have a significant impact on a study's conclusion.[3] The existence of a significant amount of missing data (1) reduces the representatives of the sample studies, (2) reduces the power of statistical tests typically performed to test hypotheses, and (3) increases the biases in the estimated parameters.

There are several methods for handling missing data. The simplest is to just omit sample observations where there are missing data. This approach is referred to as the *complete case analysis* or *listwise deletion*. The impact depends on the size of the sample. The larger the sample, the less the impact of deleting observations with missing data will have. A second approach is to replace the missing data with the mean of a variable. This method has its problems because although it does not reduce the size of the sample, it may cause biases in the estimated parameters.[4] There are also several statistical techniques that can be used for filling in missing data. These include regression imputation and the maximum likelihood method and an explanation of them is beyond the scope of this chapter.

8.2.3 Sparse and Dense Dataset

Sparse data are where a high percentage of instances of a given variable have a value of zero. That is, the data are known, but the value is zero. In terms of matrices, a matrix is said to be *sparse* if the elements of the matrix have mostly zero values. In contrast, a dense dataset is one where most of the values for the matrix elements are nonzero.

Although known, sparse data can present problems for ML algorithms. Sparse features increase the time and computational complexity of estimating predictive models, and diagnostic measures such as goodness-of-fit tests can be flawed if the data are

3. There is an extensive body of literature in the medical research area about how to handle missing data. See, for example, Rubin (1976), which explains the reason for missing data and their impact.

4. See Malhotra (1987).

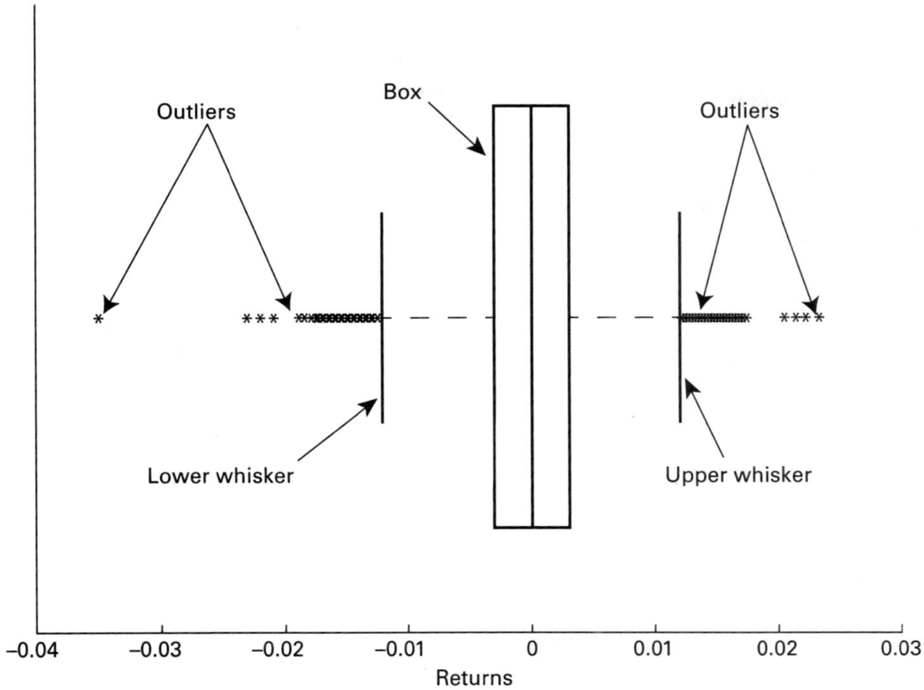

Exhibit 8.1
A box and whisker plot.

sparse.[5] Sparse data could also induce bias for estimated model parameters. The development of techniques for dealing with sparse data is an active research area in ML.[6]

8.2.4 Outliers

A dataset may contain observations that may be viewed as unusual and deemed not to represent the intended description of the data. Such values are referred to *outliers* or *extreme values*. Because outliers result in an increase in the variability of the data, they potentially can result in a decrease in the power of the statistical tests used in testing hypotheses, as well as in evaluating a proposed investment strategy.

There are several visualization methods from the field of descriptive statistics that can be used to detect outliers. Visualization methods that can be used to provide some indication of how the data are spread out, and therefore where outliers may be found. The methods include box and whisker plots, histograms, and scatterplots.

A *box and whisker plot* (also referred to as simply a *box plot*) shows on a graph the median, lower (first) and upper (third) quartiles, and the lower and upper outliers of a dataset. We will use exhibit 8.1, which plots return data to explain the construction of a box and whisker plot and the determination of outliers. First, the median and the lower and upper quartiles are determined. The middle 50% of the dataset, as represented by the interquartile range (IQR), is indicated in the graph by a horizontal box with its left and right bounds given

5. See Kuss (2002).

6. Some such techniques are described by Chickering and Heckerman (n.d.).

by lines extending vertically above the lower and upper quartiles, respectively. Another vertical line (inside the box) extends at the point where the median of the dataset is. The values in the dataset that are at or below 1.5 times the IQR to the left and right of the lower and upper quartiles define the dashed lines extending to the left and the right of the box, respectively. (These dashed lines, including their corresponding lower and upper limit values, are referred to as "whiskers" because of their appearance.) Above both these two whisker limit values, a vertical line with a shorter length than the vertical bounds of the box is extended. Finally, any values beyond the limits are referred to as "outliers." They are indicated by asterisks (*) in the exhibit.

More advanced statistical methods for detecting outliers include the Histogram-Based Outlier Score (HBOS).[7] There are also numerous advanced methods for outlier detection that take advantage of ML algorithms and are beyond the scope of this book, including nearest-neighbor-based, clustering-based, subspace-based, and classifier-based approaches.[8]

Understanding why outliers occurred in a sample is essential to determining how to deal with them. Outliers can occur due to errors in data entry or simply a natural variation in the data. Errors in data entry can be as simple as transposing digits or adding digits. During the cleansing stage of assembling a database, outliers can be checked to determine whether they were the result of an error in entering the data. If so, and if it is possible to correct the data, the problem will be resolved. However, if it is impossible to access the original data source from which the data were obtained, the outliers should be eliminated.

Outliers can be expected if a population has a wide range of values. In that case, the outlier could be a legitimate observation and should not be discarded. When there are outliers of this sort that should not be removed from the database, there are techniques that can be used to mitigate their impact on any analysis that uses them. These techniques draw from the field of robust statistics.[9]

8.2.5 Imbalanced Dataset

Suppose that an analyst is seeking to predict whether a borrower is likely to default on a loan. This is a classification problem that we describe in chapters 9 and 10 because it can also be stated as the problem of determining to which class (group) a borrower belongs: the class of borrowers who default on a loan versus the class of borrowers who do not default. To build statistical or ML models that treat each class equally, the dataset ideally should include approximately the same number of borrowers who have repaid their loans (i.e., did not default) as borrowers who defaulted on their loans. So, in a dataset of, say, 400,000 borrowers, it would be desirable to have roughly 200,000 of nondefault borrowers and 200,000 of default borrowers.

However, there are situations where the number of observations for one of the two groups may be substantially greater than the other. The number of borrowers who defaulted would be an example. It would not be unusual to find that the vast majority of borrowers did not

7. See the poster and demo track by Goldstein and Dengel (2012).

8. See Goldstein and Uchida (2016).

9. See Maronna et al. (2019).

default on their loans. Similarly, when trying to predict whether a corporation would default on the bonds that it issued, the number of nondefaulting corporations is likely to be far greater than the number of defaulting corporations. Observations in the class with a large percentage of the observations are said to be in the "majority class." In contrast, observations in the class with a small percentage of observations are said to be in the "minority class."

In instances where there is a majority class and minority class as just described, the dataset is said to be an *imbalanced dataset*. Balancing the dataset during model building often results in better model performance on data that the model has not seen. There are techniques in ML that address this issue, and some ML models actually have a parameter that allows the designation of a dataset to be balanced.[10]

8.3 Dimensionality and the Curse of Dimensionality

In the field of statistics, *dimensionality* refers to the number of variables or attributes in a dataset. The term *univariate data* refers to data that have only one dimension. *High-dimensional data* means that the number of dimensions is extremely large relative to the number of observations in the sample; that is, data are said to be high dimensional when the ratio of the number of variables to the number of observations in the sample is extremely large.

As more and more variables are added to a dataset that is used for modeling, it would seem that it would make prediction better because there are more data. However, in practice, if the number of observations stays the same, it becomes increasingly more difficult to use the dataset for predicting. This is due to what is referred to as the "curse of dimensionality." The curse of dimensionality causes problems when using certain statistical techniques (such as multiple regression analysis, which we discuss in chapter 9), the most common problem being that of multicollinearity.

Two general types of techniques in statistics and ML for reducing dimensionality are feature selection and dimensionality reduction. *Feature selection* involves using only variables that are the most relevant. *Dimensionality reduction* involves combining related variables into groups or components, and it basically identifies variables that are similar. ML algorithms that are described in chapter 9 can be used for this purpose.

8.4 Data Measurement Scales

Data are defined, measured, and grouped according to *measurement scales* or *measurement levels*. The term *scales* means a rule that is used for the assignment of numerals to properties of the variables. The five measurement scales used in data analysis are (1) nominally scaled data, (2) ordinally scaled data, (3) interval scaled data, (4) ratio scaled data, and (5) absolute scaled data.

The measurement scale provides an indication as to which algorithms and tools that we describe in later chapters can be applied to analyze the data. This listing of the measurement scales is based on a hierarchy in terms of the sophistication of the statistical tools that can be

10. For example, random forecasts are described in chapter 10.

applied, starting with the weakest measurement scale (nominally scaled data) to the strongest measurement level (absolute scaled data).

Nominally scaled data are used for classification purposes. One example concerns the qualitative data described earlier in this chapter, such as the credit rating of a bond issue or the credit rating of a corporation. Another example involves the data obtained from a survey of asset managers in response to a question about whether they might use a particular type of derivative. The reason why nominally scaled data is the weakest measurement level is that statistical analysis is limited to describing the data in terms of a frequency count or as a percentage and displayed using a pie chart or a bar chart.

One step higher in the hierarchy is *ordinally scaled data*. With this type of data, also referred to as "rank data," the values are still qualitative but follow a natural order. By "order," it means to arrange the data according to a particular sequence or method. For example, in the analysis of financial statements, current assets can be measured in terms of the degree of liquidity. On the balance sheet, the most liquid current asset is cash and short-term securities, accounts receivable, and inventory. In a bond portfolio, the holdings can be ranked based on the credit rating. Hence, we have a natural ranking or order among the values. However, the difference between two pieces of ordinally scaled data is meaningless. For example, there is no numerical meaning for the difference between a AAA-rated bond and an A-rated bond. There is limited analysis that can be performed using both nominally scaled and ordinally scaled data.

Interval scaled data can be transformed by a linear equation. Suppose that we are given values for variable x. With interval data, it is feasible to express a new variable y by the relationship $y = \mathrm{a} + \mathrm{b}x$, where the xs are from the original data. If x has a meaning, then so does y. Data have to possess a numerical meaning, and therefore be quantitative, to be measured on an interval scale.

Ratio scaled data share all the properties of interval scaled data. However, ratio scaled data have an additional property: they have a fixed or true zero point. In terms of the linear transformation, for ratio scaled data, the intercept, a, can be arbitrarily changed through transformation. Since the zero point of ratio scaled data is invariable, only the slope, b, can be transformed. So, for example, $y = \mathrm{b}x$ is always a multiple of x. In other words, there is a relationship between y and x given by ratio b (and hence, the name used to describe this type of data). This feature would be possible only for a b value that is different from zero in the transformation. For example, the bond price of some European bond, E, is given in euros. The same price in U.S. dollars, D, would be D equals E times the exchange rate between euros and U.S. dollars. But if the issuer's bond price after bankruptcy went to zero, the price in either currency would be zero even at different rates determined by the exchange rate between the U.S. dollar and the euro. This is a result of the invariant zero point.

Absolutely scaled data are given by quantitative data measured on a scale even stricter than for ratio scaled data, where along with the zero point, the units are invariant as well. Data measured on an absolute scale occurs when transformation would be mathematically feasible but lacked any interpretational implication. A common example is provided by counting numbers. All analysts would agree on the number of bond issues comprising a certain bond index. There is no ambiguity as to the zero point and the count increments. Suppose one bond issue is added to the bond index. In that case, it is immediately clear that the difference between this index and the content of the old bond index is exactly one unit of bond issue, assuming that no stock is deleted.

8.5 Big Data

Big data is a term that has been adopted to refer to data that are so large, fast, and/or complex that traditional methods of data analysis find it difficult or impossible to process them. That is, data stored in traditional databases can generally be handled by basic analytical systems. In contrast, big data are so massive, complex and varied that they are difficult to process using standard methods.

The term "big data" has been in use since the 1990s. Advancements in technology have been increasing our ability to handle complex data and thus shifting the exact meaning of the term. As pointed out by Kolanovic and Krishnamachari (2017, p. 9), the three trends that have facilitated what they refer to as the "Big Data Revolution" are

- The exponential increase in the amount of data available from a wide variety of sources, particularly the Internet of Things phenomenon, in which sensors are embedded in devices
- The significant increase in computing power and storage capacity, accompanied by reduced costs for computing and storage
- Advances in the field of ML that allow statistical methods to be applied to deal with large datasets to derive information (e.g., patterns and ways to classify) that is useful for decision making

8.5.1 Defining Big Data

The defining dimensions of big data are expressed in terms of what is referred to as the "five Vs":[11]

- *Volume* is the dimension that is most associated with big data. It basically means that the quantity of data is enormous. However, this is a relative term. As computing power increases, what may be big data at one point in time may be able to be handled by new technology with no difficulty.
- *Velocity* is a measure of the speed at which data are generated and how quickly those data become available for decision making (e.g., real-time and near real-time).
- *Variety* refers to the range of formats of data (e.g., structured data such as numeric data) that are available in traditional databases or unstructured text documents such as stock ticker data, financial filings with regulators, financial transactions, emails, videos, and audio files.
- *Veracity* refers to the quality and accuracy of the data. Data often come from multiple sources, some of which may be subjective, corrupted, or generated by humans. As a

11. Doug Laney offered the first three Vs of big data, while SAS augmented the definition with the last two Vs. See https://www.sas.com/en_us/insights/big-data/what-is-big-data.html. More Vs have been added to describe the insights that can be gained from big data.

result, it is challenging to link (bring information together to create a new database), match, cleanse (detect and correct corrupt or inaccurate data before storing), and transform data from different sources. Basically, veracity covers the level of trust that decision makers have when using the data.

- *Value* refers to the value that the data provide for decision making. That is, what can a decision maker do with the large database?

8.5.2 Alternative Data

In finance, alternative data is a category of big data utilized by active portfolio managers (i.e., quantitative and fundamental portfolio managers described in later chapters) to enhance portfolio returns. Ekster and Kolm (2021, p. 11) define alternative data as "any dataset that does not originate from securities exchanges, regulatory disclosures, or economic releases and indicators." Many large asset management firms have a team dedicated to maintaining and using alternative data. Kolanovic and Krishnamachari (2017) classify data sources into three categories:

- Data generated by individuals, which are typically unstructured data that can be classified as (1) social media posts such as X, LinkedIn, and Facebook; (2) specialized sites such as business-reviewing websites (e.g., e-commerce groups and Yelp); and (3) web searches and personalized data, such as Google searches
- Data generated by individuals through business processes such as e-commerce and financial transactions
- Data generated by sensors embedded in various devices such as satellite imagery, geographical data, weather and pollution sensors

There are a good number of data providers of information that can be used in investment decisions. According to AlternativeData.org, the number of providers has increased from about 50 in 2000 to 445 by 2018.[12] The major ones, according to Kolanovic and Krishnamachari (2017), are Gallop, Inrix, Nielson, Open Signal, Orbital Labs, Pew, SimilarWeb, Thinknum, Verizon, Yipit, and Yodlee.

For asset management, Ekster and Kolm (2021) explain the two purposes for evaluating the value of acquiring costly alternative data. First, since an asset management firm typically will acquire an alternative dataset to forecast returns for one or more asset classes, the dataset should help in forecasting returns. Second, although the alternative dataset may not be useful for forecasting returns as a stand-alone dataset, return forecasting can be improved by using the alternative dataset as an enhancement to another dataset. In practice, this is done by determining whether there is a significant correlation between the alternative dataset or transformed versions of the alternative dataset and factors such as fundamental metrics used for forecasting returns.[13]

12. https://alternativedata.org/alternative-data/.

13. Since many alternative datasets have short histories and few observations (e.g., an alternative dataset may have only four years of quarterly data for twenty companies), correlation analysis may not be sufficient to assess the value of such a dataset. Ekster and Kolm (2021) suggest a methodology that they refer to as the "golden triangle event study."

8.6 Data Visualization

To understand a dataset and its impact on the problem at hand, often it is useful to visualize the data graphically. *Data visualization* involves expressing data in a visually appealing format so that the data are easier to understand and provide insights. In a *Harvard Business Review* article, Berinato (2006) writes, "Not long ago, the ability to create smart data visualizations, or dataviz, was a nice-to-have skill. For the most part, it benefited design- and data-minded managers who made a deliberate decision to invest in acquiring it. That's changed. Now visual communication is a must-have skill for all managers, because more and more often, it's the only way to make sense of the work they do."

Effective data visualization should be not only appealing and informative, but also efficient, interactive, and predictive. By "efficient," we mean that it should save an analyst or portfolio manager time when communicating the data concisely, as well as leave no room for ambiguity. Dashboards are often used for precisely this reason. Data visualizations can also be used as analytical tools to assess how the results may change by changing different input values.

There are a large number of data visualization tools that are open-source or commercially available. The number and sophistication of such tools continue to increase.

Summary

- Data science lies at the intersection of multiple fields, including statistics, computer science, and operations research.
- Data are a collection of facts that can be obtained from observations, experimentation, and simulation and can take the form of numbers, texts, measures, symbols, images, and recordings.
- Data can be classified as (1) quantitative and qualitative; (2) structured, unstructured, and semistructured; (3) labeled and unlabeled; and (4) cross-sectional and time-series data.
- Structured data are objectively represented and conform to a tabular format, which makes them convenient for aggregation and analysis. Structured data can be quantitative or qualitative.
- Unstructured data do not have an underlying structure and therefore they are difficult to categorize.
- Unlabeled data that relate to finance could be audio recordings of webcasts by security analysts or company representatives, articles about a company by the media or by security analysts, tweets, and Securities and Exchange Commission (SEC) filings by a public company.
- Some unlabeled data can be enhanced by an expert assigning a meaningful or informative label to them.
- Time-series data are data related to a variable successively observed at a sequence of points in time.
- Cross-sectional data are values of a particular variable across some universe of items observed at a unique point in time.

- Issues with data and data collection include inaccurate data, missing data, sparse data, outliers, and imbalanced data.
- When the number of variables (dimensions) is very large relative to the number of observations in a sample, the data are said to be high dimensional.
- There are techniques in statistics and machine learning (ML) for dimensionality reduction.
- Measurement scales or measurement levels refer to different ways in which data are defined and grouped.
- Measurement scales used in data analysis are nominally scaled data, ordinally scaled data, interval scaled data, ratio scaled data, and absolute scaled data.
- Big data are characterized by dataset sizes that are massive and have high complexity. They may include structured, unstructured, and semistructured data, and are difficult to process using standard methods
- Alternative data are data from nonconventional information sources and include structured data and most unstructured data.
- Data visualization involves expressing data in a visually appealing and useful format so the data are easier to understand and provide insights relevant for decision making.

9

Regression Models

In this chapter and the two that follow, we cover analytical tools used in finance that come from the fields of statistics and computer science. Regression, the subject of this chapter, is an important fundamental tool rooted in inferential statistics and is now widely used in statistical, machine learning (ML), and artificial intelligence (AI) applications. As we will explain in more detail in our discussion of ML in chapter 10, regression is a supervised learning model.

Regression models the dependence of a variable (called the *dependent variable*) on one or more *explanatory variables* (also referred to as *independent variables* or *regressors*). In ML parlance, the dependent variable is referred to as the *response variable* or *target variable* and the explanatory variable is the *input feature* or *predictor variable.* In basic regression, the functional relationship between the dependent variable and the explanatory variables is expressed as a linear equation, and hence is referred to as a *linear regression model.* The basic linear regression model is also referred to as an *ordinary least squares (OLS) regression model* because of the methodology used to calculate the parameters of the model. There are statistical tests that describe how well the linear regression model fits the data. When the linear regression model includes only one explanatory variable, the model is said to be a *simple linear regression.* However, it is often the case in applications in finance that it is necessary to use several explanatory variables simultaneously. In that case, the model used is a *multiple linear regression.*

There are different types of regression models that depend on the type of data for the dependent and explanatory variables. In this chapter, we describe the basic OLS regression model and four specialized regression models: linear probability model, logistic regression, probit regression, and discriminant analysis. In OLS regression, the objective is to predict the expected value for the dependent variable based on an estimated model using the explanatory variables. An example would be predicting the estimated return on a portfolio given attributes of the holding of the individual stocks in the portfolio and economic conditions as the explanatory variables. The four specialized regressions described in this chapter are used to classify observations as belonging to some group or category and are accordingly referred to as "probabilistic classification regression models."

In chapter 10, we describe extensions of the basic OLS regression model, referred to as *regularization algorithms.* The purpose of regularization is to induce desirable properties of a model (e.g., to penalize the model due to its complexity so as to favor simpler models and minimize the risk of overfitting the data).

9.1 OLS Regression

In a simple linear regression model, the joint behavior of the dependent variable, denoted by y, and the explanatory variable x can be thought of as y being some function of x. That is, it is assumed that there is a functional relationship between the two variables, given by

$$y = f(x) \tag{9.1}$$

Equation (9.1) is an example of a deterministic relationship. However, the variation of y may be influenced by other factors in addition to x. To allow additional explanatory variables, an adjustment can be made to equation (9.1). The adjustment is represented by a term referred to as the *residual term* or *error term*. It is assumed that the residual term is independent (specifically, uncorrelated) with x, and it is assumed to account for any movement of y that is not accounted for by equation (9.1).

Adjusting the deterministic equation given by equation (9.1) by the residual term, the relationship assumed is

$$y = f(x) + \epsilon \tag{9.2}$$

where the residual term (or error term) is represented by the Greek letter epsilon (ϵ).

In addition to the assumption that the residual term is independent of x, the residual term is assumed to have a mean of zero, with some constant variance denoted by σ^2, and is considered to be some unforeseen information or shock. Assuming a linear functional relationship, the relationship can be expressed as follows:

$$f(x) = \alpha + \beta x \tag{9.3}$$

where parameters α and β are the intercept and slope, respectively. Equation (9.3) is referred to as a *simple linear regression* or a *univariate regression* because there is only one explanatory variable (x) that is used to explain the dependent variable (y).

9.1.1 Assumptions of the Regression Model

The explanatory variable can be a deterministic quantity or a random variable. In an experimental setting, the explanatory variable can be controlled and is therefore deterministic. The more common case in finance is where the explanatory variable cannot be directly controlled and is therefore a random variable. For example, if a portfolio manager wants to look at the relationship between the return on some stock (the dependent variable) and the return of a stock market index such as the S&P 500 (the explanatory variable), the explanatory variable is random. Similarly, if the change in the value of a bond (the dependent variable) is assumed to depend on the change in yield on a U.S. 10-year Treasury bond (the explanatory variable), the explanatory variable is a random variable.

Given a set of observations for x and y, $\{(x_1,y_1), \ldots, (x_n,y_n)\}$, the n residual terms (error terms) given by equation (9.3) are assumed to be *independent and identically distributed (i.i.d).* This assumption has two important implications. *Independent* means that each error assumes a value that is unaffected by any of the other errors, and therefore knowledge of other errors cannot be used to predict the current error term. *Identically distributed* means that all errors follow the same distribution, which is assumed to be a normal distribution. The i.i.d. assumption is important if the assertion made is that all information is contained in equation (9.1) and any deviations from equation (9.1) are purely random. In other words, the residuals are *statistical noise,* so they cannot be predicted from other quantities.

Equation (9.4) says that given a value for x, it is assumed that on average, y will be exactly equal to the value determined by the functional relationship. The only variation in equation (9.4) is attributable to the residual term. On average, the error term will have no influence on the value of y.

What if the distributional assumptions about the error terms are violated? Later in this chapter, we will discuss the implications of violating the assumptions regarding the error term, how to diagnose whether an assumption is violated, and how to deal with assumption violations.

9.1.2 Estimating the Simple Linear Regression Model

We will use exhibit 9.1 to explain the criterion used to estimate the values for α and β for a simple linear regression. The circles in the exhibit represent the 12 observations. On the horizontal axis is the value of the explanatory variable x, while the value for the dependent variable y is on the vertical axis. A graph that shows the plot of each x, y for a simple linear regression is called a *scatterplot*. Also shown in the exhibit is a straight line labeled "Regression line." This is actually the line that we want to estimate (i.e., it provides the values for the intercept α and the slope β that we seek). There is one observation shown in the exhibit to focus on. It is the observation labeled C. Notice that there is a vertical line for that observed value. That, of course, is one of the observed values for y. The value of x that corresponds with observation C is A on the horizontal axis. Therefore, the length of the line CA is the observed value for y for the observed value for x. Where the vertical line intercepts the regression line is the estimated value for y. In the exhibit, it is at point B on the regression line. The length given by BA, therefore, is the estimated value for y provided by the regression line. That is,

$$\text{CA} = \text{observed value for } y$$
$$\text{BA} = \text{estimated value for } y$$

The observed error that is made by using the regression line, therefore, is calculated by CA − BA = CB.

The objective in estimating intercept α and slope β is to find values for those two parameters that will have the smallest observed total error for all the observations. However, there is a problem with using this as a criterion for estimating α and β. Notice that the observed error shown in exhibit 9.1 is positive. There will be observed errors that will be negative. The problem with just adding up the observed error terms for all the observations is that the positive observed errors will offset the negative observed errors. To address that problem, instead of summing all of the observed errors, the observed error terms are squared and then added up. Squaring the error penalizes larger errors more strongly than smaller ones and guarantees that all individual terms are nonnegative so error terms are not canceled out in the summation. So the criterion for estimating intercept α and slope β is to

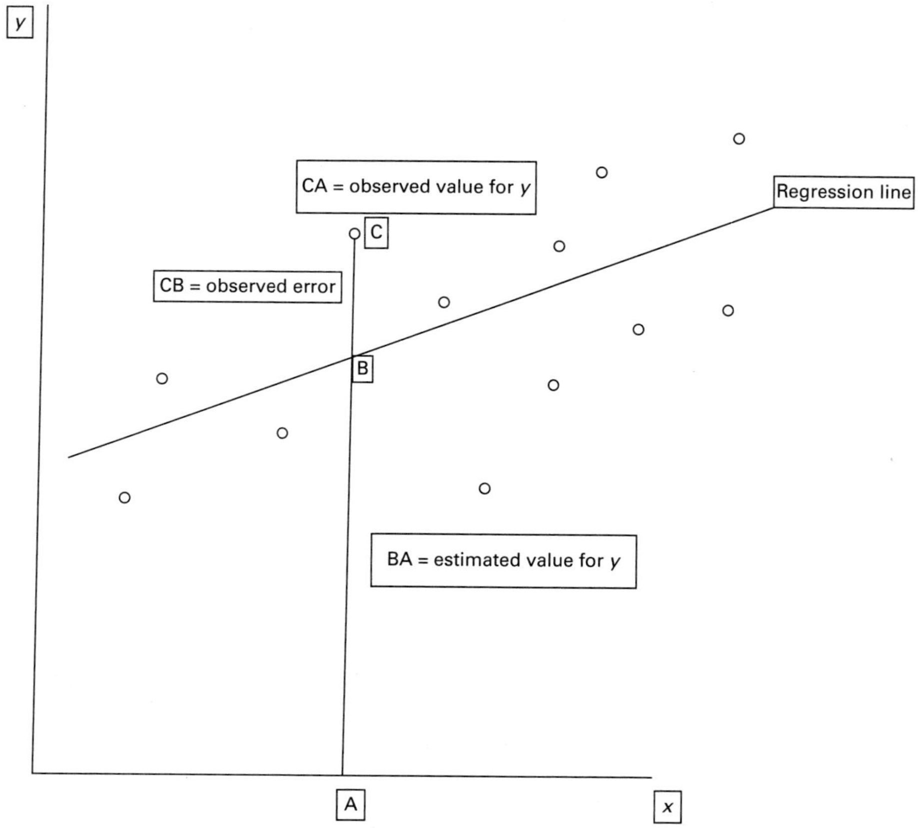

Exhibit 9.1
Graphical depiction of the observed error.

find values a and b that minimize the sum of the squared observed error terms. For this reason, the method for estimating the regression line is referred to the *method of least squares* or the *ordinary least squares* (OLS) *method.*

Mathematically, denoting the parameter estimate of α and β as a and b, respectively, the following relationship must be solved using the n observations for x and y:

$$\min_{a,b} \sum_{i=1}^{n} (y_i - a - bx_i)^2 \tag{9.5}$$

The value in brackets is the observed error term resulting from using a particular pair of a and b. The expression given by equation (9.5) indicates that the total of the squared errors should be minimized to determine the estimates a and b of parameters α and β, respectively.

In practice, it would be impossible to try every possible combination of values of a and b to determine which pair produced the minimum value for the squared observed errors. Fortunately, optimization theory and calculus can be used to determine two equations (referred to as the *normal equations*) that can be used to calculate a and b. We will not provide the equations here since statistical software easily provides the results. What is important to note, though, is that the OLS method provides the best linear estimate in the sense that no other linear estimate results in a smaller sum of squared error terms.

9.1.3 Goodness of Fit of the Model

Some statistical measure is needed to assess how good the estimated relationship is that is obtained using the OLS estimation method. A commonly used measure is the *coefficient of determination*. This goodness-of-fit measure, denoted as R^2, calculates how much of the variation in y is caused or explained by the variation in x. If the percentage explained by the coefficient of determination is small, the fit might not be reliable.

To understand this measure, let's look at the variance of the observations y by analyzing the total sum of squares of the observations for y around their mean (SST), as given by

$$SST = \sum_{i=1}^{n}(y_i - \bar{y})^2 \tag{9.6}$$

where

SST = total sum of squares, n = number of observations, and
$\bar{y}$ = mean value for observations $y_1, \ldots, y_n$.

In turn, SST can be decomposed into the *sum of squares explained by the regression (SSR)* and the *sum of squared errors* (SSE). That is,

$$SST = SSR + SSE$$

Here, SSR is that part of the total sum of squares that is explained by the regression, and SSE is the part of the total sum of squares that is unexplained. We will not show how SSR and SSE are calculated since they are easily computed by software. The coefficient of determination is defined as follows:

$$R^2 = \frac{SSR}{SST} \tag{9.7}$$

R^2 takes values between 0 and 1. The meaning of R^2 being equal to 0 is that the explanatory variable x explains no part of the variation in y; that is, there is no discernable linear relationship between x and y. Thus, the linear regression model makes little sense. If R^2 is equal to 1, all the variation in y is explained by x (i.e., the fit of the linear regression line is perfect).

9.1.4 Extension to Multiple Linear Regression Model

In real-world applications of regression analysis to finance, a simple linear regression that has only one explanatory variable is typically insufficient. The behavior of the variable of interest (i.e., the dependent variable) usually needs to be explained by two or more variables. For example, suppose that we want to determine the financial or macroeconomic variables that affect the monthly return on the S&P 500 index. Let's suppose that economic and financial theory suggest that there are six such explanatory variables. In this case, a multiple linear regression model is used.

The multiple linear regression model takes the form

$$y = \beta_0 + \beta_1 x_1 + \beta_2 x_2 + \cdots + \beta_k x_k + \varepsilon \tag{9.8}$$

where β_0 = intercept, $\beta_{1,\ldots,}\beta_k$ = regression coefficients for the k explanatory variables, and ϵ = residual or error term.

In vector notation, given a sample of n observations for the dependent and the explanatory variables, equation (9.8) can be expressed as

$$\boldsymbol{y} = \boldsymbol{X\beta} + \boldsymbol{\varepsilon} \tag{9.9}$$

where $\boldsymbol{y}$ is an $n \times 1$-column vector consisting of the n observations for the dependent variable; that is,

$$y = \begin{pmatrix} y_1 \\ \vdots \\ y_n \end{pmatrix}$$

and $\mathbf{X}$ is a $n \times (k+1)$ matrix consisting of n observations of each of the k explanatory variables and a column of 1s to account for the intercepts β_0:

$$\mathbf{X} = \begin{pmatrix} 1 & x_{11} & \ldots & x_{1k} \\ 1 & x_{21} & & x_{2k} \\ \vdots & \vdots & & \vdots \\ 1 & x_{n1} & \ldots & x_{nk} \end{pmatrix}$$

The $(k+1)$ regression coefficients, including intercept, are given by the $(k+1) \times 1$ column vector:

$$\boldsymbol{\beta} = \begin{pmatrix} \beta_0 \\ \vdots \\ \beta_k \end{pmatrix}$$

Each observation's residual is represented in the column vector ε:

$$\boldsymbol{\varepsilon} = \begin{pmatrix} \varepsilon_1 \\ \vdots \\ \varepsilon_n \end{pmatrix}$$

The regression coefficient β of each explanatory variable represents the average change in the dependent variable per unit change in the explanatory variable with the other independent variables held constant. As with simple linear regression, the same distribution assumptions about the error term are made for the multiple linear regression model. And, also as with simple linear regression, we will not derive or present the equations for estimating the regression coefficient based on OLS.

9.2 Steps in Designing a Regression Model

The building process to design a regression model consists of five steps: (1) model specification, (2) data gathering, (3) estimating the model, (4) diagnosis check, and (5) testing for statistical significance.

9.2.1 Model Specification

Given the dependent variable, in the model specification step, the explanatory variables are determined. Financial economic theory often provides guidance as to what the relevant explanatory variables might be when the dependent variable is a financial variable. There are also statistical techniques that can be used to identify relevant explanatory variables. We discuss one method (stepwise regression) later in this chapter, and other methods (referred to as *feature importance models*) in chapter 10, where we discuss ML.

9.2.2 Data Gathering

After the dependent and explanatory variables have been identified, data for all the variables are gathered. Thus, we obtain vector y for the dependent variable and matrix X for the explanatory variables. The larger the sample, the better the quality of the estimation. Although in theory the sample size n should at least be 1 more than the number of explanatory variables k, a rule of thumb is that n should be at least 4 times k.

9.2.3 Model Estimation

Model estimation involves constructing the functional linear relationship expressed by the model (i.e., solving for the intercept term β_0 and the slope coefficients $\beta_{1,\ldots,}\beta_k$). The correlation between each pair of explanatory variables is also computed in this step. As we will explain later in this chapter, this is done to test for possible interactions between the explanatory variables, which would violate the assumptions of the linear regression model. Using the parameters of the estimated model, a prediction of the value for the dependent value, given values for the explanatory variables, provides an estimate, which is referred to as a *point estimate*.

9.2.4 Diagnostic Check

Once the estimates for the parameters are obtained, the next step is to evaluate the quality of the regression with respect to the given data. This is the *diagnosis step*. Diagnosing the quality of a regression model is essential to the model building process. Thus, it is necessary to set forth criteria for determining model quality. If the fit is determined to be insufficient, the regression model must be redesigned, including potentially using different explanatory variables.

As explained in our previous discussion of the simple linear regression, the goodness-of-fit measure is the coefficient of determination (denoted as R^2). That measure is also used for a multiple linear regression model, as given by equation (9.7). The interpretation of the coefficient of determination in the case of a multiple linear regression model is that it measures the percentage of variation in the dependent variable explained by *all* the explanatory variables used in the regression. The R^2 in this case is referred to as the *multiple coefficient of determination*.

9.2.5 Testing for Statistical Significance

Following the initial assessment in the diagnosis step, the estimated model must be verified by determining its statistical significance using some test statistics. This test assesses the model's overall significance and the statistical significance of the regression coefficient of the individual explanatory variables and, if necessary, a group of explanatory variables. A final aspect is testing for the interaction of the independent variables, as explained later in this chapter.

To test whether the regression model is significant, a null hypothesis (H_0) is tested, which states that all regression coefficients are equal to zero. If the null hypothesis were true, this would mean that none of the explanatory variables plays any role in explaining the dependent variable. The alternative hypothesis (H_1) states that at least one coefficient of the explanatory variables is different from zero. Mathematically,

$$H_0: \beta_0 = \beta_1 = \ldots = \beta_k = 0$$

$$H_1: \beta_j \neq 0 \text{ for at least one } j,\ j = 1, 2, \ldots, k$$

To test the null hypothesis, a test statistic called the "F-statistic" is used. The F-statistic is usually provided with standard linear regression output from any statistical software.

If the F-statistic is found statistically significant at some predetermined significance level (this can be done by checking whether its p-value is small), the regression model as a whole does explain some variation of the dependent variable y, and the null hypothesis is rejected. Suppose it is not found to be statistically significant. In that case, the regression does not explain a meaningful amount of the variation of the dependent variable, and therefore the null hypothesis is not rejected.

The *principle of parsimony* is important for building multiple linear regression models, and the simplest suitable model should be used. Complicated models with unnecessarily many explanatory variables tend to be inflexible and costly in terms of data collection, and they often fail to work well on new data. In most cases, they are poor models for forecasting purposes. The highest R^2 is not necessarily an indicator of the most useful model because one can artificially increase the R^2 by introducing additional explanatory variables into the regression model. As new explanatory variables are added, the R^2 never goes down; however, the resulting higher R^2 may be misleading. To address this, a modified version of the coefficient of determination is used to evaluate the goodness of fit and compare the performance of models with different numbers of explanatory variables. It is called the *adjusted R-squared* (or adjusted R^2) and is computed as follows:

$$R^2_{adj} = 1 - (1 - R^2)\left(\frac{n-1}{n-k-1}\right) \tag{9.10}$$

As can be seen from equation (9.10), the adjusted R^2 takes into consideration the number of explanatory variables (k) plus the constant term in the denominator ($n-k-1$). As long as the number of observations is very large compared to k, R^2 and R^2_{adj} are approximately the same. However, in contrast to R^2, R^2_{adj} does not always increase when the number k of explanatory variables included in the regression increases—it increases only if the gain in R^2 from having more explanatory variables is high enough.

Basically, the adjusted R^2 penalizes excessive use of explanatory variables, encouraging the adoption of a model that is as parsimonious as possible. In building a model, one must balance the cost of adding explanatory variables to the model and the increase in R^2.

If the null hypothesis is rejected (i.e., the alternative hypothesis is accepted), the next test is to determine which explanatory variables contribute to explaining the variation in the dependent variable. Mathematically, the null hypothesis and alternative hypothesis for each of the k explanatory variables are expressed as follows:

$$H_0: \beta_J = 0 \qquad H_1: \beta_j \neq 0$$

conditional on the other explanatory variables already included in the regression model. The appropriate test is the Student t-test (or simply t-test) which is provided in by any software package with statistical capabilities, including Microsoft Excel. Low p-values (part of standard linear regression output obtained from statistical software) generally indicate statistical significance of the corresponding coefficients. It should be noted, however, that p-values are affected by interactions between the explanatory variables, as well as more generally by whether the residual assumptions are satisfied, so one needs to conduct careful diagnostic tests (described in more detail later in this chapter) to determine whether one can use the p-value estimates to conclude the significance of individual explanatory variables.

As explained in the next chapter, the data used to estimate or "train" the model in the parlance of ML are called the *training data.* In ML, the estimated model is then tested on data not seen while building the model. These data are referred to as the *testing data.* In the next chapter, we discuss how model performance can be evaluated using testing data for ML applications.

9.3 Determining the Number of Explanatory Variables

As noted in the previous section, it is not apparent how many and which explanatory variables to use. Simply adding more explanatory variables does not always improve the quality of the estimated regression model. There is a theorem in statistics known as *Pyrrho's lemma,* which relates to the number of explanatory variables.[1] According to this theorem, adding one particular explanatory variable to a linear regression model could arbitrarily change both the size and the sign of the regression coefficients. Consequently, without a proper design and testing methodology, simply adding explanatory variables risks producing spurious results. In building financial models in finance to forecast prices, rates of return, and interest rates, for example, Pyrrho's lemma has important implications. Because of the availability of high-performance computing applications, complex regressions that produce good results in-sample (on the data on which they were fitted) but have no real forecasting power on data that they have not seen can be easily obtained by trial-and-error.

The *stepwise regression method* is a commonly used method for determining the suitable explanatory variables to be included in a final regression model. There are three

1. See Dijkstra (1995).

types of stepwise regression methods: (1) stepwise inclusion, (2) stepwise exclusion, and (3) standard stepwise regression.

9.3.1 Stepwise Inclusion

Stepwise inclusion (also called *forward selection*) begins by selecting the explanatory variable that is most highly correlated (positive or negative) with the dependent variable.[2] Suppose that this is explanatory variable x_1. After estimating the regression using x_1 as the explanatory variable, an F-test is used to determine whether the regression model for x_1 is statistically significant. If the regression model for x_1 is not statistically significant, then no explanatory variable from the set of possible explanatory variables will be found to be statistically significant in explaining the variation in the dependent variable. Consequently, a different set of explanatory variables must be identified.

If, instead, the regression model for x_1 is significant, that explanatory variable is retained for the regression, and the next explanatory variable that best explains the remaining variation in the dependent variable is used in the regression. This additional explanatory variable (say, x_2) is the one with the highest *coefficient of partial determination.* This is a measure of the goodness of fit, given that x_1 is already included in the regression. It is defined to be the ratio of the remaining variation explained by the second explanatory variable to the total of unexplained variation before x_2 was included. This is equivalent to requiring that the additional explanatory variable be the one that provides the largest coefficient of determination once included in the regression. After the inclusion, an F-test is conducted to determine the statistical significance of x_2. The addition of explanatory variables included in some set of candidate explanatory variables is continued until either all explanatory variables are in the regression or the additional contribution to explain the remaining variation in the dependent variable is not statistically significant anymore.

9.3.2 Stepwise Exclusion

Stepwise exclusion (also called *backward elimination*) is basically the opposite of stepwise inclusion. That is, one begins by including all explanatory variables in the regression. One by one, the explanatory variables that are found to be statistically insignificant variables are eliminated until all insignificant explanatory variables have been excluded from the regression, resulting in the final regression model. An F-test for the coefficient of partial determination is used to determine which explanatory variables are insignificant and therefore eliminated. The elimination process is terminated if no explanatory variable with an insignificant F-test statistic is determined to be statistically significant.

9.3.3 Standard Stepwise Regression

With *standard stepwise regression*, explanatory variables are introduced based on their significance and explanatory power and explanatory variables that have been included at previous steps are considered for elimination from the model. The reason for eliminating previously included explanatory variables is that they may have now become insignificant

2. Sometimes other criteria such as the Akaike information criterion (AIC), explained later in this chapter, are used instead of correlation to select important explanatory variables.

after the new explanatory variables have been introduced into the regression model. Therefore, at each stage of the process the statistical significance of the regression coefficients of all explanatory variables is checked using a *t-test.*

We note that all three stepwise regression methods are greedy algorithms; that is, they are myopic in that they select the best action (variable to include or exclude) for the present without knowing whether this is the best action considering all possible combinations of variables at future stages of the process, and thus they are not guaranteed to find the best subset of explanatory variables overall.

9.4 Diagnostic Tests of Violation of the Error Term

In applying the linear regression model, two assumptions about the error terms are that their variance is constant for any level of any of the explanatory variables and the error terms are uncorrelated.

9.4.1 Constancy of the Variance of the Error Term

When the variance of the error term is constant for all levels of each explanatory variable, the error terms are said to be *homoscedastic.* If this assumption is violated, the error terms are said to be *heteroscedastic.* Several tests have been used to detect the presence of heteroscedasticity.[3] If heteroscedasticity is detected, two methodologies can be used for dealing with it: weighted least squares estimation and autoregressive conditional heteroscedastic (ARCH) models. A discussion of these models is beyond the scope of this chapter.

9.4.2 Absence of Correlation of the Error Terms

The second assumption about the error terms is that they are uncorrelated across subsequent observations. When they are correlated, it is said that the error terms are *autocorrelated* or *serially correlated.* From a model estimation perspective, correlation of the error terms is critical, as will be explained later. Autocorrelation is quite common in financial data because financial data are often *time series* data, or observations collected over time.

Like any correlation, autocorrelation can range from -1 to 1. A positive autocorrelation means that if the computed error term in period t is positive (negative), then the computed error term that follows in period $t+1$ tends to be positive (negative). *Positive autocorrelation* is said to exhibit "persistence." A *negative autocorrelation* means that a positive (negative) error term in period t tends to be followed by a negative (positive) error term in period $t+1$.

The presence of significant autocorrelation in time series data means that in a probabilistic sense, the series is predictable because future values are correlated with current and past values. From an estimation perspective, autocorrelation complicates the testing of the statistical significance of the regression coefficients because variances (which are used for testing

3. These tests include the White generalized heteroscedasticity test, the Park test, the Glejser test, the Goldfeld-Quandt test, and the Breusch-Pagan-Godfrey test (Lagrangian multiplier test).

the statistical significance of the regression coefficients) may be significantly underestimated and the resulting statistical test is therefore questionable.

Two commonly used tests for autocorrelation of residuals are the Durbin-Watson test and the Dickey-Fuller test. Statistical software provides the results of these tests. In the case of the Durbin-Watson test, the statistic that is reported is typically denoted by d. If the computed value for d is close to 2, this means that there is no autocorrelation. If the computed value is around 4, this means that there is negative autocorrelation; if it is near zero, there is positive autocorrelation.

There are models for dealing with the autocorrelation problem in time series data. These models are called *autoregressive moving average* (ARMA) *models*.

9.5 Selecting the Regression Model

Model selection relies on goodness-of-fit tests to evaluate the performance of a regression model in terms of how well it explains the variation in the dependent variable. Suppose that one wants to select the best model from among several candidate regression models. There are criteria – drawn from the field of information theory that can be applied for doing so that involve minimizing the loss of information. The two most used criteria are the *Akaike information criterion* (AIC) and the *Bayesian information criterion* (BIC).

In practice, the AIC is usually considered the first model selection criterion that should be employed. It is not important to present the formula for AIC since most statistical software calculates an AIC score, but it is important to understand that the calculation involves the number of explanatory variables used in the model and how well the model explains the data in out-of-sample prediction (i.e., on data that the model has not seen). An AIC score is computed for each regression model from among the ones that can be selected. The model that has the best fit is the one that explains the greatest percentage of the variation in the dependent variable with the smallest number of explanatory variables. Using the AIC, it is the model with the lowest AIC score. However, because the AIC score is a relative measure of the quality of a model, it could be that all the candidate regression models are poor models. In other words, the best model based on the AIC score is not necessarily good.

Similar to the AIC, the BIC is based on information theory. The difference between the BIC and the AIC is that the BIC imposes a greater penalty on the number of explanatory variables than does the AIC. As with the AIC, the best model is the one with the lowest BIC score from among the candidate models.

9.6 Use of Categorical Variables as Explanatory Variables

As explained in chapter 8, categorical variables are variables that represent group membership. For example, given a sample of stocks that are classified as either a value stock or group stock, the type of stock is a categorical variable that indicates what category each stock belongs to. Estimating a regression on categorical variables does not make sense per se. For example, it does not make sense to multiply a regression coefficient by "value" or "growth." Nor does it make sense to multiply a regression coefficient by "investment grade" and "noninvestment grade." However, in many cases, the standard regression analysis tools can be applied to categorical variables after appropriate transformations. Let's first discuss the case when categorical variables are the explanatory variables. In section 9.8, we describe four classification regression models where categorical variables are the dependent variables.

Categorical input variables are used to cluster input data into different groups. We cannot, per se, mix quantitative input variables and categorical variables. However, we can perform a transformation that allows the mixing of categorical and quantitative variables. To illustrate how, suppose that there is only one categorical explanatory variable, which we denote as D, one quantitative explanatory variable X, and one quantitative dependent variable Y. Consider our set of quantitative data, which includes quantitative observations. We organize data in a matrix form as usual:

$$Y = \begin{bmatrix} Y_1 \\ \vdots \\ Y_T \end{bmatrix}, X = \begin{bmatrix} 1 & X_{11} \\ \vdots & \vdots \\ 1 & X_{T1} \end{bmatrix}, E = \begin{bmatrix} \varepsilon_1 \\ \vdots \\ \varepsilon_T \end{bmatrix}, B = \begin{bmatrix} \beta_0 \\ \beta_1 \end{bmatrix}$$

Suppose that the data in D belong to two categories. An explanatory variable that distinguishes only two categories is called a *binary*, *dummy*, or *dichotomous* variable. The key is to represent a dichotomous categorical variable as a numerical variable D, called a *dummy variable*, which can assume only one of two values: 0 or 1. We can now add variable D to the explanatory variables to represent membership in one or the other group:

$$X = \begin{bmatrix} D_1 & 1 & X_{11} \\ D_T & 1 & X_{T1} \end{bmatrix}$$

If $D_i = 0$, the data X_i belong to the first category; if $D_i = 1$, the data X_i belong to the second category.

Consider now the regression equation

$$Y_i = \beta_0 + \beta_1 X_i + \varepsilon_i$$

where the subscript i is a time period or an index within a cross-section of assets, such as stocks or bond issues.

Three separate regression equations can be written, one for those data that correspond to $D = 1$, one for those data that correspond to $D = 0$, and one for the fully pooled data. Suppose now that the three equations differ by the intercept term but have the same slope. Let's explicitly write the two equations for those data that correspond to $D = 1$ and for those data that correspond to $D = 0$:

$$y_i = \begin{cases} \beta_{00} + \beta_1 X_{i1} + \varepsilon_1, & \text{if } D_i = 0 \\ \beta_{01} + \beta_1 X_{i1} + \varepsilon_1, & \text{if } D_i = 1 \end{cases}$$

where i defines the observations that belong to the first category when the binary variable D assumes value 0, and also defines the observations that belong to the second category when the dummy variable D assumes value 1. If the two categories are value stock and growth stock, the first equation might hold in periods of expansion and the second in periods of recession. If the two categories are investment-grade bonds and noninvestment-grade corporate bonds, the two equations apply to different cross sections of bonds.

Observe now that, under the assumption that only the intercept term differs in the two equations, the two equations can be combined into a single equation in the following way:

$$Y_i = \beta_{00} + \gamma D(i) + \beta_1 X_i + \varepsilon_i$$

where $\gamma = \beta_{01} - \beta_{00}$ represents the difference of the intercept or the two categories. In this way, we have defined a single regression equation with two independent quantitative variables, X and D, which can be estimated using OLS. By estimating the regression coefficients of this regression, a common slope and two intercepts are obtained. Note that the same results would be obtained if the categories were reversed.

So far, no interaction between the categorical and quantitative variables is assumed. That is, the slope of the regression is the same for the two categories. This means that the effect of the categorical variable is added regardless of the value taken by the quantitative explanatory variable. This can be an unrealistic assumption in some situations. Consider the regression equation $Y_i = \beta_0 + \beta_1 X_i + \varepsilon_i$ and write two regression equations for the two categories as we did before, but now $\beta_{10,}\ \beta_{11}$ are different slopes:

$$y_i = \begin{cases} \beta_0 + \beta_{10} X_{i1} + \varepsilon_1, & \text{if } D_i = 0 \\ \beta_0 + \beta_{11} X_{i1} + \varepsilon_1, & \text{if } D_i = 1 \end{cases}$$

We can combine these two equations into a single equation as follows:

$$Y_i = \beta_0 + \beta_{10} X_i + \delta(D_i X_i) + \varepsilon_i$$

where $\delta = \beta_{11} - \beta_{10}$. In fact, this equation is identical to the first equation for $D_i = 0$ and to the second for $D_i = 1$.

We can write the following regression adding two variables, the dummy D and the interaction DX:

$$Y_i = \beta_0 + \gamma\, D_i + \beta_1 X_i + \delta(D_i X_i) + \varepsilon_i$$

This regression equation, which now includes three explanatory variables, combines both effects.

This process of introducing dummy variables can be generalized to regressions with multiple explanatory variables. In our discussion, however, we have considered only two categories, allowing the use of the numerical variable 0 or 1 to identify the two categories. Fortunately, the process can be extended to multiple categories by adding multiple dummy variables. An explanatory variable that distinguishes among more than two categories is called a *polytomous variable.*

Let's discuss the case of three categories, A, B, and C. Consider a dummy variable D_1 that assumes a value of 1 if the observation belongs to category A and zero if not. A second dummy variable, D_2, can be added that assumes the value of 1 if the observation belongs to category B and zero otherwise. The three categories are now completely identified: category A is identified by the values 1,0 of the two dummy variables D_1 and D_2, category B by the values 0 and 1, and category C by the values 0 and 0. This process can be extended to any number of categories. If there are K categories, we need $K-1$ dummy variables.

As explained earlier, hypothesis testing for the statistical significance of the regression coefficients for individual explanatory variables is based on the t-test. The t-statistic applied to the regression coefficients of dummy variables offers a set of important tests to judge which regressors are significant. As mentioned earlier in this chapter, a high p-value (generally greater than 0.05) associated with a particular regression coefficient estimate indicates that the corresponding variable's coefficient in the regression is too close to 0 for the variable to be relevant. A low p-value (generally, less than 0.05) is an indication that the corresponding variable is significant.

We can also use the F-test to check the significance of the dummy variables. This is done by estimating the regression with and without the set of dummy variables and performing the corresponding F-test. The *Chow test*[4] is the F-test used to gauge if all the dummy variables are collectively statistically significant.

9.7 Multicollinearity and the Selection of Explanatory Variables

In selecting the explanatory variables to include in building a regression model, there is an important issue regarding the interaction of the explanatory variables. This issue is referred to as the *multicollinearity problem*. Multicollinearity occurs in a multiple regression model when the explanatory variables in the model are highly correlated with each other, which means that they contain common information. As a result, it is difficult to interpret the coefficients in the model in terms of the contribution of each individual independent variable to explain the variation in the dependent variable because they make the same contribution. Sometimes multicollinearity can lead to counterintuitive regression coefficients. Moreover, it creates an overfitting problem. Here, we describe how to test for the problem of multicollinearity after the model's significance has been assessed and all statistically significant explanatory variables to be used in the final regression have been determined.

Intuition can be used in assessing if the regression coefficients of the explanatory variables make sense. For example, select each explanatory variable one by one. Estimate a regression model only with this particular explanatory variable and check if the regression coefficient of this variable in the original regression model seems unreasonable should its sign be counterintuitive, or its value appear too small or too large. In such cases, consideration should be given to removing that explanatory variable from the larger regression model. The inconsistency may very well be the result of multicollinearity.

In the very extreme case where two or more explanatory variables are perfectly correlated (i.e., their pairwise correlations are equal to plus or minus 1), some vectors of observations of these variables are merely linear combinations of others. The result of this would be that some of the explanatory variables are fully explained by others and consequently provide no additional information. The case of perfectly correlated explanatory

4. See Chow (1960).

variables is very extreme. Yet, although in most problems in finance the data for the explanatory variable vectors are not perfectly correlated, they may be correlated to a high degree. In any case, the result is that, roughly, the regression estimation procedure is confused by this ambiguity of data so the distinct regression coefficients for the explanatory variables involved cannot be trusted when building a regression model.

9.7.1 Indications of Multicollinearity

There are indications that can be investigated to identify if multicollinearity might be present. First, check if there appears to be a mismatch between the sign (positive or negative) of the correlation coefficient in the large regression model and the sign of the regression coefficient of that particular explanatory variable in the simple regression model. Second, check the sensitivity of the regression coefficients of the explanatory variables in the regression model when additional explanatory variables are included. If the regression coefficients are highly sensitive, this may indicate the presence of multicollinearity. Third, check the p-values for the regression coefficients to see whether any of the regression coefficients of the explanatory variables in the regression model change from being statistically significant to statistically insignificant after new explanatory variables have been added. Finally, one can check what happens to the *standard error of the regression*. This measure indicates how far the observations tend to fall on average from the estimated values for the dependent variable (i.e., how accurate the estimate is). In the presence of multicollinearity, the standard error of the regression may increase as explanatory variables are added.

9.7.2 Remedy for the Multicollinearity Problem

A remedy that is most often suggested for the multicollinearity problem is to try to identify the explanatory variables that are likely to be causing the problem. This can be done by excluding from the regression model the identified explanatory variables.

Generally, as a result of the multicollinearity problem, the computed t-test of many explanatory variables may be too small to indicate statistical significance despite the fact that the regression model is highly statistically significant. That is because the standard error of the regression increases and that measure is used in the denominator of the t-test, resulting in a lower computed t-value. This will result in rejecting the hypothesis that the regression coefficient for an explanatory is statistically different from zero.

A commonly employed tool to analyze whether the standard error of the regression measure is too large is by computing the impact of the correlation between some explanatory variables and the jth explanatory variable. In particular, $k-1$ variables are used as explanatory variables in a linear model with the remaining (jth) explanatory variable treated as a dependent variable. The R^2 of this regression is computed and is used to divide the original variance of the jth regression coefficient estimate by a correction term called the *variance inflation factor* (VIF), which is calculated as follows:

$$\text{VIF} = \frac{1}{1 - R_j^2}$$

If the variation in the jth explanatory variable is not explained by the remaining explanatory variables (i.e., R^2 in the previous formula is 0), the t-test results will be unchanged. However, if the variation in the jth explanatory variable is mostly explained by the remaining explanatory variables, the calculated t-statistic will most likely decline, resulting in the rejection of the jth explanatory variable as statistically significant for the larger regression model.

As a rule of thumb, a benchmark for the VIF that is typically used in practice is 10. When the VIF exceeds 10, the indication is that there is a severe impact due to multicollinearity, and it would be wise to remove that explanatory variable.

9.8 Probabilistic Classification Regression Models

In the regression models described thus far, the dependent variable is quantitative. The explanatory variables can be either quantitative or qualitative. There are regression models where the dependent variable is binary or nominal. These models are known as *probabilistic classification regression models.* We describe four of them here: the linear probability model, the probit model, the logistic model, and the discriminant model. Other models for classification are described in the next chapter. Probabilistic classification regression models are primarily used in bankruptcy prediction and in credit analysis, as explained in chapter 15.

9.8.1 Linear Probability Model

Equation (9.8) shows the multiple linear regression market. When the dependent variable y in the equation is binary, then the regression model is called a *linear probability model.* More specifically, when y is a binary variable, then the linear probability model can be expressed as

$$P(y=1|x_1, x_2, \ldots, x_k)=\beta_0+\beta_1 x_1+\beta_2 x_2+\cdots+\beta_k x_k$$

This equation says that the probability that $y=1$ is conditional on the values for the explanatory variables. Exhibit 9.2 provides a plot of the linear probability model.

A β value in the linear probability model can be interpreted as follows: it is the change in the probability that the dependent variable is 1 when an explanatory variable increases by 1 unit, assuming all other explanatory variables are held constant. Although the coefficient of the linear probability model can be estimated using OLS and the statistical significance

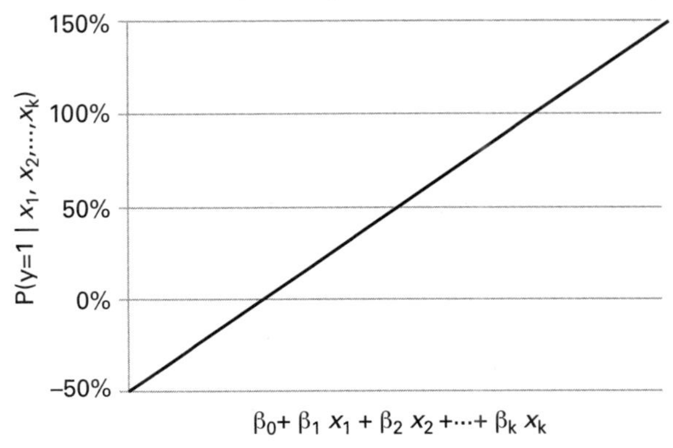

Exhibit 9.2
Linear probability model.

of each β can be tested, the goodness-of-fit coefficient (R^2) is meaningless, given that the dependent variable is binary.

There are three problems with the linear probability model. The first is that the predicted value for y may fall outside the range of 0 and 1, which is the range expected for a probability. That is, the predicted value for y can be nonsensical. The models described next deal with this flaw of linear probability models by using a nonlinear function to model the conditional probability. More specifically, these models take a linear model and feed it into a mathematical function that is nonlinear, such that a linear regression estimation can be used but the predicted value for y is always between 0 and 1. Second, in a linear probability model, the assumption that the error term is normally distributed is violated. This is because the error term when the dependent variable is binary will follow a binomial distribution. As a result, the standard statistical tests for testing for the significance of the coefficients will not be valid. Finally, the error term in a linear probability model will not be constant. That is, the error term will be heteroscedastic, depending on the value of the explanatory variable.

9.8.2 Logistic Regression

Logistic regression (also called *logit regression*) overcomes the flaw with the linear probability model that nonsensical values for the dependent variable y may be predicted. In logistic regression, a linear combination of the explanatory variables is transformed into an output that is always between 0 and 1. This is done by using a *link function*.[5] The link function upon which the logistic regression is based is the *logistic function* (also called the *logistic curve* or *sigmoid curve*), given by

$$y = \frac{L}{1 + e^{-k(x - x_0)}}. \tag{9.11}$$

where e = the Euler constant, approximately equal to 2.71828, L = maximum curve value, k = steepness of the curve, and $x_0 = x$ value of the sigmoid's midpoint value.

Since equation (9.11) is used to obtain a probability, the maximum value is 1, so L is set equal to 1. Letting $x_0 = 0$ and $k = 1$, we obtain the logistic function used in logistic regression models:

$$y = \frac{1}{1 + e^{-x}} \tag{9.12}$$

where the predicted value for y can take any real value between 0 and 1.

Exhibit 9.3 shows the S-shape of the logistic curve.

The basic question that the logistic regression seeks to answer is how likely it is that an observation belongs to a category. The logistic regression equation looks just like the multivariate linear regression model given by equation (9.8):

$$\log\left(\frac{p}{1-p}\right) = \beta_0 + \beta_1 x_1 + \beta_2 x_2 + \cdots + \beta_n x_k \tag{9.13}$$

5. In an OLS regression and in the linear probability model, the link function is called the *identity link function* because no transformation is required to obtain the parameters of the linear regression model to the normal distribution.

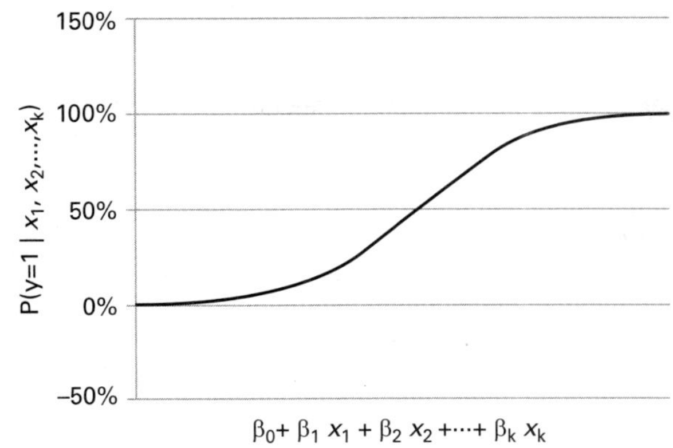

Exhibit 9.3
Logistic function.

However, the left side is the logarithm of the *odds* of y occurring, where the odds are the ratio of the event $y=1$ occurring and $y=1$ not occurring; that is, $\left(\frac{p}{1-p}\right)$. An alternative way to represent the relationship is through equation (9.14):

$$P(y=1|x_1, x_2,\ldots, x_k)=\frac{1}{1+e^{-(\beta_0+\beta_1x_1+\beta_2x_2+\cdots+\beta_kx_k)}} \tag{9.14}$$

For example, suppose that $y=1$ is the event that an observation—a particular corporate bond with features $x_1, x_2, \ldots, x_k$—is an investment-grade bond; and $y=0$ is the event that the corporate bond is a noninvestment-grade bond. Suppose that $P(y=1|x_1, x_2, \ldots, x_k)$, calculated from equation (9.14), is 80%. This result can be interpreted as "the bond is more likely to be investment grade than noninvestment grade," and the information may be sufficient. However, suppose instead that the objective is to classify the observation as either an investment-grade or noninvestment-grade corporate bond. Then, the probability calculated from equation (9.14) would be used to classify the observation as being in one of those two categories, given a particular cutoff value specified by the decision maker. In this scenario, 50% could be considered the standard cutoff value, with estimated probabilities larger than 50% considered indicative of the observation belonging to the class $y=1$. In this example, 80% > 50%, so the bond would be categorized in the class $y=1$ (i.e., as investment grade). It is worth pointing out, however, that there could be drawbacks to using the standard 50% cutoff for classification based on the prediction from the logistic regression model.

Suppose that the logistic regression model is used to determine whether a substantial corporate loan should be made. The event $y=1$ corresponds to a highly creditworthy borrower, whereas the event $y=0$ corresponds to a weak credit borrower. In such a situation, the lender is unlikely to find a probability that the borrower is creditworthy of 51% sufficient to extend the loan. A more appropriate cutoff value would be higher and would take into consideration both the costs and benefits of misclassification using the particular cutoff. Consequently, the appropriate value for the cutoff depends on the problem at hand.[6]

When there are more than two categories, the logistic regression can still be used. In such cases, the model is referred to as a *multinomial logistic regression*.

9.8.3 Probit Regression

Like logistic regression, *probit regression* seeks to answer how likely it is that an observation belongs to a particular category or group. As with the logistic regression, the goal in a probit regression is to predict the outcome of a categorical dependent variable by modeling a nonlinear function of a linear combination of the explanatory variables. In logistic regression, the link function is the logit function. In probit regression, the link function is based on the inverse standard normal distribution, and the value for the prediction is again guaranteed to be between 0 and 1 because it is interpreted as a cumulative probability.[7]

The inverse standard normal distribution is in fact not a probability distribution. It is the *z*-score corresponding to a particular cumulative probability value (i.e., the value of the random variable on the horizontal axis for a known standard normal cumulative probability).[8] That is, when using the standard normal distribution and given the value of the random variable, the cumulative probability, or the probability of getting a value for the random variable less than or equal to that value, can be found by determining the area under the curve. In the case of an inverse standard normal distribution, one is given the area under the standard normal curve, and one wants to calculate the value for the random variable. The NORM.INV function in Excel can compute this value for a given mean and standard deviation, and the NORM.S.INV function calculates it directly for the standard normal distribution. For example, suppose that one is interested in the value of a variable that gives a cumulative probability of 80% in a standard normal distribution. The inverse standard normal distribution value is 0.8416.

Statistical software packages can calculate the prediction based on the probit link function, and the results are used similarly to how the results from logistic regression are used. When there are more than two categories for the dependent variable, a *multinomial probit model* is used.

9.8.4 Linear Discriminant Analysis

Linear discriminant analysis is a statistical classification technique used to distinguish between or among groups or categories and to identify the characteristics of objects responsible for the objects' inclusion in one or another group. Linear discriminant analysis permits a simultaneous consideration of a large number of characteristics and does not restrict the investigator to a sequential evaluation of each individual attribute. For example, linear

6. See Provost and Fawcett (2013) for a discussion of costs and benefits in determining cutoff values. A detailed illustrative example is developed in Kopcso and Pachamanova (2017).

7. Recall from chapters 3 and 5 that the standard normal distribution has a mean of zero and a standard deviation of 1 and the cumulative probability distribution calculates the probability up to a value. The maximum value for cumulative probability is 1.

8. See also the discussion on the inverse transform in simulation in chapter 5.

discriminant analysis permits a credit analyst studying ratings of corporate bonds to examine simultaneously the total and joint impact on ratings of multiple financial ratios, financial measures, and qualitative factors. Thus, the analyst is freed from the cumbersome and possibly misleading task of looking at each characteristic in isolation from the others. Linear discriminant analysis seeks to form groups that are internally as similar as possible while maximizing the differences among the groups. Logistic and probit regressions estimate the likelihood that an observation belongs to a category or group. In contrast, linear discriminant analysis addresses which category or group is the most likely one an observation belongs to. The difficulty with using linear discriminant analysis is that there are serious assumptions about the data. Specifically, it is assumed that the data are sampled from a multivariate normal distribution, the variance/covariance matrices for the explanatory variables are the same across all categories, and the means for the explanatory variables for each category are uncorrelated with the variances. If the data fail to satisfy these assumptions, logistic regression is preferable because it has less stringent assumptions about the data.

Summary

- Regression is a fundamental statistical tool employed to model the dependence of a variable (called the dependent variable, response variable, or target variable) on one (or more) explanatory variables (also referred to as independent variables, explanatory variables, predictors, or regressors).
- The basic linear regression model is referred to as an ordinary least squares (OLS) regression model because of the methodology used to calculate its parameters .
- In a simple linear regression model, there is only one explanatory variable.
- A regression model includes a residual (error) term incorporating unforeseen information or shocks.
- There are two assumptions about the residual term in linear regression: (1) it is independent of the explanatory variables and (2) it is assumed to have a mean of zero with a constant variance.
- The method of OLS is used for estimating the parameters (intercept and slope coefficients) of the regression model.
- The coefficient of determination (denoted by R^2) is a goodness-of-fit measure used to assess how good the estimated relationship in the linear regression model is. This measure indicates the percentage of the variation in the dependent variable that is explained by the explanatory variables. If the R^2 is small, the fit might not be reliable.
- In real-world applications of regression analysis to finance, a simple linear regression that has only one explanatory variable in typically insufficient. When there is more than one explanatory variable, a multiple linear regression model is used.
- The building process to design a regression model consists of five steps: (1) model specification, (2) data gathering, (3) estimating the model, (4) diagnosis check, and (5) testing for statistical significance.
- The stepwise regression method is commonly used for determining the suitable explanatory variables to be included in a final regression model. There are three methods of

stepwise regression: the stepwise inclusion method, the stepwise exclusion method, and the standard stepwise regression method.

- When the variance of the error term is constant for all levels of each explanatory variable, the error terms are said to be *homoscedastic*. If this assumption is violated, the error terms are said to be *heteroscedastic*. There are several tests that can be used to detect the presence of heteroscedasticity.
- Another assumption about the error terms is that they are uncorrelated across subsequent observations. When they are correlated, it is said that the error terms are autocorrelated or serially correlated. Positive autocorrelation is said to exhibit persistence, while a negative autocorrelation means that a positive (negative) computed error term in period t tends to be followed by a negative (positive) computed error term in period $t+1$.
- In selecting from among several candidate regression models, two commonly used criteria are the Akaike information criterion (AIC) and the Bayesian information criterion (BIC).
- Categorical variables, variables that represent group membership, can be included in a multiple linear regression by transformation into dichotomous (dummy) variables.
- Multicollinearity occurs in a multiple regression model when the explanatory variables in the model are highly correlated with each other, which means that they contain common information. As a result, it is difficult to interpret the coefficients in the model in terms of the contribution of each individual independent variable to explaining the variation in the dependent variable.
- Regression models where the dependent variable is binary or nominal are referred to as probabilistic classification regression models, and they include linear probability models, logistic model, probit models, and discriminant models.
- In a linear probability model, the dependent variable is binary.
- Three problems with the linear probability model are that (1) the predicted value for y may fall outside the range of 0 and 1, which is the range expected for a probability; (2) the assumption that the error term is normally distributed is violated; and (3) the error term will not be constant.
- Logistic regression (also called logit regression) overcomes the flaw with the linear probability model that nonsensical values for y may occur by using a link function (the logistic or sigmoid curve).
- As with logistic regression, probit regression seeks to answer how likely it is that an observation belongs to a particular category or group and the goal is to predict the outcome of a categorical dependent variable by transforming a linear combination of the explanatory variables through a link function. The link function is based on the inverse standard normal distribution.
- As with logistic regression, probit regression seeks to answer how likely it is that an observation belongs to a particular category or group and the goal is to predict the outcome of a categorical dependent variable by transforming a linear combination of

the explanatory variables through a link function. The link function is based on the inverse standard normal distribution.

- Linear discriminant analysis is a statistical classification technique that is used to distinguish between or among groups or categories and to identify the characteristics of objects responsible for their inclusion in one or another group. Although linear discriminant analysis permits a simultaneous consideration of a large number of characteristics and does not restrict the investigator to a sequential evaluation of each individual attribute, it has limitations in that it makes serious assumptions about the data.

10

Machine Learning

Machine learning (ML) is the science of developing algorithms and statistical models to analyze and draw inferences from patterns in data, which computer systems can use to perform complex tasks. ML is a subfield (i.e., a set of tools) of artificial intelligence (AI) that enables computer systems to mimic human cognitive processes. Natural language processing (NLP), which sometimes draws on tools from ML, is another subfield of AI, and it will be covered in chapter 11. Because ML is a modeling framework that does not depend on any specific financial theory, when applied to problems in finance, it is a purely statistical analysis of financial phenomena. In this chapter, we provide an introductory, nontechnical treatment of ML methods. Later chapters explain how ML is applied to various activities in portfolio management.

10.1 ML Terminology

Although ML utilizes many algorithms with roots in statistics, such as linear regression and logistic regression, it has its own terminology, which we describe next. In the field of statistics, the term *statistical learning* is referred to in ML terminology as *classical machine learning.* When a model is estimated, the term *fitting a model* is used in statistics, whereas the equivalent term in ML is to *learn a model.* Similarly, in statistics, when a model is estimated, the objective is to determine the value of the *model parameters*. The term *model weights* is used in ML.

Statistical models often involve hypothesis testing (described in chapter 4), and the performance of the model is assessed by evaluating whether the hypothesis about the population is supported or refuted by statistical testing using data or experimentation. When performing hypothesis testing, *observations* or *data points* are used in statistics. In ML, the terms *examples* and *instances* are used instead, and the focus is less on statistical testing than on creating models that perform well on data that they have not seen before.

In statistics, the term *sample* refers to the available set of observations or data points, and it is the sample that is used to perform statistical analysis in hypothesis testing. Classical inferential statistics focuses on generalizing insights from analysis of the sample to the population. When models are fitted in statistics, their performance on the dataset on which they were fitted is referred to as *in-sample* performance, and their performance on data not used for fitting the model is referred to as *out-of-sample* performance. The terms corresponding to *in-sample* and *out-of-sample* in ML are *training set* and *test set.* The model weights used in ML are learned from the training set. The algorithm's performance is assessed using the test set, which contains data that have not been seen by the model (i.e., that have not been used to train the model).

The terminology used in the context of linear regression also differs between statistics and ML. As explained in chapter 9, in statistics, the terms *dependent variable* and *explanatory variables* (or *independent variables*, *predictors*, and *regressors*) are commonly used. In ML, by contrast, the dependent variable is often called the *response*, *output*, or *target*, while the independent variables are referred to as *attributes*, *features*, or *inputs*.

An important concept in ML discussed in this chapter is *overfitting*. It is possible to train an ML model on data so exceptionally well that it fails to perform well on the test data. This outcome is referred to as *overfitting* because the ML model learns the unique pattern and noise (i.e., randomness or irrelevant information) in the training data, causing it not to be able to generalize to the test data or, more generally, fail to perform well on new data. Overfitting can be a direct result of the *curse of dimensionality*—when too many features are used in the model—but it can also be related to characteristics of the specific ML methods used. We will describe such examples later in this chapter. In contrast, if the model is not complex enough, it will result in *underfitting*.

10.2 Categorizing ML Algorithms

There are several ways in which ML algorithms can be categorized. They include (1) task performed, (2) learning behavior, and (3) model parameterization.

10.2.1 Task Performed

Four common ML tasks are (1) regression, (2) classification, (3) clustering, and (4) dimensionality reduction.

10.2.1.1 Regression *Regression* (sometimes referred to as *prediction*) in ML refers to the task of predicting the value of a continuous, numeric variable; the term is often used to describe a model or address a problem that requires predicting. In an ML sense, the term *regression* is sometimes used interchangeably with *prediction* to describe this type of task rather than a particular algorithm. We discuss some specific regression models later in this section: the least absolute shrinkage and selection operator (LASSO), ridge regression, and elastic net regression.

10.2.1.2 Classification In ML, *classification* refers to the task of assigning a category or a class to an observation (i.e., predicting a categorical variable). As explained in the previous chapter, prediction can be used for classification by specifying a cutoff value (e.g., logistic regression) that predicts a numerical value (the probability of an observation belonging to a class) that can be used as a classification method if the predicted numeric value is assigned to a category based on its magnitude relative to the cutoff value. Other ML algorithms, such as classification trees, deep learning, support vector machines (SVMs), and naive Bayes, focus directly on the classification task.

10.2.1.3 Clustering The task of clustering involves identifying natural groupings of observations for a dataset. *K*-means and hierarchical clustering are commonly used algorithms for this task.

10.2.1.4 Dimensionality Reduction *Dimensionality* refers to the number of input variables or features contained in the dataset. In the previous chapter, we discussed the curse of dimensionality, when the number of input variables is large relative to the number of observations. Some of the input variables may be irrelevant for prediction purposes, or redundant in that the information that they contain is provided by other input variables in the dataset or a combination of other variables. The ML task of reducing the number of input variables in the dataset by identifying input variables that are irrelevant or contain the same information as a combination of other input variables is referred to as *dimensionality reduction*.

The ML task of dimensionality reduction can be further categorized based on feature selection and feature extraction. *Feature selection* involves determining the subset of the input variables in the dataset to retain for the analysis. In contrast, *feature extraction* involves creating a new set of input variables from the dataset, which is a combination of the input variables in the dataset. The resulting dataset is a smaller set of input variables containing information that is most useful for predicting.

Stepwise regression is one ML technique for feature selection, as described in chapter 9. Techniques for dealing with multicollinearity (also described in chapter 9) are another method for dealing with feature selection. Finally, search algorithms called *genetic algorithms* are also commonly used for feature selection. ML algorithms used for feature extraction include linear discriminant analysis, principal component analysis (PCA), autoencoders, and certain types of linear regularization models, such as LASSO and Elastic Net.

10.2.2 Learning Behavior

How does a machine (i.e., a computer) learn? Consider the process of how someone learns any activity. The individual may fail many times to perform the activity before becoming proficient. Similarly, a machine will go through many iterations before discovering the optimal solution to a problem. The machine will continue to learn through trial-and-error, with the objective of identifying the best model for a particular problem.

In the field of education, there are five main theories of learning: (1) cognitive, (2) behaviorism, (3) constructivism, (4) humanism, and (5) connectivism. Similarly, in the field of ML, there are different types of statistical learning processes, the four main ones being (1) unsupervised, (2) supervised, (3) semisupervised, and (4) reinforcement.

The information used by the ML algorithm during the training period differentiates each of the four learning processes. More specifically, the key is the feedback provided to the algorithm during the training phase. Consequently, each learning process produces answers to different types of questions and can be used for different applications in finance.

Next, we describe each of these learning styles.

10.2.2.1 Supervised Learning Algorithms The learning behavior style that allows the ML algorithm to learn from training data that is labeled for each input is supervised learning. Using labeled data, the computer will identify patterns that link the input variables (i.e., features) to the output variable (response variable). The term *supervised learning* describes this type of learning because the algorithm is "guided" in discovering patterns. Since the dataset contains the answers to the question under consideration, the algorithm can search for patterns in the features so as to distinguish between categories or values for the output variable (which are known/labeled in the training data).

Supervised learning algorithms are used for the first two types of ML tasks: regression and classification (section 10.2.1). Linear regression, which was described in chapter 9, is one type of supervised learning algorithm, which predicts the expected value of the output from the values of the features. The output is a numerical variable and the labeled output data are continuous values. In classification, the "label," or value of the output variable for each training example, will belong to a category or group. The algorithm then learns to identify patterns and associate features with rules to differentiate between categories or groups for the output variable. As explained earlier, a *regression* supervised learning algorithm can be used for the purposes of classification if cutoffs, or thresholds, are specified in advance, such that the continuous labels (values predicted by the algorithm) can be converted to categories based on their magnitude relative to the cutoff.

There are supervised learning models that combine several ML algorithms into one predictive model with the objective of (1) decreasing the variance of an estimate, (2) reducing the bias, or (3) improving the predictive power. These methods are called *ensemble methods*, the most common of which are bootstrap aggregation and boosting. *Bootstrap aggregation* decreases the variance of an estimate by averaging multiple estimates. *Boosting* is a method to reduce bias. To understand boosting, it is necessary to understand the concept of a "weak learner" and a "strong learner." Weak learners (also referred to as *base learners*) are models that produce predictions that are just slightly better than guessing. Strong learners, in contrast, are good or near-optimal models, as measured by their predictive ability. The objective of boosting is to convert weak learners to strong learners. In other words, boosting seeks to create a stronger classifier algorithm from several weak classifier algorithms. A commonly used boosting algorithm is AdaBoost (Freund and Schapire 1997).

The most popular supervised learning algorithms used in finance are

- Linear regression
- *k*-nearest neighbors (kNN)
- Naive Bayes classifier
- Support vector machines (SVMs)
- Linear regularization models
- Neural networks (NNs)
- Decision trees
- Random forest

In the previous chapter, we described regression. The last algorithm is an ensemble method. Next, we briefly describe the other methods.

K-nearest neighbors (kNN) A supervised learning algorithm that is used for both regression and classification is kNN. The key idea is that the value or class of an observation is determined by the observations around it (i.e., its nearest neighbors). The number of neighbors (k) is specified in advance. To find the kNN for a given observation, a distance metric must be used. The two most common distance metrics are Euclidean distance and Manhattan distance.

Given input features for a new observation whose value or class is to be determined, one measures the distance between that observation and all the observations in the training set. Once all distances have been calculated, the kNN are identified as the observations (from the training set) with k minimum distances from the new observation.

The predicted value or class for the new observation is then based on the values or labels of those nearest k-neighbors. When used in classification, the predicted category or group will be the label that appears most frequently among those k-neighbors. For example, if $k=5$ (i.e., if five nearest neighbors are used), and their labels (categories) are "high," "medium," "medium," "low," and "medium," the predicted class for the new observation will be "medium" (the prevalent class among the five nearest neighbors, which is the class of three out of the five neighbors). In a regression problem with a numerical output value, the predicted value for the new observation will be the average of the labels (values) of the kNN. For example, if five nearest neighbors are used and their values are 10, 20, 15, 12, and 18, the predicted value for the new observation will be 15 (the average of the output labels of the five nearest neighbors).

In summary, two parameters that need to be specified for a kNN algorithm: the number of neighbors (k) and the distance metric used to identify the nearest neighbors. Because the specification of these parameters affects algorithm performance, the best values for these parameters can be identified through hyperparameter tuning and cross-validation (described in section 10.4). It is also worth noting that the features used for calculating the distance are prespecified (i.e., they are features the modeler has decided are important), rather than determined by the algorithm.

Naive Bayes classifier This supervised learning algorithm is used for classification tasks when there are two or more categories for the output variable. It works especially well with NLP, which we describe later in this chapter. The key assumption in applying this ML classification algorithm is that the features (predetermined by the modeler) are independent of each other. In the real word, it is highly unlikely that the features will be independent, and for this reason, this ML classification algorithm is referred to as *naive*.

The underlying theory in probability on which this ML classification algorithm is based is Bayes's theorem. To understand this important theorem, let's introduce some notation. We will denote as B the evidence prior to observing new information or observed data and suppose that a decision maker's belief can be expressed by the unconditional probability $P(B)$. What Bayes's theorem tells the decision maker is that after observing new information, denoted as A, the belief in B can be adjusted as follows, assuming that $P(A)$ is greater than zero:

$$P(B \mid A) = \frac{P(A \mid B)\, P(B)}{P(A)} \tag{10.1}$$

where the following are true:

- $P\,(B \mid A)$ = the revised probability of B given the new information or observed data; commonly referred to as the *posterior probability.*
- $P(B)$ = unconditional probability of B before observing the new information or observed data; commonly referred to as the *prior probability.*
- $P\,(A \mid B)$ = conditional probability of the new information or observed data, given that the prior evidence, B, is true; referred to as the *likelihood.*
- $P(A)$ = unconditional probability of the new information or observed data
- $P(A)$ is computed as follows: $P(A) = P(A \mid B)\, P(B) + P(A \mid B^c)\, P(B^c)$, where the superscript c denotes the complement (or complementary event) of B. That is, c is all possible outcomes that could occur if B is not realized.

The sum of $P(B)$ and $P(B^c)$ is equal to 1. Intuitively, $P(A)$ calculates the likelihood of the new evidence A happening as the sum of the probability of A happening when B is true and the probability of A happening when B is not true (i.e., when B^c happens); that is, across all the possible ways in which A could have happened. Bayes's theorem then calculates the relative chance that B is true as a ratio of instances of A happening among outcomes in which B happened over all the possible ways A could have happened.

Let's denote the features as X_i ($i = 1, 2, \ldots, n$), and let y_j be the jth target (output) class label (out of J possible labels). For a new observation, the naive Bayes classifier seeks to determine the posterior probability of the classification of that observation being in class j, given the values for the new observation's n features ($x_1, x_2, \ldots, x_n$), which are the new data or evidence A in the description of Bayes's theorem. This can be expressed as

$$P\,(y_j \mid X_1 = x_1, X_2 = x_2, \ldots, X_n = x_n) \tag{10.2}$$

The likelihood probability, which is the probability of a specific combination of the features given a label set j, can be expressed as

$$P\,(x_1, x_2, \ldots, x_n \mid y_j) \tag{10.3}$$

The probability of the particular values of the set of features for the new observation occurring is

$$P(x_1, x_2, \ldots, x_n) = \sum_{j=1}^{J} P(x_1, x_2, \ldots, x_n \mid y_j)\, P(y_j) \tag{10.4}$$

The probability of class j is equal to

$$P(y_j) = \frac{\text{Number of observations with class } y_j}{\text{Total number of observations}} \tag{10.5}$$

Substituting the probability given by equation (10.2) for $P\,(B \mid A)$ in equation (10.1), the probability given by equation (10.3) for $P\,(A \mid B)$ in the numerator in equation (10.1), $P\,(y_j)$ for $P(B)$ in the numerator in equation (10.1), and the probability given by equation (10.4) in the denominator in equation (10.1), we get

$$P(y_j|x_1, x_2, \ldots, x_n) = \frac{P(x_1, x_2, \ldots, x_n | y_j)\, P(y_j)}{\sum_{j=1}^{J} P(x_1, x_2, \ldots, x_n | y_j)\, P(y_j)} \tag{10.6}$$

Note that $P\,(x_1, x_2, \ldots, x_n \mid y_j)$ calculates the probability that the exact combination of values of the features for the new observation happens among the observations with label j in the training set. Similarly, calculating the value of the denominator in equation (10.6) requires counting the number of times that this exact combination of feature values happens within the observations for each label class j in the training data. This presents several problems. For example, when there is a large number of features, the chance that one will find one or more observations with the same combination of features in the training set as the new observation whose class one is trying to predict is virtually zero. Even if some such observations are found, this estimate of the probabilities has high volatility because it is based on a small number of training observations. This is the reason why the features are assumed to be independent. With the assumption of independence of the features, the joint conditional probability of all feature values occurring together in equation (10.3) can be written as a product of the individual features' conditional probabilities:

$$P\,(x_1, x_2, \ldots, x_n \mid y_j) = P\,(x_1 \mid y_j)\; P\,(x_2 \mid y_j) \ldots P\,(x_1 \mid y_j)$$

Calculating the probability of a feature's occurrence given class j is far easier. The expression multiplies the percentage of times that the value of each individual feature for the new observation happened in class j. Therefore, it requires far fewer observations.

After calculating the probability in equation (10.6), a determination is made about whether it is within a range of predefined cutoff values so as to decide whether the new observation should be classified as class j. We note that assuming independence of the features biases the exact value calculated for the probability in equation (10.6), and therefore this estimate is not used as an exact value, but only to determine the class of the new observation. We also note that assuming independence of features is more reasonable in some situations than others. Suppose that we seek to classify a stock as "value" or "growth" based on the growth of earnings over the past three years and the price-earnings ratio. Using the naive Bayes classifier for this task would assume that the growth of earnings is independent of the price-earnings ratio, which may not be reasonable.

Assumptions must be made about the probability distribution for the features. For example, when the features are binary (0 or 1), the Bernoulli distribution is used (see chapter 3). If a feature has more than two discrete classes, the multinomial distribution is used. The normal (Gaussian) distribution is used when there are continuous values for the features.

A naive Bayes classifier is often less accurate than other more sophisticated ML classification algorithms; however, it is very fast and computationally efficient. When there is a low correlation among the features, the naive Bayes classifier is competitive with other classifiers, such as logistic regression, while requiring less training data. Moreover, when categorical variables are used as inputs, the naive Bayes classifier performs better than when the features are numerical variables. A numerical difficulty with using this classifier is that there is a possibility that there are no observations for a particular class in the training set so in the testing phase, a probability of zero will be assigned to an observation that is in the test set. A simple fix is to ensure that all classes represented in the test set are also represented in the training set.

Support vector machines (SVMs) This algorithm is primarily used for classification but can be used for regression problems. The way that SVM differentiates classes is by constructing a *decision boundary,* which is used to classify the data into distinct categories. The process begins by plotting each data point in an *n*-dimensional space, where *n* is the number of features. For example, suppose that we want to classify a dataset that consists of two input features. Then, each data point can be plotted in a two-dimensional space, and a straight line would be used to draw a decision boundary. Exhibit 10.1 shows an example with two features (represented on the axes of the scatterplot) and two categories for the output, 1 (represented by dark gray for the observations/points) and 0 (represented by white for the observations/points). When there are three features, each data point is drawn on a three-dimensional space and a plane is used to draw a boundary. Going beyond three features, we cannot visualize the plotting of the data points. In this case, a hyperplane is used conceptually to create the decision boundary.

Once the decision boundary is obtained, an observation is classified depending on which side of the boundary it falls on. The SVM algorithm can be used for nonlinear classification as well by employing a technique known as a "kernel trick" to identify a boundary. The kernel trick involves taking a low-dimensional feature space and transforming it into a higher-dimensional feature space.

Linear regularization algorithms Most generally, *regularization* refers to guiding an algorithm toward solutions with desirable properties. In ML applications in finance, the term typically refers to including penalty terms in the loss function minimized to train the algorithm (e.g., the sum of squared errors used in OLS regression) to shrink the coefficients of the model features (or to retain only the most informative features). This is an important concept, as it helps with overfitting and feature selection. For this reason, regularization is particularly useful when working with a large set of features.

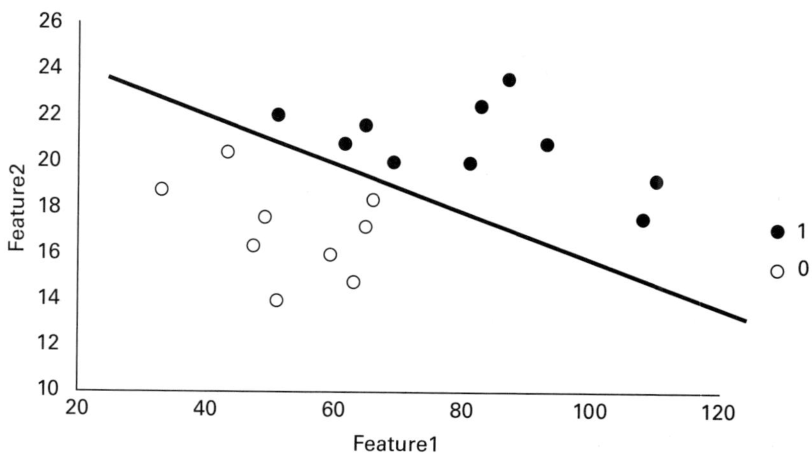

Exhibit 10.1
SVM example.

Commonly used regularization methods include L1-regularization, L2-regularization, and a combination of the two. In the case of OLS regression, the equation for L1-regularization is

$$\sum_{i=1}^{n}(y_i - \hat{y})^2 + \lambda \sum_{j=1}^{p} |\beta_j| \tag{10.7}$$

and for L2-regularization, it is

$$\sum_{i=1}^{n}(y_i - \hat{y})^2 + \lambda \sum_{j=1}^{p} \beta_j^2 \tag{10.8}$$

The key difference between the two loss functions is the penalty function (starting with the λ term). L2-regularization penalizes the squared magnitude of the coefficients, whereas L1-regularization penalizes the absolute value of the sum of coefficient values. The λ term determines the degree to which regularization (i.e., coefficient shrinkage) occurs. The value of the λ term can be determined through cross-validation and hyperparameter tuning.

The three most common regularization models are *least absolute shrinkage and selection operator (LASSO)* (Tibshirani 1996), *ridge regression*, and *Elastic Net* (Zou and Hastie 2005). Lasso regressions use L1-regularization to allow some coefficients to shrink to zero, which means that certain features will not influence model predictions; thus, Lasso provides some form of feature selection as well. Ridge regressions use L2-regularization and do not shrink coefficients to zero, but they will result in less important features having a smaller impact on predictions. Finally, Elastic Net is a combination of the Lasso and ridge regression models (i.e., uses both L1- and L2-regularization); thus, it simultaneously shrinks coefficients and eliminates uninformative features.

Neural networks (NNs) In general, NNs aim to replicate how the human brain learns. There are many types of NNs that are used in ML. NNs work by using an input layer (which contains the set of features), one or more hidden layers, and an output layer. Each of the layers has a set of nodes (like neurons in the brain) that connect to each of the nodes in the subsequent layer based on what is referred to as an *activation function*. Based on the accuracy of the model, which is determined by the loss function (typically mean-squared error for regression or cross-entropy for classification), the model will use gradient descent to adjust model parameters for better predictions. For regression problems, the output layer will consist of a single node with the numerical value of the prediction. This is also the case for binary classification problems except that the value of the output layer will either be 0 or 1. When three or more categories or groups are used for classification, the output layer will have the same number of nodes as the number of categories, with the predicted probability that the observation belongs to each of the categories.

Decision trees Decision trees can be used for both classification and regression. A decision tree is grown by iteratively partitioning the space spanned by the features of the observations in the training set into "boxes" that can be mapped to rules along the branches of the tree. At each stage, a decision is made about which feature to split on and whether to partition further (i.e., grow the tree) by measuring the reduction in impurity that happens after the split. There are different measures of impurity, such as the Gini Index and entropy (used for classification). The impurity measure represents how different the labels of the observations in the training data are that fall within a particular partition of the feature space. If left unchecked, the decision tree will grow (i.e., continue to split the training data features into partitions) until all partitions are as pure as possible, leading to overfitting. Therefore, in practice, checks need to be used to stop the tree from growing fully, or, alternatively, to prune the tree back after the algorithm is done.

Decision trees are useful for visualizing decisions that must be made and are viewed as one of the most interpretable ML algorithms because the decision rules are explicitly spelled out in the tree. The final node of the tree (the so-called leaf node) is the class (for classification tasks) or the average (for prediction tasks). The paths from the root of the tree to the leaf (leaf node) represent the rules for prediction.

A simple example of a decision tree is provided in exhibit 10.2(A). The output variable has two classes: 1 and 0. There are two features, Featurel and Feature2. A small training dataset of 24 observations (points) plotted in the plane spanned by the two features is shown in exhibit 10.2(B). Their colors are gray (for observations whose output value is 1) and white (for observations whose output value is 0). The partitions represented in the decision tree in exhibit 10.2(A) are also represented in the scatterplot in exhibit 10.2(B)—there are six rectangles ("boxes") in the feature space that correspond to the six leaf nodes of the decision tree. For example, the leftmost branch of the decision tree can be interpreted as the following rule: "Observations where the value of Featurel is less than 60 and the value of Feature 2 is less than 21 should be classified as 0 (the value in the leftmost leaf node of the decision tree)." This rule is based on the fact that there are seven observations with these characteristics in the training data, and they are the white (class = 0) points in the partition at the bottom-left corner of the scatterplot in exhibit 10.2(B). Because every observation in that partition is white (class = 0), future observations with the combinations of features that determine that partition will be classified as 0. The second-leftmost leaf of the decision tree corresponds to the following rule: "Observations where the value of Featurel is less than 60 and the value of Feature 2 is greater than or equal to 21 are classified as 1." There is one such observation, and it is the gray point in the partition at the top-left corner of the scatterplot in exhibit 10.2(B).

The decision tree in exhibit 10.2(B) illustrates potential overfitting. For example, there is a tiny partition defined by the rule for the fourth-leftmost (third-rightmost) leaf, where if Featurel is greater than or equal to 60, Feature2 is less than 20, Featurel is less than 85, and Featurel is less than 62, the predicted class should be 0. However, there is only a single gray observation (class 1) surrounded by white (class 0) observations, and it is not necessary to define a rule specifically for one point. It is likely this rule will not perform well on new data. Because the decision tree's goal is to minimize the impurity within every partition, when not stopped, it partitions the data in such a way that each partition is maximally pure (i.e., each partition contains only points of the same color (class)).

Decision trees are often overly sensitive to small changes in the data, and their predictions are volatile. However, they are very useful building blocks of ensemble algorithms where outcomes of multiple decision trees are combined, such as *random forests* and *gradient boosted decision trees (GBDTs)*. The latter family of ensemble methods employs boosting and includes methods such as GBM, XGBoost, Light GBM, and CatBoost.[9] Random forests are explained in more detail next.

9. See Swalin (2018).

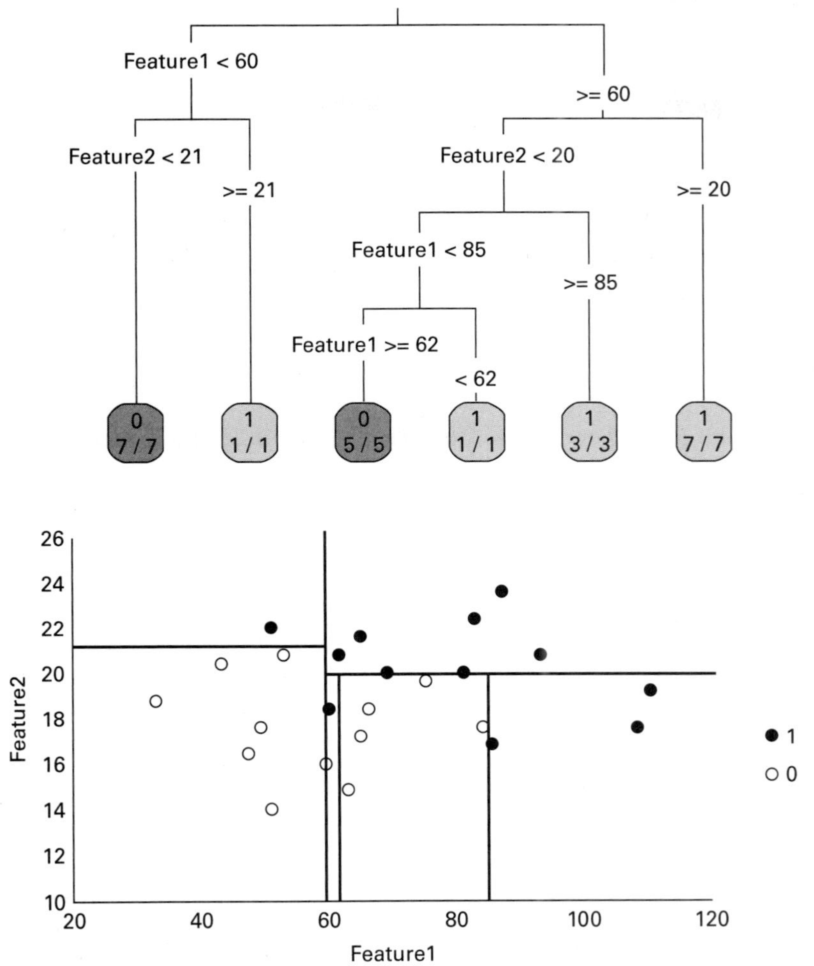

Exhibit 10.2
An example of a decision tree (A) and corresponding partitions in the feature space (B).

Random forests First suggested by Ho (1995), random forest is an ensemble method used for both prediction and classification. Random forests average multiple decision trees, trained on different parts of the same training set, to reduce the variance characteristic of decision tree predictions. They also utilize, at every step, a random selection of features rather than the entire set of features. When the method is used for prediction, the mean values of the output from the many decision trees are used as the predicted value. When used for classification, the majority class from the output from the decision trees is used as the predicted label.

An important aspect of building effective random forests is to create uncorrelated decision trees since using similar decision trees will not provide any significant information compared to using a single decision tree. Using bootstrapping (i.e., sampling from the training data) and feature randomness (i.e., selecting a random subset of features at each step) help achieve this objective.

Random forests are typically much more accurate than single decision trees, although not necessarily more accurate than boosting methods. They are not as interpretable as single decision trees, but they provide a natural way to summarize the importance of different features and are implemented as packages in a number of modeling languages, making them widely used in practice.

10.2.2.2 Unsupervised Learning In contrast to supervised learning, *unsupervised learning algorithms* do not require training data to have labels that correspond to the input features. The objective of unsupervised learning algorithms is to identify the structure of the data based solely on the statistical properties of the unlabeled data. For example, using a set of training data that is unlabeled, the objective of an unsupervised learning algorithm could be to learn how to group data that exhibit similar statistical characteristics. Unsupervised learning algorithms can be applied to datasets that have both labeled and unlabeled data and are often utilized for exploratory analysis to identify hidden patterns that can be generalized to the group. For example, unsupervised learning could be used in pricing illiquid bonds by identifying other bonds with similar characteristics for which the price is known. This is explained further in chapter 15.

Two commonly used unsupervised learning algorithms in finance are PCA and clustering analysis, discussed next.

Principal component analysis (PCA) This unsupervised learning algorithm is used to represent data parsimoniously. It starts with a response output variable that the modeler seeks to explain and a large number of features that are believed to explain the output variable. PCA involves transforming the large number of features into a smaller number of uncorrelated features called *principal components (PCs)*, which are a linear combination of the feature set. Once the PCs are identified, the challenge is to provide an economic interpretation for each one.

Clustering analysis This unsupervised learning algorithm is used to segment data points into specific clusters or groups so members of the same cluster have similar properties (or features), while at the same time, members of different clusters have very dissimilar properties (or features). Methods used for clustering analysis include hierarchical clustering, *k*-means clustering, mean-shifting clustering, density-based spatial clustering, and expectation–maximization clustering using Gaussian mixture models. The two methods most commonly used in finance are hierarchical clustering and *k*-means clustering and we briefly describe each next.

The objective of *hierarchical clustering* is to construct a hierarchy of clusters. Agglomerative hierarchical clustering and divisive hierarchical clustering are two techniques that are typically used, with the former being the more commonly used method in finance. *Agglomerative hierarchical clustering* begins by treating each data point as an individual cluster. With each iteration, clusters that are most similar or close according to a prespecified distance metric are combined. The method stops when all points have been joined into a single cluster, or when a desired number of clusters is reached. The agglomerative hierarchical clustering method is therefore referred to as the "bottom-up" approach to hierarchical clustering. The iterative process of cluster mergers is summarized in a tree diagram visualization called a *dendrogram,* which can be used by a modeler to determine an appropriate stopping point for the algorithm (see exhibit 10.3). *Divisive hierarchical clustering* starts

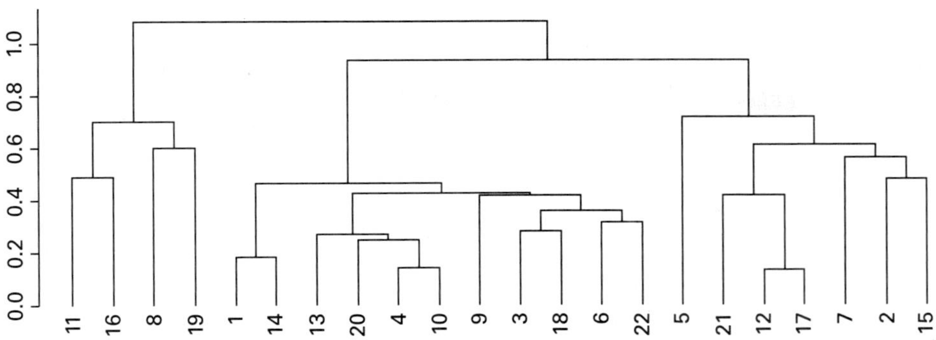

Exhibit 10.3

Example of a dendrogram obtained through agglomerative hierarchical clustering of 22 observations.
Notes: Observations 12 and 17 have the shortest distance between them and are brought together into a cluster first. Next, observations 4 and 10 are combined into a cluster, and then 1 and 14. Next, observation 20 joins the cluster of observations 4 and 10, and so on, in order of increasing height of the lines connecting the clusters in the dendrogram. The top of the dendrogram is where all observations have been merged into a single cluster, but the process can be stopped earlier. For instance, if two clusters are desired, then observations 11, 16, 8, and 19 will be placed in the first cluster, and the remaining observations will be placed in the second cluster.

with all data points assigned to one cluster and then, at each iteration, a cluster is split to create smaller clusters. The divisive hierarchical clustering method is therefore referred to as the "top-down" approach to hierarchical clustering.

The *k-means clustering analysis* requires that the user prespecify the number of clusters (*k*) to identify. The process then randomly initializes their respective center points (referred to as *centroids*). The distance (using some unit of measure) between each data point and each centroid is calculated for each data point in the dataset. The data point then gets assigned or reassigned to the group with the closest centroid. The centroids for the newly formed groups (clusters) are calculated, and the distances between each point and the new centroids are calculated again so that each data point can again be reassigned to the group (cluster) with the closest centroid. The algorithm stops when every data point's current assignment is to the cluster with the closest centroid, where no data points can be reassigned to shrink the distances between each data point and the centroids. Although *k*-means can involve multiple iterations, the method has lower storage requirements and is more computationally efficient for large datasets than hierarchical clustering methods.

10.2.2.3 Semisupervised Learning Algorithms The goal of *semisupervised learning algorithms* is to evaluate how combining labeled and unlabeled data may alter the learning behavior and then to produce algorithms that benefit from using both data types. The appeal of semisupervised learning is that it can utilize unlabeled data to improve supervised learning algorithms either when there are limited labeled data available or when it is too costly to obtain additional labeled data. Another potential advantage of semisupervised learning algorithms is that they can start with unlabeled and labeled data but eventually predict labels for new unlabeled data.

10.2.2.4 Reinforcement Learning *Reinforcement learning (RL)* differs from the other forms of ML discussed in this chapter, which learn patterns from provided labeled or unlabeled data. Although there is a field within RL called *off-policy learning* that learns from a given set of data, the learning process for RL algorithms is most generally interactive. Given a state of the world, the RL algorithm's objective is to identify the optimal action a learning agent should take based on current data and learn from new data collected after the action has been taken. Since subsequent states of the world depend on the actions previously taken by the agent, RL algorithms are structured to explore different states of the world to gain new information for model updates.

Utilizing a commonly employed metaphor, the learning behavior of a reinforcement learning algorithm can be likened to the relationship between a pet and its owner. In this analogy, the pet serves as the agent, interacting with its environment, while the owner assumes the role of providing rewards as feedback, akin to guiding the pet's behavior. Just as a pet explores its surroundings without prior knowledge, the agent freely interacts with its environment. Positive actions are rewarded, whereas suboptimal actions result in negative reinforcement. Over time, through repeated interactions, the agent learns to optimize its behavior, much like a pet learning to navigate an unfamiliar world under the guidance of its owner.

Consequently, RL is characterized by the set of actions that the algorithm can take, the environment (which sets the rules of the game), the learning agent (which interacts with the environment), and the state (which is the current position or landscape). The goal of the algorithm is to choose the actions that maximize the cumulative reward, which is an user-defined function that determines how well the algorithm is performing. Based on the action taken in each state, the algorithm's agent is provided feedback via the reward function in order to update the model to make the best decisions moving forward.

RL algorithms are much more difficult to implement than standard supervised and unsupervised algorithms due to the fact that there is not a single label applied to the dataset. Instead, RL attempts to link the state of the world to optimal actions that help to maximize some reward. RL and dynamic programming (DP), which was discussed in chapter 7, have some overlapping concepts and methodologies. Most generally, however, DP methods assume that the environment is known. RL is associated with not only solving for the optimal strategy or values (like DP), but also simultaneously learning the environment (transition structure) and reward structure, often through experimentation.

10.2.3 Parametric versus Nonparametric ML

The mapping of the input variables to the output variables in ML is done using a function called the *learning function*. Different assumptions are made about the form of the learning function and how learning takes place.

A *parametric ML algorithm* is an algorithm that summarizes data with a set of parameters where the number of parameters does not change, no matter how large the dataset.[10] A parametric ML algorithm begins by specifying the form of the learning function and then estimating the model's parameters. For example, in OLS regression, described in chapter 9, the learning function is described in equation (9.8). The OLS method is then used to estimate the parameters (i.e., coefficients) of the learning function based on the training data. When the learning function is linear, the parametric ML algorithm is called a *linear ML algorithm*.

10. Russell and Norvig (2016, p. 737).

The advantage of a parametric ML algorithm is that the results are easy to interpret, and estimation is generally easier. A disadvantage is the threat that the model is constrained by the learning function assumed (i.e., there is in fact a nonlinear relationship between input features and labels). Examples of parametric ML algorithms include three algorithms described in the previous chapter (OLS regression, logistic regression, and linear discriminant analysis) and simple NNs as described earlier.

In contrast to parametric ML algorithms, nonparametric ML algorithms do not make any strong assumptions about the learning function, allowing any functional form to be identified from the training data. Nonparametric ML algorithms are employed when there is a large dataset but no prior knowledge of what the learning function should be. The advantages of nonparametric ML algorithms are that they allow a large number of learning functions to be estimated and can result in a predictive model that has superior performance relative to parametric ML algorithms. Examples of nonparametric ML algorithms are kNN and decision trees.

10.3 Hyperparameter Tuning

In creating an ML model, parameters that control the behavior of the learning process must be specified. A parameter whose value is selected prior to the beginning of the learning process is referred to as a *hyperparameter.* The process of determining the optimal set of hyperparameters is referred to as *hyperparameter tuning.* Because hyperparameter tuning can involve an optimization process, it is also referred to as *hyperparameter optimization.* The maximum effectiveness of an ML model will depend on the set of hyperparameters used. There are several methods for hyperparameter tuning. In selecting the best set of hyperparameters, it is necessary to assess the trade-off between the performance (i.e., improvement in accuracy of an ML model) and the computational time.

It is important to note that the hyperparameters are not model parameters (i.e., weights or coefficients determined by fitting the model). The model builder sets hyperparameters before the training begins. A simple way of thinking about the difference between model parameters and hyperparameters is that if in formulating an ML model, a parameter must be manually provided, it is a hyperparameter; otherwise, it is a model parameter. In practice, these are the set of choices that one can make before fitting the model.

For example, as mentioned earlier in this chapter, kNN requires specification of the number of neighbors k (i.e., k is a hyperparameter). Hyperparameters in the case of a decision-tree ML algorithm could be the minimum number of observations needed to allow the algorithm to split (partition) further, or the amount of reduction in impurity after a split that would be considered too small to split further, so the decision tree does not grow so much that it overfits the data, as it did in the example in exhibit 10.2. These are not outputs of the decision-tree model, but rather inputs that the modeler specifies before running a decision-tree model.

The typical process for determining the best set of hyperparameters is to create a training set, validation set, and test set. The model builder selects different combinations of hyperparameters and fits the model on the training set for each set of hyperparameters. Instead of directly forecasting on the test set, the model builder looks at the set of hyperparameters that performed best on the out-of-sample validation set. Based on the set of hyperparameters selected, the model builder then fits the model again (with the selected hyperparameters) on both the training and validation sets together. That fitted model is then used for forecasting on the test set.

10.3.1 Search Methods for Hyperparameter Tuning

Three popular hyperparameter tuning methods are the grid search method, random search method, and Bayesian optimization method. With the *grid search method*, every possible combination of values for each hyperparameter is used to identify the best set of hyperparameters. This method is probably the most used for hyperparameter tuning in practice. The *grid space* contains all possible combinations of the hyperparameters and as it pertains to hyperparameter tuning, it is referred to as the *hyperparameter space*. Based on a number of criteria, the grid search method selects the best set for the hyperparameters from the hyperparameter space. Of course, the size of the hyperparameter space depends on the number of combinations that must be examined and can be quite large. This method is referred to as an *exhaustive sampling method* since it considers all combinations of the hyperparameters. Consequently, in terms of computational time, it is more expensive than the two other search methods described next.

In contrast to the grid search method, the *random search method* does not compare every possible combination of hyperparameter values from the hyperparameter space. Instead, it randomly selects the sample of the set of hyperparameters analyzed. To do this, a sampling distribution must be provided for every hyperparameter. For example, it can be assumed that the values for the hyperparameter follow a normal distribution. Then, in each iteration, a value for every hyperparameter is randomly selected based on the probability distribution.

Since random search evaluates fewer hyperparameter values in the hyperparameter space, it requires less computational time than the grid search method. The drawback of random search is that, unlike grid search, it does not guarantee that the best set of hyperparameters will be selected. However, Bergstra and Bengio (2012) show empirically and theoretically that there are cases where the random search method performs just as well as the grid search method, but only requires a fraction of the computation time as grid search. One reason, according to Bergstra and Bengio (2012, p. 281), is that "for most datasets only a few of the hyper-parameters really matter, but that different hyper-parameters are important on different datasets. This phenomenon makes grid search a poor choice for configuring algorithms for new datasets." In practice, the computational cost of grid search may restrict the set of hyperparameters the model builder decides to test, limiting the scope of the search, whereas starting with a random grid search can allow the model builder to test a wider range of hyperparameters, possibly resulting in a superior model.

As more iterations are used to determine the optimal hyperparameters, data about the hyperparameter values from previous iterations provide information in the search process in the next iteration. This information about the hyperparameter values in the prior iteration can be used to limit searching for some of the hyperparameters that may be less important. Both the grid search method and random search method ignore prior information. *Bayesian optimization* for searching the hyperparameter tuning is a constrained global optimization method based on inferences from Bayes's theorem that uses information from prior iterations in subsequent iterations so as to improve the sampling method for the next iteration. After a model with a particular set of hyperparameters is constructed, it is evaluated in the first iteration using some performance metric. (We will describe performance metrics in section 10.3.2.) The hyperparameter values are then used to estimate a posterior expectation of the hyperparameter space. The next hyperparameter values are then based on the optimal hyperparameter values based on the posterior expectation. The process continues using the results from previous iterations to identify the next hyperparameters in an informed way until there is convergence to the optimal hyperparameter values. This process can identify better hyperparameters, while reducing computational time at the same time.

10.3.2 Performance Metrics and Model Evaluation

In selecting the best set of hyperparameters, a performance metric must be used. The choice of the performance metric will depend on the algorithm and the task that algorithm is trying to perform. In particular, performance metrics will depend on whether the task is regression- or classification-based. In this section, we will discuss various performance metrics, as well as other evaluation metrics that can aid in model selection.

A performance metric provides a score of the model's fit to the data, which allows one to select among different models. The loss function used for fitting an ML model can also be considered a performance metric.

10.3.2.1 Regression Metrics There are five main performance metrics that are used when evaluating regression models. These metrics may be familiar as these are also used in standard ordinary least squares (OLS) regressions or other common financial regression models. We note, however, that sometimes they are used differently on the training and the test data.

The five metrics are R-squared, adjusted R-squared, mean squared error (MSE), root mean squared error (RMSE), and mean absolute error (MAE). The first two (R-squared and adjusted-R-squared) are regression performance metrics. They measure the fit of the model compared to a constant baseline—the average of the true labels. R-squared (also known as the *coefficient of determination*) and adjusted R-squared were discussed more rigorously in chapter 9. R-squared values will range between 0 and 1, where higher values indicate a stronger fit. A slightly modified version of R-squared, referred to as *out-of-sample R-squared*, is used when evaluating the fit of the model on the test data. While R-squared is between 0 and 1 in sample, out-of-sample R-squared values can become negative.

Adjusted R-squared performs a similar function to that of standard R-squared, but it penalizes the number of features used. This is mostly used for standard OLS regression because as the number of features used increases, the in-sample R-squared will increase but may not result in a superior model because of overfitting. For this reason, adjusted R-squared penalizes for the number of features used (k) relative to the number of total observations (n). Adjusted R-squared is typically used when comparing regression models in sample because overfitting becomes more apparent when a validation or test set is used.

The three-performance metrics MSE, RMSE, and MAE are used to measure fit for both training and test data. These three metrics measure the difference between the model's prediction ($\hat{y}$) and the true values (y). Thus, lower scores for these values are desired, as they indicate a stronger fit. The equations for these three metrics are as follows:

$$MSE = \frac{1}{n}\sum(y - \hat{y})^2 \tag{10.9}$$

$$RMSE = \sqrt{\frac{1}{n}\sum(y - \hat{y})^2} \tag{10.10}$$

$$MAE = \frac{1}{n}\sum|y - \hat{y}| \tag{10.11}$$

MSE is most used because it is differentiable and can thus be optimized better, for example, in fitting an NN. RMSE is the square root of MSE and is preferred when large errors may exist since the differences in the prediction are large relative to the true values.

MAE is the average of the absolute values of the differences between the predicted and the true values. MAE does not penalize errors as much as MSE since all errors are weighted equally (i.e., not squared). Thus, MAE is less desirable when there are extreme errors or outliers.

10.3.2.2 Classification Metrics *Classification metrics* are straightforward to calculate and interpret; however, they need to be used with care, as they can be misleading. Consider the most common classification performance metric, *total accuracy* (also referred to simply as *accuracy*), which is the percentage of correctly labeled predictions. If an ML algorithm correctly classifies 90 observations out of 100 observations in a test dataset, the total accuracy of the algorithm would be 90%, which sounds like high accuracy.

Suppose now that 90 observations in the test data belong to class 1 and 10 observations belong to class 0. A naive algorithm that simply classifies all 100 observations as class 1 would have identified 90 observations correctly and would have an accuracy of 90% as well. However, the naive model would have no ability to differentiate between observations of class 1 and class 0. Thus, even though an accuracy score of 90% may seem high at first, a closer investigation of the predictions would show that this is a poor model.

For this reason, other classification performance metrics are used in addition to accuracy for a more nuanced view of model performance. One of the most used tools for evaluating a classification model's performance is the *confusion matrix* shown in exhibit 10.4, which can be calculated from the training data (to determine model performance in sample) or from the test data (to determine model performance out of sample). The confusion matrix gives a breakdown of model predictions versus true data labels.

Exhibit 10.4 shows the confusion matrix for a binary classification model (i.e., when only two classes are predicted). The value in the upper-left quadrant of the confusion matrix represents true positives (TPs)—that is, the number of observations that the model labeled as class 1 and whose true value was class 1. The upper-right quadrant shows the number of false positives (FPs) where the model predicts a class label of 1 but the true

		True values	
		Positive (1)	Negative (0)
Predicted values	Positive (1)	True Positive (TP)	False Positive (FP)
	Negative (0)	False Negative (FN)	True Negative (TN)

Exhibit 10.4
Confusion matrix.

label is actually 0. The sum of the TP and FP quadrants corresponds to the number of observations for which the model predicts a class label of 1.

The lower-left quadrant shows the number of false negatives (FNs), which is the number of times that the model predicts a class label of 0, but the true class label is 1. The lower-right quadrant shows the number of true negatives (TNs), which is the number of class 0 observations that the model correctly classifies as being in class 0.

While the confusion matrix itself does not provide a single performance metric that can be used for model evaluation and hyperparameter tuning, the values in the confusion matrix are used to construct metrics that better evaluate the performance of the classification model. We discuss four performance metrics commonly used for ML classification models.

Precision determines the proportion of labels that are predicted as "positive" (i.e., a label of 1) that actually are positive. For example, if we are trying to predict bond defaults with defaults corresponding to a class label of 1, we would look at the proportion of bonds correctly labeled as default versus the total number of bonds predicted to default by the model. That is, we look at the fraction of TP divided by the total number of predicted positives (i.e., TP + FP). The equation for precision is

$$Precision = \frac{TP}{TP + FP} \tag{10.12}$$

Recall (also referred to as *sensitivity*) is a classification metric that calculates the proportion of observations that are actually positive (class 1) in the data versus the number of observations that are correctly classified as positive (class 1) by the model. This helps evaluate the percentage of the actual positives in the data that the algorithm discovered. Going back to the previous example, this would be the proportion of bonds that were correctly classified to default divided by the number of bonds that actually defaulted. The equation for recall is

$$Recall = \frac{TP}{TP + FN} \tag{10.13}$$

Specificity measures the proportion of observations that the model correctly classified as negative (class 0) out of the total number of observations that were negative. The equation for specificity is

$$Specificity = \frac{TN}{TN + FP} \tag{10.14}$$

In the bond example, the specificity would be the number of bonds that the model classified as not defaulting by the model divided by the number of bonds that actually did not default.

The naive model from the example at the beginning of this section that classified all 100 observations as class 1 has a recall or sensitivity of 100% (because it identified all observations labeled class 1 in the dataset) and a precision of 90% (because 90 out of the 100 observations that it identified as class 1 were indeed class 1), but its specificity is 0% (because it identified 0 out of the 10 class 0 observations in the data).

It is useful to have a single performance metric that encompasses several of these measures so that it can be used to compare models. The $F1$ *score* is calculated as follows:

$$F1\ Score = \frac{2 \times Precision \times Recall}{Precision + Recall} \tag{10.15}$$

The $F1$ score is the "harmonic mean" of the precision and recall scores. Using the harmonic mean ensures that a poor score for either of the two metrics (precision or recall) will result in a poor $F1$ score, which is desirable. The traditional arithmetic mean might be biased by a high score on one of the metrics and appear high even if the other metric is close to 0.

10.4 Cross-Validation

As mentioned before, once an ML algorithm has been constructed ("trained") on the training data, it must be validated. *Validation* begins by looking at how well the algorithm performs on the training data. A *prediction error* is calculated for each observation in the training data, where the prediction error is the difference between the prediction the algorithm provides (i.e., the output) and the observed value. This difference is also referred to as the *residual error* or the *training error.* Then standard statistical techniques such as goodness-of-fit tests are used to evaluate performance. The process for doing so is referred to as *validation.*

Although validation is a starting point for assessing a model, it is not a good gauge of how effective the model's predictions will be on data not seen by the model during the training process. The process of evaluating the performance of the model on unseen data (i.e., the testing data which has the training data removed) is referred to as *cross-validation, out-of-sample testing,* or *rotation estimation.* The cross-validation method selected will depend on the size of the dataset, the number of features (i.e., the dimensionality of the data), and whether the use of ML is for classification or regression.

10.4.1 Cross-Validation Methods

When we discuss cross-validation methods, we are referring to methods for splitting the dataset into training and test sets. We list several commonly used such method next. We note that in addition to validating model performance, cross-validation is useful for hyperparameter tuning.

Holdout method The most straightforward method for validating a model is to split the dataset into two samples: a training and a test set. Each model under consideration, as well as the hyperparameters, are fit on the training set, and the performance is computed on the test set. The model that results in the best score in terms of a prespecified performance metric (e.g., highest accuracy or lowest MSE) is then selected as the best model. Since the testing data are observations that were held out during the training process, this method is referred to as the *holdout method.* The problem with using this method for cross-validation is that there is sampling bias, and the performance may be unstable because it depends on which observations from the dataset are included in the training and test sets. Moreover, removing a portion of the dataset to train the algorithm results in a loss of information. It is desirable to retain as much of the data as possible for model estimation to reduce the risk that information about patterns or relationship is lost.

k-fold cross-validation This method is typically used to overcome the issue of sampling bias that results from the holdout method. It starts with partitioning the dataset into k subsets ("folds"). From these k folds, k pairs of training and test sets are constructed using each fold as a test set with remaining folds as the training data. Exhibit 10.5 shows the training and test sets for five-fold cross-validation. Each model under consideration and the hyperparameters are estimated from the five training sets, and an average prediction error is calculated across the five folds. The model that results in the best average score across the five folds is then selected.

As the number of folds increases, the issue of sampling bias is reduced. In the extreme case where the number of folds is equal to the number of training observations, this method is referred to as *Leave One Out Cross-Validation (LOOCV)* because the test set is then a single observation from the dataset. While LOOCV can help to estimate better values for the hyperparameters due to less sampling bias, this comes at the cost of computation speed, and can be infeasible on large datasets.

Stratified k-fold cross-validation When using ML for classification purposes, there are situations where one category of the output variable may dominate a large portion of the

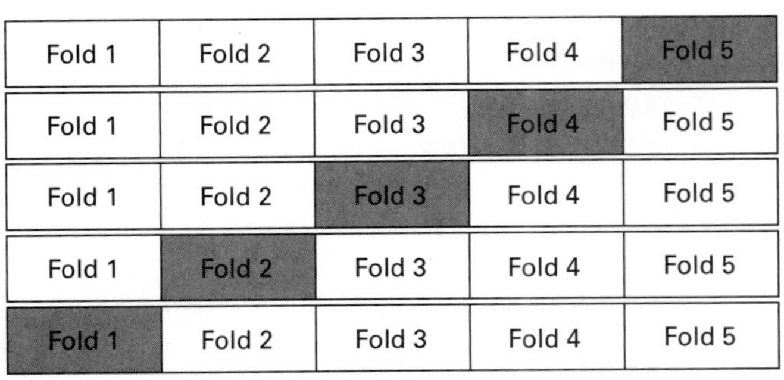

Folds in gray represent test set and folds in white represent training set.

Exhibit 10.5
Five-fold cross-validation.

dataset. As explained in chapter 8, this refers to an *imbalanced dataset.* When there are such imbalances in the classes that are used in the classification, a variation of the k-fold cross-validation method known as *stratified k-fold cross-validation* can be used. The idea is that we want the training and test set to have an equal representation of each of the classes. For example, if a dataset consists of 90% class 1 and 10% class 0, the model's predictions may be biased toward class 1. To remedy this, we use *stratified sampling* for each of the folds, which ensures that there is an equal representation of each of the classes. Thus, the model will be better able to detect the differences between classes. This approach can also be used with the holdout method.

Repeated random subsampling validation With the *repeated random subsampling validation*, also referred to as *Monte Carlo (MC) cross-validation*, the dataset is randomly split into training and test sets. The splits are not into folds, but simply into two different groups. For example, in the first trial in the process, the simulation may select g observations from the dataset of size n to create a training sample of size g as the training set and $n-g$ as the testing set; in the second trial, h as the training set and $n-h$ as the testing set, and so on. This method is unsuitable for an imbalanced dataset because it is possible to select a sample (either training or test) that may include primarily one of the classification labels.

Rolling cross-validation When dealing with time-series data, the order of the observations is important. Failing to recognize this and splitting the data using one of these cross-validation methods would produce misleading results. To deal with time-series data, the method of *rolling cross-validation* is used. With this method, the next observation is used for validation. That is, denoting T as the number of observations, in testing for the ability to predict the tth observation, the first $t-1$ observations are used as the training data and the tth observation is the testing data (i.e., one observation). Then to test for the $(t+1)$th observation, the first t observations are used as the testing data and the $(t+1)$th observation is the testing data, and so on.

10.5 Challenges of Implementing Machine Learning in Finance

There are several challenges in applying ML to financial problems. Here, we briefly describe three of them.

Financial data often contain a high degree of inherent noise. This poses challenges for accurate predictions. Specifically, financial time-series data can display characteristics resembling a random walk which we describe in chapter 17, presenting obstacles to prediction accuracy. Furthermore, issues like incomplete data, missing values, outliers, and labeling errors can adversely affect model performance. In addition, acquiring essential data can be complicated, influenced by factors such as data protection regulations such as privacy laws.

ML models are often highly complex analytical models referred to as "black box" models. Examples of such models are deep NNs and ensemble models. An important attribute of an ML model is the ease with which a human can understand, trust, and make sense of the model's output, which could be a decision or a prediction. This important attribute of an ML model is referred to as its *interpretability*. Model interpretability is a continuum, with some models being highly interpretable (like a linear regression) and others being pure black boxes (like a deep NN). This "black box" characteristic can present legal issues. For example, in cases where ML is employed for tasks like loan approvals or credit scoring, consumer laws may require a transparent explanation of the underlying rationale for the decision to deny credit to a loan applicant.

Financial markets are renowned for their inherent volatility, susceptible to a multitude of external influences spanning macroeconomic indicators, political occurrences, and financial crises, among others. This perpetual instability results in the unpredictability of the performance of predictive models because their usefulness is naturally linked to prevailing market conditions and the ability to adapt to rapidly changing dynamics. Consequently, the challenge lies not only in crafting robust models, but also in devising strategies to contend with the ever-fluctuating financial market conditions.

Summary

- Machine learning (ML) is the subfield within data science that studies how algorithms learn automatically from experience.
- Three ways to categorize ML algorithms are by the task performed, the types of learning behavior, and model parameterization.
- The four most common ML tasks are regression, classification, clustering, and dimensionality reduction.
- A regression model is used to describe a model or problem that requires predicting a continuous, numeric variable.
- A classification model predicts the class for categorical variables.
- The clustering task involves identifying natural groupings of observations for a dataset.
- The dimensionality reduction task involves reducing the number of input variables in the dataset by identifying input variables that are irrelevant or contain the same information as a combination of other input variables.
- Categorization of ML by learning behavior refers to how machines learn with each learning style differing based on the information provided to the machine during the training period.
- The four main categories of ML are supervised learning, unsupervised learning, semisupervised learning, and reinforcement learning.
- Supervised learning algorithms allow the computer to learn from training data that already contain the correct label for each input so the computer will identify patterns that link the input variables to the output variable.
- There are two types of supervised learning: regression and classification algorithms.
- The most popular supervised learning algorithms used in finance are linear regression, logistic regression, *k*-nearest neighbors (kNN), naive Bayes classifier, support vector machines (SVMs), linear regularization models (Least Absolute Shrinkage

and Selection Operator (LASSO), ridge regression, and Elastic Net), neural networks (NNs), decision trees, and random forests.

- In unsupervised learning, there are no labels provided for the inputs, and the objective of the algorithm is to determine the structure of the data based on their statistical properties.
- Clustering is a typical example of unsupervised learning.
- In semisupervised learning algorithms, the training data may include both labeled and unlabeled data. The objective is to understand how combining unlabeled and labeled data may alter the learning behavior, and then create algorithms to benefit from using both data types.
- The two commonly used unsupervised learning algorithms in finance are principal component analysis (PCA) and clustering analysis.
- The focus of reinforcement learning algorithms is learning interactively with the objective of maximizing a measure of cumulative reward.
- A parametric ML algorithm is an algorithm that summarizes data with a set of parameters where the number of parameters does not change, no matter how large the dataset.
- In contrast to parametric ML algorithms, nonparametric ML algorithms do not make any strong assumptions about the learning function, allowing any functional form to be identified from the training data.
- A hyperparameter is a parameter whose value is specified prior to the beginning of the learning process for the ML algorithm.
- The process of determining the optimal set of hyperparameters is referred to as hyperparameter tuning or hyperparameter optimization.
- The three most popular hyperparameter tuning methods are the grid search method, random search method, and Bayesian optimization method.
- In selecting the best set of hyperparameters, a performance metric must be used.
- The main distinction between performance metrics in selecting the set of hyperparameters will depend on whether the task is regression- or classification-based.
- The idea of a performance metric is to provide a score of the model's fit to the dataset that can allow one to select between different model constructions.
- There are five main performance metrics that are used when evaluating regression models: R-squared, adjusted R-squared, mean squared error (MSE), root mean squared error (RMSE), and mean absolute error (MAE).
- One of the most used tools for evaluating a classification model's performance is the confusion matrix, which provides a breakdown of model predictions versus true data labels.
- The values in the confusion matrix can help to construct other performance metrics that better evaluate the performance of the model.
- Four performance metrics that are commonly used for ML classification models are precision, recall (sensitivity), specificity, and F1 score.

- Once an ML algorithm has been constructed based on the training data, the next step is to test its performance, which involves assessing whether the model is not just picking up noise and as a result, the model's output fails to perform well with the out-of-sample data. The process for doing so is referred to as validation.
- Cross-validation (also referred to as out-of-sample testing, or rotation estimation) is the process of evaluating performance of the model on unseen data (i.e., the testing data which has the training data removed).
- The goal of cross-validation is to select the best set of hyperparameters for a given model by defining a performance metric that will be used for model selection, and then constructing different samples of the dataset, fitting the model on the training sets using each set of hyperparameters, and selecting the set of hyperparameters that performed best.
- Common methods for validating a model are the holdout method, *k*-fold cross-validation, stratified *k*-fold cross-validation, repeated random subsampling validation (also referred to as Monte Carlo (MC) cross-validation), and rolling cross-validation.
- There are a number of challenges in implementing ML to solve financial problems, including (1) data quality and availability, (2) interpretability, and (3) data availability and instability.

11

Natural Language Processing

Natural language processing (NLP) aids computers to understand, interpret, and apply human language to build models that can be used for decision-making purposes. It is an interdisciplinary field bridging computer science and linguistics.[1] Its applications span various domains, including finance, where it has been utilized for sentiment analysis, fraud detection, reporting, and compliance. Given its broad applicability, NLP encompasses a wide range of tools and techniques that have been tailored to specific tasks. In finance, the machine learning (ML) techniques described in chapter 10 are frequently used within NLP to develop models and systems capable of processing and understanding natural language, using supervised, unsupervised, and reinforcement learning algorithms for text analysis and generation. This chapter explains the fundamentals of NLP and its relevance to finance, primarily asset management. At its heart lies the *corpus*, a carefully compiled set of text documents used as the raw material for analysis and training models.

11.1 A Brief History of NLP

The roots of NLP can be traced to the 1950s through the pioneering work of Alan Turing, who sought to answer the question, "Can machines think?" In attempting to answer this question of whether a machine is intelligent, he devised the "Turing test," a benchmark used in artificial intelligence (AI) for assessing whether a machine can demonstrate humanlike intelligence. According to this test, a machine is considered intelligent if its conversational responses can convincingly deceive humans into believing that they are interacting with another human. Turing's seminal contributions earned him recognition as a foundational figure in the field of AI.

The idea that further inspired NLP came from the works of Alan L. Hodgkin and Andrew F. Huxley, who demonstrated in a series of five papers first published in 1952 how

1. *Linguistics* is the scientific study of language, and it has a number of subfields. The three of these that are most relevant for NLP are *morphology* (the study of word structure), *syntax* (the study of linguistic units), and *semantics* (the study of meaning). A further subfield within each of these three subfields, which employs the techniques of computer science, is *computational linguistics,* which involves quantitatively measuring the properties and logical characteristics of a language.

the brain utilizes neurons to create an electrical network. Two years later, advancing concepts in the field of linguistics, Noam Chomsky demonstrated that for a computer to be able to understand a language, the sentence structure had to be changed. From the late 1950s to the late 1980s, NLP was primarily based on the rules developed by linguists. Until 1990, chatbots, conversational tools for performing routine tasks, particularly for communicating with online users, were rule-based, in that thousands of phrases had to be programmed so the chatbots could effectively respond to user statements.

It was not until the late 1980s through 1995 that there was a major shift to what is known as a *corpus-based, statistical/machine learning approach.* This approach, fostered by the increase in computer speed and the substantial increase in machine-readable text and speech data, replaced the rule-based approach. Rather than having a linguist create the rules, linguistics statistics (language statistics) were used to create them. Continuing with the chatbot application, linguistic statistics using ML were used for chatbots by the 1990s, handling substantially more human-to-human potential conversations. As the amount of data provided increased, chatbots became more effective.

The 2020s saw the advance of generative AI and large language models (LLMs), which revolutionized NLP across various domains, including finance. LLMs, a subset of generative AI tools emphasizing specifically text-based outputs, are initially trained on vast amounts of Internet data, learning to predict the next word in a sentence based on the context. They create dense vector representations for each word in the vocabulary, capturing semantic meanings and contexts for all of them. LLMs also consider the surrounding words, learning to represent them in a way that reflects their relationships. These models can then be fine-tuned on a smaller dataset specific to particular tasks, such as finance applications.

We next describe the NLP techniques in more detail.

11.2 NLP Techniques

In NLP, several approaches are used for the purpose of understanding and interpreting human language. We briefly describe them next.

11.2.1 Dictionary-Based Approaches

Dictionary-based, or *rule-based, approaches* involve compiling a list of words and categorizing them as positive or negative based on their associated sentiments. A *sentiment score* is then assigned by counting the number of occurrences of positive and negative words. Let C_+ be the count of positive words in a text document and C_- be the count of negative words in a text document. Then, a common formulation for calculating a sentiment score is

$$Sentiment = \frac{C_+ - C_-}{C_+ + C_-} \tag{11.1}$$

Sentiment analysis can also be quantified by first computing the difference between the number of positive words and the number of negative words in a given text and then dividing by the total word count. Nevertheless, the exact methodology for calculating the sentiment score can differ and should be customized to fit the specific application.

When we refer to "dictionaries" in this context, we're talking about the predefined sets of words categorized as positive or negative. There are two commonly utilized dictionaries used for sentiment analysis. The first, the Harvard IV-4 Psychosociological Dictionary, a well-known resource in the field of content analysis, categorizes words based on various psychological and sociological criteria, including their sentiment. This dictionary is particularly useful for general-purpose sentiment analysis across a wide range of texts. Loughran and McDonald (2011), however, discovered that many words in general dictionaries do not properly classify the sentiment of certain words in a financial context. For example, the word "debt" may hold a negative context more generally, but in finance, it does not necessarily hold either positive or negative sentiment.

As an example, consider the task of sentiment analysis of the following text: "Company XYZ reported a significant increase in assets, but acknowledged an increase in liabilities due to recent acquisitions." The implementation process can be facilitated by the open-source package **pysentiment2**. This program operates by utilizing a dictionary of sentiment-laden words, scanning the text for these words, and subsequently using the occurrence of positive and negative words to compute a sentiment score given by equation (11.1).

The *subjectivity score* is another output. This score, indicative of the objectivity of the text, is derived by comparing the total count of positive and negative words to the overall word count in the text. In other words, subjectivity measures the ratio of sentiment-laden words to the total word count, after eliminating uninformative words (commonly referred to as *stop words*) from the text. We will delve into stop words in the following section.

While dictionary-based approaches provide a simplistic and easy-to-interpret methodology for calculating sentiment scores, there are several issues with this approach, which is why this methodology is rarely used in practice today. First, the practice of predefining a set of positive and negative words is inherently subjective. Moreover, dictionary-based approaches are not adept at handling negations effectively. For example, consider the following two sentences: "The company did not have strong performance" and "The company had strong performance." Using dictionary-based sentiment analysis, both sentences would produce the same sentiment score because the word "not" is typically not considered when calculating sentiment scores.

11.2.2 Statistical Approaches

Dictionary-based approaches fall under the category of *bag-of-words models* because they involve extracting individual words and using those word counts for formulating sentiment scores or other scores based on predefined word dictionaries. Another bag-of-words approach involves applying ML or econometric models to the individual counts of words.

11.2.2.1 Count Vectors A *count vector* is a numerical representation of text data that transforms text into a vector or array of numbers. Each number in the vector represents the frequency of a specific word in the text. This approach simplifies text by ignoring grammar and word order while retaining the information about word frequency (i.e., the number of times that each word appears).

Typically, multiple documents (i.e., text inputs) are used to formulate a *document-term matrix*, where each document appears as a row and the set of words used across all

	NLP	is	a	great	tool	for	finance	I	like	using
Document 1	1	1	1	1	1	1	1	0	0	0
Document 2	1	0	0	0	0	1	1	1	1	1

Exhibit 11.1
Count vectorization.

documents appear as the columns. Exhibit 11.1 provides an example of a document-term matrix for two input texts.

Document 1: "NLP is a great tool for finance"

Document 2: "I like using NLP for finance"

As can be seen from exhibit 11.1, each element of the document-term matrix corresponds to the number of times that the word in the column appeared in the document shown in the row. The challenge with using count vectors for statistical analysis arises as the number of documents and the total vocabulary size increase, leading to a rapid growth in the number of input features. The disadvantages of using count vectors are that (1) it fails to distinguish between more and less important words for analysis, (2) it treats frequently occurring words in a corpus as the most statistically significant ones, and (3) it fails to recognize relationships between words.[2]

11.2.2.2 Term Frequency-Inverse Document Frequency The count vector technique has been refined by considering not just the frequency of words in a single document, but also how unique a word is across all the documents in the corpus. This technique, referred to as the *term frequency-inverse document frequency* (TF-IDF), assigns greater importance to words that appear often in a single document but are rare across all the documents.

TF-IDF is computed as the product of two statistics. The first is the term frequency (*TF*), which is calculated as follows:[3]

$$TF = \frac{\text{No. of times the term appears in the document}}{\text{Total number of terms in the document}}$$

The second term is the inverse document frequency (*IDF*), which is calculated as follows:

$$IDF = \text{Log}\left(\frac{\text{Total no. of documents in the corp}}{\text{No. of documents that mention the term}}\right)$$

2. These disadvantages are mentioned in a LinkedIn post by Sheel Saket, "Count Vectorizer vs TFIDF Vectorizer | Natural Language Processing," dated January 12, 2020 (https://www.linkedin.com/pulse/count-vectorizers-vs-tfidf-natural-language-processing-sheel-saket/).

3. See Saket (2022).

The TF-IDF score is then found by multiplying the *TF* and *IDF*. That is,

$$TF - IDF = \left(\frac{\text{No. of times the term appears in the document}}{\text{Total number of terms in the document}} \right) \times \text{Log}\left(\frac{\text{Total no. of documents in the corpus}}{\text{No. of documents that mention the term}} \right).$$

The TF-IDF score varies between 0 and 1. The smaller the score, the more common the term; the higher the score, the less common the term.

To illustrate the calculation of the TF-IDF score, suppose that the term appears 10 times in a document that has 5,000 words, and there are 4,000 documents (i.e., the corpus), with 400 of them mentioning the term. Then

$$TF = \frac{10}{5{,}000} = 0.002$$

$$IDF = \text{Log}\left(\frac{4{,}000}{400} \right) = 1$$

Therefore,

$$TF - IDF = 0.002 \times 1 = 0.002$$

Suppose instead that the term appears 400 times in the document instead of 10 times, and the term appears in 3,000 documents (i.e., the corpus). Then

$$TF = \frac{400}{5{,}000} = 0.08$$

$$IDF = \text{Log}\left(\frac{4{,}000}{3{,}000} \right) = 0.301$$

Therefore,

$$TF - IDF = 0.08 \times 0.301 = 0.041$$

TF-IDF vectors and count vectors are essential NLP techniques for converting text to numbers that ML models can understand. The TF-IDF vectors technique is a more sophisticated one that has several advantages over count vectors. First, it enhances count vectors by assigning importance-based weights to words, not merely counting their frequency, and identifying those terms that are likely to be more relevant to the document's content. Second, by assigning greater importance to words that are rare or unique, the TF-IDF vectors technique allows more effective differentiation between documents with shared vocabulary. Finally, unlike count vectors, where all words are treated equally (which means that words appearing frequently across many documents can dominate), TF-IDF reduces the importance of words that appear frequently across the corpus, ensuring that less informative words are not overemphasized. This results in better capturing of the unique content of the documents.

11.2.3 Neural Network Models

Count vectors and other bag-of-words approaches require extensive text preprocessing, which we explain in section 11.3, where the preprocessing will make or break the performance of the resulting model. More recently, NLP applications have focused on neural network (NN) models to represent text and enhance the models' abilities to understand context.

There is a wide range of methods that use the ML method of NNs for representing text. Without going into detail about the various methodologies for doing so, we will describe the general idea of how these models represent text in a way that allows the model to understand the context and relationships between words.

The most common NN method involves using transformer models (Vaswani, 2017) models to embed text based on the context of that word within a sentence. Transformers offered improvements over sequential models like RNNs and LSTMs by allowing the model to look across entire text sequences, capturing long-range dependencies amongst words and sentences. These models utilize a number of training techniques, with the most common being *masked language modeling* (MLM), where an NN obscures a specific word in the input sentence and then attempts to predict or reconstruct the hidden word based on the surrounding words in the sentence. In this way, these models can embed information from other words and can extract an understanding of context and relationships between words. The vector representations are typically produced by taking hidden layers within the neural network that are trained during MLM. This produces a vector representation for each word in the corpus, which then can be used in another model for some predictive tasks.

The two classes of NN models found in modern-day NLP applications, generative language models and contextual embedding models, are briefly described next.

11.2.3.1 Generative Language Models *Generative language models* are NN models that aim to predict the next word or subword (i.e., token) in a sequence of textual input. For this reason, they are commonly utilized as AI assistants, such as ChatGPT, as they anticipate the most suitable words to generate based on the user's input prompt. Generative language models have shown impressive capabilities in a range of tasks due to the flexibility granted by outputting text. However, using generative language models requires extensive computational resources, precluding those that do not have access to institutional-level computing infrastructures.

Generative language models can employ expert annotators for training the model to improve the model's performance, accuracy, and reliability. These models are referred to as *expert-augmented generative models, annotator-enhanced generative models,* and *human-in-the-loop models*. They are used for specific domains. The involvement of expert annotators can vary, from providing high-quality training data to evaluating and correcting the model's outputs. The use of expert annotators in the development of generative language models combines AI with human expertise.

11.2.3.2 Contextual Embedding Models *Contextual embedding models*, also called *embedding models*, are NN models trained to predict missing tokens, which are words, subwords, or individual characters, in an input text. By training the model to use the context of the surrounding words to predict a missing word gives these models a strong understanding of relationships across words, effectively capturing the context of the entire sequence.

While contextual embedding models are trained to predict missing words, they are rarely used in this way. Instead, one will extract a hidden layer of the NN and use that as the input feature. That is, the text is passed through the model one time, and the output of one of the hidden layers is extracted and used along with a secondary statistical model. This process is referred to as *feature extraction,* and the resulting vector representations are referred to as *embeddings*.

These embeddings can function similarly to count vectors, but with a key difference. They encapsulate the entire text sequence within a single vector, capturing not just individual word counts, but also the deeper context, relationships, and semantic information of the text as a whole. Studies have demonstrated the superiority of using these embeddings compared to count vector methods, highlighting their effectiveness in capturing more nuanced textual information.

Because these NN models require extensive training on a large corpus of text to give the model its ability to capture context and meaning, they are typically trained by large technology companies or institutions and provided to users via open-source repositories such as Huggingface (https://huggingface.co/). These models are trained for a generic understanding of text and then are typically further trained on a specific task or domain-specific text. This process is referred to as *fine-tuning*.

A common contextual embedding model is the Bidirectional Encoder Representation from Transformers (BERT) model. Again, the performance and abilities of this model are due to the extensive pre-training process applied. There are many variants of the BERT model, which differ based on the pre-training approach applied. Robust Optimized BERT (RoBERTa) and Sentence BERT (SBERT) are examples of common variants of pre-trained BERT models.

11.3 Preprocessing Text Data

Cleansing text data is crucial to the performance of an NLP model. There are two broad categories of preprocessing text data: general text preprocessing and preprocessing for vectorization.[4]

11.3.1 General Text Preprocessing

General text preprocessing synthesizes and normalizes text into its most informative components, removing any uninformative words and grouping words by their roots. Many programming languages, including Python, have libraries for text preprocessing. This is done prior to any form of vectorization or more advanced processing by performing the tasks described next.

11.3.1.1 Lowercasing and Removing Punctuations/Special Characters All text must be converted to lowercase to avoid having multiple copies of the same words. For example, consider "apple" and "Apple." If lowercasing were not employed, there would be confusion between the word referring to a fruit and referring to the company. In situations where this distinction should be preserved, the occurrences of the word can be preprocessed or

4. There are many online resources that explain text preprocessing for NLP and how to implement it. See, for example, Hilkmah (2023) and Weng (2019).

recoded. It is often the case that punctuation and special characters fail to contribute to the meaning of a text for analysis purposes and can be removed. For instance, Uniform Resource Locators (URLs) are removed.

11.3.1.2 Removing Stop Words *Stop words* appear frequently in a language but are insignificant in and of themselves. To filter the noise and narrow the focus on important words, NLP removes stop words before any statistical analysis is performed on the text. Some examples of words that would be treated as stop words are "a," "as," "the," "and," "of," "are," "as," "if," and "will." Such words would be included in a stop list (also called a *negative dictionary*).[5]

11.3.1.3 Text Stemming and Lemmatization Languages consist of words that appear in different forms or are derived from one another. For example, in English, "manage," "manages," and "managed" are modified forms of the same word that would be used in different grammatical contexts. A language with changes in the form or ending of some words is referred to as an *inflected language*. All inflected words in such a language share a *common root form*, which provides an efficient, cost-effective way of identifying meaning. Two techniques are used to analyze an inflected word to determine its root: stemming and lemmatization. Collectively, they are referred to as *text normalization techniques*.

Stemming analysis reduces an inflected word to its stem. Consider the words "universe," "universal," and "university." Stemming analysis would reduce these three inflected words to their stem word, "univers." That is, stemming analysis simply removes several letters at the end of an inflected word. As another example, the words "operate," "operates," "operating," and "operational" are inflected words. Stemming analysis would identify the root "oper" as being common to these words.[6] However, there is a drawback to stemming analysis: roots in isolation do not always help understand the original word. For example, the root "univers" is not sufficient for uncovering the meaning of the original word. *Lemmatization analysis* helps overcome this drawback.

Lemmatization groups together inflected forms of words such that they are treated as a single word. That is, it analyzes the context of an inflected word and converts it to its understandable form (referred to as a *lemma*). This process assists the predictive model's learning such that the group of inflected forms of words can be employed in similar contexts. For example, lemmatizing "managing" would return "manage." Thus, in contrast to stemming analysis that provides the root of an inflected word, lemmatization provides a new, full word. Lemmatization analysis is far more computationally expensive than stemming analysis: the latter simply drops letters at the end of a word, while lemmatization requires building and running look-up tables to find the accurate word to return.

11.3.1.4 Noun Phrase Chunking Grouping together words to represent a single idea or concept is referred to as *noun phrase chunking*. This task relies on output from dependency

5. Stop words can be removed using the Natural Language Toolkit (NLTK) library, which provides a list of stop words in sixteen languages.

6. Such analysis can be performed by **nltk.sten** software, from the library **WordNetLemmatizer**.

parsing and groups a string of words together to form an idea or concept. Noun phrases, at a minimum, consist of a noun and a verb or a noun with its descriptor (e.g., adjective). Examples of a noun phrase in asset management would be "active manager," "volatile market," and "bull market." Noun phrases are then used to form parts of longer sentences in further analysis.

11.3.1.5 Named Entity Recognition *Named entity recognition (NER)* refers to the task of identifying and then categorizing key entities (information) in text. In this task (also known as *entity chunking*), the term "entity" means a word or string of words that refers to the same thing throughout a piece of text. Every identified entity is classified into a category that has previously been determined for the application at hand.

NER involves two steps. The first detects an entity, which subsequently is treated as a token. It can be a single word or a string of words. For example, "New York Stock Exchange" might appear in a text several times. Once identified and flagged, this four-word string would be treated as a token in the analysis.

The second step creates entity categories, such as the following:

- *Individuals*: Examples are Harry Markowitz, Eugene Fama, and Fischer Black.
- *Companies*: Examples are Amazon, 3M, Vanguard, and Fidelity.
- *Sectors of the financial markets*: Examples are technology, consumer durables, energy, and industrials.
- *Indices*: Examples are S&P 500, Dow Jones, Russell 2000, FTSE 100, and Nikkei 225.
- *Locations*: Examples are New York City, London, Singapore, and Hong Kong
- *Times*: Examples are 1929 and 1990.
- *Events*: Examples are Great Depression, Great Recession, and dot-com bubble.

After the two steps are completed, the entity categories can be used to label the data and then used to create a training dataset for ML applications.

11.3.1.6 Co-reference Resolution The final task in NLP is *co-reference resolution,* in which all word strings or groups of words that refer to the same entity in a text are identified. The task outputs a co-reference chain, or a collection of all NERs in a text that refer to the same entity. By identifying all the references, sentences become self-contained and do not require additional context. Hence, this task is very helpful for extracting information, summarizing the contents of a document, and especially answering questions.

11.3.2 Preprocessing for Vectorization

In section 11.2.2.2, we described two vectorization techniques: count vectors and TF-IDF vectors. After completing the general text preprocessing tasks as just described, the process of preparing for vectorization involves converting the cleaned text into structured, numerical formats suitable for input into ML algorithms. This preparation includes tokenization and the creation of N-grams.

11.3.2.1 Tokenization Critical to the process of generating count vectors or document-term matrices is breaking the text into smaller units, referred to as *tokens*. The purpose of this task, referred to as *tokenization*, is to decompose text into manageable pieces for further processing and analysis. Transforming text into tokens enables NLP techniques to more effectively understand the syntax and semantic meaning of the text, which are crucial for the applications described in section 11.4. Typically, a token represents a word. While *word tokenization* is the most common type of tokenization, depending on the application's required level of detail, there is *sentence tokenization*, *subword tokenization*, and *character tokenization*. While tokenization may seem straightforward, it is challenging because of the complexity of human languages.

11.3.2.2 N-Grams Bag-of-words models have difficulty dealing with negation and multiword phrases because sometimes two or more words are used as a single feature. While single words (unigrams) are the most basic elements, combining words into bigrams (two-word sequences), trigrams (three-word sequences), and higher *n*-grams can capture more nuanced language features. However, doing so increases the number of words in the feature space immensely.

11.3.3 Vectorization and the Curse of Dimensionality

As the number of words grows, the curse of dimensionality becomes an issue. The *curse of dimensionality* refers to the performance of ML models deteriorating as the number of input features grows, causing overfitting. Researchers address the curse of dimensionality through three primary methods: (1) text preprocessing, (2) decomposition algorithms, and (3) using models specifically designed for high-dimensional input features.

Dimensionality reduction can employ methods such as principal component analysis (PCA), correlation screening, and singular value decomposition to reduce the number of features while at the same time preserving the most relevant information.

11.3.3.1 Principal Component Analysis As explained in chapter 10, the statistical tool of PCA transforms the original features in a dataset into a new set of uncorrelated features (i.e., a new set of orthogonal features). These new features are referred to as *principal components* (PCs) and transformed so that the first PC explains the maximum variance of the data, the second PC explains the maximum remaining variance, and so on. The determination of the number of PCs to use to describe the dataset involves evaluating the balance between maintaining a sufficient variance in the dataset and reducing dimensionality.[7]

11.3.3.2 Correlation Screening In text, there may be features (words or tokens) that are highly correlated, in that they convey the same information. For example, in sentiment analysis, words such as "good" and "excellent" convey the same positive sentiment, and words such as "poor" and "bad" convey the same negative sentiment. Correlation analysis can be used to identify and remove words or tokens that are highly correlated, thereby reducing dimensionality.

7. The use of PCA for NLP is explained in Drikvandi and Lawal (2023).

11.3.3.3 Singular Value Decomposition *Singular value decomposition (SVD)* is a matrix factorization technique (i.e., a technique for decomposing a matrix into the product of two or more simpler matrices). The objective is to represent the original matrix in a more compact form that captures its underlying relationships or structures. When used in NLP to reduce dimensionality, the matrices involved are the document-term matrices.[8]

11.4 Applications of NLP to Asset Management

Three common applications of NLP in asset management are detecting material events, event extraction, market sentiment analysis, and modeling document topics. We describe each next.

11.4.1 Detecting Material Events: Event Extraction

An occurrence of something that has resulted in a certain time and in a certain space that is associated with one or more participants is referred to as an *event*.[9] *Event extraction* refers to the process of detecting one or more events in a text.[10] The first use of event extraction was by the U.S. Defense Advanced Projects Agency in the late 1980s. Once an event is identified, the goal is to classify the type of event and all the participants. Basically, there are five well-known event-related questions that should be answered for an identified event summarizing a report or document: Who? When? Where? Why? and How?

There are events in financial markets that can move the price of a security, such as a stock or bond or the market overall. Examples include the announcement of a new product, the signing of a major sales agreement, and the signing of a labor agreement. This information is transmitted to the market via a text or a company spokesperson announcement.

A real-world example of six identified events that resulted in a major movement in Tesla's stock price is provided by the Man Institute.[11] The six events are identified here and shown in exhibit 11.2:

- *Event 1*: On August 2, 2018, Tesla announced that its production for its least expensive model is growing, and Elon Musk, the company's chief executive officer, would not raise funds from investors. The result was a significant increase in the stock price.
- *Event 2*: On August 7, 2018, a tweet by Musk stated that he was seeking to take the public company private. He estimated that such a transaction would substantially

8. For an online resource that illustrates how SVD is used in NLP, see Toczkowska (2023).

9. Ace (Automatic Content Extraction). *English Annotation Guidelines for Events*, Linguistic Data Consortium, Philadelphia, 2005.

10. There are two event extraction methods: closed-domain event extraction method and open-domain event extraction. Using predefined events, *closed-domain event extraction* seeks to identify and extract events from text. To do so, ML, deep learning, semisupervised learning algorithms, and pattern matching are used. For example, Ding, et al. (2015) used deep learning for stock price movements. A semantic frame parser method for predicting stock price movements from news is employed by Xie et al. (2013). Open-event extraction focuses on identifying either new events or for a known event, tracking its change. One algorithm that can be used is semisupervised learning.

11. See Marinov (2019).

increase the value of the company. The result was a significant increase in the stock price.

- *Event 3:* Musk appeared on a podcast with comedian Joe Rogan on September 8, 2018, and during the interview, both Musk and Rogan smoked marijuana. Shortly after the podcast, both Tesla's chief accounting officer and the head of human resources announced that they were leaving the firm. This departure of key members of the senior management team resulted in a significant drop in the stock price.
- *Event 4:* The August 7, 2018, announcement that Musk wanted to take the company private, and thereby increase shareholder value, resulted in an action by the Securities and Exchange Commission (SEC) on September 27, 2018. The SEC viewed Musk's statement as misleading investors. Because this SEC action raised concerns about Musk's future, the stock significantly declined.
- *Event 5:* On January 18, 2019, Musk announced that Tesla was going to find it challenging to generate a profit in the first quarter of 2019. To reduce operating costs, the company announced that it was cutting 3,000 employees. The result of this announcement was a sharp decline in Tesla's stock price.
- *Event 6:* On March 1, 2019, Musk confirmed his forecast of January 18, 2019, that Tesla would not realize a profit in the first quarter, resulting in another decline in the stock price.

Such material events occur frequently in financial markets. Analysts monitor markets to identify such events, an activity that is extremely time-consuming. Moreover, there is the risk that a material event will be missed, resulting in a lost opportunity to profit from a significant price movement or from selling a holding whose price may be adversely affected. NLP can be used to monitor financial markets to detect events that are material enough to move markets without an analyst needing to monitor the markets.

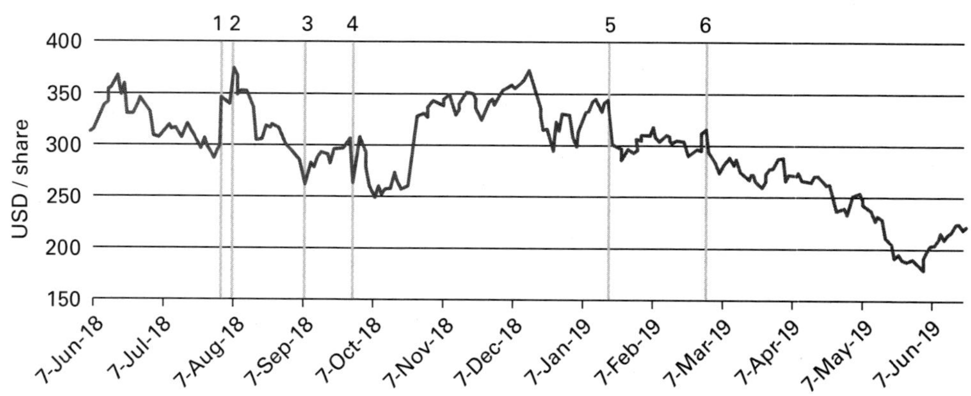

Exhibit 11.2
An example of how events affected Tesla.
Data source: Bloomberg; as of June 21, 2019.
Reprinted from Figure 2 of Marinov (2019, p. 3), with permission from the Man Institute.

11.4.2 Market Sentiment Analysis

In finance, market sentiment is the attitude of investors concerning the financial market overall or to the security of a specific company. Typically, market sentiment is described as bullish (the expectation that the market or a security's price will increase) or bearish (the expectation that the security's price will decrease). Investors use indicators to measure market sentiment. These measures include the Chicago Board Options Exchange Volatility Index (CBOE VIX), the Bullish Percent Index, and the High-Low Exchange. These sentiment indicators are based on market price movements.

Using unstructured data, NLP allows investors to gauge the sentiment of the financial market overall or a particular security. In the case of a particular security, such data include filings by the issuer of a security to regulatory authorities (e.g., SEC filings and state or industry regulatory filings), reports by analysts, company speeches at investor meetings, earnings call transcripts, and social media. In this section, we describe how sentiment from the text can be used to predict the direction of stock price movements. This is referred to as *sentiment analysis*.

The following are three examples of how asset management firms have employed sentiment analysis as reported on the Internet:

- To formulate a view on fiscal policy, BlackRock Financial Management, the world's largest asset management firm, used NLP to generate sentiment signals to gain insights into how fiscal policy is moving across countries. Given the sentiment signals, the firm's portfolio managers then tilt their portfolio composition to countries that are easing fiscal policy.
- As a result of the COVID-19 pandemic, security analysts were slow to update their earnings estimates for the first quarter of 2020. However, senior portfolio managers of the firm's equity funds held the view that despite analysts' delay in updating their earnings estimates, insights can be gained by using NLP to look at the tone of analysts' reports to gain insight of their view of companies even without an earnings forecast (Decimal Point Analytics 2020).
- Since the monetary policy of the Board of Governors of the Federal Reserve (Fed) has a significant impact on the value of assets in financial markets, investors closely monitor the minutes of the Federal Open Market Committee (FOMC). The practice of monitoring the actions of the Fed is referred to as "Fed watching." Two Sigma, a large hedge fund, used NLP to analyze the Fed's minutes for decision-making. We'll discuss this application further later in this section.

Several researchers have demonstrated how asset managers can use sentiment analysis. Here are three examples:

- Azar and Lo (2016), for example, assign a polarity score to Twitter (now X) messages. They find that the sentiment score performed well in predicting the return on a well-known stock index, even when the articles and tweets were published at least 24 hours before the FOMC meetings. Based on the Tweet sentiment index, the authors formulate trading strategies and find that the portfolio constructed outperformed a buy-and-hold (i.e., passive index) strategy.

- Liew and Budavari (2017) create a tweet sentiment index based on stock market tweets available from the website StockTwits.com, and find that the index can explain stock market returns over time, beyond that which can be explained by commonly used factor models.

11.4.3 Modeling Document Topics

The information contained in a document is more than just its tone. It can be used also to identify themes or topics, referred to as *modeling document topics*. NLP can be used to do so from financial documents such as regulatory filings, earnings reports, news articles, and analyst reports.

Marinov (2019) uses the following snippet from a news article to illustrate this: "Oil prices fell on Monday after climbing to their highest this year earlier in the session as China reported automobile sales in January fell for a seventh month, raising concerns about fuel demand in the world's second-largest oil user." This discusses three key topics. The first key topic is oil, as suggested by the words "prices," "fuel," "fell," and "climb," not to mention the word "oil." The second key topic is the global economy, as suggested by the words "world," "China," "demand," and "sales." A third topic is various sectors of the economy, as suggested by the words "automobiles," "utilities," and "banking." The importance of each topic, as provided by the algorithm used to identify each one, is as follows: 50% for the global economy, 45% for oil, and only 5% for sectors.

An actual application of NLP for modeling document topics is its use by the hedge fund Two Sigma for Fed-watching purposes, as discussed earlier (also see Turner 2016). Analyzing the FOMC minutes from the 1990s to 2016 for content, the hedge fund found the following, which helped it in making investment decisions: (1) the FOMC devoted about 37% of the minutes of the meeting in late 2008 on the topic of financial markets (based on the words "securities," "credit," "dollar," "rates," and "mortgage"); (2) since late 2008, the time devoted to financial market has declined but remained above 20%; (3) since late 2008, the time devoted to economic growth had declined; (4) during the Global Financial Crisis of 2007–2009, the topic of inflation accounted for only 15% of the FOMC minutes; (5) since mid-2014, the topic of inflation increased to as much as 30%, while the topic of employment received considerably less attention (5%); and (6) in the later part of their study, there were four topics—inflation, growth, policy, and financial markets—which individually represented 20% of the minutes, suggesting that the topics are more interrelated than they had been in the past.

Although there are several approaches to modeling document topics, the most common is the *latent Dirichlet allocation* (LDA) *model*, a generative statistical model (i.e., a statistical model that generates synthetic data similar to the observed data). LDA assumes that (1) a document contains a mixture of a small number of topics and (2) each word in the document is generated from one of the topics. LDA, as well as other models for identifying topics, is trained on vectorized text data to identify the underlying topics and generates several topic clusters, where each cluster is a probability distribution over the words in the corpus. Identifying topics and monitoring them dynamically help categorize news sources. Moreover, the information that they contain can be used to generate alerts or enhance predictive models of market behavior.

11.5 Using NLP in Financial Applications

The field of NLP is ever evolving. Recent advances in generative AI have opened further opportunities for applications in investment management. New NLP algorithms can scan and make sense of vast amounts of data, identifying investment and new product opportunities, analyzing connections between traditionally disparate sources of information, and generating deeper insights. There are known challenges, such as the need for substantial computing resources, inherited model bias because of bias in the available training data, interpretability, and the inclination for hallucinations (i.e., models generating plausible but incorrect information). Although the risks of using the newer generations of NLP models are still being evaluated, firms are developing proprietary models to take advantage of the sophistication of today's NLP tools, finding both traditional and new, creative ways to employ such tools in the investment industry. This is made easier by the development of open-source tools, including Python libraries, that can aid with generative AI/NLP model development, testing, and deployment.

Summary

- Natural language processing (NLP), an interdisciplinary field that bridges computer science and linguistics, enables computers to understand, interpret, and utilize human language to create models that support decision-making processes.
- In NLP, several approaches are used for understanding and interpreting human language: dictionary-based (rule-based) approaches, statistical approaches (count vectors and term frequency-inverse document frequency), and neural network (NN) models.
- Count vectors and other bag-of-words approaches require extensive text preprocessing, in which the preprocessing will make or break the performance of the resulting model.
- NLP applications focus on NN models to represent text and enhance the models' abilities to understand context.
- The most common NN method involves using transformer models to embed text based on word context within a sentence. Transformers are able to capture longer-range dependencies among words over that of sequential models like long short-term memory (LSTM) and recurrent neural networks (RNNs).
- NN models utilize a number of training techniques, with the most common technique being masked language modeling (MLM), where an NN obscures a specific word in the input sentence and then attempts to predict or reconstruct the hidden word based on the surrounding words in the sentence. In this way, these models can embed information from other words and extract an understanding of the context and relationships between words.
- The vector representations in NN models are typically produced taking hidden layers within the NN, which are trained during MLM to produce a vector representation for each word in the corpus, which can then be used in another model for some predictive tasks.

- The two classes of NN model found in modern-day NLP applications are generative language models and contextual embedding models.
- Generative language models are NN models that aim to predict the next word or subword (i.e., token) in a sequence of textual input.
- Generative language models have shown impressive capabilities in a range of tasks due to the flexibility granted by outputting text.
- Generative language models require extensive computational resources, precluding those who do not have access to institutional-level computing infrastructures.
- Generative language models can employ expert annotators for training the model with the objective of improving the model's performance, accuracy, and reliability. These models are referred to as expert-augmented generative models, annotator-enhanced generative models, and human-in-the-loop models.
- Contextual embedding models, or embedding models, are NNs trained to predict missing words, subwords, or characters in a text. This training enables the models to understand and capture the context and relationships between words effectively.
- Although contextual embedding models are trained to predict missing words, they are often used differently in practice. Typically, a hidden layer of the NN is extracted and used as input features for another model. This process, known as feature extraction, generates vector representations called embeddings, which capture the contextual information of the text.
- Cleansing text data is crucial to the performance of an NLP model. There are two broad categories of preprocessing text data: general text preprocessing and preprocessing for vectorization.
- General text preprocessing synthesizes and normalizes text into its most informative components, removing uninformative words, and grouping words by their root.
- Three common applications of NLP in asset management are detecting material events, market sentiment analysis, and modeling document topics.
- Event extraction refers to the process of detecting one or more events in a text.
- NLP is used to measure market sentiment (via a sentiment score), reflecting investors' attitudes toward the overall financial market or a specific company's security.
- The information in a document extends beyond its tone; it can also identify themes or topics, known as document topic modeling. NLP can be used to extract these themes from financial documents such as regulatory filings, earnings reports, news articles, and analyst reports.

III

Applications to Asset Management

12

Asset Allocation Models

The investment management process involves determining how an investor's funds should be allocated among the major asset classes, as explained in chapter 2. The choice as to how much to put in each asset class is referred to as the *asset allocation decision*. Once that decision is made, a portfolio consisting of the specific assets in each asset class must be created. That is, the portfolio must be constructed (assembled) from the universe of assets comprising that asset class. This is referred to as the *portfolio construction decision*. For example, suppose that only three asset classes are being considered (stocks, bonds, and cash), and the total amount to be invested in those three asset classes is $1 billion. The asset allocation decision involves determining how much to allocate to each of the three asset classes. Suppose the decision is to allocate $450 million to stocks, $500 million to bonds, and $50 million to cash. Given this allocation, three portfolios must be constructed: a stock portfolio, a bond portfolio, and a cash portfolio. The stock portfolio, for example, will be built by selecting from the universe of company stocks to meet the investor's investment objective.

Historically, the asset allocation decision was not based on any rigorous analysis. For many decades, the "60/40 rule" was recommended by financial advisors. This rule says that an investor should allocate wealth by investing 60% in stocks and 40% in bonds. The reasoning is that a diversified portfolio of publicly traded stocks provided the portfolio with growth potential and the volatility that an investor faces for the return on the stocks would be dampened by investing in highly credit rated bonds. Clearly, the 60/40 rule is naive. It ignores how many years remain before the investor retires, the investor's risk tolerance, and the investor's investment objective.

There are two other reasons why this naive asset allocation rule is no longer appropriate (if it ever was). First, when interest rates are at a historically low level, as they have been in recent years, bonds are no longer the dampener that they were when the 60/40 rule was first proposed. Second, today there are more than two asset classes. In particular, the rule ignores traditional asset classes, such as high-yield bonds and inflation-protected bonds, as well as alternative asset classes such as commodities, residential and commercial real estate, hedge funds, and private equity available to investors. For example, Bekkers, Doeswijk, and Lam (2009) report that investing in real estate, commodities, and high-yield bonds can add value to an asset allocation based only on stocks and bonds.

How important is the asset allocation decision? That is, is the asset allocation decision a major factor in the performance of a financial strategy? The importance of the asset allocation decision in the investment management process has been supported by two major studies that investigated the historical performance of a portfolio due to its asset class mix. The first study, by Brinson, Hood, and Beebower (1995), investigated the performance of U.S. pension plans over the period 1974–1983. They found that the asset class mix can explain about 94% of the average return variation. The second study, by Ibbotson and Kaplan (2000), found that about 90% of returns can be explained by the asset class mix, confirming the findings from fourteen years earlier. Subsequent studies further confirm the critical importance of the asset allocation decision.

In this chapter, we will focus on the asset allocation decision, describing three models that are used for making this decision: the mean-variance optimization model, the robust portfolio optimization model, and the risk-parity model. Models for portfolio construction for stocks and bonds are described in chapters 14 and 15, respectively. As we will see in this chapter, the definition of risk as the variance of returns leads to the conclusion that *diversification* is preferable as an investment strategy. Therefore, we begin with a discussion of the notion of diversification.

12.1 Asset Allocation and Diversification

One often hears financial advisors tell clients that they should "diversify" their portfolios. The argument is that an investor who diversifies constructs a portfolio in such a way as to reduce portfolio risk without sacrificing returns. While this is certainly a reasonable investment goal that investors should seek, the question is how to do this in practice. Some financial advisors argue that including assets across all asset classes could diversify a portfolio. That might be reasonable, but the question is how much should be allocated to each asset class.

Prior to the development of the first model for asset allocation that we will present in this chapter, the mean-variance model, while financial advisors often talked about diversification in general terms, they did not have command of the analytical concepts and tools with which to determine the best asset allocation. In 1952, Harry Markowitz formulated an investment theory that quantified the notion of diversification by using basic statistical concepts and optimization models to determine the optimal asset allocation (Markowitz 1952). Markowitz's investment theory, popularly referred to as *mean-variance analysis*, *mean-variance portfolio optimization*, and *modern portfolio theory*, is primarily concerned with the degree of covariance/correlation between asset class returns in a portfolio as a measure of portfolio risk, rather than with the risk of each asset class in isolation. In 1990, Markowitz was awarded the Nobel Memorial Prize in Economic Sciences in recognition of his seminal work.

To illustrate Markowitz's concept of diversification consider the following example. Suppose an investor is evaluating an allocation of wealth to two asset classes over the next year. The expected returns for the two asset classes are $E[\tilde{r}_1] = \mu_1 = 9.1\%$ and $E[\tilde{r}_2] = \mu_2 = 12.1\%$, and their standard deviations are $\sigma_1 = 16.5\%$ and $\sigma_2 = 15.8\%$.

At first glance, asset class 2 is the clear winner. Its expected return is higher than that of asset class 1, and its standard deviation is lower than that of asset class 1. Thus, by investing 100% of the investor's wealth in asset class 2, the investor could achieve a better return for less risk, if risk is defined as the standard deviation of possible outcomes.

Now suppose that the investor is given the additional information that the correlation coefficient between the two returns of the two asset classes is $\rho_{12}=-0.22$. Let us denote the weight of asset class 1 in the portfolio as w_1, and the weight of asset class 2 as w_2. Note that the sum of the weights of the two asset classes must be 100% (i.e., $w_2=1-w_1$).
The portfolio return, which is a random variable and denoted by a tilde (~) over the return variable r, can be expressed as

$$\tilde{r}_p = w_1\tilde{r}_1 + w_2\tilde{r}_2$$

The portfolio's expected return and the variance can be computed from the rules listed in section 3.9. In particular, the portfolio expected return is

$$\begin{aligned} E[\tilde{r}_p] &= E[w_1\tilde{r}_1 + w_2\tilde{r}_2] = E[w_1\tilde{r}_1] + E[w_2\tilde{r}_2] \\ &= w_1 E[\tilde{r}_1] + w_2 E[\tilde{r}_2] = w_1\mu_1 + w_2\mu_2. \end{aligned}$$

The portfolio variance is

$$\begin{aligned} \sigma_p^2 &= \text{Var}(w_1\tilde{r}_1 + w_2\tilde{r}_2) = \text{Var}(w_1\tilde{r}_1) + \text{Var}(w_2\tilde{r}_2) + 2\text{Covar}(w_1\tilde{r}_1, w_2\tilde{r}_2) \\ &= w_1^2\sigma_1^2 + w_2^2\sigma_2^2 + 2w_1w_2\sigma_{12} \end{aligned}$$

Since we are given the correlation coefficient instead of the covariance, we can express the portfolio variance through the correlation coefficient (see the definition of correlation coefficient in section 3.8):

$$\sigma_p^2 = w_1^2\sigma_1^2 + w_2^2\sigma_2^2 + 2w_1w_2\sigma_1\sigma_2\rho_{12}.$$

The portfolio standard deviation is the square root of the portfolio variance computed here.

Exhibits 12.1(A) and 12.1(B) illustrate how the portfolio return and standard deviation change with the fraction of the portfolio invested in asset class 1. (All these calculations are contained in the worksheet **Diversification** in the file **Ch12-Diversification2Stocks.xlsm**.) We can observe that while the portfolio expected return is highest when 0% is invested in asset class 1, the portfolio standard deviation when the weight of asset class 1 is 0% is not the lowest one possible. By investing in both asset class 1 and asset class 2, the investor can reduce the portfolio standard deviation to a level that is lower than the level of any of the individual asset classes.

In the previous two-asset class example, the fact that the asset classes were negatively correlated made the effect of diversification particularly dramatic in terms of reducing the overall portfolio standard deviation. The same conclusion—that diversification decreases the portfolio standard deviation—holds when returns for the asset classes are uncorrelated or exhibit weak correlations. The conclusion holds true in observed asset class return behavior as well.

12.2 The Classical Mean-Variance Optimization Model

With an understanding of Markowitz's notion of diversification, let's describe the classical mean-variance optimization model. Suppose that an investor would like to invest in N

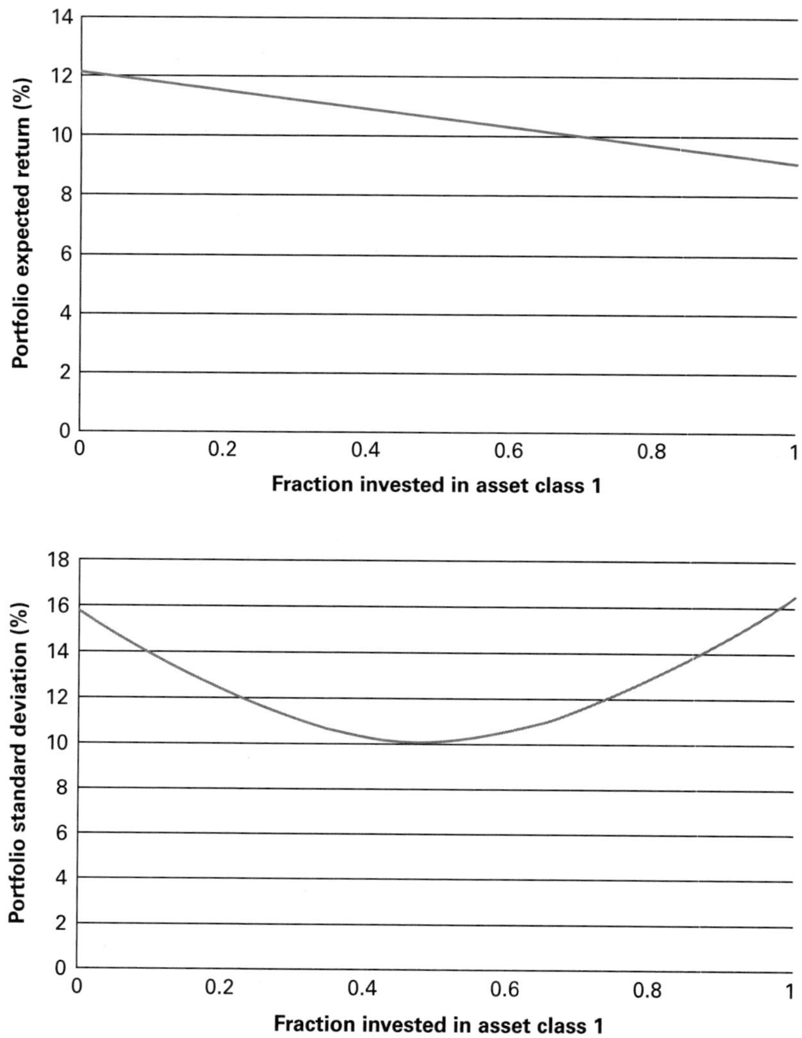

Exhibit 12.1
(A) Change in portfolio expected return as the fraction invested in asset class 1 increases from 0 to 1; (B) change in portfolio standard deviation as the fraction invested in asset class 1 increases from 0 to 1.

asset classes. The investor's choice can be represented as an $N \times 1$ vector array $\mathbf{w} = (w_1, \ldots, w_N)'$ of asset class weights.[1] Each weight w_i represents the proportion of asset class i held in the portfolio, and the total portfolio weight needs to be 100%; that is,

$$\sum_{i=1}^{N} w_i = 1$$

In vector notation, this requirement can be written as[2]

$$\mathbf{w}'\iota = 1$$

1. See online appendix A for a review of matrix notation and the definition of matrix transpose (').
2. See online appendix A for a review of matrix array multiplication.

where $\boldsymbol{\iota}$ is an $N \times 1$ vector array of 1s. If short selling is allowed,[3] then the weights can be negative.

Markowitz's framework assumes that the investor is making an asset allocation decision for a specified time period. The investor is concerned with the portfolio return *at the end* of that time period, but not during it or after the end of it. The returns of the N asset classes in the portfolio during that time period can be represented as a vector array of random variables: $\tilde{\mathbf{r}}=(\tilde{r}_1,\ldots,\tilde{r}_N)'$. Suppose that the expected returns on the N assets are $\boldsymbol{\mu}=(\mu_1,\ldots,\mu_N)'$, and the covariance matrix of returns is

$$\Sigma = \begin{bmatrix} \sigma_{11} & \cdots & \sigma_{1N} \\ \vdots & \ddots & \vdots \\ \sigma_{N1} & \cdots & \sigma_{NN} \end{bmatrix}$$

where σ_{ij} denotes the covariance between asset class i and asset class j, and the diagonal element σ_{ij} is the variance of asset class i (i.e., $\sigma_{ii}=\sigma_i^2$). (Note that $\sigma_{ij}=\sigma_{ji}$—that is, the covariance matrix is symmetric—because the covariance between i and j is the same as the covariance between j and i.) Then the expected return on a portfolio that has allocations of $\mathbf{w}=(w_1,\ldots,w_N)'$ is

$$\mu_p = \sum_{i=1}^{N} \mu_i \cdot w_i = \boldsymbol{\mu}'\mathbf{w}$$

and the portfolio variance σ_p^2 is

$$\sigma_p^2 = \mathbf{w}'\Sigma\,\mathbf{w}.$$

If, instead of the covariance matrix, we know the correlation matrix

$$\mathbf{K} = \begin{bmatrix} 1 & \cdots & \rho_{1N} \\ \vdots & \ddots & \vdots \\ \rho_{N1} & \cdots & 1 \end{bmatrix}$$

and the standard deviations of the individual asset classes, we can either convert the correlation matrix into a covariance matrix element by element by using the following relationship:[4]

$$\rho_{ij} = \frac{\sigma_{ij}}{\sigma_i \sigma_j}$$

or we can directly use the correlation matrix in the expression for portfolio variance. To do that, we need to construct a vector $\mathbf{w}^s$ of products of the weights of the asset classes and the corresponding standard deviations, $\mathbf{w}^s=(w_1\sigma_1,\ldots,w_N\sigma_N)'$. Then, the portfolio variance can be computed as $\sigma_p^2=(\mathbf{w}^s)'\mathbf{K}\mathbf{w}^s$.

3. See chapter 2 for a definition of the term *short selling*.

4. See section 3.8.

To provide some intuition, let us go back to the case of two asset classes with weights w_1 and w_2. The portfolio return can be written in vector notation as

$$\tilde{r}_p = [w_1 \quad w_1] \cdot \begin{bmatrix} \tilde{r}_1 \\ \tilde{r}_2 \end{bmatrix} = \mathbf{w}'\tilde{\mathbf{r}}$$

The portfolio expected return in matrix notation is

$$E[\tilde{r}_p] = E[\mathbf{w}'\tilde{\mathbf{r}}] = \mathbf{w}'E[\tilde{\mathbf{r}}] = [w_1 \quad w_1] \cdot \begin{bmatrix} E[\tilde{r}_1] \\ E[\tilde{r}_2] \end{bmatrix} = \mathbf{w}'\boldsymbol{\mu}$$

The portfolio variance in matrix notation is

$$\sigma_p^2 = \mathbf{w}'\sum \mathbf{w} = [w_1 \quad w_2] \cdot \begin{bmatrix} \sigma_1^2 & \sigma_{12} \\ \sigma_{21} & \sigma_2^2 \end{bmatrix} \cdot \begin{bmatrix} w_1 \\ w_2 \end{bmatrix}$$
$$= [w_1\sigma_1^2 + w_2\sigma_{21} \quad w_1\sigma_{12} + w_2\sigma_2^2] \cdot \begin{bmatrix} w_1 \\ w_2 \end{bmatrix}.$$

Note that the last expression equals

$$w_1^2\sigma_1^2 + w_2^2\sigma_2^2 + 2w_1w_2\sigma_{12}$$

which is the same expression as the expression for variance derived in section 10.1.

If we are given the correlation matrix rather than the covariance matrix, then we can compute the portfolio variance as

$$\sigma_p^2 = [w_1\sigma_1 \quad w_2\sigma_2] \cdot \begin{bmatrix} 1 & \rho_{12} \\ \rho_{21} & 1 \end{bmatrix} \cdot \begin{bmatrix} w_1\sigma_1 \\ w_2\sigma_2 \end{bmatrix}$$
$$= [w_1\sigma_1 + w_2\sigma_2\rho_{12} \quad w_1\sigma_1\rho_{12} + w_1\sigma_2] \cdot \begin{bmatrix} w_1\sigma_1 \\ w_2\sigma_2 \end{bmatrix} = w_1^2\sigma_1^2 + w_2^2\sigma_2^2 + 2w_1w_2\sigma_1\sigma_2\rho_{12},$$

which again is equivalent to the expression for variance derived in the previous section, because $\sigma_1\sigma_2\rho_{12} = \sigma_{12}$.

The classical mean-variance portfolio allocation problem is formulated as follows:

$$\begin{aligned} \min_{\mathbf{w}} \quad & \mathbf{w}'\sum \mathbf{w} \\ \text{s. t.} \quad & \mathbf{w}'\boldsymbol{\mu} = r_{\text{target}} \\ & \mathbf{w}'\boldsymbol{\iota} = 1 \end{aligned}$$

Note that the objective function of this optimization problem is quadratic in the decision variables **w**.[5] This minimization problem is *convex* because the objective function is convex

5. See chapter 6 for a review of optimization problem formulations, classification, and terminology.

and all the constraints are linear functions of the decision variables.[6] To see that the objective function is a convex function of the decision variables **w**, consider the portfolio of two asset classes. The weight of the second asset class, w_2, can be expressed through the weight of the first asset class, w_1, as $w_2 = 1 - w_1$. Plugging into the expression for the portfolio variance, we obtain

$$\begin{aligned}\sigma_p^2 &= w_1^2\sigma_1^2 + (1-w_1)^2\sigma_2^2 + 2w_1(1-w_1)\rho_{12}\sigma_1\sigma_2 \\ &= w_1^2(\sigma_1^2 + \sigma_2^2 - 2\rho_{12}\sigma_1\sigma_2) + w_1(-2\sigma_2^2 + 2\rho_{12}\sigma_1\sigma_2) + \sigma_2^2.\end{aligned}$$

The sign of the coefficient in front of the decision variable w_1^2 determines whether the quadratic objective function will be concave or convex (see exhibit 6.3). Note that the coefficient can be written as

$$\begin{aligned}\sigma_1^2 + \sigma_2^2 - 2\sigma_1\sigma_2 + 2\sigma_1\sigma_2 - 2\rho_{12}\sigma_1\sigma_2 &= (\sigma_1^2 + \sigma_2^2 - 2\sigma_1\sigma_2) + 2\sigma_1\sigma_2(1-\rho_{12}) \\ &= \underbrace{(\sigma_1 + \sigma_2)^2}_{\geq 0\,(\text{squared term})} + \underbrace{2\sigma_1\sigma_2(1-\rho_{12})}_{\geq 0\,(\text{because } -1 \leq \rho_{12} \leq 1)},\end{aligned}$$

so it is always nonnegative. Therefore, the objective function has the shape in exhibit 6.3(A) and, as a result, minimization will bring us to the global minimum at the tip of the curve.[7]

The optimal solution for the classical mean-variance portfolio allocation problem can be found in closed form by using Lagrange multipliers. The optimal weights are

$$\mathbf{w}^* = \mathbf{g} + \mathbf{h} \cdot r_{\text{target}},$$

where

$$\mathbf{g} = \frac{1}{ac - b^2} \cdot \Sigma^{-1} \cdot [c \cdot \iota - b \cdot \mu], \ \mathbf{h} = \frac{1}{ac - b^2} \cdot \Sigma^{-1} \cdot [a \cdot \mu - b \cdot \iota]$$

and

$$a = \iota'\Sigma^{-1}\iota \qquad b = \iota'\Sigma^{-1}\mu \qquad c = \mu'\Sigma^{-1}\mu.$$

Typically, however, the classical mean-variance optimization is modified to include additional constraints or to express the objective in a different way, so no closed-form solution exists, and an optimization solver must be used to find the optimal weights. In the online appendices, we provide instructions and code for implementing the mean-variance problem with Microsoft Excel Solver, MATLAB's Optimization Toolbox, and Python.

The problem of minimizing the portfolio variance is equivalent to the problem of minimizing the portfolio standard deviation (which is the square root of the portfolio variance) in the sense that the optimal weights will be the same. Minimizing the portfolio variance,

6. See chapter 6 for a discussion of the use of convex functions in optimization.

7. This statement is a bit simplified because the function plotted in exhibit 6.3 is a function of a single variable x, whereas here, we have a function of two variables, so the picture would be three-dimensional. The general conclusion, however, is the same.

however, is more solver friendly. It is preferable that the minimum variance formulation is implemented with optimization software. The optimal portfolio standard deviation can then be derived easily from the optimal portfolio variance.

12.2.1 Efficient Frontiers

Let us consider again the two-asset class example from the beginning of section 12.2, which is illustrated in the worksheet **Diversification** in the file **Ch12-Diversification2Stocks.xlsm**. As the weight of asset class 1 in the portfolio increases, the portfolio expected return and risk trace the solid curve in exhibit 12.2(A). Each point on this curve is obtained for a different combination of the weights for each asset class. The point at the top-right part of the curve is the portfolio that is obtained if 100% is invested in asset class 2. Note that that portfolio's expected return is 12.1% (the expected return of asset class 2), and its standard deviation is 15.8% (the standard deviation of asset class 2). At the other end (the point at the bottom-right part of the curve) is a portfolio in which 100% is invested in asset class 1.

As we trace the curve between its top-rightmost point and its bottom-rightmost point, we obtain different portfolio risk-return characteristics. It is difficult to say which risk-return combination is "optimal"—that will depend on the individual's risk tolerance. What we can say, however, is that no rational investor would prefer portfolios located on the lower part of the curve, such as portfolio B in exhibit 12.2(A). For the same level of portfolio risk (standard deviation of 13.0%), the investor could obtain a higher expected return—that of portfolio A. Therefore, portfolio A dominates portfolio B. Exhibit 12.2(B) illustrates the *efficient frontier*—the upper part of the curve, which contains the set of portfolios that dominate all other portfolios given a specific tolerance for the level of risk or the level of expected return.

Consider now an investor who is considering N asset classes, where N is greater than 2. The set of all asset class risk-return pairs obtained when varying the weights of the individual assets fills the shaded area in exhibit 12.3. The Markowitz mean-variance formulation explained in section 12.2 helps us find the portfolios along the upper part of the curve (between portfolios D and E on the graph)—that is, the portfolios along the efficient frontier. Those portfolios offer the lowest standard deviation for a given level of expected return and provide the best possible trade-off between return and risk. All portfolios in the shaded area (such as portfolio C) and along the lower part of the curve (such as portfolio B) are dominated by the portfolios on the efficient frontier. All portfolios above the efficient frontier (i.e., higher on the graph than the curve defined by portfolios A, D, and E) are unattainable. Portfolio D has the lowest possible standard deviation among all combinations of weights for the assets in the portfolio. It is called the *minimum variance portfolio.*

If more asset classes are added to the portfolio, there is obviously a higher number of possible combinations of weights for these assets in the portfolio. The feasible set in exhibit 12.3 widens, and the efficient frontier gets pushed outward to reflect the fact that there are now more possibilities for diversification.

To construct the efficient frontier, we simply solve the portfolio optimization problem from this section and plot the optimal standard deviation obtained for any level of targeted expected return. The code for calculating the efficient frontier is provided in the online appendix to this chapter.

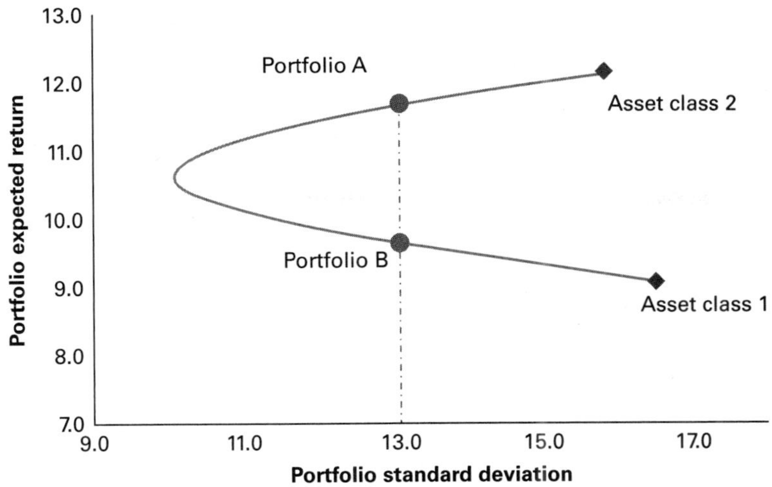

Exhibit 12.2a
(A) Possible pairings of portfolio expected return and standard deviation as the weights of the two asset classes vary between 0 and 1.

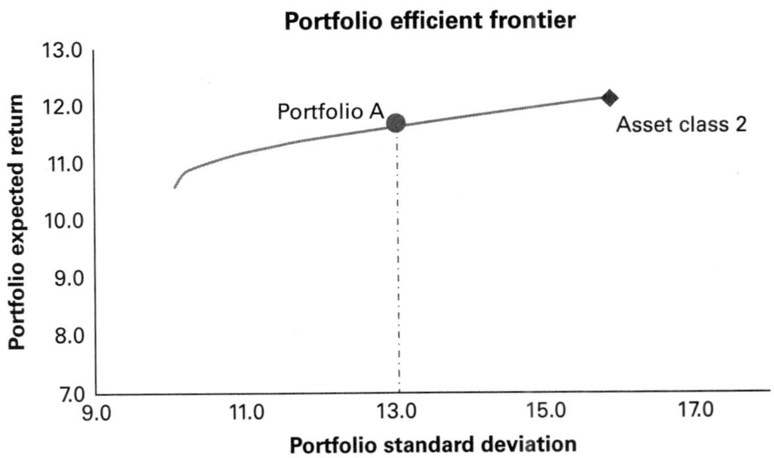

Exhibit 12.2b
(B) Portfolio efficient frontier.

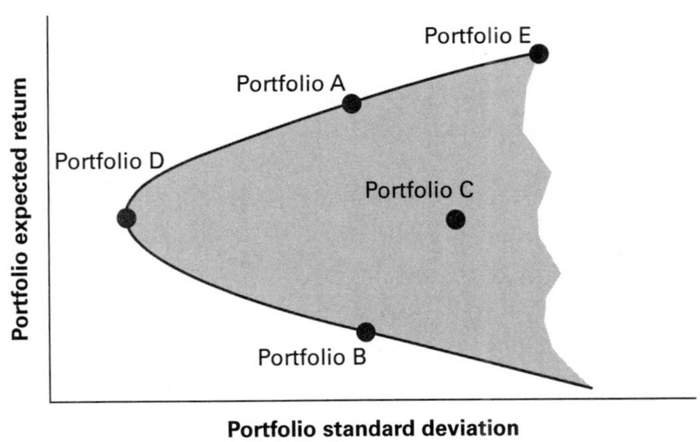

Exhibit 12.3
Feasible and mean-variance efficient portfolios.

12.2.2 Alternative Formulations of the Classical Mean-Variance Optimization Problem

The mean-variance optimization problem introduced in section 10.2 has a couple of alternative but equivalent formulations used in practice.

12.2.2.1 Expected Return Formulation Instead of imposing a constraint on the expected return and minimizing the portfolio variance, we could impose a constraint on the portfolio variance and maximize the expected return. The optimization formulation, then, is

$$\begin{aligned} \max_{\mathbf{w}} \quad & \mathbf{w}'\boldsymbol{\mu} \\ \text{s. t.} \quad & \mathbf{w}'\Sigma\mathbf{w} = \sigma^2_{\text{target}} \\ & \mathbf{w}'\boldsymbol{\iota} = 1 \end{aligned}$$

This formulation, which we will refer to as the *expected return maximization formulation* of the classical mean-variance optimization problem, is especially used by portfolio managers whose goal is to limit their risk relative to a benchmark.

12.2.2.2 Risk Aversion Formulation Another possible formulation is to model the trade-off between risk and return directly through the objective function. This can be accomplished by assigning a penalty term for high portfolio variance (i.e., a risk-aversion coefficient λ). The *risk aversion mean-variance formulation* is stated as follows:

$$\begin{aligned} \max_{\mathbf{w}} \quad & \mathbf{w}'\boldsymbol{\mu} - \lambda \cdot \mathbf{w}'\Sigma\mathbf{w} \\ \text{s. t.} \quad & \mathbf{w}'\boldsymbol{\iota} = 1 \end{aligned}$$

The risk aversion coefficient λ is referred to as the *Arrow-Pratt risk aversion coefficient.* When λ is small, the aversion to risk is also small, leading to more risky portfolios because the portfolio variance is not penalized as much in the objective of the optimization problem. If we gradually increase λ starting from 0 and solve the optimization problem for each value of λ, we in fact calculate every portfolio along the efficient frontier. It is common practice to calibrate λ so the portfolio has the desired risk-return characteristics (i.e., the "risk profile"). The calibration is often performed via backtests with historical data. For most portfolio allocation decisions in practice, the risk aversion coefficient is somewhere between 2 and 4.

12.2.3 Selecting the Asset Allocation

It makes economic sense that the asset allocation that should be selected by an investor lies somewhere on the efficient frontier. Efficient portfolios represent a trade-off between expected portfolio return and portfolio risk. How does the investor determine the asset class allocation?

Financial economic theory offers one solution for determining the *optimal* asset allocation based on expected utility theory, and that is the approach explained in investment management textbooks. In practice, this approach is not used. There are more practical ways of selecting the asset allocation from the portfolios on the efficient frontier.

One way to select an *optimal* asset allocation without relying on expected utility theory is to base the decision on a reward-risk ratio (i.e., risk-adjusted return ratio). The most used reward-risk ratio is the *Sharpe ratio*,[8] given by

8. See Sharpe (1966).

$$\text{Sharpe ratio} = \frac{\text{Realized portfolio return} - \text{Risk-free rate}}{\text{Standard deviaion of the realized portfolio return}}$$

The higher the Sharpe ratio is, the greater the return per unit of risk, where risk is measured by the standard deviation. So the criterion would be to select the asset allocation that maximizes the Sharpe ratio.

Another reward ratio that can be used is the *Sortino ratio*.[9] This ratio addresses a major criticism of the Sharpe ratio when it comes to employing the standard deviation of returns. The Sortino ratio uses as the measure of relative performance a *client-specified minimum acceptable return*. The risk measure is not the standard deviation of the realized returns, but the standard deviation of the realized returns that are below the client-specified minimum acceptable return. Effectively, rather than looking at total volatility (i.e., standard deviation), the risk measure only considers bad volatility, which consists of returns below the minimum acceptable return.[10]

Another criterion to select the asset allocation is to select the one with the minimum risk from among all the efficient portfolios. Since risk is measured by the variance in the mean-variance model, the criterion used is to select the asset allocation with the smallest variance. This portfolio is called the *global minimum variance* (GMV) *portfolio*.

When roboadvisors employ the mean-variance model for allocating a client's wealth, it is based on what the roboadvisor believes is the client's risk tolerance. That estimate of the client's risk is based on a series of questionnaires that the client completes at the start.

Additional advanced risk measures and portfolio allocation formulations are discussed in chapter 13.

12.2.4 Illustrations

To illustrate the mean-variance optimization model, we will use actual data and the online portfolio optimization software from Portfolio Visualizer (https://www.portfoliovisualizer

9. Sortino and van der Meer (1991) and Sortino and Price (1994).

10. Other measures have been proposed as a criterion for selecting the optimal portfolio. One risk associated with an asset allocation is *drawdown risk*. Investors are concerned with capital preservation if they invest in a select portfolio based on a particular asset allocation. The concern is that the portfolio will incur a significant decline in value. *Drawdown* is the difference in the portfolio value if an investor selected a portfolio based on an asset allocation at its peak value, maintained it until it declined to the time before it rose in value again, and then sold it before it turned up in value. The difference between any peak value that was reached and the low value before the portfolio value increased is the drawdown. A drawdown can be computed for a specific time period such as quarterly or annually. For example, suppose that an investor invests $125 million in a portfolio based on a particular asset allocation and the portfolio doubles in value to $250 million, then declines to $150 million, and then rises in value again. The drawdown in this case is $150 million ($250 million – $100 million). However, drawdown is typically calculated not in dollar terms, but as a percentage of the peak portfolio value. In our example, it would be 60% ($150 million/$250 million). Maximum drawdown is the decline in the portfolio's value from its maximum value over some time period. The maximum value for this measure is 100%. The larger the maximum drawdown, the greater the risk. Let's use the previous illustration to explain this measure. Suppose that after the investment value reaches $100 million, it rises in value to $300 million and then declines to $75 million before it rises in value again. The maximum value in this illustration is $300 million. The drawdown from this maximum value is 75% (($300 million – $75 million)/$300 million), and thus it is the maximum drawdown. The maximum drawdown is expressed as a negative value. Thus, in our illustration, the maximum drawdown would be expressed as –75%.

Asset Class	Expected Return (%)	Standard Deviation (%)
US Large Cap	11.66	15.33
US Mid Cap	11.86	17.81
US Small Cap	12.19	19.89
Short-Term Treasury	2.23	1.50
Intermediate-Term Treasury	4.19	4.27
Corporate Bonds	6.03	6.03
Commodities	−3.27	23.72

Exhibit 12.4a
Data for mean-variance model (monthly returns from January 1, 2007 to August 31, 2021).
Part A: Expected Returns and Standard Deviations

Asset class	US Large Cap	US Mid Cap	US Small Cap	Short-Term Treasury	Intermediate-Term Treasury	Corporate Bonds	Commodities
US Large Cap	1	0.96	0.93	−0.31	−0.27	0.33	0.55
US Mid Cap	0.96	1	0.97	−0.33	−0.28	0.37	0.57
US Small Cap	0.93	0.97	1	−0.34	−0.31	0.32	0.55
Short-Term Treasury	−0.31	−0.33	−0.34	1	0.85	0.33	−0.2
Intermediate-Term Treasury	−0.27	−0.28	−0.31	0.85	1	0.47	−0.27
Corporate Bonds	0.33	0.37	0.32	0.33	0.47	1	0.1
Commodities	0.55	0.57	0.55	−0.2	−0.27	0.1	1

Exhibit 12.4b
Part B: Correlations

.com/). We will assume that the investor is considering an allocation of funds to the following seven asset classes: U.S. large cap, U.S. mid cap, U.S. small cap, short-term Treasury, intermediate-term Treasury, corporate bonds, and commodities

Using monthly returns for the period January 2007 to August 31, 2021, the expected return and standard deviation of monthly returns for each asset class are shown in exhibit 12.4(A), and the monthly pairwise correlations between each asset class are shown in exhibit 12.4(B).

Exhibit 12.5(A) shows the asset allocation based on different criteria, including maximization of the Sharpe ratio, minimum variance portfolio, and minimum maximum drawdown. There is no allocation to all seven asset classes. Although the allocations are different, they are heavily weighted toward short-term Treasuries.

Typically, there are constraints imposed on the minimum and maximum amounts that can be allocated to each asset class, as well as limitations on the allocation for a group of asset classes. In our illustration, we will impose the following constraints:

Asset class	Asset allocation (%)	
Criterion	Max. Sharpe ratio	Min. Variance
US Large Cap	7.93	1.01
US Mid Cap	0.00	0.31
US Small Cap	0.00	1.77
Short-Term Treasury	90.74	96.66
Intermediate-Term Treasury	1.33	0.00
Corporate Bonds	0.00	0.00
Commodities	0.00	0.24
Portfolio expected return	2.97	2.50
Portfolio standard deviation	1.55	1.37
Max Sharpe ratio	1.39	
Min variance		1.87

Exhibit 12.5a
Asset allocation based on data from January 1, 2007 to August 31, 2021.
Part A: No Constraints

Asset class	Asset allocation (%)	
Criterion	Max. Sharpe ratio	Min. Variance
US Large Cap	20.73	20.00
US Mid Cap	5.00	5.00
US Small Cap	5.00	5.00
Short-Term Treasury	15.44	37.84
Intermediate-Term Treasury	44.56	22.16
Corporate Bonds	5.00	5.00
Commodities	5.00	5.00
Portfolio expected return	5.81	5.36
Portfolio standard deviation	5.57	5.53
Max Sharpe ratio	0.86	
Min variance		30.58

Exhibit 12.5b
Part B: Constraints

1. A minimum allocation of 5% to all asset classes except U.S. large cap stocks and intermediate-term Treasuries
2. A minimum of 30% allocated to equities (U.S. large cap stocks + U.S. mid cap stocks + U.S. small cap stocks)
3. A maximum allocation of 50% to equities
4. A maximum allocation to the total allocated to intermediate-term Treasuries and corporate bonds

Exhibit 12.5(B) shows the asset allocations based on the four constraints using the same two criteria as in exhibit 12.5(A).

Asset class	Asset allocation (%)			
Inputs estimated based on:	1/1/2007-8/31/2021	1/1/2009-8/31/2021	1/1/2013-8/31/2021	1/1/2017-8/31/2021
US Large Cap	7.93	8.38	10.53	10.35
US Mid Cap	0.00	0.32	0.00	0.00
US Small Cap	0.00	0.00	0.00	0.00
Short-Term Treasury	90.74	90.58	89.47	73.88
Intermediate-Term Treasury	1.33	0.39	0.00	15.77
Corporate Bonds	0.00	0.33	0.00	0.00
Commodities	0.00	0.00	0.00	0.00
Portfolio expected return	2.97	2.74	2.89	3.92
Portfolio standard deviation	1.55	1.48	1.42	1.60
Max Sharpe ratio	1.39	1.49	1.54	1.67

Exhibit 12.6
Different periods for estimating the inputs: asset allocation using maximizing Sharpe ratio (no constraints).

In exhibit 12.6, we show the sensitivity of the unconstrained mean-variance optimization model based on the maximization of the Sharpe ratio using the estimation periods for the various inputs.

12.3 Robust Optimization for Mean-Variance Analysis

The inputs to the mean-variance model must be estimated, typically from historical data. An issue with the mean-variance optimization model when used for asset allocation is that asset classes with estimated mean returns that are large and standard deviations that are low relative to other asset classes will be overweighted in the portfolios on the efficient frontier. Conversely, asset classes with low estimated returns and high standard deviations will be underweighted for portfolios on the efficient frontier. Therefore, large estimation errors in the estimates of expected returns and variances/covariances will introduce errors in the optimal weights obtained from mean-variance optimization. For this reason, some portfolio managers refer to optimizers as "error maximizers."[11]

Researchers have examined the problem of misestimation of inputs (expected return and variance/covariance) on the optimal weights, and specifically which input misestimation has the greatest impact on the optimal weights for the asset classes. Best and Grauer (1991, 1992) report that the uncertainty from estimation error in expected returns tends to have more influence than in the variance/covariance matrix in a mean-variance optimization. Although the relative importance of input estimation error depends on the investor's risk aversion, as a general rule of thumb, errors in the expected returns are about 10 times more important than errors in the covariance matrix, and errors in the variances are about

11. See Michaud (1989).

Asset class	Robust	Classic	Robust	Classic
US Large Cap	9.54%	10.15%	18.18%	20.00%
US Mid Cap	0.14%	0	5.88%	5.00%
US Small Cap	0.55%	0	5.94%	5.00%
Short-Term Treasury	80.65%	82.72%	20.43%	15.00%
Intermediate-Term Treasury	8.77%	7.13%	37.09%	45.00%
Corporate Bonds	0.21%	0.00%	6.74%	5.00%
Commodities	0.15%	0.00%	5.00%	5.00%

Exhibit 12.7
Robust mean-variance portfolio optimization versus classic mean-variance portfolio optimization.
Note: Based on month returns from January 1, 2007, to August 31, 2021.

twice as important as errors in the covariances. (See Chopra and Ziemba, 1993.) The relative impact of estimation errors in the expected returns becomes even more important as the risk tolerance increases. Conversely, the relative impact between errors in expected returns and the covariance matrix becomes smaller as the risk tolerance decreases. For this reason, good estimates for the expected returns are critically important, followed by the variances.

Several approaches have been proposed for dealing with this problem of errors in estimating the inputs. We describe these approaches in detail in sections 14.7-14.9. Here, we provide high-level intuition by extending the example from section 12.2 to illustrate one of them: robust mean-variance optimization.[12]

We will assume that the input that is most uncertain is the expected returns of the asset classes. Although the variance and covariance are also uncertain, as just explained, the optimal weights are most sensitive to the expected returns. We will use μ_i to denote the unknown but true expected return and $\hat{\mu}_i$ to denote the estimated expected return. As explained in section 7.3.1, one possible choice for the uncertainty set is to assume that the true expected return belongs to an interval around the estimated value,

$$\hat{\mu}_i - d_i \leq \mu_i \leq \hat{\mu}_i + d_i$$

where d_i is a positive number selected for each asset class. If the expected return of an asset class is characterized by higher uncertainty, then a larger d_i for that asset class should be selected.

The objective in the optimization problem is then reformulated so the asset classes with more uncertain expected returns on a relative basis are penalized:

$$w_1\ \hat{\mu}_1 + \cdots + w_K\ \hat{\mu}_K - |w_1\,|\,d_1 - \cdots - |\,w_K\,|\,d_K$$

The constraints are not modified.

We use the robust portfolio optimization software by Portfolio Visualizer to illustrate robust portfolio optimization for the asset allocation decision for the seven asset classes in this example in section 12.2.4. Exhibit 12.7 shows the optimal allocation based on

12. See chapter 7 for an introduction to robust optimization as a technique for optimization under uncertainty.

maximizing the Sharpe ratio for the robust optimization model. The second and third columns compare the unconstrained case for the classic mean-variance optimization and robust optimization, respectively. The last two columns of the exhibit show the corresponding allocation for the constrained case.

Sections 7.3.1 and 14.9 present rigorous mathematical derivations of a general robust optimization formulation and the robust portfolio optimization formulation, respectively, and contain a more detailed discussion of alternative uncertainty sets and robust formulations.

12.4 Risk Parity Model

An alternative to the mean-variance framework for determining asset allocation is the *risk parity model*.[13] With this asset allocation model, the idea is not to allocate to different asset classes based on capital allocation using an optimization that targets a specific return with a minimal level of risk, but rather to generate a portfolio where the contribution of an asset class to the portfolio risk is equal, regardless of the expected return for the asset classes. Unlike mean-variance optimization, a risk parity model for asset allocation does not require a forecast of the expected return of each asset class. In this section, we briefly describe the basic workings of the risk parity model.[14]

12.4.1 Essential Elements of a Risk Parity Model

The risk parity model does not seek to identify the optimal portfolio from mean-variance analysis for a given level of expected return, but instead to construct a portfolio such that each asset's risk contribution to the portfolio is roughly the same. Mean-variance analysis often provides an efficient portfolio that is heavily concentrated in a few risk assets, such as equities and commodities. Therefore, the efficient portfolio identified is such that there is considerable exposure to volatility spikes since the latter asset classes expose investors to more near-term downside than other asset classes such as bonds. From the standpoint of theory and practice, the risk parity model can be viewed as yet another framework offering diversification in the asset allocation process.

Formal descriptions[15] of the risk parity strategy typically begin by defining the volatility contribution of risk for each asset:

$$\sigma_i(\mathbf{w}) = w_i \times \partial_{w_i}\sigma(\mathbf{w})$$

where portfolio volatility $\sigma(\mathbf{w}) = \sqrt{\mathbf{w}^T \Sigma \mathbf{w}}$.

13. The foundations for the risk parity strategy appeared in publications by Ray Dalio and his portfolio management team at the Bridgewater Associates hedge fund. Bridgewater developed risk parity as the core investment strategy for the firm's All Weather Fund, which started in 1996. It was not until 2005 when the term "risk parity" was coined by Edward Qian of PanAgora Asset Management. Various risk parity strategies were subsequently marketed by several major asset management firms.

14. For a more detailed discussion of the risk parity model, its history, and the various risk parity strategies marketed by several major asset management firms, see Fabozzi, Simonian, and Fabozzi (2021).

15. Maillard, Roncalli, and Teïletche (2010) provide a detailed discussion of some of the mathematical properties of risk parity portfolios.

Given this, it is clear that $\sigma(\mathbf{w}) = \sum_{i=1}^{n} \sigma_i(\mathbf{w})$, and the vector of marginal contributions $\partial_{w_i}\sigma(\mathbf{w})$ is derived as follows:

$$mc(w) = \frac{\sum \mathbf{w}}{\sqrt{\mathbf{w}^T \sum \mathbf{w}}}$$

Accordingly, for N assets, the objective function to determine the risk parity portfolio weights is

$$\arg\min_{\mathbf{w}} \sum_{i=1}^{N} \left[\frac{\sqrt{\mathbf{w}^T \sum \mathbf{w}}}{N} - w_i \times mc(\mathbf{w})_i \right]^2$$

Risk parity is more diversification-focused than mean-variance analysis, and it is empirically driven based on historical evidence about how assets are priced. The key is that portfolios should be structured so there is an equal marginal risk contribution from each asset class. From an implementation standpoint, perhaps the most criticized aspect of a risk parity model is its use of leverage, specifically the leveraging of the entire portfolio to enhance returns. For most investors or plan sponsors, the expected return of an unleveraged risk parity strategy is insufficient compared to their required return goals. The application of leverage to a risk parity helps align the portfolio with an investor's return objectives without compromising its stability objectives.

The implementation of a risk parity model involves six decisions that must be made by the investor:

- Selection of the risk measure and the target level of risk
- Selection of the asset classes to be included in the portfolio
- How to estimate the risk contribution of each selected asset class
- How to construct an equally risk-weighted portfolio with no leverage (i.e., an unlevered risk parity portfolio)
- How to construct a leveraged risk parity portfolio
- How to make tactical expressions away from the strategic risk allocation of the portfolio

What is the appropriate risk measure in a risk parity strategy? While most risk parity managers use the standard deviation of asset class returns as the risk measure, other risk measures can be used. (These other measures are the subject of chapter 13.) Despite the well-known problems with using standard deviation as a measure of risk, it appears to be the risk measure of choice in most risk parity models used in practice because it is convenient for decomposing a portfolio's volatility into volatility contributions from each of the candidate asset classes. The target level of risk and leverage can be based on a variety of considerations, primarily client suitability.[16]

The universe of potential asset classes to include in a risk parity portfolio has grown over the years. The universe of assets today sometimes includes alternative asset classes. The

16. Creating a leveraged portfolio is also part of the selection of an optimal portfolio using mean-variance analysis to achieve a target return. In this case, what is being leveraged is the market portfolio.

inclusion of extended asset classes will typically necessitate the augmenting of the basic risk parity framework to account for additional types of risk, including illiquitiy and event risk.

Leverage can be applied to a risk parity portfolio, either explicity or implicitly. Explicit leverage is created through borrowing funds from a counterparty (e.g., prime broker) and fund assets are used to collateralize the loan. Prime broker financing and repurchase agreements are examples of explicit leverage. Implicit leverage is created through the use of derivative instruments where the notional exposure is greater than the margin required to collateralize the position. Futures, forwards, swaps, and options are all examples of implicit leverage and are discussed further in chapter 18.

Various empirical studies on asset pricing have been useful in refining investors' implementation of risk parity strategies, in particular studies dealing with what is referred to as the "low-volatility anomaly." The latter has shown evidence that relatively low-volatility asset classes exhibit a better return per unit of risk than high-volatility asset classes. This was also found to be true within asset classes.[17] Risk parity therefore involves constructing an unleveraged portfolio that may have a low expected return because of a relative overweighting of bonds and then uses leverage to increase exposure to bonds, which have a better return per unit of risk relative to other asset classes. At one time, the bond sector of choice that offered the most desirable investment attributes for risk parity was fixed-rate U.S. Treasury bonds. However, in the current low interest-rate environment, some portfolio managers have gravitated toward U.S. Treasury inflation protection securities or risky sovereign market bonds to enhance returns. While there is a potential return benefit from the latter tactic, it also burdens risk parity portfolios with increasing liquidity risk.

In the selection of the specific assets for each asset class, a risk parity strategy can be done through a passive strategy using a low-cost collective investment, such as an exchange-traded fund (ETF), or an active strategy, such as one using a factor model.

There are three practical issues in implementing a risk parity model. The first involves the use of leverage. Risk parity strategies typically attempt to use leverage to increase their expected returns. Because leverage involves borrowing, risk parity strategies are susceptible to sudden and/or significant jumps in borrowing costs. (This is true only for explicit leverage.) A second implementation challenge is that in some market environments, such as the one since 2019, most reasonable leverage levels would not be able to provide a level of expected returns that would justify the additional risk of leveraging the portfolio . This is primarily due to the ultra-low yields we observe in the bond market. A third implementation challenge is that asset correlations (namely, those between stocks and bonds) may not behave as expected. This is also true for the mean-variance model.

12.4.2 Illustration of the Risk Parity Model

To illustrate the risk parity model, we will use the same seven asset classes as in section 12.2.3 and the software and data for monthly returns from Portfolio Visualizer. The results are shown in the second column of exhibit 12.8. For comparison purposes, the third column of the exhibit shows the results for the classical mean-variance model, assuming no

17. See Frazzini and Pedersen (2014).

Asset class	Risk parity	Classic
US Large Cap	3.72%	10.15%
US Mid Cap	3.15%	0
US Small Cap	2.97%	0
Short-Term Treasury	60.17%	82.72%
Intermediate-Term Treasury	19.88%	7.13%
Corporate Bonds	6.99%	0.00%
Commodities	3.11%	0.00%

Exhibit 12.8
Risk parity model results.
Note: Based on month returns from January 1, 2007, to August 31, 2021.

constraints and using maximization of the Sharpe ratio as the criterion for selecting the optimal weights.

12.5 Using ML Models for Asset Allocation

The asset allocation problem involves two steps. The first is estimating the required inputs, and the second involves using an optimization model to determine the weights (i.e., allocations) for the various asset classes. As explained in section 12.2, one of the major drawbacks of the mean-variance approach to the asset allocation problem is the difficulty of estimating the inputs. As noted by López de Prado (2016), this estimation difficulty is why mean-variance optimization can result in optimal performance when using the training dataset but perform poorly when using the testing dataset. As explained in section 12.2, the risk-parity approach does not require forecasts of the inputs. Alternatively, ML techniques can be used that do not require the forecasting of inputs.

Two ML methodologies that are commonly used for asset allocation are hierarchical clustering and deep learning models. These will be discussed next.

12.5.1 Correlation Clustering for Asset Allocation

As explained in chapter 10, one of the tasks where ML can be used is in clustering analysis (i.e., grouping observations such as stocks into clusters). One type of ML algorithm used for clustering is correlation clustering. An input that is used in portfolio optimization is the correlation matrix.

12.5.2 Deep Learning Models for Asset Allocation

Zhang, Zohren, and Roberts (2020) demonstrate how deep learning models can be used to obtain an optimized portfolio allocation that maximizes the Sharpe ratio. Deep learning models circumvent the requirement that expected returns for asset classes be forecasted, allowing the model to produce the optimal asset class weights directly by updating model parameters.

The objective function in their model is the maximization of the Sharpe ratio. There are three main building blocks in their model, as shown in exhibit 12.9: the input layer, the neural layer, and the output layer. In the exhibit, A_i denotes the asset class, w_i is the weight

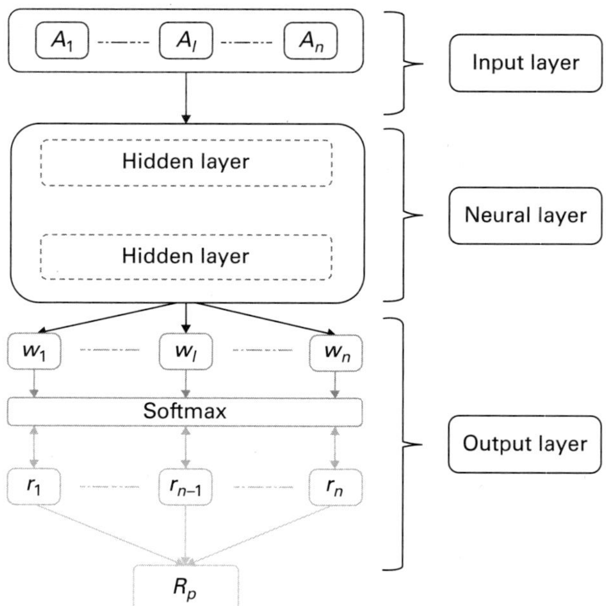

Exhibit 12.9
Model architecture schematics.
Source: Exhibit 2 in Zhang et al. (2020, p. 12).
Note: A_i denotes the asset class, w_i is the weight of asset class i, r_i is the return for asset class i, and R_p is the portfolio return.

of asset class i, r_i is the return for asset class i, and R_p is the portfolio return. The purpose is to use neural networks to extract cross-sectional features from the four asset classes. Using the extracted features, the portfolio weights (i.e., the allocations to the various asset classes) are outputted by the model, and then the realized returns that will maximize the Sharpe ratio are obtained. Here, we summarize the three main components.

The input layer accepts the data for each asset class and passes them on to the rest of the model. There are two dimensions to the input. The first is the number of lookback windows used to compute the second dimension, which in the model is past prices and returns. This is denoted by (k, 2), and since there are n asset classes, the dimension of the input is (k, $2{\times}n$). The features are said to be "stacked," which requires an ensemble ML algorithm. As explained in chapter 10, this involves combining the forecasts from several ML models using the same dataset.[18] When the input is fed into the model shown in exhibit 12.9, the expected features can be extracted. These features are not restricted to being linear.

The neural layer is the layer between the input and output layers that contains one or more hidden layers.[19] There are several ways of specifying the hidden layers. Zhang et al. (2020) used a convolutional neural network (CNN) for determining the hidden layers, which takes input from the input layer and assigns importance to each feature.

18. As explained in chapter 10, techniques for combining these forecasts include bagging and boosting.

19. They are referred to as "hidden layers" because they cannot be directly observed from either the inputs or the outputs of the model.

Finally, it is in the output layer where the asset allocation is determined (i.e., the weight w_i is determined). The authors used the *softmax* activation function[20] in this layer. The *softmax* activation function imposes the constraint that the portfolio weights are positive (i.e., no short-selling position for an asset class) and the sum of the weights must be 1.

The four asset classes used in their experiment to compare the deep learning model to other asset allocations were equities, bonds, fixed income, and volatility. Rather than market indices for these four asset classes, the authors used an ETF for each asset class because these funds offer high liquidity and relatively small expense ratios. The ETFs were the U.S. total stock index (VTI), the U.S. aggregate bond index (AGG), the U.S. commodity index (DBC), and the Volatility Index (VIX).

The authors' experiment used daily observations for the period 2006 to 2020, retraining the model every two years. The testing period was January 2011 to April 2020. Closing prices and daily returns for each ETF with a time window of the past 50 days of these observations formed a single input at the input layer.

The baseline asset allocations to which the authors compare their deep learning model fell into two categories. The first were common asset allocation used by pension funds. The second was a baseline portfolio constructed with mean-variance analysis.[21]

In their training scheme, the authors used a simple hidden layer. The only features used in their model were prices and returns. To optimize hyperparameters and control overfitting problems, they used 10% of any training data as a separate validation set. The training process was stopped after 100 times that the learning algorithm worked through the entire training database. A stochastic gradient descent algorithm was used as an optimizer.[22]

The results of the experiment support the authors' position that deep learning models for asset allocation can outperform various benchmark portfolios, including mean-variance analysis.

Summary

- The asset allocation decision involves allocating funds to each asset class under consideration.
- Once the asset allocation decision is made, the portfolio construction decision must be made for each asset class. This involves selecting specific assets from the individual asset classes.
- The critical importance of the asset allocation decision in the investment management process has been supported by major studies that investigated the historical performance of Markowitz's mean-variance model for allocation and quantified the idea of diversification as a prudent strategy.

20. An activation function defines the output, and software is one of the commonly used activation functions.

21. Other optimization constructed portfolios were also used as baseline portfolios (maximum diversification and diversity weighted), but the conclusions were not changed.

22. More specifically, the Adam optimizer is an extension of the classical stochastic gradient descent algorithm.

- Mathematically, the portfolio variance is a sum of terms including both the variances of the returns of the individual assets and the covariances (alternatively, the correlations) between those returns.
- In a well-diversified portfolio, the weak performance of a single asset will be compensated for by the performance of other assets that are not strongly correlated with that asset.
- The basic principle of the mean-variance model for asset allocation, formulated by Markowitz in 1952, is that for a given level of expected return, a rational investor would select the portfolio with the minimum variance among all possible portfolios.
- There are three equivalent formulations of the classic mean-variance model: (1) the portfolio variance minimization formulation; (2) the expected return maximization formulation; and (3) the risk-aversion formulation.
- Portfolio allocations obtained by minimizing the portfolio variance are called mean-variance efficient portfolios. The set of all mean-variance efficient portfolios is called the efficient frontier. The portfolio on the efficient frontier with the smallest variance is called the global minimum variance portfolio.
- Financial economic theory offers a solution for determining the optimal asset allocation based on expected utility theory. However, this approach is not used in practice.
- Another way to select is an optimal asset allocation without relying on expected utility theory is to base the decision on the maximization of some reward-risk ratio (e.g., Sharpe or Sortino ratio) or selecting the global minimum variance portfolio.
- Classical mean-variance optimization is sensitive to estimation error and small changes in the inputs.
- Empirical studies have shown that errors in the expected returns are about 10 times more important than errors in the covariance matrix, and errors in the variances are about twice as important as errors in the covariances.
- There are different approaches that can be used to make the classical mean-variance framework more robust. These approaches include (1) improving the accuracy of the inputs, (2) using constraints for the portfolio weights, and (3) applying a robust framework to the portfolio allocation process.
- In the robust portfolio optimization approach, the objective function is modified to include parameters that represent the uncertainty in returns.
- Unlike the mean-variance optimizaton model, a risk parity strategy allocates across asset classes such that contribution to portfolio risk of each asset class is equal, regardless of their expected returns.

13

Advanced Portfolio Risk Measures

In the asset allocation models described in chapter 12, we used the variance of returns as a measure of portfolio risk. However, as we saw in section 3.6.2, the variance of a probability distribution is a measure of the spread or the dispersion of the distribution. Using the variance in the portfolio optimization context means that outcomes that are above the expected portfolio return are deemed as risky as outcomes that are below the expected portfolio return. This is counterintuitive to many, as investors are more likely to be concerned about outcomes that fall short of expectations rather than exceed expectations. Moreover, there is considerable evidence that return distributions are not symmetric and are characterized by tails for distributions that are larger (i.e., fatter) than that of the normal distribution.[1]

Using the portfolio variance as a risk measure has been a subject of considerable debate in both academic circles and in practice. The goal of this chapter is to discuss the issue in more detail and present alternative risk measures that have been proposed. Since about the mid-1990s, considerable thought and innovation in the financial industry have been directed toward creating a better understanding of risk and its measurement and improving the management of risk in financial portfolios. Here, we review some important types of risk measures, such as semivariance, Roy's safety-first criterion, and quantile-based risk measures. Also discussed in detail are the history of, estimation of, and portfolio allocation under *value-at-risk* (VaR) and *conditional value-at-risk* (CVaR), two important risk measures that are widely used in practice.

13.1 Classes of Risk Measures

Most generally, risk measures can be divided into two classes: *dispersion* and *downside*. This section provides examples of risk measures from the two categories.

13.1.1 Dispersion Risk Measures

Dispersion risk measures measure the amount of dispersion of the returns around the expected portfolio return. Hence, they are measures of uncertainty in the estimate of the expected portfolio return. Uncertainty, however, does not necessarily quantify risk.

1. See Cont (2001) for a summary of the evidence on stylized facts about asset returns. One of these facts is that asset returns do not follow the properties of a normal distribution and asset returns are asymmetric.

Dispersion measures consider both positive and negative deviations from the mean and treat those deviations as equally risky. In other words, outperformance relative to the mean is penalized as much as underperformance.

Variance and Standard Deviation Because of the key role that they play in the theory of portfolio selection as set forth by Markowitz more than 55 years ago, the portfolio *variance* and *standard deviation* are the best-known dispersion measures. The portfolio variance is defined as

$$\sigma_p^2 = E[(\tilde{r}_p - E[\tilde{r}_p])^2] = E\left[\left(\sum_{i=1}^{N} w_i\tilde{r}_i - \sum_{i=1}^{N} w_i\mu_i\right)^2\right]$$

and the portfolio standard deviation is defined as

$$\sigma_p = (E[(\tilde{r}_p - E[\tilde{r}_p])^2])^{1/2} = \left(E\left[\left(\sum_{i=1}^{N} w_i\tilde{r}_i - \sum_{i=1}^{N} w_i\mu_i\right)^2\right]\right)^{1/2}$$

where $\tilde{r}_i$ are the returns of the N individual assets in the portfolio, μ_i are their means, and

$$\tilde{r}_p = \sum_{i=1}^{N} w_i\tilde{r}_i$$

is the return of the portfolio.

As explained in chapter 12, the expressions for the portfolio variance and standard deviation can be written using matrix notation as follows:

$$\sigma_p^2 = \mathbf{w}'\Sigma\,\mathbf{w}$$

and

$$\sigma_p = \sqrt{\mathbf{w}'\Sigma\,\mathbf{w}},$$

respectively, where Σ is the covariance matrix of the portfolio.

Absolute Deviation Konno and Yamazaki (1991) introduced the *absolute deviation* (AD) portfolio risk measure. Instead of the portfolio standard deviation, which is the average of the squared deviations of the possible realizations of portfolio returns from the expected portfolio return, the AD measures the average absolute value of the deviations of the possible realizations of portfolio returns from the expected portfolio return. Formally, the AD risk measure can be written as

$$\mathrm{AD}(\tilde{r}_p) = E[|\tilde{r}_p - E[\tilde{r}_p]|] = E\left[\left|\sum_{i=1}^{N} w_i\tilde{r}_i - \sum_{i=1}^{N} w_i\mu_i\right|\right]$$

where $\tilde{r}_i$ are the returns of the N individual assets in the portfolio, μ_i are their means, and $\tilde{r}_p$ is the return on the portfolio, as before.[2]

2. Here, |.| is the standard notation for absolute value.

The computation of the optimal mean-AD portfolio is substantially simplified because the resulting optimization problem is linear and can be solved by standard linear programming (LP) algorithms. Another advantage of estimating the portfolio AD compared to the portfolio standard deviation is that there is no need to estimate the portfolio's covariance matrix. Finding a reliable and stable estimate of the covariance matrix is challenging in practice.

It can also be shown that if the individual asset returns are multivariate normally distributed, the AD is a multiple of the standard deviation of the portfolio (σ_p). Namely,

$$AD(\tilde{r}_p) = \sqrt{\frac{2}{\pi}} \cdot \sigma_p$$

Hence, if asset returns are multivariate normally distributed, mean-variance and mean-AD portfolio optimization result in equivalent allocations.

Absolute Moment The *absolute moment risk measure* of order q is defined as[3]

$$AM_q(\tilde{r}_p) = (E[|\tilde{r}_p - E[\tilde{r}_p]|^q])^{1/q} = \left(E\left[\left| \sum_{i=1}^{N} w_i \tilde{r}_i - \sum_{i=1}^{N} w_i \mu_i \right|^q \right] \right)^{1/q}, \quad q \geq 1.$$

It is basically a generalization of the standard deviation ($q = 2$) and the AD ($q = 1$) portfolio risk measures.

13.1.2 Downside Risk Measures

As we mentioned in the introduction to this chapter, most investors are concerned about outcomes that fall short of expectations rather than exceed expectations. The portfolio variance and other dispersion measures cannot accurately represent this fact. Markowitz (1959) acknowledged this shortcoming of his model and suggested a downside dispersion risk measure, semivariance, as an alternative way of measuring portfolio risk. The same realization prompted research into several other *downside dispersion risk measures*, many of which are special cases of the lower-partial moment risk measure (also called the *Fishburn risk measure*). This section describes several such risk measures.

Lower-Partial Moment The lower-partial moment risk measure is defined as

$$(E[(\min\{\tilde{r}_p - t, 0\})^q])^{1/q} = \left(E\left[\left(\min\left\{ \sum_{i=1}^{N} w_i \tilde{r}_i - \sum_{i=1}^{N} w_i \mu_i, 0 \right\} \right)^q \right] \right)^{1/q}$$

In the case of a continuous probability distribution for the portfolio return, this expression is equivalent to

$$\int_{-\infty}^{t} (t - r)^k f(r) dr$$

3. See section 3.6.1 for a brief definition of the moments of a probability distribution.

whereas in the case of a discrete probability distribution for the portfolio return, it is equivalent to[4]

$$\sum (t-r)^k \cdot P(\tilde{r}=r)$$

where the sum is over all the values of the random variable that are less than or equal to t.

The constant t represents a cutoff point between the downside, of concern to the investor, and the upside, which is not of concern. In practice, the value of t is often selected to be the short-term interest rate, the expected return, or a minimum required return. The notation $\tilde{r}$ stands for the random variable representing portfolio return.

On an intuitive level, you can think of the lower partial moment as the "weighted average" of the portfolio return deviations from the threshold (raised to a specific power k) when the return is less than the threshold t. Fishburn (1977) showed that $q=1$ corresponds to a risk-neutral investor, $0<q\leq 1$ corresponds to a risk-seeking investor, and $q>1$ corresponds to a risk-averse investor.

Semivariance *Semivariance* is defined as the average of the squared deviations from the mean of all values that are below the mean. Thus, it is a special case of the lower partial moment risk measure when $k=2$ and t equals the mean of the probability distribution for the portfolio return. The portfolio semivariance can be written as

$$E\left[\min\left\{\left(\sum_{i=1}^{N} w_i\tilde{r}_i - \sum_{i=1}^{N} w_i\mu_i\right)^2, 0\right\}\right]$$

Roy's Safety-First Criterion The theory behind *Roy's safety-first criterion* is that rather than thinking in terms of overall portfolio risk, the investor first makes sure that a certain amount of the invested principal is preserved. Hence, the investor tries to minimize the probability that the return earned is less than or equal to the threshold t.[5] Mathematically, it can be expressed as an optimization problem:

$$\min_{\mathbf{w}} P(\tilde{r}_p \leq t)$$

That is,

$$\min_{\mathbf{w}} P\left(\sum_{i=1}^{N} w_i\tilde{r}_i \leq t\right)$$

Note that Roy's safety-first criterion is actually a special case of the lower-partial moment formula when $k=0$.

In the financial industry, Roy's safety-first criterion is often referred to as *shortfall risk*. When the threshold t is zero, the shortfall risk is called the *risk of loss*.

4. See sections 3.6.1 and 3.6.2 of chapter 3 for an introduction to the notation in these expressions. Section 3.6.1 introduced briefly the concept of moments of a probability distribution.

5. See Roy (1952).

Quantile-Based Risk Measures The theory of stochastic dominance, which gained popularity in the 1970s, provided new tools for comparing probability distributions and drew attention to quantile-based risk measures. *Quantile-based risk measures* evaluate volatility in terms of the percentiles of a distribution. They are justified from a theoretical point of view in the sense that they are consistent with the preferences of risk-averse investors. The most widely used quantile-based risk measure in practice is VaR. A related risk measure, CVaR (also encountered as *expected shortfall*), however, has gained popularity because of its desirable theoretical and computational properties. CVaR is in fact a multiple of the lower-partial moment formula with $k=1$.

VaR and CVaR are two very important developments in the theory of risk measures. In the remainder of this chapter, we elaborate on the history, estimation, and portfolio allocation under these two risk measures.

13.2 Value-at-Risk

VaR is related to the percentiles of probability distributions and measures the predicted maximum portfolio loss at a specified probability level over a certain time horizon. Commonly used probability levels include 0.95 and 0.99, and the corresponding VaR is referred to as 95% VaR or 99% VaR (in other words, the probability is stated as a percentage). Typical time horizons include 1 day and 10 days. The portfolio loss is defined as the difference between the portfolio's initial value at the current time t, V_t, and the future value of the portfolio at time $t+1$, V_{t+1}.[6]

VaR can be used for individual assets, trading positions, and portfolios. Mathematically, VaR at a probability level $100(1-\varepsilon)\%$ is defined as the value γ such that the probability that the negative of the portfolio return will exceed γ is not more than a small number ε as follows:

$$\mathrm{VaR}_{(1-\varepsilon)}(\tilde{r}) = \min\{\gamma \mid P(-\tilde{r} > \gamma) \le \varepsilon\} \tag{13.1}$$

(In the preceding expression, $\tilde{r}$ denotes the random variable representing the portfolio return and $-\tilde{r}$ is associated with the portfolio loss, as we will see shortly.) For example, when $\varepsilon=0.05$, then $(1-\varepsilon)=0.95$, $100(1-\varepsilon)\%=95\%$, and we are interested in the 95% VaR, which is the level of the portfolio losses that will not be exceeded with probability of more than 5%.

Asset managers often use a modified version of VaR, which measures the loss relative to a benchmark.[7] The formula for VaR in equation (13.1) still stands, but $\tilde{r}$ is the *excess return* relative to the benchmark; that is, the difference between the return on the portfolio and the return on the benchmark.

VaR is reported as a *dollar amount of losses*. Let us see how the definition of VaR in terms of the return can be stated in dollar terms.

6. Note that the difference $V_t + V_{t+1}$ is a positive number if there is a loss and a negative number if there is a profit.

7. A *benchmark* is a hypothetical portfolio of assets that functions as a performance standard against which portfolio management is measured. See Siegel (2003) for a review of benchmarks and their uses.

Suppose that $\tilde{r}$ is the arithmetic portfolio return.[8] It is easy to see that if we know the value γ and would like to obtain VaR as a dollar amount for possible losses, we simply need to multiply γ by the portfolio value at the beginning of the time period of interest. In particular, the negative of the arithmetic return over time period t, $-\tilde{r}_{t,t+1}$, is

$$-\tilde{r}_{t,t+1} = \frac{V_t - \tilde{V}_{t+1}}{V_t}$$

where V_t is the portfolio value at time t. The numerator in this expression is the loss over time period t, $V_t - \tilde{V}_{t+1}$. Hence, the loss over time period t can be written as

$$V_t - \tilde{V}_{t+1} = -\tilde{r}_{t,t+1} \cdot V_t$$

The portfolio value at time t, V_t, is known; it can be treated as a constant. Therefore, the probability distribution of the loss is the same as the probability distribution of the negative of the return $-\tilde{r}_{t,t+1}$, scaled by a constant. If we know γ, the $100(1-\varepsilon)$th percentile of the latter distribution, the $100(1-\varepsilon)$th percentile of the former can be computed as $\gamma \cdot V_t$.

Let us now compute VaR in dollar terms if we are working with geometric returns $\tilde{r}$. We have

$$-\tilde{r}_{t,t+1} = -\ln\left(\frac{\tilde{V}_{t+1}}{V_t}\right) = -(\ln(\tilde{V}_{t+1}) - \ln(V_t)) = \ln(V_t) - \ln(\tilde{V}_{t+1})$$

Just as before, the portfolio value at time t, V_t, can be treated as a constant. Therefore, the probability distribution of $\ln(\tilde{V}_{t+1})$ is the same as the probability distribution of $\tilde{r}$. We can rewrite the previous equality as

$$\ln(\tilde{V}_{t+1}) = \tilde{r}_{t,t+1} + \ln(V_t)$$

or, equivalently, as

$$\tilde{V}_{t+1} = e^{\tilde{r}_{t,t+1} + \ln(V_t)} = e^{\tilde{r}_{t,t+1}} \cdot V_t$$

Therefore, the loss $(V_t - \tilde{V}_{t+1})$ can be expressed as

$$V_t - \tilde{V}_{t+1} = (1 - e^{\tilde{r}_{t,t+1}}) \cdot V_t$$

So if we know the value of γ, we can compute the VaR as

$$(1 - e^{-\gamma}) \cdot V_t$$

The difference in estimating VaR from the two different assumptions for returns is not very large for short holding periods and realistic return parameters. For example, suppose that we computed $\gamma = 0.004000$. (We will explain how to obtain an estimate of γ later in this chapter.) Then $(1 - e^{-\gamma}) = (1 - e^{-0.004000}) = 0.003992$. For an initial portfolio value of \$100 million, we have VaR = \$400,000 for arithmetic returns and VaR = \$399,201.07 for geometric returns.

8. See chapter 2 for a definition of geometric returns.

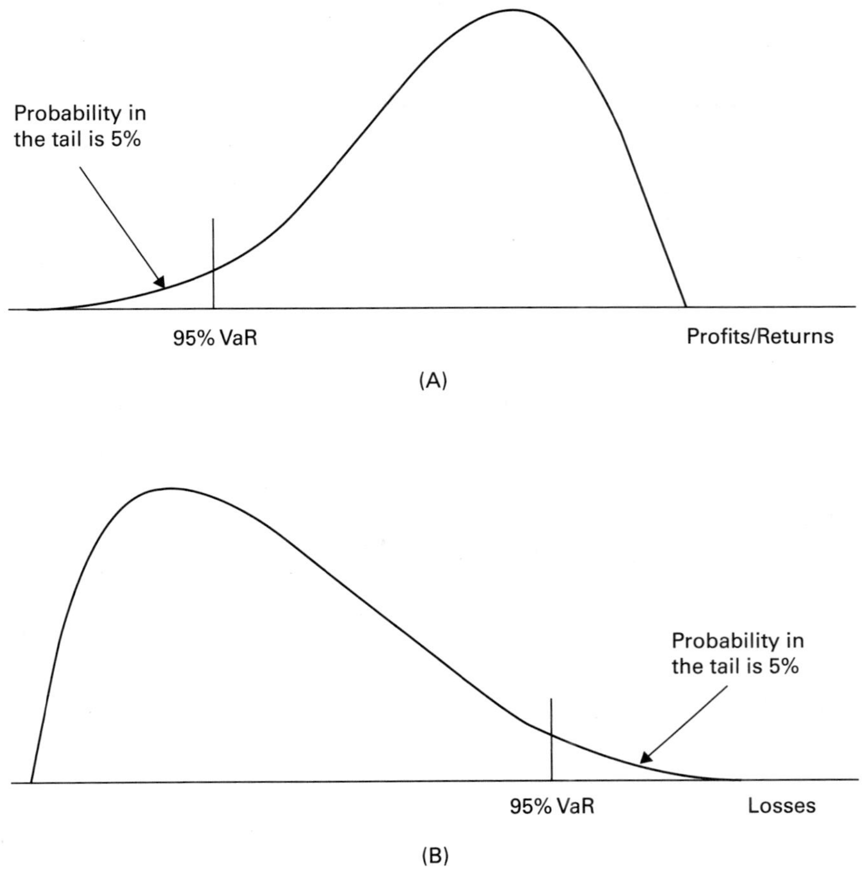

Exhibit 13.1
(A) 95% VaR computed from P/L data; (B) 95% VaR computed from L/P data.

In practice, VaR is often computed directly as a dollar amount because historical data are available in the form of cash flows. More specifically, it is in either profit/loss (P/L) or loss/profit (L/P) form.

The P/L generated by an asset or a portfolio of assets is the value of the asset (or portfolio) at the end of time period t plus any interim cash flows (dividends, interest, realized capital gain or loss on disposal of assets) and minus the asset value at the beginning of period t:

$$(P/L)_{t+1} = V_{t+1} + D_{t+1} - V_t$$

(As a general rule, the amounts should be properly discounted so all dollar amounts are commensurate, but if the time periods themselves are short, the adjustment will be small.) When the data are in P/L form, positive values indicate profits and negative values indicate losses. The $100(1-\varepsilon)\%$ VaR is then the εth percentile of the distribution of the P/L values. (See exhibit 13.1(A).)

The loss/profit (L/P) form is basically the negative of the profit/loss (P/L) data:

$$(L/P)_t = -(P/L)_t.$$

In that case, the $100(1-\varepsilon)\%$ VaR is the $100(1-\varepsilon)$th percentile of the distribution of the L/P values. (See exhibit 13.1(B).)

13.2.1 The History of the VaR Metric

Among banks, the consensus to use the maximum likely loss as a way to look at risk evolved gradually and was established formally in 1996, when the Basel Committee on Banking Supervision of the Bank for International Settlements (BIS) proposed several amendments to the original 1988 Basel Accord for minimal capital requirements for banks of its member-countries. While the original accord covered only credit risk (deposits and lending), the new proposal in 1998 also covered market risk, including organizationwide commodities exposure (measured by the 10-day 95% VaR).

The deliberate effort among the central banks that were members of the Basel Committee to come up with better risk management schemes at the firm level, however, had started almost two decades earlier. The impetus for this effort was the realization that there was little connection between the limits that were imposed on trading positions and the risk that banks were taking. Good trades were passed over because of arbitrary trading limits, and good capital allocation was missed for the same reason. In addition, banks, whose primary business had been loans, were beginning to meld with investment banks, whose primary business was trading stocks, bonds, and complex financial instruments, and with asset management companies, whose focus was investments. There was a need for an integrated approach to risk management that allowed banks to evaluate their exposure across divisions and for increasingly complex positions. Hence, a number of banks began developing internal systems for measuring firmwide risk.

J.P. Morgan was one of the early leaders in this endeavor. Industry legend has it that J.P. Morgan's integrated risk management system was started when Dennis Weatherstone, the company's chairman at the time, asked his staff to give him a daily one-page report describing the firmwide risk over the next 24 hours, taking into consideration the bank's entire trading portfolio. The "4:15" report, as the report became widely known because it was to be delivered at the close of trading every day, used VaR to estimate the maximum loss with a given probability over the next trading day. The fact that VaR was quoted as a dollar amount, rather than a percentage or a probability, made it convenient for reporting results to management and eliminated the need to explain complex mathematics.

The original calculation of VaR was based on a normal approximation to the distribution of the firm's profits over the next day, similar to the calculation of VaR under a normal distribution we will show in section 13.2.2. While, theoretically, the calculation was straightforward, its practical implementation was immensely time consuming and complicated, as it involved compiling data and estimating several statistical parameters, such as expected returns, variances, and covariances among different complex trading positions. Still, the system was completed by 1990. In 1993, J.P. Morgan presented the system at their research conference and witnessed a great deal of interest from potential clients. Instead of leasing it or attempting to generate fees from consulting, however, J.P. Morgan decided to make a simplified version of their internal system, RiskMetrics, available online in 1994, along with the data necessary for the statistical estimation of VaR. This move generated a huge amount of publicity for the company and accelerated the adoption of VaR as a risk measure across financial institutions. By the mid-1990s, VaR had established itself as the dominant measure of risk. As computer equipment became cheaper and faster and developers more experienced, VaR systems continued to spread and became more elaborate, including not only measures of market risks, but also credit risks, liquidity risks, and operational risks.

Unfortunately, as we will see later in this chapter, VaR was not well understood, and its simplicity as a single dollar amount risk estimate could be very misleading. Complicating matters, while all banks reported and monitored VaR, there were no established regulations on how to compute it. Some banks used the original RiskMetrics approach, incorporating estimates of standard deviations and correlations between the returns of different traded instruments. Others opted for historical simulation approaches that estimated VaR from histograms of past P/L data. Yet others used forward-looking Monte Carlo (MC) simulation, generating future scenarios for the underlying drives of uncertainty in their companies' positions. We explain these methods for estimating VaR in more detail in sections 13.2.2 and 13.2.3. A higher-level discussion of applications of VaR in portfolio risk management with complex financial instruments is provided in chapter 20.

13.2.2 Calculation of Value-at-Risk for a Normal Distribution

Let us assume that our P/L data follow a normal distribution. To estimate $100(1-\varepsilon)\%$ VaR, we need to find the value of the $100(1-\varepsilon)$th percentile of the distribution. In the case of the normal distribution, there is a closed-form expression for the percentiles. Every percentile can be expressed as a sum of the mean of the distribution and the standard deviation scaled by a multiplier—namely,

$$\mathrm{VaR}_{(1-\varepsilon)} = -\mu_{P/L} + z_{(1-\varepsilon)} \cdot \sigma_{P/L}$$

where $\mu_{P/L}$ is the mean and $\sigma_{P/L}$ is the standard deviation of the P/L distribution. The number $z_{(1-\varepsilon)}$ is the $100(1-\varepsilon)$th percentile of a standard normal distribution. A widely used notation for the same expression is $\Phi^{-1}(1-\varepsilon)$.[9] The concept is used in so many applications that most spreadsheet and statistical software packages contain a function for computing it. As we mentioned earlier in this book, $z_{(1-\varepsilon)}$ is computed with the formula NORMSINV$(1-\varepsilon)$ in Microsoft Excel. So, for example, $z_{0.95}$ corresponding to the 95th percentile is computed as NORMSINV(0.95), which is 1.6445. Similar functions for computing $z_{(1-\varepsilon)}$ exist in MATLAB and Python.

If, instead, we have normally distributed L/P data, then we would use the formula

$$\mathrm{VaR}_{(1-\varepsilon)} = \mu_{L/P} + z_{(1-\varepsilon)} \cdot \sigma_{L/P}$$

If we are given data on asset returns and assume arithmetic returns, the formula for VaR would be

$$\mathrm{VaR}_{(1-\varepsilon)} = (-\mu_r + z_{(1-\varepsilon)} \cdot \sigma_r) \cdot V_t$$

where V_t is the portfolio value at the beginning of the period over which VaR is estimated.

9. See section 3.4 for a definition of the standard normal distribution, section 4.1.3 for the use of a similar notation of percentile in the context of confidence interval estimation, and section 7.2.3 for use in stochastic programming.

If, instead, we assume geometric returns, then it can be easily shown (as in the derivation at the beginning of section 13.2) that

$$\text{VaR}_{(1-\varepsilon)} = (1 - e^{\mu_r - z_{(1-\varepsilon)} \cdot \sigma_r}) \cdot V_t$$

If we are trying to estimate the VaR for a portfolio, the μ and the σ in the formulas above would be the portfolio mean and standard deviation. (Depending on the data, they may be reported as dollar amounts or percentage returns.) You can now see why we need information on the covariance structure of the various assets in the portfolio if the VaR is to be computed this way: as we showed in chapter 12, the covariances are an input to the computation of the portfolio variance, which is then used to compute the portfolio standard deviation.

There are some serious problems with the assumption of normality in the VaR estimation context:

- Using normal-distribution-based VaR is technically correct for elliptical distributions for returns, of which the normal distribution is an example. This is because such distributions are entirely described by their means and variances. Most real-world data, however, exhibit "fat tails" and are not normally distributed. When a distribution has fatter tails than the normal distribution, the VaR computed with the normal approximation can grossly underestimate the real VaR.
- Even when returns are assumed to be normally distributed, inaccuracies in estimating the input parameters to the model can render the risk evaluation process meaningless. Accurate estimation of the covariance structure even for equities—the simplest assets—is challenging because the covariance structure varies over time.
- Recall from chapter 3 that covariance and correlation measure only the strength of *linear* dependence between random variables. A bank may have thousands of positions in complex types of financial securities with payoffs that are not linearly correlated. Thus, estimating the risk of a firm's portfolio by using only the correlation structure and the mean for estimating the risk leaves out important information about the actual distribution of returns for the entire portfolio.

Even though the normal-distribution-based VaR suffers from a number of problems, it is unfortunately widely used. It was the model underlying the RiskMetrics system when it became freely available, and many financial companies adopted it, not understanding (or choosing to ignore) its drawbacks. The whole point of using a risk estimation framework that is different from the traditional mean-variance framework, however, is that it should enable financial institutions to evaluate risk in highly nonnormal situations. Thus, it is not satisfactory to measure tail risk as a multiple of the standard deviation, as the normal approximation to the VaR does.

13.2.3 Calculation of Value-at-Risk Using Historical and Simulated Data Scenarios

A more realistic way to estimate VaR is to use scenarios for the possible realizations of the uncertainties underlying the prices of the various securities in the portfolio. The scenario approach allows us to incorporate dependencies between uncertainties implicitly, as well as to estimate the actual percentile of the probability distribution of future portfolio losses, eliminating strong assumptions such as normality.

Suppose that we have S scenarios for the possible losses (L/P) over the time period of interest stored in an array named LossData. The $100(1-\varepsilon)\%$ VaR is found by sorting the data (in an increasing order) and selecting a scenario with index $(S-\varepsilon \cdot S+1)$ in the sorted data array.[10] Intuitively, we select the scenario that results in the highest magnitude of loss so the total number of scenarios in which the loss is greater is not more than $\varepsilon \cdot S$.

In Excel, the data can be sorted by clicking on the **Data** tab, selecting **Sort**, and referencing the array where the data are stored. Similar sort functions exist in MATLAB and Python. Be careful with the default for the sort function in different software packages. If the default for the *sort* function is to order the elements of the array that is passed to it in increasing order, the $100(1-\varepsilon)\%$ VaR is the $(S-\varepsilon \cdot S+1)$st element of the resulting sorted array.

For example, if we have 1,000 L/P scenarios, then the 95% VaR will be the 951st-highest scenario $((1000-0.05 \cdot 1000+1)=951)$. If we have 1,005 L/P scenarios, then the 95% VaR will be the 956th-highest scenario $((1005-0.05 \cdot 1005+1)=956)$.[11]

How do we decide on the set of scenarios to consider for the VaR estimation procedure? The most straightforward approach is to use historical scenarios over a given window (e.g., 1,000 observations), updating the most recent scenarios and dropping scenarios that happened before the most recent 1,000 observations. Such scenarios may be bootstrapped; that is, simulation techniques may be used to sample from the set of scenarios and generate a new set with the same general risk profile.[12] The advantage of bootstrapping is that the bootstrapped datasets are also useful for gauging the accuracy of the VaR estimate.

The obvious drawback of this approach is that important insights from scenarios that happened outside the window may be lost. For example, the VaR computed from scenarios for market performance during the year 2006 or 2019 would be quite low because the market generally rose during those time periods. However, including scenarios from previous financial crises would have enabled us to obtain a better estimate for what was to come in the crises that followed those risking markets.

Even when such extreme scenarios are included in the dataset, an important cause for concern is that some events, such as the market crash of October 1987, are single events that will not affect the VaR unless the confidence level is set very high. One way in which this situation can be mended is by assigning weights to different historical observations and preserving a longer-term memory of possible events. The weights can be determined in different ways. One possible assignment is to do it based on age; that is, to discount older observations relative to newer ones.

Another possible assignment of weights is based on the current volatility forecast. Namely, if recent market volatility has been 1% and the forecasted volatility over the time

10. As explained earlier in this book, the notation a stands for the integer part of the number a (i.e., for the nearest integer less than or equal to a).

11. Note that the value of the VaR computed with the described method of sorting the data first may be different from the value returned by the commands for computing percentiles in Excel, MATLAB, or Python. While for continuous data, the value of the percentile is the value of the VaR, conventions for computing VaR may vary for discrete data. The approach for estimation of VaR from discrete data described in this chapter picks a conservative estimate of VaR—that is, it considers the value of the smallest loss that is greater than the value for the percentile.

12. See chapter 4 for an introduction to the bootstrapping technique.

horizon of risk estimation is higher, then we can adjust all historical returns by a coefficient to reflect the greater anticipated market volatility.

Other approaches for determining scenario weights include incorporating considerations for the correlations between different assets and so-called semiparametric bootstrap approaches.[13] In practice, a thoughtful approach to risk estimation would combine two sets of scenarios: a "moderate" set of scenarios, based on the current situation in the market and recent history, and an "extreme" set of scenarios, which repeats major stock, bond, and currency market crises, weighing scenarios in a sensible way. To smooth the gaps in the VaR estimates obtained from historical data, especially in the tails of the distribution, practitioners also often fit a probability distribution to observed historical data, so the tails of the distribution can be explicitly modeled when VaR is simulated.[14]

There are multiple advantages to using historical observations to generate scenarios for the purposes of risk evaluation. First, the fact that these scenarios have actually occurred gives them plausibility. Second, they are easy to understand and generate. A statement like "If a market crash similar to the crash in October 2008 happens, our portfolio stands to lose $X" is easy to communicate and conceptualize. However, this approach is inherently backward looking. Simulation of random processes can instead be used to generate forward-looking risk models based on modeling the uncertainty in a set of underlying market risk factors. Such approaches are discussed in more detail in chapter 19, after introducing random processes and financial derivatives in chapters 14 through 18. Unfortunately, traditional MC simulation approaches can be very time consuming. In chapters 17 and 19, we will introduce some methodologies for reducing the number of scenarios while still achieving an accurate risk estimate.

13.2.4 VaR Calculation Example

To illustrate how VaR can be calculated under the assumptions in sections 13.2.2 and 13.2.3, let us consider two sets of P/L data in column D in worksheets **VaR 1** and **VaR 2**, respectively, in the file **Ch13-VaRCalculation.xlsx**.

The P/L distribution for the dataset in worksheet **VaR 1** is shown in exhibit 13.2. The data in this sample are symmetrically distributed (i.e., the mean and the median are approximately the same, and the skewness is close to 0), with a distribution that is not as peaked as (i.e., is flatter than) the normal distribution. The VaR calculation directly from historical data is presented in cells F32:F33 in worksheet **VaR 1**. The 99% VaR from historical data is $9.50 (cell F32), whereas the normal approximation to the 99% VaR based on the estimate of the mean and the standard deviation of the P/L data is $13.27 (cell F33). In this case, the normal approximation to the 99% VaR overestimates the true 99% VaR, computed as a percentile of the P/L historical data.

Often, however, historical P/L graphs look like the graph in exhibit 13.3. This historical distribution was obtained from the daily stock prices of a major financial institution (Citigroup) between the beginning of 2005 and the end of 2008, after the major financial crisis in the fall of 2008, and is stored in worksheet **VaR 2** of the file **Ch13-VaRCalculation**

13. See chapter 4 in Dowd (2005).

14. Many software packages have functions for fitting probability distributions to data. See chapters 4 and 5.

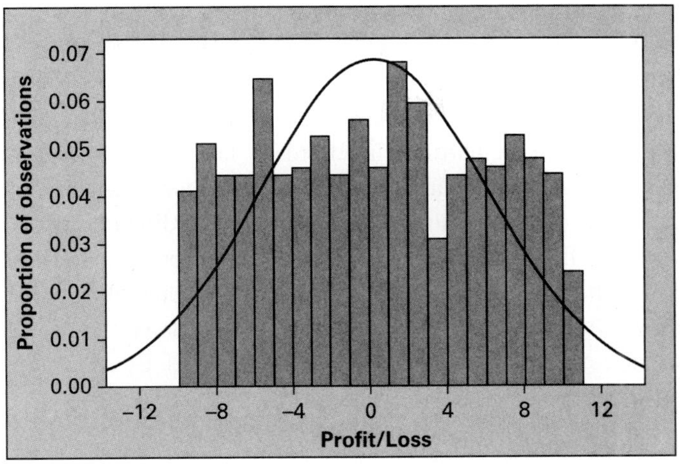

Mean: 0.20
Standard deviation: 5.79
Skewness: 0.03
Kurtosis: −1.17
Minimum: −9.57
Maximum: 10.39
Median: 0.19

Exhibit 13.2
P/L distribution of the data in worksheet **VaR 1** of the file **Ch13-VaRCalculation.xlsx**.

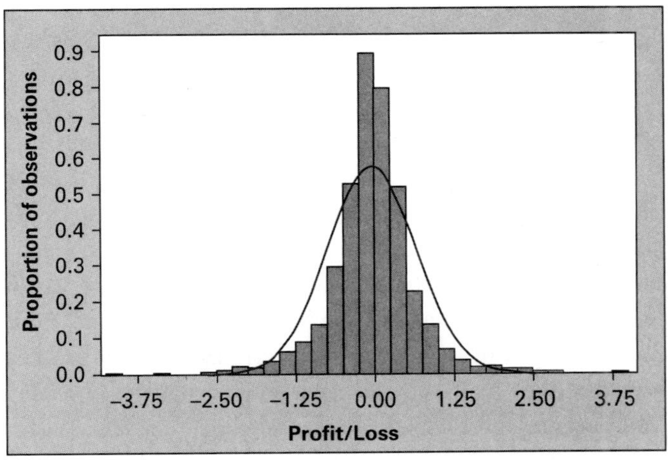

Mean: −0.04
Standard deviation: 0.70
Skewness: 0.01
Kurtosis: 4.89
Minimum: −4.15
Maximum: 4.00
Median: −0.04

Exhibit 13.3
P/L distribution of the data in worksheet **VaR 2** of the file **Ch13-VaRCalculation.xlsx**.

.xlsx. Although the distribution still appears symmetric (the skewness is close to 0), the distribution has fat tails—it has a lot more observations in the tails than a normal distribution would have. This is confirmed also by the high positive value for the kurtosis. In this case, the normal approximation to the 99% VaR severely underestimates the 99% VaR obtained as a percentile of the historical data. The normal approximation 99% VaR is $1.67 (cell F33), whereas the VaR computed directly from historical data is $2.12 (cell F32).

Worksheets **VaR 1** and **VaR 2** also contain a calculation of the 99% VaR based on a bootstrapping procedure and simulating portfolio losses (rather than P/L). There are 500 realizations for L/P (which is the negative of P/L) that are drawn randomly from the set of historical data (column D in both worksheets) and are sorted in ascending order in column O in both worksheets. The 99% VaR is the 496th observation in each dataset. The bootstrapped 99% VaR in **VaR 1** is $9.50, whereas the bootstrapped 99% VaR in **VaR 2** is $2.12.

13.2.5 Selection of VaR Parameters and Regulatory Requirements

VaR calculation requires two arbitrary input parameters: the confidence level $(1-\varepsilon)$ and the time horizon. How are these parameters selected?

Theoretically, the best length to use for the time horizon is the amount of time that it would take to liquidate all positions in the portfolio in an orderly fashion.[15] It is typically assumed that a time period of two weeks (10 business days) is sufficient, and this is the holding period specified by regulation. (BIS capital requirements state a holding period of 10 days.) The time horizons used by financial institutions for internal purposes may be one trading day or one month, and some financial institutions operate on longer holding periods (e.g., a quarter). To convert VaR estimates for a short time period (e.g., a day) into a VaR estimate for a long time period (e.g., 10 days) for the same confidence level, BIS regulations sanction the use of the approximation

$$\text{VaR}_{(1-\varepsilon),10} = \text{VaR}_{(1-\varepsilon),1}\sqrt{10}$$

The mathematics behind this conversion will become clearer in part III, but the intuitive reasoning is that for certain types of random processes used to model security prices, variability over time increases with the square root of the length of the time period. Thus, the VaR over T time periods should be larger than the VaR over one time period by a factor of a square root of the elapsed time (i.e., by $\sqrt{T}$). In practice, this is an approximation rather than an exact conversion; it is an exact conversion only when prices of securities indeed follow the specific type of random process.

Banks can use any confidence level for estimating VaR for internal purposes, but when they report VaR externally, they typically use a confidence level that is consistent with other banks (typically, a number in the range 95%–99%). A very useful technique for setting the VaR parameters for internal risk management purposes is to analyze the value of VaR for pairs of values of the confidence level parameter and the length of the time horizon. Thus, a VaR surface rather than a single value of VaR is examined to determine if the risk is acceptable for any values of the two parameters. As the confidence level increases (i.e., ε becomes smaller), the estimation of VaR becomes more challenging because there are fewer historical observations in the "tail" that can be used to calibrate VaR models accurately.

The official capital adequacy standards for banks prescribed by the 1996 Amendment to the 1988 Basel Accord include the following:

- Banks in the Group of Ten (G10) countries[16] should report a 10-day VaR at the 99% level.
- Banks are free to calculate their VaR using their own models under certain conditions:
- The models used for internal risk management should be the same as the ones used for reporting to regulators.
- The models must be approved by the regulating body.

15. A quick liquidation of positions may have an effect on the current market prices of the different securities, which will change the estimate of the VaR. Therefore, the estimation of VaR is done on the assumption that markets behave as usual; that is, positions are liquidated in an orderly fashion.

16. The G10 actually include 11 industrial countries. They are Belgium, Canada, France, Germany, Italy, Japan, the Netherlands, Sweden, Switzerland, the UK, and the U.S.

- The models must meet certain technical conditions on computing the risks of relatively complex positions.
- Banks must calibrate their daily VaR measures to daily P/L observations. They must perform backtesting daily and identify the number of trading days in which losses exceed the VaR.
- The results of these backtests are used to assess VaR models and to determine a value for a *hysteria factor*, or a *multiplier* to apply to standard VaR estimation results. In particular, the VaR value reported for regulatory purposes should be always the greater of the standard VaR value and the average of the VaR values over the last 60 days, multiplied by the hysteria factor, which is a number between 3 and 4. For example, if there are fewer than five exceptions to the VaR models over the last 250 days, then the multiplier is 3; if there are five exceptions, the multiplier is 3.40, and so on.

More recent Basel Accords have retained these main features but also included new provisions on credit risk and operational risk models.

It is important to note that while the point of these regulations is to improve bank solvency, these capital requirements do little to achieve this goal. Not only are some of the rules arbitrary, but there is also a lot of leeway given to the individual banks in backtesting and reporting VaR, which can make the whole process of reporting VaR for regulatory purposes meaningless.

13.2.6 Optimization of Value-at-Risk

In addition to risk management, VaR can be used in making decisions for portfolio allocation purposes.

The portfolio VaR optimization problem is in fact a problem with chance constraints, which we introduced in section 7.2.3. To see this, note that we can state the VaR minimization problem as

$$\begin{aligned} \min_{\gamma, \mathbf{w}} \quad & \gamma \\ \text{s.t.} \quad & P(-\tilde{\mathbf{r}}'\mathbf{w} > \gamma) \leq \varepsilon, \\ & \mathbf{w}'\boldsymbol{\iota} = 1 \end{aligned}$$

where $\tilde{\boldsymbol{r}}$ is the N-dimensional vector of uncertain asset returns over the time horizon for portfolio optimization, and $\mathbf{w}$ is the N-dimensional vector of asset weights in the portfolio. Stated in words, this optimization formulation says that we would like to minimize a number γ (which is a decision variable) such that the probability that the portfolio losses exceed γ is less than or equal to a small number ε. We also have the standard budget constraint that the portfolio weights must add up to 1, or 100%.

Given our discussion about optimization problems with chance constraints in section 7.2.3, optimizing a portfolio allocation so the resulting VaR is the lowest among all possible distributions is nontrivial. Suppose, for example, that we are given data on S possible scenarios for vectors of individual asset returns $\mathbf{r}^{(1)}, \ldots, \mathbf{r}^{(S)}$. The VaR optimization problem can be written as[17]

17. See section 7.2.3.

$$\begin{aligned}
\min_{\gamma,\mathbf{w}} \quad & \gamma \\
\text{s.t.} \quad & (-\mathbf{r}^{(s)})'\mathbf{w} \leq \gamma + M \cdot y_s, \quad s = 1,\ldots,S \\
& \sum_{s=1}^{S} y_s \leq \varepsilon \cdot S \\
& \mathbf{w}'\boldsymbol{\iota} = 1 \\
& y_s \in \{0,1\}, \quad s = 1,\ldots,S
\end{aligned}$$

where M is a "large" constant. Since the input data in the formulation are asset returns (which are small in magnitude), a value of 100 for M is large enough for all practical purposes. The optimal value of γ returned by the solver will be the minimum value for the VaR.

Note that for a dataset consisting of 1,000 scenarios, this problem formulation involves solving a mixed-integer optimization problem[18] with 1,000 binary variables, which can take a very long time. In practice, the optimization of VaR can be done with approximations or with additional assumptions. For example, if we assume that the asset returns follow a multivariate normal distribution with a vector of means μ and a covariance matrix Σ, then the portfolio VaR optimization problem can be written as

$$\begin{aligned}
\min_{\gamma,\mathbf{w}} \quad & \gamma \\
\text{s.t.} \quad & -\boldsymbol{\mu}'\mathbf{w} + z_{(1-\varepsilon)} \cdot \sqrt{\mathbf{w}'\Sigma\mathbf{w}} \leq \gamma \\
& \mathbf{w}'\boldsymbol{\iota} = 1
\end{aligned}$$

where $z_{(1-\varepsilon)}$ is the $100(1-\varepsilon)$th percentile of a standard normal distribution, as explained in section 13.2.2. Notice that this formulation is equivalent to the optimization formulation

$$\begin{aligned}
\min_{\mathbf{w}} \quad & -\boldsymbol{\mu}'\mathbf{w} + z_{(1-\varepsilon)} \cdot \sqrt{\mathbf{w}'\Sigma\mathbf{w}} \\
\text{s.t.} \quad & \mathbf{w}'\boldsymbol{\iota} = 1
\end{aligned}$$

which can also be written as

$$\begin{aligned}
\max_{\mathbf{w}} \quad & \boldsymbol{\mu}'\mathbf{w} - z_{(1-\varepsilon)} \cdot \sqrt{\mathbf{w}'\Sigma\mathbf{w}} \\
\text{s.t.} \quad & \mathbf{w}'\boldsymbol{\iota} = 1
\end{aligned}$$

This formulation involves optimizing the portfolio allocation using only the portfolio mean ($\boldsymbol{\mu}'\mathbf{w}$) and the portfolio standard deviation $\sqrt{\mathbf{w}'\Sigma\mathbf{w}}$. Thus, the portfolio allocations resulting from solving this will suffer from the same drawbacks as allocations obtained with mean-variance formulations.

13.2.7 Arguments for and against Value-at-Risk

At its introduction, VaR was hailed as an advanced and comprehensive way to handle portfolio risk. Its appeal was due to the following features, not shared by basic measures used to estimate risk before VaR and its ultimate endorsement by the Basel Committee:

- As we mentioned earlier, VaR is expressed as a dollar amount, making it easier to convey information about risk exposure to a wide range of decision makers.

18. See chapter 6.

- VaR estimates downside risk rather than dispersion, and it is a probabilistic measure of risk in the sense that implicit in the number reported for VaR is an estimate of the probability that the loss will exceed that amount. This is not the case with other measures of risk, such as variance.
- Before VaR, measures of the risk of trading and portfolio positions included duration (see chapter 2), option Greeks, which are sensitivity measures for option prices (discussed in chapter 18), and others. Those risk measures, however, do not give a sense of the entire distribution of possible outcomes; in a sense, they are based on a "what-if" analysis.
- VaR could be applied to any type of asset and position. This is not the case for variance (which is meaningful mostly for equity and commodity positions and portfolios, not for complex financial securities with highly nonnormal distributions of possible returns), duration (which applies only to fixed-income portfolios), or Greeks (which apply to financial option positions). Thus, VaR provides a consistent way to compare the risks of equity, fixed-income, and other positions, and it also can be used to aggregate risks across the entire firm.

Even early on, however, many criticisms of VaR surfaced. Two of the most vocal early critics of VaR included Nassim Taleb (1997a, 1997b), who summarized many of his arguments in his best-selling book *The Black Swan* (Taleb 2007), and Richard Hoppe (1998). They criticized the literal transfer of techniques from the mathematical and the physical sciences to model social systems in which processes are not stationary and depend on the complex dynamic interactions of rational and irrational market agents. Taleb (1997a) said, "You are worse off relying on misleading information than not having any information at all. If you give a pilot an altimeter that is sometimes defective, he will crash the plane. Give him nothing and he will look out the window."

Such criticisms are valid for all risk management systems—indeed, risk estimates are subject to errors, model risk (i.e., making wrong assumptions about the underlying processes), and implementation risk (i.e., risk of errors because of the way that systems are implemented). However, VaR suffers from some unique disadvantages that should be understood before it is used as a risk measure.

First, as has become clear by now, VaR does not tell us *how much* we could lose if a low-risk tail event occurs. A trading strategy that has the loss distribution in exhibit 13.4(A) appears just as risky as the trading strategy in exhibit 13.4(B) in terms of VaR. It is clear, however, that we stand to lose more, and more often, with the trading strategy in exhibit 13.4(B). Thus, using VaR as the threshold for approving an investment strategy can leave investors exposed to extreme losses.

Second, VaR's reporting of the loss at a certain percentile of the distribution without consideration for the size of the losses in the tail of the distribution encourages traders to take more low-probability, high-impact bets. Such risks do not show up in the VaR estimates but can have a devastating effect on the firm;, in fact, they can destabilize the entire financial system, as the financial system collapse in the fall of 2008 demonstrated. Taleb (1997a) predicted this long before it was a reality. He pointed out that if everybody uses VaR as a risk measure, taking on low-probability risks in the tail, then the events in the tail become highly correlated and are no longer low-probability risk events if the financial system is considered as a whole. Danielsson and Zigrand (2001) also showed that VaR

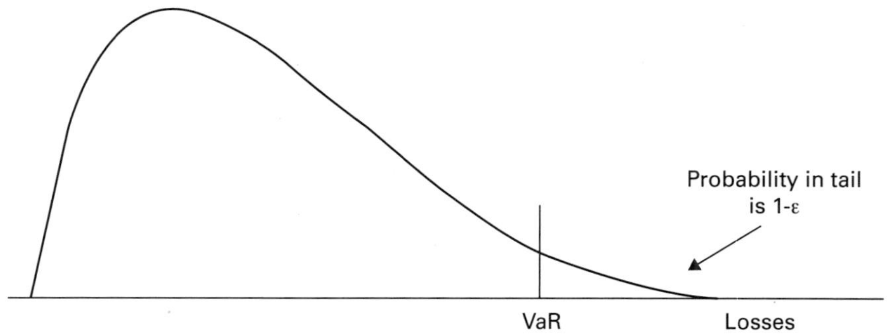

(A)

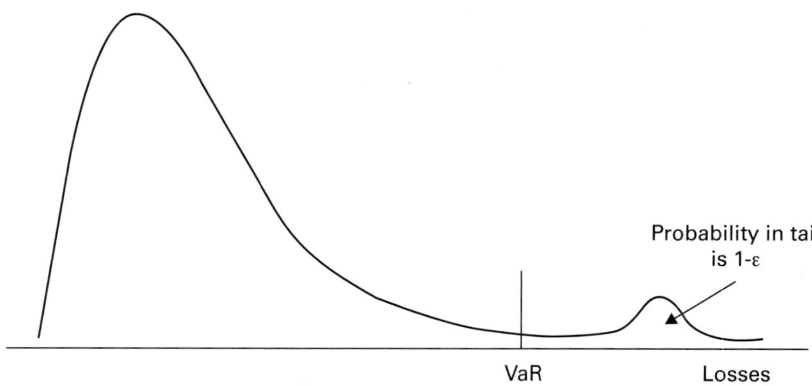

(B)

Exhibit 13.4
Two trading strategies (A) and (B) with the same VaR and different losses in the tail. In (B), the VaR is the same, but the potential losses in the tail are greater on average.

regulatory constraints on financial institutions can aggravate financial crises, and even cause them, because the markets cannot clear properly.

Third, VaR computation and optimization are difficult. Using a mean-variance framework to estimate or optimize VaR does not make sense because that eliminates the whole purpose of using a tail-risk measure. However, estimating VaR by simulation and optimizing VaR can be very computationally intensive. VaR optimization based on particular scenarios has nonsmooth and nonconvex constraints, which means that we cannot trust the solutions from the optimization solver even if the solver takes a long time to search for the optimal solution.

Finally, problems exist with the theoretical foundation of VaR as well. In a seminal article, Artzner, Delbaen, Eber, and Heath (1999) pointed out that the use of VaR actually discourages diversification, which goes against intuition and established portfolio management practices. Let us consider a simple example to illustrate this fact.

Suppose that we can invest in two zero-coupon bonds, A and B, both with \$100 face value.[19] Bond A costs \$97 today and will pay \$111.55 one year from now. Bond B costs

19. See chapter 2 for a definition of zero-coupon bonds.

			Distribution of Losses		
	Position Today	End Payment	Probability	Amount of Loss	95% VaR
Bond A	$97.00	$111.55	0.96	$(14.55)	$(14.55)
			0.04	$ 97.00	
Bond B	$90.00	$103.50	0.96	$(13.50)	$(13.50)
			0.04	$ 90.00	

Exhibit 13.5
Calculation of the VaRs of two individual positions in zero-coupon bonds with 4% probability of default.

$90 today and will pay $103.50 one year from now. Both bonds, however, have a 4% probability of default. If a particular bond defaults, we will lose our entire original investment in that bond and therefore will not receive any payment. The original value of the individual bonds, the distribution of the individual bond's losses, and the 95% VaR for the position in each bond are shown in exhibit 13.5.

Let us show the calculations for bond A. The loss on bond A is computed as ($97 – Final payment) and is therefore –$14.55 (a profit) if the bond pays as promised, and $97 (an actual loss) if the bond defaults. Since the loss of $97 happens with probability of 4%, which is in the tail of the distribution, the 95% VaR does not account for it, and hence the 95% VaR equals –$14.55. The interpretation is that we will realize a profit of $14.55 on our position in bond A with a probability of no less than 5%. Similarly, we can obtain the 95% VaR of the individual position in bond B—it is again a profit (a loss of –$13.50).

The sum of the VaRs of the two positions, therefore, is –$14.55 (–$13.50) = –$28.05; that is, it is a profit of $28.05.

Now let us compute the probability distribution of the losses on a portfolio consisting of a long position in bond A and a long position in bond B:

- With probability 92.16% (= 0.96^2), both bond A and bond B will make their final payments, in which case the loss on the portfolio will be –$14.55 + (–$13.50) = –$28.05; that is, there will be a profit of $28.05.
- With probability 3.84% (= $0.96 \cdot 0.04$), bond B will default and bond A will pay, in which case the loss on the portfolio will be (–$14.55) + $90 = $75.45.
- With probability 3.84% (= $0.04 \cdot 0.96$), bond A will default and bond B will pay, in which case the loss on the portfolio will be $97 + (–$13.50) = $83.50.
- With probability 0.16% (= 0.04^2), both bonds will default, in which case the loss will be $97 + $90 = $187.

The probability distribution of the portfolio losses is illustrated in exhibit 13.6. Note that the cumulative probability becomes 95% at a value of $75.45 for losses, which determines the value of the 95% VaR.

Hence, in this example, the 95% VaR of the portfolio, $75.45, is higher than the sum of the individual 95% VaRs (–$28.05). In fact, a risk manager who uses the 95% VaR portfolio as a risk measure for this portfolio would prefer to increase the portfolio's holdings in one of these bonds rather than diversify and invest in both at the same time. Ironically, VaR, which

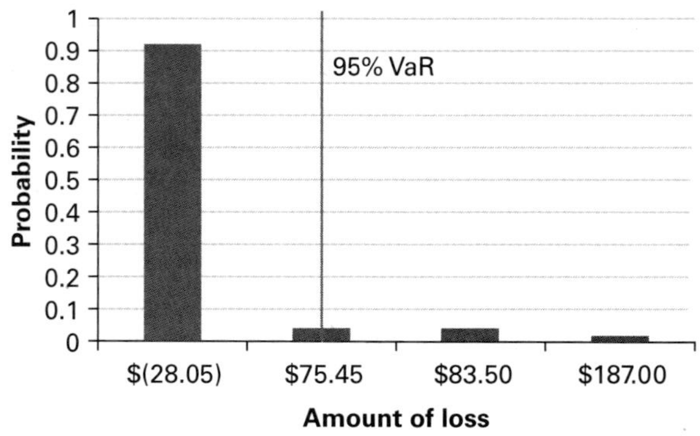

Probability	Cumulative probability	Amount of loss
92.16%	92.16%	$ (28.05)
3.84%	96.00%	$ 75.45
3.84%	99.84%	$ 83.50
0.16%	100.00%	$ 187.00

Exhibit 13.6
Probability distribution of portfolio losses and 95% VaR.

gained popularity because of its ability to summarize firmwide risk based on compounding risk reports from different parts of the firm, is ill suited for calculating compounded risks.

13.3 Conditional Value-at-Risk and the Concept of Coherent Risk Measures

In view of the conceptual difficulties associated with classical measures of risk, Artzner, Delbaen, Eber, and Heath (2001) suggested a new class of risk measures that they called *coherent measures of risk*. A risk measure ρ is a coherent measure of risk if it satisfies the following conditions for any two random variables $\tilde{x}$ and $\tilde{y}$:

1. *Monotonicity.* If $\tilde{x} \geq 0$, then $\rho(\tilde{x}) \leq 0$.
2. *Subadditivity.* $\rho(\tilde{x} + \tilde{y}) \leq \rho(\tilde{x}) + \rho(\tilde{y})$.
3. *Positive homogeneity.* For any positive real number, $c, \rho(c \cdot \tilde{x}) = c \cdot \rho(\tilde{x})$.
4. *Translational invariance.* For any real number, $c, \rho(\tilde{x} + c) \leq \rho(\tilde{x}) - c$.

Stated in words, these properties can be interpreted as follows:

1. If there are only positive returns, then the risk should be nonpositive.
2. The risk of a portfolio of two assets should be less than or equal to the sum of the risks of the individual assets.
3. If the amount of assets in the portfolio is increased c times, the risk becomes c times larger.
4. Cash or another risk-free asset does not contribute to portfolio risk.

Conditions (1), (3), and (4) are rather technical, and arguments have been presented in the literature that not all of them need to be satisfied for a risk measure to be considered acceptable in practice. Condition (2), however, is worth noting. It expresses the principle of diversification: aggregating different risks should diversify them away, not increase the overall risk.

As we saw in the example at the end of the previous section, VaR violates the second condition. There are instances in which the sum of the risks of two individual investments as represented by their VaRs is less than the risk (as represented by the VaR) of the portfolio of the two investments.

Taken together, the four conditions for coherence are rather restrictive. The standard deviation does not satisfy them either—it violates the monotonicity property. Artzner, Delbaen, Eber, and Heath (2001) suggested a tail-based risk measure that we mentioned earlier, CVaR, which satisfies all four conditions and is related to the popular risk measure VaR. The intuitive explanation behind CVaR and the easy way in which the portfolio allocation problem could be solved rapidly increased its popularity in practice.

While $100(1-\varepsilon)\%$ VaR considers the maximum loss only with a given probability ε, the $100(1-\varepsilon)\%$ CVaR asks what happens on average if the losses exceed the $100(1-\varepsilon)\%$ VaR; that is, what is the *expected loss in the tail*? Thus, CVaR addresses a major problem associated with VaR, which is that VaR ignores losses that may happen with low probability.

The formal definition of the $100(1-\varepsilon)\%$ CVaR is

$$\text{CVaR}_{(1-\varepsilon)}(\tilde{r}) = E[-\tilde{r} \,|\, -\tilde{r} \geq \text{VaR}_{(1-\varepsilon)}(\tilde{r})]$$

Note that this definition implies that the $100(1-\varepsilon)\%$ CVaR is always greater than or equal to the $100(1-\varepsilon)\%$ VaR. In other words, if we manage our portfolio risk using CVaR, we will be implicitly minimizing our portfolio VaR as well.[20]

It is difficult to estimate the CVaR for a general distribution but, similar to VaR, there are methods for estimating CVaR in special cases, such as the case in which we assume that future losses are normally distributed, or when we are given a set of scenarios for possible realizations of the portfolio returns.

13.3.1 Estimation of Conditional Value-at-Risk from a Normal Distribution

Let us first illustrate the calculation of CVaR for a normal distribution when the data are in P/L format and are assumed to follow a normal distribution. In this case, $100(1-\varepsilon)\%$ CVaR is given by the expression

$$\text{CVaR}_{(1-\varepsilon)} = -\mu_{P/L} + \frac{\varphi(z_{(1-\varepsilon)})}{\varepsilon} \cdot \sigma_{P/L}$$

where

$\mu_{P/L}$ is the mean of the P/L distribution

$\sigma_{P/L}$ is the standard deviation of the P/L distribution.

The number $z_{(1-\varepsilon)}$ is the $100(1-\varepsilon)$th percentile of a standard normal distribution, as before, and we use $\varphi(z_{(1-\varepsilon)})$ to denote the value of the normal probability density at the point $z_{(1-\varepsilon)}$. For any z, the value of $\varphi(z)$ can be found with the command NORMDIST(z,0,1,0) in Excel, or similar commands in MATLAB and Python. For example, let $\varepsilon = 0.05$. Therefore, $1-\varepsilon = 0.95$ and $z_{(1-\varepsilon)} = \text{norminv}(0.95) = 1.6448$. The value of $\varphi(z_{(1-\varepsilon)})$ is then 0.1031 (computed as NORMDIST(1.6448,0,1,0) in Excel).

If, instead, we have normally distributed L/P data, then we would use the formula

$$\text{CVaR}_{(1-\varepsilon)} = \mu_{L/P} + \frac{\varphi(z_{(1-\varepsilon)})}{\varepsilon} \cdot \sigma_{L/P}$$

20. The latter fact can be proved more formally; see, for example, Rockafellar and Uryasev (2002).

Finally, if we are given data on asset returns and assume arithmetic returns, the formula for CVaR would be

$$\mathrm{CVaR}_{(1-\varepsilon)} = \left(-\mu_r + \frac{\varphi(z_{(1-\varepsilon)})}{\varepsilon} \cdot \sigma_r \right) \cdot V_t$$

where V_t is the portfolio value at the beginning of the period over which CVaR is estimated.

13.3.2 Estimation of Conditional Value-at-Risk from a Discrete Distribution

Suppose that we have a discrete distribution of scenarios for portfolio losses, and a loss amount of l_j occurs with probability p_j. The $100(1-\varepsilon)\%$ CVaR is given by

$$\mathrm{CVaR}_{(1-\varepsilon)} = \frac{1}{\varepsilon} \cdot \sum_{j \text{ such that } l_j \geq \mathrm{VaR}(1-\varepsilon)} p_j \cdot l_j$$

One special case of a discrete distribution that is encountered often in practice is a discrete uniform distribution, in which every scenario in a set of S scenarios could happen with the same probability $1/S$. This happens, for example, when we use historical scenarios as a basis for our CVaR calculations. In this case, CVaR is the average of all scenarios that exceed the VaR, or, equivalently, the average of the highest $\varepsilon \cdot S$ scenarios. For simplicity, suppose that we have sorted the S scenarios for losses in increasing order (i.e., scenario S is the scenario with the highest loss). We can compute the $100(1-\varepsilon)\%$ CVaR as

$$\mathrm{CVaR}_{(1-\varepsilon)} = \frac{1}{\lfloor \varepsilon \cdot S \rfloor} \cdot \sum_{s=S-\lfloor \varepsilon \cdot S \rfloor+1}^{S} l_s$$

For example, if there are 215 scenarios and $\varepsilon = 0.05$, then $\lfloor \varepsilon \cdot S \rfloor = \lfloor 0.05 \cdot 215 \rfloor = \lfloor 10.75 \rfloor = 10$. The 95% CVaR is the average of the 10 scenarios with highest losses. If the scenarios are sorted in increasing order, we take the average of the losses in scenarios 206, 207, . . . , 215.

If the data take the form of arithmetic returns, we can compute the CVaR by using the same expression as the previous equation, but replacing the loss with the negative of the return in each scenario and multiplying the resulting amount by the portfolio value at the beginning of the time period under consideration.

13.3.3 Optimization of Conditional Value-at-Risk

The CVaR of a portfolio of N assets is a function of both the uncertain returns of the different assets in the portfolio (the N-dimensional vector $\tilde{\mathbf{r}}$), and the weights $\mathbf{w}$ that these assets have in the portfolio. For any given set of weights $\mathbf{w}$, the portfolio return is given by $\tilde{r}_p = \tilde{\mathbf{r}}'\mathbf{w}$. Suppose that the portfolio return $\tilde{r}_p$ follows a probability distribution with density function f. Then, we can express the $100(1-\varepsilon)\%$ CVaR mathematically as

$$\mathrm{CVaR}_{(1-\varepsilon)} = \frac{1}{\varepsilon} \cdot \int_{-r \geq \mathrm{VaR}_{(1-\varepsilon)}} (-r) \cdot f(r)\, dr.$$

We can recognize the term inside the integral as the expected value of the portfolio loss (as a percentage of amount invested) in the tail of the distribution.

In fact, CVaR is a function of the portfolio weights for the different assets $\mathbf{w}$, which determine the probability distribution of $\tilde{r}_p$. The existence of expected value in the definition of CVaR suggests the possibility of using stochastic programming methods if we want to find the asset allocation that results in the minimum portfolio CVaR.[21] Unfortunately, the definition of CVaR in terms of VaR makes it hard to optimize the CVaR because we need to go through the VaR, which itself suffers from computational difficulties when it comes to optimization. Rockafellar and Uryasev (2000) suggested using an auxiliary objective function instead of CVaR which has better computational properties. Namely, consider the function

$$F_{1-\varepsilon}(\mathbf{w},\xi)=\xi+\frac{1}{\varepsilon}\cdot\int_{-r\geq\xi}(-r-\xi)\cdot f(r)\,dr$$

which can be equivalently written as

$$F_{1-\varepsilon}(\mathbf{w},\xi)=\xi+\frac{1}{\varepsilon}\cdot\int_{-\infty}^{\infty}\max\{-r-\xi,0\}\cdot f(r)\,dr$$

It turns out that if we try to minimize this function by varying $\mathbf{w}$ and ξ, the minimum value of the function will in fact equal the $100(1-\varepsilon)\%$ CVaR. Mathematically, this is expressed as

$$\min_{\mathbf{w}}\ \text{CVaR}_{1-\varepsilon}=\min_{\mathbf{w},\xi}\ F_{1-\varepsilon}(\mathbf{w},\xi)$$

Hence, we can find the minimum value of CVaR without finding VaR first.[22] The value of ξ in the optimal solution will actually equal the VaR of the optimal portfolio found by optimizing the CVaR. However, the weights for the portfolio that minimizes CVaR will not necessarily be those for the portfolio that minimizes VaR.

Note that the integral in the expression for $F_{1-\varepsilon}(\mathbf{w},\xi)$ is multidimensional, and its calculation depends on knowing the joint probability density function of the returns of all assets in the portfolio. This is not only difficult to estimate, but is often undesirable to use, as multidimensional integration is very time consuming. There is a specific case in which the minimization of CVaR is a tractable optimization problem: when the joint probability density function of the returns for the assets in the portfolio is represented in a set of scenarios. This is typically the kind of data that we have in practice: we can use historical data or generate scenarios by simulation. Suppose also that each scenario in the set is equally likely. In that case, the function can be written as

$$F_{(1-\varepsilon)}(\mathbf{w},\xi)=\xi+\frac{1}{\lfloor\varepsilon\cdot S\rfloor}\cdot\sum_{s=1}^{S}\max\{-(\mathbf{r}^{(s)})'\mathbf{w}-\xi,0\}$$

where the N-dimensional vector $\mathbf{r}^{(s)}$ is the vector of returns on the N assets in the sth scenario. (Note here that $(\mathbf{r}^{(s)})'\mathbf{w}$ is the portfolio return in the sth scenario.)

21. See chapter 7 for an introduction to stochastic programming.

22. The $100(1-\varepsilon)\%$ VaR is a minimizer of the function $F_{1-\varepsilon}(\mathbf{w},\xi)$. In other words, in some cases, the value of ξ that results in the minimum of the function $F_{1-\varepsilon}(\mathbf{w},\xi)$ will in fact be the $100(1-\varepsilon)\%$ VaR, and thus VaR will be computed as a by-product of computing CVaR. However, there is an additional nontrivial amount of work involved in verifying that the value of ξ obtained in the optimization is indeed the $100(1-\varepsilon)\%$ VaR, and hence it cannot be assumed that CVaR optimization would provide a computationally efficient way of computing VaR. (For more details, see Rockafellar and Uryasev, 2000.) Still, knowing that CVaR minimization implies VaR minimization (rather than computing the actual value of VaR) is useful when making portfolio allocation decisions.

To make this function more optimization-solver friendly, we get rid of the expression

$$\max\{-(\mathbf{r}^{(s)})'\mathbf{w} - \xi, 0\}$$

by introducing the auxiliary decision variables $y_1, \ldots, y_S$—one for each scenario. We write the portfolio CVaR minimization problem as

$$\begin{aligned} \min_{\mathbf{w},\xi,\mathbf{y}} \quad & \xi + \frac{1}{\lfloor \varepsilon \cdot S \rfloor} \cdot \sum_{s=1}^{S} y_s \\ \text{s.t.} \quad & y_s \geq -(\mathbf{r}^{(s)})'\mathbf{w} - \xi, \quad s = 1, \ldots, S \\ & y_s \geq 0, \quad s = 1, \ldots, S \\ & \mathbf{w}'\boldsymbol{\iota} = 1 \end{aligned}$$

To understand the meaning of the first two sets of constraints, note that the objective function contains a minimization of the sum of the variables y_s. The optimization solver will try to make the values of these variables as small as possible. The first two sets of constraints, however, restrict the auxiliary variables y_s to be greater than both $-(\mathbf{r}^{(s)})'\mathbf{w} - \xi$ and 0. Thus, to satisfy both sets of constraints, the solver will set them equal to the larger of the two values; that is, to the maximum of $-(\mathbf{r}^{(s)})'\mathbf{w} - \xi$ and 0, which is the expression in $F_{(1-\varepsilon)}(\mathbf{w}, \xi)$. An alternative derivation of the optimization formulation can be obtained using optimization duality theory instead of the auxiliary function $F_{(1-\varepsilon)}(\mathbf{w}, \xi)$.

The previous formulation is a linear optimization problem, which makes sample CVaR optimization a particularly attractive option from a computational perspective. Adding portfolio constraints encountered in practice, such as number of positions, trading costs, and so on (see chapter 14) generally results in equally tractable (linear or mixed-integer) optimization formulations. For example, we can formulate an optimization problem of maximizing the expected portfolio return subject to a constraint on the portfolio CVaR by rewriting the previous problem as

$$\begin{aligned} \max_{\mathbf{w},\xi,\mathbf{y}} \quad & \boldsymbol{\mu}'\mathbf{w} \\ \text{s.t.} \quad & \xi + \frac{1}{\lfloor \varepsilon \cdot S \rfloor} \cdot \sum_{s=1}^{S} y_s \leq b_{1-\varepsilon} \\ & y_s \geq -(\mathbf{r}^{(s)})'\mathbf{w} - \xi, \quad s = 1, \ldots, S \\ & y_s \geq 0, \quad s = 1, \ldots, S \\ & \mathbf{w}'\boldsymbol{\iota} = 1 \end{aligned}$$

where $\boldsymbol{\mu}$ is the N-dimensional vector of expected returns on the N assets, and $b_{1-\varepsilon}$ is the average loss in the tail the portfolio manager is willing to tolerate. The online appendix to this chapter contains examples of the implementation of sample portfolio CvaR optimization.

Summary

- The mean-variance portfolio optimization framework takes into consideration only the first two moments of the distribution of portfolio returns, the mean and the variance; it does not take into consideration higher moments. Thus, it omits important information about the skewness, kurtosis, and higher moments of the distribution.

- A number of advanced risk measures have been suggested to incorporate such considerations better. In particular, many advanced portfolio risk measures look at the potential for downside risk. Such risk measures include semivariance, Roy's safety-first criterion, and quantile-based risk measures such as value-at-risk (VaR) and conditional value-at-risk (CVaR).
- VaR measures the maximum portfolio loss at a specified probability level over a given time horizon. Specifically, it is defined as the value such that the probability that the portfolio loss will exceed it is not more than some small number.
- The position or portfolio VaR can be estimated via three methods: (1) based on an approximation by the normal distribution; (2) via historical simulation; (3) via Monte Carlo (MC), or forward-looking simulation.
- Despite its advantages as a comprehensive measure of risk that can be applied to any type of asset and position, VaR suffers from a number of drawbacks. From a practical perspective, VaR does not convey information about the size of the possible extreme losses. Moreover, employing it as a risk management tool in an institution may encourage undesirable behavior, as traders have an incentive to take low-probability, high-impact bets that do not show up on the VaR radar screen. From a theoretical perspective, VaR does not support the principle of diversification.
- CVaR corrects some of the undesirable properties of VaR, in that CVaR is concerned with measuring extreme losses and supports the principle of diversification. It is defined as the expected loss in the tail of the probability distribution of portfolio losses; that is, it reports the expected loss if the losses exceed the VaR.
- CVaR can be estimated similarly to VaR: (1) based on an approximation by the normal distribution; (2) via historical simulation; (3) via MC simulation.
- Portfolio allocation with the goal of minimizing VaR is a difficult stochastic optimization problem with chance constraints. It is generally very computationally intensive to solve, and the solution that gets returned is not guaranteed to be optimal.
- The portfolio CVaR optimization problem is a difficult problem except in a case that is widely the context in practice: when the data for the problem take the form of scenarios for the possible realizations of asset returns. In the latter case, the portfolio CVaR minimization problem has a tractable linear programming (LP) formulation.

14

Equity Portfolio Selection in Practice

In investment management, an important decision is how to allocate funds among asset classes, and the quantitative frameworks for doing so were explained in chapter 13. The funds are then managed within the asset classes. As explained in chapter 2, the two major asset classes are equities and fixed-income securities. Equity portfolio management differs from fixed-income portfolio management in substantive ways, and fixed-income portfolio management is discussed separately in chapter 15. Regardless of the asset class being managed, however, the investment process follows the same integrated activities. These activities can be defined as follows:[1]

- An investor's objectives, preferences, and constraints are identified and specified to develop explicit investment policies.
- Strategies are developed and implemented through the choice of optimal combinations of financial and real assets in the marketplace.
- Market conditions, relative asset values, and the investor's circumstances are monitored.
- Portfolio adjustments are made as appropriate to reflect significant changes in any or all of the relevant variables.

In this chapter, we focus on the second activity of the investment process, developing and implementing a portfolio strategy. We introduce quantitative formulations of portfolio allocation problems widely used in equity portfolio management. Quantitative equity portfolio selection often involves extending the classical Markowitz framework (see chapter 12) or the more advanced tail-risk portfolio allocation frameworks (see chapter 13) to include different constraints that take specific investment guidelines and institutional features into account.

We begin by discussing the activities involved in the investment process in more detail, so we can provide context for the rest of the discussion. We then provide a classification of the most common portfolio constraints used in practice, and discuss extensions such as index tracking formulations, the inclusion of transaction costs, optimization of trades across

1. See Maginn and Tuttle (1990, pp. 1–3 and 1–5).

multiple client accounts, tax-aware strategies, and incorporating robustness in portfolio allocation procedures by using robust statistics, simulation, and robust optimization techniques.

14.1 The Investment Process

In practice, portfolio management consists of four activities:[2]

1. Setting the investment objectives
2. Developing and implementing a portfolio strategy
3. Monitoring the portfolio
4. Adjusting the portfolio

This section discusses each of these activities in more detail.

14.1.1 Setting Investment Objectives

Investment objectives vary by the type of financial institutions and are essentially dictated by the nature of an institution's liabilities. For banks, the objective is to earn a return on invested funds that is higher than the cost of acquiring those funds. For defined benefit pension plans, the investment objective is to generate sufficient cash flow from the investment portfolio to satisfy the plan's pension obligations. Life insurance companies sell a variety of products guaranteeing a dollar payment or a stream of dollar payments at some time in the future. They charge policyholders premiums that depend on the interest rate that the company can earn on its investments. To realize a profit, the company must earn a higher return on the premium that it invests than the implicit (or explicit) interest rate that it has guaranteed policyholders. Finally, for regulated investment companies (i.e., mutual funds and closed-end funds), hedge funds, and managed accounts by trust departments, the main objective of portfolio selection is often to maximize expected returns at a certain level of risk. The target return and risk level can be defined as absolute or relative to a benchmark, where a benchmark is a collection of securities against which the portfolio manager's performance can be evaluated.

We therefore divide investors into two general categories based on the characteristics of their benchmark. The first category of investors specifies the benchmark as a function of its liability structure. The investment objective is to generate a cash flow from their portfolio that, at a minimum, satisfies the liability structure. This is often referred to as *asset-liability management.* The second investor category specifies the benchmark as a target level of return or as an index such the S&P 500 or the Russell 1000. The investment objective, then, is to outperform the target. In this chapter, we will focus on investors in the second category, but we will provide some background on fixed-income, liability-driven portfolio management in chapter 15.

14.1.2 Developing and Implementing a Portfolio Strategy

Typically, the investor develops an investment policy in conjunction with a consultant. Given the investment policy, investment guidelines are established for individual managers

2. See Fabozzi (2007).

hired by the investor. The portfolio allocation among various asset classes (such as bonds and stocks) is usually decided in advance, and then each portfolio manager is hired to manage a specific asset class, or a subset of an asset class. In this chapter as well as chapter 15, we discuss the actual implementation of portfolio strategies for two specific asset classes—equities and fixed-income securities, respectively.

14.1.2.1 Active versus Passive Investment Strategies In pursuing an equity investment strategy, an investor will pursue or retain the services of an asset manager to pursue either an *active investment strategy* or a *passive investment strategy.* A portfolio manager who pursues an active management strategy utilizes available information and forecasting techniques to earn a higher return (after adjusting for risk, transaction costs, and management fees) than simply investing in a broadly diversified stock portfolio. Essential to all active investment strategies are expectations about the factors that have been found to materially affect the performance of stocks. Once those factors are identified, the portfolio management team must be able to produce realistic and reasonable return expectations and forecasts, construct the portfolio and rebalance it when necessary to manage its risk exposure, and manage trading and transaction costs. The construction process involves identifying efficient portfolios (as described in chapter 12) and then selecting the portfolio that the portfolio manager believes has the greatest likelihood of outperforming a broadly based stock market index after considering risk and fees.

In contrast to an active equity investment strategy, a passive equity investment strategy involves minimal expectational input. Instead, this approach to equity portfolio management relies on matching the performance of some client-designated stock index. The underlying assumption here is that the stock market will rapidly and efficiently embody all available information in the prevailing price of traded stocks. There are two passive management strategies: buy-and-hold and indexing. As the name suggests, a *buy-and-hold strategy* involves constructing a portfolio and holding it over some long (but undefined) period of time. By far, the more common passive strategy today that portfolio managers pursue is *indexing.* The objective is to manage the performance of some designated stock market index. What is done is to buy all stocks in the stock market index in proportion to their market value relative to the index's market value. So if the market value of an index is $\$W$ and stock A has a market value (i.e., market capitalization) of $\$w$, the amount of portfolio funds allocated to stock A will be $\$w/\$W$. Quantitative formulations of the portfolio indexing problem are discussed in section 14.3.

We can distinguish an active investment strategy from indexing (the most popular passive investment strategy) in terms of the portfolio construction (i.e., deciding on the stocks to include in the portfolio) and trading of stocks. Portfolio managers who follow an active equity investment strategy devote most of their time to portfolio construction, whereas those following an indexing strategy devote very little time to this activity. There is portfolio trading (buying and selling stocks) with an active strategy to take advantage of what the portfolio manager believes to be stocks or groups of stocks that are expected to perform better than the designated index.

Which should be selected, given the choice between active and passive equity investment strategies? The answer depends on the client's (1) view of how price efficient the market is, (2) investment beliefs, and (3) risk tolerance. *Price efficiency* means how difficult it would be to earn a greater return than a passive investment strategy after adjusting for the risk associated with a strategy, the transaction costs associated with implementing that strategy, and the fee charged by the portfolio manager.

14.1.2.2 Fundamental versus Quantitative Portfolio Management Active equity portfolio managers can pursue either a fundamental or quantitative approach. The *fundamental approach*, also referred to as *discretionary approach,* to equity portfolio management emphasizes human judgment of the stock analysts and portfolio manager who are part of the asset management team. The fundamental approach starts by gaining an understanding of the company based on the company's filings with the Securities and Exchange Commission (SEC), information about the major industries in which the company operates, and social media information with the goal of making forecasts (estimates) of the company's value. Although the valuation analysis utilizes both qualitative and quantitative data, that does not classify it as a quantitative approach.

Equity portfolio managers are said to pursue a *quantitative approach* when they apply a systematic, model-driven approach to managing a portfolio. The quantitative approach is said to be "systematic" with respect to (1) how the stock of companies are selected from among a universe of company stocks and (2) how portfolios are constructed from the universe of company stocks. The quantitative approach is also referred to as a *systematic approach.* Quantitative equity strategies include multifactor strategies, factor strategies, event-based strategies, statistical arbitrage strategies, textual strategies, and alternative data strategies. Our focus in this chapter is on quantitative equity portfolio management.

Broadly, here is how one distinguishes the fundamental and systematic approaches. A fundamental portfolio manager begins the stock selection process by screening a list of candidate stocks for inclusion in the portfolio. For example, the portfolio manager may only want to include stocks comprising the Russell 1000 stock index, an index that includes the 1,000 largest market capitalization stocks in the U.S. The stocks in this index then represent the investment universe. Given this universe, the portfolio manager selects characteristics for filtering the investment universe to create a shorter list of acceptable stocks from which the portfolio manager can select. For example, the portfolio manager may establish as its criteria for an acceptable company one that has had earnings growth of at least 12% per annum in each of the past five years and a price-earnings ratio over the past three months that does not exceed 15.

The filtering rules are based on what indicators the fundamental manager has found to be useful in identifying stocks that have superior company value and potential mispricing. The view is that these characteristics will create long-term value. The portfolio management team will then focus on the list of companies that satisfy the criteria. Suppose that there are 150 companies from seven industries that are on the list of acceptable stocks. The senior portfolio manager will then assign to each industry analyst's group the stocks from that list. The stock analysts will then perform traditional equity analysis to determine which stocks to recommend to the senior portfolio manager as potential acquisitions. The next step in the process is for the portfolio manager to construct the portfolio (i.e., select the stocks to be included in the portfolio and how much should be allocated to each stock). Most of the portfolio team's time is devoted to traditional equity analysis.

Now let's look at how this contrasts with the quantitative approach to equity portfolio management. As with a fundamental portfolio approach, the quantitative approach begins the investment process by screening the investment universe based on characteristics that are believed, based on the team's research and academic studies, to achieve the portfolio's investment objective. A quantitative manager believes that the characteristics provide sufficient information for selecting a company based on the firm's value and the biases that investors show in the market. The bulk of the portfolio team's time is spent on using models to decide on the characteristics to be used in filtering the investment universe. Suppose that the screen produces 200 stocks. The portfolio manager then will purchase all those stocks.

Consequently, both approaches use characteristics in screening to create a list of acceptable stocks. In the quantitative approach, the characteristics are used in a manner that is systematic and automated. In the fundamental approach, the characteristics are used as a more qualitative criterion.

Bukowski (2011) provides the following five differences between the two approaches to equity portfolio management:

- *Company versus characteristic focus:* The principal focus of the fundamental approach is on the companies that are filtered based on characteristics that create the acceptable list, while in the quantitative, there is no further screening of the companies on the filtered list since the characteristics used for the screening are those that the portfolio manager believes are sufficient to warrant the portfolio manager to allocate funds.
- *Narrow versus broad focus:* The acceptable list is used by a fundamental portfolio manager for further narrowing the potential stocks to be included in the portfolio, while for a quantitative portfolio manager, the characteristics are believed to contain all the information that will result in superior returns.
- *Position concentration/size of bets:* The position size in stocks tends to be larger with the fundamental approach than with the quantitative approach. This is because the in-depth analysis performed by the stock analysts in identifying attractive stocks gives the portfolio manager a higher level of confidence in selecting a stock. As a result, portfolio managers pursing a fundamental approach are essentially making larger bets on stocks. A quantitative portfolio manager relies on an optimization model to determine position size. The quantitative approach therefore prioritizes diversification in portfolio construction, which results in spreading the portfolio over a larger number of stocks. For this reason, the bet is lower for each stock.
- *Risk perspective:* Because of the way that the portfolio is constructed, a portfolio manager following the fundamental approach focuses on the risk of the individual companies comprising the portfolio. The portfolio risk following the quantitative approach is the perspective taken by the manager.
- *Past versus future focus:* In selecting stocks from the acceptable list, the portfolio management team relies not just on past information in selecting the stocks, but also the company's future prospects. In contrast, while a portfolio manager pursuing a quantitative approach relies on current and past information, less consideration is given to qualitative future prospects for the companies in selecting the stocks.

14.1.2.3 Machine Learning and Active Equity Investment Strategies Big data,[3] and more specifically alternative data[4] coupled with traditional financial databases, are commonly utilized by machine learning (ML) algorithms[5] and used to create data-driven models for active equity investment strategies. Bartram et al. (2020) describe the potential benefits of ML in the investment management process because of the ability of the ML algorithms to identify nonlinear relationships and make predictions. They also describe why the use of ML will continue to grow due to advances in computing power, and they identify potential pitfalls that portfolio managers should consider.

Bartram et al. (2021) provide a survey of ML potential applications to active equity portfolio management. They identify the three activities in the investment management process where ML has the potential to add value:

- Signal generation
- Portfolio construction
- Trade execution

Signal generation In active equity portfolio management, portfolio managers seek to generate signals for factors[6] that are relevant in driving returns. These factors can be technical factors (e.g., momentum) and fundamental factors (e.g., book-to-price ratio). Empirically, studies applying standard statistical tools have identified a large number of factors, but the out-of-sample estimates for many of these identified factors have been found to have poor predictive power.[7] ML algorithms for selecting the most important features (i.e., factors) such as least absolute shrinkage and selection operator (LASSO), elastic nets, tree-based regression, and artificial neural networks can be used to build multifactor signals.

Exhibit 14.1 lists the studies and ML algorithms used for signal generation. These studies have generally found that ML algorithms provided better performance in forecasting some factors than standard regression analysis. However, not all the studies support the position that ML algorithms outperform regression analysis in forecasting future stock returns. A study by Vanguard's Investment Strategy Group used several ML algorithms (including random forest and gradient boosting machine) to determine if ML could outperform a regression-based approach in forecasting 10-year stock returns.[8] The study found that ML algorithms could improve the performance only modestly relative to a regression model. In fact, the performance was even worse than when a commonly used econometric technique for that analysis of time-series data (vector autoregressive (VAR) model) was used for forecasting. However, when ML algorithms that allowed unspecified nonlinear relationships were combined with VAR, the forecasting ability of this hybrid model (ML-VAR model) improved the forecasting accuracy for 10-year stock returns.

3. See chapter 8.

4. Recall from chapter 8 that alternative data are nontraditional sources of data such as satellite imagery, Internet web traffic, and patent filings.

5. See chapter 10.

6. We discuss factors and factor models in chapter 16.

7. See Harvey, Liu, and Zhu (2016).

8. Wang et al. (2021).

Study	ML Algorithm(s) Used
Messmer and Audrino (2017)	LASSO
Rapach et al. (2019)	LASSO
Feng, Giglio, and Xiu (2020)	LASSO
Freyberger, Neuhierl, and Weber (2020)	LASSO
Rapach et al. (2013)	elastic nets
Coqueret and Guida (2018)	tree-based regression
Bryzgalova, Pelger, and Zhu (2020)	decision trees and tree-based regression
Leung et al. (2021)	gradient-boosted trees
Gu, Kelly, and Xiu (2020)	elastic nets, tree-based regression models using gradient-boosted regression trees.
Studies Using Machine Learning for Signal Generation	

Exhibit 14.1
Studies using ML for signal generation.

Ensemble models, which as explained in chapter 10 are averages of the forecasts of several ML algorithms, have been used for signal generation. For example, Borghi and De Rossi (2020) found that in forecasting stock returns, an ensemble of forecasts from four ML algorithms (random forest, neural networks, gradient-boosted trees, and regularized regressions) outperformed that of any individual ML algorithm. Similar findings were reported by Wolff and Echterling (2020) in predicting the weekly return for the stocks included in the S&P 500.

To forecast equity returns from textual social media data, natural language processing (NLP) and sentiment analysis can be used (for more, see chapter 11). The following five examples of key applications of NLP by asset management firms are provided in a 2020 article by Decimal Point Analytics:[9]

- BlackRock Financial Management used NLP during the pandemic to obtain insights from research documents based on the assumption that other asset managers would be relatively slow to update the earnings estimates for the first quarter of 2020. In addition, this asset management firm used NLP to generate sentiment signals to position its portfolio based on text material on fiscal policy.
- To complement its equity research process, American Century Investments uses NLP to create a sentiment model. The objective of the NLP sentiment model is to detect deception by management during quarterly earnings calls. Examples of management deception during earnings calls include omission of information such as the failure to disclose key details, spinning the facts to make performance look better than it actually was, obfuscation by management's use of complex explanations/storytelling to explain simple concepts, and deflecting responsibility.

9. "How Asset Managers Are Leveraging Natural Language Processing (NLP) Techniques," December 2020. Decimal Point Analytics. Available at https://decimalpointanalytics.medium.com/how-asset-managers-are-leveraging-natural-language-processing-nlp-techniques-b83aa91cf9dd.

- Deutsche Bank used NLP to evaluate sustainability reports (i.e., commitments made by companies to reduce carbon emission) rather than rely on standard ESG reports for rating companies.
- UBS Wealth Management uses NLP to detect negative news for the purpose of performing due diligence. This frees its analysts from reading and assessing a large number of documents.
- AIG and Citadel use NLP in analyzing alternative data in attempting to enhance returns.

Portfolio construction With respect to portfolio construction, the problems discussed in chapter 1 regarding the drawbacks of applying mean-variance analysis for asset allocation also apply to the construction of equity portfolios. ML has been used to deal with these drawbacks. One example, proposed by Lòpez de Prado (2016), is to implement a decision-tree structure with hierarchical clustering analysis instead of estimating portfolio risk from the covariance matrix of returns. This ML algorithm requires far fewer estimates for the inputs and as a result, it provides better stability and robustness compared to constructing a portfolio using mean-variance analysis. Neural networks are used by Chapados and Bengio (2001) to learn the optimal asset allocation using value-at-risk (VaR) constraints. Yu, Wang, and Li (2008) demonstrate how neural networks can be built to identify efficient portfolios using skewness in addition to mean and variance.

Trade execution Market impact cost (also referred to as *price impact cost*) is the deviation of the transaction price from the market price that would have prevailed had the trade not occurred. The price movement is the market impact cost of liquidity. Equity investors have used ML algorithms to estimate market impact costs since they can deal with complex dynamics in the equity market and nonlinearity of relationships. Logistic regressions using potential predictors as derived from LASSO were used by Zheng, Moulines, and Abergel (2013) to estimate the relationship between market impact and a large set of potential predictors. Booth, Gerding, and McGroarty (2015) apply performance-weighted random forests to predict market impact, finding that their approach significantly outperforms out-of-sample linear regressions, neural networks, and support vector machines (SVMs). Following a similar analysis, Park, Lee, and Son (2016) find that neural networks, Bayesian neural networks, Gaussian process regressions, and SVM regression significantly outperform a standard parametric benchmark with SVM regression generating the least unambiguous conclusions.

14.1.3 Monitoring the Portfolio

Once the portfolio has been constructed, it must be monitored. Monitoring involves two activities. The first is to assess whether there have been changes in the market that might suggest that any of the key inputs used in constructing the portfolio may not be realized. The second task is to monitor the performance of the portfolio.

The portfolio performance is monitored in two phases. The first is *performance measurement*, which involves the calculation of the return realized by the manager over a specified time interval (the *evaluation period*). The second is performance evaluation, which determines whether the manager has added value and how the manager achieved the observed return. The decomposition of the performance results to explain why those results were achieved is called *return attribution analysis*.

14.1.4 Adjusting the Portfolio

Investment management is an ongoing process, and portfolio strategies are in fact performed in a multiperiod context. Portfolio selection strategies are designed to take advantage of market conditions, but those conditions exist temporarily, and as the conditions change, the portfolio manager must perform *portfolio rebalancing*. In doing so, the manager typically takes the steps discussed in the following sections.

By monitoring developments in the capital market, the portfolio manager determines whether to revise the inputs used in the portfolio construction process. Based on the new inputs, the manager then constructs a new portfolio. In constructing that portfolio, the costs of trading are often evaluated against the benefits of rebalancing. Such costs include transaction costs and taxes and are discussed in more detail in sections 14.4 and 14.5.

14.2 Portfolio Constraints Commonly Used in Practice

Institutional features and investment policy specifications often lead to more complicated requirements than simple minimization of risk (whatever the definition of risk may be) or maximization of expected portfolio return. For example, as mentioned earlier, there can be constraints that limit the number of trades, the exposure to a specific industry, and the number of stocks to be kept in the portfolio. Some of these constraints are imposed by the clients, while others are imposed by regulators. For example, in the case of regulated investment companies, restrictions on asset allocation are set forth in the prospectus and may be changed only with the approval of the fund's board of directors. Pension funds must comply with Employee Retirement Income Security Act (ERISA) requirements.[10] The objective of the portfolio optimization problem can also be modified to consider specifically the trade-off between risk and return, transaction costs, or taxes.

In this section, we will take a single-period view of investing, in the sense that the goal of the portfolio allocation procedure will be to invest optimally over a single predetermined period of interest, such as one month.[11] We will use $\mathbf{w}_0$ to denote the vector array of stock weights in the portfolio at the beginning of the period, and $\mathbf{w}$ to denote the weights at the end of the period (which are to be determined).

Many investment companies, especially institutional investors, have a long investment horizon. However, in reality, they treat that horizon as a sequence of shorter-period horizons. Risk budgets are often stated over a time period of a year, and return performance is monitored quarterly or monthly.

14.2.1 Long-Only (No-Short-Selling) Constraints

Many funds and institutional investors face restrictions or outright prohibitions on the amount of short selling they can do. When short selling is not allowed, the portfolio allocation optimization model contains the constraints $\mathbf{w} \geq \mathbf{0}$.

10. ERISA was enacted in 1974 as a federal regulatory scheme for private-sector employee benefit plans, including health care plans. It sets forth requirements for benefit plan participation, funding, and vesting of benefits.

11. Multiperiod portfolio optimization models are not always used in practice, not because the value of multiperiod modeling is questioned, but because such models are often too intractable from a computational perspective.

14.2.2 Holding Constraints

Diversification principles argue against investing a large proportion of the portfolio in a single asset or having a large concentration of assets in a specific industry, sector, or country. Limits on the holdings of a specific stock can be imposed with the constraints

$$\mathbf{l} \leq \mathbf{w} \leq \mathbf{u}$$

where **l** and **u** are vectors of lower and upper bounds of the holdings of each stock in the portfolio.

Consider now a portfolio of 10 stocks. Suppose that the issuers of assets 1, 3, and 5 are in the same industry, and that we would like to limit the portfolio exposure to that industry to be between 20% and 40%. To limit exposure to that industry, we add the constraint

$$0.20 \leq w_1 + w_3 + w_5 \leq 0.40$$

to the portfolio allocation optimization problem.

More generally, if we have a specific set of stocks I_j out of the investment universe I consisting of stocks in the same category (such as by industry or by country), we can write the constraint as

$$l_j \leq \sum_{j \in I_j} w_j \leq u_j$$

Stated in words, this constraint requires that the sum of all stock weights in the particular category of investments with indices I_j is greater than or equal to a lower bound l_j and less than a maximum exposure of u_j.

14.2.3 Turnover Constraints

High portfolio turnover can result in large transaction costs that make portfolio rebalancing inefficient and costly. Thus, some portfolio managers limit the amount of turnover allowed when trading their portfolios. (Another way to control transaction costs is to minimize them explicitly, and the appropriate formulations are discussed later in this chapter.)

Most commonly, turnover constraints are imposed for each stock as follows:

$$|w_i - w_{0,i}| \leq u_i$$

that is, the absolute magnitude of the difference between the final and the initial weight of stock i in the portfolio is restricted to be less than some upper bound u_i. Sometimes a constraint is imposed to minimize the portfolio turnover as a whole:

$$\sum_{j \in I_j} |w_j - w_{0,j}| \leq U_j$$

that is, the total absolute difference between the initial and the final weights of the stocks in the portfolio is restricted to be less than or equal to an upper bound U_j. Under this constraint, some stock weights may deviate a lot more than others from their initial weights, but the total deviation is limited.

Turnover constraints are often imposed relative to *average daily volume (ADV)* of a stock.[12] For example, we may want to restrict turnover to no more than 5% of the ADV. (In the latter case, the upper bound u_i is set to a value of 5% of the ADV.) Modifications of these constraints, such as limiting turnover in a specific industry or sector, are also frequently applied.

14.2.4 Risk Factor Constraints

In practice, it is very common for quantitatively oriented portfolio managers to use *factor models* to control for risk exposures to different risk factors, which could include the market return, size, and style.[13] Let us assume that the return on stock i has a factor structure with K risk factors; that is, it can be expressed through the equality

$$r_i = \alpha_i + \sum_{k=1}^{K} \beta_{ik} \cdot f_k + \varepsilon_i$$

The factors f_k are common to all securities. The coefficient β_{ik} in front of each factor f_k shows the sensitivity of the return on stock i to factor k. The value of α_i shows the expected excess return of the return on stock i, and ε_i is the idiosyncratic (called *nonsystematic*) part of the return of stock i. The coefficients α_i and β_{ik} are typically estimated by multiple regression analysis.[14]

To limit the exposure of a portfolio of N stocks to the kth risk factor, we impose the constraint

$$\sum_{i=1}^{N} \beta_{ik} \cdot w_i \leq U_k.$$

The mathematics behind risk factor models will become more intuitive in chapter 16, but this constraint formulation is easy to understand at this stage as well. The total return on the portfolio can be written as

$$\begin{aligned}\sum_{i=1}^{N} w_i \cdot r_i &= \sum_{i=1}^{N} w_i \cdot \left(\alpha_i + \sum_{k=1}^{K} \beta_{ik} \cdot f_k + \varepsilon_i \right) \\ &= \sum_{i=1}^{N} w_i \cdot \alpha_i + \sum_{i=1}^{N} \left(w_i \left(\sum_{k=1}^{K} \beta_{ik} \cdot f_k \right) \cdot \right) + \sum_{i=1}^{N} w_i \cdot \varepsilon_i\end{aligned}$$

The sensitivity of the portfolio to the various factors is represented by the second term, which can also be written as

$$\sum_{k=1}^{K} \left(\left(\sum_{i=1}^{N} w_i \cdot \beta_{ik} \right) \cdot f_k \right).$$

Therefore, the exposure to a particular factor k is the coefficient in front of f_k; that is,

12. As the term intuitively implies, the ADV measures the total amount of a given asset traded in a day on average over a prespecified time period.

13. Risk factors and factor models are discussed in more detail in chapter 16.

14. See chapter 16.

$$\sum_{i=1}^{N} \beta_{ik} \cdot w_i.$$

On an intuitive level, the sensitivity of the portfolio to factor k will be larger, the larger the presence of factor k in the portfolio through the exposure of the individual stocks. Thus, when we compute the total exposure of the portfolio to factor k, we need to consider both how important this factor is for determining the return on each of the securities in the portfolio, and how much of each security we have in the portfolio.

A commonly used version of the maximum factor exposure constraint is

$$\sum_{i=1}^{N} \beta_{ik} \cdot w_i = 0.$$

This constraint forces the portfolio optimization algorithm to find portfolio weights so that the overall risk exposure to factor k is 0; that is, so the portfolio is neutral with respect to changes in factor k. Portfolio allocation strategies that claim to be "market-neutral" typically employ this constraint, and the factor is in fact the return on the market.

14.2.5 Cardinality Constraints

Depending on the portfolio allocation model used, sometimes the optimization subroutine recommends holding small amounts of a large number of stocks, which can be costly when one considers the transaction costs incurred when acquiring these positions. Alternatively, a portfolio manager may be interested in limiting the number of stocks used to track a particular index. Mathematically, modeling the constraint of a limited number of stocks to be held in the portfolio is actually very similar to modeling the number of projects to be selected in the capital budgeting example discussed in section 6.3.3. To formulate the constraint on the number of stocks to be held in the portfolio (called *cardinality constraint*), we introduce binary variables, one for each of the N stocks in the portfolio. Let us call these binary variables $\delta_1, \ldots, \delta_N$. The variable δ_i will take the value 1 if stock i is included in the portfolio, and 0 otherwise.

Suppose that out of the N stocks in the investment universe, we would like to include a maximum of K stocks in the final portfolio. K here is a positive integer, less than N. This constraint can be formulated as

$$\sum_{i=1}^{N} \delta_i \leq K, \ \delta_i \text{ binary}, \ i = 1, \ldots, N.$$

We need to make sure, however, that if a stock is not selected in the portfolio, then the binary variable that corresponds to that stock is set to 0, so the stock is not counted as one of the K stocks left in the portfolio. When the portfolio weights are restricted to be non-negative, this can be achieved by imposing the additional constraints

$$0 \leq w_i \leq \delta_i, \ i = 1, \ldots, N.$$

If the optimal weight for stock i turns out to be different from 0, then the binary variable δ_i associated with stock i is forced to take the value 1, and stock i will be counted among the K stocks to be kept in the portfolio. If the optimal weight for stock i is 0, then the binary variable δ_i associated with stock i can be either 0 or 1, but that will not matter for all practical purposes because the solver will set it to 0 if there are too many other attractive stocks that will be counted as the K stocks to be kept in the portfolio. At the same time, since the portfolio weight w_i is between 0 and 1 and δ_i is 0 or 1, the constraint $w_i \leq \delta_i$ does not restrict the values that the stock weight w_i can take.

The constraints are a little different if short sales are allowed, in which case the weights may be negative. We have

$$-M \cdot \delta_i \leq w_i \leq M \cdot \delta_i, i = 1, \ldots, N,$$

where M is a large constant (relative to the size of the inputs in the problem, so in this portfolio optimization application, $M = 10$ can be considered "large"). You can observe that if weight w_i is anything but 0, the value of the binary variable δ_i will be forced to be different from 0; that is, δ_i will need to be 1 since it can take only the value 0 or 1.

15.2.6 Minimum Holding and Transaction Size Constraints

Cardinality constraints are often used in conjunction with minimum holding/trading constraints. The latter set a minimum limit on the amount of a specific stock that can be held in the portfolio, or the amount of a stock that can be traded, effectively eliminating small trades. Both cardinality and minimum holding/trading constraints aim to reduce the amount of transaction costs.

Threshold constraints on the amount of stock i to be held in the portfolio can be imposed with the constraint

$$|w_i| \geq L_i \cdot \delta_i$$

where L_i is the smallest holding size allowed for stock i, and δ_i is a binary variable, analogous to the binary variables δ_i defined in the previous section—it equals 1 if stock i is included in the portfolio, and 0 otherwise. (All additional constraints relating to δ_i and w_i described in the previous section still apply.)

Similarly, constraints can be imposed on the minimum trading amount for stock i. As we explained earlier in this section, the size of the trade for stock i is determined by the absolute value of the difference between the current weight of the stock, $w_{0,i}$, and the new weight w_i that will be found by the solver: $|w_i - w_{0,i}|$. The minimum trading size constraint formulation is

$$|w_i - w_{0,i}| \geq L_i^{\text{trade}} \cdot \delta_i$$

where L_i^{trade} is the smallest trading size allowed for stock i.

As we explained in section 6.2.5, adding binary variables to an optimization problem makes the problem more difficult for the solver, and it can also increase the computation time substantially. That is why in practice, portfolio managers often omit minimum holding and transaction size constraints from the optimization problem formulation, electing instead to manually eliminate weights and trades that appear too small after the optimal portfolio is determined by the optimization solver. It is important to realize, however, that modifying the optimal solution for the simpler portfolio allocation problem (the optimal solution, in this case, is the weights/trades for the different stocks) by eliminating small positions manually does not necessarily produce the optimal solution to an optimization problem that contained the minimum holding and transaction size constraints from the beginning. In fact, there can be pathological cases in which the solution is very different from the true optimal solution. However, for most cases in practice, the small manual adjustments to the optimal portfolio allocation do not cause tremendous discrepancies or inconsistencies.

14.2.7 Round Lot Constraints

So far, we have assumed that stocks are infinitely divisible; that is, that we can trade and invest in fractions of stocks, bonds, and the like. This is not true, of course—in reality, securities are traded in multiples of minimum transaction lots, or *rounds* (e.g., 100 or 500 shares).

To represent the condition that securities should be traded in rounds, we need to introduce additional decision variables (let us call them z_i, $i = 1, \ldots, N$) that are integers and will correspond to the number of lots of a particular security that will be purchased. Each z_i will then be linked to the corresponding portfolio weight w_i through the equality

$$w_i = z_i \cdot f_i,\ i = 1, \ldots, N$$

where f_i is measured in dollars and is a fraction of the total amount to be invested. For example, suppose that there is a total of \$100 million to be invested, and stock i trades at \$50 in round lots of 100. Then

$$f_i = \frac{50 \cdot 100}{100{,}000{,}000} = 5 \cdot 10^{-7}$$

All remaining constraints in the portfolio allocation can be expressed through weight w_i, as usual. However, we also need to specify for the solver that the decision variable z_i is an integer.

An issue with imposing round lot constraints is that the budget constraint

$$\mathbf{w'\iota} = 1,$$

which is in fact

$$\sum_{i=1}^{N} z_i \cdot f_i = 1,$$

may not be satisfied exactly. To understand this better, recall the capital budgeting example from section 6.3.3, which illustrated a similar situation in a different context—when projects with different budgets were added up without the ability to adjust their budgets up or down, they did not necessarily use the entire available budget (or else they could end up over budget).

One possibility to handle this problem is to relax the budget constraint. For example, we can state the constraint as

$$\mathbf{w'\iota} \leq 1,$$

or, equivalently,

$$\sum_{i=1}^{N} z_i \cdot f_i \leq 1.$$

This will ensure that we do not go over budget.

If our objective is stated as expected return maximization, the optimization solver will attempt to make this constraint as tight as possible; that is, we will end up using up as much of the budget as we can. Depending on the objective function and the other constraints in the formulation, however, this may not always happen. We can try to force the solver to minimize the slack in the budget constraint by introducing a pair of nonnegative decision variables (let us call them ε^+ and ε^-) that account for the amount that is "overinvested" or "underinvested," respectively. These variables will pick up the slack left over because of the inability to round the amounts for the various investments. Namely, we impose the constraints

$$\sum_{i=1}^{N} z_i \cdot f_i + \varepsilon^- - \varepsilon^+ = 1$$
$$\varepsilon^- \geq 0,\ \varepsilon^+ \geq 0$$

and subtract the following term from the objective function:

$$\lambda_{\text{rl}} \cdot (\varepsilon^- + \varepsilon^+),$$

where λ_{rl} is a penalty term associated with the amount of overinvestment or underinvestment that the portfolio manager is willing to tolerate (selected by the portfolio manager). In the final solution, the violation of the budget constraint will be minimized. Note, however, that this formulation technically allows the budget to be overinvested.

Note that the optimal portfolio allocation that we obtain after solving this optimization problem will not be the same as the allocation that we would obtain if we solve an optimization problem without round lot constraints, and then round the amounts to fit the lots that can be traded in the market.

Cardinality constraints, minimum holding/trading constraints, and especially round lot constraints require more sophisticated binary and integer programming (IP) solvers. In addition, they are difficult problems to solve for large portfolios.

14.3 Benchmark Exposure and Tracking Error Minimization

Expected portfolio return maximization under the mean-variance framework or other risk measure minimization are examples of active investment strategies; that is, strategies that identify a universe of attractive investment, and ignore inferior investment opportunities. As we explained in section 14.1.2, a different approach, referred to as a *passive investment strategy*, argues that in the absence of any superior forecasting ability, investors might as well resign themselves to the fact that they cannot beat the market. From a theoretical perspective, the analytics of portfolio theory tell them to hold a broadly diversified portfolio anyway. Many mutual funds are managed relative to a particular benchmark or stock universe, such as the S&P 500 or the Russell 1000. The portfolio allocation models are then formulated in such a way that the tracking error relative to the benchmark is kept small.

14.3.1 Standard Definition of Tracking Error

To incorporate a passive investment strategy, we can change the objective function of the portfolio allocation problem so that instead of minimizing a portfolio risk measure, we minimize the tracking error with respect to a benchmark that represents the market, such as the Russell 3000 or the S&P 500. Such strategies are often referred to as *indexing*. The *tracking error* can be defined in different ways. However, practitioners typically mean a specific definition: the variance (or standard deviation) of the difference between the portfolio return, $\mathbf{w}'\tilde{\mathbf{r}}$, and the return on the benchmark, $\mathbf{w}_b'\tilde{\mathbf{r}}$. Mathematically, the tracking error (TE) can be expressed as

$$\begin{aligned}\text{TE} &= Var(\mathbf{w}'\tilde{\mathbf{r}} - \mathbf{w}_b'\tilde{\mathbf{r}}) \\ &= Var((\mathbf{w} - \mathbf{w}_b)'\tilde{\mathbf{r}}) \\ &= (\mathbf{w} - \mathbf{w}_b)'\, Var(\tilde{\mathbf{r}})\, (\mathbf{w} - \mathbf{w}_b) \\ &= (\mathbf{w} - \mathbf{w}_b)' \Sigma (\mathbf{w} - \mathbf{w}_b)\end{aligned}$$

where Σ is the covariance matrix of the stock returns. You can observe that the formula is very similar to the formula for the portfolio variance derived in chapter 12; however, the portfolio weights in the formula from chapter 12 are replaced by differences between the weights of the stocks in the portfolio and the weights of the stocks in the index.

A question that may be on some readers' minds is why we need to optimize portfolio weights to track a benchmark when technically, the most effective way to track a benchmark is by investing the portfolio in the stocks in the benchmark portfolio in the same proportions as the proportions of these securities in the benchmark. The problem with this approach is that, especially with large benchmarks such as the Russell 3000, the transaction costs of a proportional investment and the subsequent rebalancing of the portfolio can be prohibitive (i.e., they dramatically adversely affect the performance of the portfolio relative to the benchmark). Furthermore, in practice, securities are not infinitely divisible, so investing a portfolio of a limited size in the same proportions as the composition of the benchmark will still not achieve zero tracking error. Thus, the optimal formulation is to require that the portfolio follows the benchmark as closely as possible.

While indexing has become an essential part of many portfolio strategies, most portfolio managers cannot resist the temptation to identify at least some securities that will outperform others. Hence, restrictions on the tracking error are often imposed as a constraint, while the objective function is something different than minimizing the tracking error. The tracking error constraint takes the form

$$(\mathbf{w} - \mathbf{w}_b)' \Sigma (\mathbf{w} - \mathbf{w}_b) \leq \sigma^2_{\text{TE}}$$

where σ^2_{TE} is a limit (imposed by the investor) on the amount of tracking error that the investor is willing to tolerate. This is a quadratic constraint, which is convex and computationally tractable but requires specialized optimization software.

14.3.2 Alternative Ways of Defining Tracking Error

There are alternative ways in which tracking-error type constraints can be imposed.

For example, we may require that the absolute deviations (ADs) of the portfolio weights ($\mathbf{w}$) from the index weights ($\mathbf{w}_b$) are less than or equal to a given vector array of upper bounds $\mathbf{u}$:

$$|\mathbf{w} - \mathbf{w}_b| \leq \mathbf{u}$$

where the absolute values $|\cdot|$ for the vector differences are taken componentwise; that is, for pairs of corresponding elements from the two vector arrays. These constraints can be stated as linear constraints by rewriting them as

$$\begin{aligned}\mathbf{w} - \mathbf{w}_b &\leq \mathbf{u} \\ -(\mathbf{w} - \mathbf{w}_b) &\leq \mathbf{u}.\end{aligned}$$

Similarly, we can require that for stocks within a specific industry (whose indices in the portfolio belong to a subset I_j of the investment universe I), the total tracking error is less than a given upper bound U_j:

$$\sum_{j \in I_j}(w_j - w_{b,j}) \le U_j .$$

Finally, tracking error can be expressed through risk measures other than the ADs or the variance of the deviations from the benchmark. Rockafellar and Uryasev (2002) suggest using CVaR[15] to manage the tracking error. (As we know from chapter 13, CVaR is a computationally tractable risk measure so long as the data are presented in the form of scenarios.[16]) We provide here a formulation that is somewhat different from that of Rockafellar and Uryasev (2002) but preserves the main idea.

Suppose that we are given S scenarios for the return of a benchmark portfolio (or an instrument that we are trying to replicate), b_s, $s = 1, \ldots, S$. These scenarios can be generated by simulation or taken from historical data. We also have N stocks with returns $r_i^{(s)}$ ($i = 1, \ldots, N$, $s = 1, \ldots, S$) in each scenario. The value of the portfolio in scenario s is

$$\sum_{i=1}^{N} r_i^{(s)} \cdot w_i ,$$

or, equivalently, $(\mathbf{r}^{(s)})'\mathbf{w}$, where $\mathbf{r}^{(s)}$ is the vector of returns for the N stocks in scenario s. Consider the differences between the return on the benchmark and the return on the portfolio:

$$b_s - (\mathbf{r}^{(s)})'\,\mathbf{w} = -((\mathbf{r}^{(s)})'\,\mathbf{w} - b_s).$$

If this difference is positive, we have a loss; if the difference is negative, we have a gain; both gains and losses are computed relative to the benchmark. Rationally, the portfolio manager should not worry about differences that are negative; the only cause for concern would be if the portfolio underperforms the benchmark, which would result in a positive difference. Thus, it is not necessary to limit the variance of the deviations of the portfolio returns from the benchmark, which penalizes for positive and negative deviations equally. Instead, we can treat these differences in the same way as we treated absolute portfolio losses in section 13.3 and impose a limit on the amount of loss we are willing to tolerate regarding the CVaR of the distribution of losses relative to the benchmark.

From the formulation of the CVaR optimization problem from section 13.3, it is easy to see that the tracking error constraint in terms of the CVaR can be stated as the following set of constraints:

$$\begin{aligned}
&\xi + \frac{1}{(\varepsilon \cdot S)} \cdot \sum_{s=1}^{S} y_s \le U_{\mathrm{TE}} \\
&y_s \ge -((\mathbf{r}^{(s)})'\mathbf{w} - b_s) - \xi, \quad s = 1, \ldots, S \\
&y_s \ge 0, \quad s = 1, \ldots, S
\end{aligned}$$

where U_{TE} is the upper bound on the negative deviations.

15. See section 13.3 for an introduction to CVaR.

16. As explained in chapter 13, another computationally tractable situation is when the data are normally distributed. In that case, minimizing CVaR is equivalent to minimizing the standard deviation.

This formulation of tracking error is appealing in two ways. First, it treats positive and negative deviations relative to the benchmark differently, which agrees with an investor's strategy of maximizing overall returns. Second, it results in a linear set of constraints, which are easy to handle computationally, in contrast to the first formulation of the tracking error constraint in this section, which results in a quadratic constraint.

14.3.3 Actual versus Predicted Tracking Error

The tracking error calculation in practice is often backward-looking. For example, in computing the covariance matrix Σ in the standard tracking error definition in section 14.3.1, or in selecting the scenarios used in the CVaR-type tracking error constraint in section 14.3.2, we may use historical data. The tracking error calculated in this manner is called the *ex post tracking error, backward-looking error*, or *actual tracking error.*

The problem with using the actual tracking error for assessing future performance relative to a benchmark is that the actual tracking error does not reflect the effect of the portfolio manager's current decisions on the future active returns, and hence the tracking error that may be realized in the future. The actual tracking error has little predictive value and can be misleading regarding portfolio risk.

Portfolio managers need forward-looking estimates of tracking errors to reflect future portfolio performance more accurately. In practice, this is accomplished by using the services of a commercial vendor that has a *multifactor model*[17] that has identified and defined the risks associated with the benchmark, or by building such a model in house. Statistical analysis of historical return data for the stocks in the benchmark are used to obtain the risk factors and to quantify the risks. Using the manager's current portfolio holdings, the portfolio's current exposure to the various risk factors can be calculated and compared to the benchmark's exposures to the risk factors. From the differential factor exposures and the risks of the factors, a *forward-looking tracking error* for the portfolio can be computed. This tracking error is also referred to as an *ex ante tracking error* or a *predicted tracking error.*

There is no guarantee that the predicted tracking error will match exactly the tracking error realized over the future time period of interest. However, this calculation of the tracking error has its use in risk control and portfolio construction. By performing a simulation analysis on the factors that enter the calculation, the manager can evaluate the potential performance of portfolio strategies relative to the benchmark and eliminate those that result in tracking errors beyond the client-imposed tolerance for risk. The actual tracking error, on the other hand, is useful for assessing actual performance relative to a benchmark.

14.4 Incorporating Transaction Costs

Transaction costs critically affect investment performance. The costs associated with managing a portfolio go beyond brokerage costs for transacting in securities. They can be

17. See chapter 16.

generally divided into two categories: explicit (such as bid-ask spreads, commissions and fees) and implicit (such as price movement risk costs[18] and market impact costs).[19]

The typical portfolio allocation models are built on top of one or several forecasting models for expected returns and risk. Small changes in these forecasts can result in reallocations that would not occur if transaction costs are considered. In practice, the effect of transaction costs on portfolio performance is far from insignificant. If transaction costs are not considered in allocation and rebalancing decisions, they can lead to poor portfolio performance.

This section describes some common transaction cost models for portfolio rebalancing. We use the mean-variance framework to describe the various approaches. However, it is straightforward to extend the transaction cost models to other portfolio allocation frameworks.

The earliest and most widely used model for transaction costs is the mean-variance risk-aversion formulation with transaction costs.[20] The optimization problem has the following objective function:

$$\max_{\mathbf{w}} \quad \mathbf{w}'\boldsymbol{\mu} - \lambda \cdot \mathbf{w}'\boldsymbol{\Sigma}\mathbf{w} - \lambda_{\mathrm{TC}} \cdot \mathrm{TC}$$

where TC is a transaction cost penalty function and λ_{TC} is the transaction cost aversion parameter. In other words, the objective is to maximize the expected portfolio return minus the cost of risk and transaction costs. We can imagine that as the transaction costs increase, at some point it becomes optimal to keep the current portfolio rather than to rebalance. Variations of this formulation exist. For example, it is common to maximize expected portfolio return minus transaction costs and impose limits on the risk as a constraint (i.e., to move the second term in the objective function in the constraints).

Transaction cost models can involve complicated nonlinear functions. Although software exists to handle general nonlinear optimization problems, the computational time required for solving such problems is often too long for realistic investment applications, and, as explained in chapter 6, the quality of the solution is not guaranteed. In practice, an observed complicated nonlinear transaction cost function is often approximated with a computationally tractable function that is assumed to be separable in the portfolio weights; that is, it is often assumed that the transaction costs for each individual stock are independent of the transaction costs for another stock. For the rest of this section, we will denote the individual cost function for stock i by TC_i.

Next, we explain several commonly used models for the transaction cost function.

18. Price movement risk costs are the costs resulting from the potential for a change in market price between the time that the decision to trade is made and the time that the trade is actually executed.

19. Market impact is the effect that a trader has on the market price of an asset when it sells or buys it. It is the extent to which the price moves up or down in response to the trader's actions. For example, a trader who tries to sell a large number of shares of a particular stock may drive down the stock's market price.

20. Versions of this model have been suggested in Pogue (1970), Schreiner (1980), Adcock and Meade (1994), Lobo, Fazel, and Boyd (2007), and Mitchell and Braun (2004).

14.4.1 Linear Transaction Costs

Let us start simple. Suppose that the transaction costs are proportional; that is, they are a percentage c_i of the transaction size $|t| = |w_i - w_{0,i}|$.[21] Then the portfolio allocation problem with transaction costs can be written simply as

$$\max_{\mathbf{w}} \quad \mathbf{w}'\boldsymbol{\mu} - \lambda \cdot \mathbf{w}'\Sigma\,\mathbf{w} - \lambda_{\mathrm{TC}} \cdot \sum_{i=1}^{N} c_i \cdot |w_i - w_{0,1}|.$$

The problem can be made solver-friendly by replacing the absolute value terms with new decision variables y_i, and adding two sets of constraints. Hence, we rewrite the objective function as

$$\max_{\mathbf{w},\,\mathbf{y}} \quad \mathbf{w}'\boldsymbol{\mu} - \lambda \cdot \mathbf{w}'\Sigma\,\mathbf{w} - \lambda_{\mathrm{TC}} \cdot \sum_{i=1}^{N} c_i \cdot y_i$$

and add the constraints

$$\begin{aligned} y_i &\geq w_i - w_{0,i} \\ y_i &\geq -(w_i - w_{0,i}). \end{aligned}$$

This preserves the quadratic optimization problem formulation—one that can be passed to quadratic optimization solvers because the constraints are linear expressions and the objective function contains only linear and quadratic terms.

In the optimal solution, the optimization solver will in fact set the value for y_i to $|w_i - w_{0,i}|$. This is because this is a maximization problem and y_i occurs with a negative sign in the objective function, so the solver will try to set y_i to the minimum value possible. That minimum value will be the maximum of $(w_i - w_{0,i})$ or $-(w_i - w_{0,i})$, which is in fact the absolute value $|w_i - w_{0,i}|$.

14.4.2 Piecewise-Linear Transaction Costs

Taking the model in the previous section a step further, we can introduce piecewise-linear approximations to transaction cost function models. This function is more realistic than the linear cost function, especially for large trades. As the trading size increases, it becomes increasingly more costly to trade because of the market impact that it would have.

An example of a piecewise-linear function of transaction costs for a trade of size t of a particular security was illustrated in exhibit 14.1. The transaction cost function illustrated in the graph assumes that the rate of increase of transaction costs (reflected in the slope of the function) changes at certain threshold points. For example, it is smaller in the range 0 to 15% of daily volume than in the range 15% to 40% of daily volume (or some other trading volume index). Mathematically, the transaction cost function in exhibit 14.1 can be expressed as

21. Here, we are thinking of w_i as the portfolio weights, but in fact, it may be more intuitive to think of the transaction costs as a percentage of amount traded. It is easy to go back and forth between portfolio weights and portfolio amounts by simply multiplying w_i by the total amount in the portfolio. In fact, we can switch the whole portfolio optimization formulation around and write it in terms of allocation of dollars instead of weights. We just need to replace the vector of weights **w** by a vector **x** of dollar holdings.

$$\mathrm{TC}(t) = \begin{cases} s_1 t, & 0 \le t \le 0.15 \cdot \mathrm{Vol} \\ s_1(0.15 \cdot \mathrm{Vol}) + s_2(t - 0.15 \cdot \mathrm{Vol}), & 0.15 \cdot \mathrm{Vol} \le t \le 0.40 \cdot \mathrm{Vol} \\ s_1(0.15 \cdot \mathrm{Vol}) + s_2(0.25 \cdot \mathrm{Vol}) & 0.40 \cdot \mathrm{Vol} \le t \le 0.50 \cdot \mathrm{Vol} \\ \quad + s_3(t - 0.40 \cdot \mathrm{Vol}), & \end{cases}$$

where s_1, s_2, and s_3 are the slopes of the three linear segments on the graph. To include piecewise-linear functions for transaction costs in the objective function of a mean-variance (or any general mean-risk) portfolio optimization problem, we need to introduce new decision variables that correspond to the number of pieces in the piecewise-linear approximation of the transaction cost function (in this case, there are three linear segments, so we introduce the variables z_1, z_2, and z_3). We write the penalty term in the objective function for an individual stock as[22]

$$\lambda_{\mathrm{TC}} \cdot (s_1 \cdot z_1 + s_2 \cdot z_2 + s_3 \cdot z_3)$$

If there are N stocks in the portfolio, the total transaction cost will be the sum of the transaction costs for each individual stock; that is, the penalty term that involves transaction costs in the objective function becomes

$$-\lambda_{\mathrm{TC}} \sum_{i=1}^{N} (s_{1,i} \cdot z_{1,i} + s_{2,i} \cdot z_{2,i} + s_{3,i} \cdot z_{3,i}).$$

In addition, we specify the following constraints on the new decision variables:

$$0 \le z_{1,i} \le 0.15 \cdot \mathrm{Vol}_i$$
$$0 \le z_{2,i} \le 0.25 \cdot \mathrm{Vol}_i$$
$$0 \le z_{3,i} \le 0.10 \cdot \mathrm{Vol}_i$$

Note that because of the increasing slopes of the linear segments and the goal of making that term as small as possible in the objective function, the optimizer will never set the decision variable corresponding to the second segment, $z_{2,i}$, to a number greater than 0 unless the decision variable corresponding to the first segment, $z_{1,i}$, is at its upper bound. Similarly, the optimizer would never set $z_{3,i}$ to a number greater than 0 unless both $z_{1,i}$ and $z_{2,i}$ are at their upper bounds. So this set of constraints allows us to compute the amount of transaction costs incurred in the trading of stock i as $z_{1,i}+z_{2,i}+z_{3,i}$.

Of course, we also need to link the transaction costs incurred in the trading of stock i to the optimal portfolio allocation. This can be done by adding a few more variables and constraints. We introduce the variable y_i, one for each stock in the portfolio, which would represent the amount traded (but not the direction of the trade) and would be nonnegative. Then, we require that

$$y_i = z_{1,i} + z_{2,i} + z_{3,i}$$

for each stock i, and also that y_i equals the change in the portfolio position of stock i. The latter condition can be imposed by writing the constraint

22. See, for example, Bertsimas, Darnell, and Soucy (1999).

$$y_i = |w_i - w_{0,i}|$$

where $w_{0,i}$ and w_i are the initial and the final amount of stock i in the portfolio, respectively.[23]

Despite their apparent complexity, piecewise-linear transaction cost approximations are solver-friendly and save time (relative to nonlinear models) in the actual portfolio optimization. Although modeling transaction costs this way requires introducing new decision variables and constraints, the increase in the dimension of the portfolio optimization problem does not significantly affect the running time or the performance of the optimization software because the problem formulation is easy from a computational perspective.

14.4.3 Quadratic Transaction Costs

The transaction cost function is often parameterized as a quadratic function of the form

$$\mathrm{TC}_i(t) = c_i \cdot |t| + d_i \cdot |t|^2.$$

The coefficients c_i and d_i are calibrated from data, such as by fitting a quadratic function to an observed pattern of transaction costs realized for trading a particular stock under normal conditions.[24]

Including this function in the objective function of the portfolio optimization problem results in a quadratic program that can be solved with widely available quadratic optimization software.

14.4.4 Fixed Transaction Costs

In some cases, we need to model fixed transaction costs, which are incurred independent of the amount traded. To include such costs in the portfolio optimization problem, we need to introduce binary variables $\delta_1, \ldots, \delta_N$ corresponding to each stock, where δ_i equals 0 if the amount traded of stock i is 0, and 1 otherwise. The idea is similar to the idea that we used to model the requirement that only a given number of stocks can be included in the portfolio.

Suppose that the fixed transaction cost is a_i for stock i. Then the transaction cost function is

$$\mathrm{TC}_i = a_i \cdot \delta_i$$

The objective function formulation, then, is

$$\max_{\mathbf{w},\boldsymbol{\delta}} \quad \mathbf{w}'\boldsymbol{\mu} - \lambda \cdot \mathbf{w}'\boldsymbol{\Sigma}\mathbf{w} - \lambda_{\mathrm{TC}} \cdot \sum_{i=1}^{N} a_i \cdot \delta_i,$$

23. As we explained earlier, this constraint can be written in an equivalent, more optimization solver-friendly form; namely,

$$y_i \geq w_i - w_{0,i}$$
$$y_i \geq -(w_i - w_{0,i}).$$

24. Many software packages, including Microsoft Excel, have tools for fitting quadratic functions to data.

and we need to add the following constraints to make sure that the binary variables are linked to the trades $|w_i - w_{0,i}|$:

$$|w_i - w_{0,i}| \leq M \cdot \delta_i, i = 1,\ldots,N,$$
$$\delta_i \text{ binary}$$

where M is a "large" constant. When the trading size $|w_i - w_{0,i}|$ is nonzero, δ_i will be forced to be 1. When the trading size is 0, then δ_i can be either 0 or 1, but the optimizer will set it to 0, since it will try to make its value the minimum one possible in the objective function.

Of course, combinations of different trading cost models can be used in practice. For example, if the trade involves both fixed and variable quadratic transaction costs, then we could use a transaction cost function of the following kind:

$$\mathrm{TC}_i(t) = a_i \cdot \delta_i + c_i \cdot |t| + d_i \cdot |t|^2.$$

The important takeaway from this section is that when transaction costs are included in the portfolio rebalancing problem, the result is a reduced amount of trading and rebalancing and a different portfolio allocation than the one that would be obtained if transaction costs are not taken into consideration.

14.5 Incorporating Taxes

When stocks in a portfolio appreciate or depreciate in value, *capital gains* (or *losses*) accumulate. When stocks are sold, investors pay taxes on the *realized* net capital gains. The taxes are computed as a percentage of the difference between the current market value of the stocks and their tax basis, where the *tax basis* is the price at which the stocks were bought originally.[25] The percentage is less for long-term capital gains (when stocks have been held for more than a year) than for short-term capital gains (when stocks have been held for less than a year).[26] Since shares of the same stock could have been bought at different points in time (and in different *lots*), selling one lot of the stock as opposed to another could incur a different amount of tax. In addition to capital gains taxes, investors who are not exempt from taxes must pay taxes on the dividends paid on stocks in their portfolios. The tax liability of a particular portfolio therefore depends on the timing of the execution of trades, on the tax basis of the portfolio, on the accumulated short- and long-term capital gains, and on the tax bracket of the investor.

Over two-thirds of marketable portfolio assets in the U.S. are held by individuals, insurance, and holding companies that pay taxes on their returns. (Exceptions are, for example, pension funds, which do not pay taxes year over year.) Studies have indicated that taxes are the greatest expense that investors face—greater than commissions and investment management fees. To gain some intuition about the effect of taxes on the income of an investor over the investor's lifetime, consider a portfolio that has a capital appreciation of 6% per year.

25. The computation of the tax basis is different for stocks and bonds. For bonds, there are special tax rules and the original price is not the tax basis.

26. The exact rates vary depending on the current version of the tax code, but the main idea behind the preferential treatment of long-term gains to short-term gains is to encourage long-term capital investment and fund entrepreneurial activity.

After 30 years, \$1,000 invested in that portfolio will turn into $\$1{,}000 \cdot (1+0.06)^{30} = \$5{,}743.49$. Now suppose that the capital gains are realized each year, and a tax of 35% is paid on the gains (the remainder is reinvested). After 30 years, \$1,000 invested in the portfolio will turn into $\$1{,}000 \cdot (1+(1-0.35) \cdot 0.06)^{30} = \$3{,}151.13$, about half of the amount without taxes even when the tax is about one-third of the capital gains. In fact, to provide the same return as the portfolio with no taxes, the portfolio with annual realized capital gains would need to generate a capital appreciation of 9.23% per year! You can imagine that the same logic would make benchmark tracking and performance measurement very difficult on an after-tax basis.

As investors have become more aware of the dramatic impact of taxes on their returns, there is increasing pressure on portfolio managers to include tax considerations in their portfolio rebalancing decisions and to report after-tax performance. Consequently, the demand for computationally efficient and quantitatively rigorous methods for taking taxes into consideration in portfolio allocation decisions has grown in recent years. The complexity of the problem of incorporating taxes, however, is considerable, both from a theoretical and practical perspective, as follows:

- The presence of tax liabilities changes the interpretation of even fundamental portfolio performance summary measures such as market value and risk. Thus, well-established methods for evaluating portfolio performance on a pretax basis do not work well in the case of tax-aware portfolio optimization. In traditional portfolio management, for example, a loss is associated with risk and is therefore minimized whenever possible. However, in the presence of taxes, losses may be less damaging because they can be used to offset capital gains and reduce the tax burden of portfolio rebalancing strategies. Benchmarking is also not obvious in the presence of taxes: two portfolios that have the same current holdings are not equivalent if the holdings have a different tax basis.[27]
- Tax considerations are too complex to implement in a nonautomated fashion; at the same time, their automatic inclusion in portfolio rebalancing algorithms requires the ability to solve very difficult, large-scale optimization problems.
- The best approach for portfolio management with tax considerations is to use optimization problem formulations that look at return forecasts over several time periods (e.g., until the end of the year) before recommending new portfolio weights. However, the latter *multiperiod view* of the portfolio optimization problem is very difficult to handle computationally—the dimension of the optimization problem; that is, the number of variables and constraints, increases exponentially with the number of time periods under consideration.

We need to emphasize that while many of the techniques described in the previous sections of this chapter are widely known, there are no standard practices for tax-aware portfolio management that appear to be established. Different asset management firms interpret tax-aware portfolio allocation and approach the problem differently. To some firms, minimizing turnover,[28] such as by investing in index funds, or selecting strategies that minimize

27. See Stein (1998).

28. Apelfeld, Fowler, and Gordon (1996) showed that a manager can outperform on an after-tax basis with high turnover as well, if the turnover does not result in net capital gains taxes. (There are other issues with high

the portfolio dividend yield[29] qualify as tax-aware portfolio strategies. Other asset management firms employ complex optimization algorithms that incorporate tax considerations directly into portfolio rebalancing decisions, so they can keep up with the considerable burden of keeping track of thousands of managed accounts and their tax preferences. The fact is, even using simple rules of thumb, such as always selling stocks from the oldest lots after rebalancing the portfolio with classical portfolio optimization routines, can have a positive effect on after-tax portfolio returns. The latter strategy minimizes the likelihood that short-term gains will be incurred, which in turn reduces taxes because short-term capital gains are taxed at a higher rate than long-term capital gains.

Apelfeld, Fowler, and Gordon (1996) suggested a tax-aware portfolio rebalancing framework that incorporates taxes directly into the portfolio optimization process. The main idea of their approach is to treat different lots of the same stock as different securities and then penalize for taxes as if they were different transaction costs associated with the sale of each lot. (This means, for example, that Microsoft stock bought on date 1 is treated as a different security from Microsoft stock bought on date 2.) Many tax-aware quantitative investment strategies employ versions of this approach, but there are a few issues to beware of when using it in practice:

- The first is a general problem for all tax-aware approaches when they are used in the context of active portfolio management. For a portfolio manager who handles thousands of accounts with different tax exposures, it is virtually impossible to pay attention to the tax cost incurred by each individual investor. While the tax-aware method described here minimizes the overall tax burden by reducing the amount of realized short-term sales, it has no provisions for differentiating among investors in different tax brackets because it is difficult to think of each trade as divided among all the investors and adjusted for each individual investor's tax circumstances. This issue is so intractable that in practice, it is not really brought under consideration.
- The dimension of the problem can become unmanageable very quickly. For example, a portfolio of 1,000 securities, each of which has 10 lots, is equivalent to a portfolio of 10,000 securities when each lot is treated as a different security. Every time that a new purchase is realized, a new security is added to the portfolio since a new lot is created. One needs to exercise care and clean up lots that have been sold and therefore have holdings of zero each time the portfolio is rebalanced.
- As explained in section 14.2, practitioners typically use factor models for forecasting returns and estimating risk. We will explain factor models in more detail in chapter 16, but here we will mention that one of the assumptions when measuring portfolio risk through factor models is that the specific risk of a particular security is uncorrelated with the specific risk of other securities. (The only risk that they share is the risk expressed through the factors in the factor model.) This assumption clearly does not hold when different supposed securities are in fact different lots of the same stock.

turnover, however, such as higher transaction costs that may result in a lower overall portfolio return.)

29. Dividends are taxed as regular income; that is, at a higher rate than capital gains, so minimizing the portfolio dividend yield should theoretically result in a lower tax burden for the investor.

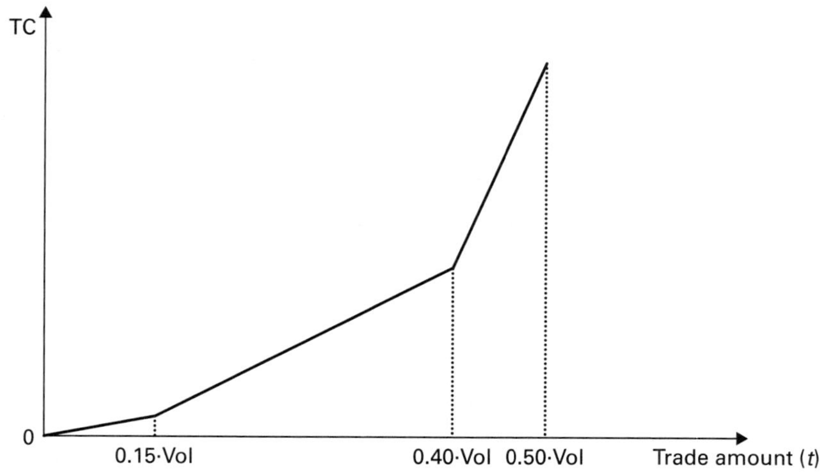

Exhibit 14.2
Example of modeling transaction costs (TC) as a piecewise-linear function of trade size t.

DiBartolomeo (2000) describes a modification to the model used by Northfield Information Service's portfolio management software that eliminates the last two problems. Instead of treating each lot as a separate security, the software imposes piecewise linear transaction costs (see section 14.4 and exhibit 14.2, where the break points on the horizontal axis correspond to the current sizes of different lots of the same security). The portfolio rebalancing algorithm goes through several iterations for the portfolio weights, and at each iteration, only the shares in the tax lot with the highest cost basis can be traded. Other shares of the same stock can be traded in subsequent iterations of the algorithm, with the appropriate tax costs attached.

The approaches described so far take into consideration the short- or long-term nature of capital gains but do not incorporate the ability to offset the capital gains and losses accumulated over the year. This is an inherent limitation of single-period portfolio rebalancing approaches and is a strong argument in favor of adopting more realistic, multiperiod portfolio optimization approaches. The rebalancing of the portfolio at each point in time should be made by considering not only the immediate consequences for the market value of the portfolio, but also the opportunity to correct for tax liabilities by realizing other capital gains or losses by the end of the taxable year. The theoretical literature on multiperiod, tax-aware portfolio optimization contains some characterizations of optimal portfolio strategies under numerous simplifying assumptions.[30] However, even under such simplifying assumptions, the dimension of the problem grows exponentially with the number of stocks in a portfolio, and it is difficult to come up with computationally viable algorithms for portfolios of realistic size.

14.6 Multiaccount Optimization

Portfolio managers who handle multiple accounts face an important practical issue. When individual clients' portfolios are managed, portfolio managers incorporate their clients'

30. See Constantinides (1983), Dammon and Spatt (1996), and Dammon, Spatt, and Zhang (2001, 2004).

preferences and constraints. However, the necessary trades for multiple diverse accounts are pooled and executed simultaneously on any given trading day. Moreover, trades typically may not be crossed; that is, it is not simply permissible to transfer an asset that should be sold on behalf of one client into the account of another client for whom the asset should be bought.[31] The trades should be executed in the market. Thus, each client's trades implicitly affect the results for the other clients: the *market impact* of the combined trades may be such that the benefits sought for individual accounts through trading are lost due to increased overall transaction costs. A robust, multiaccount management process should ensure accurate accounting and fair distribution of transaction costs among the individual accounts.

One possibility to handle the effect of trading in multiple accounts is to use an iterative process in which the market impact of the trades in previous iterations is taken into account for each iteration.[32] More precisely, single clients' accounts are optimized as usual, and once the optimal allocations are obtained, the portfolio manager aggregates the trades and computes the actual marginal transaction costs based on the aggregate level of trading. The portfolio manager then reoptimizes individual accounts using these marginal transaction costs, aggregates the resulting trades again to compute new marginal transaction costs, and so on. The advantage of this approach is that little needs to be changed in the way that individual accounts are typically handled, so the existing single-account optimization and management infrastructure can be reused. The disadvantage is that most generally, this iterative approach does not guarantee a convergence (or its convergence may be slow) to a "fair equilibrium" in which clients' portfolios receive an unbiased treatment with respect to the size and the constraint structure of their accounts.[33] The latter equilibrium is the one that would be attained if all clients traded independently and competitively in the market for liquidity, and it is thus the correct and fair solution to the aggregate trading problem.

An alternative, more comprehensive approach is to optimize trades across all accounts simultaneously. O'Cinneide, Scherer, and Xu (2006) describe such a model and show that it attains the fair equilibrium mentioned previously.[34] Assume that client k's utility function is given by u_k and takes the form of a dollar return penalized for risk. Assume also that a transaction cost model τ gives the cost of trading in dollars and τ is a convex increasing function.[35] Its exact form will depend on the details of how trading is implemented. Let $\mathbf{t}$ be the vector of trades. It will typically take the form $(t_1^+, \ldots, t_N^+, t_1^-, \ldots, t_N^-)$; that is, it

31. The Securiies and Exchange Commission (SEC) in general prohibits cross-trading, but it does provide exemptions if, prior to the execution of the cross-trade, the asset manager can demonstrate to the SEC that a particular cross-trade benefits both parties. Similarly, section 406(b)(3) of the Employee Retirement Income Security Act of 1974 (ERISA) forbids cross-trading, but there is a new cross-trading exemption in section 408(b)(19) adopted in the Pension Protection Act of 2006.

32. See Khodadadi, Tutuncu, and Zangari (2006).

33. The iterative procedure is known to converge to the equilibrium, however, under special conditions; see O'Cinneide, Scherer, and Xu (2006).

34. The issue of considering transaction costs in multiaccount optimization has been discussed by others as well. See, for example, Bertsimas, Darnell, and Soucy (1999).

35. As mentioned in section 14.4, realistic transaction costs are in fact described by nonlinear functions because costs per share traded typically increase with the size of the trade due to market impact.

will specify the aggregate buys t_i^+ and the aggregate sells t_i^- for each asset $i = 1, \ldots, N$, but it may also incorporate information about how the trade could be carried out.[36]

The multiaccount optimization problem can be formulated as

$$\max_{\mathbf{w}_1,\ldots,\mathbf{w}_K,\mathbf{t}} \quad E[u_1(\mathbf{w}_1)] + \cdots + E[u_K(\mathbf{w}_K)] - \tau(\mathbf{t})$$
$$\text{s.t.} \quad \mathbf{w}_k \in C_k, k = 1,\ldots,K$$

where $\mathbf{w}_k$ is the N-dimensional vector of asset holdings (or weights) of client k and C_k is the collection of constraints on the portfolio structure of client k. The objective can be interpreted as maximization of net expected utility; that is, as maximization of the expected dollar return penalized for the risk and net of transaction costs.

The problem can be simplified by making some reasonable assumptions. For example, it can be assumed that the transaction cost function τ is additive across different assets; that is, trades in one asset do not influence trading costs in another. In such a case, the trading cost function can be split into more manageable terms:

$$\tau(t) = \sum_{i=1}^{N} \tau_i(t_i^+, t_i^-)$$

where $\tau_i\,(t_i^+, t_i^-)$ is the cost of trading asset i as a function of the aggregate buys and sells of that asset. Splitting the terms $\tau_i\,(t_i^+, t_i^-)$ further into separate costs of buying and selling, however, is not a reasonable assumption because the simultaneous buying and selling of an asset tends to have an offsetting effect on its price.

To formulate the problem completely, let w_k^0 be the vector of original holdings (or weights) of client k's portfolio, $\mathbf{w}_k$ be the vector of decision variables for the optimal holdings (or weights) of client k's portfolio, and $\eta_{k,i}$ be constants that convert the holdings (or weight) of each asset i in client i's portfolio $w_{k,i}$ to dollars (i.e., $\eta_{k,i}w_{k,i}$ is client k's dollar holdings of asset i).[37] We also introduce new variables w_k^+ to represent an upper bound on the weight of each asset client k will buy:

$$w_{k,i} - w_{k,i}^0 \leq w_{k,i}^+, \quad i = 1,\ldots,N, k = 1,\ldots,K.$$

The aggregate amount of asset i bought for all clients can then be computed as

$$t_i^+ = \sum_{k=1}^{K} \eta_{k,i} \cdot w_{k,i}^+.$$

The aggregate amount of asset i sold for all clients can be easily expressed by noticing that the difference between the amounts bought and sold of each asset is exactly equal to the total amount of trades needed to get from the original position $w_{k,i}^0$ to the final position $w_{k,i}$ of that asset:[38]

36. For example, if asset i is a euro-pound forward, then a trade in that asset can also be implemented as a euro-dollar forward plus a dollar-forward, so there will be two additional assets in the aggregate trade vector **t**. Such concepts will become more intuitive after introducing financial derivatives in chapters 18 and 19.

37. Note that $\eta_{k,i}$ equals 1 if $w_{k,i}$ is the actual dollar holdings.

38. Note that, similar to $\mathbf{w}_k^+$, we could introduce additional sell variables $\mathbf{w}_k^-$, but that is not necessary. By expressing aggregate sales through aggregate buys and total trades, we reduce the dimension of the

$$t_i^+ - t_i^- = \sum_{k=1}^{K} \eta_{k,i} \cdot (w_{k,i} - w_{k,i}^0).$$

Here, t_i^+ and t_i^- are nonnegative variables.

The multiaccount optimization problem then takes the following form:

$$\begin{aligned}
\max_{\mathbf{w}_1,\ldots,\mathbf{w}_K,\mathbf{t}^+,\mathbf{t}^-} \quad & E[u_1(\mathbf{w}_1)] + \cdots + E[u_K(\mathbf{w}_K)] - \sum_{i=1}^{N} \tau_i(t_i^+, t_i^-) \\
\text{s.t.} \quad & \mathbf{w}_k \in C_k, k = 1,\ldots,K \\
& w_{k,i} - w_{k,i}^0 \le w_{k,i}^+, \quad i = 1,\ldots,N, k = 1,\ldots,K \\
& t_i^+ = \sum_{k=1}^{K} \eta_{k,i} w_{k,i}^+, \quad i = 1,\ldots,N \\
& t_i^+ - t_i^- = \sum_{k=1}^{K} \eta_{k,i} \cdot (w_{k,i} - w_{k,i}^0), \quad i = 1,\ldots,N \\
& t_i^+ \ge 0, t_i^- \ge 0, w_{k,i}^+ \ge 0, \quad i = 1,\ldots,N, k = 1,\ldots,K.
\end{aligned}$$

O'Cinneide, Scherer, and Xu (2006) studied the behavior of the model in simulated experiments with a simple model for the transaction cost function; namely, one in which

$$\tau(t) = \theta \cdot t^{\gamma},$$

where t is the trade size and θ and γ are constants satisfying $\theta \ge 0$ and $\gamma \ge 1$.[39] In this expression, θ and γ are specified in advance and calibrated to fit observed trading costs in the market. The transaction costs for each client k, therefore, can be expressed as

$$\tau_k = \theta \sum_{i=1}^{N} |w_{k,i} - w_{k,i}^0|^{\gamma}.$$

O'Cinneide, Scherer, and Xu observed that key portfolio performance measures, such as the information ratio (IR),[40] turnover, and total transaction costs, change under this model relative to the traditional approach. Not surprisingly, the turnover and the net IRs of the portfolios obtained with multiaccount optimization are less than those obtained with single-account optimization, under the assumption that accounts are traded separately, while transaction costs are more. These results are in fact more realistic and are a better representation of the postoptimization performance of multiple client accounts in practice.

---

optimization problem because there are fewer decision variables. This would make a difference for the speed of obtaining a solution, especially in the case of large portfolios and complicated representations of transaction costs.

39. Note that $\gamma = 1$ defines linear transaction costs. For these costs, multiaccount optimization produces the same allocation as single-account optimization because linear transaction costs assume that an increased aggregate amount of trading has no impact on prices.

40. The IR is the ratio of annualized portfolio residual return (alpha) to annualized portfolio residual risk, where risk is defined as the standard deviation. The concept of alpha is discussed in chapter 16.

14.7 Robust Parameter Estimation

The most used approach for estimating security expected returns, covariances, and other parameters that are inputs to portfolio optimization models is to calculate the sample analogs from historical data.[41] These are sample estimates for the parameters that we need. It is important to remember that when we rely on historical data for estimation purposes, we in fact assume that the past provides a good representation of the future.

It is well known, however, that expected returns exhibit significant time variation (referred to as *nonstationarity*). They are affected by changes in markets and economic conditions, such as interest rates, the political environment, consumer confidence, and the business cycles of various industry sectors and geographical regions. Consequently, extrapolated historical returns are often poor forecasts of future returns.

Similarly, the covariance matrix is unstable over time. Moreover, sample estimates of covariances for portfolios with thousands of stocks are notoriously unreliable because we need large datasets to estimate them, and such sets of relevant data are difficult to procure. Estimates of the covariance matrix based on *factor models* are often used to reduce the number of statistical estimates needed from a limited set of data. We return to this issue after discussing factor models in chapter 16.

In practice, portfolio managers often alter historical estimates of different parameters subjectively or objectively, based on their expectations and forecasting models for future trends. They also use statistical methods for finding estimators that are less sensitive to outliers and other sampling errors, such as Bayesian and shrinkage estimators. A complete review of advanced statistical estimation topics is beyond the scope of this book. We provide a brief overview of the most widely used concepts here and refer readers to chapters 6 and 8 in Fabozzi, Kolm, Pachamanova, and Focardi (2007) and Kim, Kim, and Fabozzi (2016) for further details.

Shrinkage is a form of averaging different estimators. The shrinkage estimator typically consists of three components: (1) an estimator with little or no structure (like the sample mean); (2) an estimator with a lot of structure (the shrinkage target); and (3) a coefficient that reflects the shrinkage intensity. Probably the best-known estimator for expected returns in the financial literature was proposed by Jorion (1986). The shrinkage target in Jorion's model is a vector array with the return on the minimum variance portfolio,[42] and the shrinkage intensity is determined from a specific formula.[43] Shrinkage estimators are used for estimates of the covariance matrix of returns as well (see, e.g., Ledoit and Wolf, 2003), although equally weighted *portfolios of covariance matrix estimators* have been shown to be equally effective as shrinkage estimators as well.[44]

Bayesian estimation approaches, named after the English mathematician Thomas Bayes, are based on subjective interpretations of the probability that a particular event will occur. A probability distribution, called the *prior distribution*, is used to represent the investor's

41. See chapter 4 for how to obtain sample estimates, and chapter 13 for how to use historical data to estimate VaR and CVaR.

42. See chapter 12 for a definition of the minimum variance portfolio.

43. See Fabozzi et al. (2007, 217).

44. See Disatnik and Benninga (2007) for an overview of such models.

knowledge about the probability before any data are observed. After more information is gathered (e.g., data are observed), a formula (known as *Bayes's theorem*) is used to compute the new probability distribution, called the *posterior distribution*.

In the portfolio parameter estimation context, a posterior distribution of expected returns is derived by combining the forecast from the empirical data with a prior distribution. One of the best-known examples of the application of the Bayesian framework in this context is the *Black-Litterman model*,[45] which produces an estimate of future expected returns by combining the market equilibrium returns (i.e., returns that are derived from pricing models and observable data) with the investor's subjective views. The investor's views are expressed as absolute or relative deviations from the equilibrium, together with confidence levels of the views (as measured by the standard deviation of the views).

The ability to incorporate exogenous insight, such as a portfolio manager's opinion, into quantitative forecasting models is important; this insight may be the most valuable input to the model. The Bayesian framework provides a mechanism for forecasting systems to use both important traditional information sources, such as proprietary market data, and subjective external information sources, such as analysts' forecasts.

It is important to realize that regardless of how sophisticated the estimation and forecasting methods are, they are always subject to estimation error. What makes matters worse, however, is that different estimation errors can accumulate over the activities of the portfolio management process, resulting in large aggregate errors at the final stage. It is therefore critical that the inputs evaluated at each stage are reliable and robust so the aggregate impact of estimation errors is minimized.

14.8 Portfolio Resampling

Robust parameter estimation is only one part of ensuring that the quantitative portfolio management process as a whole is reliable. It has been observed that portfolio allocation schemes are very sensitive to small changes in the inputs that go into the optimizer. In particular, a well-known study by Black and Litterman (1992) demonstrated that in the case of mean-variance optimization, small changes in the inputs for expected returns had a substantial impact on the portfolio composition. Optimal portfolios constructed under conditions of uncertainty can have extreme or nonintuitive weights for some stocks.

With advances in computational capabilities and new research in the area of optimization under uncertainty, practitioners in recent years have been able to incorporate considerations for uncertainty not only at the estimation, but also at the portfolio optimization stage. Methods for taking into consideration inaccuracies in the inputs to the portfolio optimization problem include simulation (resampling) and robust optimization. We explain portfolio resampling in this section and robust portfolio optimization in the following section.

To make portfolio allocation more robust for changes in the input parameters, *portfolio resampling*[46] involves generating different scenarios for the values that these parameters

45. See chapter 8 in Fabozzi, Kolm, Pachamanova, and Focardi (2007) for a step-by-step description of the Black-Litterman model.

46. See Michaud (1998), Jorion (1992), and Scherer (2002).

can take and finding weights that remain stable for small changes in the input parameters. Simulation is therefore a natural technique to use in this context. We explain how it is applied to portfolio mean-variance optimization as an example to illustrate the resampling technique.

Suppose that we have initial estimates for the expected stock returns, $\hat{\mu}$, and covariance matrix $\hat{\Sigma}$, for the N stocks in the portfolio. (As before, we use a "hat" to denote a statistical estimate.) Then we do the following:

1. We simulate S samples of N returns from a multivariate normal distribution with mean $\hat{\boldsymbol{\mu}}$ and covariance matrix $\hat{\boldsymbol{\Sigma}}$.
2. We use the S samples we generated in the previous step to compute S new estimates of vectors of expected returns $\hat{\boldsymbol{\mu}}_1, \ldots, \hat{\boldsymbol{\mu}}_S$ and covariance matrices $\hat{\boldsymbol{\Sigma}}_1, \ldots, \hat{\boldsymbol{\Sigma}}_S$.
3. We solve S portfolio optimization problems, one for each estimated pair of expected returns and covariances $(\hat{\boldsymbol{\mu}}_S, \hat{\boldsymbol{\Sigma}}_S)$, and save the weights for the N stocks in a vector array $\mathbf{w}^{(s)}$, where $s = 1, \ldots, S$. (The optimization problem itself could be any of the standard mean-variance formulations: maximize expected return subject to constraints on risk, minimize risk subject to constraints on the expected return, or maximize the utility function.)[47]
4. To find the final portfolio weights, we average out the weight for each stock over the S weights found for that stock in each of the S optimization problems. In other words,

$$\mathbf{w} = \frac{1}{S}\sum_{s=1}^{S} \mathbf{w}^{(s)}.$$

For example, stock i in the portfolio has a final weight of

$$w_i = \frac{w_i^{(1)} + \cdots + w_i^{(S)}}{S}.$$

Perhaps even more valuable than the average estimate of the weights obtained from the simulation and optimization iterations is the probability distribution that we obtain for the portfolio weights. If we plot the weights for each stock obtained over the S iterations, $w_i^{(1)}, \ldots, w_i^{(S)}$, we can get a sense of how variable this stock weight is in the portfolio. A large standard deviation computed from the distribution of portfolio weight i will be an indication that the original portfolio weight was not very precise due to estimation error.

An important question, of course, is how large is large enough. Do we have evidence that the portfolios obtained through resampling are statistically different from one another? We can evaluate that by using a test statistic.[48] For example, it can be shown that the test statistic

$$d(\mathbf{w}^*, \mathbf{w}) = (\mathbf{w}^* - \mathbf{w})'\Sigma(\mathbf{w}^* - \mathbf{w})$$

follows a chi-square (χ^2) distribution[49] with degrees of freedom equal to the number of securities in the portfolio. If the value of this statistic is statistically large, then there will

47. See chapter 12.

48. See chapter 4 for a brief introduction to statistical hypothesis testing.

49. See chapter 4.

be evidence that the portfolio weights $\mathbf{w}^*$ and $\mathbf{w}$ are statistically different. This is an important insight for the portfolio manager, and its applications extend beyond just resampling. Let us provide some intuition as to why.

Suppose that we are considering rebalancing our current portfolio. Given our forecasts of expected returns and risk, we could calculate a set of new portfolios through the resampling procedure. Using the previous test statistic, we determine whether the new set of portfolio weights are statistically different from our current weights and, therefore, whether it would be worthwhile to rebalance. If we decide that it is worthwhile to rebalance, we could choose any of the resampled portfolios that are statistically different from our current portfolio. Which one should we choose? A natural choice would be to select the portfolio that would lead to the lowest transaction costs. Therefore, the idea of determining statistically equivalent portfolios has much wider implications than those illustrated in the context of resampling.

Resampling does have the following drawbacks:

- Since the resampled portfolio is calculated through a simulation procedure in which a portfolio optimization problem needs to be solved at each step, the approach is computationally cumbersome, especially for large portfolios. There is a trade-off between the number of resampling steps and the accuracy of estimation of the effect of errors on the portfolio composition.
- Due to the averaging in the calculation of the final portfolio weights, it is highly likely that all stocks will end up with nonzero weights. This has implications for transaction costs that will be incurred if the final portfolio is to be attained. One possibility is to include constraints that limit both the turnover and the number of stocks with nonzero weights. As we saw in section 14.2, however, the formulation of such constraints adds another level of complexity to the optimization problem and will slow the resampling procedure.
- Since the averaging process happens *after* the optimization problems are solved, the final weights may not actually satisfy some of the constraints in the optimization formulation. In general, only convex (e.g., linear) constraints are guaranteed to be satisfied by the averaged final weights. Turnover constraints, for example, may not be satisfied. This is a serious limitation of the resampling approach for practical applications.

Despite these limitations, resampling has advantages and presents a good alternative to using only point estimates of inputs to the optimization problem.

14.9 Robust Portfolio Optimization

Another way in which uncertainty about the inputs can be modeled is by incorporating it directly into the optimization process. Robust optimization, the technique introduced in section 7.3, is an intuitive and efficient way to deal with uncertainty. Robust portfolio optimization does not use traditional forecasts, such as expected returns and stock covariances, but rather uncertainty sets containing these point estimates. An example of such an uncertainty set is a confidence interval (CI) around the forecast for expected returns. We can also formulate advanced uncertainty sets that incorporate more knowledge about the estimation error. For example, as we explained in section 7.3.1, a widely used uncertainty set is the ellipsoidal uncertainty set, which takes into consideration the covariance structure of the estimation errors.

Let us give a specific example of how the robust optimization framework can be applied in the portfolio optimization context. Consider the utility function formulation of the classical mean-variance portfolio allocation problem from chapter 12:

$$\max_{\mathbf{w}} \quad \mathbf{w}'\boldsymbol{\mu} - \lambda \cdot \mathbf{w}'\boldsymbol{\Sigma}\mathbf{w}$$
$$\text{s.t.} \quad \mathbf{w}'\boldsymbol{\iota} = 1$$

Suppose that we have estimates $\hat{\boldsymbol{\mu}}$ and $\hat{\boldsymbol{\Sigma}}$ of the vector of expected returns and the covariance matrix. Instead of the estimate $\hat{\boldsymbol{\mu}}$, however, we will consider a set of vectors $\boldsymbol{\mu}$ that are close to $\hat{\boldsymbol{\mu}}$. We define the "box" uncertainty set as follows:[50]

$$U_{\delta}(\hat{\boldsymbol{\mu}}) = \{\boldsymbol{\mu} \big| \, ||\mu_i - \hat{\mu}_i| \leq \delta_i, \; i = 1, \ldots, N\}$$

Stated in words, the set $U_{\delta}(\hat{\boldsymbol{\mu}})$ contains all vectors $\boldsymbol{\mu} = (\mu_1, \ldots, \mu_N)$ such that each component μ_i is in the interval $[\hat{\mu}_i - \delta_i, \hat{\mu}_i + \delta_i]$. The robust counterpart of the classical mean-variance problem with this uncertainty set can be found using the techniques described in chapter 12. To see the analogy, however, we can introduce an auxiliary variable v and express the expression in the objective function as a constraint:

$$\max_{\mathbf{w}} \quad v$$
$$\text{s.t.} \quad \mathbf{w}'\boldsymbol{\mu} - \lambda \cdot \mathbf{w}'\boldsymbol{\Sigma}\mathbf{w} \geq v$$
$$\mathbf{w}'\boldsymbol{\iota} = 1$$

This is a standard trick in optimization: The value of the decision variable v is to be maximized but is constrained from above by the expression $\mathbf{w}'\boldsymbol{\mu} - \lambda \cdot \mathbf{w}'\boldsymbol{\Sigma}\mathbf{w}$, so the optimizer will try to make $\mathbf{w}'\boldsymbol{\mu} - \lambda \cdot \mathbf{w}'\boldsymbol{\Sigma}\mathbf{w}$ as large as possible (i.e., maximize it) as well. The optimal solution to the problem does not change, but now we can compute the robust counterpart of the constraint

$$\mathbf{w}'\boldsymbol{\mu} - \lambda \cdot \mathbf{w}'\boldsymbol{\Sigma}\mathbf{w} \geq v$$

in the same way as we did in chapter 7 for a constraint of the general type

$$\tilde{\mathbf{a}}'\mathbf{x} \leq b$$

Namely, we first solve an optimization problem of the kind

$$\max_{\mu \in U_{\delta}(\hat{\boldsymbol{\mu}})} \{-\mathbf{w}'\boldsymbol{\mu} + \lambda \cdot \mathbf{w}'\boldsymbol{\Sigma}\mathbf{w}\} \leq -v.$$

(Note here that we multiplied both sides of the constraint by −1, which reversed the sign of the constraint. This is just to demonstrate that we can bring the constraint exactly into the general form $\tilde{\mathbf{a}}'\mathbf{x} \leq b$.) This problem is actually equivalent to

50. See exhibit 7.7(A) in chapter 7.

$$\max_{\boldsymbol{\mu} \in U_\delta(\hat{\boldsymbol{\mu}})} \{-\mathbf{w}'\boldsymbol{\mu}\} \leq -\upsilon - \lambda \cdot \mathbf{w}'\boldsymbol{\Sigma}\mathbf{w},$$

and since there is no $\boldsymbol{\mu}$ in the expression at the right side of the constraint, we can treat the whole expression as if it were a constant (with respect to $\boldsymbol{\mu}$). In other words, we have the constraint $\tilde{\mathbf{a}}'\mathbf{x} \leq b$, where $\tilde{\mathbf{a}} = \boldsymbol{\mu}$, $\mathbf{x} = \mathbf{w}$, and $b = -\upsilon - \lambda \cdot \mathbf{w}'\boldsymbol{\Sigma}\mathbf{w}$.[51]

The robust counterpart of the mean-variance optimization problem under the box uncertainty set for expected returns is therefore

$$\begin{aligned} \max_{\mathbf{w}} \quad & \mathbf{w}'\boldsymbol{\mu} - \boldsymbol{\delta}'|\mathbf{w}| - \lambda \cdot \mathbf{w}'\boldsymbol{\Sigma}\mathbf{w} \\ \text{s.t.} \quad & \mathbf{w}'\boldsymbol{\iota} = 1 \end{aligned}$$

where $|\mathbf{w}|$ denotes the absolute value of the entries of the vector of weights $\mathbf{w}$. To gain some intuition, notice that if the weight of stock i in the portfolio is negative, the worst-case expected return for stock i is $\mu_i + \delta_i$ (we lose the largest amount possible). If the weight of stock i in the portfolio is positive, then the worst-case expected return for stock i is $\mu_i - \delta_i$ (we gain the smallest amount possible). Observe that $\mu_i w_i - \delta_i |w_i|$ equals $(\mu_i - \delta_i)$ w_i if weight w_i is positive and $(\mu_i + \delta_i)$ w_i if weight w_i is negative. Hence, the mathematical expression in the objective agrees with our intuition: it minimizes the worst-case expected portfolio return. In this robust version of the mean-variance formulation, stocks whose mean return estimates are less accurate (i.e., have a larger estimation error δ_i) are therefore penalized in the objective function and will tend to have a lighter weight in the optimal portfolio allocation.

This optimization problem has the same computational complexity as the nonrobust mean-variance formulation—namely, it can be stated as a quadratic optimization problem. The latter can be achieved by using a standard trick that allows us to get rid of the absolute values for the weights. The idea is to introduce an N-dimensional vector of additional variables $\boldsymbol{\psi}$ to replace the absolute values $|\mathbf{w}|$, and to write an equivalent version of the optimization problem:

$$\begin{aligned} \max_{\mathbf{w},\, \boldsymbol{\psi}} \quad & \mathbf{w}'\hat{\boldsymbol{\mu}} - \boldsymbol{\delta}'\boldsymbol{\psi} - \lambda \cdot \mathbf{w}'\boldsymbol{\Sigma}\mathbf{w} \\ \text{s.t.} \quad & \mathbf{w}'\boldsymbol{\iota} = 1 \\ & \psi_i \geq w_i;\ \psi_i \geq -w_i,\ i = 1, \ldots, N \end{aligned}$$

Therefore, incorporating considerations about the uncertainty in the estimates of the expected returns in this example has virtually no computational cost.

51. Observe that this model incorporates the notion of aversion to estimation error in the following sense: When the interval $[\hat{\mu}_i - \delta_i, \hat{\mu}_i + \delta_i]$ for the expected return of the ith asset is large, meaning that the expected return has been estimated with a large estimation error, then the minimization problem over μ is less constrained. Consequently, the minimum is smaller than it would be in situations when the interval for the expected return is smaller. Obviously, when the interval is small enough, the minimization problem will be so tightly constrained that it would deliver a solution that is close to the optimal solution of the classical portfolio optimization problem in which estimation errors are ignored. In other words, it is the size of the intervals (in general, the size of the uncertainty set) that controls the aversion to the uncertainty that comes from estimation errors.

We can view the effect of this particular robustification of the mean-variance portfolio optimization formulation in two ways. On the one hand, we can see that the values of the expected returns for the different stocks have been adjusted downward in the objective function of the optimization problem. In other words, the robust optimization model shrinks the expected return of stocks with a large estimation error, meaning, in this case, that the robust formulation is related to statistical shrinkage methods.[52] On the other hand, we can interpret the additional term in the objective function as a risklike term that represents a penalty for the estimation error. The size of that penalty is determined by the investor's aversion to estimation risk and is reflected in the magnitude of the deltas.

More complicated specifications for uncertainty sets have more involved mathematical representations but can still be selected so they preserve an easy computational structure for the robust optimization problem. For example, a commonly used uncertainty set is the ellipsoidal uncertainty set[53]

$$U_\delta(\hat{\boldsymbol{\mu}}) = \{\boldsymbol{\mu} \mid (\boldsymbol{\mu} - \hat{\boldsymbol{\mu}})' \boldsymbol{\Sigma}_\mu^{-1} (\boldsymbol{\mu} - \hat{\boldsymbol{\mu}}) \le \delta^2\}$$

where $\boldsymbol{\Sigma}_\mu$ is the covariance matrix of estimation errors for the vector of expected returns $\boldsymbol{\mu}$. This uncertainty set represents the requirement that the scaled sum of squares (scaled by the inverse of the covariance matrix of estimation errors) between all elements in the set and the point estimates $\hat{\mu}_1, \hat{\mu}_2, \ldots, \hat{\mu}_N$ can be no larger than δ^2. We note that this uncertainty set cannot be interpreted as individual CIs around each point estimate. Instead, it captures the idea of a joint confidence region. In practical applications, the covariance matrix of estimation errors is often assumed to be diagonal. For this particular case, the set contains all the vectors of the expected returns that are within a certain number of standard deviations from the point estimate of the vector of expected returns, and the resulting robust portfolio optimization problem would protect the investor if the vector of expected returns is within that range.

It can be shown that the robust counterpart of the mean-variance portfolio optimization problem with an ellipsoidal uncertainty set for the expected return estimates is the following optimization problem formulation:

$$\begin{aligned} \max_{\mathbf{w}} \quad & \mathbf{w}'\boldsymbol{\mu} - \lambda \cdot \mathbf{w}'\boldsymbol{\Sigma}\mathbf{w} - \delta\sqrt{\mathbf{w}'\boldsymbol{\Sigma}_\mu \mathbf{w}} \\ \text{s.t.} \quad & \mathbf{w}'\boldsymbol{\iota} = 1 \end{aligned}$$

This is a second-order cone programming (SOCP) problem, and it requires specialized software to solve, but the methods for solving it are very efficient (see chapter 6).

Just as in the robust counterpart with a box uncertainty set, we can interpret the extra term in the objective function $\left(\delta\sqrt{\mathbf{w}'\boldsymbol{\Sigma}_\mu \mathbf{w}}\right)$ as the penalty for estimation risk, where δ incorporates the degree of the investor's aversion to estimation risk. By the way, note that the covariance matrix in the estimation error penalty term, $\boldsymbol{\Sigma}_\mu$, is not necessarily the same as the covariance matrix of returns $\boldsymbol{\Sigma}$. It is not immediately obvious how $\boldsymbol{\Sigma}_\mu$ can be estimated from data. $\boldsymbol{\Sigma}_\mu$ is the covariance matrix of the errors in estimating the expected average returns. Thus, if a portfolio manager forecasts 5% active return over

52. See section 14.7 for a definition of statistical shrinkage.

53. See exhibit 7.7(B) in chapter 7.

the next time period but gets only 1%, he cannot argue that there was a 4% error in his expected return—the actual error would consist of both an estimation error in the expected return and the inherent volatility in actual realized returns. Critics of this approach have argued that the realized returns typically have large stochastic components that dwarf the expected returns; hence, estimating Σ_μ from data is very hard, if not impossible.[54]

Several approximate methods for estimating Σ_μ have been found to work well in practice. For example, simpler estimation approaches, such as using just the diagonal matrix containing the variances of the estimates (as opposed to the complete error covariance matrix), often provide most of the benefit of robust portfolio optimization.[55] In addition, standard approaches for estimating expected returns, such as Bayesian statistics and regression-based methods, can generate estimates for the estimation error covariance matrix while generating the estimates themselves.[56]

Among practitioners, the notion of robust portfolio optimization is often equated with the robust mean-variance model discussed in this section, with the box or the ellipsoidal uncertainty sets for the expected stock returns. While robust optimization applications often involve one form or another of this model, the actual scope of robust optimization can be much broader. We note that the term *robust optimization* refers to incorporating information about uncertainty sets for the parameters in the optimization model and not to the specific definitions of uncertainty sets or the choice of parameters to model as uncertain. For example, we can use the robust optimization methodology to incorporate considerations for uncertainty in the estimate of the covariance matrix and the uncertainty in expected returns, and obtain a different robust portfolio allocation formulation. Robust optimization also can be applied to portfolio allocation models that are different from the mean-variance framework, such as Sharpe ratio optimization and VaR optimization.[57] Finally, robust optimization has the potential to provide a computationally efficient way to handle portfolio optimization over multiple stages—a problem for which so far there have been few satisfactory solutions.[58] There are numerous useful robust formulations, but a complete review is beyond the scope of this book. We refer interested readers to Fabozzi et al. (2007) for further details.

Is implementing robust optimization formulations worthwhile? Some tests with simulated and real market data indicate that robust optimization, when inaccuracy is assumed in the expected return estimates, outperforms classical mean-variance optimization in terms of total excess return a large percentage (70%–80%) of the time.[59] Other tests have not been as conclusive (Lee et al., 2006). The factor that accounts for much of the difference is how the uncertainty in parameters is modeled. Therefore, finding a suitable degree

54. See Lee, Stefek, and Zhelenyak (2006).

55. See Stubbs and Vance (2005).

56. See chapter 12 in Fabozzi et al. (2007) for an in-depth coverage of the topic of estimating input parameters for robust optimization formulation.

57. See, for example, Goldfarb and Iyengar (2003) and Natarajan, Pachamanova, and Sim (2008).

58. See Ben-Tal, Margalit, and Nemirovski (2000) and Bertsimas and Pachamanova (2008).

59. See Ceria and Stubbs (2006).

of robustness and appropriate definitions of uncertainty sets can have a significant impact on portfolio performance.

Independent tests by practitioners and academics using both simulated and market data appear to confirm that robust optimization generally results in more stable portfolio weights; that is, it eliminates the extreme corner solutions resulting from traditional mean-variance optimization. This fact has implications for portfolio rebalancing in the presence of transaction costs and taxes, as transaction costs and taxes can add substantial expenses when the portfolio is rebalanced. Depending on the particular robust formulations employed, robust mean-variance optimization also appears to improve worst-case portfolio performance and results in smoother and more consistent portfolio returns. Finally, by preventing large swings in positions, robust optimization typically makes better use of the turnover budget and risk constraints.

Robust optimization, however, is not a panacea. By using robust portfolio optimization formulations, investors are likely to trade the optimality of their portfolio allocation in cases in which nature behaves as they predicted in exchange for protection against the risk of inaccurate estimation. Therefore, investors using this technique should not expect to do better than classical portfolio optimization when estimation errors have little impact or when typical scenarios occur. However, they should expect insurance in scenarios in which their estimates deviate from the actual realized values by up to the amount that they have prespecified in the modeling process.

Summary

- The portfolio management process consists of four activities: (1) setting the investment objectives, (2) developing and implementing an investment strategy, (3) monitoring the portfolio, and (4) adjusting the portfolio.
- Investment strategies can be active or passive. Active strategies utilize information provided by manager intuition or quantitative models to come up with strategies that select what the portfolio manager thinks are the most attractive investment opportunities. Passive strategies require minimal management.
- The most popular type of passive investment strategy is indexing, whose objective is to replicate the performance of a designated market index.
- Active investment strategies fall into two categories: a quantitative (systematic) equity approach and a fundamental (discretionary) equity approach. The fundamental approach emphasizes the human judgment exhibited by the members of the asset management team. The quantitative approach uses a systematic, model-driven approach to equity portfolio management.
- Differences between the fundamental and quantitative approach are due to (1) company focus (fundamental) versus characteristic focus (quantitative), (2) narrow focus (fundamental) versus broad focus (quantitative), (3) position concentration/size of bets, (4) risk perspective, and (5) past focus (quantitative) versus future focus (fundamental).
- Big data and machine learning (ML) have been used in various activities in the active investment management process.

- The three activities in the investment management where ML has the potential to add value are (1) signal generation, (2) portfolio construction, and (3) trade execution.
- Commonly used constraints in practice include long-only (i.e., no short-selling) constraints, turnover constraints, holding constraints, risk factor constraints, and tracking error constraints. These constraints can be handled in a straightforward way by the same type of optimization algorithms used for solving the classical mean-variance portfolio allocation problem.
- Minimum holding constraints, transaction size constraints, cardinality constraints, and round-lot constraints are also widely used in practice, but their nature is such that they require binary and integer modeling, which necessitates the use of mixed-integer and other specialized optimization solvers.
- Transaction costs can easily be incorporated in standard portfolio allocation models. Typical functions for representing transaction costs include linear, piecewise linear, and quadratic.
- Taxes can have a dramatic effect on portfolio returns; however, it is difficult to incorporate them into the classical portfolio optimization framework. Their importance to the individual investor is a strong argument for taking a multiperiod view of investments, but the computational burden of multiperiod portfolio optimization formulations with taxes is extremely high.
- For investment managers who handle multiple accounts, increased transaction costs because of the market impact of simultaneous trades can be an important practical issue and should be taken into consideration when individual clients' portfolio allocation decisions are made to ensure fairness across accounts.
- As the use of quantitative techniques has become widespread in the investment industry, the consideration of estimation risk and model risk has grown in importance. Methods for robust statistical estimation of parameters include shrinkage and Bayesian techniques.
- Portfolio resampling is a technique that uses simulation to generate multiple scenarios for possible values of the input parameters in the portfolio optimization problem and aims to determine portfolio weights that remain stable with respect to small changes in model parameters.
- Robust portfolio optimization incorporates uncertainty directly into the optimization process. The uncertain parameters in the optimization problem are assumed to vary in prespecified uncertainty sets that are selected subjectively or based on data.

15

Fixed-Income Portfolio Management in Practice

Previous chapters of this book have introduced fundamental concepts in risk measurement and quantitative equity portfolio management. We discussed risk measures such as variance, tracking error relative to an index, value-at-risk (VaR), and conditional value-at-risk (CVaR), as well as portfolio management strategies and formulations. Many of these concepts are used in fixed-income portfolio management as well; however, fixed-income securities have some fundamental differences from equities, so the concepts cannot always be applied in the same way in which they would be applied for stock portfolios. Furthermore, fixed-income securities are strongly influenced by changes in interest rates and credit quality, which adds another dimension to portfolio analysis.

This chapter focuses on the basics of fixed-income portfolio management in practice. We begin by reviewing measures of bond portfolio risk. Many bond portfolio strategies can be understood in terms of risk and return relative to a benchmark, so we provide an overview of bond market indices and a classification of bond index strategies. We then proceed with a discussion of asset-liability portfolio strategies such as cash-flow matching and immunization. We give examples of how optimization and simulation can be applied in bond portfolio allocation and risk management.

15.1 Measuring Bond Portfolio Risk

As just mentioned, many of the risk measures that we discussed in the context of risk management of equity portfolios in chapter 14 hold in the case of bond portfolios: we can evaluate a bond portfolio's standard deviation, tracking error, VaR, and CVaR similarly to the way that we evaluated these risk measures by considering the portfolio returns in the case of equity portfolios. However, some additional measures of bond portfolio risk are not really used in equity portfolio management. To appreciate these measures, we next discuss sources of bond portfolio risk, starting with classical measures of bond portfolio risk and moving on to more recent ways to look at this risk.

15.1.1 Interest Rate Risk

A portfolio's *duration* is the measure used to quantify the portfolio's exposure to changes in the level of interest rates. This risk measure is valid only if we assume a parallel shift in the yield curve. As explained in chapter 2, the duration of an individual bond is the approximate percentage change in market value for a 100-basis-point change in interest rates. The interpretation of the duration of a portfolio is the same. A duration of 4, for example, means that the portfolio's market value will change by approximately 4% for a 100-basis-point change in the interest rate for all maturities.

As explained in chapter 2, three versions of the duration measure are modified duration, Macaulay duration, and effective duration. *Modified duration* assumes that when interest rates change, the cash flows do not change. This is a limitation when measuring the exposure of bonds with embedded options, such as callable bonds, mortgage-backed securities (MBSs), and some asset-backed securities (ABSs).[1] *Macaulay duration* is related to modified duration and suffers from the same failure to consider changes in cash flows when interest rates change. In contrast, *effective duration* takes these changes in cash flows into account and thus is the appropriate measure for bonds with embedded options. Effective duration is also referred to as *option-adjusted duration* or *adjusted duration*.[2]

The calculation of a portfolio's duration begins with the calculation of the duration for each of the individual bonds comprising the portfolio. This calculation requires using a valuation model. Duration is found by shocking (i.e., changing) interest rates up and down, computing the new value of the bond in both cases, and then computing the average percentage price change for the change in interest rates used. Consequently, the duration measure is only as good as the valuation model.

A portfolio's duration is obtained by calculating the weighted average of the various durations of the bonds in the portfolio. The weight of a bond is the proportion of the market value of the portfolio represented by the bond. Mathematically, we have

$$D_p = w_1 \cdot D_1 + w_2 \cdot D_2 + \cdots + w_N \cdot D_N,$$

where N is the number of bonds in the portfolio, w_i is the weight of the ith bond, D_i is the duration of the ith bond, and D_p is the duration of the portfolio. The duration of a bond index is computed in the same way since an index is simply a portfolio with particular weights.

A measure of the portfolio exposure to an individual issue or sector is given by its *contribution to portfolio duration*. This contribution is found by multiplying the percentage of the portfolio's market value represented by the individual issue or sector ties the duration of the individual issue or sector. That is,

$$\text{Contribution to portfolio duration} = (\text{Weight of issue or sector in portfolio}) \cdot (\text{Duration of issue or sector})$$

In chapter 2, we explained that convexity helps to improve the estimate of interest rate risk provided by the duration of an individual bond. Convexity is used for measuring the interest risk of portfolios as well.

1. See chapter 2 for definitions of callable bonds, ABSs, and MBSs. We will discuss MBSs in detail in chapter 21.

2. We come back to the concept of option-adjusted duration in chapter 21.

15.1.2 Yield Curve Risk

Duration provides a measure of a portfolio's or a benchmark index's exposure to changes in interest rates. However, duration does not indicate the portfolio's or benchmark index's exposure to changes in the shape of the yield curve.

One way to get a feel for the risk exposure resulting from yield curve shifts is to analyze the distribution of the present values of the cash flows for the portfolio under different scenarios for the yield curve. Another way is to compute the key rate durations of the portfolio and the benchmark. *Key rate duration*, which was described in chapter 2, is the sensitivity of a portfolio's value to the change in a particular key spot rate. The specific maturities on the spot rate curve for which key rate durations are measured vary from firm to firm.

15.1.3 Spread Risk

For non–U.S. Treasury securities, the yield is equal to the Treasury yield plus a spread to the Treasury yield curve. Non-Treasury securities are referred to as *spread products*. The risk that the price of a bond changes due to changes in spreads is referred to as *spread risk*. A measure of how a spread product's price changes if the spread sought by the market changes is called *spread duration*.

Spread duration measures are typically used to capture the spread risk. There are three spread duration measures: nominal spread, zero-volatility spread, and option-adjusted spread.

The *nominal spread* is the traditional spread measure. That is, it is the difference between the yield on a spread product and the yield on a comparable maturity Treasury issue. Thus, when spread is defined as the nominal spread, spread duration indicates the approximate percentage change in price for a 100-basis-point change in the nominal spread, holding the Treasury yield constant. It is important to note that, for any spread product, spread duration is the same as duration if the nominal spread is used. For example, suppose that the duration of a corporate bond is 5. This means that, for a 100-basis-point change in interest rates, the value of the corporate bond changes by approximately 5%. It does not matter whether the change in rates is due to a change in the level of rates (i.e., a change in the Treasury rate) or a change in the nominal spread.

The *zero-volatility spread*, or *static spread*, is the spread that, when added to the Treasury spot rate curve, makes the present value of the cash flows (when discounted at the spot rates plus the spread) equal to the price of the bond plus accrued interest. It is a measure of the spread over the Treasury spot rate curve. When spread is defined in this way, spread duration is the approximate percentage change in price for a 100-basis-point change in the zero-volatility spread, holding the Treasury spot rate curve constant.

The *option-adjusted spread (OAS)* is another spread measure that can be interpreted as the approximate percentage change in price of a spread product for a 100-basis-point change in the OAS, holding Treasury rates constant. So, for example, if a corporate bond has a spread duration of 3, this means that if the OAS changes by 20 basis points, then the price of this corporate bond will change by approximately 0.6% (=0.03 0.02 100). We will encounter OAS again in chapter 21, when we discuss MBSs.

The spread duration for a portfolio or a bond index is computed as a market-weighted average of the spread duration for each sector.

15.1.4 Credit Risk

The portfolio allocation to each credit rating can gauge a portfolio's credit risk on a standalone basis or relative to a benchmark index.[3] However, a better gauge is the contribution to duration by credit rating. Basically, the portfolio is divided into groups of bonds with the same credit rating, and the contribution to duration for each group is computed.

15.1.5 Estimating Value-at-Risk for Fixed-Income Securities

Even though the measures described in the previous sections in this chapter are classical measures in bond portfolio management, many bond portfolio managers use additional measures, such as VaR and CVaR,[4] to obtain a fuller picture of portfolio risk.

To estimate the VaR or the CVaR of a bond portfolio, we need to simulate the distribution of possible values for the portfolio (or the total return of the portfolio[5]) at the end of the holding period. This requires the simulation of the term structure of interest rates. As we will explain in chapter 21, there is a large body of literature on interest rate models. We will need the material in chapters 17 and 19 to explain how term structure scenarios can be generated. However, we can understand the intuition behind the simulation now as well. Consider a simple example: Suppose that we are trying to estimate the VaR of a $1 position in a bond with 10 years to maturity after a 1-year investment. We do the following:

- We calculate the initial price of the bond (given the yield curve observable today).
- We generate scenarios for the future values of interest rates, and estimate the price of the bond (given those future interest rates) after 1 year. Let us call this price the "terminal price" because it is at the end of the investment horizon.
- In each interest rate scenario, we calculate the losses from the position as the difference between the initial price and the terminal price (plus any coupon payments, appropriately discounted, that happened between today and 1 year from now).
- We now have a series of observations from losses for the bond position. The VaR or the CVaR can be estimated using the techniques described in chapter 13.

Suppose that we would like to incorporate not only interest rate risk, but also credit risk, in our VaR or CVaR estimate. To do that, we would need to take into consideration the following additional factors:

- *The default process:* A default is a binary event, and its associated cash flows are distributed far from normal. The only time that we can make the assumption of normality is if we have a lot of small, independent default events, in which case the Central Limit Theorem (CLT) applies.[6]
- *The recovery rate:* The recovery rate is the amount recovered in the event of default. (The exact specification of recovery rate depends on the credit risk model used. For example, it could be measured as a percentage of the expected cash flows.)

3. See chapter 2 for an introduction to credit ratings.
4. See chapter 13.
5. See chapter 2 for a definition of total return.
6. See chapter 4.

- *The dependence between market and default risk:* Even though the two are often assumed to be independent in many pricing models, the reality is that the price difference between credit-risky and riskless bonds will depend on both types of risks in a complex way. In addition, the default probability may change over time.
- *The complicated nature of credit enhancement agreements that often accompany credit-risky positions:* Such agreements include collateral requirements, credit triggers, credit guarantee arrangements, and the like. In practice, these agreements help the institution manage its credit risk, but they make it more complicated to assess the actual impact of a credit event on a bond portfolio.

These complications actually make simulation a good way to approach the modeling of credit-risky positions. The procedure for evaluating the VaR or CVaR of a credit-risky bond is like the procedure for a nondefaultable bond described earlier in this section. However, to evaluate future cash flows, we simulate the realizations of binary variables that tell us whether the cash flows are received. (Once a bond has defaulted, we make sure that no future cash flows are received.)

Estimating the VaR or the CVaR of a portfolio of credit-risky bonds (as opposed to a position in a single bond) is more complicated because we need to simulate the dependencies between the defaults of the different bonds. Such dependencies have been often modeled through different types of copula functions.[7] Through transformations of the original variables, *copula functions* allow for modeling dependence between the random variables in a tractable way. The Gaussian copula is one such example. Gaussian copula dependency models, however, have received bad press after their failure to account for the high tail losses observed during the financial crisis of 2008. In addition, calibrating (i.e., finding the input parameters for) such models is very difficult in practice because historically, there have been few observations of multiple defaults happening simultaneously.

Let us now consider an example that takes advantage of both simulation and optimization to manage the credit risk of a bond portfolio. Anderson et al. (2001) describe an approach to optimizing bond portfolios so as to minimize the losses stemming from credit risk exposure. They consider a portfolio of 197 bonds from 29 countries, with a market value of $8.8 billion and duration of approximately 5. The goal is to rebalance the portfolio to minimize credit risk over a 1-year horizon; that is, to minimize losses resulting from default and from a decline in market value because of downgrades in credit ratings.

To address the problem, they first generate scenarios for the future values of the losses due to credit migration (i.e., changes in the credit rating of obligors). This is done by simulation of. 20,000 scenarios of joint credit states for bond issuers and the related losses. Based on these scenarios, they can evaluate the total losses on all bonds in the portfolio, equal to the sum of the differences between the value of each bond without credit migration and the value of that bond with credit migration. Then, they solve a CVaR minimization problem using the optimization formulation presented in chapter 13.

7. See, for example, Glasserman (2004) and Pachamanova and Fabozzi (2016).

15.2 Spectrum of Bond Portfolio Strategies

The bond portfolio strategy selected by an investor or client depends on the investment objectives and policy guidelines. In general, bond portfolio strategies can be categorized into the following three groups: (1) bond benchmark-based strategies, (2) absolute return strategies, and (3) liability-driven strategies.

15.2.1 Bond Benchmark-Based Strategies

There is a wide range of bond portfolio management strategies for an investor or client who has selected a bond index as a benchmark. Volpert (2021) classifies traditional bond benchmark-based strategies as follows:

- Pure bond index matching
- Enhanced indexing: matching primary risk factors
- Enhanced indexing: minor risk-factor mismatches
- Active management: larger risk-factor mismatches
- Active management: full-blown active

15.2.1.1 Pure Bond Indexing Strategy In terms of risk and return, a pure bond index matching strategy minimizes the risk of underperforming an index. The factors that explain the popularity of bond indexing are similar to those for equity index strategies. First, the empirical evidence suggests that historically, the overall performance of active bond managers has been worse than for passive managers. Second, the advisory management fees charged for an indexed portfolio are lower compared to active management advisory fees. Advisory fees charged by active managers typically range from 15 to 50 basis points. The range for indexed portfolios, in contrast, is 1 to 20 basis points (with the upper range representing the fees for enhanced indexing discussed later in this chapter).

Critics of indexing point out that while an indexing strategy matches the performance of an index, the performance of that index does not necessarily represent optimal performance. Moreover, matching an index does not mean that the manager will satisfy a client's return requirement objective. For example, if the objective of a life insurance company or a pension fund is to have sufficient funds to satisfy a predetermined liability, indexing only reduces the likelihood that performance will not be materially worse than the index. The return on the index is not necessarily related to the liability.

Similar to equities index strategies, pure bond indexing strategies involve creating a portfolio to replicate the index's performance. Similar to equities index strategies, exact replication is too costly or impossible to perform. First, the prices for each issue used by the organization that publishes the index may not be the execution prices available to the portfolio manager. Second, the prices used by organizations reporting the value of indices are based on bid prices. However, portfolio managers must transact at asking prices when constructing or rebalancing the indexed portfolio. Third, logistical problems are unique to certain bond market sectors. For example, consider the corporate bond market. There are typically about 5,000 issues in the corporate bond sector of a broad-based market index. Because of the illiquidity of many of the issues, not only may the prices used by the organization that publishes the index be unreliable, but many of the issues may not even be available. Finally, recall that the total return[8] depends on the reinvestment rate available on the interim cash flows received prior to the end of the month. If the organization publishing the index regularly overestimates the reinvestment rate, then the indexed portfolio could underperform the index.

Portfolio managers more commonly pursue what is referred to as a *core/satellite strategy.*[9] Basically, this strategy involves building a blended portfolio using an indexed and active approach. The core component is a low-risk portfolio constructed using one of the indexing strategies. The benchmark for the core portfolio is a broad liquid bond market index, and the core component provides broad market exposure that has basically the same primary risk-factor exposure as the benchmark. The satellite component is constructed using an active strategy with a benchmark that is specialized rather than a broad liquid bond market index. It is this component of the portfolio where the manager makes bets on (i.e., takes views of) the primary risk factors.

The core component provides broad market exposure and therefore captures systematic market risk, or what is commonly referred to as a *beta.* In contrast, an active return—commonly referred to as an *alpha*—is sought in the actively managed satellite portfolio.

The advantage cited for the core/satellite strategy is that it provides a cost-efficient means for controlling portfolio risk relative to a benchmark (i.e., tracking error).

15.2.1.2 Enhanced Indexing/Matching Primary Risk Factor Approach An enhanced indexing strategy can be pursued to construct a portfolio to match the primary risk factors without acquiring each issue in the index. Smaller funds often use this strategy because of the difficulties of acquiring all the issues comprising the index. Generally, the fewer the number of issues used to replicate the index, the smaller the tracking error due to transaction costs, but the greater the tracking error risk because of the difficulties of matching the primary risk factors perfectly. In contrast, the more issues purchased to replicate the index, the greater the tracking error due to transaction costs, and the smaller the tracking error risk due to the mismatch of the primary factors between the indexed portfolio and the index.

15.2.1.3 Enhanced Indexing/Minor Risk Factor Mismatches Another enhanced strategy is one where the portfolio is constructed to have minor deviations from the risk factors that affect the performance of the index. For example, there might be a slight overweighting of issues or sectors if the manager believes that there is relative value. However, it is important to point out that the duration of the constructed portfolio is matched to the duration of the index. That is, there are no duration bets (i.e., duration is matched exactly) for the pure index match strategy and the two enhanced index strategies.

15.2.1.4 Active Management/Larger Risk Factor Mismatches Active bond strategies attempt to outperform the market by intentionally constructing a portfolio that will have a greater index mismatch than in the case of enhanced indexing. The decision to pursue an active strategy or to engage a client to request a portfolio manager to pursue an active

8. See chapter 2 for a definition of the total return of a bond.

9. For a further discussion of this strategy, see Almenc, Malaise, and Martellini (2004).

strategy must be based on the belief that there is some type of gain from such costly efforts; for there to be a gain, pricing inefficiencies must exist. The particular strategy chosen depends on why the portfolio manager believes that this is the case.

Volpert (2021) classifies two types of active strategies. In the more conservative of the two active strategies, the portfolio manager makes large mismatches relative to the index in terms of risk factors. This includes minor mismatches of duration. Typically, there will be a limitation as to the degree of duration mismatch. For example, the portfolio manager may be constrained to be within ±1 of the duration of the index. So if the duration of the index is 4, the portfolio manager may have a duration that is between 3 and 5. Alternatively, if the manager believes that he or she can take advantage of an anticipated reshaping of the yield curve, there can be significant differences in the cash-flow distribution between the index and the portfolio constructed by the manager. As another example, if the portfolio manager believes that issues rated A will outperform issues rated AA within the corporate sector, he or she may overweight the issues rated A and underweight issues rated AA.

15.2.1.5 Active Management/Full-Blown Active Management In the full-blown active management case, the portfolio manager is permitted to make a significant duration bet with no constraints. The portfolio manager can have a duration of zero (i.e., be all in cash) or can leverage the portfolio to a high multiple of the duration of the index. The portfolio manager can decide not to invest in one or more of the major sectors of the broad-based bond market indices and can make a significant allocation to sectors not included in the index. For example, there can be a substantial allocation to nonagency MBSs.[10]

Active portfolio strategies and enhanced indexing/minor risk factor mismatch strategies seek to generate additional return after adjusting for risk. As previously mentioned, this additional return is popularly referred to as *alpha*.[11] These strategies are referred to as *value-added strategies* and can be classified as strategic strategies and tactical strategies.

Strategic strategies, sometimes referred to as *top-down value-added strategies*, involve the following:

- Interest rate expectation strategies
- Yield curve strategies
- Interand intrasector allocation strategies

Tactical strategies, sometimes referred to as *relative value strategies*, are short-term trading strategies that include the following:

- Strategies based on rich/cheap analysis
- Yield curve trading strategies
- Return-enhancing strategies employing futures and options

Next, we discuss these strategies in more detail.

10. Such securities are discussed in chapter 21.

11. The concept of alpha is discussed in more detail in chapter 16.

Interest Rate Expectation Strategies A portfolio manager who believes that he or she can accurately forecast the future level of interest rates will alter the portfolio's duration based on the forecast. Because duration is a measure of interest rate sensitivity, this involves increasing a portfolio's duration if interest rates are expected to fall and reducing duration if interest rates are expected to rise. For those portfolio managers whose benchmark is a bond market index, this means increasing the portfolio duration relative to the benchmark index if interest rates are expected to fall and reducing it if interest rates are expected to rise. The degree to which the duration of the managed portfolio is permitted to diverge from that of the benchmark index may be limited by the client. Interest rate expectations strategies are commonly referred to as *duration strategies*.

A portfolio's duration may be altered in the cash market by swapping (or exchanging) bonds in the portfolio for other bonds that will achieve the target portfolio duration. Alternatively, a more efficient means for altering the duration of a bond portfolio is to use interest rate futures contracts.[12] Buying futures increases a portfolio's duration, while selling futures decreases it.

The key to this active strategy is, of course, an ability to forecast the direction of future interest rates. Academic literature does not support the view that interest rates can be forecasted so risk-adjusted excess returns can be consistently realized. It is doubtful whether betting on future interest rates will provide a consistently superior return.

Yield Curve Strategies As explained in chapter 2, the yield curve for U.S. Treasury securities shows the relationship between maturity and yield. The shape of the yield curve changes over time. A *shift in the yield curve* refers to the relative change in the yield for each Treasury maturity. A *parallel shift in the yield curve* refers to a shift in which the change in the yield for all maturities is the same. A *nonparallel shift in the yield curve* means that the yield for every maturity does not change by the same number of basis points.

Top-down yield curve strategies involve positioning a portfolio to capitalize on expected changes in the shape of the Treasury yield curve. There are three yield curve strategies: (1) bullet strategies, (2) barbell strategies, and (3) ladder strategies. In a *bullet strategy*, the portfolio is constructed so that the maturities of the bonds in the portfolio are highly concentrated at one point on the yield curve. In a *barbell strategy*, the maturity of the bonds included in the portfolio is concentrated at two extreme maturities. In practice, when managers refer to a barbell strategy, it is relative to a bullet strategy. For example, a bullet strategy might be to create a portfolio with maturities concentrated around 10 years, while a corresponding barbell strategy might be a portfolio with 5-year and 20-year maturities. In a *ladder strategy,* the portfolio is constructed to have approximately equal amounts of each maturity. So, for example, a portfolio might have equal amounts of bonds with 1 year to maturity, 2 years to maturity, and so on.

Each of these strategies will result in different performances when the yield curve shifts. The actual performance will depend on both the type of shift and the magnitude of the shift. Thus, no general statements can be made about the optimal yield curve strategy.

12. Futures contracts are derivatives. Financial derivatives are explained in chapter 18.

Interand Intrasector Allocation Strategies A manager can allocate funds among the major bond sectors in a way that is different from the allocation in the index. This is referred to as an *intersector allocation strategy*. In an *intrasector allocation strategy*, the portfolio manager's allocation of funds within a sector differs from that of the index.

In making intersector and intrasector allocations, a portfolio manager is anticipating how spreads will change. Spreads reflect differences in credit risk, call risk, and liquidity risk.[13] When the spread for a particular sector or subsector is expected to decline, or "narrow," a portfolio manager may decide to overweight that particular sector or subsector. The sector or subsector will be underweighted if the portfolio manager expects the spread to increase, or "widen."

Credit spreads change because of expected changes in economic prospects. Credit spreads between Treasury and non-Treasury issues widen in a declining or contracting economy and narrow during economic expansion. The economic rationale is that in a declining or contracting economy, corporations experience a decline in revenue and cash flow, making it difficult for corporate issuers to service their contractual debt obligations. To induce investors to hold non-Treasury securities, the yield spread relative to Treasury securities must widen. The converse is that during economic expansion and brisk economic activity, revenue and cash flow pick up, increasing the likelihood that corporate issuers will have the capacity to service their contractual debt obligations. Yield spreads between Treasury and federal agency securities will vary depending on investor expectations about the prospects that an implicit government guarantee will be honored.

A portfolio manager, therefore, can use economic forecasts of the economy in developing forecasts of credit spreads. Also, some managers base forecasts on historical credit spreads. The underlying principle is that a "normal" credit spread relationship exists. If the current credit spread in the market differs materially from that normal credit spread, then the portfolio manager should position the portfolio to benefit from a return to the normal credit spread. The assumption is that the normal credit spread is some type of average or mean value and mean-reversion will occur. If, in fact, there has been a structural shift in the marketplace, this may not occur as the normal spread may change.

A portfolio manager will also look at technical factors to assess relative value. For example, a manager may analyze the prospective supply and demand for new issues on spreads in individual sectors or issuers to determine whether they should overweight or underweight them. This commonly used tactical strategy is referred to as *primary market analysis*.

Individual Security Selection Strategies Once the allocation to a sector or subsector has been made, the portfolio manager must decide on the specific issues to select. This is because a manager will typically not invest in all issues within a sector or subsector. Instead, depending on the dollar size of the portfolio, the manager will select a representative number of issues.

It is at this stage that a portfolio manager makes an intrasector allocation decision about the specific issues. The portfolio manager may believe that there are securities that are

13. *Liquidity risk* is the risk that issues will not be traded as quickly as anticipated. See chapter 2 for definitions of credit risk and call risk.

mispriced within a subsector and therefore will outperform other issues within the same sector over the investment horizon. There are several active strategies that portfolio managers pursue to identify mispriced securities. The most common strategy identifies an issue as undervalued because either (1) its yield is higher than that of comparably rated issues or (2) its yield is expected to decline (and price therefore to rise) because credit analysis indicates that its rating will be upgraded.

Once a portfolio is constructed, a portfolio manager may undertake a swap that involves exchanging one bond for another that is similar in terms of coupon, maturity, and credit quality but offers a higher yield. This is called a *substitution swap,* depending on capital market imperfections. Such situations sometimes exist in the bond market owing to temporary market imbalances and the fragmented nature of the non-Treasury.[14]

15.2.2 Absolute Return Strategies

In an absolute return strategy, the portfolio manager seeks to earn a positive return over a time frame regardless of market conditions. Few restrictions are placed on the exposure to the primary risk factors. Absolute return strategies are typically pursued by hedge fund managers who employ leverage. Other absolute return managers set as their target a return from 150 to 400 basis points per year over the return on cash, and hence such strategies are referred to as *cash-based absolute return strategies*. "Cash" means a money market reference rate. Typically, these strategies involve the use of fixed-income derivatives.

Absolute return bond strategies have also been used as a complement to liability-driven strategies, which we will discuss next.

15.2.3 Liability-Driven Strategies

Liability-driven investing (LDI) is concerned with controlling investment risk where the benchmark for assessing performance is not in terms of an asset benchmark or a peer group, but rather by referring to a client's liabilities. These strategies involve managing both assets and liabilities to achieve a return objective or a series of liabilities that a client faces.

Life insurance companies use LDI strategies known as *immunization* and *cash-flow matching* for several products that they issue: annuities, guaranteed investment contracts, and structured contracts that guarantee a minimum rate. Defined benefit pension plans are increasingly using LDI strategies. We will discuss LDI strategies later in this chapter.

15.3 Bond Benchmarks

Typically, bond portfolio managers are given a mandate that involves performance evaluation relative to a benchmark. Given a client's desired risk exposure in seeking to meet its investment objective, a benchmark represents the portfolio that has the highest expected return, given the desired risk exposure. The construction of a benchmark requires that a set of rules be specified to determine which specific issues from the bond universe should be included and which should be excluded.

14. Swaps are financial derivative contracts, which are discussed in chapter 18.

U.S. bond market indices are classified based on one or more of the following characteristics with respect to the bonds that are included in the index: (1) sectors covered (i.e., government bonds, corporates, and securitized products); (2) credit rating (i.e., investment grade and high yield); and (3) maturity (i.e., short term, intermediate term, and long term).

The broad-based U.S. bond market index most used is the Bloomberg Barclays U.S. Aggregate Bond Index. There are around 11,500 issues in this index, which includes only investment-grade securities. Each broad-bond index is broken into sectors. The sector indices for the Bloomberg Barclays U.S. Aggregate Bond Index (with the number of issues shown in parentheses) are Bloomberg Barclays U.S. Corporate (6,425), Bloomberg Barclays U.S. High Yield (2,061), Bloomberg Barclays U.S. MBS (467), Bloomberg Barclays U.S. Agg Govt/Credit (7,817) Bloomberg Barclays U.S. Treasury (260), Bloomberg Barclays Capital High Yield Caa (327).

15.4 Using Quantitative Methods for Portfolio Allocation

The portfolio allocation strategies described so far in this section are often aided by quantitative approaches and software that enable portfolio managers to sort through alternative strategies quickly. For example, there are two methodologies used to construct a portfolio to replicate an index: the stratified sampling and the optimization approach. Both approaches assume that the performance of an individual bond depends on several systematic factors that affect the performance of all bonds and on a factor unique to the individual issue.[15] This last risk is diversifiable risk. The objective of the two approaches is to construct an indexed portfolio that eliminates this diversifiable risk.

15.4.1 Stratified Sampling Approach

In the *stratified sampling approach* (also called the *cellular approach*) to indexing, the index is divided into cells representing the primary risk factors. The objective is to select, from all the issues in the index, one or more issues in each cell that can be used to represent that entire cell. The total dollar amount purchased of the issues from each cell will be based on the percentage of the index's total market value that the cell represents. For example, consider two factors: credit quality and duration. Imagine a table with rows that correspond to the various credit ratings[16] and columns that correspond to different ranges for durations. In effect, we have "buckets," in which we place all the bonds under consideration depending on their credit quality and duration.

The number of cells that the indexer uses will depend on the dollar amount of the portfolio to be indexed. In indexing a portfolio of less than $50 million, for example, using a large number of cells would require purchasing odd lots of issues. This increases the cost of buying the issues to represent a cell, thus increasing the tracking error risk. However, reducing the number of cells to overcome this problem also increases tracking error risk because the major risk factors of the indexed portfolio may differ materially from those of the index.

15. This is referred to as a *factor model*. Factor models are discussed in detail in chapter 16.

16. See exhibit 2.1 in chapter 2.

15.4.2 Optimization Approach

In the optimization approach, the manager seeks to design an indexed portfolio that will match the cell breakdown just as described, but that will also satisfy other constraints and optimize an objective. An objective might be to maximize convexity or to maximize expected total returns or to minimize tracking error.[17] Constraints other than matching the cell breakdown might include not purchasing more than a specified amount of one issuer or group of issuers within the same strategy.

Although on the surface, the stratified sampling approach is more straightforward to use than the optimization approach, it is extremely difficult to implement the stratified sampling approach when large, diversified portfolios are taken as the benchmark. In this case, many cells are required and the problem becomes complex. Also, because the hand-picking of issues to match each cell is subjective, large tracking errors may result. Optimization modeling reduces the work for the manager, allowing efficient analysis of large quantities of data.

15.5 Liability-Driven Strategies

Thus far, the bond portfolio strategies discussed in this chapter have focused on managing funds relative to a benchmark that is a market index. In a liability-driven strategy, the goal is to manage funds to satisfy contractual liabilities. The two liability-driven strategies are immunization and cash-flow matching. Insurance companies, sponsors of defined benefit pension plans, and other institutions with liabilities often take advantage of such strategies.

15.5.1 Immunization Strategy for a Single-Period Liability

Immunization is a hybrid strategy that has elements of both active and passive strategies. Classical immunization can be defined as the process by which a bond portfolio is created such that it has an assured return for a specific time horizon regardless of interest rate changes. The following are the important characteristics:

- A specified time horizon
- An assured rate of return during the holding period to a fixed horizon date
- Insulation from the effects of potential adverse interest rate changes on the portfolio value at the horizon date

The fundamental mechanism underlying immunization is a portfolio structure that balances the change in the value of the portfolio at the end of the investment horizon with the return from the reinvestment of portfolio cash flows (coupon payments and maturing securities). That is, immunization requires offsetting interest rate risk and reinvestment risk. To accomplish this balancing act requires controlling duration and setting the present value of the cash flows from the bond portfolio to the present value of the liability. By setting the duration of the portfolio equal to the desired portfolio time horizon, the offsetting of positive and negative incremental return sources can under certain circumstances be assured. However, given the fact that duration is the tool being used, the portfolio is

17. See chapter 14 for a mathematical definition of tracking error.

Year	Spot	df	B1	PV1	B2	PV2
1	3.64%	0.965	6	5.79	10	9.65
2	4.17%	0.922	6	5.53	10	9.22
3	4.70%	0.871	6	5.23	10	8.71
4	5.21%	0.816	6	4.90	10	8.16
5	5.45%	0.767	6	4.60	110	84.36
6	6.06%	0.703	6	4.22		
7	6.43%	0.646	6	3.88		
8	6.75%	0.593	6	3.56		
9	7.10%	0.539	6	3.24		
10	7.35%	0.492	6	2.95		
11	7.57%	0.448	6	2.69		
12	7.79%	0.406	106	43.09		
Price of bond today			B1	89.66	B2	120.10

Exhibit 15.1
Current yield curve, discount factors, cash flows from bonds 1 and 2, and present values of cash flows from the two bonds.

immunized only if there is a parallel shift in the yield curve. If there is a change in interest rates that does not correspond to this shape-preserving shift, matching the duration to the investment horizon no longer assures immunization.

Let us see an example of how immunization works. Suppose that we have a liability of \$1,000,000 that must be paid five years from now. We would like to invest enough money today to meet this future obligation. Our investment universe consists of two bonds, B_1 and B_2, with face values of \$100, maturities of 12 years and 5 years, and coupon rates of 6% and 5%, respectively. For simplicity, we will assume that the coupons are paid once per year (as opposed to semiannually). How much should we invest in the two bonds so the overall portfolio (i.e., bonds and liability) is immunized against changes in interest rates?

Exhibit 15.1 contains the current yield curve (the column "Spot"), the discount factors computed from the yield curve (the column "df"), the cash flows from bonds 1 and 2 (the columns "B1" and "B2"), and the present values of the cash flows from the two bonds (the columns "PV1" and "PV2"). (See also the Microsoft Excel workbook **Ch15-Immunization.xlsx**.) The current prices of the bonds are determined by summing up the present values of the cash flows for each bond. They are \$89.66 and \$120.10, respectively.

Now let us compute the durations of the bonds and liabilities. As explained in chapter 2, duration can be interpreted as the change in the value of the bond per unit change in interest rates, and the formula can be stated as

$$D = \frac{B_{-} - B_{+}}{2 \cdot B_0 \cdot \Delta y}.$$

Exhibit 15.2 shows how the duration can be determined for bonds 1 and 2. We consider a shift in interest rates of $\Delta y = 25$ basis points,[18] and compute the new yield curves, present

18. This means that we change the interest rate for each maturity in the table in exhibit 15.2 by the amount Δy.

df–	PV1–	PV2–	df+	PV1+	PV2+
0.967	5.80	9.67	0.963	5.78	9.63
0.926	5.56	9.26	0.917	5.50	9.17
0.878	5.27	8.78	0.865	5.19	8.65
0.824	4.94	8.24	0.808	4.85	8.08
0.776	4.66	85.37	0.758	4.55	83.37
0.713	4.28		0.693	4.16	
0.657	3.94		0.636	3.82	
0.604	3.63		0.582	3.49	
0.551	3.31		0.528	3.17	
0.504	3.02		0.481	2.88	
0.460	2.76		0.437	2.62	
0.418	44.31		0.395	41.91	
	91.46	121.32		87.91	118.90

Exhibit 15.2
Effect of a shift of $\Delta y = 25$ basis points on bond prices.

values, and bond prices if interest rates shift up or down by this amount. The notation used is as follows: df– and df+ are the discount factors under a negative shift and a positive shift of the yield curve, respectively; PV1– and PV1+ are the present values of the cash flows for bond 1 under a negative shift and a positive shift of interest rates, respectively; and similarly, PV2– and PV2+ are the present values of the cash flows for bond 2 under a negative shift and a positive shift of interest rates, respectively. The bond prices are as follows: under a negative shift in interest rates, $B_{1-} = \$91.46$ and $B_{2-} = \$121.32$. Under a positive shift in interest rates, $B_{1+} = \$87.91$ and $B_{2+} = \$118.90$. This allows us to compute the durations for the two bonds. For example, for bond 1, we have

$$D_1 = \frac{91.46 - 87.91}{2 \cdot 89.66 \cdot 0.0025} = 7.91.$$

Similarly, the duration for bond 2 can be computed as 4.02.

To compute the duration of the liability of \$1,000,000, we go through a similar procedure. The 5-year spot rate is 5.45%, so the present value of the liability is

$$\frac{1{,}000{,}000}{(1 + 0.0545)^5} = \$766{,}950.05.$$

Under a negative shift in interest rates of 25 basis points, the value of the liability becomes

$$\frac{1{,}000{,}000}{(1 + 0.0545 - 0.0025)^5} = \$776{,}106.46,$$

and under a positive shift in interest rates, it becomes \$757,922.96. Therefore, the duration of the liability is 4.74.

To immunize against interest rate changes, we look for the number of units of bonds (x_1 and x_2) to invest so the present value of the cash flows from the bonds equals the present value of the liability and the duration of the portfolio of bonds matches the duration of the liability. How do we compute the duration of the portfolio of bonds? Recall from section 15.1.1 that the duration of the portfolio is the weighted average of the durations of the individual bonds, where the weights are the weights of the bonds in the portfolio. In this case, the weights can be expressed as $x_1/(x_1+x_2)$ and $x_2/(x_1+x_2)$. (This is because (x_1+x_2) is the total amount invested.)

We need to solve the following system of equations, in which the unknowns are the number of units x_1 and x_2 to invest in bond 1 and bond 2, respectively:

$$B_1 \cdot x_1 + B_2 \cdot x_2 = PV(\text{Liability})$$

$$D_1 \cdot \frac{x_1}{(x_1+x_2)} + D_2 \cdot \frac{x_1}{(x_1+x_2)} = D(\text{Liability})$$

To make this a linear system of equations, we will multiply both sides of the second equation by (x_1+x_2). Hence, we want to find values of x_1 and x_2 that satisfy

$$B_1 \cdot x_1 + B_2 \cdot x_2 = PV(\text{Liability})$$

$$D_1 \cdot x_1 + D_2 \cdot x_l = D(\text{Liability}) \cdot (x_1 + x_2)$$

This can be done with a simple linear optimization solver or a numerical procedure. (In the case of two bonds, the problem is easy to solve by hand, but with larger portfolios, it would require numerical implementation.) If we have an optimization solver, the decision variables will be the number of units to invest in bond 1 and bond 2, x_1 and x_2, respectively. We can minimize, for example, the expression on the left side of the first equation, subject to constraints that are represented by the two equations.[19] This will make sure that the two equations are satisfied. In our example, the optimal solution is to purchase $1,239.14 of bond 1 and $5,460.68 of bond 2.

Let us now verify that this investment will indeed cover the liability if there are parallel shifts in the yield curve. Exhibit 15.3 summarizes the information on the price of the bonds, the value of the liability, and the total portfolio value under a positive and a negative shift of 1% (i.e., 100 basis points) in interest rates. We can see that the portfolio remains largely (although not perfectly) immunized against changes in interest rates.[20]

Further Issues How often should the portfolio be rebalanced to adjust its duration? On the one hand, more frequent rebalancing increases transaction costs, thereby reducing the likelihood of achieving the target return. On the other hand, less frequent rebalancing results in the portfolio's duration wandering from the target duration, which will also reduce the likelihood of achieving the target return. Thus, a portfolio manager faces a trade-off:

19. See the Solver dialog box in the file **Ch15-Immunization.xlsx**.

20. Try different investment amounts to illustrate that the change in the portfolio value for a different number of units invested in the two bonds is worse. For example, a combination of 1,000 units of bond 1 and 5,639.21 units of bond 2 also results in a present value of $766,950.05, which offsets the present value of the liability. However, if interest rates shift by 100 basis points, the value of the overall portfolio is –$1,952.73 (in the case of a negative shift) and $2,094.94 (in the case of a positive shift), which is a larger discrepancy than in the case of the immunized portfolio found in this section.

	Δy = 0	Δy = 100 bp	Δy = –100 bp
Bond 1			
Units	1,239.14	1,239.14	1,239.14
Price	$89.66	$82.93	$97.15
Bond 2			
Units	5,460.68	5,460.68	5,460.68
Price	$120.10	$115.40	$125.07
Liability value	$766,950.05	$731,596.59	$804,373.54
Portfolio value (Bonds – Liability)	0	$1,324.19	–$1,048.30

Exhibit 15.3
Immunization results.

some transaction costs must be accepted to prevent the portfolio duration from wandering too far from its target, but a certain amount of misalignment in the portfolio duration must be tolerated, or transaction costs will become prohibitively high.

In the actual process leading to the construction of an immunized portfolio, the selection of the investment universe is extremely important. Immunization theory assumes that there will be no defaults and securities will be responsive only to overall changes in interest rates. The lower the credit quality permitted in the portfolio, the greater the likelihood that these assumptions will not be met. Furthermore, securities with embedded options such as call features or mortgage-backed prepayments complicate, and may even prevent, the accurate estimation of cash flows and hence the duration, which prevents immunization from achieving the desired effect. Finally, liquidity is a consideration for immunized portfolios because, as just noted, they must be rebalanced over time.

A natural extension of classical immunization theory is a technique for modifying the assumption of parallel shifts in the yield curve. One approach is a strategy that can handle any arbitrary interest rate change so it is not necessary to specify an alternative duration measure. The approach, developed by Fong and Vasicek (1984), establishes a measure of immunization risk against any arbitrary interest rate change. The immunization risk measure can then be minimized subject to the constraint that the duration of the portfolio is equal to the investment horizon, resulting in a portfolio with minimum exposure to any interest rate movements.

One way of minimizing immunization risk is shown in exhibit 15.4. The spikes in the two panels of the exhibit represent actual portfolio cash flows. The taller spikes depict the actual cash flows generated by matured securities, while the smaller spikes represent coupon payments. Both portfolio A and portfolio B are composed of two bonds with durations equal to the investment horizon. Portfolio A is, in effect, a barbell portfolio—a portfolio comprising of both short and long maturities and interim coupon payments. For portfolio B, the two bonds mature very close to the investment horizon and the coupon payments are nominal over the investment horizon, so portfolio B is a bullet portfolio. It is not difficult to see why the barbell portfolio should be riskier than the bullet portfolio. Assume that both portfolios have durations equal to the horizon length, so both portfolios are immune to parallel rate changes. This immunity is attained from balancing the effect of changes in reinvestment rates on payments received during the investment horizon

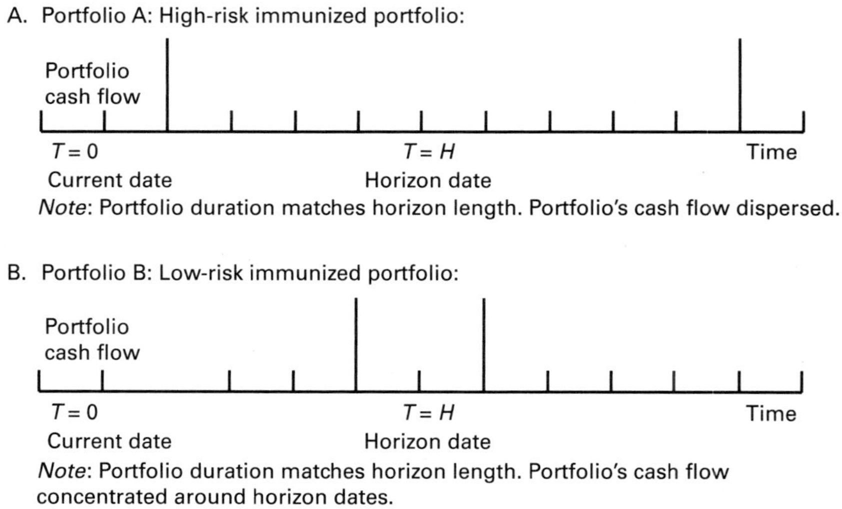

Exhibit 15.4
Immunization risk measure.

against the effect of changes in market value of the portion of the portfolio still outstanding at the end of the investment horizon.

When interest rates change in an arbitrary nonparallel way, however, the effect on the two portfolios is very different. Suppose, for instance, that short rates decline while long rates go up. Both portfolios would realize a decline of the portfolio value at the end of the investment horizon below the target investment value since they experience a capital loss as well as lower reinvestment rates. The decline, however, would be substantially higher for the barbell portfolio for two reasons. First, the lower reinvestment rates are experienced on the barbell portfolio for longer time intervals than on the bullet portfolio, so the opportunity loss is much greater. Second, the portion of the barbell portfolio still outstanding at the end of the investment horizon is much longer than that of the bullet portfolio, which means that the same rate increase would result in a much greater capital loss. Thus, the bullet portfolio has less exposure to whatever the change in the interest rate structure may be than the barbell portfolio.

It should be clear from the foregoing discussion that immunization risk is the risk of reinvestment. The portfolio that has the least reinvestment risk will have the least immunization risk. When there is a high dispersion of cash flows around the horizon date, as in the barbell portfolio, the portfolio is exposed to higher reinvestment risk. However, when the cash flows are concentrated around the horizon date, as in the bullet portfolio, the portfolio is subject to minimum reinvestment risk.

15.5.2 Cash-Flow Matching Strategy

The immunization strategy described in the previous section is used to immunize a portfolio created to satisfy a single liability in the future against adverse interest rate movements. However, it is more common to have multiple future liabilities. One example is the liability structure of pension funds. Another example is a life insurance annuity contract. It is possible to extend the principles of immunization to multiple future liabilities.

However, it is more common in practice to use a *cash-flow matching strategy*. This strategy is used to construct a portfolio that can fund a schedule of liabilities from portfolio return and asset value, with the portfolio's value diminishing to zero after payment of the last liability.

A cash-flow matching strategy can be described intuitively as follows. A bond is selected with a maturity that matches the last liability. An amount of principal equal to the amount of the last liability is then invested in this bond. The remaining elements of the liability stream are then reduced by the coupon payments on this bond, and another bond is chosen for the next-to-last liability, adjusted for any coupon payments of the first bond selected. Going backward in time, this sequence is continued until all liabilities have been matched by payments on the securities selected for the portfolio. However, optimization techniques are more effective for constructing a least-cost cash-flow matching portfolio from an acceptable universe of bonds. We saw an example of a using optimization to design a cash-flow matching strategy in chapter 6.

15.6 Machine Learning Applications in Bond Portfolio Management

In chapter 10, we covered machine learning (ML). In this section, we describe how ML can be used in bond portfolio management.

15.6.1 Application to Corporate Bond Credit Risk Management

A critical aspect of bond portfolio management is credit risk management, which involves credit evaluation and credit risk assessment, Traditional credit evaluation of bonds did not involve sophisticated quantitative models but merely relied on the credit analyst's assessment of the bond issuer's ability to pay based on underwriting guidelines established by the asset management firm's internal credit policies.

Corporate bond credit risk management involves two types of credit risk: default risk and credit spread risk. *Downgrade risk* is the risk that a corporation's bond issues will be assigned a lower credit rating in the future. *Credit spread risk* is the risk that the spread between the yields on a non-Treasury security and a Treasury security of comparable maturity will widen. In the analysis of these types of risk, forecasts of factors that affect these two risks are required, and this is where ML algorithms have been extensively applied.

15.6.1.1 Predicting Credit Ratings For a corporate bond, *default risk* is the risk that the issuer will fail to satisfy the terms of the obligation with respect to the timely payment of interest and repayment of the amount borrowed. To gauge default risk, individual investors use as their starting point the credit ratings of commercial rating companies such as Moody's Investors Service, Standard & Poor's (S&P), and Fitch.

A major problem with credit ratings is that rating agencies are slow to change ratings. The question is whether credit ratings can be predicted and used by portfolio managers in anticipation of a rating change to minimize downgrade risk (i.e., the risk that an issuer will be downgraded by a rating agency). Although credit rating agencies have long argued that their rating process is subjective, numerous studies have used ML models to predict credit ratings for a bond issue. In fact, a study by one of the credit rating agencies, Moody's, found that

ML techniques to model credit risk for medium-sized borrowers make a considerable contribution that improves the accuracy ratio for certain types of corporate borrowers.[21]

Ahn and Kim (2011) describe three stages in the development of credit rating prediction models. In the first stage, multiple discriminant analysis (MDA) and logistic regression analysis (LogR) described in chapter 10 were used. The pioneer of MDA was Altman (1968). The original Altman model for predicting corporate bankruptcy was refined by Altman, Haldeman, and Narayanan (1977), with the refined MDA model using seven predictors to produce a bankruptcy score. Given the value of the seven predictors for a given bond issuer, a Z-score is computed. It is the Z-score that is used to classify firms with respect to whether there is potentially a serious credit problem that would lead to bankruptcy.

In the second stage, researchers employed neural networks (NN). Ahn and Kim (2011) apply several ensembles of NNs and support vector machines (SVMs) to predict credit ratings using only company fundamentals. Unfortunately, in applying NN for credit rating prediction, two problems arose. The first was that selecting the relevant input variables, hidden layer size, and learning rate was difficult. The second problem is that NNs required a large amount of data for the training model. The model used to overcome this problem is SVM, the third stage of the development of credit rating prediction models.

A study by Wallis et al. (2019) compared the most popular ML algorithms to predict the long-term credit rating assigned by Moody's. Applying these ML algorithms to 308 of the S&P 500 companies from January 2016 to November 2017, they found that the three top-performing models were random forest, NN, and SVM. Random forest outperformed the others, with a 64.6% accuracy rate. Four ML models—SVM, random forest, decision trees, and NN (more specifically, multiple-layer perceptron)—were used to predict corporate credit ratings by Golbayani, Florescu, and Chatterjee (2020). Evaluating performance using a onefold cross-validation technique, they reported the superiority of decision tree–based models.

Using stepwise regression to extract relevant financial variables from a bond dataset as a benchmark for categorizing a bond's credit rating, Kwon and Lim (1998) compared this method of classification to that obtained from NN and SVM to predict credit ratings. Because credit ratings involve more than one classification, the authors could not use traditional NN and SVM. Rather, they applied multiclass NN and SVM, which allow more than one classification. They reported that the best results came from a multiclass NNs.

The problem with applying the more popular ML models such as NN and SVM for predicting credit ratings is that these models have been used for binary classification. Yet there are more than twenty-three credit ratings that can be assigned by a credit rating agency. The new generation of ML models has been extended to allow multiclassifications. In multiclassification models, there are several approaches, including the "one versus all approach" and the "one versus one approach." The former approach, also referred to as the "one versus rest approach," splits the multiclass dataset into multiple binary classifications. Each binary classifier is trained and treated as a binary classification problem. For example, suppose that there are only three rating classifications: A, B, and C. There are then three binary classifications problems:

21. See Bachar and Zhao (2017).

- Binary classification problem 1: A rating versus {B and C rating}
- Binary classification problem 2: B rating versus {A and C rating}
- Binary classification problem 3: C rating versus {A and B rating}

Predictions are then made by using the binary classification that provides the most confidence. The drawback of this approach is that it is difficult to apply to large datasets. With the one versus one approach, the dataset is split into one dataset for each class, and then all the combinations are analyzed. In our example of three classifications, there would be three binary classification problems (A versus B, A versus C, and B versus C). If there were four rating categories, then there would be six binary classification binary problems.

The first such study to use a multiclassification NN and SVM models was by Huang et al. (2004) for predicting bond ratings in the U.S. and Taiwan markets. The accuracy of the forecasts for both ML models was 80%. There was not much improvement by using SVM compared to NN. However, three later studies—Cao, Guan, and Jingqing (2006), Chen and Shih (2006), and Lee (2007)—did report the superiority of multiclassification SVM compared to multiclassification NN and traditional methods for bond rating prediction.

15.6.1.2 Predicting Corporate Defaults and Recoveries Bond portfolio managers who invest in corporate bonds use bankruptcy forecasting models, particularly when the portfolio includes noninvestment-grade (i.e., high-yield) corporate bonds. Models for predicting corporate bankruptcy are of two types. Some models produce a probability of the corporation going bankrupt within a specified period of time. The second type provides a binary classification—"bankrupt" or "not bankrupt"—based on the model developer's predefined threshold.

Beaver (1966) identified thirty financial ratios that affect bankruptcy, which he used in a univariate discriminant model to predict bankruptcy. Altman (1968) used five financial ratios obtained from the company's financial statements to predict corporate bankruptcy. All these early models ignored any information about a corporation beyond that obtained from financial statements. The standard credit scoring models for predicting corporate bond bankruptcy that use ML are those based on logistic regression and discriminant analysis.

Since the late 1990s, models using other ML algorithms have been proposed. Zhang, Hu, Patuwo, and Indro (1999), for example, provided a general framework for explaining how artificial neural networks can play a role in bankruptcy prediction. They find that NNs are significantly better than logistic regression models in predicting bankruptcy.

Random forest was used by Hanna (2016) to predict defaults of noninvestment-grade corporate bonds (i.e., high-yield corporate bonds). The author finds that random forest had better predictive ability than traditional metrics that have used to predict defaults. Mai, Tian, Lee, and Ma (2019) propose a deep learning model that uses textual disclosures as a feature as well as financial ratios. Using layers of NNs from a deep learning model, the authors extract features from textual data that can be used to predict bankruptcy. Using a database of almost 12,000 U.S. publicly traded corporations, they report that the prediction performance of their model is superior to other models that do not use textual disclosures, but only financial ratios. Their results are the first to provide large-sample evidence of how financial ratios supplemented by textual disclosures can improve the performance of bankruptcy prediction models.

Predicting the likelihood of bankruptcy is one aspect of corporate credit risk evaluation. The other is predicting the recovery rate should there be a bankruptcy. Nazemi, Heidenreich, and Fabozzi (2018) studied the performance gain by using SVM techniques, linear regression, and regression trees for predicting the recovery rates of defaulted corporate bonds with different explanatory variables. They reported that the support vector regression (SVR) approaches outperform linear regression. Nazemi, Baumann, and Fabozzi (2022) applied ML algorithms for intertemporal analysis of U.S. corporate bonds' recovery rates. They showed that ML algorithms significantly outperform traditional approaches to predicting corporate bond recovery rates.

15.6.1.3 Credit Spread Forecasting Active bond portfolio managers will position a portfolio to take advantage of expected changes in credit spreads. For example, keeping all other factors constant, a decrease (increase) in the credit spread of a corporate bond will increase (decrease) the value of that bond. So forecasting changes in the credit spreads is essential in constructing a portfolio.

Studies have sought to forecast corporate bond credit spreads using ML algorithms. The question is whether models can be developed to forecast both the direction and magnitude of the change in credit spreads. Kim, Kim, and Jung (2021) assessed the use of four ML algorithms – ridge regression, NN, random forecast, and SVR– to forecast corporate bond spreads and compare their performance to traditional forecasting methods. They reported that for both short- and long-term horizons, the forecasts using NN forecasts are superior to the other methods that they investigated in their study. Xiong et al. (2019) used ML to predict the direction of the next-day movement in the credit spread. Several ML models were investigated, including random forest, regression trees, and long short-term memory (LSTM). They test these ML models for the credit spread between U.S. investment-grade corporate bonds for the period between December 1996 and January 2019. Although regression trees performed well in predicting the size of the change in the credit spread, it did not accurately predict the direction of the change. The ML model that performed the best in predicting the next-day credit change using a 3-day lookback was the LSTM model.

15.6.2 Applications to Mortgage-Backed Securities

As we will explain in more detail in chapter 21, MBSs share features with bond portfolios. There are two types of MBSs: residential mortgage-backed securities (RMBSs) and commercial mortgage-backed securities (CMBSs). Agency RMBSs are backed by a pool of residential mortgage loans (i.e., loans to purchase one- to four-family homes), while CMBSs are backed by a pool of loans for income-producing properties. Next, we describe how ML has been applied to predicting prepayments for RMBSs and how it is used for predicting defaults for CMBSs.

15.6.2.1 Mortgage Prepayment Modeling for RMBS As will be explained in chapter 21, valuing agency RMBS requires predicting mortgage prepayments. The complexities associated with RMBS valuation models are due to the need to analyze a large dataset (i.e., availability of both pool- and loan-level data), a large set of risk factors, and difficulties in model specification and estimation. ML models are beginning to be applied to replace traditional prepayment models, resulting in what can be described as "second-generation" mortgage prepayment models.

Zhang et al. (2019) demonstrate how NN models can be used for the modeling of the 30-year RMBS pool-level prepayment modeling. NN models were shown to accurately replicate the overall prepayment rates with training by using only 10% of the pool sample data between 2016 and 2018.

A gradient boosting classifier, trained at the loan level and generalized to the pool level, was used by Schultz and Fabozzi (2022).[22] They applied the model to the Freddie Mac loan-level dataset, which represents the more comprehensive release of loan-level data of the two government sponsored enterprises (Freddie Mac and Fannie Mae). Well-known features that affect mortgage prepayments are used:

- *External time-dependent variables*: Housing turnover rate; seasonal factors; updated borrower loan-to-value ratio
- *Internal time-dependent variables*: Loan age; borrower incentive
- *Continuous variables*: Debt-to-income ratio; credit score
- *Categorial variables*: Variables related to borrower or loan characteristics, such as loan purpose, property type, property location, and servicer

The classifier is trained on 101,202,381 transaction records covering the period from January 2006 to December 2020. Each feature is scored based on its contribution to the predictive accuracy of the model. The dominate features of the model are borrower incentive, loan age, lagged mortgage curve, and home appreciation. A backtest of the test data for origination years 2011 to 2020 indicated that the model performed well overall, despite some notable exceptions such as 2011 and 2012.

15.6.2.2 Forecasting Defaults for CMBS Commercial loans are loans for the purchase of income-producing properties. The loan can be retained by the originator, sold to other investor groups, or packaged to create CMBSs. In a CMBS transaction, several bond classes are created. Active bond portfolio managers who invest in CMBS attempt to identify relative value in the deal's various bond classes. Relative value analysis involves investigating the underlying collateral and loan details for each individual commercial property within a deal. The collateral must be analyzed for its potential to default on future payments to assess the potential performance of the properties in the loan pool.

By investigating default potential among the different properties within a loan pool, a portfolio manager can identify CMBS bond classes that contain properties that have lower projected default risk than other bond classes of CMBS deals. If portfolio managers find that the default risks involved have been incorrectly embedded into the CMBS's price for a bond class, there is an opportunity to enhance portfolio returns. To predict defaults and the future performance of property loans, a model has to be developed that incorporates

22. More specifically, they propose a gradient boosting classifier, which is a tree-based model using an ensemble of weak learners to create a strong committee for prediction.

the characteristics of the individual properties. A good number of studies have proposed models to predict future default probabilities of residential and commercial properties.

Episcopos, Pericli, and Hu (1998) compared logistic regression and NNs to predict commercial mortgage defaults using seven independent variables from property types and regions. They concluded that NN predicts loan defaults better than the logistic regression benchmark.

Several ML algorithms were analyzed by Cowden, Fabozzi, and Nazemi (2019) to predict commercial real estate loan defaults for loans in CMBS. They assessed the performance of the following ML classification techniques: SVM, random forest, boosting, and classification tree, comparing the performance to the typical statistical technique. The principal finding of their study is that the SVM technique for predicting defaults on commercial property loans significantly outperforms other methods. This ML model enables an optimization program to attribute significance to many individual property metrics that affect defaults, the two most popular metrics being the loan-to-value ratio and the debt-service coverage ratio, to find the best classifier between defaulting and nondefaulting commercial loans. SVM allows for the testing of several property metrics instead of focusing attention on only one or two individual components of a property's financial attributes. The boosting technique identified the ratio of the capitalization rate spread to the average capitalization rate spread of property type as the most important driver of defaults in commercial real estate loans.

15.6.3 Identifying Risk Factors

In constructing and controlling risks associated with a bond portfolio, it is critical to be able to identify and quantify risk. The two major types of risk are associated with changes in the term structure of interest rates. The first is more popularly referred to as *yield curve risk*. The yield curve shows the relationship between a bond's yield and its maturity. The second type of risk is nonterm structure risk; that is, risks that affect the performance of a bond portfolio not associated with a change in the yield curve. The ML tool used for identifying of bond portfolio risk is principal component analysis (PCA).

15.6.3.1 Identifying and Measuring Yield Curve Risk Several studies applying PCA have investigated the factors that have affected how changes in the shape of the yield curve affect portfolio returns. The focus of these studies has been on the historical returns on Treasury portfolios. Examining Treasury portfolios allows the identification of only interest rate changes, not changes in credit spreads.

The pioneering study was by Litterman and Scheinkman (1991), who found that three factors explain historical bond returns for U.S. zero-coupon Treasuries. The first principal component (PC) is changes in the level of rates, the second PC is changes in the slope of the yield curve, and the third PC is changes in the curvature of the yield curve. On average, almost 90% of the return was found to be explained by PC1 (changes in the level of interest rates), 8% by PC2 (changes in the slope of the yield curve), and 2% by PC3 (changes in the curvature of the yield curve). Two subsequent studies supported these finding using PCA, Applying PCA to U.S. Treasury yields from 1984 to 2020, Phoa (2021) reported that the first PC explains 92%, the second PC about 5%, the third PC about 1%, and the fourth PC about 0.5%.

The PCA application described in these two studies focused on the U.S. Treasury market. In contrast, Phoa (2021) applied PCA to government securities issued in Canada, the UK, Germany, and Japan, covering maturities ranging from 3 months to 10 years. He found that, compared to the U.S. Treasury market, the impact of changes in the level of interest rates was smaller for the first principal component (PC) in these markets. Once yield curve risk is measured in terms of PCs, the factor loadings can be used to do the following:

- Construct hedges that neutralize exposure to changes in the direction of interest rates;
- Construct hedges that neutralize exposure to changes in nonparallel shifts in the yield curve;
- Structure yield curve trades.

Axel and Vankudre (2002) illustrated how this is done. They also presented evidence that using PCA to measure and control interest-rate risk is superior to the traditional approaches using duration and key rate duration.

15.6.3.2 Measuring and Identifying Non–Yield Curve Risk Factors Gauthier and Goodman (2003) empirically identified the risk factors that generate excess returns for a popular bond index at the time for the period from January 1992 to March 2003. The results of their PCA for the first six PCs were as follows: the first three PCs explained 98.1% of the variation in excess returns. However, these three components are different from those found in the studies just described, which focused only on explaining the factors that explain yield curve movements.

The first PC explains 92.7% of the variation. They find that the factor loading on each of the sectors of the bond index looks very much like the average duration for each sector. That is, it is related to a parallel shift in the yield curve. The second PC explained 3.1% of nominal excess returns. Gauthier and Goodman identify this factor as credit specific, while the third PC was identified as an optionality factor.

15.6.4 Pricing of Illiquid Bonds

Unlike equities, which are traded either on an organized exchange or in the over-the-counter (OTC) market, bonds are traded primarily in the OTC market. Moreover, corporate bonds, municipal bonds, and MBSs are traded infrequently. Moreover, private debt or private credit, which refers to loans that are typically negotiated among private parties where the ultimate credit risk is held by an investor other than a bank or financial intermediary, is increasingly included in bond portfolios. According to the foremost provider of data for the alternative asset community, Preqin, private debt is the second-fastest alternative asset class, behind private equity.

Consequently, information for pricing these bonds that is needed for (1) marking-to-market portfolio holdings (i.e., recording the fair market value of each bond held in the portfolio); (2) making decisions about buying and selling bonds in terms of their relative value; and (3) applying optimization models for portfolio constructions that requires accurate prices. Not only is accuracy critical for these applications, but computational time is also important in dealing with large datasets since timely information is needed. Note that pricing a bond is equivalent to determining its yield. That is, given the characteristics of a bond and its price, its yield to maturity (YTM; or simply *yield*) can be determined.

Prior to the application of ML for determining the price of illiquid corporate bonds, third-party vendors used standard statistical tools based on characteristics such as sector of the bond market, number of years to maturity, coupon rate, embedded options (i.e., callable and/or putable) benchmark yield curve, credit rating, and issuer fundamentals such as leverage and coverage ratios. Pricing using these third-party prices produced what is referred to as a *matrix price.* More recently, several ML algorithms are either used or being proposed to price illiquid securities.

Ganguli and Dunnmon (2017) demonstrate how various supervised learning algorithms followed by ensemble methods can be used to predict up-to-date bond prices. Their dataset of 762,678 bonds includes sixty-one bond attributes (i.e., features) and trade data history. They evaluate all the ML models that they investigate for both accuracy and speed. Three methods were used for feature selection: correlation analysis, PCA, and a scoring function from ensemble methods. Correlation analysis was not found to be particularly useful in identifying features. Using the full dataset, PCA was used with the objective of determining if there is a reduced feature set that retains the majority of the explanatory power of the full feature set. The random forest model was used to obtain a scoring function for ensemble methods. The supervised learning algorithms that they use are generalized linear models and regression trees. They also assess methods such as PCA, regression, and SVR. To mitigate the risk of overfitting and potentially benefit from their large dataset, Ganguli and Dunnmon employ three ensemble methods: bagging, boosting, and random forests. Because NNs can deal with this problem, as they are known to fit even highly nonlinear data, the authors also experimented with applying this ML algorithm to predict bond prices. With respect to relative performance of the tested models in predicting bond prices, they reached the following conclusions:

- Not only did general linear models perform well, but computational costs were also low (order of seconds).
- The results improved when feature selection was employed time series models.
- Not only was more computational investment required with ensemble methods, but they failed to improve results significantly.
- Very accurate results were obtained with NNs with overfitting.

The U.S. municipal bond market is far larger than the corporate and Treasury bond markets in terms of the number of bonds. However, there is little trading of issues in this sector of the bond market. Consequently, in the absence of many trades, pricing is challenging in this illiquid market.

Several studies have looked at the pricing of municipal bonds based on their features. Raman and Leidner (2018) estimated the yield on municipal bonds based on actual municipal bond transactions. That is, given the features of those municipal bonds traded, one can apply a yield prediction model to determine how well the yield produced by a model matches that of the actual yield of a traded bond. Assessing more than 100,000 municipal bond transactions, the authors find that by employing a hierarchical clustering approach based on a smaller subset of bond features, this ML approach does an effective job in estimating the yield. The model can then be applied to municipal bonds that are not actively traded.

Kolm and Purushothaman (2022) also propose a systematic approach to price municipal bonds using several models, including ridge regression (an ML model tuning approach used in analyzing data when there are highly correlated predictors) and Kalman filter (a learning algorithm that updates estimation sequentially as new data become available). They report that these two ML models perform well in pricing compared to non-ML models used for the pricing of illiquid bonds. Moreover, they show how to incorporate their pricing model to relative value trading strategies to generate excess returns (or alpha). Relative value trades seek to capture excess returns by identifying how bonds trade relative to each other and to position a portfolio to benefit from mispricing when the relationship is out of line with its historical relationship.

Summary

- Most generally, bond portfolio management strategies can be classified into five categories: pure bond index matching, enhanced indexing/matching primary risk factor approach, enhanced indexing/minor risk factor mismatches, active management/larger risk factor mismatches, and active management/full-blown active management.
- The difference between indexing and active management is the extent to which the portfolio can deviate from the primary risk factors associated with the index. The primary risk factors associated with an index are (1) the duration of the index, (2) the present value distribution of the cash flows, (3) the duration contribution of the sector, (4) the duration contribution of credit quality, (5) sector/coupon/maturity cell weights, and (6) issuer exposure control.
- Value-added strategies seek to enhance return relative to an index and can be strategic or tactical. Strategic strategies include interest rate expectations strategies, yield curve strategies, and intersector and intrasector allocation strategies. Tactical strategies are short-term trading strategies that include strategies based on rich/cheap analysis, yield curve trading strategies, and return-enhancing strategies employing derivatives (futures and options).
- Interest rate expectation strategies involve adjusting the duration of the portfolio relative to the index based on expected movements in interest rates. Top-down yield curve strategies involve positioning a portfolio to capitalize on expected changes in the shape of the Treasury yield curve by following either a bullet strategy, a barbell strategy, or a ladder strategy.
- An intersector allocation strategy involves a manager's allocation of funds among the major bond sectors. In making intersector and intrasector allocations, a manager is anticipating how spreads due to differences in credit risk, call risk, and liquidity risk will change.
- Immunization and cash-flow matching are two liability-driven strategies whose goal is to make sure that the investor can meet a schedule of future liabilities.
- *Classical immunization* can be defined as the process by which a bond portfolio is created so that it has an assured return for a specific time horizon regardless of interest rate

changes. It is accomplished by matching the present value of the liability, as well as the duration of the liability. In practice, however, immunization protects only against parallel changes in the yield curve.

- A cash-flow matching strategy is used to construct a portfolio that can fund a schedule of liabilities from portfolio return and asset value, with the portfolio's value diminishing to zero after payment of the last liability.
- Optimization and simulation are valuable tools for bond portfolio risk management. Optimization is used in portfolio allocation under different measures of risk, such as tracking error relative to a benchmark, or conditional value-at-risk (CVaR). Simulation aids in estimating portfolio interest rate risk and portfolio credit risk by allowing the portfolio manager to understand the performance of the portfolio in different scenarios.
- Machine learning (ML) can be used in corporate bond credit risk management to predict changes in credit ratings, corporate defaults, and recovery rates, and changes in credit spreads.
- In the analysis of mortgage-backed securities (MBSs), ML has been used to project prepayments for residential mortgage-backed securities (RMBSs) and forecast defaults for commercial mortgage-backed securities (CMBSs),

IV

Asset Pricing Models

16

Factor Models

Quantitative portfolio managers use statistical models to forecast future returns to construct portfolios and measure portfolio risk. Models for forecasting returns and risk are based on asset pricing models, which estimate the link between asset returns and variables and have been found to be useful in forecasting returns. Those variables that have been found to systematically affect the returns of all assets within an asset class (e.g., stocks and bonds) are referred to as *factors*.

Factor models are the key models used in quantitative asset management. There are two basic applications of such models. The first is to forecast an asset's expected return. Given forecasted returns for individual assets from a factor model, a portfolio that is expected to outperform a benchmark can be constructed. These models represent one type of factor model, referred to as *expected-return forecasting factor models.* The second application is a model to forecast risk and then use the forecasts to construct a portfolio with the desired risk level, identify the sources of risk, and then control that risk. Factor models used for this purpose are referred to as *risk-forecasting factor models.*

In this chapter, we discuss various aspects of factor models, beginning with how the factors are determined using several statistical techniques: regression analysis, principal component analysis (PCA), and factor analysis. We describe two economic theories that provide the theoretical foundation for factor models. Then the various expected-return forecasting factor models and risk-forecasting factor models are described.

16.1 Identifying Factors

There are two philosophically different approaches to identifying factors from a large number of variables that are potential candidates. The first is to start by stating a hypothesis about which variables would be expected to influence returns, and then test whether the data confirm the hypothesis. Fortunately, there have been a good number of studies suggesting variables that would qualify as factors. The statistical technique used to test the hypothesis is *regression analysis.*

The second approach is to let the data speak for themselves. We start with data on security returns and try to identify underlying factors by observing groups of securities that exhibit strong correlations in returns. The statistical methodology used to identify such factors is called *factor analysis*. While factor analysis helps to identify sources of risk common to groups of securities, it does not identify these sources.

PCA is also used in empirical factor model building. It also attempts to identify factors that underlie asset return processes, but its general goal is to reduce the dimension of the representation; that is, to identify factors one by one in such a way that the first factor explains the largest percentage of the variability in the data; the second factor explains the second-largest percentage of the variability in the data, and so on. This enables the modeler to drop from consideration factors that contribute relatively little to the explanatory power of the model. The factors discovered by PCA are also uncorrelated to each other, which can be very useful for modeling purposes.

A comprehensive review of these approaches is beyond the scope of this chapter, but we provide some intuition and detail next.

16.1.1 Regression Analysis

In chapter 9, we discussed and illustrated regression analysis. To identify factors, multiple regression analysis is employed, where the variables in the model are those that are thought to drive asset returns. Those variables that are determined to be statistically significant based on the statistical tests described in chapter 9 are selected as factors.

The regression model assumes that the return on a particular stock i (r_i) can be represented as

$$r_i = \alpha_i + \sum_{k=1}^{K} \beta_{ik} f_k + \varepsilon_i \tag{16.1}$$

where α_i is the mean return, $f_1, \ldots, f_K$ are the K factors, β_{ik} are the coefficients of the factors, and ε_i is the residual error. In practice, the linearity assumption is not very restrictive because nonlinear relationships can be represented by transforming the data.

The factors f_k in this regression are the *explanatory variables* (also called *independent variables*). They help explain the variability in the *response variable* (also called *dependent variable*) r_i.

In addition to the statistical tests to determine which variables are statistically significant and therefore qualify as factors, there are other tests explained in chapter 9 that must be checked to determine if the model is valid. Specifically, there are three tests regarding the assumptions about the residuals (ε): (1) they follow a normal distribution; (2) they exhibit homoscedasticity (i.e., they have the same variability independent of the values of the response and the explanatory variables); and (3) they are not autocorrelated (i.e., they do not exhibit patterns with the order of the data in the dataset).

16.1.2 Factor Analysis

Factor analysis is a statistical tool. To illustrate the main idea behind it, let us begin with a simple, nonfinance example. Suppose that we have the grades for 1,000 students in nine subjects: literature, composition, Spanish, algebra, calculus, geometry, physics, biology, and chemistry. If we compute the pairwise correlations for grades in each subject, we would expect to find higher correlations among grades within the literature, composition, and Spanish group than between grades in, say, literature and calculus.

Suppose that we observe that we have high correlations for grades in the literature, composition, and Spanish group, high correlations for grades in the algebra, calculus, and geometry group, and high correlations for grades in the physics, biology, and chemistry group. There will still be some correlations among grades in different groups, but suppose that they are not nearly as high as the correlations within the groups. This may indicate that three factors determine a student's performance in these subjects: a verbal aptitude, an aptitude for math, and an aptitude for science. A single factor does not necessarily determine a student's performance; otherwise, all correlations would be 0 or 1. However, some factors will be weighted more than others for a particular student. Note, by the way, that these factors (the aptitudes for different subjects) are invisible. We can observe the strength of the correlations only within and between the groups, and we need to provide interpretation for what the factors might be based on our intuition.

How does this example translate to financial applications? Suppose that we have data on the returns of N stocks. You can think of them as the grades recorded for the various students. We compute the pairwise correlations between the stock returns and look for patterns. There may be a group of stocks for which the returns are highly correlated. All the stocks in the group receive a large portion of their earnings from foreign operations, so we may conclude that exchange risk is one underlying factor. Another group of highly correlated stocks may have high debt-to-equity ratios, so we may conclude that the level of interest rates is another underlying factor. We proceed in the same way, trying to identify common factors from groups that exhibit high correlations.

There is a specific statistical technique for computing such underlying factors. Most advanced statistical packages have a function that can perform the calculations. Microsoft Excel's statistical capabilities are unfortunately not as advanced, but MATLAB's Statistical Toolbox and Python libraries such as sklearn have functions that allow a user to provide the data, specify the number of factors (which the user can try to guess based on the preliminary analysis and intuition), and obtain the factor loadings. The *factor loadings* are the coefficients in front of the factors that determine how to compute the value of the observation (the grade or the stock return) from the hidden factors, and they can be interpreted as the sensitivities of the stock returns to the various factors.

A factor model equation in fact looks like the familiar regression given in equation (16.1). The difference is in the way that the factors are computed. The output from running factor analysis with statistical software on our dataset of stock returns will be a model. It is expressed in terms of the vector of returns for the assets in the portfolio:

$$\mathbf{r} = \boldsymbol{\alpha} + \mathbf{B} \cdot \mathbf{f} + \varepsilon$$

where $\boldsymbol{\alpha}$ is the N-dimensional vector of mean returns, $\mathbf{f}$ is the K-dimensional vector of factors, $\mathbf{B}$ is the $K \times N$ matrix of factor loadings (the coefficients in front of every factor), and $\boldsymbol{\varepsilon}$ is the N-dimensional vector of residual errors.

The problem with factor analysis for identifying the factors from the candidate variables is that even if we have accounted for all the variability in the data and have identified the factors numerically, we may not be able to provide a good interpretation of their meaning. This makes the factors identified from factor analysis difficult to apply in practice for constructing portfolios, understanding portfolio risk, and evaluating performance.

16.1.3 Principal Component Analysis

We also discussed principal component analysis (PCA) in chapter 10. PCA is similar to factor analysis in the sense that the goal of the statistical procedure is to compute factors, referred to as *principal components (PCs)*, out of a given set of return data that explain the variability in the data. These factors are statistical; that is, they are not input by the user but computed by software. However, the difference is that the main goal of PCA is to find *uncorrelated* factors in such a way that the first factor explains as much of the variability in the data as possible, the second factor explains as much of the remaining variability as possible, and so on. PCA is even less concerned with the interpretation of the factors than factor analysis is, and this is a drawback in the sense that it is difficult to use the results from PCA for understanding portfolio risk. However, PCA models are helpful for modeling purposes and can be used as a way to reduce the dimensionality of the data. Let us explain the latter point in more detail.

As mentioned earlier, each subsequent PC explains a smaller portion of the variability in the original data. If we observe that a large percentage of the variability in the original data is explained by the first few components, we can drop the remaining components from consideration. For example, if we have data for the returns on 1,000 stocks and find that the first 7 PCs explain 99% of the variability, we can drop the other PCs and model with only 7 variables (instead of the original 1,000). The representation of the data will in a sense be inverse to the original representation: each PC will be expressed as a linear combination of the original data. For example, if we are given N stock returns $r_1, \ldots, r_N$, the PCs $x_1, \ldots, x_N$ will be given by

$$x_k = \sum_{i=1}^{N} \beta_{ik}\, r_i \tag{16.2}$$

As with factor analysis, most advanced statistical packages have a function that can compute the PCs for a set of data. There is no such function in Excel; however, MATLAB's Statistical Toolbox and Python's sklearn library contain functions that allow a user to provide the data and obtain useful output such as the coefficients in front of the original data; that is, β_{ik} in equation (16.2), the scores (i.e., the PCs themselves), and the percentage of the variability of the original data explained by each PC.

16.2 Equity Factors and Market Anomalies

For many years, the dominant financial theory regarding what drives the return on equity was the capital asset pricing model (CAPM), derived independently by Sharpe (1964), Lintner (1965), and Mossin (1966). According to the CAPM, the only driver of the return on an asset is the market. The entire finance profession was so held captive by this economic model that any empirical study that discovered there was another variable was difficult to accept. When empirical studies reported other factors affecting equity returns, such findings were labeled "market anomalies." Today, however, some of these so-called anomalies are recognized as systematic factors that affect equity returns. In fact, the pendulum has swung in the opposite direction. In the past twenty years or so, the finance literature has gone overboard with discoveries of factors that are believed to systematically drive equity returns, leading to what some describe as "factor proliferation." Some practitioners have used hundreds of factors to describe equity returns. This led Cochrane (2011) to coin the phrase "factor zoo" to describe the collection of factors reported in the finance literature.

Studies have reexamined the factors reported in the literature. In trying to determine whether factors were useful in capital budgeting decisions, Levi and Welch (2014) investigated 600 factors and found that a little less than half the proposed factors were in fact factors. Focusing on 82 factors appearing in the literature, McLean and Pontiff (2016) were able to confirm the empirical results for 72 of the factors, while the remaining 10 seemed to be due to error. Studying 315 factors, Harvey, Liu, and Zhu (2016) reported that only a handful of the factors in the factor zoo were statistically significant in explaining stock returns.

16.3 Expected-Return Forecasting Factor Models in Practice

Factor models used in the equity space can be categorized as *single-factor* and *multifactor*. These models will be discussed next.

16.3.1 Single-Factor Equity Model

As mentioned earlier, the theory underlying a single-factor model is the CAPM, which was the first asset pricing model. Sharpe (1964), Lintner (1965), and Mossin (1966) extended the microview of risk and return taken by Harry Markowitz (1952) in his statement of the individual investor's mean-variance problem to a statement about the entire economy. Their model holds if every investor optimizes his portfolio allocation by taking into consideration only the portfolio's mean return and the return variance, subject to some additional assumptions.[1]

The CAPM asserts that if the assumptions of the model are met, then the only factor that affects the return on an asset in equilibrium is the market return. The formula for the CAPM when applied to equities is

$$E(\tilde{r}_i) = r_f + \beta_i \left[E(\tilde{r}_M) - r_f\right] \tag{16.3}$$

where

$E(\tilde{r}_i)$ = expected return on stock i,

$E(\tilde{r}_M)$ = expected return on a broad based stock market index, and

r_f = risk-free rate.

The β_i coefficient, referred to as *beta*, is estimated empirically for a stock or a portfolio using regression analysis based on historical return data. The single-factor model given in equation (16.3) states that the expected return on stock i is equal to the risk-free rate plus a premium. The premium, in turn, is based on beta, which is a measure of *systematic risk*, multiplied by the difference between the expected return on the market and the risk-free rate.

The CAPM requires that an expectation of the return on the market is provided. While the model is used in corporate finance in the context of determining the cost of equity of a

1. These assumptions are that (1) investors are rational and risk-averse, (2) investors all invest for the same period of time, (3) there is a risk-free asset, (4) all investors can borrow or lend any amount at the risk-free rate, and (5) capital markets are perfectly competitive and frictionless.

May 2018-April 2023	60 observations	
	Factor	
	Loading	p-Value
Market (Rm-Rf) (beta)	0.57	0.002
Alpha (intercept)	18.92 bps	0.846
Annualized alpha	2.27%	
Cofficient of determination R2	15.80%	
Adjusted R2	14.30%	
F statistics	10.85%	0.002

Exhibit 16.1
Single-factor model estimate for Pfizer (PFE).

company, it is not used in portfolio management to construct a portfolio and determine its risk exposure. Instead, the CAPM is used as justification for the use of only one factor as driving the return on a stock or a stock portfolio. That factor is the return on the market.

The single-factor model that is estimated in practice is a variant of equation (16.3), in which instead of expectations, actual returns for the market and the stock or portfolio are used. The single-factor model (which is also referred to as the *single-index market model*) is

$$r_{it} - r_{ft} = \alpha_i + \beta_i + (r_{mt} - r_{ft}) + \varepsilon_{it} \tag{16.4}$$

where r_{it} is the observed return for stock in period t, r_{mt} is the observed return for the market in period t, time r_{ft} is the risk-free rate for period t, and ε_{it} is the error term. The parameters to be estimated by the regression are α_i and β_i Although technically, equation (16.4) is not the CAPM, some practitioners will refer to as such.

To illustrate this point, we have estimated the single-factor model given by equation (16.4) for Pfizer (ticker symbol PFE) using data from May 2018 to April 2023 (sixty observations) and using the S&P 500 index as a proxy for the market. The results are reported in exhibit 16.1.[2] The intercept term (alpha) is 18.92 basis points, which is a monthly value. Multiplying 18.92 basis points by 12, the annualized alpha is 2.27%. The beta is 0.57 and the coefficient of determination (R^2) is 15.8%. The market factor is statistically significant, as can be seen from the beta coefficient's p-value of less than 1%. The value of 15.8% means that over the 60-month time period, 15.8% of the variance in Pfizer's monthly return is explained by the return on the S&P 500. The value 0.57 of beta indicates that if the S&P 500's return increases by one unit, the Pfizer stock will increase on average by one-half (0.57 times the increase in the S&P 500's).

The estimated single-factor model for an exchange-traded fund (ETF), the SPDR S&P 500 High Dividend ETF Trust, for the same period used for Pfizer is shown in exhibit 16.2. The ETF is a well-diversified portfolio that contains those stocks in the S&P 500

2. The return data for all the regressions estimated in this chapter, as well as the results reported in the exhibits, were obtained from Portfolio Visualizer, https://www.portfoliovisualizer.com/.

May 2018-April 2023	60 observations	
	Factor Loading	p-Value
Market (Rm-Rf) (beta)	0.95	0
Alpha (intercept)	–27.53 bps	0.571
Annualized alpha	–1.16%	
Cofficient of determination R2	67.80%	
Adjusted R2	67.20%	
F-statistics	121.98	0

Exhibit 16.2
Single-factor model estimate for the SPDR S&P 500 High Dividend ETF Trust.

that pay high dividends. The beta here is very close to 1 (the coefficient is 0.95), indicating that the ETF returns track the market returns on average. R^2 (67.80%) is also considerably higher than it is for the single stock, Pfizer, as expected.

16.3.2 Multifactor Equity Models

Most investors were surprised by the implications of the CAPM that only the movements in the market drove the return on stocks and equity portfolios. Fortunately, an economic theory provided support for the practitioners' intuition—that the market may not be the only factor that drives returns. However, the theory did not identify those other factors. In this section, we describe that theory, which is called the *arbitrage pricing theory* (APT). We then explain multifactor equity models and how these models are used in practice.

16.3.2.1 The Arbitrage Pricing Theory The APT, developed by Stephen Ross (1976), starts from a different vantage point than the CAPM. Instead of making assumptions on investment behavior or asset return distributions, APT assumes that there are a limited number of independent factors that influence returns. Namely, asset returns can be expressed as

$$\tilde{r}_i = E(\tilde{r}_i) + \beta_{i1}\,\tilde{f}_1 + \cdots + \beta_{iK}\,\tilde{f}_K + \varepsilon_i \tag{16.5}$$

The CAPM is a special case of the APT, in which there is only one factor—the market. However, the APT provides a more flexible and general framework that is more consistent with numerous studies on returns.

The derivation of the APT is based purely on arbitrage principles. We will explain the basics of arbitrage as a concept in detail in chapter 18, so we will not go through the formal derivation of the APT here. Instead, let us discuss several major advantages of the APT over the CAPM. First, the APT makes less restrictive assumptions about investor preferences toward risk and return than the CAPM. While the CAPM requires that investors consider trade-offs between risk and return solely on the basis of the expected returns and standard deviations of prospective investments, the APT simply requires that some bounds be placed on investors' utility functions.[3] Second, the APT is a relative pricing model, in the sense that it prices securities on the basis of the prices of other securities. By contrast, the CAPM is an absolute pricing model, in the sense that it relates returns on the securities to the fundamental source of risk inherent in the portfolio of total wealth. Finally, the APT does not rely on identifying the market portfolio and does not require any assumptions about the distribution of asset returns except for the factor structure.

While the APT provides strong theoretical support for more than one factor, it is silent on what those factors are. Academics and third-party vendors have developed models used by portfolio managers and researchers in academic studies. Academic models include the Fama-French models and macroeconomic factor models.

16.3.2.2 Fama-French Factor Models In a series of published papers, Eugene Fama, the 2013 co-recipient of the Nobel Prize in Economic Science, and Kenneth French developed several models that have been extensively used by practitioners in formulating investment strategies and in performing academic studies.

16.3.2.2.1 Fama-French Three-Factor Model The *Fama-French three-factor model,* first proposed in Fama and French (1992), included the market, size factor, and value factor. The market factor is measured by the difference between the market (as measured by a stock market index) and the risk-free rate. Fama and French denote this measure by RMRF, which means "market return minus the risk-free rate."

Empirical support for the size factor was provided in a study by Banz (1981) that found that small-company stocks (i.e., companies with small market capitalization) outperform large-company stocks on a risk-adjusted basis. This empirical observation became known as the "size effect." Small firms are said to be riskier, for two reasons. First, stocks of smaller companies tend to be less liquid than the stocks of larger companies. This could be attributable to the fact that small-cap firms make up less of the market or that there tends to be less investor demand because the stock of smaller companies are not as well known as the stock of larger companies (i.e., neglected by market analysts giving rise to the "neglected firm effect"). The second reason offered is that smaller stocks are more sensitive to market movements. If the company has a lower price per share and experiences an increase in demand, the price appreciation will be greater than that for the stock of a larger company.

In their model, Fama and French do not use size in terms of market capitalization (i.e., market cap). Rather, they use the difference between small and large firms, which they denote by *SMB* (which stands for "small minus big") as the factor.

Turning to the value factor, value investing has been one of the longest-lasting stock selection techniques in investment management. The idea behind value investing is that investors should buy stocks that are undervalued compared to their fundamental values. Value investors use certain financial measures that compare the stock's price to certain firm-specific variables that provide a good indicator of a stock's future performance to identify underpriced stocks. They include price-to-earnings ratio, price-to-book ratios, and debt

3. See the discussion of investor utility functions in chapter 12.

ratios. Essentially, value investing is the idea that if two stocks have the same fundamental indicators, the stock with the lower price is expected to outperform the stock with the higher price. Conversely, stocks that are priced high compared to their fundamental indicators are called "growth stocks" because the high price indicates that investors expect the firm to grow in the future. Fama and French (1988) found international evidence that value firms outperform growth firms.

The measure used in the Fama-French three-factor model as a proxy for value is the difference between stocks classified as value stocks and those classified as growth stocks. Stocks are *value stocks* if they have a high book-to-market ratio and *growth stocks* if they have a low book-to-market ratio. In Fama and French's model, the value factor is the difference between the return on high and low book-to-market ratio stocks, and it is denoted by HML which means "high minus low."

The Fama-French three factor model for a stock or a portfolio, then, is

$$r_t - r_{ft} = \alpha + \beta_1 \text{ RMRF}_t + \beta_2 \text{ SMB}_t + \beta_3 \text{ HML}_t + \varepsilon_t \tag{16.6}$$

where RMRF, SMB, and HML are as defined earlier; the subscript t indicates the time period.

r_t is the return on the stock or portfolio for period t; r_{ft} is the risk-free rate for period t; and ε_t is the error term in period t. α is the intercept term, and β_1, β_2, and β_3 are the factor loadings.

Exhibits 16.3 and 16.4 show the estimated Fama-French three-factor model for Pfizer and the SPDR S&P 500 High Dividend ETF Trust, respectively. Notice how Pfizer's exposure to the market has increased from 0.57 to 0.71 by introducing the two factors: size (SMB) and value (HML). The R^2 increased from 15.8% to 24.3%, and the adjusted R^2 increased from 14.4% to 20.2%. The market factor and the size factor are statistically significant, as can be seen from their p-values, while the value factor is not. In the case of the size factor, note that the factor loading is negative. For the ETF, the factor loading for the market factor is roughly the same. All three factors are statistically significant. The adjusted R^2 increased from 67.2% in the single-factor model to 91.4% in the Fama-French three-factor model.

16.3.2.2.2 Fama-French-Carhart Four-Factor Model The tendency of a stock's price to follow an upward or downward trend is referred to as *momentum*. Jegadesh and Titman (1993) reported that a momentum strategy—namely, purchasing stocks that have had high returns in the prior 3–12 months and selling stocks with low returns during that same time period—produced an average return of 1% per month. Subsequent studies found that a momentum strategy continued to provide above-average returns.

Carhart (1997) included momentum as a factor in the Fama-French three-factor model. In this model, referred to as the *Fama-French-Carhart four-factor model,* momentum is measured by the difference between winner stocks and loser stocks, denoted by WML (winner minus loser). The model then becomes

$$r_t - r_{ft} = \alpha + \beta_l \text{ RMRF}_t + \beta_2 \text{ SMB}_t + \beta_3 \text{ HML}_t + \beta_4 \text{ WML}_t + \varepsilon_t \tag{16.7}$$

Several studies have reported that the model with momentum outperforms that of the model that does not have momentum.

May 2018-April 2023	60 observations	
	Factor	
	Loading	p-Value
Market (Rm-Rf)	0.71	0
Size (SMB)	−0.85	0.016
Value (HML)	0.04	0.827
Alpha	5.90 bps	0.846
Annualized alpha	−0.71%	
Cofficient of determination R2	24.30%	
Adjusted R2	20.20%	
F statistics	5.99%	0.001

Exhibit 16.3
Estimate of the Fama-French three-factor model for Pfizer.

May 2018-April 2023	60 observations	
	Factor	
	Loading	p-Value
Market (Rm-Rf)	0.91	0
Size (SMB)	0.18	0.057
Value (HML)	0.68	0
Alpha	−5.19 bps	0.836
Annualized alpha	−0.62%	
Cofficient of determination R2	91.90%	
Adjusted R2	91.40%	
F statistics	210.82	0

Exhibit 16.4
Estimate of Fama-French three-factor model for the SPDR S&P 500 High Dividend ETF Trust.

An estimate of the Fama-French four-factor model for Pfizer and the ETF are shown in exhibits 16.5 and 16.6, respectively. For Pfizer, the only factor that is statistically significant is the market factor. Adding the size factor, value factor, and momentum factor did not add significantly to the explanatory power of the model. For the ETF, the only factor that is not statistically significant is the size factor.

16.3.2.2.3 Fama-French Five-Factor Model Empirical studies on factors led Fama and French (2015) to add two more factors to their original three-factor model, creating the *Fama-French five-factor model.* These two factors are the profitability factor and investment factor.

Novy-Marx (2012) reported that strategies based on a firm's gross profitability performed well in explaining the average returns for stocks. In the study, the specific measure used was

May 2018-April 2023	60 observations	
	Factor Loading	p-Value
Market (Rm-Rf)	0.84	0
Size (SMB)	–0.74	0.035
Value (HML)	0.13	0.536
Momentum (MCM)	0.37	0.129
Alpha	–13.50 bps	0.846
Annualized alpha	–1.62%	
Cofficient of determination R2	27.40%	
Adjusted R2	22.10%	
F statistics	5.19%	0.001

Exhibit 16.5
Estimate of the Fama-French four-factor model for Pfizer.

May 2018-April 2023	60 observations	
	Factor Loading	p-Value
Market (Rm-Rf)	0.86	0
Size (SMB)	0.13	0.142
Value (HML)	0.65	0
Momentum (MCM)	–0.15	0.022
Alpha	–2.18 bps	0.928
Annualized alpha	–1.62%	
Cofficient of determination R2	92.60%	
Adjusted R2	92.10%	
F statistics	172.50	0

Exhibit 16.6
Estimate of Fama-French four-factor model for the SPDR S&P 500 High Dividend ETF Trust.

the ratio of a firm's gross profits to its assets. (Gross profits are calculated by reducing a company's revenue by its cost of goods sold.) The argument for using gross profits is that using gross profits-to-assets complements the value factor because it identifies the profitable stocks that are also priced at a discount (i.e., value stocks). Therefore, the gross profits-to-assets ratio acts as a form of quality control when buying stocks that are considered cheap. Novy-Marx reported that the gross profits-to-assets ratio has a significant and positive relationship with average stock returns. Fama and French measure this ratio, denoted by RMW (which stands for "robust minus weak"), which is calculated as the excess return of stock with high profitability over stocks with low profitability.

Fama and French (2015) found that firms with lower capital investments tended to have higher returns than those with high capital investments. The idea behind what they refer to as the *investment factor* is that, on average, when a firm increases investment expenditures, the future return generated on investment tends to be less than the present value of the investment expenditure. Essentially, this means that capital investments tend to produce less value than the cost of the project or capital investment itself. Thus, when the level of capital investment increases, the stock price tends to decline. Conservative stocks tend to be stocks of companies with little investment during the past period. In contrast, aggressive stocks are stocks of companies that have increased their investment expenditures in the last period. In their model, Fama and French denote the investment factor by CMA (which stands for "conservative minus aggressive"), which is measured by the difference between the return for firms with low capital investments and high capital investment.

The Fama-French five-factor model, then, is

$$r_t - r_{ft} = \alpha + \beta_1 \text{ RMRF}_t + \beta_2 \text{ SMB}_t + \beta_3 \text{ HML}_t + \beta_4 \text{ RMW}_t + \beta_5 \text{ CMA}_t + \varepsilon_t \qquad (16.8)$$

Note that the Fama-French five-factor model does not include the momentum factor.

Now let's look at the impact of adding the profitability factor and investment factor on the Pfizer and ETF. In the case of Pfizer, the market factor is statistically significant in the three-factor models that we reported on and the size factor is statistically significant in the three- and four-factor models. However, as can be seen in exhibit 16.7, after including the profitability factor and investment factor, the size factor is no longer statistically significant. The other four factors, however, are all statistically significant.

In the case of the ETF, the size factor was not significant in the four-factor model. Adding the two factors results in the size factor becoming statistically significant. However, these two factors (profitability factor and investment factor) are not statistically significant.

16.3.2.3 Macroeconomic Factor Models In a *macroeconomic factor model,* the factors used are observable macroeconomic variables. Chen, Roll, and Ross [1986] proposed the first macroeconomic factor model. They found that the following macroeconomic variables were statistically significant in explaining stock returns: industrial production, changes in the risk premium, and changes in the shape of the U.S. Treasury yield curve. Other macroeconomic variables found to be less strongly related in explaining stock returns were unanticipated inflation and changes in expected inflation.

Subsequent macroeconomic multifactor models have analyzed additional macroeconomic factors. Tangjitprom (2012) notes that the macroeconomic factors that have been used are (1) general economic condition and business cycle factors (e.g., gross domestic product, employment, industrial production); (2) financial market–related factors (e.g. yield curve, corporate bond spreads, stock market index, key commodity indices); (3) monetary policy–related factors (e.g., key money market rates, inflation rate); and (4) internationally related factors (i.e., foreign exchange rate).

In macroeconomic factor models used today, the macroeconomic variables in the model are not the observed value. Instead, what is used is a "factor surprise," which is the difference between the observed value for the macroeconomic variable and the forecasted value for that macroeconomic variable. The forecasted value can be from government forecasts, from proprietary econometric models provided by a consulting firm, or from internal forecasts by the economics group of an asset management firm.

May 2018-April 2023	60 observations	
		Factor
	Loading	p-Value
Market (Rm-Rf)	0.63	0.001
Size (SMB)	–0.01	0.985
Value (HML)	–0.54	0.070
Profitability (RMW)	1.30	0.005
Investment (CMA)	1.08	0.018
Alpha	–115.57 bps	0.207
Annualized alpha	–1.62%	

Exhibit 16.7
Estimate of Fama-French five-factor model for Pfizer.

May 2018-April 2023	60 observations	
	Factor	
	Loading	p-Value
Market (Rm-Rf)	0.90	0.001
Size (SMB)	0.26	0.027
Value (HML)	0.60	0.000
Profitability (RMW)	0.04	0.731
Investment (CMA)	0.08	0.524
Alpha	–9.95 bps	0.706
Annualized alpha	–1.19%	
Cofficient of determination R2	92.20%	
Adjusted R2	91.50%	
F statistics	128.47	0

Exhibit 16.8
Estimate of Fama-French five-factor model for the SPDR S&P 500 High Dividend ETF Trust.

16.3.3 Applications to Portfolio Management

In this section, we review several applications of factor models in portfolio management. The list of applications is by no means exhaustive. We discuss a classical portfolio performance measure, as well as mean-variance optimization. Factor models are widely used when pricing fixed-income securities and financial derivative contracts by Monte Carlo (MC) simulation.

16.3.3.1 Portfolio Performance Measurement In evaluating the performance of a portfolio manager, one must adjust for the risks accepted by the manager in generating return. Asset pricing models such as the CAPM or a multifactor model provide the expected return after adjusting for risk.

Various measures have been used to assess performance based on the excess return. One such measure is the *Jensen measure* (also called the *Jensen index*). In 1968, Michael

Jensen used simple linear regression to analyze the performance of mutual fund managers. Basically, using time-series data for the return on the portfolio managed by the particular fund manager and the market index, he estimated the regression given by equation (16.3), which assumes that the only factor is the market (i.e., single-factor model). The intercept term, α_i, is the estimated value of the Jensen measure and is interpreted as the unique return realized by the portfolio manager. A statistically significant intercept term that is positive means that the portfolio manager outperformed the market; a negative value means that the portfolio manager underperformed the market. The Jensen measure is appropriate only when the portfolio is diversified.

When Jensen proposed the model for measuring performance, he used the Greek letter *alpha* to represent the intercept term in the regression equation, as in equation (16.3). Hence, the Jensen measure is also called the *Jensen alpha*. Consequently, the market sometimes refers to the "alpha" of a portfolio manager as a measure of performance. However, the concept of alpha used today in the investment industry is not the Jensen measure but rather the average excess return (also called *active return*) over a period of time. The active return is the difference between a portfolio's return and a benchmark index's return. Notice that unlike the Jensen measure, measuring performance by the average active return does not adjust for market risk.

Let's look at the Jensen alpha for Pfizer and SPDR S&P 500 High Dividend ETF Trust. Exhibits 16.1 and 16.2 show the single-factor model estimates and the p-values for alpha in both cases. In neither case is the alpha significant.

While the Jensen measure was proposed for use for the single-factor model, it has also been used for treating the intercept terms in the Fama-French models as a performance measure. Looking at exhibits 16.3, 16.5, and 16.7, it can be seen that alpha is not significant for any of the Fama-French factor models for Pfizer. The same is true for the ETF (see exhibits 16.4, 16.6, and 16.8).

Musumeci (2023) investigated the appropriateness of using the intercept term as a measure of performance in factor models. The accuracy of intercept measures for detecting abnormal performance is critically dependent on accurately estimating the factor loadings of the other factors. The failure of the intercept to detect abnormal performance is that the same unsystematic perturbation to stock or portfolio returns that causes abnormal performance typically distorts the estimate of the factor. He identifies necessary and sufficient conditions for higher returns to produce lower intercepts, erroneously implying lower performance.

16.3.3.2 Efficient Mean-Variance Optimization Consider a portfolio with N stocks. As explained in chapter 12, risk is traditionally defined as the variance of the portfolio's returns. So, in this case, we need to find the covariance matrix of the N stocks, which would require the portfolio manager to estimate N variances (one for each of the N stocks) and $N \cdot (N-1)/2$ covariances. If we have a portfolio of 400 stocks, this means that we need to estimate 400 variances and 79,800 covariances. Adding the 400 estimates of expected returns (one for each stock), this is a total of 80,200 values to estimate—a very difficult undertaking.

Instead, suppose we use the Fama-French three-factor model to represent stock returns. Then, we need to estimate (1) the three-factor loadings (the beta coefficients) for each of the

400 assets (i.e., 1,200 values); (2) the 6 values of the factor variance-covariance matrix; and (3) the 400 residual variances (one for each stock). That is, we need to estimate only 1,600 values in all. This represents an almost 99% reduction from the original number of 80,200 values—a huge improvement. Hence, with well-chosen factors, the work involved in estimating a portfolio's risk can be substantially reduced. From a statistical estimation point of view, factor covariance matrices also tend to be much more stable and reliable than stock return covariance matrices.

Let us explain how the portfolio optimization would be performed when stock returns are expressed through factors. Suppose that the vector of N stock returns $\mathbf{r}$ can be written as

$$\mathbf{r} = \boldsymbol{\alpha} + \mathbf{B} \cdot \mathbf{f} + \varepsilon \tag{16.9}$$

where $\boldsymbol{\alpha}$ is the N-dimensional vector of mean returns, $\mathbf{f}$ is the K-dimensional vector of factors, $\mathbf{B}$ is the $K \times N$ matrix of factor loadings (the coefficients in front of every factor), and $\boldsymbol{\varepsilon}$ is the N-dimensional vector of residual errors.

If the portfolio weights invested in each asset are represented by the N-dimensional vector $\mathbf{w}$, it is easy to see that the expected excess portfolio return can be written as

$$\boldsymbol{\alpha}' \cdot \mathbf{w} + \mathbf{B} \cdot \mathbf{f}$$

where $\mathbf{f}$ is the vector of factor means; and the variance of the portfolio return can be written as

$$\mathbf{w}' \cdot (\mathbf{B}' \cdot \boldsymbol{\Sigma}_{\mathbf{f}} \cdot \mathbf{B} + \mathbf{D}) \cdot \mathbf{w}$$

where $\boldsymbol{\Sigma}_{\mathbf{f}}$ is the factor covariance matrix and $\mathbf{D}$ is the diagonal matrix (with zeros in all off-diagonal elements) that contains the variance of the error terms These expressions for the mean and the variance of the portfolio return can be used directly in the mean-variance portfolio optimization problem introduced in chapter 12.

16.4 Risk-Forecasting Factor Models

The factor models described thus far were developed for forecasting expected returns; that is, they are expected-return forecasting factor models. The application to risk forecasting was recognized by Rosenberg (1974).[4] Once a portfolio manager controls the portfolio's risk, the team could use one of many approaches to identify stocks that would outperform so as to generate "alpha"; that is, performance relative to a benchmark after adjusting for risk. The model could be an expected-return forecasting multifactor model or traditional fundamental security analysis.

Grinold and Kahn (1994) describe the three phases in building a risk-forecasting factor model: (1) selecting the factors, (2) estimating factor returns, and (3) forecasting risk. The basic relationship to be estimated in a risk-forecasting factor model is the same, but the factors are risk factors. As with expected-return forecasting factor models, portfolio

4. Barr Rosenberg went on to found Barr Rosenberg & Associates (BARRA, Inc.), a quantitative consulting firm that developed several fundamental factor models, one of which is used in the illustration in exhibit 16.9. In 2004, BARRA, Inc. was acquired by Morgan Stanley Capital International (MSCI) and the name changed to MSCI BARRA.

managers will either create their own risk-forecasting factor models or use the services of a third-party vendor that has developed such a model.

Examples of commercial vendors of risk-forecasting factor models for equity include Northfield Information Services, FactSet, and MSCI. The Northfield model, which it calls the "U.S. Fundamental Equity Risk Model," uses 67 factors: market beta, 11 fundamental characteristics (e.g., firm size, dividend yield, and growth orientation), and 55 industry groups. The FactSet Equity Model is a global model that has 11 style factors, 89 industry factors, and 52 country factors.

16.4.1 Illustration of a Risk-Forecasting Factor Model

To illustrate a risk-forecasting factor model, we will use an old version of a model developed by Barra, the "E3 model." While the model has been significantly upgraded,[5] the discussion and illustrations provide the essential points for appreciating the value of risk-forecasting factor models in portfolio management.

The E3 model uses company and industry attributes and market data as descriptors. Examples of descriptors include earnings/price ratios, book/price ratios, estimated earnings growth, and trading activity. An analysis of historical stock returns and descriptors about a company is the starting point in building this model. The process of identifying the risk factors to be included in the model begins with historical monthly returns for hundreds of stocks that its descriptors must explain. These descriptors are not the "risk factors" but instead are the candidates for risk factors to be included in the final model. The descriptors are selected in terms of their ability to explain stock returns. That is, all the descriptors are potential risk factors, but only those that appear to be important in explaining stock returns are used to construct risk factors.

The descriptors that are statistically significant in explaining stock returns are then grouped into risk indices or factors to capture related company attributes. For example, in the E3 model, the descriptors market leverage, book leverage, debt-to-equity ratio, and the company's debt rating are combined to obtain a risk index or factor referred to as "leverage." Consequently, a risk index is a combination of descriptors that captures a particular attribute of a company.

The E3 model used 13 risk indices and 55 industry groups. The 13 risk indices and the descriptor used to construct each risk for the E3 model are shown in exhibit 16.9. The 55 industry classifications are further classified into sectors.

Given the risk factors, information about the factor loading for every stock to each risk factor is estimated using statistical analysis. For a given time period, the return for each risk factor (R_{Fj}) also can be estimated using statistical analysis. The prediction for the expected return can be obtained from equation (16.3) for any stock. The nonfactor return (i.e., the error term) is found by subtracting the actual return for the period for a stock from the return as forecasted by the risk factors.

Moving from the individual stocks to portfolios, the forecasted return for a portfolio can be computed. The factor loading for a given risk factor of a portfolio is simply the

5. For a description of the latest version of what is now the MSCI BARRA model, see https://www.msci.com/our-solutions/factor-investing/factor-models.

Descriptors in risk index	Risk index
Beta times sigma Daily standard deviation High-low price Log of stock price Cumulative range Volume beta Serial dependence Option-implied standard deviation	Volatility
Relative strength Historical alpha	Momentum
Log of market capitalization	Size
Cube of log of market capitalization	Size nonlinearity
Share turnover rate (annual) Share turnover rate (quarterly) Share turnover rate (monthly) Share turnover rate (five years) Indicator for forward split Volume to variance	Trading activity
Payout ratio over five years Variability in capital structure Growth rate in total assets Earnings growth rate over the last five years Analyst-predicted earnings growth Recent earnings change	Growth
Analyst-predicted earnings-to-price Trailing annual earnings-to-price Historical earnings-to-price	Earnings yield
Book-to-price ratio	Value
Variability in earnings Variability in cash flows Extraordinary items in earnings Standard deviation of analyst-predicted earnings-to-price	Earnings variability
Market leverage Book leverage Debt to total assets Senior debt rating	Leverage
Exposure to foreign currencies	Currency sensitivity
Predicted dividend yield	Dividend yield
Indicator for firms outside US-E3 estimation universe	Non-estimation Universe indicator

Exhibit 16.9
BARRA E3 model risk definitions.

weighted average of the factor loading of each stock in the portfolio to that risk factor. For example, suppose that a portfolio has 62 stocks and that stocks 1–60 are equally weighted in the portfolio at 1.5%, while stock 61 is 4% of the portfolio and stock 62 is 6% of the portfolio. Then the exposure of the portfolio to risk factor *j* is

$$0.015\,\beta_{1,j} + 0.015\,\beta_{2,j} + \cdots + 0.015\,\beta_{60,j} + 0.040\,\beta_{61,j} + 0.060\,\beta_{62,j}$$

The nonfactor error term is measured in the same way as in the case of an individual stock. However, in a well-diversified portfolio, the nonfactor error term will be considerably less for the portfolio than for the individual stocks in the portfolio. The same analysis can be applied to a stock market index because an index is nothing more than a portfolio of stocks.

Next, we provide more information about two applications of risk-forecasting factor models to portfolio management: risk decomposition and portfolio construction.

16.4.2 Application to Risk Decomposition

Once estimated, a risk-forecasting factor model can be used to decompose risk to assess the potential exposure of a portfolio to the factors and the potential performance of a portfolio relative to a benchmark. This is the portfolio construction and risk control application of the model. Also, the actual performance of a portfolio relative to a benchmark can be assessed.

Barra (1998) suggests that there are various ways that a portfolio's total risk can be decomposed when employing a risk-forecasting multifactor model. Each decomposition approach can be useful to managers depending on the equity portfolio management that they pursue. The four approaches are (1) total risk decomposition, (2) systematic-residual risk decomposition, (3) active risk decomposition, and (4) active systematic–active residual risk decomposition. In all these approaches to risk decomposition, the total return is divided into the risk-free return and the total excess return. The total excess return is the difference between the actual return realized by the portfolio and the risk-free return. The risk associated with the total excess return, called *total excess risk,* is what is further partitioned in the four approaches.

Now we briefly describe each of these and explain how managers pursuing different strategies will find the decomposition helpful in portfolio construction and evaluation:[6]

- *Total risk decomposition:* Some portfolio managers seek to minimize total risk and construct a portfolio accordingly. For such managers, total risk decomposition, which divides the total excess risk into two components, common factor risks (e.g., capitalization and industry exposures) and specific risk, is useful. There is no provision for market risk, only risk attributed to the factor risks and company-specific influences (i.e., risk unique to a particular company and therefore uncorrelated with the specific risk of other companies). Thus, the market portfolio is not a risk factor considered in this decomposition.
- *Systematic-residual risk decomposition:* Some portfolio managers seek to time the market or intentionally make bets to create a different exposure than that of a market portfolio. Such managers would find it useful to decompose total excess risk into systematic risk and residual risk. Unlike the total risk decomposition approach, this view brings market risk into the analysis.
- *Active risk decomposition:* Portfolio managers assess a portfolio's risk exposure and actual performance relative to a benchmark index. The active risk decomposition approach is useful for that purpose. In this type of decomposition, the total excess return is divided into benchmark risk and active risk. *Benchmark risk* is defined as the risk associated with the benchmark portfolio. *Active risk* results from the manager's attempt to generate a return that will outperform the benchmark. Active risk is further partitioned into common factor risk and specific risk.
- *Active systematic–active residual risk decomposition:* There are portfolio managers who overlay a market-timing strategy on their stock selection. That is, they not only

6. This discussion draws from Barra (1988).

try to select stocks they believe will outperform but also try to time the purchase of each stock. For a portfolio manager who pursues such a strategy, it will be important to evaluate performance to separate market risk from common factor risks. In the active risk decomposition approach just discussed, lack of market risk is identified as one of the risk factors. Since market risk (i.e., a systematic risk) is an element of active risk, its inclusion as a source of risk is preferred by portfolio managers. When market risk is included, we have the active systematic residual risk decomposition approach. Total excess risk is again divided into benchmark risk and active risk. However, active risk is divided into active systematic risk (i.e., active market risk) and active residual risk. Then, active residual risk is divided into systematic risk factors and specific risk.

The four approaches to risk decomposition are just different ways of slicing up the risk to help a portfolio manager to construct and control the risk of a portfolio.

16.4.3 Application to Portfolio Construction and Risk Control

Given the risk factors and their factor loadings, a portfolio's risk exposure profile can be quantified and controlled using a risk-forecasting factor model. More specifically, it can be used to (1) assess the risk exposure of a portfolio, (2) control risk against a stock market index, and (3) tilt a portfolio based on a portfolio manager's view:

- *Assessing the risk exposure of a portfolio:* By assessing the risk exposure of the current portfolio using a risk-forecasting factor model, a manager can determine whether the portfolio is consistent with the strength of its management team. For example, suppose that the model shows that the portfolio has (1) a high active exposure to the momentum factor (i.e., the stocks held in the portfolio have significant momentum); (2) stocks were smaller than the benchmark average in terms of market capitalization; and (3) industry factor exposures with exceptionally high active exposure to the semiconductor industry and electronic equipment industry. Such large bets can expose the portfolio to large swings in returns. An important use of such information from a risk-forecasting multifactor model is the identification of explicit and implicit portfolio bets. If, for example, the portfolio manager did not want to place such a large technology sector bet or momentum risk index bet, then the portfolio can be rebalanced to minimize any such bets.
- *Controlling risk against a stock market index:* The objective of equity indexing is to match the performance of some specified stock market index with little tracking error. To do this, the risk profile of the indexed portfolio must match the risk profile of the designated stock market index. That is, the factor risk exposure of the indexed portfolio must match as closely as possible the exposure of the designated stock market index to the same factors. Any differences in the factor risk exposure result in tracking error. Identification of any differences allows the portfolio manager seeking to pursue an indexed portfolio to rebalance the portfolio to reduce tracking error.
- *Tilting a portfolio:* An active manager can employ a risk-forecasting multifactor model to construct a portfolio to make intentional bets. Suppose, for example, that a portfolio manager seeks to construct a portfolio that generates superior returns relative to the S&P 500 by tilting it toward stocks with a low price-earnings ratio but does not want to

increase tracking error significantly. An obvious approach may seem to be to identify all the stocks in the universe that have a lower-than-average price-earnings ratio. The problem with this approach is that it introduces unintentional bets with respect to the other risk factors. Instead, an optimization method combined with a risk-forecasting multifactor model can be used to construct the desired portfolio. The necessary inputs to this process are the tilt exposure sought and the benchmark stock market index. Additional constraints can be placed, for example, on the number of stocks to be included in the portfolio.

Summary

- Models for forecasting returns and risk are based on asset pricing models.
- Factors are variables that have been found to systematically affect the returns of all assets within an asset class (e.g., stocks and bonds).
- There are two basic applications of factor models: expected-return forecasting factor models and risk-forecasting factor models.
- Factor models can be constructed by using regression analysis, factor analysis, or principal component analysis (PCA).
- Factor analysis is a statistical technique for identifying unobservable factors that drive correlations between observable quantities.
- PCA is a statistical technique for identifying uncorrelated factors that are linear combinations of the original data.
- The capital asset pricing model (CAPM) is an equilibrium model of asset prices that links the expected return on an asset or a portfolio to the expected return of the market.
- Based on the CAPM, there is only one factor, the market, and hence the appropriate factor model is the single-factor version.
- Empirical studies have suggested a large number of systematic factors.
- The arbitrage pricing theory (APT) provides justification for more than one systematic factor, but it does not identify these factors.
- Commonly used expected return forecasting factor model are the Fama-French three-factor model, Fama-French-Carhart four-factor model, and Fama-French five-factor model.
- The market factor, size factor, and value factor are present in all the Fama-French models.
- The Fama-French-Carhart four-factor model includes the momentum factor.
- The Fama-French five-factor model includes the profitability factor and the investment factor.
- In a macroeconomic factor model, the factors used are macroeconomic variables.
- In macroeconomic factor models, the macroeconomic variables in the model are not the observed values but instead are *factor surprises*, the differences between the

observed value for the macroeconomic variable and the forecasted value for that macroeconomic variable.

- Expected-return forecasting factor models are used for portfolio performance evaluation, portfolio risk decomposition, and portfolio optimization.
- For factor models, the intercept term (alpha) measures performance if it is statistically sufficient.
- When applied to a single-factor model, the intercept term is referred to as the Jensen alpha.
- When the factors are used in mean-variance optimization, it reduces the number of variances and covariances significantly.
- In a risk-forecasting factor model, the factors are risk factors.
- A risk-forecasting factor model, once estimated, can be used to decompose risk to assess the potential performance of a portfolio to the factors and to assess the potential performance of a portfolio relative to a benchmark.
- A risk-forecasting factor model can decompose the risk in one of four ways: (1) total risk decomposition, (2) systematic-residual risk decomposition, (3) active risk decomposition, and (4) active systematic-active residual risk decomposition.
- Given the risk factors and their factor loadings, a portfolio's risk exposure profile can be quantified and controlled using a risk-forecasting factor model.
- A risk-forecasting model can be used to (1) assess the risk exposure of a portfolio, (2) control risk against a stock market index, and (3) tilt a portfolio based on a portfolio manager's view.

17

Modeling Asset Price Dynamics

Our discussion so far has focused mostly on models that take a myopic view. For example, the capital asset pricing model (CAPM) and the arbitrage pricing theory (APT) consider events that happen one time period ahead of the present time, where the length of the time period is determined by the investor. In practice, asset prices are subject to ever-present uncertainty, and fluctuate continuously. Investors' decisions are updated dynamically. The volatility of asset prices is accounted for in market participants' views of the fair prices to pay for financial securities that depend on the realizations of continuing uncertainties. Therefore, we need to introduce a new apparatus that can handle asset dynamics and volatility over time. The roots of the techniques described in this chapter are in physics and the other natural sciences. They were first applied in finance at the beginning of the twentieth century and have represented the foundations of asset pricing ever since.

The dynamics of price processes in discrete time increments are typically described by two kinds of models: *trees* (such as *binomial trees*) and *random walks*. When the time increment used to model the asset price dynamics becomes infinitely small, we talk about *stochastic processes in continuous time*. We will discuss the special notation and terminology associated with stochastic processes later in this chapter; however, our focus in this book in general will be on interpretation and simulation of processes in discrete time.

This chapter introduces the fundamentals of these models and provides examples of how they can be used in practice. Specifically, we will discuss arithmetic random walks, geometric random walks, mean reverting walks, and more complex combinations of walks.

Let us first introduce some definitions and notation. A financial *time series* is a sequence of observations of the values of a financial variable, such as an asset price (index level) or asset (index) returns, over time. Exhibit 17.1 shows an example of a time series consisting of weekly observations of the S&P 500 price level over a period of five years (August 19, 2005, to August 19, 2009). This period included the Global Financial Crisis and the Great Recession.

When we describe a time series, we talk about its drift and volatility. The term *drift* indicates the direction of any observable trend in the time series. In the example in exhibit 17.1, it appears that the time series has a positive drift upward from August 2005 until about the middle of 2007, as the level of prices appears to have been generally increasing over that time period. From the middle of 2007 until the beginning of 2009, there is a negative drift. The

Exhibit 17.1
S&P 500 index level between August 19, 2005, and August 19, 2009. Data obtained from Dow Jones Factiva.

volatility was smaller (the time series was less "squiggly") from August 2005 until about the middle of 2007, but it increased dramatically between the middle of 2007 and the beginning of 2009.

We also are usually interested in whether the volatility increases when the price level increases, decreases when the price level increases, or remains constant independent of the current price level. In this example, the volatility was lower when the price level was increasing and higher when the price level was decreasing. Finally, we talk about the *continuity* of the time series—is the time series smooth, or are there jumps whose magnitude appears to be large relative to the price movements the rest of the time? From August 2005 until about the middle of 2007, the time series is quite smooth. However, some dramatic drops in price levels can be observed between the middle of 2007 and the beginning of 2009—most notably in the fall of 2008.

For the remainder of the chapter, we will use the following notation:

- S_t is the value of the underlying variable (price, interest rate, index level) at time t.
- S_{t+1} is the value of the underlying variable (price, interest rate) at time $t+1$.
- ω_t is a random error term observed at time t. (For the applications in this chapter, it will follow a normal distribution, with mean equal to 0 and standard deviation equal to σ.)
- ε_t is a realization of a normal random variable with mean equal to 0 and standard deviation equal to 1 at time t. (We will use this in the context of modeling the random error term.)

17.1 Binomial Trees

We introduced *binomial trees* (also called *binomial lattices*) earlier in this book, in section 6.6.1, in the context of formulating dynamic programming problems. They provide a natural way to model the dynamics of a random process over time. The initial value of security S_0 (at time 0) is known. The length of a time period, Δt, is specified before the tree is built.[1]

1. In general, we use the symbol Δ to denote *difference*. The notation Δt, therefore, means time difference; that is, length of one time period.

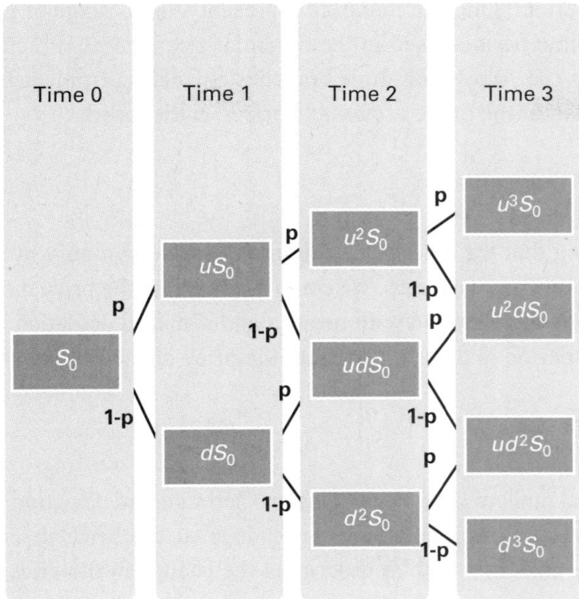

Exhibit 17.2
Example of a binomial tree.

The binomial tree model assumes that during the next time period, only two values are possible for the price; that is, the price may go up with probability p or down with probability $(1-p)$. Usually, these values are represented as multiples of the price at the beginning of the period. The factor u is used for an up movement, and d is used for a down movement. For example, the two prices at the end of the first time period are $u \cdot S_0$ and $d \cdot S_0$. If the tree is recombining, there will be three possible prices at the end of the second time period: $u^2 \cdot S_0$, $u \cdot d \cdot S_0$, and $d^2 \cdot S_0$. Proceeding in a similar manner, we can build the tree shown in exhibit 17.2.

The binomial tree model may appear simple because, given the current price, it only allows for two possibilities for the price at each time period. However, if the length of the time period is small, it is possible to represent a wide range of values for the price after only a few steps. To see this, notice that each step in the tree can be thought of as a Bernoulli trial[2]—it is a success with probability p and a failure with probability $(1-p)$. (The definitions of *success* and *failure* here are arbitrary because a price increase is not always desirable, but we define them in this way for the sake of this example.) After n steps, each value for the price will be reached by realizing k successes and $(n-k)$ failures, where k is a number between 0 and n. The probability of reaching each value for the price after n steps will be[3]

$$P(k \text{ successes}) = \frac{n!}{k!(n-k)!} p^k (1-p)^{n-k}$$

As exhibit 3.5 illustrated, for large values of n, the shape of the binomial distribution becomes more and more symmetric, and looks like a continuum. In fact, it approximates

2. In other words, it is generated from a Bernoulli distribution (see section 3.2).

3. See section 3.3.

the normal distribution.[4] One can therefore represent a large range of values for the price if the number of time periods used in the binomial tree is large. Practitioners often also use trinomial trees (i.e., trees with three branches emanating from each node) to obtain a better representation of the range of possible prices in the future.

17.2 Arithmetic Random Walks

Instead of assuming that the asset price can move up or down only by a certain multiple with a given probability at each step, we could assume that the price moves by an amount that follows a normal distribution with mean μ and standard deviation σ. In other words, the price for each period is determined from the price of the previous period by the following equation:

$$S_{t+1} = S_t + \mu + \tilde{\omega}_t \tag{17.1}$$

where $\tilde{\omega}_t$ is a normal random variable with mean 0 and standard deviation σ. We also assume that the random variable $\tilde{\omega}_t$ describing the change in the price in one time period is independent of the random variables describing the change in the price in any other time period.[5] A sequence of independent and identically distributed (i.i.d.) random variables $\tilde{\omega}_0, \ldots, \tilde{\omega}_t, \ldots$ with zero mean and finite variance σ^2 is sometimes referred to as *white noise.*

The movement of the price expressed by equation (17.1) is called an *arithmetic random walk with drift.* The drift term, μ, represents the average change in price over a single time period. Note that for every time period t, we can write the equation for the arithmetic random walk as

$$\begin{aligned}
S_t &= S_{t-1} + \mu + \tilde{\omega}_{t-1} \\
&= (S_{t-2} + \mu + \tilde{\omega}_{t-2}) + \mu + \tilde{\omega}_{t-1} \\
&= (S_{t-3} + \mu + \tilde{\omega}_{t-2}) + 2 \cdot \mu + \tilde{\omega}_{t-1} + \tilde{\omega}_{t-2} \\
&= \cdots \\
&= S_0 + \mu \cdot t + \sum_{i=0}^{t-1} \tilde{\omega}_i.
\end{aligned}$$

Therefore, an arithmetic random walk can be thought of as a sum of two terms: a deterministic straight line $S_t = S_0 + \mu \cdot t$ and a sum of all past noise terms (see exhibit 17.3).

17.2.1 Simulation

The equation for the arithmetic random walk also can be expressed as

$$S_{t+1} = S_t + \mu + \sigma \cdot \tilde{\varepsilon}_t, \tag{17.2}$$

where $\tilde{\varepsilon}_t$ is a standard normal random variable.[6]

4. See section 3.4.

5. This is known as *the Markov property.* It implies that past prices are irrelevant for forecasting the future, and only the current value of the price is relevant for predicting the price in the next time period.

6. To show this, we need to mention that every normal distribution can be expressed in terms of the standard normal distribution. Namely, if $\tilde{\varepsilon}$ is a standard normal variable with mean 0 and standard deviation 1, and $\tilde{x}$ is a normal random variable with mean μ and standard deviation σ, we have

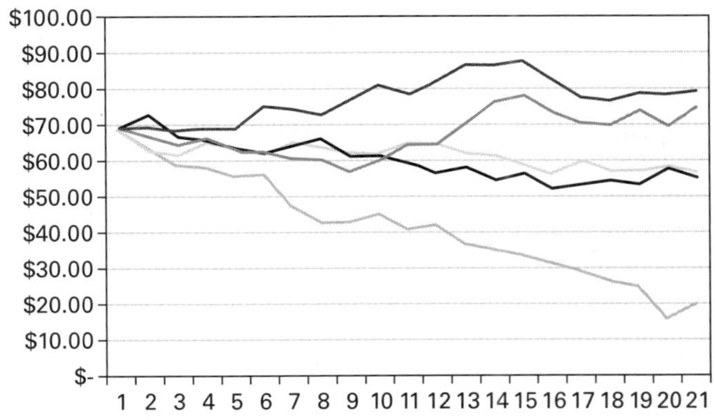

Exhibit 17.3
Five paths of an arithmetic random walk with $\mu = -0.1697$ and $\sigma = 3.1166$. See the **ARW** worksheet in **Ch17-RandomWalks.xlsx**, or the **RandomWalks** and **ARWPaths** Python and MATLAB files in the online appendices.

This equation makes it easy to generate paths for the arithmetic random walk by simulation. All we need is a way of generating the normal random variables $\tilde{\varepsilon}_t$. We start with an initial price S_0, which is known. To generate the price at the next time period, S_1, we add μ to S_0, simulate a normal random variable from a standard normal distribution, multiply it by σ, and add it to $S_0 + \mu$. At the next step (time period 2), we take the price at the time period 1 that we already generated, S_1, add μ to it, simulate a new random variable from a standard normal distribution, multiply it by σ, and add it to $S_1 + \mu$. We proceed in the same way until we generate the desired number of steps of the random walk. For example, given a current price S, in Microsoft Excel, the price for the next time period can be generated with the formula

$$S + \mu + \sigma * NORMINV(RAND(), 0, 1)$$

Similar formulas can be used in @RISK, MATLAB, and Python. (See this chapter's online appendix and accompanying files, such as **Ch17-RandomWalks.xlsx**.)

17.2.2 Parameter Estimation

To simulate paths of the arithmetic random walk, we need to have estimates of parameters μ and σ. We need to assume that these parameters remain constant over the time period of estimation. Note that the equation for the arithmetic random walk can be written as

$$S_{t+1} - S_t = \mu + \sigma \cdot \tilde{\varepsilon}_t. \tag{17.3}$$

Given a historical series of T prices for an asset, therefore, we can do the following to estimate μ and σ:

(continued)

$$\tilde{\varepsilon} = \frac{\tilde{x} - \mu}{\sigma} \text{(equivalently, } \tilde{x} = \sigma \cdot \tilde{\varepsilon} + \mu)$$

This is a property unique to the normal distribution—no other family of probability distributions can be transformed in the same way. In the context of the equation for the arithmetic random walk, we have a normal random variable $\tilde{\omega}_t$ with mean 0 and standard deviation σ. It can be expressed through a standard normal variable $\tilde{\varepsilon}_t$ as $\sigma \cdot \tilde{\varepsilon} + 0$.

1. Compute the price changes $S_{t+1} - S_t$ for each time period t, $t=0, \ldots, T-1$.
2. Estimate the drift of the arithmetic random walk, μ, as the average of all the price changes.
3. Estimate the volatility of the arithmetic random walk, σ, as the standard deviation of all the price changes.

(See this chapter's online appendix for the implementation of an example.)

An important point to remember is the units in which the parameters are estimated. If we are given time series in monthly increments, then the estimates of μ and σ that we will obtain through steps 1–3 will be for a monthly drift and monthly volatility, respectively. If we then need to simulate future paths for monthly observations, we can use the same μ and σ. However, if, for example, we need to simulate weekly observations, we will need to adjust μ and σ to account for the difference in the length of the time period. In general, the parameters should be stated as annual estimates. The annual estimates can then be adjusted for daily, weekly, monthly, and other increments.

17.2.3 Arithmetic Random Walk: Some Additional Facts

In general, if we use the arithmetic random walk model, any price in the future, S_t, can be expressed through the initial (known) price S_0 as

$$S_t = S_0 + \mu \cdot t + \sigma \sum_{i=0}^{t-1} \tilde{\varepsilon}_t. \tag{17.4}$$

The random variable corresponding to the sum of t independent normal random variables $\tilde{\varepsilon}_0, \ldots, \tilde{\varepsilon}_{t-1}$ is a normal random variable with a mean equal to the sum of the means and standard deviation equal to the square root of the sum of variances. Since $\tilde{\varepsilon}_0, \ldots, \tilde{\varepsilon}_{t-1}$ are independent standard normal variables, their sum is a normal variable with mean 0 and a standard deviation equal to

$$\sqrt{\underbrace{1 + \cdots + 1}_{t \text{ times}}} = \sqrt{t}.$$

Therefore, we can have a closed-form expression for computing the asset price at time t given the asset price at time 0:

$$S_t = S_0 + \mu \cdot t + \sigma \cdot \sqrt{t} \cdot \tilde{\varepsilon} \tag{17.5}$$

where $\tilde{\varepsilon}$ is a standard normal random variable.

Based on the discussion so far in this section, we can state the following observations about the arithmetic random walk:

- The arithmetic random walk has constant drift μ and volatility.
- At every time period, the change in price is normally distributed, on average equal to μ, with a standard deviation of σ.
- The overall noise in an arithmetic random walk never decays. The price change over t time periods is distributed as a normal distribution with mean equal to $\mu \cdot t$ and standard deviation equal to $\sigma\sqrt{t}$. That is why the phrase "The uncertainty grows with the square root of time" is often used in industry.
- Prices that follow an arithmetic random walk meander around a straight line $S_t = S_0 + \mu \cdot t$. They may depart from the line and then cross it again.

- Because the distribution of future prices is normal, we can theoretically find the probability that the future price at any time will be within a given range.
- Because the distribution of future prices is normal, future prices can theoretically take infinitely large or infinitely small values. Thus, they can be negative, which is an undesirable consequence of using the model.

Asset prices cannot be negative, of course. In practice, the probability of the price becoming negative can be made quite small, as long as the drift and the volatility parameters are selected carefully. However, the possibility of generating negative prices with the arithmetic random walk model is real.

Another problem with the assumptions underlying the arithmetic random walk is that the change in the asset price is drawn from the same random probability distribution, independent of the current level of the prices. A more natural model assumes that the parameters of the random probability distribution for the change in the asset price vary depending on the current price level. For example, a \$1 change in a stock price is more likely when the stock price is \$100 than when it is \$4. Empirical studies confirm that over time, asset prices tend to grow, as do fluctuations. Only returns appear to remain stationary; that is, to follow the same probability distribution over time. A more realistic model for asset prices, therefore, may be that *returns* are an i.i.d. sequence. We will describe such a model in the next section.

17.3 Geometric Random Walks

Consider the following model:

$$r_t = \mu + \sigma \cdot \tilde{\varepsilon}_t, \tag{17.6}$$

where $\tilde{\varepsilon}_0, \dots, \tilde{\varepsilon}_t$ is a sequence of independent normal variables and r_t, the return, is computed as[7]

$$r_t = \frac{S_{t+1} - S_t}{S_t}. \tag{17.7}$$

Returns are therefore normally distributed, and the return over each interval of length 1 has mean μ and standard deviation σ. How can we express future prices if returns are determined by equations (17.6) and (17.7)?

Suppose that we know the price at time t, S_t. The price at time $t+1$ can be written as

$$\begin{aligned} S_{t+1} &= S_t \cdot \frac{S_{t+1}}{S_t} \\ &= S_t \cdot \left(\frac{S_t}{S_t} + \frac{S_{t+1} - S_t}{S_t} \right) \\ &= S_t \cdot \left(1 + \frac{S_{t+1} - S_t}{S_t} \right) \\ &= S_t \cdot (1 + \tilde{r}_t) \\ &= S_t + \mu \cdot S_t + \sigma \cdot S_t \cdot \tilde{\varepsilon}_t \end{aligned} \tag{17.8}$$

7. See chapter 2.

Equation (17.8) is very similar to equation (17.5), except that the price from the previous time period appears as a factor in all the terms.

The equation for the geometric random walk makes it clear how paths for the geometric random walk can be generated. As in the case of the arithmetic random walk, all we need is a way of generating the normal random variables $\tilde{\varepsilon}_t$. We start with an initial price S_0, which is known. To generate the price at the next time period, S_1, we add $\mu \cdot S_0$ to S_0, simulate a normal random variable from a standard normal distribution, multiply it by σ and S_0, and add it to $S_0 + \mu \cdot S_0$. At the next step (time period 2), we use the price at time period 1 that we already generated, S_1, add $\mu \cdot S_1$, simulate a new random variable from a standard normal distribution, multiply it by σ and S_1, and add it to $S_1 + \mu \cdot S_1$. We proceed in the same way until we generate the desired number of steps of the geometric random walk. Given a current price S, in Excel, the price for the next time period can be generated with the formula

$$S + \mu{*}S + \sigma{*}S{*}\ NORMINV\,(RAND(), 0, 1)$$

A similar formula can be used with @RISK, MATLAB, and Python.

We can express the price at any time t in terms of the known initial price S_0. Note that we can write the price at time t as

$$S_t = S_0 \cdot \frac{S_1}{S_0} \cdot \cdots \cdot \frac{S_{t-1}}{S_{t-2}} \cdot \frac{S_t}{S_{t-1}}.$$

Therefore,

$$S_t = S_0 \cdot (1 + \tilde{r}_0) \cdot \cdots \cdot (1 + \tilde{r}_{t-1}).$$

In the case of arithmetic random walk, we determined that the price at any time period follows a normal distribution. That is, if we know the starting price S_0, then the price at any time period could be obtained by adding a sum of independent normal random variables to a constant term and S_0. The sum of independent normal random variables is a normal random variable itself. In the equation for the geometric random walk, each of the terms $(1 + \tilde{r}_0), \ldots, (1 + \tilde{r}_{t-1})$ is a normal random variable as well (it is the sum of a normal random variable and a constant). However, these terms are multiplied together. The product of normal random variables is not a normal random variable, which means we cannot have a nice closed-form expression for computing the price S_t based on S_0.

To avoid this problem, let us consider the logarithm of prices.[8] If we take natural logarithms of both sides of the equation for S_t, we get

$$\begin{aligned}\ln(S_t) &= \ln(S_0 \cdot (1 + \tilde{r}_0)(\cdot \cdots \cdot (1 + \tilde{r}_{t-1}))\\ &= \ln(S_0) + \ln(1 + \tilde{r}_0) + \cdots + \ln(1 + \tilde{r}_{t-1}).\end{aligned}$$

Log returns are in fact differences between log prices. To see this, recall the definition of the log return from chapter 2:

8. Unless otherwise specified, we use the term *logarithm* to refer to the natural logarithm; that is, the logarithm of base e. In many references, as well as software packages such as Excel, the abbreviation used for the natural logarithm is `ln`.

$$\ln(1+r_t) = \ln\left(1+\frac{S_{t+1}-S_t}{S_t}\right)$$
$$= \ln\left(\frac{S_{t+1}}{S_t}\right)$$
$$= \ln(S_{t+1}) - \ln(S_t).$$

Now assume that log returns (not returns) are independent and follow a normal distribution with mean μ and standard deviation σ:

$$\ln(1+\tilde{r}_t) = \ln(S_{t+1}) - \ln(S_t) = \mu + \sigma \cdot \tilde{\varepsilon}_t$$

As a sum of independent normal variables, the expression

$$\ln(S_0) + \ln(1+\tilde{r}_0) + \cdots + \ln(1+\tilde{r}_{t-1})$$

is also normally distributed. This means that $\ln(S_t)$ is normally distributed; that is, S_t is a lognormal random variable.[9,10]

In fact, similar to the case of an arithmetic random walk, we can compute a closed-form expression for the price S_t given S_0 as follows:

$$\ln(S_t) = \ln(S_0) + \left(\mu - \frac{1}{2}\cdot\sigma^2\right)\cdot t + \sigma\cdot\sqrt{t}\cdot\tilde{\varepsilon} \tag{17.9}$$

or, equivalently,

$$S_t = S_0 \cdot e^{\left(\mu - \frac{1}{2}\cdot\sigma^2\right)\cdot t + \sigma\cdot\sqrt{t}\cdot\tilde{\varepsilon}}$$

where $\tilde{\varepsilon}$ is a standard normal variable.

Notice that the only inconsistency with the formula for the arithmetic random walk is the presence of the extra term

$$\left(-\frac{1}{2}\cdot\sigma^2\right)\cdot t$$

in the drift term

$$\left(\mu - \frac{1}{2}\cdot\sigma^2\right)\cdot t.$$

9. See chapter 3, where we stated that if $\tilde{Y}$ is a normal random variable, then the random variable $\tilde{X} = e^{\tilde{Y}}$ is lognormal. In this case, $\log(S_t)$ is a normal random variable. Therefore, $e^{\ln(S_t)}$ (i.e., S_t) is lognormally distributed.

10. In general, if the logarithm of a random variable is normally distributed, then the random variable itself follows a lognormal distribution. The lognormal distribution has a very convenient property, which is that products of independent lognormal random variables are themselves lognormal random variables. This is another way to say that S_t is a lognormal random variable given S_0; it is a product of lognormal random variables, scaled by a constant (S_0) as follows:

$$S_t = (1+\tilde{r}_{t-1})\ldots(1+\tilde{r}_0)\cdot S_0$$

Why is there an adjustment of half of the variance in the expected drift? In general, if $\tilde{Y}$ is a normal random variable with mean μ and variance σ^2, then the random variable, which is an exponential of the normal random variable $\tilde{Y}$, $\tilde{X} = e^{\tilde{Y}}$, has the mean

$$E[\tilde{X}] = e^{\mu + \frac{1}{2}\cdot\sigma^2}.$$

At first, this seems counterintuitive—why is the expected value of $\tilde{X}$ not

$$E[\tilde{X}] = e^{\mu}?$$

As we discussed in chapter 3, the expected value of a linear function of a random variable is a linear function of the expected value of the random variable. For example, if a is a constant, then

$$E[a \cdot \tilde{Y}] = a \cdot E[\tilde{Y}].$$

However, determining the expected value of a nonlinear function of a random variable (in particular, the exponential function, which is the function that we are using here) is not as trivial. For example, there is a well-known relationship, the *Jensen inequality*, which states that the expected value of a convex function of a random variable is less than the value of the function at the expected value of the random variable.

In our example, $\tilde{X}$ is a lognormal random variable, so its probability distribution has the shape shown in exhibit 3.15. The random variable $\tilde{X}$ cannot take values less than 0. Since its variance is related to the variance of the normal random variable $\tilde{Y}$, as the variance σ^2 of $\tilde{Y}$ increases, the distribution of $\tilde{X}$ will spread out in the upward direction. This means that the mean of the lognormal variable $\tilde{X}$ will increase not only as the mean of the normal variable $\tilde{Y}$, μ, increases, but also as $\tilde{Y}$*'s* variance, σ^2, increases. In the context of the geometric random walk, $\tilde{Y}$ represents the normally distributed log returns, and $\tilde{X}$ is in fact the factor by which the asset price from the previous period is multiplied to generate the asset price in the next time period. To make sure that the geometric random process grows exponentially at the average rate μ, we need to subtract a term (that term turns out to be $\sigma^2/2$), which will correct the bias.

Specifically, suppose that we know the price at time t, S_t. We have

$$\ln(S_{t+1}) = \ln(S_t) + \ln(1 + \tilde{r}_t)$$

that is,

$$S_{t+1} = S_t \cdot e^{\ln(1+\tilde{r}_t)}$$

Note that we are explicitly assuming a *multiplicative model* for asset prices here—the price in the next time period is obtained by multiplying the price from the previous time period by a random factor. In the case of an arithmetic random walk discussed in section 17.2, we had an *additive model*—a random shock was added to the asset price from the previous time period.

If the log return $\log(1 + \tilde{r})$ is normally distributed with mean μ and standard deviation σ, then the expected value of

$$e^{\ln(1+\tilde{r})}$$

is

$$e^{\mu+\frac{1}{2}\cdot\sigma^2}.$$

and hence

$$E[S_{t+1}] = S_t \cdot e^{\mu+\frac{1}{2}\cdot\sigma^2}. \tag{17.10}$$

To make sure that the geometric random walk process grows exponentially at an average rate μ rather than $(\mu + 0.5 \cdot \sigma^2)$, we need to subtract the term $0.5 \cdot \sigma^2$ when we generate the future price via this process. This argument can be extended to determining prices for more than one time period ahead of the present time.

In section 17.6, we will understand better why equation (17.10) holds.

17.3.1 Simulation

It is easy to see that future prices can be simulated based on the initial price S_0. In general, for a current price of S, in Excel, the price t periods from now can be generated as

$$S * \exp((\mu - 0.5 * \sigma\hat{}2) * t - \sigma * \sqrt{t} * NORMINV(RAND(),0,1))$$

(See also this chapter's online appendix and accompanying files.)

One might wonder whether this approach for simulating realizations of an asset price following a geometric random walk is equivalent to the simulation approach mentioned earlier in this section, which is based on the discrete version of the equation for a random walk. The two approaches are different (e.g., the approach based on the discrete version of the equation for the geometric random walk does not produce the expected lognormal price distribution), but it can be shown that the differences in the two simulation approaches tend to cancel over many steps.

17.3.2 Parameter Estimation

To simulate paths of the geometric random walk, we need to have estimates of parameters μ and σ. The implicit assumption here, of course, is that these parameters remain constant over the time period of estimation. (We will discuss how to incorporate considerations for changes in volatility in section 17.5.) Note that the equation for the geometric random walk can be written as

$$\ln(S_{t+1}) - \ln(S_t) = \ln(1 + \tilde{r}_t).$$

Equivalently,

$$\log\left(\frac{S_{t+1}}{S_t}\right) = \mu + \sigma \cdot \tilde{\varepsilon}_t.$$

Given a historical series of T prices for an asset, therefore, we can do the following to estimate μ and σ:

1. Compute $\ln(S_{t+1}/S_t)$ for each time period t, $t = 0, \ldots, T-1$.
2. Estimate the volatility of the geometric random walk, σ, as the standard deviation of all $\ln(S_{t+1}/S_t)$.

3. Estimate for the drift of the arithmetic random walk, μ, as the average of all $\ln(S_{t+1}/S_t)$, plus half of the standard deviation squared.

Note that

$$\log\left(\frac{S_{t+1}}{S_t}\right) = \log\left(1 + \frac{S_{t+1} - S_t}{S_t}\right) = \log(1 + \tilde{r}_t).$$

Therefore, if we are given data on returns rather than asset prices, we can compute $\ln(1 + \tilde{r}_t)$ and use the result to replace $\ln(S_{t+1}/S_t)$ in steps 1–3.

17.3.3 Geometric Random Walk: Some Additional Facts

To summarize, the geometric random walk has several important characteristics:

- It is a multiplicative model; that is, the price at the next time period is a multiple of a random term and the price from the previous time period.
- It has constant drift μ and volatility σ. At every time period, the *percentage change* in price is normally distributed; on average, it is equal to μ, with a standard deviation of σ.
- The overall noise in a geometric random walk never decays. The *percentage price change* over t time periods is distributed as a normal distribution, with mean equal to $\mu \cdot t$ and standard deviation equal to $\sigma\sqrt{t}$.
- The exact distribution of the future price knowing the initial price can be found. The price at time t is lognormally distributed with specific probability distribution parameters.
- Prices that follow a geometric random walk in continuous time never become negative.

The geometric random walk model is not perfect. However, its computational simplicity makes the geometric random walk and its variations the most widely used processes for modeling asset prices. The geometric random walk defined with log returns never becomes negative because future prices are always a multiple of the initial stock price and a positive term (see exhibit 17.4). In addition, observed historical stock prices can be quite close to lognormal.

It is important to note that the assumption that log returns are normal is not required to justify the lognormal model for prices. If the distribution of log returns is nonnormal but the log returns are i.i.d. with finite variance, the sum of the log returns is asymptotically normal.[11] Stated differently, the log return process is approximately normal if we consider changes over sufficiently long periods of time.

Price processes, however, are not always geometric random walks, even asymptotically. A very important assumption for the geometric random walk is that price increments are independently distributed; if the time series exhibits autocorrelation, the geometric random walk does not represent it well. We will see some models that incorporate considerations for autocorrelation and other factors later in this chapter.

11. This is based on a version of the Central Limit Theorem (see chapter 4).

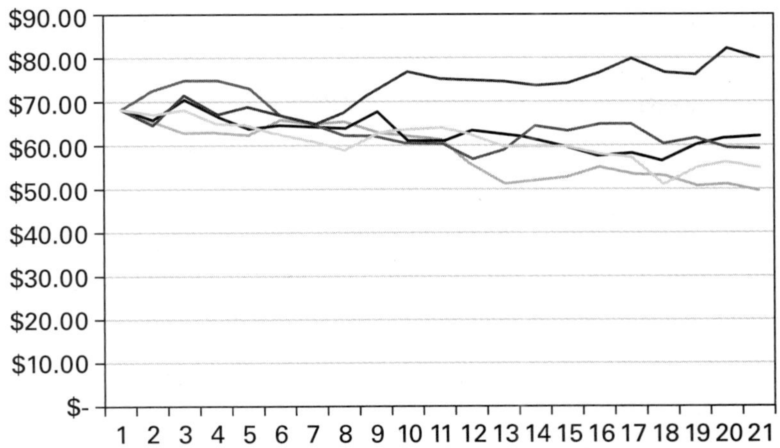

Exhibit 17.4
Five paths of a geometric random walk with $\mu = -0.0014$ and $\sigma = 0.0411$. Note that although the drift is slightly negative, it is still possible to generate paths that generally increase over time. See the worksheet **GRW** in **Ch17-RandomWalks.xlsx**, or the **RandomWalks** and **GRWPaths** files in Python and MATLAB.

17.4 Mean Reversion

The geometric random walk provides the foundation for modeling the dynamics for asset prices of many different securities, including stock prices. In some cases, however, it is not justified to assume that asset prices evolve with a particular drift or can deviate arbitrarily far from a representative value. Interest rates, exchange rates, and the prices of some commodities are examples of when the geometric random walk does not provide a good representation over the long term. For example, if the price of copper becomes high, copper mines would increase production to maximize profits. This would increase the supply of copper in the market, therefore decreasing the price of copper and returning it to some equilibrium level. Consumer demand plays a role as well—if the price of copper becomes too high, consumers may look for substitutes, which would return the price of copper back to its equilibrium level.

Exhibit 17.5 illustrates the behavior of the one-year U.S. Treasury bill yield from the beginning of January 1962 through the end of July 2009. It can be observed that even though the variability of Treasury bill rates has changed over time, there is a long-term average level of interest rates to which they return after deviating up or down. This behavior is known as *mean reversion* (MR).

The simplest MR model is like an arithmetic random walk, but the means of the increments change depending on the current price level. The price dynamics are represented by the equation

$$S_{t+1} = S_t + \kappa \cdot (\mu - S_t) + \sigma \cdot \tilde{\varepsilon}_t,$$

where $\tilde{\varepsilon}_t$ is a standard normal random variable. Parameter κ is a nonnegative number that represents the *speed of adjustment* of the mean-reverting process—the larger its magnitude, the faster the process returns to its long-term mean. Parameter μ is the long-term

Exhibit 17.5
Weekly data on 1-year Treasury yield rates, January 5, 1962, to July 31, 2009.

mean of the process. When the current price S_t is lower than the long-term mean μ, the term $(\mu - S_t)$ is positive. Hence, on average, there will be an upward adjustment to obtain the value of the price in the next time period, S_{t+1}. We add a positive number, $\kappa \cdot (\mu - S_t)$, to the current price current price S_t. By contrast, if the current price S_t is higher than the long-term mean μ, the term $(\mu - S_t)$ is negative. Hence, on average, there will be a downward adjustment to obtain the value of the price in the next time period, S_{t+1}. We add a negative number, $\kappa \cdot (\mu - S_t)$, to the current price S_t. Thus, the mean-reverting process will behave in the way that we desire—if the price becomes lower or higher than the long-term mean, it will be returned to the long-term mean.

In the case of arithmetic and geometric random walks, the volatility of the process increases over time. The volatility for one step of the mean-reverting process is σ^2; however, as the number of steps increases, the volatility peaks at

$$\frac{\sigma^2}{\kappa \cdot (2 - \kappa)}.$$

In continuous time, this basic mean-reversion process is called the *Ornstein-Uhlenbeck process* (see section 17.5 for more information). It is widely used when modeling interest rates and exchange rates in the context of computing bond prices and prices of more complex fixed-income securities. When used in the context of modeling interest rates, this simple mean-reversion process is also referred to as the *Vasicek model*.[12]

The mean-reversion process suffers from some of the disadvantages of the arithmetic random walk—for example, it can technically become negative. However, if the long-run mean is positive and the speed of mean reversion is large relative to the volatility, the price will be pulled back to the mean quickly if it becomes negative. Exhibit 17.6 contains an example of five paths generated from a mean-reverting process.

12. See Vasicek (1977).

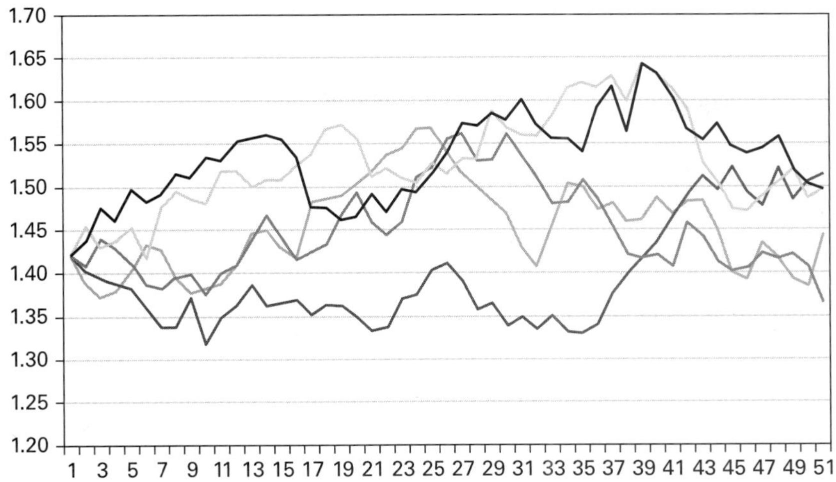

Exhibit 17.6
Five paths with 50 steps each of a mean-reverting process with $\mu = 1.4404$, $\kappa = 0.0347$, and $\sigma = 0.0248$. See the worksheet **MR** in **Ch17-RandomWalks.xlsx**, or the **MRPaths** file in the online appendices.

17.4.1 Simulation

The formula for the mean-reverting process makes it clear how paths for the mean-reverting random walk can be generated with software. Given a current price S, in Excel, the price for the next time period can be generated with the formula

$$S + \kappa^* \ (\mu - S) + \sigma^* \ NORMINV\,(RAND(), 0{,}1).$$

(See also this chapter's online appendices and accompanying model files.)

17.4.2 Parameter Estimation

To simulate paths of the geometric random walk, we need to have estimates of the parameters (κ, μ, and σ) of the mean-reverting process. Again, we assume that these parameters remain constant over the time period of estimation. The equation for the mean-reverting process can be written as

$$S_{t+1} - S_t = \kappa \cdot (\mu - S_t) + \sigma \cdot \tilde{\varepsilon}_t$$

or, equivalently,

$$S_{t+1} - S_t = \kappa \cdot \mu - \kappa \cdot S_t + \sigma \cdot \tilde{\varepsilon}_t \tag{17.11}$$

This equation has the characteristics of a linear regression model, with the absolute price change ($S_{t+1} - S_t$) as the response variable and S_t as the explanatory variable. Given a historical series of T prices for an asset, therefore, we can do the following to estimate κ, μ, and σ:

1. Compute the price changes ($S_{t+1} - S_t$) for each time period t, $t = 0, \ldots, T-1$.
2. Run a linear regression with ($S_{t+1} - S_t$) as the response variable and S_t as the explanatory variable. For example, in Excel, click the **Data** tab, click **Data Analysis**, and select **Regression** from the Analysis Tools.

3. Verify that the estimates from the linear regression model are valid by doing the following:

   a. Plot the values of S_t versus $(S_{t+1} - S_t)$. The points in the scatterplot should approximately vary around a straight line, with no visible cyclical or other patterns.

   b. The p-value for the coefficient in front of the explanatory variable S_t should be small, preferably less than 0.05.

4. An estimate for the speed of adjustment of the mean-reversion process, κ, can be obtained as the negative of the coefficient in front of S_t. Since the speed of adjustment cannot be a negative number, if the coefficient in front of S_t is positive, the regression model cannot be used for estimating the parameters of the mean reverting process.

5. An estimate for the long-term mean of the mean-reverting process, μ, can be obtained as the ratio of the intercept term estimated from the regression and the slope coefficient in front of S_t (if that slope coefficient is valid; that is, negative and with low p-value).

6. An estimate for the volatility of the mean-reverting process, σ, can be obtained as the standard error of estimate in the regression.[13]

(See this chapter's online appendices and accompanying model for implementation of an example.)

17.4.3 The Cox-Ingersoll-Ross Model for Interest Rates Dynamics

More advanced mean-reversion processes have been used to avoid the pitfalls of the simple mean-reversion process. A commonly used model for interest rates, called the *Cox-Ingersoll-Ross (CIR) model*,[14] includes the square root of the current asset price as a factor in the random term of the mean reversion, where we use r to denote the short-term interest rate:

$$r_{t+1} = r_t + \kappa \cdot (\mu - r_t) + \sigma \cdot \sqrt{r_t} \cdot \tilde{\varepsilon}_t$$

The effect is that if the current interest rate is low, the variability of the process is relatively low, thus reducing the probability that the mean-reverting random walk will become negative. When the current interest rate is high, the variability of the process can afford to be higher without the risk that the interest rate will become negative. Future interest rates are easy to simulate with this model. Historically, the appeal of this model has been that a closed-form solution for the future interest rates is available, knowing that the current interest rate can be found. It turns out that

$$r_1 = r_0 + \frac{(1 - e^{-\kappa \cdot t}) \cdot \sigma^2}{2 \cdot \kappa} \cdot \tilde{\eta}$$

where $\tilde{\eta}$ has a chi-square distribution with $4 \cdot \kappa \cdot \mu / \sigma^2$ degrees of freedom and a noncentrality parameter[15]

13. The standard error of estimate in the regression measures the standard deviation of the points around the regression line.

14. See Cox, Ingersoll, and Ross (1985).

15. See chapter 3 for a definition of the chi-square random variable.

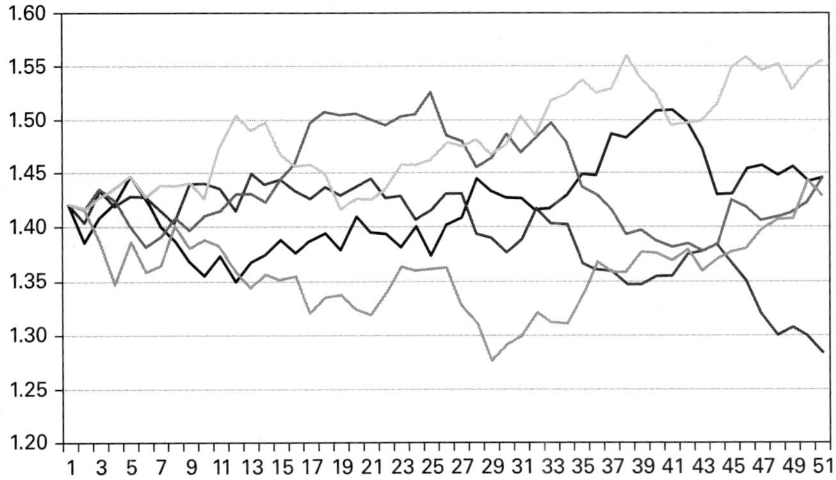

Exhibit 17.7
Five paths with 50 steps each of a geometric mean-reverting process with $\mu = 1.4464$, $\kappa = 0.0253$, and $\sigma = 0.0177$. See the worksheet **GMR** in **Ch17-RandomWalks.xlsx**, or the **GMRPaths** file in the online appendices.

$$2 \cdot r_0 \cdot e^{-\kappa \cdot t} \cdot \frac{(1 - e^{-\kappa \cdot t}) \cdot \sigma^2}{2 \cdot \kappa}$$

It is worth noting that while the random processes described in previous sections are used for modeling stock and commodity prices, they cannot be directly applied to modeling bond prices. The prices of fixed-income securities, such as bonds, evolve in a substantially more complex fashion than the evolution of stock or commodity prices described in this chapter. In some cases, such as in the case of the CIR model, there is a closed-form formula for bond prices based on the assumptions for the process, followed by the short-term interest rate. This enables us to generate the entire yield curve[16] and calculate the price of a fixed-income security tied to these interest rates.

17.4.4 Geometric Mean Reversion

A more advanced mean-reversion model that bears some similarity to the geometric random walk is the *geometric mean reversion* (GMR) *model*:[17]

$$S_{t+1} = S_t + \kappa \cdot (\mu - S_t) \cdot S_t + \sigma \cdot S_t \cdot \tilde{\varepsilon}_t \qquad (17.12)$$

The intuition behind this model is like the intuition behind the discrete version of the geometric random walk—the variability of the process changes with the current level of the price, and we think of the change in price as a percentage change (roughly) rather than an absolute change. However, the GMR model allows for incorporating mean reversion. Exhibit 17.7 contains an example of five paths generated with a geometric mean-reversion model.

Even though it is difficult to estimate the future price from this model analytically, it is easy to simulate. As before, $\tilde{\varepsilon}_t$ is a standard normal random variable, which can be

16. See chapter 2 for a definition of *yield* and *yield curve*.

17. This is a special case of the mean reversion model $S_{t+1} = S_t + \kappa \cdot (\mu - S_t) \cdot S_t + \sigma \cdot S_t^{\gamma} \cdot \tilde{\varepsilon}_t$, where parameter γ is selected in advance. The most used model has $\gamma = 1$.

generated with standard commands in Excel, @RISK, MATLAB, or Python. Given the current price S, in Excel, the price for the next time period can be generated with the formula

$$S+\kappa^*(\mu-S)^*\ S+\sigma^*S^*\ NORMINV(RAND(), 0, 1).$$

We can use a series of T observations to estimate the parameters κ, μ, and σ that will be used in the simulation. Assume that the parameters of the geometric mean reversion remain constant during the time period of estimation.

Note that the equation for the geometric mean reversion can be written as

$$\frac{S_{t+1}-S_t}{S_t}=\kappa\cdot(\mu-S_t)+\sigma\cdot\tilde{\varepsilon}_t$$

or, equivalently, as

$$\frac{S_{t+1}-S_t}{S_t}=\kappa\cdot\mu-\kappa\cdot S_t+\sigma\cdot\tilde{\varepsilon}_t$$

Again, this equation bears characteristics of a linear regression model, with the percentage price change $(S_{t+1}-S_t)/S_t$ as the response variable, and S_t as the explanatory variable. Given a series of T asset prices, therefore, we can do the following to estimate κ, μ, and σ:

1. Compute the percentage price changes $(S_{t+1}-S_t)/S_t$ for each time period t, $t=0, \ldots, T-1$.
2. Run a linear regression with $(S_{t+1}-S_t)/S_t$ as the response variable and S_t as the explanatory variable. In Excel, click the **Data** tab, click **Data Analysis,** and then select **Regression** from the Analysis Tools.
3. Verify that the estimates from the linear regression model are valid by doing the following:
   a. Plot the values of S_t versus $(S_{t+1}-S_t)/S_t$. The points in the scatterplot should approximately vary around a straight line, with no visible cyclical or other patterns.
   b. The p-value for the coefficient in front of the explanatory variable S_t should be small (preferably less than 0.05).
4. An estimate for the speed of adjustment of the mean-reverting process, κ, can be obtained as the negative of the coefficient in front of S_t. Since the speed of adjustment cannot be a negative number, if the coefficient in front of S_t is positive, the regression model cannot be used for estimating the parameters of the geometric mean-reverting process.
5. An estimate for the long-term mean of the mean-reverting process, μ, can be obtained as the ratio of the intercept term estimated from the regression and the slope coefficient in front of S_t (if that slope coefficient is valid; that is, negative and with low p-value).
6. An estimate for the volatility of the mean-reverting process, σ, can be obtained as the standard error of estimate in the regression.[18]

18. As explained earlier in this chapter, the standard error of estimate in the regression measures the average variability of the points around the line.

(See this chapter's online appendices and accompanying files for implementation of an example.)

17.5 Advanced Random Walk Models

The models described so far in this chapter provide building blocks for representing the asset price dynamics. However, observed real-world asset price dynamics has features that cannot be incorporated into these basic models. For example, asset prices exhibit correlation—both with each other and with themselves over time. Their volatility typically cannot be assumed constant. This section reviews several techniques for making asset price models more realistic depending on observed price behavior.

17.5.1 Correlated Random Walks

So far, we have discussed models for asset prices that assume that the dynamic processes for the prices of different assets evolve independent of each other. This is an unrealistic assumption—it is expected that market conditions and other factors will have an impact on the prices of groups of assets simultaneously. For example, it is likely that stock prices for companies in the oil industry will generally move together, as will stock prices for companies in the telecommunications industry.

The argument that asset prices are codependent has theoretical and empirical foundations as well. If asset prices were independent random walks, then large portfolios would be fully diversified, would have no variability, and, therefore, would be completely deterministic. Empirically, this is not the case. Even large aggregates of stock prices, such as the S&P 500, exhibit random behavior. If we assume that log returns are jointly normally distributed, then their dependencies can be represented through the covariance matrix (equivalently, through the correlation matrix).[19]

Let us give an example of how one can model two correlated stock prices assumed to follow geometric random walks. Suppose that we are given two series of T observations for each observed asset prices for stock 1 and stock 2. We follow steps 1 and 2 from section 17.3.2 to estimate the drifts and volatilities for the two processes. To estimate the correlation structure, we find the correlation between

$$\ln\left(\frac{S_{t+1}^{(1)}}{S_t^{(1)}}\right)$$

and

$$\ln\left(\frac{S_{t+1}^{(2)}}{S_t^{(2)}}\right)$$

19. Recall from chapter 3 that covariance and correlation are, in general, not equivalent with dependence of random variables. Covariance and correlation measure only the strength of linear dependence between two random variables. However, in the case of a multivariate normal distribution, covariance and correlation are sufficient to represent dependence.

where the indices (1) and (2) correspond to the stock number. In Excel, the correlation between two data series can be computed with the function

CORREL(Arrayl, Array2)

for two vertical arrays, Arrayl and Array2.

This correlation can then be incorporated into the simulation. Excel cannot generate correlated normal random variables without special add-ins, but software like @RISK, MATLAB, and Python have functions for it. For example, as explained in chapter 5's online appendices, to generate two correlated random variables in @RISK, use the formula

RISKCORRMAT(CorrMx, RowNumber, InstanceNumber),

where

CorrMx is the array in which the correlation matrix is stored.

RowNumber is the row number in the correlation matrix that stores the correlations that correspond to that stock.

InstanceNumber basically refers to whether the random variables that are generated need to be correlated across time periods. If we do not want them to be correlated across time periods (only within one time period), then we need to specify a different instance number for every time period for which we generate a new price.

To generate the price for stock 1 t periods from now, given a current price of S, in @RISK, use

$$S^*exp((\mu_1 - 0.5^*\sigma_1\hat{\ }2)^*t - \sigma_1{}^*\sqrt{t}^*RISKNORMAL(0, 1, RISKCORRMAT(CorrMx, 1, t))$$

To generate the price for stock 2 t periods from now, given a current price of S, use

$$S^*exp((\mu_2 - 0.5^*\sigma_2\hat{\ }2)^*t - \sigma_2{}^*\sqrt{t}^*RISKNORMAL(0, 1, RISKCORRMAT(CorrMx, 2, t)))$$

In the case of arithmetic or geometric random walk, we will need to simulate correlated standard normal random variables, so we will enter a vector of expected values of zero, a covariance matrix, and the number of steps that we need to generate.

When we consider many different assets, the covariance matrix becomes very large and cannot be estimated accurately. Instead, factor models[20] can be used to reduce the dimension of the covariance structure. Multivariate random walks are in fact *dynamic factor models* for asset prices. A multifactor model for the return of asset i can be written in the following general form:

$$r_t^{(i)} = \mu^{(i)} + \sum_{k=1}^{K} \beta^{(i,k)} \cdot f_t^{(k)} + \varepsilon_t^{(i)}$$

where the K factors $f^{(k)}$ follow random walks, $\beta^{(i,k)}$ are the factor loadings, and $\varepsilon_t^{(i)}$ are normal random variables with zero mean.

It is important to note that the covariance matrix cannot capture correlations at lagged times (i.e., correlations of dynamic nature). Furthermore, the assumption that log returns behave as multivariate normal variables is not always applicable—some assets exhibit a nonlinear

20. See chapter 16 for an introduction to factor models.

dependency, which cannot be captured by the covariance or correlation matrix. Alternative tools for modeling covariability include *copula functions* and *transfer entropies*.[21]

17.5.2 Incorporating Jumps

Many of the dynamic asset price processes used in industry assume continuous sample paths, as was the case with the arithmetic, geometric, and the different mean-reverting random walks considered earlier in this chapter. However, there is empirical evidence that the prices of many securities incorporate jumps. The prices of some commodities, such as electricity and oil, are notorious for exhibiting spikes. The logarithm of a price process with jumps is not normally distributed but is instead characterized by a high peak and heavy tails, which are more typical of market data than the normal distribution. Thus, more advanced models are needed to incorporate realistic price behavior.

A classical way to include jumps in models for asset price dynamics is to add a Poisson process to the process (geometric random walk or mean reversion) used to model the asset price. A *Poisson process* is a discrete process in which arrivals occur at random discrete points in time, and the times between arrivals are drawn from an exponential distribution with the average time between arrivals equal to $1/\lambda$.[22] Recall from chapter 3 that this means that the number of arrivals in a specific time interval follows a Poisson distribution with mean arrival rate λ. The jump Poisson process is assumed to be independent of the underlying smooth random walk.

The Poisson process is typically used to determine the times when the jumps occur. The magnitude of the jumps itself could come from any distribution, although the lognormal distribution is often used for tractability.

Let us explain how one would model and simulate a geometric random walk with jumps. At every point in time, the process moves as a geometric random walk and updates the price S_t to S_{t+1}. If a jump happens, its size is added to S_t as well, to obtain S_{t+1}. To avoid confusion about whether we have included the jump in the calculation, let us denote the price right before we find out whether a jump has occurred as $S_{t+1}^{(-)}$, and keep the total price for the next time period as S_{t+1}. We therefore have

$$S_{t+1}^{(-)} = S_t + \mu \cdot S_t + \sigma \cdot S_t \cdot \tilde{\varepsilon}_t$$

that is, $S_{t+1}^{(-)}$ is computed according to the normal geometric random walk rule. Now suppose that a jump of magnitude $\tilde{J}_t$ occurs between time t and time $t+1$. Let us express the jump magnitude as a percentage of the asset price; that is, let

$$S_{t+1} = S_{t+1}^{(-)} \cdot \tilde{J}_t$$

If we restrict the magnitude of the jumps $\tilde{J}_t$ to be nonnegative, we will make sure that the asset price itself does not become negative.

Let us now express the changes in price in terms of the jump size. Based on the relationship between S_{t+1}, $S_{t+1}^{(-)}$, and $\tilde{J}_t$, we can write

21. See, for example, chapter 17 and appendix B in Fabozzi, Focardi, and Kolm (2006).

22. See chapter 3 for a definition of an exponential distribution.

$$S_{t+1} - S_{t+1}^{(-)} = S_{t+1}^{(-)} \cdot (\tilde{J}_t - 1)$$

and therefore,

$$S_{t+1}^{(-)} = S_{t+1} - S_{t+1}^{(-)} \cdot (\tilde{J}_t - 1)$$

Thus, we can substitute this expression for $S_{t+1}^{(-)}$ and write the geometric random walk with jumps model as

$$S_{t+1} = S_t + \mu \cdot S_t + \sigma \cdot S_t \cdot \tilde{\varepsilon}_t + S_{t+1}^{(-)} \cdot (\tilde{J}_t - 1)$$

How would we simulate a path for the jump-geometric random walk process? Note that given the relationship between S_{t+1}, $S_{t+1}^{(-)}$, and $\tilde{J}_t$, we can write

$$\ln(S_{t+1}) = \ln(S_{t+1}^{(-)}) + \ln(\tilde{J}_t)$$

Since $S_{t+1}^{(-)}$ is the price resulting only from the geometric random walk at time t, we already know what $\ln(S_{t+1}^{(-)})$ is. Based on our discussion of the geometric random walk in section 17.3, recall that

$$\ln(S_{t+1}^{(-)}) = \ln(S_t) + (\mu - 0.5 \cdot \sigma^2) + \sigma \cdot \tilde{\varepsilon}_t.$$

Therefore, the overall equation will be

$$\ln(S_{t+1}) = \ln(S_t) + (\mu - 0.5 \cdot \sigma^2) + \sigma \cdot \tilde{\varepsilon}_t + \sum_i \ln(J_t^{(i)})$$

where $J_t^{(i)}$ are all the jumps that occur during the time period between t and $t+1$. This means that

$$S_{t+1} = S_t \cdot e^{\mu - 0.5 \cdot \sigma^2 + \sigma \cdot \tilde{\varepsilon}_t} \cdot \prod_i J_t^{(i)}$$

where the symbol Π denotes the product. (If no jumps occurred between t and $t+1$, we set the product to 1.)

Hence, to simulate the price at time $t+1$, we need to simulate the following:

- A standard normal random variable $\tilde{\varepsilon}_t$, as in the case of a geometric random walk
- How many jumps occur between t and $t+1$
- The magnitude of each jump

The exact simulation procedure is as follows:

1. Generate a standard normal random variable $\tilde{\varepsilon}_t$. With @RISK, for example, this can be done with the command RISKNORMAL(0, 1).
2. Simulate the number of arrivals in the time period (t, $t+1$) by drawing a number from a Poisson distribution with an arrival rate per unit period λ. In @RISK, use RISKPOISSON(λ).
3. Suppose that the number of arrivals generated in step 2 was K. For each arrival, generate a random number from the probability distribution that the jump size $\tilde{J}_t$ is assumed to follow. For example, if the jumps are assumed to come from a lognormal distribution

with mean m and standard deviation s, then use the function RISKLOGNORM(m, s) in @RISK to generate K random numbers $J_1, \ldots, J_K$ from that distribution.

4. Compute the sum of the natural logarithms of the random numbers generated in step 3: $\ln(J_1) + \cdots + \ln(J_K)$.
5. Compute the natural logarithm of the price at the next time period as

$$\ln(S_{t+1}) = \ln(S_t) + (\mu - 0.5 \cdot \sigma^2) + \sigma \cdot \varepsilon_t + \ln(J_1) + \cdots + \ln(J_K)$$

Note that we could compute S_{t+1} directly as well. However, if we are simulating a path for the random walk with jumps, we will need $\ln(S_{t+1})$, rather than S_{t+1}, for the calculation of the next step, so this equation is sufficient.

As Merton (1976) noted, if we assume that the jumps follow a lognormal distribution, then $\ln(\tilde{J}_t)$ is normal and the simulation is even easier. For more advanced examples, see Glasserman (2004).

17.5.3 Stochastic Volatility

All the models that we have considered so far assumed that the volatility of the stochastic process remains constant over time. Empirical evidence suggests that volatility changes over time, and more advanced models recognize that fact. Such models assume that the volatility parameter σ itself follows a random walk of some kind. Since there is some evidence that volatility tends to be mean-reverting, often different versions of mean-reversion models are used. For more details on stochastic volatility models and their simulation, see sources such as Glasserman (2004) and Hull (2008).

17.6 Stochastic Processes

In this section, we introduce what is known as *stochastic calculus.* Our goal is not to achieve a working knowledge in the subject, but rather to provide context for some of the terminology and formulas encountered in the literature on modeling asset prices with random walks.

So far, we have discussed random walks for which every step is taken at a specific discrete point in time. When the time increments are very small, almost zero in length, the equation of a random walk describes a *stochastic process in continuous time.* In this context, the arithmetic random walk model is known as a *generalized Wiener process* or *Brownian motion.* The geometric random walk is referred to as *geometric Brownian Motion (GBM)*, and the arithmetic mean-reverting walk is the Ornstein-Uhlenbeck process mentioned earlier.

Special notation is used to denote stochastic processes in continuous time. Increments are denoted by d or Δ. For example, $(S_{t+1} - S_t)$ is denoted as dS_t, meaning a change in S_t over an infinitely small interval. The equations describing the process, however, take a very similar form to the equations we introduced earlier in this section:

$$dS_t = \mu\, dt + \sigma dW$$

Equations involving small changes (differences) in variables are referred to as *differential equations.* Stated in words, this equation reads, "The change in the price S_t over a small time period dt equals the average drift μ multiplied by the small time change plus a random term equal to the volatility σ multiplied by dW, where dW is the increment of a Wiener process." The Wiener process, or Brownian motion, is the fundamental building block for many classical asset price processes. A standard Wiener process $W(t)$ has the following properties:

- For any time $s < t$, the difference $W(t) - W(s)$ is a normal random variable with mean zero and variance $(t-s)$. It can be expressed as $\sqrt{t-s} \cdot \tilde{\varepsilon}$, where $\tilde{\varepsilon}$ is a standard normal random variable.[23]
- For any times $0 \le t_1 < t_2 \le t_3 < t_4$, the differences $(W(t_2) - W(t_1))$ and $(W(t_4) - W(t_3))$, which are random variables, are independent.[24] Note that independent implies uncorrelated.
- The value of the Wiener process at the beginning is zero: $W(t_0) = 0$.

Using the new notation, the first two properties can be restated as follows:

Property 1. The change dW during a small period of time dt is normally distributed with mean 0 and variance dt and can be expressed as $\sqrt{dt} \cdot \tilde{\varepsilon}$.
Property 2. The values of dW for any two nonoverlapping time intervals are independent.

The arithmetic random walk can be obtained as a generalized Wiener process, which takes the form

$$dS_t = a\,dt + b\,dW$$

The appeal of the generalized Wiener process is that we can find a closed-form expression for the price at any time period. Namely,

$$S_t = S_0 + a \cdot t + b \cdot W(t)$$

The generalized Wiener process is a special case of the more general class of *Ito processes*, in which both the drift term and the coefficient in front of the random term are allowed to be nonconstant. The equation for an Ito process is

$$dS_t = a(S, t)dt + b(S, t)dW$$

GBM and the Ornstein-Uhlenbeck process are both special cases of Ito processes.

In contrast to the generalized Wiener process, the equation for the Ito process does not allow us to write a general expression for the price at time t in closed form. However, an expression can be found for some special cases, such as GBM. We now show how this can be derived.

The main relevant result from stochastic calculus is the *Ito lemma*, which states the following. Suppose that variable x follows an Ito process:

23. To show this, recall that if $\tilde{\varepsilon}$ is a standard normal variable with mean 0 and standard deviation 1, and $\tilde{x}$ is a normal random variable with mean μ and standard deviation σ, we have

$$\tilde{\varepsilon} = \frac{\tilde{x} - \mu}{\sigma} \text{(equivalently, } \tilde{x} = \sigma \cdot \tilde{\varepsilon} + \mu\text{).}$$

In the context of property 1 of the Wiener process, we have a normal random variable $(W(t) - W(s))$ with mean 0 and standard deviation $\sqrt{t-s}$. It can be expressed through a standard normal variable $\tilde{\varepsilon}$ as $\sqrt{t-s} \cdot \tilde{\varepsilon} + 0$.

24. These differences are the actual increments of the process at different points in time.

$$dx_t = a(x, t)dt + b(x, t)\, dW$$

and let y be a function of x; that is,

$$y_t = f(x, t)$$

Then, y evolves according to the following differential equation:

$$dy = \left(\frac{\partial f}{\partial x} \cdot a + \frac{\partial f}{\partial t} + \frac{1}{2} \cdot \frac{\partial^2 f}{\partial x^2} \cdot b^2 \right) dt + \frac{\partial f}{\partial x} \cdot b \cdot dW$$

where the symbol ∂ is standard notation for the partial derivative of function f with respect to the variable in the denominator. For example,

$$\frac{\partial f}{\partial t}$$

is the derivative of function f with respect to t, assuming that all the terms in the expression for f that do not involve t are constant. Respectively, ∂^2 denotes the second derivative of function f with respect to the variable in the denominator; that is, the derivative of the derivative.

This expression shows that a function of a variable that follows an Ito process also follows an Ito process.

A rigorous proof of Ito's lemma is beyond the scope of this book, but let us provide some intuition. Let us see how we would compute the expression for y in Ito's lemma.

In ordinary calculus, we could obtain an expression for a function of a variable in terms of that variable by writing the Taylor series extension as follows:

$$dy = \frac{\partial f}{\partial x} \cdot dx + \frac{\partial f}{\partial t} \cdot dt + \frac{1}{2} \cdot \frac{\partial^2 f}{\partial x^2} \cdot dx^2 + \frac{1}{2} \cdot \frac{\partial^2 f}{\partial t^2} \cdot dt^2 + \frac{\partial^2 f}{\partial x \partial x} \cdot dx\, dt + \cdots.$$

We will eliminate all terms of order dt^2 or higher, deeming them "too small." However, we need to expand the terms that contain dx because they will contain terms of order dt. We have

$$\begin{aligned} dy = {} & \frac{\partial f}{\partial x} \cdot (a(x,t)\, dt + b(x,t)\, dW) + \frac{\partial f}{\partial t} \cdot dt \\ & + \frac{1}{2} \cdot \frac{\partial^2 f}{\partial x^2} \cdot (a(x,t)\, dt + b(x,t)\, dW)^2 \end{aligned}$$

The last expression in parentheses, when expanded, becomes (dropping the arguments of a and b for notational convenience)

$$\begin{aligned} (a\, dt + b\, dW)^2 &= a^2(dt)^2 + b^2(dW)^2 + 2ab \cdot dt \cdot dW \\ &= b^2 dt \end{aligned}$$

To obtain this expression, we dropped the first and the last terms in the expanded expression because they are of higher orders than dt. The middle term, $b^2 \cdot (dW)^2$, in fact equals $b^2 \cdot dt$ as dt goes to 0. The latter is not an obvious fact, but it follows from the properties of the standard Wiener process. The intuition behind it is that the variance of $(dW)^2$

is of order dt^2, so we can ignore it and treat the expression as deterministic and equal to its expected value. The expected value of $(dW)^2$ is in fact dt.[25]

Substituting this expression back into the expression for dy, we obtain the expression in Ito's lemma.

Using Ito's lemma, let us derive the equation for the price at time t, S_t, that was the basis for the simulation method in section 17.3.1. Suppose that S_t follows the GBM:

$$dS_t = (\mu \cdot S_t)\, dt + (\sigma \cdot S_t) dW$$

We will use Ito's lemma to compute the equation for the process followed by the logarithm of the stock price. In other words, in the notation we used in the definition of Ito's lemma, we have

$$y_t = f(x, t) = \ln S_t$$

We also have

$$a = \mu \cdot S \text{ and } b = \sigma \cdot S$$

Finally, we have

$$\frac{\partial f}{\partial x} = \frac{\partial (\ln S)}{\partial S} = \frac{1}{S}$$

and

$$\frac{\partial^2 f}{\partial x^2} = \frac{\partial (1/S)}{\partial S} = -\frac{1}{S^2}$$

Plugging into the equation for y in Ito's lemma, we obtain

$$\begin{aligned} d\ln S &= \left(\frac{1}{S} \cdot a + 0 + \frac{1}{2} \cdot \left(-\frac{1}{S^2} \right) \cdot b^2 \right) dt + \frac{1}{S} \cdot b \cdot dW \\ &= \left(\mu - \frac{1}{2} \cdot \sigma^2 \right) dt + \sigma \cdot dW \end{aligned}$$

which is the equation presented earlier. This also explains the presence of the term in the expression for the drift of the GBM.

As we will see in chapters 18 and 19, some stochastic processes lead to closed-form formulas for the prices of the underlying securities and *financial derivatives* on those

25. To see this, recall from the properties of the standard Wiener process that the difference between the values of the process between any two points in time is distributed as a normal random variable with mean 0 and variance equal to the time difference itself. Therefore, dW (the difference over a very small time interval dt) is distributed as a normal random variable with mean 0 and variance dt; that is,

$$dW = \varepsilon \cdot \sqrt{dt},$$

where ε is a standard normal random variable. Finding the distribution of the squared difference $(dW)^2 = \varepsilon^2 \cdot dt$ is not as easy (it is no longer normal). However, we can say something about the mean and the variance of that distribution. The variance of a standard normal variable ε equals 1 and can be expressed as $E[\varepsilon^2] - (E[\varepsilon])^2$ (see chapter 3). Since $E[\varepsilon] = 0$, we must have $E[\varepsilon^2] = 1$. Therefore, the expected value of $(dW)^2 = E[\varepsilon^2] \cdot dt = 1 \cdot dt = dt$.

securities. When the pricing is instead done by simulation, we refer to the *discretization* of the underlying stochastic process and talk about the *discretization error*, which occurs because in practice, it is computationally intractable (and in fact impossible) to simulate future prices at infinitely small time intervals. We need to resign to using time intervals of finite length, and the longer the time intervals, the greater the divergence between the range of simulated prices and the prices that we would expect based on the closed-form formula; that is, the larger the discretization error.

To illustrate the concept of discretization error, let us go back to the example of simulation of a geometric random walk in section 17.3. The real process for the price is described by the differential equation

$$dS_t = \mu S_t dt + \sigma S_t dW$$

To simulate paths for the price, we need to find an approximation of the terms dS_t, dt, and dW. The simplest scheme for doing that is the Euler scheme.[26] Then we would get

$$S_{t+\Delta t} - S_t = \mu \cdot S_t \cdot \Delta t + \sigma \cdot S_t \cdot \sqrt{\Delta t} \cdot \tilde{\varepsilon}_t$$

As mentioned in section 17.3.2, however, the distribution of each $S_{t+\Delta t}$ generated in this manner is normal, not lognormal. (This is because each S_{t+vt} is the sum of constants and a normal random variable, $\tilde{\varepsilon}_t$.) If Δt is very small, this discretization error can be reduced, and the price distribution after many steps will approximate a lognormal distribution with the correct parameters. However, this is computationally intensive and time consuming. We can eliminate the discretization error altogether by using Ito's lemma and the exact expression for the asset price derived in this section:

$$S_t = S_0 \cdot e^{\left(\mu - \frac{1}{2} \cdot \sigma^2\right) \cdot t + \sigma \cdot \sqrt{t} \cdot \tilde{\varepsilon}}$$

However, such closed-form results are not readily available for all stochastic processes. Thus, when simulating in practice, we must tolerate some discretization error. With complicated stochastic differential equations, we can reduce the error by generating the whole path of the underlying variable (e.g., the stock price), even if we are interested only in what happens at the end of the time horizon. Such refined discretization schemes are widely used in practice.

Summary

- Models of asset dynamics include trees (such as binomial trees) and random walks (such as arithmetic, geometric, and mean-reverting random walks). Such models are called discrete when the changes in the asset price are assumed to happen at discrete time increments. When the length of the time increment is assumed infinitely small, we refer to them as stochastic processes in continuous time.
- The arithmetic random walk is an additive model for asset prices—at every time period, the new price is determined by the price at the previous time period plus a

26. The Euler scheme replaces small terms with discrete differences.

deterministic drift term and a random shock that is distributed as a normal random variable with mean equal to zero and a standard deviation proportional to the square root of the length of the time period. The probability distribution of future asset prices conditional on a known current price is normal.

- The arithmetic random walk model is analytically tractable and convenient; however, it has some undesirable features, such as a nonzero probability that the asset price will become negative.
- The geometric random walk is a multiplicative model for asset prices—at every time period, the new price is determined by the price at the previous time period multiplied by a deterministic drift term and a random shock that is distributed as a lognormal random variable. The volatility of the process grows with the square root of the elapsed amount of time. The probability distribution of future asset prices conditional on a known current price is lognormal.
- The geometric random walk is not only analytically tractable but it is also more realistic than the arithmetic random walk because the asset price cannot become negative. It is widely used in practice, particularly for modeling stock prices.
- Mean reversion models assume that the asset price will meander but tend to return to a long-term mean at the speed of adjustment. They are particularly useful for modeling prices of some commodities, interest rates, and exchange rates.
- The codependence structure between the price processes for various assets can be incorporated directly (by computing the correlation between the random terms in their random walks), by using dynamic multifactor models, or by more advanced means such as copula functions and transfer entropies.
- A variety of more advanced random walk models are used to incorporate different assumptions, such as time-varying volatility and spikes, or jumps, in the asset price. They are not as tractable analytically as the classical random walk models but can easily be simulated.
- The Wiener process, a stochastic process in continuous time, is a fundamental building block for many of the stochastic processes used to model asset prices. Its increments are independent, normally distributed random variables with variances proportional to the length of the time period.
- An Ito process is a generalized Wiener process with drift and volatility terms that can be functions of the asset price and time.
- A main result in stochastic calculus is Ito's lemma, which states that a variable that is a function of a variable that follows an Ito process follows an Ito process itself, with specific drift and volatility terms.

V

Financial Derivatives and Mortgage-Backed Securities

18

Introduction to Derivatives

Earlier in this book, chapters 12 and 13 introduced the concept of risk management in the context of investment management. We saw that diversification was instrumental and a key statistical determinant of risk management policies was the ratio between the bulk of the risk and the risk of the tails of the probability distribution of portfolio returns.

Financial firms and insurance companies have taken the concept of risk management in three different directions: (1) by recognizing that the kind of risk is an important determinant of the risk-return trade-off; (2) by engineering contracts (known as *derivatives*) able to transfer selected portions of risk; and (3) by trading these contracts. This part of the book focuses on item 2.

Derivative instruments, or simply *derivatives*, are contracts that derive their value from underlying financial securities such as stocks or bonds, market indices, interest rates, currencies, or commodities. There are many applications of financial derivatives, but the two main purposes of including them in an investor's portfolio are risk management (with hedging as a special case) and return enhancement (speculation). *Risk management* refers to investment strategies whose goal is to control risk, and *hedging* is a special case in which the goal is to eliminate risk. *Return enhancement* or *speculation* refer to investment strategies that bet on the direction in which the underlying uncertainties will be resolved, or that attempt to take advantage of perceived discrepancies in pricing to make a profit. We discuss advanced portfolio strategies that involve derivatives in chapter 20.

Derivatives are either traded on an exchange or in the *over-the-counter (OTC)* market. In other words, there are *exchange-traded derivatives* (also referred to as *listed derivatives*) and *OTC derivatives*. OTC derivatives offer portfolio managers customized solutions to deal with an investment strategy. Exchange-traded derivatives are standardized contracts, and thus they may not provide the exact strategy the investment manager needs. However, exchange-traded derivatives are guaranteed by the exchange, whereas OTC derivatives are the obligation of a nonexchange entity that is the counterparty in the contract. Thus, the user of an OTC derivative is subject to the risk that the counterparty will not fulfill its contractual obligations. This is referred to as *credit risk* or *counterparty risk*.

This chapter introduces the basic types of derivatives and explains some standard principles for pricing these derivatives. A fundamental concept underlying the construction and trading of derivatives is arbitrage, which we discuss in detail in this chapter. In chapter 19, we discuss pricing derivative contracts by simulation.

18.1 Basic Types of Derivatives

There are three general classes of derivatives: forwards and futures, options, and swaps. We review each class in this section.

18.1.1 Forwards and Futures

A *forward contract* is perhaps the simplest derivative. It is an agreement to buy or sell an asset at a specific time in the future for a specific price. Forward contracts are sold in the OTC market; that is, they are nonstandard and negotiated directly between a buyer and a seller. The buyer of a forward contract assumes a *long position* in the forward contract and agrees to buy the underlying asset at the prespecified price and date in the future. The seller of a forward contract assumes a *short position* in the contract and agrees to sell the underlying asset at the prespecified price and date in the future. The prespecified price (or *delivery price*) in the future is called the *forward price*. When the underlying is a rate such as an interest rate or a foreign exchange rate, the prespecified rate is referred to as a *forward rate*.

Forward contracts on currencies and commodities such as oil are particularly popular. For example, an American company that needs to make a payment of €1 million in six months can eliminate its exchange rate risk by buying a forward contract from a bank with settlement date six months from now for €1 million (i.e., by assuming a long position in a forward contract on euros at a U.S. dollar/euro forward exchange rate). The bank that holds the short position in the forward contract will have to sell €1 million in six months at the U.S. dollar/euro forward exchange rate.

Let T be the time to delivery of the forward contract, K be the forward price at which the underlying asset will be traded at time T, and S_T be the cash market price of the underlying asset at T. It is easy to see that the final payoff from a long position in a forward contract is

$$S_T - K$$

This is because if the cash market price of the underlying asset S_T is higher than the forward price K, the holder of the long position will have made a positive profit by locking in the lower price through the contract. If, on the other hand, the cash market price of the underlying asset S_T is lower than the forward price K, the holder of the long position will realize a loss by locking in the higher price for the underlying asset. By similar reasoning, the final payoff from a short position in a forward contract will be

$$K - S_T$$

Futures are very similar to forwards, but they are standardized contracts traded on exchanges. Associated with every futures exchange is a clearinghouse, which performs several functions, one of which is to guarantee that the two parties to the transaction will perform. Because of the clearinghouse, one party does not need to worry about the financial strength and integrity of the party taking the opposite side of the contract. After the initial execution of an order, the relationship between the two parties ends. The clearinghouse interposes itself as the buyer for every sale and as the seller for every purchase.

Thus, the two parties are then free to liquidate their positions without involving the other party in the original contract and without worrying that the other party may default.

When a position is first taken in a futures contract, the investor must deposit a minimum dollar amount per contract as specified by the exchange. This amount, called *initial margin*, is required as a deposit for the contract. The initial margin may be in the form of an interest-bearing security such as a U.S. Treasury bill. The initial margin is placed in an account, and the amount in this account is referred to as the *investor's equity*. As the price of the futures contract fluctuates each trading day, the value of the investor's equity in the position changes.

At the end of each trading day, the exchange determines the *settlement price* for the futures contract. The settlement price is different from the closing price, which is the price of the security in the final trade of the day (whenever that trade occurred during the day). By contrast, the settlement price is that value that the exchange considers to be representative of trading at the end of the day. The exchange uses the settlement price to mark-to-market the investor's position, so any gain or loss from the position is quickly reflected in the investor's equity account.

Since futures contracts are marked-to-market at the end of each trading day, they are subject to interim cash flows because additional margin may be required in the case of adverse price movements or cash may be withdrawn in the case of favorable price movements. In contrast, a forward contract may or may not be marked-to-market.[1] Thus, when a forward contract is marked-to-market, there are interim cash flows, just as with a futures contract. When a forward contract is not marked-to-market, then there are no interim cash flows. Because no clearinghouse guarantees the performance of a counterparty in a forward contract, the parties to a forward contract are exposed to *counterparty risk*. As we explained earlier, this is not the case for futures contracts. Once a futures contract is traded between two parties, the exchange (or the clearinghouse associated with the exchange) becomes the counterparty to the trade. That is, neither party to the trade needs to be concerned with the other party to the original trade. Rather, both parties are exposed to the counterparty risk of the exchange.

However, by being standardized contracts, futures contracts may not meet the precise needs of portfolio managers. For example, most financial futures contracts have March, June, September, and December settlement dates. Thus, if an investment manager needs to lock in the price for the underlying asset at dates that do not coincide with the standardized settlement dates, he needs to find a futures contract with terms closest to the terms he would like to have.

18.1.2 Options

An *option* is a contract in which the option seller grants the option buyer the right, but not the obligation, to enter a transaction with the seller to either buy or sell an underlying asset at a specified price on or before a specified date. The specified price is called the *strike price*, or *exercise price*, and the specified date is called the *expiration date*, or the

1. When the counterparties are two high-credit-quality entities, the two parties may agree not to mark positions to market. However, if one or both of the parties are concerned with the counterparty risk of the other, then positions may be marked-to-market.

maturity date. The option seller grants this right in exchange for a certain amount of money, called the *option premium* or *option price*.

The option seller is also known as the *option writer*, while the option buyer is known as the *option holder*. The asset that is the subject of the option is called the *underlying*. It can be an individual stock, a stock index, a bond, an interest rate, an exchange rate, or even another derivative instrument such as a futures contract. The option writer can grant the option holder one of two rights. If the right is to purchase the underlying, the option is called a *call option*. If the right is to sell the underlying, the option is called a *put option*.

An option can also be categorized according to when the buyer may exercise it; that is, by its *exercise style*. A *European option* can be exercised only at the option's expiration date. An *American option*, in contrast, can be exercised any time on or before the expiration date. An option that can be exercised before the expiration date, but only on specified dates, is called a *Bermuda option* or an *Atlantic option*.

Complex option contracts are referred to as *exotic options* or *exotics*. Examples of exotic options include *Asian options*, which pay the difference between the strike price and the average price of the underlying over a prespecified period, and *barrier options*, whose payoff is determined by whether the price of the underlying reaches a certain barrier over the life of the option. There is, however, virtually no limit to the possibilities for designing nonstandard derivatives.

Like other financial instruments, options may be traded on an organized exchange or in the OTC market. An option that is traded on an exchange is referred to as a *listed option* or an *exchange-traded option*. An option traded in the OTC market is called an *OTC option* or a *dealer option*. The advantages of a listed option are as follows. First, the exercise price and expiration date of the contract are standardized, making them more liquid (i.e., easier to trade before the expiration date). Second, as in the case of futures contracts, the direct link between buyer and seller is severed after the trade is executed because of the interchangeability of the listed options. Finally, the transaction costs are lower for listed options than for OTC options.

The higher cost of an OTC option reflects the cost of customizing the option for an investor whose investment objectives are not satisfied by the standardized listed options. While an OTC option is less liquid than a listed option, this is typically not of concern to the user of such an option. The explosive growth in OTC options suggests that portfolio managers find that these products serve an important investment purpose.

Note that, unlike in a forward or a futures contract, one party to an option contract is not obligated to transact—specifically, the option buyer has the right, but not the obligation, to transact. The option writer does have that obligation. In the case of a forward or futures contract, both buyer and seller are obligated to transact. Of course, at the outset of the trade, a forward or a futures buyer does not pay the seller to accept the obligation, while an option buyer pays the seller the option price. Consequently, option contracts' risk/reward characteristics are also different from those of futures and forwards. In the case of a forward or a futures contract, the buyer of the contract realizes a dollar-for-dollar gain when the price of the futures contract increases and suffers a dollar-for-dollar loss when the price of the contract decreases. The opposite occurs for the seller of a forward or futures contract. Because of this relationship, forward and futures contracts are said to have a *linear payoff*.

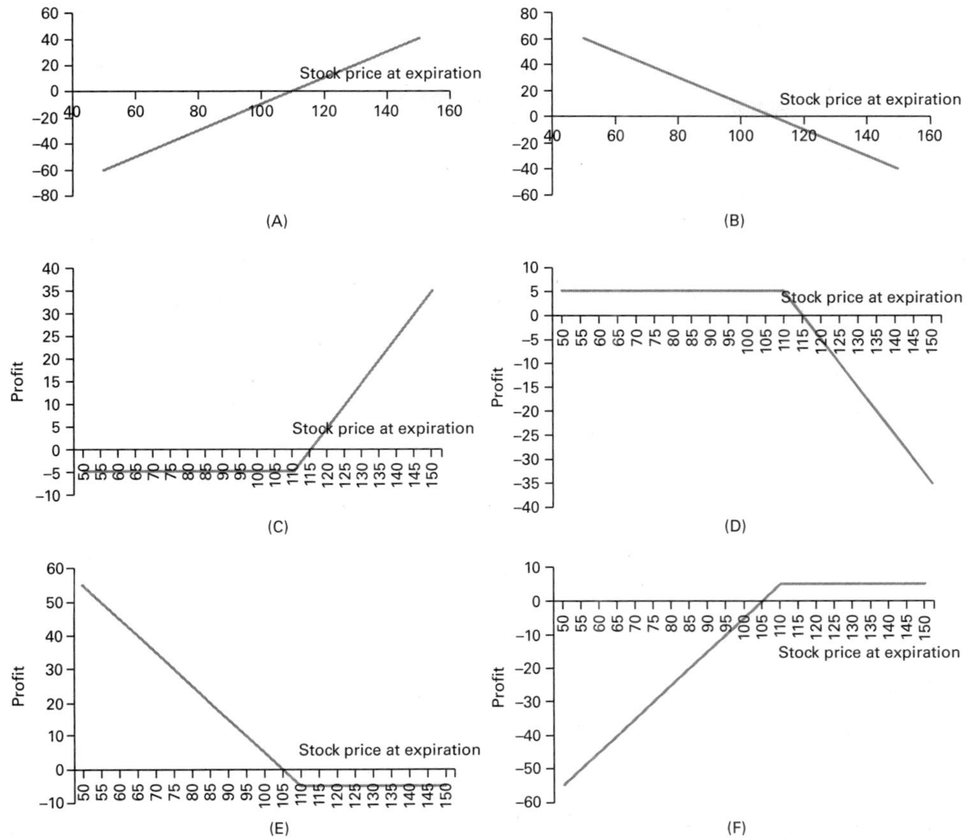

Exhibit 18.1
(A), (B): Payoffs of a long and a short position in a forward contract, respectively, at their expiration date. Forward price = \$110. (C), (D), (E), (F): Payoffs of a call and a put option at their expiration dates, with an assumed market price of \$5 each. Strike price = \$110; initial stock price = \$100. (C) Long call. (D) Short call. (E) Long put. (F) Short put.

Options do not provide this symmetric risk/reward relationship. The most the option buyer can lose is the option price. While the option buyer retains all the potential benefits from a favorable price movement of the underlying, the gain is always reduced by the amount of the option price. The maximum profit that the writer may realize is the option price; this is offset against substantial downside risk. Because of this characteristic, options are said to have a *nonlinear payoff.* The difference in the type of payoff between futures and options is very important because market participants can use futures to protect against symmetric risk and options to protect against asymmetric risk.[2]

Exhibit 18.1 graphically shows the payoffs of different options. For comparison, the payoffs from a long and a short position in a forward contract are also shown in exhibits 18.1(A) and 18.1(B).

2. This statement will become clearer when we discuss risk management strategies with derivatives in chapter 20.

Let us explain how the payoff of the basic option contract is determined at the expiration date. We will denote the time to maturity of the option as T, the underlying asset's price at maturity as S_T, and the strike price as K.

18.1.2.1 Buying a European Call Option (Long a Call Option) A European call option gives the option holder the right to buy the underlying asset for a price K at maturity. If the market price S_T at the expiration date is lower than the strike price, the option holder will not exercise the option because it will be cheaper to buy the underlying in the market; that is, the payoff from the option will be zero and the profit from holding the option will be $-C$, where C is the price of the call. If the market price S_T at expiration date is higher than the strike price, the option holder will exercise the option and the payoff will be $S_T - K$. Summarizing, the payoff from a European call option to the option holder is

$$\max\{S_T - K, 0\}$$

and the profit from the position is

$$\max\{S_T - K, 0\} - C$$

Also see exhibit 18.1(C).

18.1.2.2 Selling a Call Option (Short a Call Option) A European call option obligates the option writer to buy the underlying asset for a price K at the expiration date if the option holder desires to buy it. Thus, the payoff and profit are the exact mirror images of the payoff and profit of the call option holder. If the market price S_T at the expiration date is less than the strike price, the option holder will not exercise the option because it will be cheaper to buy the underlying in the market. Therefore, the payoff from the option to the writer will be C, the call option price. If the market price S_T at the expiration date is higher than the strike price, the option holder will exercise the option, resulting in a payoff to the option writer will be $-(S_T - K)$ before considering the option price received. Summarizing, the payoff from a European call option to the option writer is

$$-\max\{S_T - K, 0\}$$

and the profit is

$$C - \max\{S_T - K, 0\}$$

Also see exhibit 18.1(D).

18.1.2.3 Buying a Put Option (Long a Put Option) A European put option gives the option holder the right to sell the underlying asset for a price K at the expiration date. If the market price S_T at the expiration date is higher than the strike price, the option holder will not exercise the option because it will be more profitable to sell the underlying in the market; that is, the payoff from the option will be zero, and the profit from holding the option will be $-P$, where P is the price paid for the put. If the market price S_T at the expiration date is less than the strike price, the option holder will exercise the option (i.e., the payoff will be $K - S_T$), before considering the cost of acquiring it. Summarizing, the payoff from a European put option to the option holder is

$$\max\{K - S_T, 0\}$$

and the profit from the position is

$$\max\{K - S_T, 0\} - P$$

Also see exhibit 18.1(E).

18.1.2.4 Selling a Put Option (Short a Put Option) A European put option obligates the option writer to buy the underlying asset for a price K at the expiration date if the option holder desires to sell it. Thus, the payoff and profit of the put option writer are the exact mirror images of the payoff and profit of the put option holder. If the market price S_T at the expiration date is higher than the strike price, the option holder will not exercise the option because it will be more profitable to sell the underlying in the market. Thus, the payoff from the option will be zero, and the profit from holding the option to the option writer will be P, where P is the price of the put. (When the market price S_T is higher than the strike price K for a European put option, we say that the option is *out of the money*.) If the market price S_T at maturity is less than the strike price, the option holder will exercise the option; that is, the payoff to the option writer will be $-(K - S_T)$. (When the market price S_T is less than the strike price K for a European put option, we say that the option is *in the money*.) Summarizing, the payoff from a European put option to the option writer is

$$-\max\{K - S_T, 0\}$$

and the profit from the position is

$$P - \max\{K - S_T, 0)$$

Also see exhibit 18.1(F).

18.1.3 Swaps

Most generally, *swaps* are contractual agreements in which two counterparties agree to exchange returns on different assets over a prespecified period of time. There are numerous types of swaps, including equity swaps, interest rate swaps, and credit default swaps (CDS). We review some important examples of these next.

18.1.3.1 Equity Swaps *Equity swaps* are contractual agreements between two counterparties that provide for the periodic exchange of cash flows over a specified time period. At least one of the two payments is linked to the performance of an equity index, a basket of stocks, or a single stock. In a standard or plain vanilla equity swap, one party agrees to pay the other the total return of an equity index in exchange for receiving either the total return of another asset or a fixed or floating interest rate. All the payments are based on a notional amount, and payments are made over a fixed time period.

Equity swap structures are very flexible, with maturities ranging from a few months to 10 years. The returns of virtually any asset can be swapped for another without incurring the transaction costs associated with trading in the cash market. Payments that are exchanged between the two parties can be denominated in any currency regardless of the underlying equity asset, and payments can be exchanged monthly, quarterly, annually, or at maturity. The equity asset can be any equity index or portfolio of stocks. An example of an equity swap is a one-year agreement in which one party agrees to pay the counterparty the total return on the S&P 500 index on a quarterly basis, in exchange for receiving a reference interest rate plus a specified spread. Both payments would be based on the notional amount of the contract. This type of equity swap is the economic equivalent of financing a long position in the S&P 500 index at a spread to the reference interest rate. The advantages of using the swap are no transaction costs, no sales or dividend withholding tax, and no tracking error or basis risk versus the index.[3]

The basic mechanics of equity swaps are the same regardless of the structure. However, the rules governing the exchange of payments may differ. For example, U.S. investors who want to diversify internationally can enter an equity swap and, depending on their investment objective, exchange payments in such a way that they are protected against currency fluctuations. If the investment objective is to reduce U.S. equity exposure and increase Japanese equity exposure, for example, an equity swap could be structured to exchange the total returns to the S&P 500 index for the total returns to the Nikkei 225 index. If, however, the investment objective is to gain access to the Japanese equity market, an equity swap can be structured to exchange the reference interest rate plus a spread for the total returns to the Nikkei 225 index. The latter is an example of diversifying internationally, and the cash flows can be denominated in either yen or dollars. The advantages of entering an equity swap to obtain international diversification are that the investor exposure is devoid of tracking error and the investor incurs no sales tax, custodial fees, withholding fees, or market impact cost associated with entering and exiting a market. This swap is the economic equivalent of being long; the Nikkei 225 is financed at a spread to the reference interest rate at a fixed exchange rate.

18.1.3.2 Interest Rate Swaps *Interest rate swaps* are far more common than equity swaps. Different types of interest rate swaps exist, including plain vanilla (or generic) swaps, basis swaps, indexed-amortizing swaps, and callable swaps, to name a few.

In its most basic form, an interest rate swap is an agreement between two parties to exchange cash flows periodically. In a plain vanilla swap, one party pays a fixed rate of interest based on a notional amount in return for the receipt of a floating rate of interest based on the same notional amount from the counterparty. These cash flows are exchanged periodically for the life (also known as the *tenor*) of the swap. Typically, no principal is exchanged at the beginning or end of a swap.

The fixed rate on a swap is ordinarily set at a rate such that the net present value (NPV) of the swap's cash flow is zero at the start of the swap contract. This type of swap is known as a *par swap*, and the fixed rate is called the *swap rate*. The difference between the swap rate and the yield on an equivalent-maturity Treasury is called the *swap spread*.

The floating rate on a swap is benchmarked off short-term reference rate. In a plain vanilla swap, the floating rate is the three-month reference rate, which resets and pays out quarterly.

Interest rate swaps can be callable or putable prior to the swap's maturity by one of the parties. They can also be part of popular interest rate options called *swaptions*. We will discuss swaptions in section 19.4.4.

3. We will explain basis risk in more detail in chapter 20.

18.1.3.3 Credit Default Swaps *Credit default swaps (CDSs)* are the simplest example of a credit derivative.[4] They are contracts in which one party (the *protection buyer*) pays a periodic premium to the counterparty (the *protection seller*) in exchange for protection against a prespecified credit event. That is, a CDS has a payout that is contingent on the occurrence of a *credit event*. The documentation on CDSs provides a list of eight possible credit events: bankruptcy, credit event upon merger, cross acceleration, cross default, downgrade, failure to pay, repudiation/moratorium, and restructuring.

Bankruptcy is defined as a variety of acts that are associated with bankruptcy or insolvency laws. *Failure to pay* results when a reference entity does not make one or more required payments when due. When a reference entity breaches a covenant, it has *defaulted* on its obligation. When a default occurs, the obligation becomes due and payable prior to the original scheduled due date (had the reference entity not defaulted). This is referred to as an *obligation acceleration*. A reference entity may disaffirm or challenge the validity of its obligation. This is a credit event that is covered by *repudiation/moratorium*. *Restructuring* occurs when the terms of the obligation are altered to make the new terms less attractive to the debt holder than the original terms.

The settlement of the contract can be physical or through a cash valuation mechanism. With physical settlement, the protection buyer transfers the reference obligations, typically bonds or loans, to the protection seller. In return, the protection seller pays to the protection buyer a cash amount equal to 100% of the notional amount of the transaction. In the case of cash settlement, the protection seller pays to the protection buyer the difference between the notional amount of the transaction and a final value for the reference obligations. The final value is typically determined through a dealer poll. Cash settlement is less popular than physical settlement because of the wide bid-offer spread on the obligation once the reference credit is distressed.

CDSs can be more complex—for example, they can be written on multiple reference obligations. In the latter case, they are referred to as *basket credit default swaps*. In chapter 20, we will discuss CDSs further in the context of managing portfolio credit risk.

18.2 Important Concepts for Derivative Pricing and Use

In the rest of this chapter, we will review classical approaches to the valuation of a number of plain types of financial derivatives to introduce important pricing concepts and terminology. These classical methods will be contrasted with simulation methods for pricing classical and exotic derivatives in chapter 19.

Two concepts that underlie all derivative pricing methods are arbitrage and hedging, explained next.

18.2.1 Arbitrage

Most generally, *arbitrage* is the opportunity to make "free money"; that is, to realize a profit with no risk. Academic definitions are more technical; they generally refer to the

4. As the name implies, *credit derivatives* are contracts whose payoff depends on the creditworthiness of the underlying asset.

opportunity to hold a portfolio of securities that can realize positive cash flows today or at some point in the future without realizing negative cash flows at any point in time. *Type A arbitrage* is associated with a situation in which an investor can make money immediately and never has to pay anything in the future. You can think of it as investing in a security that pays zero with certainty but has a negative price today. *Type B arbitrage* is associated with a situation in which an investment has a nonpositive cost but a positive probability of yielding a positive payoff and no probability of yielding a negative payoff.

When investors attempt to make money by taking advantage of a perceived arbitrage opportunity, they are said to have an *arbitrage strategy*. Originally, realizing arbitrage opportunities was all about accessing the right information. *Classic arbitrage* involved buying a currency or a commodity in one market and selling it as close to simultaneously as possible in another market. Improved communications and increased competition have eroded meaningful profit opportunities in such traditional forms of arbitrage. Many traders, however, have switched to *relative value arbitrage*, which involves watching for distortions in the price relationship between different commodities or currencies, or between them and financial derivative instruments whose payoff is based on them, using interest rates and other factors to estimate the appropriate relative values.

In this and the following chapters, we will often talk about *pricing a financial instrument by arbitrage*. A financial instrument can be either a security or a derivative. What this means is that we can construct a portfolio of other securities with observable prices that mimic the payoff of the financial instrument whose price we are trying to find. If such a *replicating portfolio* exists, then the price of the financial instrument should equal the cost of the replicating portfolio. If this is not the case, there will be an arbitrage opportunity. Namely, if the price of the replicating portfolio is higher than the price of the financial instrument, then investors will choose to short the replicating portfolio and buy the financial instrument (which will be cheaper relative to the replicating portfolio). This will create an immediate positive cash flow, with no future obligations, since the payoffs of the two securities will be the same. Inversely, if the price of the replicating portfolio is lower, then investors will choose to short the security and buy the replicating portfolio, again realizing a riskless profit.

Typically, for pricing purposes, it is assumed that no arbitrage exists in the market; otherwise, investors would have already taken advantage of the arbitrage opportunities and brought the prices of the securities involved into alignment. Obviously, this assumption does not always hold in practice, and some investment managers focus explicitly on identifying and exploiting such arbitrage opportunities.

To illustrate the concept of arbitrage, let us consider a simple example. Exhibit 18.2 presents a strategy for taking advantage of a type A arbitrage opportunity. The prices of five bonds are \$102.36, \$110.83, \$96.94, \$114.65, and \$96.63. Their coupon payments at eight future dates are listed in columns underneath the prices. For example, bond 1 has a principal value of \$100, a 5% coupon rate paid semiannually, and a maturity of 2.5 years. It makes four coupon payments of \$2.50, after which it pays the principal value and the last coupon payment.

	Bond 1	Bond 2	Bond 3	Bond 4	Bond 5			
Amounts	0.00	1,400.25	70.01	(14,927.40)	14,999.15			
Prices	$102.36	$110.83	$96.94	$114.65	$96.63	Cash flow today $(100,000.00) Total		
t=1	$2.50	$5.00	$3.00	$4.00	$3.50	$(0.00)	>=	0
t=2	$2.50	$5.00	$3.00	$4.00	$3.50	$(0.00)	>=	0
t=3	$2.50	$5.00	$3.00	$4.00	$3.50	$(0.00)	>=	0
t=4	$2.50	$5.00	$3.00	$4.00	$3.50	$(0.00)	>=	0
t=5	$102.50	$5.00	$3.00	$4.00	$3.50	$(0.00)	>=	0
t=6	$–	$105.00	$3.00	$4.00	$3.50	$140,025.33	>=	0
t=7	$–	$–	$103.00	$4.00	$3.50	$(0.00)	>=	0
t=8	$–	$–	$–	$104.00	$103.50	$(0.00)	>=	0

Exhibit 18.2
Five bonds that are priced in such a way that they allow an arbitrage strategy.

Based on the output in exhibit 18.2, consider the following portfolio:

Bond	Amount Invested
1	0
2	1,400.25
3	70.01
4	−14,927.40
5	14,999.51

The negative sign for the amount invested in bond 4 means that this bond was shorted.

This portfolio provides a nonnegative cash flow at each coupon date ($0.00 on coupon payment dates 1, 2, 3, 4, 5, 7, and 8; and $140,025.33 on date 6), and a cash flow of $100,000 today. The cash flow today appears with a negative sign, but it is in fact a net inflow of cash generated by short-selling bond 4 (i.e., borrowing it and selling it in the market) and buying the other bonds. The net cash flows at the future coupon dates consist of the positive cash flows from long bond positions and the negative cash flows for the short position in bond 4.

To find the arbitrage strategy, we used linear programming (LP), imposing the constraints that at each coupon payment date, the cash flow generated from coupons should be nonnegative, and we minimized the cash flow today. In this example, we arbitrarily imposed a limit of $100,000 on the cash flow today. If an arbitrage strategy exists in this situation, technically, we could make as much money as we wish since we can just invest multiples of the amounts invested here. (See this chapter's online appendices and accompanying files for an actual implementation of this strategy.)

Of course, we ignored many issues in this example. We assumed that the bonds were infinitely divisible (i.e., we could trade portions of actual issues).[5] We assumed that the bid and ask prices for the bonds were the same. We also ignored transaction costs, issue size, and possible differences in the credit quality of these bonds that could account for the apparent discrepancy. These issues should be carefully considered before a strategy is implemented.

Sophisticated analytical models can be built to explore mispricing in baskets of assets or derivatives on multiple assets, and optimization modeling is a handy technique to help identify such opportunities. (See, e.g., Cornuejols and Tutuncu (2007) for an example of using optimization to identify mispricing in options on the same stock with different strike prices.)

A special kind of arbitrage strategy often used in practice is the *risk arbitrage strategy*, or *equity arbitrage strategy*. This strategy involves the simultaneous purchase of shares in one company and the short sale of shares in another. Such strategies are typically used in the expectation of a pending announcement of a takeover by a company or a merger of two companies. By purchasing shares in the company that is expected to be taken over (with the anticipation that its market value will increase) and selling short shares in the acquiring company (with the anticipation that its market value will decrease), an investor hopes to gain from both sides of the trade.

5. This issue can be fixed by restricting the amounts to be invested in the bonds to be integers. For computational issues with integer programming (IP), see chapter 6.

Risk arbitrage strategies are not textbook arbitrage strategies because they do not guarantee riskless profit. The profit depends on several uncertain events. Simulation can be helpful for evaluating the risk of such strategies. By incorporating assumptions about the behavior of the stock prices and the likelihood that the deal goes through, an investor can obtain an estimate of the risk involved in betting on the deal.

18.2.2 Hedging

A *hedging strategy* is a trading or investment strategy that reduces risk. For example, consider an airline that will lose $1 million for every cent increase in the price of jet fuel and gain $1 million for every cent decrease in the price. The airline sells tickets well in advance of the date of travel and incurs the risk of fuel price increases. To reduce that risk, suppose that the airline buys futures on the price of jet fuel, which will guarantee that it can buy jet fuel at a particular price. If the price of jet fuel increases, the airline will lose money when it buys jet fuel but will make money on the futures because they will be more valuable.[6] So the airline will be able to offset its risk.

If there were jet fuel futures in the market with the appropriate settlement date, the airline may have been able to achieve a perfect hedge. A *perfect hedging strategy* eliminates risk completely. However, in practice, perfect hedge opportunities rarely exist. Even in cases in which one can find a counterparty to take the opposite side in a contract with the desired specifications, one incurs counterparty risk.

In the airline example, the airline would not be able to achieve a perfect hedge. Two important reasons are that, first, there are no futures on jet fuel, and second, futures contracts are traded in the market and have specified delivery dates that may not coincide with dates that are relevant to the airline. The airline could purchase futures on crude or heating oil with longer settlement dates than it needs. Generally, jet fuel and oil prices go hand in hand, although they are not perfectly correlated. If the price of jet fuel goes up, the airline could sell the oil futures, which should go up in value as well, and make up for at least some of its losses.

Who would take the opposite side of the futures contracts that the airline buys? Companies that risk incurring losses if the price of oil goes down. For example, an oil and gas company such as ExxonMobil would hedge its risk by selling futures on oil.

The hedging strategy discussed here involved a hedge that was constructed once, at the beginning. Hedging strategies can also be *dynamic*; that is, assets can be traded over the duration of time for which the hedge is needed. The celebrated Black-Scholes formula for pricing European options, which we will discuss later in this chapter, relies on such a hedging strategy to arrive at the fair price of an option.

We will discuss more advanced portfolio hedging strategies in chapter 20.

18.3 Pricing Forwards and Futures

The classical models for pricing futures are models for pricing forwards. Different adjustments can be made depending on the specific features of the contracts, as well as the type of underlying asset. We will use the following notation:

6. Note that since we are talking about futures contracts, no physical delivery of jet fuel takes place. Instead, the futures contracts will be traded or settled in cash at the delivery date.

- T is the time until the delivery date of the forward or futures contract (in years).
- S_0 is the cash price of the asset underlying the futures or forward contract at time 0 (today).
- F_0 is the price of the forward or futures contract at time 0 (today).
- r is the annual risk-free interest rate (with continuous compounding) for an investment maturing at the delivery date T.

The simplest forward contract is one written on an asset with no income, such as a zero-coupon bond or a stock that does not pay dividends. In this case, the forward price is given by

$$F_0 = S_0 \cdot e^{r \cdot T}$$

To see this, observe that if $F_0 > S_0 \cdot e^{r \cdot T}$, an investor can borrow S_0 at time 0 at the risk-free rate r, buy the asset, and take a short position in the forward contract. At time T, the investor can deliver the asset under the forward contract for a price of F_0 and repay the loan, which at that time is $S_0 \cdot e^{r \cdot T}$. The investor will realize a riskless positive profit $F_0 - S_0 \cdot e^{r \cdot T}$ at the settlement date; that is, there will be an arbitrage opportunity.

If the opposite holds (i.e., $F_0 < S_0 \cdot e^{r \cdot T}$), an investor can take a long position in the forward contract and short the asset. By shorting the asset, the investor realizes a cash flow of S_0, which can then be invested at the risk-free rate of r for a time period T. At the delivery date, the investor can buy the asset for F_0 under the terms of the forward contract and close out the short position in the asset. The profit realized at maturity is $S_0 \cdot e^{r \cdot T} - F_0$.

Even though we used shorting in this argument, the forward price formula also holds when shorting is not allowed.[7]

The formula can be generalized to include the case when the underlying asset provides an income whose present value discounted at the risk-free rate is I during the life of the forward contract. A similar argument can be used to show that in that case, the fair forward price should be

$$F_0 = (S_0 - I) \cdot e^{r \cdot T}$$

If, instead, we know that the asset will pay a continuous dividend yield of q per annum, the formula is

$$F_0 = S_0 \cdot e^{(r-q) \cdot T}$$

These pricing formulas also apply to futures prices; however, in such cases, they are only approximations. It can be shown that if the risk-free interest rate is constant during the life of the contract and the same for all maturities, the prices of forward and futures contracts will be the same. However, when interest rates vary, which is the case in the real world, we no longer have such guarantees. For example, when interest rates increase and the price of the underlying asset is strongly positively correlated with the level of interest rates, futures prices tend to be higher than forward prices. This is because an investor who holds a long futures position gains due to the daily settlement procedure, which then allows the investor

7. See Hull (2008).

to invest the gains at a higher interest rate, whereas an investor holding a forward contract is not necessarily affected in the same way. There are also a number of factors that affect the theoretical prices of forward and futures contracts and the actual trading price, such as the interim cash flows, differences in borrowing and lending rates, taxes, transaction costs, and treatment of margins.[8] However, for futures and forward contracts with short times to delivery (up to several months), the price differences are often small enough to be disregarded.

18.4 Pricing Options

Now let us look at the general principles of pricing options. The price of an option is made of two components: the intrinsic value and the time premium over the intrinsic value.

The *intrinsic value* of an option is the maximum of zero and the value that the option would have if exercised immediately. The intrinsic value for an American call option at any point in time t before its expiration, for example, is $\max\{S_t - K, 0\}$. When the intrinsic value of an option is positive, we say that the option is *in the money*. When the intrinsic value is 0, we say that the option is *out of the money*.

The *time premium*, also called the *time value* of an option, is so named because of the possibility of future favorable movements in the underlying's price. It equals the amount by which the market price of the option exceeds its intrinsic value. For example, if the price of a call option with a strike price of \$100 is \$12 when the market price of the underlying is \$104, the time premium of this option is \$8 (\$12 minus its intrinsic value of \$4). Had the market price of the underlying been \$95 instead of \$104, the time premium of this option would be the entire \$12 because the option has no intrinsic value. All other things being equal, the time premium of an option will increase with the amount of time remaining to expiration. The time value of the option equals zero after the expiration date, or when it is optimal to exercise the option.

One can come up with bounds on the price of an option based on its intrinsic value and its time premium. It can be shown, for example, that the minimum price of an American call option at any point in time is its intrinsic value. However, for most practical purposes, this is not enough. Traders and investors need a way to calculate the exact price of an option.

For a long time, practitioners did not know how to approach pricing options. It was not until the Black and Scholes option pricing model was introduced in 1973 that the tools for tackling problems of pricing options of all kinds became available, including the following:

- *No-arbitrage pricing:* The idea that the only kind of pricing that can be stable is one that does not give rise to arbitrage opportunities
- *Perfect hedging:* The idea of creating a replicating portfolio that mimics the payoffs of the option to be priced in all states of the world
- *Ito's stochastic calculus:* A previously obscure tool for modeling random processes in physics that allowed certain types of options to be priced exactly given assumptions about the random process, followed by the price of the underlying asset

8. For more details, see Fabozzi (2009).

Basically, the idea behind deriving option pricing models is that if the payoff from owning, say, a call option can be replicated by (1) purchasing the underlying for the call option and (2) borrowing funds, after which the price of the option will be (at most) the cost of creating the replicating strategy.

This section introduces the binomial method for pricing European and American equity options, as well as the Black-Scholes formula for European options. Chronologically, binomial methods appeared after the Black-Scholes model—they were suggested by Sharpe (1978), Cox, Ross, and Rubinstein (1979), and Rendleman and Bartter (1979). However, the binomial methods provide an intuitive introduction to the main ideas of option pricing, so we discuss the binomial tree method first.

18.4.1 Using Binomial Trees to Price European Options

Binomial trees are a very popular method for pricing both European and American options. In this section, we focus on European options. In section 18.4.3, we will illustrate how the same concepts, together with the dynamic programming technique, can be applied to pricing American options.

18.4.1.1 A Simple One-Period Example Suppose that we would like to find the fair price of a European call option with strike price $K = \$52$ and time to maturity $T = 6$ months (0.5 years) on a stock whose current price is \$50. Let us start simply. Suppose that at the end of $T = 0.5$ years, the stock price can be in only one of two states: it can go up to \$60 or it can go down to \$42. The probability of the stock price going up is 60%. The probability of the stock price going down is 40%. The risk-free rate is 10%.

In what follows, we use the assumption that there is no arbitrage in the market to derive the price of the option. The main idea is the following: We set up a portfolio of the stock and the option in such a way that there is no uncertainty about the value of the portfolio at the end of six months. We then argue that because there is no risk, the return that the portfolio will earn should equal the risk-free rate (otherwise, there will be an arbitrage opportunity). This will enable us to work out the cost of setting up the portfolio, and therefore the price of the option. Since there are two assets (the stock and the option) and only two possible outcomes (up or down), it is always possible to set up a riskless portfolio. While this is a simple argument, it can be extended to a more general setting in which there are infinitely many possible states for the stock price. This is the idea behind the Black-Scholes formula, which we will introduce in the next section.

Consider a portfolio that consists of a long position in Δ shares of stock and a short position in one call option. What is the value of Δ that makes the portfolio riskless?

If the stock price goes up from \$50 to \$60, the value of the shares is $\$60\Delta$, and the value of the call option is $\max\{\$60 - \$52, 0\} = \$8$. Therefore, the total value of the portfolio is $(\$60\Delta - \$8)$.

If the stock price goes down from \$50 to \$42, then the value of the shares is $\$42\Delta$, and the value of the call option is $\max\{\$42 - \$52, 0\} = \$0$. Therefore, the total value of the portfolio is $\$42\Delta$. This scenario is illustrated in exhibit 18.3.

For the portfolio to be riskless, its future value should be the same independent of the state of the world in which the stock price ends up. Therefore, we have the condition

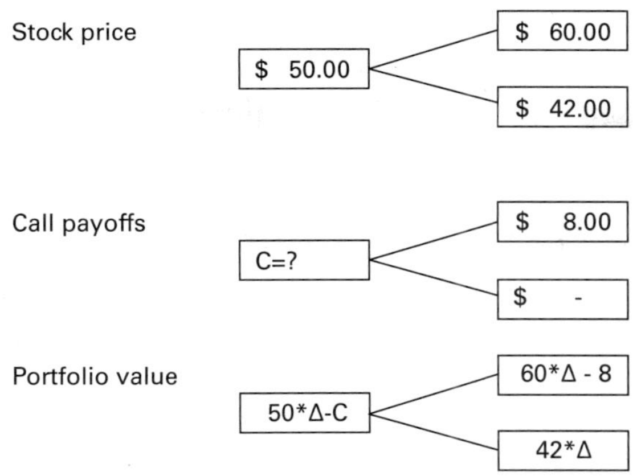

Exhibit 18.3
One-period binomial tree with values for the stock, payoffs for the call option, and the value of a portfolio consisting of a long position in Δ shares of stock and a short position in the option.

$$\$60\Delta - \$8 = \$42\Delta$$

That is, $\Delta = \$8/\$18 = 0.4444$. Therefore, a riskless portfolio would consist of a long position in 0.4444 shares of the stock and a short position in 1 call option. The value of the portfolio is $\$60 \cdot 0.4444 - \$8$ (or $42 \cdot 0.4444$) $= \$18.67$ in both states of the world.

Since the portfolio is riskless, it must earn the risk-free rate of interest, 10%. Given that the portfolio value is \$18.67 a half-year from the current date, the present value of the portfolio can be calculated by discounting its future value, \$18.67, by the risk-free rate. Therefore, the value of the portfolio today is

$$\$18.67 \cdot e^{-0.10 \cdot 0.5} = \$17.76$$

We know the value of the stock part of the portfolio today—it is the current price of the stock (\$50) times the number of shares (0.44). Therefore, we can find the value of the call option (C) today. Namely, we have

$$\$50 \cdot 0.4444(\text{the value of the shares today}) - 1 \cdot C$$
$$= \$17.76 \text{ (the present value of the portfolio), or}$$
$$C = \$4.46.$$

Notice that we never used the information about the probabilities of the stock price going up or down. In fact, all the information we needed about the stock was already incorporated into the values of the stock prices in the up and the down states. It turns out that there are different probabilities that are at play, and these determine the possible values for the stock price one period from now. We will explain the intuition behind this fact next.

18.4.1.2 Risk-Neutral Probabilities Now let us generalize the method from the previous section. Suppose that the stock price today is S_0, and it can go up to uS_0 or down to dS_0 over a given period Δt. We would like to find the value f of an option written on the stock. Let the payoffs of the derivative in the up and the down states of the world be f_u and f_d, respectively.

We take a long position in Δ shares of stock and a short position in one call option. The portfolio values in the up and the down states are

$$(uS_0) \cdot \Delta - f_u \text{ and } (dS_0) \cdot \Delta - f_d$$

respectively. The two portfolio values are the same when

$$(uS_0) \cdot \Delta - f_u = (dS_0) \cdot \Delta - f_d$$

that is, when

$$\Delta = \frac{f_u - f_d}{uS_0 - dS_0}$$

This equation shows that Δ is the ratio of the change in the option price and the change in the stock price. We will come back to this observation in section 18.4.4.

The present value of the portfolio is

$$((uS_0) \cdot \Delta - f_u) \cdot e^{-r \cdot (\Delta t)}$$

The value of the portfolio today is also $(S_0 \cdot \Delta - f)$; therefore, $((uS_0) \cdot \Delta - f_u) \cdot e^{-r \cdot (\Delta t)} = (S_0 \cdot \Delta - f)$.

From here, we deduce that the fair value of the option today is

$$f = S_0 \cdot \Delta - ((uS_0) \cdot \Delta - f_u) \cdot e^{-r \cdot (\Delta t)}$$

Substituting the value for Δ, we get

$$f = e^{-r \cdot (\Delta t)} \cdot (p \cdot f_u + (1 - p) \cdot f_d)$$

where

$$p = \frac{e^{r \cdot (\Delta t)} - d}{u - d}$$

Parameter p in this equation can be viewed as a special probability. It is in fact called a *risk-neutral probability*. Note that if we use this new probability, the value of the option today equals the expected value of its future payoffs, f_u and f_d. In fact, this is the same probability that makes the value of the stock today equal to the expected value of its discounted future values when the discount rate is the risk-free rate. To see this, note that in our example in the previous section, we had the following:

$$\begin{aligned}
u &= \$60 / \$50 = 1.20 \\
d &= \$42 / \$50 = 0.84 \\
\Delta t &= 0.5 \\
f_u &= \$8 \\
f_d &= \$0 \\
p &= \frac{e^{0.10 \cdot (0.5)} - 0.84}{1.20 - 0.84} = 0.5869 \\
1 - p &= 0.4131
\end{aligned}$$

The value of the call option today was[9]

$$C = e^{-0.10 \cdot 0.5} \cdot (0.5869 \cdot \$8 + (1 - 0.5869) \cdot \$0) = \$4.47$$

The expected value of the stock under this probability distribution today, assuming that the return on the stock is the risk-free rate, is

$$e^{-0.10 \cdot 0.5} \cdot (0.5869 \cdot \$60 + (1 - 0.5869) \cdot \$42) = \$50$$

which was indeed its current value.

18.4.1.3 Generalization to Multiple Periods The formula for the price of the option as an expected value of its discounted payoffs under a risk-neutral probability measure can be derived for multiple time periods. For example, if we have two time periods, we get

$$f = e^{-2r \cdot (\Delta t)}[p^2 \cdot f_{uu} + 2 \cdot p \cdot (1 - p) \cdot f_{ud} + (1 - p)^2 \cdot f_{dd}]$$

Note that the coefficients in front of the terms containing the probabilities p count how many ways there are to get to the particular end node in the tree. For example, there are two ways to get a payoff of f_{ud}: the stock price can go up first and then down (probability $p \cdot (1-p)$), or down first and then up (probability $(1-p) \cdot p$). So the probability of getting a payoff of f_{ud} is $2 \cdot p \cdot (1-p)$. To get f, the expected value of the option today, we take the weighted average of all possible future payoffs (with weights that are products of the risk-neutral probabilities) and discount it to the present.

Exhibit 18.4 shows the example of pricing the same call option as in the previous section, but over two time periods rather than one. The parameters u, d, and p are slightly different—they are adjusted for the fact that each time period is shorter than the time period considered in the previous section. Now $u = 1.13$, $d = 0.88$, and $p = 56.99\%$. We will explain their exact computation in section 18.4.2.

At time 0, we start with an initial stock price of \$50. At time 1, we have two possible prices: $\$50 \cdot 1.19 = \$56.67$ and $\$50 \cdot 0.88 = \$44.12$. At the option's expiration date, we have three (instead of two) possible values for the underlying stock price: \$64.22, \$50, and \$38.93.[10] You can imagine that as you continue to divide the time to maturity into shorter and shorter intervals, you will obtain a large number of possible stock prices at the expiration date, which will represent the possible states of the world better.

In exhibit 18.4, we show the values of the options in the possible states of the world at times 0, 1, and 2. At time 2, we simply compute the payoffs of the option. For example, the top payoff at time 2 is $\$12.22 = \max\{\$64.22 - \$52.00, 0\}$. We fill out the remaining two nodes at time 2 similarly. If we use the formula for the value of the option at the beginning of this section, we get the following value for the European call price:

9. There is a one-cent difference compared to the previous estimate due to a rounding error.

10. We have three final nodes because we built the binomial tree to be *recombining*. This keeps the dimension of the problem manageable. With a recombining tree, we have $t + 1$ nodes at time t. With a nonrecombining tree, we have 2^t nodes at time t. Thus, the number of nodes quickly becomes unmanageable with a nonrecombining tree.

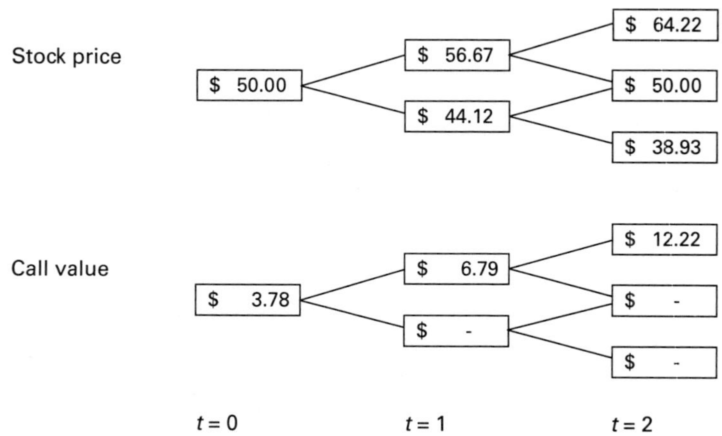

Exhibit 18.4
Pricing of a European call option using a two-period binomial tree.

$$C = e^{-0.10 \cdot 0.5} \cdot \big(0.5699^2 \cdot \$12.22 + 2 \cdot 0.5699 \cdot (1 - 0.5699) \cdot \$0 + (1 - 0.5699)^2 \cdot \$0\big) = \$3.78.$$

Basically, we weighed all final payoffs at time 2 by the probabilities of obtaining them and discounted the weighted average to time 0. For example, the payoff of \$12.22 was weighted by 0.5699^2 because to obtain it, the stock price needs to go up at time period 1, and then up again at time period 2.

Let us show how we would compute the option value at each time period. Although we do not need to do it in the case of European options, it is instructive for when we discuss American options in section 18.4.3.

The value of \$6.79 obtained at time 1 in exhibit 18.4 is the discounted expected payoff from the two nodes at time 2 that are reachable from the node at time 1:

$$\$6.79 = e^{-0.10 \cdot (0.5/2)} \cdot (0.5699 \cdot \$12.22 + (1 - 0.5699) \cdot \$0)$$

Note that the discount factor takes into consideration the fact that the time period has length $T/2$. Similarly, we can compute the second possible value for the option at time 1. (It turns out that value is 0 since it is the expected value of two zero payoffs.)

At time 0, we compute the discounted expected value of the option values at time 1; that is,

$$e^{-0.10 \cdot (0.5/2)} \cdot (0.5699 \cdot \$6.79 + (1 - 0.5699) \cdot \$0)$$

This gives us the price of the option, \$3.78.

We can similarly compute the price of a put option on the same stock. The only thing that we need to change is how we compute the option payoffs at time 2, which in turn changes the option values at times 0 and 1 (see exhibit 18.5).

What if there were more time periods? Suppose that there are n time periods, each of length Δt (i.e., $\Delta t = T/n$, where T is the maturity of the option). Then

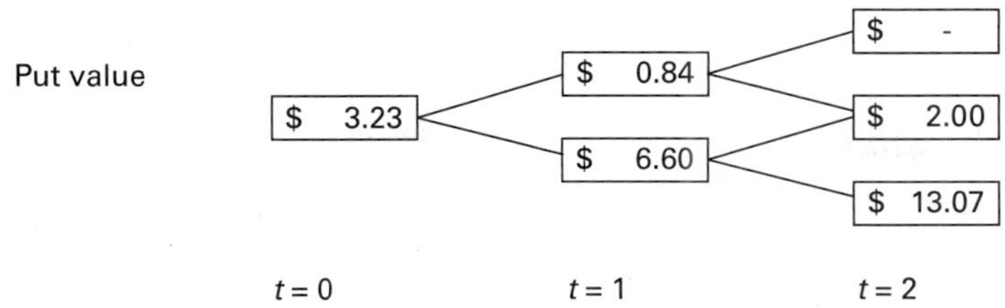

Exhibit 18.5
Pricing a European put option with a two-period binomial tree.

$$
\begin{aligned}
f &= e^{-n\cdot r\cdot(\Delta t)}\left[p^n \cdot f_n + \binom{n}{n-1}\cdot p^{n-1}\cdot(1-p)\cdot f_{n-1} + \cdots \right.\\
&\quad \left. + \binom{n}{1}\cdot p\cdot(1-p)\cdot{}^{n-1}\cdot f_1 + (1-p)^n\cdot f_0\right]\\
&= e^{-n\cdot r\cdot(\Delta t)}\left[\sum_{j=0}^{n}\binom{n}{j}\cdot p^j\cdot(1-p)^{n-j}\cdot f_j\right].
\end{aligned}
$$

In this formula, $f_j = \max(u^j d^{n-j} S_0 - K, 0)$ for a European call option; and $f_j = \max(K - u^j d^{n-j} S_0, 0)$ for a European put option ($j = 0, 1, \ldots, n$).[11]

As we mentioned earlier, even though we assume that the stock price can take only a discrete set of values, if we divide the time to maturity of the option T into many small time periods, there will be many possible values (end nodes) for the final stock price. This allows us to price the option quite accurately.

18.4.2 The Black-Scholes Formula for European Options

Instead of assuming that the future stock price can take only two values—uS_0 or dS_0—the Black-Scholes model assumes that the future stock price can take a continuous range of values with a specific probability distribution: the lognormal distribution. The Black-Scholes formulas for a European call (C) and put (P) option are as follows:

$$C = S_0\cdot e^{-qT}\cdot\Phi(d_1) - K\cdot e^{-rT}\cdot\Phi(d_2)$$

and

$$P = K\cdot e^{-rT}\cdot\Phi(-d_2) - S_0\cdot e^{-qT}\cdot\Phi(-d_1)$$

where

$$d_1 = \frac{\ln(S_0/K) + (r - q + \sigma^2/2)\cdot T}{\sigma\cdot\sqrt{T}}$$

$$d_2 = d_1 - \sigma\cdot\sqrt{T}$$

11. As we saw in chapter 3, the numbers $\binom{n}{k}$ (pronounced "n choose k") are *binomial coefficients*. They count how many ways there are to choose k objects out of n. (In the context of option pricing, they count how many ways there are to get k "up" moves of the stock price out of n possible moves.) These coefficients appear in the formula for the binomial probability distribution. (Recall from chapter 3 that the binomial distribution associates a probability with k successes out of n trials.)

and

K is the strike price.

T is the time to maturity.

q is the percentage of stock value, paid annually in dividends.

Φ denotes the cumulative probability density function for the normal distribution.[12]

To illustrate the Black-Scholes option pricing formula, assume the following values:

Current stock price $(S_0) = \$50$

Strike price $(K) = \$52$

Time remaining to expiration $(T) = 183$ days $= 0.5$ years (183 days/365, rounded)

Stock return volatility $(\sigma) = 0.25$ (25%)

Short-term risk-free interest rate $= 0.10$ (10%).

Plugging into the formula, we obtain

$$d_1 = \frac{\ln(50/52) + (0.10 - 0 + 0.25^2/2) \cdot 0.5}{0.25 \cdot \sqrt{0.5}} = 0.1502$$

$$d_2 = 0.1502 - 0.25 \cdot \sqrt{0.5} = -0.0268$$

$$\Phi(0.1502) = 0.5597$$

$$\Phi(-0.0268) = 0.4893$$

$$C = 50 \cdot 1 \cdot 0.5597 - 52 \cdot e^{-0.10 \cdot 0.5} \cdot 0.4893 = \$3.79$$

(See this chapter's online appendices and accompanying files for an implementation of the formula.)

It is a good idea to check how sensitive the Black-Scholes price is to the values of different inputs. We have implemented that using Excel **Data Tables**[13] in the worksheet **B-S** of file **Ch18-BlackScholes.xlsx**, and you can also easily create a script in MATLAB or Python that computes the value of the Black-Scholes call price for different values of one of the input parameters, such as time to expiration or volatility.

Prices of European call and put options using the Black-Scholes formula for different values of the time to maturity T and the volatility σ, are given in Exhibit 18.6.

It is easy to observe that both calls and puts become more valuable as the volatility of the process for the underlying price increases. Also, the call option becomes more valuable as the time to expiration increases.

While the Black-Scholes formula is still widely used in practice, it is not always well understood. It is important to realize that the formula applies only under very specific assumptions, as follows:

- *Assumption 1.* The option to be priced is a European option.

12. As explained previously in this book, the value for $\Phi(d)$ can be found with the formula `=NORMDIST(d,0,1,1)` in Excel and similar formulas in MATLAB and Python.

13. Data tables are a very useful tool in Excel. They allow one to reference a formula and compute the values of the formula for different input values of one of the arguments in the formula. See this chapter's online appendices.

Time to Expiration					
(Years)	Call	Put	Volatility	Call	Put
0.5	\$3.78	\$3.24	10%	\$1.69	\$1.15
1.0	\$6.44	\$3.49	20%	\$3.09	\$2.54
1.5	\$8.76	\$3.51	30%	\$4.48	\$3.94
2.0	\$10.86	\$3.43	40%	\$5.88	\$5.33
2.5	\$12.81	\$3.31	50%	\$7.26	\$6.72
3.0	\$14.63	\$2.15	60%	\$8.64	\$8.10
3.5	\$16.35	\$2.99	70%	\$10.10	\$9.46
4.0	\$17.97	\$2.82	80%	\$11.36	\$10.82

Exhibit 18.6
Prices of European call and put options for different values of the time to maturity T and the volatility σ.

The Black-Scholes model assumes that the call option is a European call option. Using the Black-Scholes model (except as a part of approximation schemes) is inappropriate when derivatives with American features are priced. The binomial option pricing model described in the previous section can easily handle American call options.

- *Assumption 2.* The stock return volatility σ is constant over the life of the option and known with certainty.
  If the first part of the assumption does not hold, an option pricing model can be developed that allows the variance to change. The violation of the second part of the assumption, however, is more serious. Because the Black-Scholes model depends on the riskless hedge argument, and in turn the stock return volatility must be known to construct the proper hedge, if the stock return volatility is uncertain, the hedge will not be riskless.

- *Assumption 3.* The risk-free rate r is constant over the life of the option and is the same for borrowing and lending.
  The first part of the assumption is unrealistic because interest rates change daily. As we will show in section 19.1.1, simulation can make the model more realistic. The second part of the assumption is unlikely to hold as well because in real-world financial markets, borrowing rates are higher than lending rates. Realistically, the market price for a call option would be between the call prices derived from the Black-Scholes model using the two interest rates.

- *Assumption 4.* The stochastic process generating stock prices is a diffusion process.
  To derive an exact option pricing model, an assumption is needed about the way that stock prices move. As we will show shortly, the Black-Scholes model assumes that stock prices follow a diffusion process (a geometric random walk). In other words, the future stock price is assumed to be determined from the following equation:

$$S_T = S_0 e^{\left(r - q - \frac{1}{2}\sigma^2\right)\cdot T + \sigma \cdot \sqrt{T} \cdot \tilde{\varepsilon}}$$

where $\tilde{\varepsilon}$ is a standard normal random variable, $\tilde{\varepsilon} \sim \Phi(0, 1)$. Recall that the stock price can take on any positive value in a diffusion process, but it does not jump from one stock price to another, skipping over interim prices. The Black-Scholes formula does not apply when stock prices follow a jump process; that is, when prices are not continuous and smooth but rather exhibit jumps. Merton (1973) and Cox, Ross, and Rubinstein (1979) have developed alternative option-pricing models, assuming a jump process for the underlying price.

- *Assumption 5.* There are no transaction costs and taxes.

  The Black-Scholes model ignores taxes and transaction costs. The model can be modified to account for taxes, but the problem is that there is not just one tax rate. Transaction costs include commissions, the bid-ask spreads for the stock and the option, and other costs associated with trading options.

18.4.2.1 Estimating the Parameters in the Black-Scholes Formula Most of the parameters in the Black-Scholes formula—like the initial stock price, the time to maturity, and the short-term risk-free interest rate—can be observed directly. The one parameter that needs to be estimated is the underlying asset's price volatility. Market participants determine this input into the Black-Scholes option pricing model in one of two ways: (1) by calculating the implied volatility from current option prices or (2) by calculating the standard deviation using historical daily stock returns.

Calculating the *implied probability* relies on the fact that an option pricing model relates a given volatility estimate to a unique price for the option. If the option price is known, the same option pricing model can be used to determine the corresponding volatility. Therefore, the volatility in the pricing model for an option we seek to value can be *implied* from observed market prices for other options on the same stock. (See this chapter's online appendices for the implementation of an example.)

In addition to its use as input in an option pricing model, implied volatility has other applications in strategies that employ options. The most straightforward application is a comparison of implied volatility with the volatility estimate using historical return data, which we will describe shortly. Suppose an investor believes that the estimated volatility using historical data is a better estimate than implied volatility. In that case, the two volatility estimates can be compared to assess whether an option is cheap or expensive. Specifically, if the estimate of volatility using historical data is greater than implied volatility, then the option is cheap; if it is less than implied volatility, then the option is expensive.

A further use for implied volatility is to compare put and call options on the same stock at the same time to expiration. Implied volatility also can be used to compare options on the same underlying stock and time to expiration but with different strike prices. For example, suppose that the implied volatility for a call option with a strike price of 90 is 8% when a call option with a strike of 100 has an implied volatility of 12%. Then, on a relative basis, the call option with a strike of 90 is cheaper than the call option with a strike of 100. One fact to keep in mind for latter application, however, is that a phenomenon called *volatility smile* is often naturally observed in option markets. Namely, implied volatilities for options on the same stock but with different strike prices exhibit a pattern like that shown in exhibit 18.7. More specifically, options that are at the money (i.e., options where the underlying's price is the same as the strike price) tend to have a lower implied volatility than options that are out of the money or in

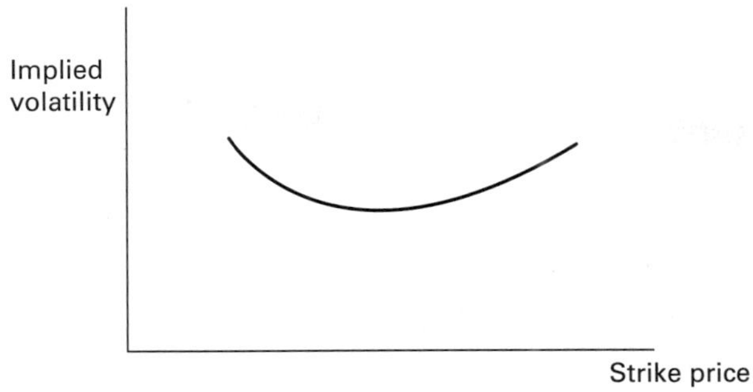

Exhibit 18.7
Volatility smile for in-the-money call options.

the money. When trying to determine the correct volatility to use for pricing a new option, practitioners often use a quick-and-dirty approach: they interpolate between volatility values on the smile.[14]

The second method used to estimate stock return volatility is to calculate the standard deviation of historical daily stock returns. Market practices with respect to the number of trading days that are used to calculate the daily standard deviation vary. The number of trading days can be as few as 10 or as many as 100. Since market participants are interested in annualized volatility, the daily standard deviation is annualized as follows:

$$\text{Daily standard deviation} \cdot \sqrt{\text{Number of trading days in a year}}$$

Conventions about the number of trading days in a year to use vary as well. Typically, either 250, 260, or 365 trading days are used. The first two are used because they represent the number of actual trading days for certain options. Given the different conventions about the number of trading days of data to use for the estimation and the number of trading days in a year to use for annualizing the estimated historical daily volatility, estimates of historical volatility can vary significantly.

Whereas historical volatility estimates are backward-looking, implied volatility estimates are forward-looking, in the sense that the latter incorporate market participants' expectations about where the volatility will be. Generally, implied volatility estimates are preferred, but sometimes they are not easy to produce. Sometimes a combination of historical and implied volatilities is used.

18.4.2.2 The Black-Scholes Option Pricing Formula and Geometric Random Walks We will now show that the assumption that the underlying asset price follows a geometric random walk leads to the Black-Scholes formula. We will focus on deriving the formula for the price of a European call option. (The formula for the price of a European put option can be derived in a similar way.) Recall that the assumption that the stock price follows a geometric

14. Note that if the Black-Scholes model truly applied to markets, the volatility smile phenomenon should not occur. The fact that it exists implies that practitioners do not believe that the lognormal probability distribution correctly represents extreme events. In the real world, extreme events (those that happen in the tails of the distribution) are more likely than the lognormal distribution would imply.

random walk means that the future stock price at time T is lognormally distributed (i.e., that the log of the stock returns at time T is normally distributed).

The call value equals the discounted expected value of the call payoffs under the risk-neutral probability distribution. We can write

$$C = e^{-rT} E[\max(S_T - K, 0)]$$

This expression can be rewritten as

$$C = e^{-rT} E[S_T | S_T > K] - e^{-rT} E[K | S_T > K]$$

As explained in chapter 3, $E[. \mid .]$ denotes conditional expectation. For example, $E[S_T | S_T > K]$ is the expectation of the possible values for the future stock price conditional on the fact that the future stock price value is greater than the strike price K. (This is because we do not worry about the case when the stock price is less than the strike price; the payoff from the call option in the latter case is zero.)

As mentioned before, the fact that the log of the stock returns is normally distributed means that $S_T = S_0 e^{\tilde{\omega}_T}$, where $\tilde{\omega}_T$ is a normal random variable with mean $m = (r - q - 0.5 \cdot \sigma^2) \cdot T$ and standard deviation $s = \sigma \cdot \sqrt{T}$. (Note that we replaced μ, the drift of the geometric random walk for the stock price, with r, the risk-free rate. This is because we will be doing the computations in a risk-neutral world, where the rate of return for all assets is assumed to be the risk-free rate.)

Recalling the fact that an expectation is a weighted average, the expected value in the second term of the formula for the call price can be written as $K \cdot \mathrm{P}(S_T > K)$, where P stands for "probability." Since $S_T = S_0 e^{\tilde{\omega}_T}$, the expectation can be written as

$$K \cdot P(S_0 e^{\tilde{\omega}_T} > K) = K \cdot P(\tilde{\omega}_T > \ln(K/S_0))$$

This expression implies that the option will be exercised only if the value of $\tilde{\omega}_T$ is greater than $\ln(K/S_0)$.

Here, $\tilde{\omega}_T$ can be converted to a standard normal variable, $\tilde{\varepsilon}_T$, by subtracting its mean and dividing by its standard deviation.[15] Thus, the variable

$$\tilde{\varepsilon}_T = \frac{\tilde{\omega}_T - m}{s}$$

has a standard normal distribution. The cumulative normal distribution function, $\Phi(d)$, gives the probability in the left tail of the distribution; that is, $P(\tilde{\varepsilon}_T < d)$. The expression $\Phi(-d)$ then gives the probability in the right tail of the standard normal distribution. (Here, we are using the fact that the normal distribution is symmetric.)

We can write

$$\begin{aligned} P(\tilde{\omega}_T > \ln(K/S_0)) &= P\left(\tilde{\varepsilon}_T > \frac{\ln(K/S_0) - m}{s}\right) \\ &= P\left(\tilde{\varepsilon} < -\frac{-\ln(K/S_0) - m}{s}\right) = P\left(\tilde{\varepsilon} < \frac{-\ln(K/S_0) + m}{s}\right) \end{aligned}$$

15. See chapter 3.

$$= P\left(\tilde{\varepsilon} < \frac{\ln(S_0/K) + \left(r - q - \frac{1}{2}\sigma^2\right)T}{\sigma\sqrt{T}} \right) = P(\tilde{\varepsilon} < d_2).$$

This is where the second term in the Black-Scholes call option pricing formula comes from. The first term can be derived similarly, but it involves more complicated mathematical transformations, so we will omit it here.

18.4.2.3 Relationship between the Black-Scholes Option Pricing Formula and the Binomial Tree Pricing Model We showed in section 18.4.1 that

$$f = e^{-n \cdot r \cdot (\Delta t)} \cdot \left[\sum_{j=0}^{n} \binom{n}{j} \cdot p^j \cdot (1-p)^{n-j} \cdot f_j \right]$$

is the generalized expression for the price of a call or put option with the binomial tree model with n steps. Let us focus on the call option price. In that case,

$$f_j = \max(u^j d^{n-j} S_0 - K, 0)$$

We will show that as the number of time periods increases, the binomial option pricing formula and the Black-Scholes pricing formula produce the same option price.

We are not interested in states of the world in which the future stock price is less than the strike price (the option payoffs in those cases are zero), so we would like to eliminate them from consideration. Then we would no longer have to deal with a clumsy formula of the kind max{., 0}, and we can compute the expression for the option price in closed form. Let a =the minimum number of steps that the payoff is nonnegative; that is, the option is in the money. We have

$$u^a d^{n-a} S_0 > K > u^{a-1} d^{n-(a-1)} S_0$$

Dividing both sides of the inequalities by $d^n S_0$, we have

$$\left(\frac{u}{d}\right)^a > \frac{K}{d^n S_0} > \left(\frac{u}{d}\right)^{a-1}$$

Taking natural logarithms of both sides, we get

$$a \cdot \ln\left(\frac{u}{d}\right) > \ln\left(\frac{K}{d^n S_0}\right) > (a-1) \cdot \ln\left(\frac{u}{d}\right)$$

This trick allows us to compute the value of a. Since

$$a > \frac{\ln\left(\frac{K}{d^n S_0}\right)}{\ln\left(\frac{u}{d}\right)} > (a-1)$$

it follows that

$$a = \left\lfloor \frac{\ln\left(\dfrac{K}{d^n S_0}\right)}{\ln\left(\dfrac{u}{d}\right)} \right\rfloor + 1$$

Here, $\lfloor\cdot\rfloor$ stands for "the largest integer less than or equal to the number inside the brackets."

Knowing a allows us to rewrite the call option pricing formula as

$$f = e^{-n \cdot r \cdot (\Delta t)} \cdot \left[\sum_{j=a}^{n} \binom{n}{j} \cdot p^j \cdot (1-p)^{n-j} \cdot (u^j d^{n-j} S_0 - K) \right]$$

which in turn can be written as

$$\begin{aligned} f &= e^{-n \cdot r \cdot (\Delta t)} \cdot \left[\sum_{j=a}^{n} \binom{n}{j} \cdot p^j \cdot (1-p)^{n-j} \cdot u^j d^{n-j} S_0 \right. \\ &\quad \left. - \sum_{j=a}^{n} \binom{n}{j} \cdot p^j \cdot (1-p)^{n-j} \cdot K) \right] \\ &= \sum_{j=a}^{n} \binom{n}{j} \cdot \left(p \cdot u \cdot e^{-r \cdot (\Delta t)}\right)^j \cdot ((1-p) \cdot d \cdot e^{-r \cdot (\Delta t)})^{n-j} \cdot S_0 \\ &\quad - \left[\sum_{j=a}^{n} \binom{n}{j} \cdot p^j \cdot (1-p)^{n-j} \right] \cdot K \cdot e^{-n \cdot r \cdot (\Delta t)} \\ &= \sum_{j=a}^{n} \binom{n}{j} \cdot \left(p \cdot u \cdot e^{-r \cdot (\Delta t)}\right)^j \cdot (1 - p \cdot u \cdot e^{-r \cdot (\Delta t)})^{n-j} \cdot S_0 \\ &\quad - \left[\sum_{j=a}^{n} \binom{n}{j} \cdot p^j \cdot (1-p)^{n-j} \right] \cdot K \cdot e^{-n \cdot r \cdot (\Delta t)} \\ &= S_0 \cdot B(n, a, \text{probability of success} = p \cdot u \cdot e^{-r(\Delta t)}) \\ &\quad - K \cdot e^{-n \cdot r \cdot (\Delta t)} \cdot B(n, a, \text{probability of success} = p) \end{aligned}$$

where B(.) stands for "1 minus the cumulative binomial probability distribution up to a."

As illustrated in chapter 3, as n becomes larger, the binomial distribution starts looking more symmetric and approximates the normal distribution more and more closely. Therefore, for the carefully selected parameters u and d, the formula derived with the binomial tree will approximate the call option price derived using the assumption of a geometric random walk (i.e., the original Black-Scholes formula).

While it is reassuring to know that two popular models for pricing European options lead to consistent estimates, one may ask why we need to work with binomial trees when the Black-Scholes expression provides such a nice closed-form formula. More complicated options and other derivatives (American options are one example) cannot be priced in closed form. So trees are often used to come up with a set of possible values for the stock price, evaluate the possible payoffs for these types of options, and discount the payoffs to the present to obtain a fair price.

18.4.2.4 Matching Parameters How can we make the parameters used in constructing a binomial tree consistent with the parameters used in the Black-Scholes model, and at the same time ensure that the tree will be recombining? One can derive specific formulas by *moment matching,* where the parameters in the binomial tree model are selected in such a way that the first and the second moments of the stock price (i.e., its expected value and its variance) are the same in both models. For example, the expected stock price for the first time period on the tree is

$$(p \cdot u \cdot S_0 + (1-p) \cdot d \cdot S_0)$$

where p and $(1-p)$ are the risk-neutral probabilities. The expected stock price at the end of the first step if the stock price follows a geometric random walk (the assumption behind the Black-Scholes model) is

$$S_0 \cdot e^{\mu \cdot (\Delta t)}$$

(When pricing the actual option under the risk-neutral probability measure, the drift parameter μ will be replaced by the risk-free rate r.) These two expressions must be equal.

Similarly, we can come up with a condition that links the volatility in the binomial tree model and the Black-Scholes model. From these two conditions and the condition that the tree should be recombining, we can derive the following equivalency relationships:

$$u = e^{\sigma \cdot \sqrt{\Delta t}}$$

$$d = \frac{1}{u} = e^{-\sigma \cdot \sqrt{\Delta t}}$$

$$p = \frac{e^{r \cdot (\Delta t)} - d}{u - d}$$

Here, σ is the observed (implied or historical) volatility.

So, for instance, the example that we gave to illustrate the Black-Scholes formula can be matched directly to the one-period and the two-period binomial trees considered in section 18.4.1. That is also why the option prices computed with both the Black-Scholes and the binomial tree models turned out to be close. (The binomial tree with two periods gave us an estimate closer to the price of the Black-Scholes option than the single-period binomial tree. The more time periods we consider for the binomial tree, the closer the approximation will be.)

18.4.2.5 The Black-Scholes Formula and Bonds While the Black-Scholes formula is still widely used in the valuation of European options on equities, it is not as straightforward to apply it to the valuation of options on bonds. There are three assumptions underlying the Black-Scholes model that limit its use in pricing options on Treasury securities.

First, the probability distribution for the prices assumed by the Black-Scholes model permits some probability—no matter how small—that the price can take any positive value. But in the case of a zero-coupon bond, for example, the price cannot take a value above the maturity value. In the case of a coupon bond, the price cannot exceed the sum of the coupon payments plus the maturity value. Thus, unlike stock prices, bond prices have a maximum value. So any probability distribution for prices assumed by an option pricing model that permits bond prices to be higher than the maximum value could generate nonsensical option prices. For instance, the Black-Scholes model allows bond prices to exceed the maximum bond value.

The second assumption of the Black-Scholes model is that the short-term interest rate is constant over the option's life. Yet the price of a bond will change as interest rates change. A change in the short-term interest rate changes the rates along the yield curve. Therefore, to assume that the short-term rate will be constant is inappropriate for options where the underlying is a bond.

The third assumption is that price variance is constant over the life of the option. However, price volatility declines as a bond moves closer to maturity. This is a fundamental mathematical property of fixed-rate coupon bonds. Therefore, the assumption that price variance is constant over the life of a bond option is inappropriate.

The most common type of bond options are on Treasury futures. For such options, referred to as *futures options*, the option buyer has the right to establish a position in a bond futures contract (a long futures position if the case of a call futures option and a short futures position in the case of a put futures option). The model used for valuing bond futures options is the one developed by Black (1976). The Black model was initially developed for valuing European options on forward contracts. There are two problems with this model. First, the Black model does not overcome the problems that were just identified for the Black-Scholes model. Failing to recognize the yield curve means that there will not be a consistency between pricing Treasury futures and options on Treasury futures. Second, the Black model was developed for pricing European-exercise style options on futures contracts. Treasury futures options that are exchange traded, however, are American-exercise-style options. The second problem can be overcome. The Black model was extended by Barone-Adesi and Whaley (1987) to American options on futures contracts. This is the model used by the exchange where Treasury futures options are traded, the Chicago Board of Trade, to settle the certain types of Treasury futures options. However, this model was also developed for equities and is subject to the first problem noted previously. Despite its limitations, the Black model is a very popular model for pricing options on Treasury futures.

18.4.3 Pricing American Options with Binomial Trees

As we explained in section 18.1.2, American-exercise-style options can be exercised at any time, up to and including the expiration date. This makes pricing them more challenging because we need to model not only the possible probability distribution of underlying asset prices at the expiration date, but also the dynamics of the asset price between time 0 and the expiration date. In practice, the possible paths for the asset price between time 0 and the expiration date are discretized—that is, the option value is computed at a finite number of intermediate time periods. If the number of such time periods is large, the approximation is reasonable. In chapter 19, we will show how to use simulation to generate paths for the price of the underlying and price the option using this information. The classical methods for pricing American options include binomial (or trinomial) trees and finite difference methods. In this section, we show the idea behind a traditional pricing method for American options: binomial trees. The main technique underlying the methodology is dynamic programming—that is, finding an optimal solution over multiple stages.[16]

16. See sections 6.6 and 7.1 for an introduction to dynamic programming.

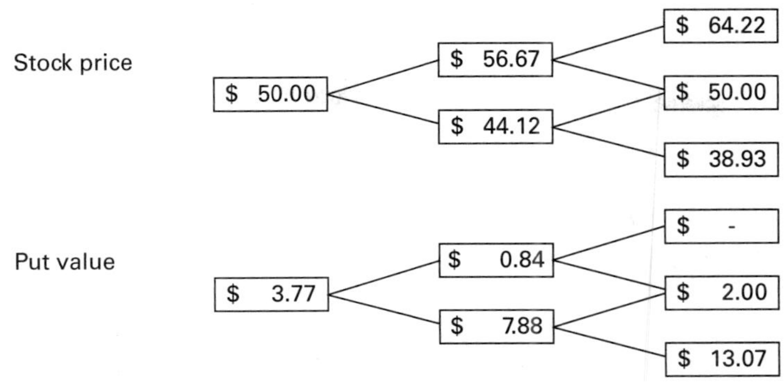

Exhibit 18.8
Pricing an American put option in a two-period binomial tree.

To illustrate this approach, let us consider the same example as in section 18.4.1, which discussed a two-period binomial tree for pricing a European call option. Instead of the call option, however, let us consider a put option with the same strike price. (The price of an American call option on a nondividend-paying stock is the same as the price of a European call option on the stock, so let us consider the put option to make the example more interesting.)[17] In exhibit 18.8, we show the value of the American put option in the possible states of the world at times 0, 1, and 2. To compute the price of the option, we start at the last time period (i.e., the expiration date), and work our way backward.

Similarly, to the case of the European option, for the last time period (time 2), we simply compute the payoffs of the option. For example, the top payoff at time 2 is $\$0 = \max\{\$52.00 - \$64.22, 0\}$. The idea is that if the option holder has not exercised the option before the expiration date, he will exercise it only if the intrinsic value of the option is greater than 0. In the latter case, the payoff to the option holder will be the discounted payoff of the intrinsic value.

Computing the values for the option at time 1 is not as straightforward as at time 2. At time 1, we need to determine whether to exercise the option or continue to hold it (i.e., not exercise it), and the payoff will depend on our decision. We will exercise if the intrinsic value of the option (i.e., the immediate payoff from exercising the option) is greater than the expected value of continuing to hold it. Note that here, we are dealing with a relatively simple value function in a dynamic program: the value function is the maximum of the intrinsic value of the option, and the discounted expected payoff if we do not exercise.[18]

17. The price of an American call option in the two-period binomial tree example is computed in the worksheet **American** in the file **Ch18-BinomialTrees.xlsm**. You can observe that the price of the American call is the same as the price of the European call. This is not a coincidence. The price of an American call option on a nondividend-paying stock is the same as the price of a European call option on the stock because it is never optimal to exercise early; that is, one would never take advantage of the early exercise feature of the American call option. There are a couple of reasons for this, one of which is the time value of money—from the perspective of the option holder, the later the strike price is paid, the better. See Hull (2008) for a detailed explanation.

18. See section 7.1 for a definition and examples of value function in dynamic programming.

For example, the value of \$0.84 obtained at the top node at time 1 in exhibit 18.8 is the maximum of the discounted expected payoff from the two nodes at time 2 that are reachable from the node at time 1, and the intrinsic value of the option:

$$\$0.84 = \max\{\$52.00 - \$56.67, e^{-0.10\cdot(0.5)/2}\cdot(0.5699\cdot\$0.00 + (1-0.5699)\cdot\$2.00)\}$$

Note that the discount factor takes into consideration the fact that the time period has a length of $T/2$. It turns out that the intrinsic value of the option is negative, and less than the value of continuing to hold it, so the option holder would not choose to exercise the option at that node.

Similarly, we can compute the second possible value for the option at time 1. The computation is as follows:

$$\$7.88 = \max\{\$52.00 - \$44.12, e^{-0.10\cdot(0.5)/2}\cdot(0.5699\cdot\$2.00 + (1-0.5699)\cdot\$13.07)\}$$

In this case, it turns out that it is optimal to exercise the option. The intrinsic value is \$7.88 (= \$52.00 – \$44.12), whereas the discounted expected payoff of continuing is

$$e^{-0.10\cdot(0.5/2)}\cdot(0.5699\cdot\$2.00 + (1-0.5699)\cdot\$13.07) = \$6.60$$

At time 0, we similarly compute the value of the option as

$$\max\{\$52.00 - \$50.00, e^{-0.10\cdot(0.5/2)}\cdot(0.5699\cdot\$0.84 + (1-0.5699)\cdot\$7.88)\}$$

This gives us the price of the option, \$3.77. It is not optimal to exercise at time 0—the intrinsic value of the option is \$2, whereas the value of continuing to hold it is \$3.77.

Exhibit 18.5 in section 18.4.1 shows that the price of the European put option was \$3.23. The American put option on the same stock was more expensive—this is to be expected since the American option gives the option holder more flexibility than the European option.

The binomial tree technique for pricing American options can be extended to multiple periods. (See this chapter's online appendices for code for implementing the dynamic programming algorithm.) Moreover, the binomial tree model can be advanced to incorporate more than one underlying factor. However, as the number of factors grows, the dimension and the tractability of the tree become more and more problematic. For example, if we have two factors (e.g., suppose that the American option payoff depends on the performance of two stocks rather than one), then at time 1, we have 4 nodes; at time 2, we have 9 nodes, and the number of nodes becomes larger and larger after that. Simulation techniques are useful in such applications. We will discuss one class of simulation techniques for pricing American options, regression-based methods, in chapter 19.

18.4.4 Measuring Sensitivities

In employing option strategies, an investor needs to know how sensitive the option price is to changes in any of the factors that determine it. Measures for the sensitivity of the option price with respect to the underlying factors are denoted by Greek letters and are usually referred to as "the Greeks." Here, we discuss measures of the sensitivity of the option price with respect to the underlying stock, the time to expiration, and the volatility in the underlying stock price.

18.4.4.1 Delta We have seen the importance of understanding the relationship between the option price and the price of the underlying stock in developing the option pricing model. Option traders and portfolio managers employing options to control the price risk of a portfolio need to know how the option position will change as the price of the underlying stock changes. The ratio of the change in the option price and the change in the price of the underlying is referred to as *delta* (Δ). On an intuitive level, Δ is the number of units of the stock that we should hold for each option, shorted to create a riskless hedge. (The selection of the notation Δ in section 18.4.1 was not by chance.) The option delta is formally defined as

$$\Delta = \frac{\partial f}{\partial S}$$

where f is the derivative price and S is the price of the underlying.

18.4.4.2 Gamma Often, it is of interest to estimate the rate of change of the option delta as the stock price changes. The ratio of the change in delta and the change in the underlying stock price is commonly referred to as *gamma* (Γ), and it is formally defined as

$$\Gamma = \frac{\partial \Delta}{\partial S} = \frac{\partial^2 f}{\partial S^2}$$

Gamma can therefore also be viewed as the second derivative of the option price with respect to the price of the underlying.

18.4.4.3 Theta All other factors remaining constant, the longer the time to expiration, the greater the option price. Because each day the option moves closer to the expiration date, the time to expiration decreases. The theta (Θ) of an option measures the change in the option price relative to the decrease in the time to expiration, or, equivalently, it is a measure of *time decay*. Formally, theta is defined as follows:

$$\Theta = \frac{\partial f}{\partial T}$$

If the price of the underlying stock does not change (which means that the intrinsic value of the option does not change), theta measures how quickly the time premium of the option changes as the option moves toward expiration. Theta is usually negative for an option (although there are exceptions) because as the time to maturity decreases, the option tends to become less valuable.

Buyers of options prefer a low theta so the option price does not decline quickly as it moves toward the expiration date. An option writer, on the other hand, benefits from an option that has a high theta.

18.4.4.4 Vega The option pricing models considered so far assume that the volatility of the price of the underlying, σ, remains constant over time. In reality, this is not the case. The *vega* (V) of a derivative is the rate of change of the derivative value with respect to the volatility of the underlying stock price:[19]

19. Even though *vega* is the term used in the context of option "Greeks," there is no actual letter with that name in the Greek alphabet.

$$V = \frac{\partial f}{\partial \sigma}$$

If the vega is high, the option value is very sensitive to small changes in the volatility of the underlying stock price.

18.4.5 Pricing Options Using Machine Learning

The concern in using the option pricing models just discussed is that they are parametric models, meaning that they require estimation of inputs such as volatility. Moreover, these models are based on unrealistic statistical and economic assumptions. For example, the assumptions on the stochastic behavior of the underlying asset depend on the option price model employed. Machine learning (ML), the subject of chapter 10, is a data-driven approach, and therefore a nonparametric model. Consequently, several researchers have suggested and analyzed the use of ML algorithms to improve the modeling of option prices, as well as to increase the speed of doing so. Moreover, ML algorithms provide more modeling flexibility and can be used to value more complex (i.e., exotic) options. The main idea is for ML algorithms to learn option prices directly from data, using features that could determine the shape of the option pricing function, such as the underlying asset price, the strike price, and the time to maturity.

One of the first studies to propose ML for pricing options is by Hutchinson, Lo, and Poggio (1994), who analyzed the use of neural networks for doing so. They found not only that neural networks provided more accurate option prices than the Black-Scholes option pricing model but also that they were more computationally efficient. Hutchinson, Lo, and Poggio's findings regarding the superiority of neural networks for option pricing were supported by several other studies, including, most recently, Liu, Oosterlee, and Bohte (2019), who tested the use of ML against several extensions of the Black-Scholes pricing model.

ML algorithms other than neural networks (NNs) have been applied for pricing options. For example, Park, Kim, and Lee (2014) investigated the use of support vector regression (SVR), NNs, and genetic algorithms for pricing options on the Korea Composite Stock Price Index (KOSPI) and found that they perform better than parametric models. Ivaşcu (2021) studied the same three ML algorithms as Park, Kim, and Lee (2014) and looked at the performance of random forest, XGBoost, and LightGBM on pricing European call options on crude oil futures contracts (i.e., futures options) traded on the Chicago Mercantile Exchange. One of the reasons for selecting options with this underlying was that it exhibited a high degree of nonlinearity because of its stochastic volatility. Ivaşcu (2021) concluded that the ML algorithms that were studied dramatically outperformed the two parametric models used as a benchmark (the Black-Scholes model and one extension of it), and for the ML algorithms that were studied, the best models were the two boosting models (XGBoost and LightGBM).

Cao et al. (2022) showed how to use NNs for pricing exotic options. They argued that when valuing exotic options, information about volatility (specifically, the volatility surface) is lost in the calibration process. The exotic option used is a knock-in and knockout option where the underlying is the S&P 500 index.

If the pricing dynamics are accurately modeled, then there is no advantage to using ML algorithms. The difficulty with applying ML algorithms is the large amount of data needed for training the model. This limits their application for pricing limited/infrequent traded options, such as exotic options and nontraded customized options.

18.5 Pricing Swaps

As we explained in section 18.1.3, there is a wide variety of swaps. The main idea when pricing all of them, however, is that the fair value of a swap should be the difference between the present values of the expected cash flows exchanged between the two parties in the swap.

By far, the type of swaps most often used by asset managers and traders is interest rate swaps. Specifically, it is the generic interest rate swap (i.e., swapping of fixed rate for floating rate interest rate payments). We discuss the pricing of a generic interest rate swap in detail in this section.

In a generic interest rate swap, the cash flows on the fixed component (i.e., the fixed-rate payments) are known at the inception of the swap. However, the future cash flows on the floating component are unknown since they depend on the future value of the reference rate. The future floating rates for valuing a swap are derived from forward rates embedded in the current yield curve.

By utilizing forward rates, a swap net cash flow can be derived throughout the life of a swap. The sum of these cash flows discounted at the corresponding forward rate for each time period is the current value of the swap. Mathematically, the value of a swap position is

$$\text{Swap value} = \sum_{t=1}^{T} PV(\text{Fixed cash flow}_t - \text{Floating cash flow}_t)$$

where $PV(x)$ denotes the present value of x and t are the dates at which payments are made. The fair swap rate is the fixed rate that makes the swap value zero.

An alternative approach to pricing a generic interest rate swap is to view it as two simultaneous bond payments made by the two parties. Namely, think of the fixed-rate payer as paying the notional amount to the floating-rate payer at the termination date, and of the floating-rate payer as paying the notional amount to the fixed-rate payer at the termination date. This slight modification does not change the actual cash flows and value of the swap because the payments of the notional amounts are canceled out at the termination date. However, it does help us imagine the stream of payments from the fixed-rate payer as the value of a fixed coupon bond, and the stream of payments from the floating-rate payer as the value of a floating-rate bond.

Let the notional amounts be 100, and let v denote the premium (per annum) paid by the fixed-rate payer. Assume that the payments happen at dates $1, 2, \ldots, T$, and that the time interval between payments is Δt. (The latter time interval is typically a quarter.)

At time 0, the value of the fixed-rate bond is

$$100 \cdot v \cdot (\Delta t) \cdot \sum_{t=1}^{T} B(0,t) + 100 \cdot B(0,T)$$

where $B(0, t)$ denotes the value (at time 0) of a zero-coupon bond with a face value of 1 and maturity t. (This is because the collection of payments during the life of the swap can be thought of as a portfolio of zero-coupon bonds of face value 1, with time to maturity equal to the times of the swap payments.)

The value of the floating-rate bond at time 0 is 100. To see this, note that the floating-rate payer can replicate the value of the bond by investing 100 today at the current interest rate, and earning just enough interest to pay the first coupon on the floating-rate bond to the fixed-rate payer. Then, the floating-rate payer can invest 100 again at the prevailing interest rates after the first swap payment and earn enough interest to pay the second floating-rate coupon, with 100 left over. Continuing in the same way, the floating-rate payer can reinvest the 100 until the last time period, when he pays the 100 to the fixed-rate payer. Therefore, the present value of the investment from the perspective of the floating-rate payer is 100. From the perspective of the floating-rate payer, the value of the swap today is the difference between the fixed-rate payer's payments and his or her payments; that is,

$$100 \cdot v \cdot (\Delta t) \cdot \sum_{t=1}^{T} B(0,t) + 100 \cdot B(0,T) - 100$$

The fixed rate v that makes the value of the swap equal to zero at time 0 is the fair price of the swap at time 0. It is easy to see that the value of v should be

$$v = \frac{1 - B(0,T)}{(\Delta t) \cdot \sum_{t=1}^{T} B(0,t)}$$

The values of $B(0, t)$ can be determined from today's yield curve. (In practice, they are determined from the swap rate curve, which is a plot of swap rates against maturities in much the same manner as the bond yield curve.) They are in fact the discount factors that apply to different maturities.

Summary

- Derivatives are contracts that derive their value from underlying financial securities, such as stocks, bonds, market indices, currencies, and commodities.
- There are three general classes of derivatives: forwards and futures, options, and swaps.
- A forward contract is an agreement to buy or sell an asset at a specific time in the future for a specific price. Forward contracts are sold in the over-the-counter (OTC) market; that is, they are nonstandard and negotiated directly between a buyer and a seller.
- Futures are very similar to forwards, but they are standardized contracts traded on exchanges.
- An option is a contract in which the option seller grants the option buyer the right to enter into a transaction with the seller to either buy or sell an underlying asset at a specified price on or before a specified date. If the right is to purchase the underlying, the option is referred to as a call option. If the right is to sell the underlying, the option is referred to as a put option.
- An option can also be categorized according to when it may be exercised by the buyer. A European option can be exercised only at the option's expiration date, while an American option can be exercised any time on or before the expiration date.

- More sophisticated option contracts are referred to as exotic options or exotics. Examples of exotic options include Asian options and barrier options.
- Options do not have a linear payoff, while futures and forwards do. The difference in the type of payoff between futures and options is important because market participants can use futures to protect against symmetric risk and options to protect against asymmetric risk.
- Swaps are contractual agreements in which two counterparties agree to exchange returns on different assets over a prespecified period of time.
- Arbitrage is the opportunity to make "free money"; that is, to realize a profit with little or no risk of losing money in the future.
- A hedging strateg*y* is a trading or investment strategy that reduces risk.
- The concept of no arbitrage and the idea of creating a replicating portfolio that mimics the payoff of a financial derivative provide the foundation for pricing complex financial instruments.
- Classical methods for pricing European options include binomial trees and the Black-Scholes formula. Those two methods result in similar estimates for appropriately chosen model parameters.
- The Black-Scholes formula holds under very specific conditions and assumes that the price of the underlying asset follows a geometric random walk. It is not appropriate for use when pricing fixed-income securities.
- Binomial and trinomial trees are widely used for pricing American options.
- Measures for the sensitivity of the option price with respect to underlying factors (such as the stock price, the time to maturity, and the volatility of the underlying) are denoted by Greek letters and are usually referred to as *Greeks*. Such sensitivity measures include delta, gamma, theta, and vega.
- The value of a swap can be found by computing the difference between the discounted cash flows (DCFs) on the floating leg and the DCFs on the fixed leg of the swap. The value of a swap can also be viewed as the difference between the value of a floating-rate bond and a fixed-rate bond.
- The fair swap rate is the fixed premium that makes the value of the swap zero.
- Machine learning (ML) algorithms can be used to value options.

19

Pricing Derivatives with Simulation

In chapter 18, we introduced the main ideas behind the pricing of standard financial derivative instruments, or simply *derivatives*. We saw that the main assumption underlying derivative pricing schemes is that there is no arbitrage in the markets. When there is no arbitrage, the price of a derivative can be found as the expected value of its discounted payouts, where the expected value is taken with respect to a transformation of the original probability distribution of outcomes, called the *risk-neutral probability measure*.

The same principles that guide the computation of the fair price of standard derivatives extend to the pricing of more complex derivatives. However, the difference is that closed-form formulas of the Black-Scholes type cannot necessarily be found for complex derivatives. Such derivatives must be priced with different numerical techniques, and simulation is one of those.

We begin this chapter by showing how simulation can be used to price some of the simple derivatives discussed in chapter 18, such as European call options. Although simulation does not need to be applied in this context, techniques that make the simulation procedures more efficient can be demonstrated in a familiar setting and benchmarked against a known final price. These examples help us illustrate more advanced simulation techniques, called *variance reduction methods*, whose goal is to make the simulation process as efficient as possible and minimize the estimate's variance. We review several such methods, including antithetic variables, stratified sampling, importance sampling, and control variates. We also review quasirandom (also called *quasi-Monte Carlo*) methods for simulation that use low-discrepancy number sequences to obtain a good representation for the probability distribution being simulated. We then give examples of pricing more complex derivatives, such as barrier options and American options, by simulation, and discuss evaluating the sensitivity of derivatives to changes in underlying parameters by crude and pathwise simulation methods.

19.1 Computing Option Prices with Crude Monte Carlo Simulation

As we mentioned at the beginning of this chapter, the main idea behind computing prices of options (and other financial securities) by simulation is to generate a set of payoffs and discount them to the present to find the expected value of all discounted payoffs under the risk-neutral probability measure. The expected payoff value is the derivative's "fair" price. Typically, when pricing financial derivatives, the prices of the underlying securities are assumed to follow specific kinds of random walks.[1] The most straightforward way to price a derivative is to create paths of realizations of the random walks for the derivative's underlying, compute the payoff along each path, discount to the present, and find the appropriate weighted average of the payoffs as an estimator for the expected value of the payoff. This is referred to as using *crude Monte Carlo* (MC). It is not always the most efficient way to find a derivative's price, but it is tangible and easy to implement.

In this section, we give a couple of examples of how crude MC can be used for pricing options. Smart ways to simulate the prices of options that exploit knowledge about the simulation process or the underlying distributions are discussed in section 19.2.

19.1.1 Pricing a European Call Option by Simulation

As explained in chapter 18, a widely used formula for European options is the Black-Scholes formula.[2] It provides a closed-form expression for computing the price of the option. In chapter 18, we also showed that the underlying assumption used in the derivation of the Black-Scholes formula is that the underlying asset price follows a geometric Brownian motion.[3] The evolution of the asset price can then be described by the equation

$$dS_t = \mu S_t dt + \sigma S_t dW_t$$

where W_t is standard Brownian motion and μ and σ are the drift and the volatility of the process, respectively. For technical reasons (absence of arbitrage), when pricing an option, the drift μ is replaced by the risk-free rate r in the Black-Scholes formula.

Under the assumption for the random process followed by the asset price, the value of the asset price S_T at time T, given the asset price S_t at time t, can be computed as

$$S_T = S_t e^{\left(r - \frac{1}{2}\sigma^2\right)\cdot(T-t) + \sigma\cdot\sqrt{(T-t)}\cdot\tilde{\varepsilon}}$$

where $\tilde{\varepsilon}$ is a standard normal random variable.[4]

Hence, the option price obtained from the Black-Scholes formula can be approximated by simulation if a large number of values for the normal random variable $\tilde{\varepsilon}_t$ are generated. By creating scenarios for the stock price S_T at time T, we can compute the discounted payoffs of the option, and find the expected payoff. Suppose that we generate N scenarios for $\tilde{\varepsilon}$: $\varepsilon^{(1)}, \ldots, \varepsilon^{(N)}$. Then the price of a European call option with strike price K will be

$$C_t = e^{-r\cdot(T-t)} \cdot \sum_{n=1}^{N} \frac{1}{N} \cdot \max\left\{ S_t e^{\left(r - \frac{1}{2}\sigma^2\right)\cdot(T-t) + \sigma\cdot\sqrt{(T-t)}\cdot\varepsilon^{(n)}} - K, 0 \right\}$$

1. See chapter 17 for an introduction to different types of random walks.

2. See Black and Scholes (1973).

3. See chapter 17.

4. If the stock pays a continuously compounded dividend yield of q, then we use $(r - q - 0.5 \cdot \sigma^2)$ instead of $(r - 0.5 \cdot \sigma^2)$ as the drift term.

This expression is the expected value of the option payoffs; that is, the weighted average of the option payoffs. The weight, or the probability of each scenario, is assumed to be $1/N$ since the scenarios are picked at random, and the frequency of their occurrence already incorporates the probability distribution of $\tilde{\varepsilon}$. (See this chapter's online appendices and accompanying model files (e.g., **Ch19-PricingBySimulation.xlsx, Ch19-OptionPricingVBA.xlsm, EuropeanCall**) for an actual implementation of the simulation.)

It appears unnecessarily complicated to price the option this way, and indeed, simulation is rarely used for this kind of simple problem in practice. There are more complex derivatives and more sophisticated models for asset price behavior; in such cases, it can be simpler to generate scenarios and evaluate prices by simulation than to derive closed-form analytical formulas mathematically. For example, if the underlying asset follows a mean reversion process, the Black-Scholes formula will not work for a European call option, but simulation can help us evaluate the option price easily. In addition, in the case of portfolios and baskets of multiple assets, generating joint scenarios for multiple securities through simulation can help capture the otherwise complicated effect of interactions among different risk factors influencing the future value of the portfolio or derivatives.

Let us illustrate another advantage of simulating the price of a European call option rather than using the Black-Scholes formula. Recall that one of the assumptions in the Black-Scholes formula is that the interest rate r remains constant during the life of the option, which is a limitation of the model. Simulation makes it easy to calibrate model parameters to observed market factors and to incorporate additional layers of modeling complexity. For example, suppose that at time 0, we observe a term structure[5] of zero-coupon bond prices $B(0, 1), \ldots, B(0, T)$ that is not necessarily consistent with a single interest rate r. In other words, we cannot find a short rate r such that

$$B(0, t) = e^{-r \cdot t}$$

for all intermediate time periods t. It would be difficult to correct for this in a closed-form formula such as the Black-Scholes formula. However, the correction can be easily implemented in the simulation: we only need to simulate future asset prices at each step as

$$S_{t+1} = S_t \cdot \frac{B(0,t)}{B(0,t+1)} \cdot e^{-\frac{1}{2}\cdot\sigma^2\cdot 1+\sigma\cdot\sqrt{1}\cdot\tilde{\varepsilon}_t}$$

Similarly, if we have information about a collection of observed forward prices[6] $F(0, t), \ldots, F(0, T)$ on the underlying asset, we can obtain a more accurate representation of the possible scenarios in the simulation by using the formula

$$S_{t+1} = S_t \cdot \frac{F(0,t+1)}{F(0,t)} \cdot e^{-\frac{1}{2}\cdot\sigma^2\cdot 1+\sigma\cdot\sqrt{1}\cdot\tilde{\varepsilon}_t}$$

The complexity of the simulation model can be increased further by incorporating random walk models for the volatility σ. The simulation technique therefore offers a great

5. See chapter 2 for a definition of term structure of interest rates.

6. See chapter 18 for a definition of forward price.

range of modeling capabilities. The need for such a technique will hopefully become more evident in the Asian option pricing example in the next section.

19.1.2 Pricing an Asian Option by Simulation

As mentioned in chapter 18, an Asian option is a contract whose value is determined by the average price of the underlying asset either continuously over the option's time to maturity or at a prespecified set of monitoring dates $t_1, \ldots, t_T$. In particular, the payoff of an Asian call option is

$$V_T = \max\{S_{\text{average}} - K, 0\}$$

The average is usually defined as the arithmetic average; that is, as

$$\frac{S_1 + \cdots + S_T}{T}$$

where T is the number of discrete time periods until the option's expiration date. The specific characteristics of an Asian option vary depending on how the average price is calculated (instead of the arithmetic average, it could be the geometric average),[7] whether there are early exercise features (in which case the average of the underlying asset price over the life of the option so far is calculated), and whether the option is a put or a call.

To find the value of an Asian option, we need information not only on the value of the asset at the expiration date (time T), but also on the possible paths that the asset could take to reach its terminal value. This is referred to as *path dependency*, and it is a context in which simulation is particularly useful.

If the underlying asset price S is assumed to follow a geometric random walk, and if the average is computed as a geometric rather than arithmetic average, there are analytical formulas for pricing continuous Asian options.[8] However, there are no exact formulas in the case of an arithmetic average Asian call option with discrete monitoring dates or different assumptions on the process followed by the asset price.

Pricing the option is rather straightforward if we use crude MC simulation. We simulate possible paths for the underlying asset price. Let $S_{t_i}(n)$ be the simulated asset price at time t_i, $i = 1, \ldots, T$, for path n, $n = 1, \ldots, N$. For example, if the underlying asset price S is assumed to follow a geometric random walk, then the asset price at time t_1 can be simulated given the asset price at time 0 as

$$S_{t_1} = S_0 e^{\left(r - \frac{1}{2}\sigma^2\right)\cdot(t_1 - 0) + \sigma \cdot \sqrt{(t_1 - 0)} \cdot \tilde{\varepsilon}_0}$$

where, as defined earlier, $\tilde{\varepsilon}_0$ is a random variable following a normal distribution with mean 0 and standard deviation 1 (the subscript 0 stands for the fact that this realization of $\tilde{\varepsilon}_0$ is for the time period $(0, t_1)$. Having generated a realization of S_{t_1}, we simulate a possible value for S_{t_2} by using the formula

7. Recall that the geometric average would be computed as $(S_1 \cdot \ldots \cdot S_T)^{1/T}$.

8. See the example in section 19.2.4.

$$S_{t_2} = S_{t_1} e^{\left(\mu - \frac{1}{2}\sigma^2\right)\cdot(t_2 - t_1) + \sigma\cdot\sqrt{(t_2 - t_1)}\cdot\tilde{\varepsilon}_1}$$

and generating a realization of the normal random variable $\tilde{\varepsilon}_1$. After repeating this T times, we have generated a path for the asset price. Averaging the properly discounted option payoff over N paths produces the fair price of the Asian option. (See this chapter's online appendices and accompanying files (e.g., **Ch19-PricingBySimulation.xlsx, Ch19-OptionPricingVBA.xlsm, ArithmeticAsianCall.m**) for an implementation of an example.) There are more efficient ways to estimate the price of an arithmetic average Asian option. We will discuss one such method in section 19.2.4.

19.2 Variance Reduction Techniques

As explained in chapter 5, paradoxically, truly random numbers can be too random for practical purposes. Recall that the error in the average estimate obtained from "truly random" MC simulation is proportional to $\frac{1}{\sqrt{N}}$, where N is the number of scenarios for the random variable (this fact would be approximately true for good pseudorandom number generators as well).[9] To estimate a European call option price twice as accurate, for example, we would have to increase the number of generated scenarios for the underlying asset price four times. Much research has been dedicated in recent years to finding ways to reduce that error and to be computationally savvy when generating scenarios. Techniques for increasing the accuracy of the estimate from simulation are often referred to as *variance reduction methods* because their goal is to reduce the variability of the estimator. Stratified sampling, which was discussed in chapter 5, is one such method. In this section, we define and provide intuition for several variance reduction methods that are used in financial applications. There are numerous ways to achieve computational efficiency in specific situations, and we cannot review all of them here. For a detailed introduction to other advanced variance reduction techniques, see Glasserman (2004), Brandimarte (2006), and McLeish (2005).

19.2.1 Antithetic Variables

Simulating a random number is computationally expensive. One technique that is used to reduce the error in the average estimate in derivative pricing without increasing the number of simulated values is to incorporate the generated random number twice in computing the derivative payoff: once as the original simulated number and another time as its antithetic number.

For example, recall from the option pricing example in section 19.1 that the value of the stock price S_T at time T can be computed from the equation for a geometric random walk. In that expression, $\tilde{\varepsilon}$ is a random variable that follows a standard normal distribution. Suppose that N values for the normal random variable $\tilde{\varepsilon}$ are generated. With the antithetic variable method, the value of the derivative payoff in each of the N scenarios is computed as the average of two payoffs: one obtained by plugging in the simulated value for $\tilde{\varepsilon}$, and

9. See chapter 5 for a discussion of estimator efficiency and bias.

another obtained by plugging in the negative of the simulated value for $\tilde{\varepsilon}$ (the "antithetic" number). These N adjusted payoffs are otherwise treated in the same way as in the traditional simulation method described earlier in this chapter: at the end, the N payoffs are averaged and properly discounted to obtain the fair estimate of the derivative price. The difference is that this approach substantially reduces the standard error in the average estimate, while keeping the number of simulation trials at N.

The antithetic variable approach is not limited to normal random variables. As explained in chapter 5, random number generation from an arbitrary probability distribution is often done by the inverse transform method; that is, a random number is generated in two stages. At the first stage, a uniform random number U between 0 and 1 is simulated. At the second stage, this random number is inverted to obtain a random number from the desired probability distribution. Thus, we can apply the antithetic technique at the first stage and treat the randomly generated number U as two realizations: U and its antithetic number $1 - U$. For example, if a number generated within the interval [0, 1] is 0.7, then the antithetic counterpart would be 0.3. Both these numbers can then be inverted to obtain a pair of antithetic variables from a prespecified distribution such as the normal distribution.

It is important to realize, however, that antithetic sampling is not a cure-all. In some cases, the variance of the estimator of the expected price may actually increase if we use antithetic sampling. For the antithetic approach to work, the payoffs generated with the antithetic variables must have a negative correlation. Specifically, the antithetic variables approach relies on generating two sets of N realizations each of a random variable simultaneously:

$$\varepsilon_1^{(1)}, \dots, \varepsilon_1^{(N)}$$

and

$$\varepsilon_2^{(1)}, \dots, \varepsilon_2^{(N)}$$

In the example of the European call option, we had $\varepsilon_2^{(n)} = -\varepsilon_1^{(n)}$, $n = 1, \dots, N$, which was a cheap way to produce another realization of the random variable given a generated observation $\varepsilon_1^{(n)}$. The vertical dependencies between the sets of observations were perfectly negatively correlated; that is, each $\varepsilon_1^{(n)}$ was perfectly negatively correlated with $\varepsilon_2^{(n)} = -\varepsilon_1^{(n)}$, and that fortunately also meant that the resulting option payoffs ended up negatively correlated.

We produced a new sample of payoffs based on pairwise averages of the payoffs corresponding to each of the two samples of realizations for $\tilde{\varepsilon}$:

$$pf^{(1)} = \frac{pf_1^{(1)} + pf_2^{(1)}}{2}, \dots, pf^{(N)} = \frac{pf_1^{(N)} + pf_2^{(N)}}{2}$$

Since the original observations for $\tilde{\varepsilon}$ were horizontally independent (we drew an independent and identically distributed [i.i.d.] sample $\varepsilon_1^{(1)}, \dots, \varepsilon_1^{(N)}$), the pairwise averaged observations $pf^{(1)}, \dots, pf^{(N)}$ are also i.i.d. The variance of the average of the new sample of observations $pf^{(1)}, \dots, pf^{(N)}$ is

$$\begin{aligned}
\operatorname{Var}(\overline{pf}) &= \operatorname{Var}\left(\frac{pf^{(1)} + \cdots + pf^{(N)}}{N}\right) \\
&= \frac{1}{N^2} \cdot \left[N \cdot \operatorname{Var}\left(pf^{(n)}\right)\right] \\
&= \frac{1}{N} \cdot \operatorname{Var}\left(\frac{pf_1^{(n)} + pf_2^{(n)}}{2}\right) \\
&= \frac{1}{4N} \cdot (\operatorname{Var}(pf_1^{(n)}) + \operatorname{Var}(pf_2^{(n)}) + 2 \cdot \operatorname{Covar}(pf_1^{(n)}, pf_2^{(n)})) \\
&= \frac{1}{2N} \cdot \operatorname{Var}(pf_1^{(n)}) + \frac{1}{2N} \cdot \operatorname{Covar}(pf_1^{(n)}, pf_2^{(n)}) \\
&= \frac{1}{2N} \cdot \operatorname{Var}(pf_1^{(n)}) + \frac{1}{2N} \cdot \underbrace{\sigma_{pf_1^{(n)}} \cdot \sigma_{pf_2^{(n)}}}_{\operatorname{Var}(pf_1^{(n)})} \cdot \rho(pf_1^{(n)}, pf_2^{(n)}) \\
&= \frac{\operatorname{Var}(pf_1^{(n)})}{2N} \cdot (1 + \rho(pf_1^{(n)}, pf_2^{(n)})).
\end{aligned}$$

If we did not generate N regular and N antithetic variables, but instead simply took a sample of $2N$ i.i.d. random variables, the variance of the estimate of the average payoff would have been

$$\frac{\operatorname{Var}(pf_1^{(n)})}{2N}$$

Thus, to reduce the variance of the average estimator $\operatorname{Var}(\overline{pf})$, we would ideally want the correlation $\rho(pf_1^{(n)}, pf_2^{(n)})$ to be less than zero. This was true in the case of European option payoffs; however, there are some cases for which this will not happen:

- *The payoffs are not monotonic functions of the random variables.* In the case of the European call option simulation, the formula for the payoff had the random variable $\tilde{\varepsilon}$ in the power of the exponential, and the exponential function is a monotonic function—it increases as its exponent increases. However, imagine a payoff function that increases and then decreases with the values of the random variable so U and $1-U$ generate the same value for the payoff. In this case, the antithetic variables method backfires, resulting in increased variance because the correlation between $pf_1^{(n)}, pf_2^{(n)}$ is 1. Therefore, the payoffs for some derivatives may not end up negatively correlated even if the antithetic variables based on the uniform random numbers U and $1-U$ are negatively correlated. An example of a payoff function that is nonmonotonic is that of a butterfly spread.
- *The generated random variables and their antithetic variables are not negatively correlated.* We assumed that we would use the inverse transform method to generate the random numbers and the antithetic random numbers. However, as mentioned in chapter 5, other simulation methods, such as the acceptance-rejection method and the Box-Muller method, are used as well. The inverse transform method uses a monotonic function—the cumulative distribution function—to produce random variable realizations from different distributions based on the realization of the uniform random numbers U and $1-U$. With the acceptance-rejection and Box-Muller methods, we no longer have the same guarantees.

19.2.2 Stratified Sampling

In chapter 5, we introduced stratified sampling as a technique that allows us to create a representative sample of the entire range of outcomes. Variations of stratified sampling are already incorporated into many random number generator software products, so it is not always necessary to implement the algorithm manually. For example, as mentioned in chapter 5, an enhanced version of stratified sampling, Latin Hypercube Sampling, is the default option for simulation with @RISK.

Nevertheless, it is instructive to see a specific, relatively simple example of how stratified sampling would be implemented. Here, we will price a European option with maturity T and a strike price K under the assumption that the asset price follows a geometric random walk.

When the underlying price follows a geometric random walk, we can simulate the price at maturity T using the equation

$$S_T = S_0 e^{\left(r - \frac{1}{2}\sigma^2\right) \cdot T + \sigma \cdot \sqrt{T} \cdot \tilde{\varepsilon}}$$

where $\tilde{\varepsilon}$ is a standard normal variable. Stratified sampling is applied for random numbers on the interval [0, 1]. We generate the values for $\tilde{\varepsilon}$ by using the inverse transform method as follows: first, generate N scenarios for realizations of a uniform random variable $\tilde{U}$ on the interval [0, 1], and then use the inverse cumulative normal distribution function Φ^{-1} to get the values for $\tilde{\varepsilon}$.[10]

The scenarios $U_1, \ldots, U_N$, representing realizations of the uniform random variable $\tilde{U}$, will be generated such that each realization falls within its own stratum n, $n = 1, \ldots, N$. To have N strata of equal probabilities, we divide the unit interval into N small intervals, each with length $1/N$. If we then consider the inverse cumulative normal distribution function,

$$\Phi^{-1}\left(\frac{n-1}{N} + \frac{U_n}{N}\right), n = 1, \ldots, N$$

we will have divided the standard normal distribution into N strata of equal probability. (Note that this does not mean that the corresponding intervals on the horizontal axis of the normal distribution will have equal lengths, only that the areas above them under the normal distribution PDF will be the same.) Thus, if we generate N scenarios for $\tilde{\varepsilon}$ using the formula

$$S_T = S_0 e^{\left(r - \frac{1}{2}\sigma^2\right) \cdot T + \sigma \cdot \sqrt{T} \cdot \Phi^{-1}\left(\frac{n-1}{N} + \frac{U_n}{N}\right)}, \quad n = 1, \ldots, N$$

we will obtain a representative sample of values for the final asset price.[11] To compute the price of the option, we would then compute the payoffs in all scenarios, discount them to the present, and find their average as usual:

10. Recall that this function can be called with the command `=NORMINV(number, mean, standard deviation)` in Microsoft Excel, and with similar functions in MATLAB and Python. In the case of the standard normal distribution, `mean` = 0 and `standard deviation` = 1.

11. The formula for Φ^{-1} can be entered as `=NORMINV((n-1+U_n)/N,0,1)` in Excel. The subscripts are not entered, of course: U_n represents the value for the nth simulated number from the uniform distribution.

$$C_0 = e^{-r \cdot T} \cdot \sum_{i=1}^{N} \frac{1}{N} \max\left\{ S_0 e^{(r - \frac{1}{2}\sigma^2) \cdot T + \sigma \cdot \sqrt{T} \cdot \Phi^{-1}\left(\frac{n-1}{N} + \frac{U_n}{N}\right)} - K, 0 \right\}.$$

19.2.3 Importance Sampling

Importance sampling is an alternative to stratified sampling for dealing with rare events, or extreme observations, and for reducing the number of simulation trials needed to achieve a particular level of accuracy. The method changes the underlying scenario probabilities to give more weight to important outcomes in the simulation. Such outcomes are generated with greater frequency than they otherwise would. At the end, the observations' weights are scaled back in the computation of the expression of interest so the estimation is correct.

There is no single recipe for constructing good importance sampling methods. The specific construction depends on the underlying random process dynamics. Let us consider the example of pricing European call options in the Black-Scholes setting, in which generating paths that are out of the money is wasteful.[12] This is because only paths that are in the money count in the final computation of the option price—the contribution of out-of-the-money paths to the option price is zero. Although in practice, one would not use importance sampling to price a European call option for which there is a closed-form formula, we use the European call example to provide some intuition about the idea behind the importance sampling method.

First, note that in-the-money paths will occur only if the asset price at the expiration date is greater than the strike price; that is, they will result from realizations of the standard normal random variable $\tilde{\varepsilon}$ such that

$$S_T = S_t e^{\left(r - \frac{1}{2}\sigma^2\right) \cdot (T-t) + \sigma \cdot \sqrt{(T-t)} \cdot \tilde{\varepsilon}} > K$$

From this inequality, we can derive that only normal random numbers higher than

$$\frac{\ln\left(\frac{K}{S_t}\right) - \left(r - \frac{\sigma^2}{2}\right) \cdot (T-t)}{\sigma \cdot \sqrt{T-t}}$$

will lead to in-the-money paths. Equivalently, this means that only random numbers between

$$\Phi\left(\frac{\ln\left(\frac{K}{S_t}\right) - \left(r - \frac{\sigma^2}{2}\right) \cdot (T-t)}{\sigma \cdot \sqrt{T-t}}\right)$$

and 1 on the unit interval [0, 1], when inverted to obtain normal random numbers, will lead to in-the-money paths. Here, Φ (.) denotes the cumulative normal distribution, as before. Thus,

12. See chapter 18 for a definition of in-the-money and out-of-the-money options.

we need to simulate random numbers only in that range of the [0, 1] interval. When computing the option price at the end, instead of weighing each payoff equally by multiplying it by $1/N$ as we would do in standard MC sampling, we would multiply the sum of the payoffs obtained from the simulation by the probability that a particular random path would be in the money, assuming truly random sampling, which is the standard MC method. The latter probability is

$$1-\Phi\left(\frac{\ln(K/S_t)-(r-\sigma^2/2)\cdot(T-t)}{\sigma\cdot\sqrt{T-t}}\right)$$
$$=\Phi\left(\frac{\ln(S_t/K)+(r-\sigma^2/2)\cdot(T-t)}{\sigma\cdot\sqrt{T-t}}\right)$$

The call option price is then

$$C_t = e^{-r(T-t)}\cdot\Phi\left(\frac{\ln(S_t/K)+(r-\sigma^2/2)\cdot(T-t)}{\sigma\cdot\sqrt{T-t}}\right)\cdot$$
$$\sum_{i=1}^{n}\max\left\{S_t e^{\left(r-\frac{1}{2}\sigma^2\right)\cdot(T-t)+\sigma\cdot\sqrt{(T-t)\cdot\varepsilon^{(i)}}}-K,0\right\},$$

where $\varepsilon(1), \ldots, \varepsilon(N)$ are random numbers generated from the range of a normal distribution higher than

$$\frac{\ln\left(\frac{K}{S_t}\right)-\left(r-\frac{\sigma^2}{2}\right)\cdot(T-t)}{\sigma\cdot\sqrt{T-t}}$$

Now let us formalize the importance sampling approach.

When we attempt to find the expected value of the discounted payoffs from a derivative, we are, in effect, trying to evaluate an integral of a specific function over all the values that the random variable can take.[13] We evaluate that integral approximately—we generate the value of the function at multiple points and multiply those values by the probabilities that they will happen. (With crude MC simulation, each scenario that we generate happens with the same probability, so we multiply the estimated value of the payoff function by 1 over the number of scenarios.)

The main idea of the importance sampling method is to introduce an *importance distribution* that rescales the original distribution and makes important scenarios more likely to appear. Suppose that the original integral we were trying to evaluate was

$$E[h(X)] = \int h(x)\cdot f(x)dx$$

where $\mathbf{X}$ is a vector of random variables with joint probability density $f(\mathbf{x})$ and $h(\mathbf{X})$ is the discounted payoff function. If we can find another probability density function g such that $f(\mathbf{x})=0$ whenever $g(\mathbf{x})=0$, we have

13. See chapter 3 for the definition of expected value as an integral over all the values that the random variable can take.

$$\begin{aligned} E_f[h(\mathbf{X})] &= \int h(\mathbf{x}) \cdot f(\mathbf{x})\, d\mathbf{x} \\ &= \int \frac{h(\mathbf{x}) \cdot f(\mathbf{x})}{g(\mathbf{x})} \cdot g(\mathbf{x})\, d\mathbf{x} \\ &= \int h^*(\mathbf{x}) \cdot g(\mathbf{x})\, d\mathbf{x} \\ &= E_g[h^*(\mathbf{X})] \end{aligned}$$

In other words, we can find the expected value of the payoff $h(\mathbf{X})$ with respect to the original probability density function $f(\mathbf{x})$ by finding the expected value of the modified payoff function

$$h^*(x) = \frac{h(x) \cdot f(x)}{g(x)}$$

with respect to the new probability density $g(\mathbf{x})$. The ratio

$$\frac{f(x)}{g(x)}$$

adjusts for the change in the probability measure. It is called the *likelihood ratio* but is also referred to as the *Radon-Nikodym derivative* in the context of stochastic calculus.

We see that on average, we will get the same answer by using importance sampling as when we use crude MC sampling. How can we guarantee, however, that the function $g(\mathbf{x})$ that we select will indeed reduce the variance of the estimator? Let us compute the variances of the two estimators $h(\mathbf{X})$ and $h^*(\mathbf{X})$. Using the equality[14]

$$\text{Var}(\tilde{X}) = \int_{-\infty}^{\infty} x^2 \cdot f(x)dx - \left(\int_{-\infty}^{\infty} x \cdot f(x)dx \right)^2$$

we get

$$\begin{aligned} Var_f[h(\mathbf{X})] &= \int h^2(\mathbf{x}) \cdot f(\mathbf{x})d\mathbf{x} - (E_f[h(\mathbf{X})])^2 \\ Var_g[h^*(\mathbf{X})] &= \int h^2(\mathbf{x}) \cdot \frac{f^2(\mathbf{x})}{g^2(\mathbf{x})} \cdot g(\mathbf{x})d\mathbf{x} - (E_g[h^*(\mathbf{X})])^2 \\ &= \int h^2(\mathbf{x}) \cdot \frac{f(\mathbf{x})}{g(\mathbf{x})} \cdot f(\mathbf{x})d\mathbf{x} - (E_f[h(\mathbf{X})])^2. \end{aligned}$$

The difference between the two variances is

$$\text{Var}_f[h(X)] - \text{Var}_g[h^*(X)] = \int h^2(x) \cdot \left(1 - \frac{f(x)}{g(x)}\right) \cdot f(x)dx$$

Therefore, to ensure that the variance becomes smaller when we use important sampling, we should select $g(\mathbf{x})$ to be large (greater than $f(\mathbf{x})$) when the term $h^2(\mathbf{x}) \cdot f(\mathbf{x})$ is large, and select $g(\mathbf{x})$ to be small (smaller than $f(\mathbf{x})$) when the term $h^2(\mathbf{x}) \cdot f(\mathbf{x})$ is small. In other words, we emphasize important observations.

14. See chapter 3.

How is this procedure applied to the European call option? The discounted payoff function in the case of a European call option is

$$h(x) = e^{-rT} \cdot \max\{S_T - K, 0\}$$

We observed that important scenarios would be generated only if the simulated paths end up in the money; that is, above the strike price K. Suppose that we decide to generate the values for the final price S_T from a probability distribution that is more likely to produce scenarios above the strike price K. Suppose further that instead of the original probability distribution f for the logarithm of the final asset price, which was normal with mean $(r-\sigma^2/2)\cdot T$ and variance $\sigma^2 \cdot T$, we consider a normal distribution with mean $\ln(K/S_0) - \sigma^2 \cdot T/2$ and the same variance, $\sigma^2 \cdot T$. In other words, in the notation used in this section,

$$f(x) = N(x,(r-\sigma^2/2)\cdot T, \sigma^2 \cdot T) = \frac{1}{\sigma\sqrt{2\pi}} e^{-\frac{(x-(rT-\sigma^2 T/2))^2}{2(\sigma^2 T)}},$$

$$g(x) = N(x, \ln(K/S_0) - \sigma^2 \cdot T/2, \sigma^2 \cdot T) = \frac{1}{\sigma\sqrt{2\pi}} e^{-\frac{(x-(\ln(K/S_0)-\sigma^2 T/2))^2}{2(\sigma^2 T)}}.$$

The likelihood ratio is then simply the ratio of two normal-density functions with different means. Therefore,

$$\begin{aligned} E_f[h(x)] &= E_f[e^{-rT} \cdot \max\{S_T - K, 0\}] \\ &= E_g\left[e^{-rT} \cdot \max\{S_T - K, 0\} \cdot \frac{f(x)}{g(x)}\right]. \end{aligned}$$

Hence, the estimator from the simulation is the average for all the scenarios generated with the formula

$$e^{-rT} \cdot \max\{S_0 \cdot e^Z - K, 0\} \cdot \frac{\frac{1}{\sigma\sqrt{2\pi}} \cdot e^{-\frac{\left(Z-\left(rT-\frac{\sigma^2 T}{2}\right)\right)^2}{2(\sigma^2 T)}}}{\frac{1}{\sigma\sqrt{2\pi}} \cdot e^{-\frac{\left(Z-\left(\ln\left(\frac{K}{S_0}\right)-\frac{\sigma^2 T}{2}\right)\right)^2}{2(\sigma^2 T)}}}$$

where Z is simulated as a normal random variable with mean $\ln(K/S_0) - \sigma^2 \cdot T/2$ and variance $\sigma^2 \cdot T$. The paths generated in this manner will be less likely to produce zero payoff.

As we mentioned at the beginning of this section, we presented European call pricing with importance sampling only as a simple example to illustrate the main idea of importance sampling. More practical (albeit more technically challenging) applications can be found, for instance, in section 4.6 in Glasserman (2004). One such important application is importance sampling in the context of estimating value-at-risk (VaR). As discussed in chapter 13, the estimation of VaR is very sensitive to the quality of sampled observations in the tail of the distribution of portfolio losses, but by definition, observations in the tail of the distribution are very unlikely to happen during a simulation unless we generate an enormous number of scenarios. Importance sampling can be applied in this context, and the importance distribution is often selected to be a member of the exponential family of distributions, which increases the tilt in the right tail of the original distribution for specific values of its input parameters. See chapter 4 in McLeish (2005) for a more detailed introduction to this application.

19.2.4 Control Variates Method

Like importance sampling, the *control variates method* uses knowledge about a function that is related somehow to the original function that we are trying to estimate by simulation. Also, like importance sampling, the choice of function is subjective.

The main idea of the control variates method is to find the expected value of the discounted payoffs of a derivative for which no analytical formula is known by using knowledge about an expected value of a related variable that is known. Such a situation would arise, for example, if we are trying to price an Asian call option. Intuitively, the price of an Asian call option for which the payoff involves the arithmetic average of stock prices over the life of the option should be related to the price of an Asian call option for which the payoff involves the geometric average of stock prices over the life of the option. While there is no closed-form formula for the price of an Asian call option with an arithmetic average, there is a closed-form formula for the price of an Asian call option with a geometric average when the underlying asset follows a geometric random walk, so we can exploit this knowledge.

More generally, suppose that we would like to estimate the expected value of a random variable X, $E[X]$, and there is another random variable Y with the expected value $E[Y]$, which is somehow correlated to X. Variable Y is called the *control variate*. The estimator for X can be written as

$$X(b) = X - b \cdot (Y - E[Y])$$

where b is a parameter that must be specified. To do this, we employ the following procedure. We simulate N observations for variable X, and along with those, we compute N observations for variable Y. Think of the observations $X_1, \ldots, X_N$ as the payoffs for the arithmetic average Asian call option, and of the observations $Y_1, \ldots, Y_N$ as the payoffs for the geometric average Asian call option. Both sets of payoffs are generated based on N sample paths for the underlying asset price S_t.

Now, instead of computing $E[X]$ directly as the average of $X_1, \ldots, X_N$, consider the average of $X_i(b)$, obtained as

$$\frac{1}{N} \cdot \sum_{i=1}^{N} (X_i - b \cdot (Y_i - E[Y])) = \bar{X} - b \cdot (\bar{Y} - E[Y])$$

where we use the standard notation $\bar{X}$ to denote the sample average, as opposed to the true expected value.[15] Again, note that we assume that $E[Y]$ is known. In the example of computing the arithmetic average Asian call option price, $E[Y]$ is the price of the geometric mean Asian call option.

It turns out that the optimal value for the constant b (the value that will minimize the variance of the estimator $X(b)$) is actually

15. See chapters 3 and 4.

$$b^* = \frac{Cov(X,Y)}{Var(Y)}$$

When we use this value of b, it can be shown that

$$\frac{Var(\bar{X} - b^* \cdot (\bar{Y} - E[Y]))}{Var(\bar{X})} = 1 - \rho^2(X,Y)$$

where ρ is the correlation coefficient between X and Y.

Therefore, the stronger the correlation between the variable of interest X and the control variate Y, the more significant is the impact of using the control variable method for reducing the variance in the estimation of $E[X]$. Note, however, that whereas a correlation of 0.95 between X and Y results in a tenfold decrease in variance of the estimator for $E[X]$ ($1 - 0.95^2 = 0.0975$, which is approximately $1/10$), a correlation of 0.70, which would be considered a strong correlation for all practical purposes, results in a twofold decrease in the variance of the estimator ($1 - 0.70^2 = 0.51$, which is approximately $1/2$). Therefore, a rather strong correlation between the original variable and the control variate is needed to achieve a significant improvement. For example, using the geometric mean Asian option price as a control variate for the estimation of the arithmetic average Asian option price is a very successful approach, whereas using other quantities that are generally related to the Asian option payoff, such as the price of a European call option on the underlying asset, or the average of the asset prices realized with a geometric random walk, is not worth the additional computational effort.

We did not elaborate on how one may compute the actual estimate of coefficient b. In practice, since we do not know $E[X]$ (we are trying to estimate it), it is unlikely that we will know the covariance between X and Y. The best we can do is estimate b. Typically, a preliminary simulation is run (with fewer trials than would be necessary to estimate the quantity of interest, $E[X]$, accurately), and the coefficient b is estimated as

$$\hat{b} = \frac{\sum_{i=1}^{N_P} (X_i - \bar{X}) \cdot (Y_i - \bar{Y})}{\sum_{i=1}^{N_P} (Y_i - \bar{Y})^2}$$

where N_p is the number of preliminary simulation trials.

To make the control variates method more intuitive, let us go through the Asian option pricing example in detail. We will take the following steps:

1. Compute the price of a geometric Asian call option, which will serve as our control variate.

   The price at time 0 of a geometric average Asian call option with time to maturity T and M intermediate evaluation steps of length Δt can be shown to be

$$C_{A,G} = e^{-r \cdot T}\left(e^{a + \frac{1}{2} \cdot c} \cdot \Phi(x) - K \cdot \Phi(x - \sqrt{c})\right)$$

where

$$\Delta t = \frac{T}{M}$$
$$v = r - q - \frac{1}{2} \cdot \sigma^2$$
$$a = \ln(S_0) + v \cdot (\Delta t) + \frac{1}{2} \cdot v \cdot (T - \Delta t)$$
$$c = \sigma^2 \cdot (\Delta t) + \sigma^2 \cdot (T - \Delta t) \cdot (2 \cdot M - 1) / (6 \cdot M)$$
$$x = \frac{a - \ln(K) + c}{\sqrt{b}}.$$

2. Run a preliminary simulation to estimate the value of coefficient b. Namely, we will simulate N_p paths for the underlying asset price, find the discounted payoffs for the geometric and the arithmetic Asian call along each path, compute their covariance, compute the variance of the discounted payoffs of the geometric Asian call, and use the formula $Cov(X,Y)/Var(Y)$ to estimate the value of b.
3. Simulate the number of paths for the price of the underlying stock that we originally intended and evaluate the payoffs for the geometric and the arithmetic Asian call options along each path. For each of these paths, knowing the exact price for the geometric Asian call from step 1 and a value for b from step 2, we can calculate an estimate for the arithmetic Asian call payoff as follows:

$$\text{Estimate} = \text{Arithmetic Asian payoff} - b * \left(\text{Geometric Asian payoff} - \text{Exact geometric price}\right)$$

4. The average of the estimates from step 3 over all the paths is the estimate of the arithmetic Asian call price with the control variates method.

(See this chapter's online appendices and accompanying model files (e.g., **Ch19-Option PricingVBA.xlsm, ArithmeticAsianCallCV**) for an exact implementation.)

As mentioned earlier, using the geometric Asian call price as a control variate is a very successful method for reducing the overall variance in computing the price of an arithmetic Asian call option by simulation. Let us do a simple comparison of the estimation of the arithmetic Asian option price with and without control variates. Consider the example of an arithmetic Asian call option with strike price \$65, time to maturity 1 year, and monthly intermediate dates (i.e., we will simulate a geometric random walk with 12 steps between time 0 and the maturity of the option). The annual risk-free rate is 10%. The volatility of the underlying stock is 40%, and the initial stock price is \$60. We will generate 100 paths for a geometric random walk for the underlying asset and evaluate the price of the Asian option using crude MC and the control variates method with 20 preliminary scenarios. The whole estimation will be repeated 30 times, and we will record the mean and the standard deviation of the 30 arithmetic Asian option prices generated with the crude MC method and the 30 arithmetic Asian option prices generated with the control variates method. (See this chapter's online appendices and accompanying files (e.g., **Ch19-OptionPricingVBA.xlsm, ArithmeticAsianCallEstimationComparison**) for the actual code.)

The results will vary from simulation to simulation, of course, but the order of magnitude of the difference between the variability of the prices obtained with the crude MC and control variates methods remains the same. In our trial run, we obtained \$5.40 for the mean price with the crude MC method, and the variability of the 30 prices was 1.4046. With the control variates method, we obtained $5.02 for the mean price and 0.0037 for the variability. The reduction in the variability of the estimate of the option price was approximately 380 times, and that happened with only 20 preliminary simulations to estimate coefficient b in the control variates method.

19.3 Quasirandom Number Sequences

In some sense, quasi-MC methods fit into the section on variance reduction methods. You can think of them as an extreme version of stratification methods. As explained in chapter 5, quasi-MC methods rely on number theory to produce sequences of numbers that do not pretend to be random but instead cover the unit interval in a uniform way, so every part of the probability distribution is represented when simulating. Some quasi-MC methods work better than others for pricing specific derivatives, but there is no comprehensive way to determine that in advance without testing. In this section, we review some of the most common types of quasi-MC sequences used in derivative pricing and give an example of how the actual implementation would work.

The exposition in this section is rather technical because quasirandom methods for pricing derivatives draw on concepts from calculus, statistics, and number theory. In fact, many of the techniques described in this section are based on research in the most efficient ways to integrate a function. As we mentioned earlier in this chapter, integrals show up in derivative pricing because the expected value of a random variable can be expressed as a sum or an integral.[16] In the context of derivative pricing, the random variable is the discounted payoff from the derivative. Under conditions of no arbitrage, the expected value of that random variable provides the derivative's fair value. MC simulation has been a technique for numerical integration for a long time. The main idea is to simulate a representative set of points and to evaluate the values of the function at the simulated points. As the concept of ever-more representative samples of points over which to evaluate the function has been pushed to its limit, the idea of low-discrepancy sequences emerged. Such sequences must be evenly distributed in some sense and cover the range [0, 1] in a way that minimizes the discrepancies between the points.

We begin with the most fundamental sequence, the *Van der Corput sequence*. More advanced sequences, such as Halton and Faure, build on the Van der Corput sequence. There are three parameters that we will associate with a quasirandom sequence (some sequences may require more): N, the number of points from the sequence to generate; d, the dimension (i.e., how many random variables are we generating at the same time); and b, the *base*, which we will explain in more detail next.

19.3.1 Van der Corput Sequence

In chapter 5, we showed an example of the Van der Corput sequence of base 2:

$$\frac{1}{2}, \frac{1}{4}, \frac{3}{4}, \frac{1}{8}, \frac{5}{8}, \frac{3}{8}, \frac{7}{8}, \ldots$$

16. See chapter 3.

Let us see how such a sequence would be generated. Consider a sequence of natural numbers in base 10:[17]

$$1, 2, 3, 4, 5, 6, 7, 8, 9, 10, 11, 12, 13, \ldots.$$

The same sequence in base 2 is

$$1, 10, 11, 100, 101, 110, 111, 10000, 1001, 1010, 1011, 1100, 1101, \ldots$$

Constructing the Van der Corput sequence in base b involves two steps:

1. Express every natural number n in the sequence in base b; that is, as

$$(a_m(n) \quad a_{m-1}(n) \quad \cdots \quad a_2(n) \quad a_1(n) \; a_0(n))_b = \sum_{k=0}^{m} a_k(n) \cdot b^{(k+1)}$$

where $a_m(n), \ldots, a_0(n)$ are the digits in the representation of the number n in base b. For example, the number 13 in base 10, $(13)_{10}$, converted to base 2, is $(1101)_2$. In this case, $m = 3$ and $a_3(13) = 1$, $a_2(13) = 1$, $a_1(13) = 0$, $a_0(13) = 1$.

2. Reverse the digits and add a decimal point to obtain a number within the interval [0, 1] (we dropped the index n for notational convenience):

$$(0.a_0 a_1 a_2 a_3 \cdots a_m)_b = \sum_{k=0}^{m} a_k \cdot b^{-(k+1)}$$

For example, the digits of the number $(13)_{10} = (1101)_2$ get reversed to 1011, and then we transform that number to

$$1 \cdot 2^{-1} + 0 \cdot 2^{-2} + 1 \cdot 2^{-3} + 1 \cdot 2^{-4} = \frac{11}{16}$$

Applying this method to the entire sequence of natural numbers 2, 3, 4, 5, . . . , we obtain

$$\frac{1}{2}, \frac{1}{4}, \frac{3}{4}, \frac{1}{8}, \frac{5}{8}, \frac{3}{8}, \frac{7}{8}, \frac{1}{16}, \frac{5}{16}, \frac{13}{16}, \frac{3}{16}, \frac{11}{16} \ldots$$

As mentioned in chapter 5, these values tend to fill the unit interval evenly. The larger the base, the greater the number of points needed to achieve uniform coverage of the interval. You can test this by using the Van der Corput sequence–generating code in the model files (e.g., **Ch19-OptionPricingVBA.xlsm, VanDerCorput**) provided with the online appendices for this chapter.

19.3.2 Halton Sequence

The *Halton sequence* is basically the multivariate extension of the Van der Corput sequence. If we need to simulate multiple random variables (e.g., if there are d of them, we

17. The base is essentially how many digits are used to express a number. The conventional way to work with numbers is in base 10—it derives from the fact that humans have 10 fingers, and the earliest counting systems were often based on that fact. We use 10 digits—0, 1, 2, 3, 4, 5, 6, 7, 8, 9 to express every number in base 10. Nothing prevents us, however, from working with numbers in different bases. The idea is to express the number as a sum of powers of the base. For example, the number 13 in base 10 can be written as $13 = 1 \cdot 10^1 + 3 \cdot 10^0$. The same number, 13, in base 2 will contain only two digits—0 and 1—and will be expressed as 1101: $1 \cdot 2^3 + 1 \cdot 2^2 + 0 \cdot 2^1 + 1 \cdot 2^0$.

need to construct a sequence in dimension d), we choose d distinct prime numbers, $b_1, \ldots,$ b_d, to serve as bases. (Usually, we select the smallest possible prime numbers.) For example, if we need to generate three random variables, $d=3$. Suppose that we select bases $b_1=2$, $b_2=3$, and $b_3=5$ (2, 3, and 5 are the smallest three prime numbers). We have three sequences:

Base 2

$$\frac{1}{2}, \frac{1}{4}, \frac{3}{4}, \frac{1}{8}, \frac{5}{8}, \frac{3}{8}, \frac{7}{8}, \frac{1}{16}, \frac{9}{16}, \frac{5}{16}, \ldots$$

Base 3

$$\frac{1}{3}, \frac{2}{3}, \frac{1}{9}, \frac{4}{9}, \frac{7}{9}, \frac{2}{9}, \frac{5}{9}, \frac{8}{9}, \frac{1}{27}, \frac{10}{27}, \ldots$$

Base 5

$$\frac{1}{5}, \frac{2}{5}, \frac{3}{5}, \frac{4}{5}, \frac{1}{25}, \frac{6}{25}, \frac{11}{25}, \frac{16}{25}, \frac{21}{25}, \frac{2}{25}, \ldots$$

The points generated with the Halton sequence of dimension 3 will have three coordinates that correspond to the points with the same index in each Van der Corput sequence given here; that is, the Halton sequence will be

$$\left(\frac{1}{2}, \frac{1}{3}, \frac{1}{5}\right), \left(\frac{1}{4}, \frac{2}{3}, \frac{5}{5}\right), \left(\frac{3}{4}, \frac{1}{9}, \frac{3}{5}\right), \ldots$$

(See this chapter's online appendices and accompanying files (e.g., **Ch19-OptionPricing VBA.xlsm, Halton**) for an implementation of the algorithm.)

19.3.3 Faure Sequence

As the dimension d of the Halton sequence grows large, the uniformity of covering the unit cube worsens. This is because the increasing value of base b makes the coverage more and more sparse. The *Faure sequence* attempts to rectify that by keeping the base the same regardless of the number of dimensions. The value for the base needs to be at least as large as the number of dimensions d, and it is usually selected to be the smallest prime number that is greater than or equal to d. For example, if d is 15, the Halton sequence uses the 15th prime number (which is 47) to generate the values of the sequence in its 15th dimension, whereas the Faure sequence uses the first prime number after 15 (which is 17). Thus, the components of the Faure sequence fill in the gaps faster than the components of the Halton sequence when dimension d is large. (If $d=1$, however, notice that the Van der Corput, Halton, and Faure sequences are equivalent.)

Instead of matching points with the same index in the individual Van der Corput sequences to create the coordinates of a point in d dimensions, the Faure sequence uses permutations of the indices for each of the coordinates. In fact, the coordinates of a Faure sequence are constructed by permuting segments of a single Van der Corput sequence.

Recall that when generating a Van der Corput sequence, we expressed the nth point in the form

$$(a_m(n) \quad \cdots \quad a_3(n) \quad a_2(n) \quad a_1(n) \quad a_0(n))_b = \sum_{k=0}^{m} a_k(n) \cdot b^k$$

and those numbers were then transformed into

$$(0.a_0(n) \quad a_1(n) \quad a_2(n) \quad a_3(n) \quad \cdots \quad a_m(n))_b = \sum_{k=0}^{m} a_k(n) \cdot b^{-(k+1)}$$

When generating the ith coordinate in a Faure sequence, the transformation uses different coefficients in front of $b^{-(k+1)}$ for every dimension. These coefficients (let us denote them as $c_k^{(i)}(n)$) are related to the coefficients $a_k(n)$, but they use only the last $(m-k+1)$ values of the coefficients a. In particular, to generate the nth point in the ith coordinate in a Faure sequence, we use the expression

$$\sum_{k=0}^{m} c_k^{(i)}(n) \cdot b^{-(k+1)}$$

where the coefficients $c_k^{(i)}(n)$, $k=0, \ldots, m$ are computed as[18]

$$c_k^{(i)}(n) = \sum_{j=k}^{m} \binom{j}{k} \cdot (i-1)^{j-k} \cdot a_j(n) \bmod b$$

Because of these adjustments, the Faure sequence has better uniformity properties than the Halton sequence for moderately high dimensionality.

19.3.4 Sobol Sequence

The *Sobol sequence* is a yet more sophisticated quasirandom sequence that uses *direction numbers* to generate the terms of the sequence. Similarly to the Faure sequence, it incorporates the idea of permuting the coordinates of the points generated by Van der Corput sequences in a clever way, but it uses base 2 independent of the number of dimensions. Working in a small base has certain computational advantages.

The computation of the Sobol sequence is more technical than the computation of the Van der Corput, Halton, and Faure sequences, so we omit the details here and refer

18. Here, we have used several standard notations. The expression $a \bmod b$ returns the remainder of a after division with b; that is, the amount by which a exceeds the largest multiple of b that is less than a. The notation

$$\binom{j}{k}$$

(read as "j choose k") returns a number that equals the number of ways in which k items can be selected out of j items. As we saw in the context of pricing options with binomial trees, it equals

$$\frac{j!}{k!(j-k)!}$$

if $j \geq k$, and 0 otherwise. The expression $j!$ (read as "j factorial") equals the product $1 \cdot 2 \cdot \ldots \cdot j$. If $j=0$, $j!=1$ by convention.

readers to chapter 6 in McLeish (2005) and section 5.2.3 of chapter 5 in Glasserman (2004) for a comprehensive exploration of the topic. Some software packages have built-in capabilities for computing the elements of the Sobol sequence. (See this chapter's online appendices.)

19.3.5 Illustrations

To illustrate how quasi-MC methods can be used, let us implement a simple example. We know the exact value of a European call option when the underlying asset price is assumed to follow a geometric random walk—the value is given by the Black-Scholes formula (see chapter 18). Let us compute the price of the European call option with crude MC simulation and with quasi-MC simulation, using the Halton and the Sobol sequences. Calculating the price of the European call option requires generating only one random variable—the normal random variable that represents the change in the underlying asset's price. Therefore, the quasirandom sequences have only one dimension. It follows that the Halton, Faure, and Van der Corput sequences all give the same result.

To implement the algorithm, we generate the price of the underlying asset at maturity T as

$$S_T = S_t e^{\left(r - \frac{1}{2}\sigma^2\right)\cdot(T-t)+\sigma\cdot\sqrt{(T-t)}\cdot\tilde{\varepsilon}}$$

where $\tilde{\varepsilon}$ is a standard normal random variable.

When using the crude MC method, $\tilde{\varepsilon}$ can be generated with the formula =NORMINV (rand()) in Excel, =RISKNORMAL(0,1) in @RISK, and similar formulas in MATLAB and Python, as explained earlier in this book. We create N scenarios for $\tilde{\varepsilon}$, and average out the discounted payoffs over the scenarios.

When using quasi-MC simulation, we generate N values from one of the low-discrepancy sequences that we have discussed—Halton or Sobol—and use the norminv function in Excel to convert those values to values from a standard normal distribution. For example, to generate the number from the standard normal distribution that corresponds to the value 0.5 from the Halton sequence in one dimension, we will enter NORMINV(0.5,0,1) in Excel. Repeating this for each of the N values in the quasirandom sequence, we obtain N scenarios for $\tilde{\varepsilon}$, which can be used to compute N stock prices at maturity. These N stock prices in turn can be used to compute the discounted payoffs of the option over all scenarios, and the discounted payoffs are then averaged out to compute the price of the option.

Exhibit 19.1 illustrates the performance of the crude MC and a quasi-MC method with the Halton sequences with base 2. We generated 1, 2, 3, . . . , 100 scenarios with each of the methods and evaluated the option price in each case. The Black-Scholes price is also given on the graph for reference. It can be observed that the crude MC simulation method produces rather volatile estimates of the option price, especially for a small number of scenarios. The quasi-MC method produces price estimates that tend to the real option price relatively monotonically.

(See this chapter's online appendices and model files (e.g., **Ch19-OptionPricingVBA.xlsm, EuropeanCallHalton, EuropeanCallSobol**) for details on implementing the algorithms with software.)

Now let us think through a somewhat more complicated example. Suppose that we would like to price an Asian option by simulation. The time to maturity of the option is

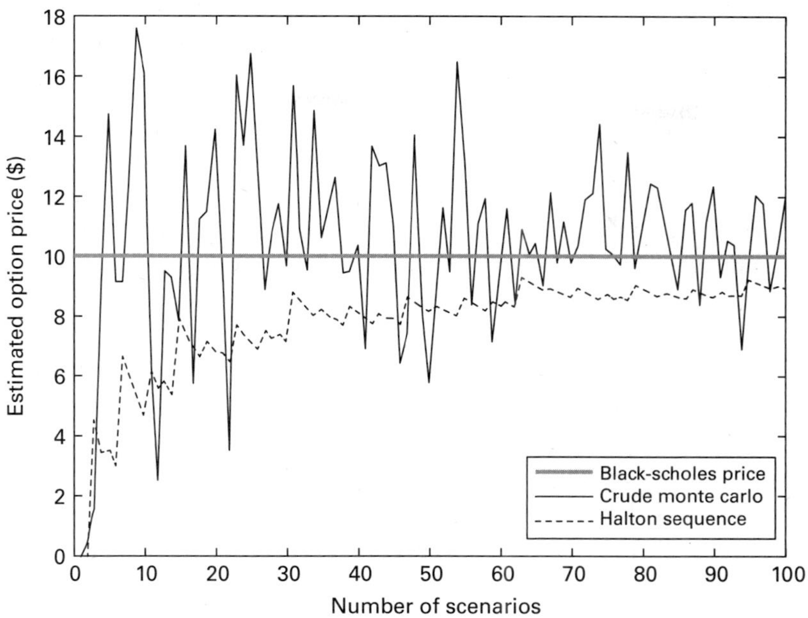

Exhibit 19.1
Comparison of performance of crude MC and a quasi-MC method (Halton sequence of base 2) for evaluating the price of a European call option. The initial stock price is assumed to be \$60, the strike price is \$65, the maturity of the option is 1 year, the volatility of the underlying stock is 0.4, and the risk-free rate is 10%. The true (Black-Scholes) price of the option is \$10.02.

1 year, and we would like to sample the price of the underlying asset monthly. This means that we want to generate N paths for the price of the underlying with 12 points each. Suppose also that we would like to use a Halton sequence. How many dimensions should the Halton sequence have? Since we are sampling at 12 time instances, and at each time instance we are drawing a price for the underlying that is assumed to follow a specific lognormal probability distribution, we need to generate a Halton sequence of dimension 12; that is, we need to generate 12 Van der Corput sequences of length N. Note that each Van der Corput sequence (each dimension of the Halton sequence) is associated with a time instance, not with a path. The length of each Van der Corput sequence equals the number of scenarios that we desire, which is N.

As mentioned earlier, the advantages of using one quasirandom sequence versus another are not clear. There is a substantial amount of literature comparing the performance of different sequences, but the comparisons are typically for a small number of select applications. There is not strong evidence that if the dimension of the problem is small (e.g., less than 15), it makes a big difference whether we use the Halton, Faure, or Sobol sequence.

19.4 More Simulation Application Examples

While the features of derivatives are different, the main ideas behind using simulation to price them remain the same. This section contains several additional examples that illustrate the main ideas and show some further twists in the implementation.

19.4.1 Pricing a Barrier Option

There are many types of barrier options, but their common feature is that there is a trigger event that activates or cancels the option contract. For *knock-in options*, the option contract is activated if a barrier value is crossed by the underlying during the life of the option. For *knockout options*, the option contract is canceled if the barrier value is crossed. When barrier S_b is above the initial asset price S_0, the barrier option is an *up option*. When barrier S_b is below the initial asset price S_0, the barrier option is a *down option*.

As an example, consider a down-and-out put option. This option contract becomes void if the asset price falls below barrier S_b. Such an option provides a payoff to the option holder for relatively small drops in the asset price. It also protects the option writer from large risks, so the option would be cheaper than a regular, or "vanilla," put option. From the point of view of the option holder, the down-and-out put option provides cheaper insurance than a vanilla put option, although the drawback is that the option holder will not be able to realize a large payoff if the price of the underlying drops substantially.

Let us now price a down-and-out put option with a strike price K and time to maturity T. To find its value, we need to keep track of whether the barrier has been crossed. We simulate paths for the underlying asset, assuming it follows a geometric random walk. For each path, we use a variable named *crossed* (in Excel, this could be represented by a dedicated cell) that takes the value 0 if the barrier has not been crossed, and 1 if it has. When we compute the final payoffs, we set the payoff for a particular path to 0 if the value of the crossed variable for that path is 1, and we compute the payoff as max $\{K-S_T, 0\}$, similar to the payoff of a vanilla put option, when the value of the crossed variable for that path is 0. (See this chapter's online appendices and accompanying model files (e.g., **Ch19-OptionPricingVBA.xlsm, DownAndOutPut**) for the implementation of an example.)

19.4.2 Pricing an American Option

As mentioned in chapter 18, in contrast to European options, American options are contracts in which the option holder has the right to exercise the option *at any time* during the life of the option, rather than only at maturity.[19] The payoff of American options, therefore, depends on the time at which the option holder decides to exercise the option. Under certain conditions (no transaction costs and equal borrowing and lending costs), it can be shown that the price of an American call option should always be equal to the price of a European call option.[20] This, however, is not the case for American and European put options.

Until recently, simulation was not considered a viable technique for pricing American options. The dynamic programming technique applied on binomial and trinomial trees, as illustrated in chapter 18, as well as finite difference methods,[21] were the dominant techniques for pricing securities with early exercise features. However, binomial trees

19. When the option holder has the right to exercise the option contract at specific, preset dates, the options are referred to as *Bermudan options* or *Mid-Atlantic options* since their features are somewhere between European and American option features.

20. See, for example, Hull (2008).

21. See, for example, Brandimarte (2006).

and finite difference methods become impractical when there are multiple stochastic factors that drive the price of the underlying security. Simulation, on the other hand, can handle multiple factors and their codependencies. There are now various techniques for applying simulation to American option pricing.[22] In this section, we present a simple example of a regression-based technique for approximating the price of an American option. Regression-based methods for approximating the value function in a dynamic program are a well-known *approximate dynamic programming technique* that has its roots in control theory.

Regression-based methods for pricing derivatives with American features have been suggested by Longstaff and Schwartz (2001) and Tsitsiklis and Van Roy (1999, 2001), among others. The main idea in these approaches is to generate possible scenarios for the future price by simulation and use regression analysis to produce an approximate estimate of the dynamic programming value function.[23] This estimate is a function only of the time period, not of the specific state (price). Based on that estimate, we decide whether to exercise early or hold the option for another time period.

When pricing American options by simulation, as with pricing any other option by simulation, we discretize the time and possible space of outcomes; thus, we do not obtain a complete picture of the range of uncertainties that can occur. Furthermore, with regression-based methods for value function estimation, only an approximation of the state space is obtained to decide whether to exercise. The price estimate that we obtain is in fact a lower bound on the true price of the American option.

Several approaches have been suggested for producing an upper bound on the true price of the American option, but they are more technical than the exposition of this book, so we will not discuss them in detail. The simplest method is actually to assume that we have perfect vision: that is, to compute the optimal strategy and payoff along each path that we have simulated, and to find the expected value of the discounted payoffs along all the simulated paths.[24] This upper bound on the option price is not particularly tight. More sophisticated approaches based on duality and resulting in tighter bounds have been suggested in Haugh and Kogan (2004) and Rogers (2002).

Let us now explain regression-based methods for estimating a lower bound on the price of the American option in more detail. For simplicity, assume that we have a vanilla American put option on a single stock. (The approach obviously applies to, and is more useful for, the pricing of more complex securities with American features.) We generate N sample paths for the stock price $S^{(1)}, \ldots, S^{(N)}$. Each of these paths contains T observations of the stock price. If we used the dynamic programming approach to find the price of the American option (see chapter 18), we would proceed backward from the last time period. At every time period, we would compare the intrinsic value of the option (i.e., the value of

22. For an overview, see Glasserman (2004).

23. Recall that the value function measures the expected reward going forward from the current state. See the introduction to dynamic programming in section 7.1 and the introduction to American option pricing with binomial trees in chapter 18.

24. Readers may wonder why we did not do this to estimate the value of the option to begin with. Note that assuming perfect vision means that you can anticipate what happens in the future when you make the decision of whether to exercise today. In practice, we do not have that knowledge, so it would be incorrect to assume that we can use the knowledge to compute the optimal price of the option.

exercising the option at that time) to the expected value of continuing. The latter quantity is difficult to estimate because in practice, we can have an infinite number of possible values for the stock price. Instead of evaluating that quantity precisely, we replace it with an estimate from a regression model. In the regression model, we use the conditional expectation of the value of continuing (based on the generated scenarios) as the response variable, as well as a collection of *basis functions* of the current stock price to create the explanatory variables. The simplest basis functions of stock price S are $\varphi_0(S)=1$, $\varphi_1(S)=S$ and $\varphi_2(S)=S^2$. It turns out, actually, that the choice of basis functions does not make a big difference in the end.[25]

At expiration, the value function in the dynamic program is

$$V_T(S_T(i))=\max\{K-S_T(i),\,0\}$$

for each sample path i, $i=1,\ldots,N$.

During the second-to-last time period (time $T-1$), we need to compare the value of exercising the option, or the intrinsic value

$$I_{T-1}(i)=\max\{K-S_{T-1}(i),\,0\}$$

to the value of continuing,

$$E[e^{-r\cdot\Delta t}\cdot V_T(\tilde{S}_T)]$$

(Note that we have discounted the payoff at time T to compare both cash flows in time $[T-1]$ dollars.)

We run a regression in which the values estimated from the last time period, max $\{K-S_T(i),0\}$, are the response variable (Y) values, and each generated scenario represents a data point. The regression equation is

$$e^{-r\cdot\Delta t}\cdot\max\{K-S_T(i),0\}=\beta_0\cdot\varphi_0(S_{T-1}(i))+\beta_1\cdot\varphi_1(S_{T-1}(i))$$
$$+\beta_2\cdot\varphi_2(S_{T-1}(i)),\ i=1,\ldots,N$$

or, for our choice of basis functions,

$$e^{-r\cdot\Delta t}\cdot\max\{K-S_T(i),0\}=\beta_0+\beta_1\cdot S_{T-1}(i)+\beta_2\cdot S_{T-1}^2(i),\ \ i=1,\ldots,N$$

After determining the regression coefficients β_0, β_1, and β_2, we have a way of approximating the value of continuing from every state for the stock price, i, $i=1,\ldots,N$, at time $T-1$. This approximate value can then be compared to the intrinsic value at that state to figure out whether to continue.

The procedure is repeated going backward in time, including at time period 0.

To improve the speed of the calculations, we may want to run the regressions only for the subsets of paths at each time period for which the option is in the money because these are the only paths for which a decision needs to be made. For paths that are not in the money, it is clearly not optimal to exercise.

The best way to illustrate the approach is to show an example. We will use a simple example from Longstaff and Schwartz (2001). Consider a three-year American put option

25. See Longstaff and Schwartz (2001).

Path	$t=0$	$t=1$	$t=2$	$t=3$
1	1.00	1.09	1.08	1.34
2	1.00	1.16	1.26	1.54
3	1.00	1.22	1.07	1.03
4	1.00	0.93	0.97	0.92
5	1.00	1.11	1.56	1.52
6	1.00	0.76	0.77	0.90
7	1.00	0.92	0.84	1.01
8	1.00	0.88	1.22	1.34

Exhibit 19.2
Eight simulated paths for the price of the underlying stock.

Path	$t=0$	$t=1$	$t=2$	$t=3$
1	–	–	–	0.00
2	–	–	–	0.00
3	–	–	–	0.07
4	–	–	–	0.18
5	–	–	–	0.00
6	–	–	–	0.20
7	–	–	–	0.09
8	–	–	–	0.00

Exhibit 19.3
Cash flows at expiration.

that can be exercised at the end of year 1, at the end of year 2, and at the end of year 3. The current stock price is \$1 and the strike price is \$1.10. The interest rate is 6% per annum. The discount factor for one time period, therefore, is $e^{-0.06 \cdot 1} = 0.9418$.

Suppose that we have simulated eight paths for the price of the underlying stock. (In practice, we would simulate many more paths, but we want to keep the example tractable.) The values for the stock prices in the paths are shown in exhibit 19.2.

We begin at the last time period, $t=3$. The cash flows at expiration are easy to compute (see exhibit 19.3).

We next figure out which paths are in the money one period earlier (at time 2). There are five of them: paths 1, 3, 4, 6, and 7. For those paths, we compute the discounted values of the final cash flows and use them as the response variable Y in a regression. (For example, the Y variable in the case of path 1 equals $0.00 \cdot 0.9418$.) The explanatory variables data in the regression are given by a constant, the stock price in the corresponding path at that time period, and the square of the stock price. Exhibit 19.4 contains the regression input data.

The estimated regression equation from the data in exhibit 19.4 is

$$Y = -1.070 + 2.983 \cdot X - 1.813 \cdot X^2$$

Path	Regression Data at Time 2			
	Y	Constant	X	X^2
1	0.00*0.9418	1.00	1.08	1.17
2	–	–	–	–
3	0.07*0.9418	1.00	1.07	1.14
4	0.18*0.9418	1.00	0.97	0.94
5	–	–	–	–
6	0.20*0.9418	1.00	0.77	0.59
7	0.09*0.9418	1.00	0.84	0.71
8	–	–	–	–

Exhibit 19.4
Input data for the regression at time 2. Only paths 1, 3, 4, 6, and 7 are considered because they are in the money.

Path	Exercise	Continue	*Strategy?*	Cash Flow Matrix at Time 2		
				$t=1$	$t=2$	$t=3$
1	0.02	0.0369	Continue	–	0.00	0.00
2	–	–	–	–	0.00	0.00
3	0.03	0.0461	Continue	–	0.00	0.07
4	0.13	0.1176	Exercise	–	0.13	0.00
5	–	–	–	–	0.00	0.00
6	0.33	0.1520	Exercise	–	0.33	0.00
7	0.26	0.1565	Exercise	–	0.26	0.00
8	–	–	–	–	0.00	0.00

Exhibit 19.5
Value of continuing and exercising at time 2, optimal strategy at time 2, and cash flows for the eight simulated paths at time periods 2 and 3.

Using this regression equation, we compute the estimates for the expected value of continuing at time $t=2$.[26] For example, the approximate expected value of continuing at time 2 for path 1 is

$$-1.070+2.983\cdot 1.08-1.813\cdot 1.08^2=0.0369$$

(We used the simulated stock price at time 2 for path 1, \$1.08.) We can now compare the intrinsic value of the option (the value of exercise at that time period) with the expected value of continuing. The value of exercising is given by max $\{K-S_2(i), 0\}$; that is, by $1.10-S_2(i)$ for the five paths of interest. The results are presented in exhibit 19.5, which

26. Typically, we would care about the validity of the regression equation and pay attention to the significance of the regression coefficients, as well as to multicollinearity issues (i.e., whether the explanatory variables are correlated among themselves, which would produce poor estimates of the regression coefficients). However, in this application, we use the regression equation for forecasting purposes, so we are concerned with the model as a whole, not with the significance of the individual explanatory variables.

Path	Y	Regression Data at Time 3		
		Constant	X	X^2
1	0.00*0.9418	1.00	1.09	1.19
2	–	–	–	–
3	–	–	–	–
4	0.13*0.9418	1.00	0.93	0.86
5	–	–	–	–
6	0.33*0.9418	1.00	0.76	0.58
7	0.26*0.9418	1.00	0.92	0.85
8	0.00*0.9418	1.00	0.88	0.77

Exhibit 19.6
Input data matrix for the regression at time 1.

also shows the cash flows at time periods 2 and 3 based on the optimal strategy computed so far and conditional on not exercising the option before time 2. Observe that if the option is exercised at time 2, the cash flow in the column for time 3 becomes 0. Once the option is exercised, there are no further cash flows because the option can be exercised only once. Note also that if the optimal strategy is to continue at time period 2, the cash flow is 0 (no immediate cash flow is realized), and the cash flow in time period 3 is determined independently based on whether it is optimal to exercise at that time or not. For example, for path 1, it is not optimal to exercise neither at time period 2, not at time period 3. In both cases, the cash flow is 0.

Now let us take a step back and consider time period 1. From the simulated data in exhibit 19.2, there are again five paths where the option is in the money at times 1, 4, 6, 7, and 8. For these paths, we create the regression data matrix in exhibit 19.6. The values for response variable Y are the discounted cash flows (DCFs) from time period 2. Note that we use the actual cash flows (computed in the table in exhibit 19.5), rather than the approximate expected values for Y computed for time period 2 (computed in the column with the title "Exercise" in the table in exhibit 19.5). This is because there can be only one stopping (exercise) time per path.

The estimated regression equation from the data in exhibit 19.6 is

$$Y = 2.038 - 3.335 \cdot X + 1.356 \cdot X^2$$

Again, using this regression equation, we compute the estimates for the expected value of continuing at time $t = 1$. For example, the approximate expected value of continuing at time 1 for path 1 is

$$2.038 - 3.335 \cdot 1.09 + 1.356 \cdot 1.09^2 = 0.0139$$

(We used the simulated stock price at time 1 for path 1, \$1.09.) We can now compare the intrinsic value of the option with the expected value of continuing. The results are presented in exhibit 19.7, which also shows the cash flows at time periods 1, 2, and 3 based on the optimal strategy computed so far and conditional on not exercising the option before time 1.

				Cash Flow Matrix at Time 1		
Path	Exercise	Continue	*Strategy?*	$t=1$	$t=2$	$t=3$
1	0.01	0.0139	Continue	0.00	0.00	0.00
2	–	–	–	0.00	0.00	0.00
3	–	–	–	0.00	0.00	0.07
4	0.17	0.1092	Exercise	0.17	0.00	0.00
5	–	–	–	0.00	0.00	0.00
6	0.34	0.2866	Exercise	0.34	0.00	0.00
7	0.18	0.1175	Exercise	0.18	0.00	0.00
8	0.22	0.1533	Exercise	0.22	0.00	0.00

Exhibit 19.7
The value of continuing and exercising at time 1, optimal strategy at time 1, and cash flows for the eight simulated paths at time periods 1, 2, and 3.

Path	$t=0$	$t=1$	$t=2$	$t=3$
1	0	0	0	0
2	0	0	0	0
3	0	0	0	1
4	0	1	0	0
5	0	0	0	0
6	0	1	0	0
7	0	1	0	0
8	0	1	0	0

Exhibit 19.8
Optimal exercise times. (One denotes the optimal stopping time along each path.)

The matrix of optimal stopping (exercise) times is given in exhibit 19.8. For paths 4, 6, 7, and 8, it is optimal to exercise the option at time 1. For path 3, it is optimal to exercise at time 3.

Discounting all cash flows in the table in exhibit 19.7 with the appropriate discount factor and averaging over the eight sample paths, we obtain

$$\left(\frac{0.07\cdot e^{-0.06\cdot 3}+0.17\cdot e^{-0.06\cdot 1}+0.34\cdot e^{-0.06\cdot 1}+0.18\cdot e^{-0.06\cdot 1}+0.22\cdot e^{-0.06\cdot 1}}{8}\right)=0.1144$$

This is the value of continuing at time 0. The intrinsic value of the option at time 0 is $1.10-1.00=0.10$, which is less than 0.1144. Therefore, 0.1144 is the fair value of the option.

The file **Ch19-OptionPricingVBA.xlsm** and equivalent MATLAB and Python model files (**AmericanPutLS**) for implementing the generalized algorithm with Microsoft Visual Basic for Applications (VBA) and other software are included with this chapter's online appendices. You may also want to modify the inputs to the programs to test whether the results in the example presented in this section are correct and to check how American put price estimates obtained with regression-based methods compare to American put price estimates obtained with binomial trees from chapter 18.

As we mentioned at the beginning of this section, simulation-based methods for pricing derivatives with American features are most valuable in situations in which multiple factors drive the price of the underlying. Such situations often present themselves in fixed-income markets, where modeling basic building blocks like the yield curve can require the specification of tens of factors. The pricing of a *swaption*—a widely used type of derivative in fixed-income markets—is one such application described in Longstaff and Schwartz (2001). We discuss swaptions in more detail later in this section. For more examples, see Longstaff and Schwartz (2001) and Glasserman (2004).

19.4.3 Evaluating Greeks

Measuring price sensitivities is an important aspect of trading and risk management. In fact, while prices of securities can be observed in the market, so the prices of new securities can be calibrated, sensitivities are not directly observable, so one may argue that their estimation is even more important than pricing applications.

Simulation is a valuable tool for producing estimates for the various Greeks, but a few important issues related to estimation bias and tractability need to be considered. To illustrate these issues, let us discuss the estimation of the delta parameter (Δ) in the Black-Scholes setting.[27] In this example, we will use f to denote the price of the financial derivative in general and C to denote the price of a call option in the Black-Scholes setting.

By definition,

$$\Delta = \frac{df}{dS} = \lim_{\delta S \to 0} \frac{f(S + \delta S) - f(S)}{\delta S}$$

This is called a *forward-difference approximation* because we are using the difference between the current price and a price that is slightly higher than the current price. The formula given here suggests a quick-and-dirty approach to estimating Δ: simulate sample paths and estimate Δ as the mean of the differences of the payoffs from an option with an initial price equal to the current stock price and an option with an initial price equal to the current stock price plus a small increment δS, divided by the increment δS.

This approach suffers from several problems. First, it is not very efficient. An immediate improvement that comes to mind is to use the same random numbers for computing the paths for both $f(S+\delta S)$ and $f(S)$.[28] This would reduce the variability of the estimate.

Second, in statistical terms, we are using a *biased estimator* for Δ. Recall that the fair prices of the financial derivatives can be viewed as the expected values of the discounted payoffs. We are interested in estimating

$$\lim_{\delta S \to 0} \frac{E[pf(S + \delta S)] - E[pf(S)]}{\delta S}$$

where pf is the discounted payoff. In fact, however, what we are estimating is

$$E\left[\frac{pf(S + \delta S) - pf(S)}{\delta S}\right]$$

27. See chapter 18 for a definition of delta.

28. See chapter 5 for a justification for this approach.

At first sight, the two expressions appear similar. However, in effect, we are exchanging the order of the limit and the expectation, which is not generally allowed.

The quality of the estimator can be improved somewhat if we use central, rather than forward, differences. In other words, we should be computing

$$\frac{pf(S+\delta S)-pf(S-\delta S)}{2\cdot\delta S}$$

The problem is that this involves many, many simulations. We need to repeat the same computations three times—once for $S+\delta S$, once for $S-\delta S$, and (since we are typically also interested in pricing the option itself) once for S.

So-called pathwise derivative estimates solve many of the problems listed here. They differentiate each simulated outcome with respect to the parameter of interest, such as the underlying stock price, and produce unbiased estimates. The problem is that they use information about the simulated stochastic process to produce exact calculations and can be applied only under specific circumstances. Fortunately, such estimators exist for many important options. The Black-Scholes delta, for example, can be determined in this way.

As we have noted several times, the price of a European call option in the Black-Scholes setting C equals the discounted payoff

$$e^{-r\cdot T}\cdot\max\{S_T-K,0\}$$

where

$$S_T=S_0e^{\left(r-\frac{1}{2}\sigma^2\right)T+\sigma\sqrt{T}\cdot\tilde{\varepsilon}}$$

Using the chain rule of differentiation, we get

$$\frac{dC}{dS_0}=\frac{dC}{dS_T}\cdot\frac{dS_T}{dS_0}$$

To evaluate the first factor in this product, we note that

$$\frac{d}{dS_T}\max\{S_T-K,0\}=\begin{cases}0, & S_T<K\\ 1, & S_T>K\end{cases}$$

There is no derivative at $S_T=K$, but we will ignore that because the assumption that S_T follows a continuous probability distribution means that the probability that S_T actually takes the value K is 0.[29] Therefore,

$$\frac{dC}{dS_T}=e^{-r\cdot T}\cdot\mathbf{1}\{S_T>K\}$$

where **1** (sometimes **I**) is standard notation for the indicator function. The indicator function equals 1 over the set specified in the brackets that follow it, and 0 otherwise.

29. See chapter 3.

To evaluate the second factor, observe that S_T is a linear function of S_0. (S_T equals S_0 multiplied by a number.) Therefore,

$$\frac{dS_T}{dS_0} = \frac{S_T}{S_0}$$

Putting everything together, we have the following estimator:

$$\frac{dC}{dS_0} = e^{-r \cdot T} \cdot \mathbf{1}\{S_T > K\} \cdot \frac{S_T}{S_0}$$

The option's delta is the average of these quantities computed over all simulated paths for the stock option price. The expression here shows that an estimate of Δ can be produced in the process of simulating the price at maturity S_T, which is very efficient. The code for implementing this approach, as well as the naive approach described at the beginning of this section, can be found in this chapter's online appendix.

In the Black-Scholes setting, we had a closed-form formula for the option price, which is rarely the case with more complex derivatives. Interestingly, however, we may be able to obtain similarly convenient pathwise estimators of the Greeks in some cases even when there is no closed-form formula for the price of the financial derivative. As we discussed in section 19.1.2, there is no closed-form expression for the price of an arithmetic Asian option. However, there is a formula for computing the delta of such an option in closed form when the price of the underlying asset is assumed to follow a geometric random walk. It is

$$\frac{dC_A}{dS_0} = e^{-r \cdot T} \cdot \mathbf{1}\{\overline{S} > K\} \cdot \frac{\overline{S}}{S_0}$$

where $\overline{S}$ is the average price over the life of the option.[30] The latter is a quantity that is easy to track during the simulation, so estimating the sensitivity of the option with respect to the initial price comes at virtually no additional computational cost.

19.4.4 Examples of Pricing Interest Rate Derivatives

In this section, we briefly introduce two popular interest rate[31] derivatives: interest rate caps and swaptions. Also, we discuss how simulation can be useful in modeling their prices.

19.4.4.1 Interest Rate Caps An *interest rate cap* is a portfolio of options that limits the interest paid on a floating-rate note over a set of consecutive payment (reset) dates. Suppose that the cap resets every three months. The interest rate paid for the first three months is the three-month U.S. Treasury bill rate observed at time 0; the interest rate paid for the second three months is the three-month Treasury bill rate observed at the first payment date (at three months); and so on. If the cap rate has been set to, say, 5%, and the three-month Treasury bill rate at a particular date is greater, then only 5% (appropriately scaled

30. See chapter 7.2 in Glasserman (2004).

31. See chapter 2 for a definition of term structure.

for the time between payments) will be paid by the floating-rate note, resulting in a positive payoff to the issuer of the floating-rate note.

Each individual option is referred to as a *caplet* and can be valued separately. The value of the cap is the sum of the values of the individual caplets. Let c be the cap rate, Δt be the time between reset dates, r_t be the interest rate for the period between reset dates t and $t+1$, and the value of the principal be L. At time $t+1$, the payoff to the floating-rate issues is

$$L \cdot (\Delta t) \cdot \max\{r_t - c, 0\}$$

Thus, a caplet is a call option on the reference rate observed at time t. (By convention, the payoff occurs at time $t+1$.)

To price the caplet, we need to make an assumption about the movement of the interest rate r_t. There are a number of interest rate models that we can use, such as the Vasicek model and the Cox-Ingersoll-Ross (CIR) model.[32] In some cases (e.g., if we assume that the interest rate follows a geometric random walk), we can derive a closed-form formula for the price of the caplet.[33] When this is not possible, we can value the option by simulation in much the same way in which we valued European options on stocks earlier in this chapter.

19.4.4.2 Swaptions Swaptions are a widely used type of interest rate derivative. There are two types of swaptions—a payer swaption and a receiver swaption. A *payer swaption* entitles the option buyer to enter an interest rate swap in which the buyer of the option pays a fixed rate and receives a floating rate. In a *receiver swaption*, the buyer has the right to enter into an interest-rate swap that requires paying a floating rate and receiving a fixed rate.

Consider a receiver swaption with a notional amount of 1 that consists of an option (expiring at time T^o) to enter into a swap with payment dates (T^o+1), (T^o+2), . . . , T^s. Following the notation and the discussion in section 19.5, we know that the value of the underlying swap at time T^o to the option holder is

$$\upsilon \cdot (\Delta t) \cdot \sum_{t=T^0+1}^{T^S} B(T^0, t) + 1 \cdot B(T^0, T^S) - 1$$

The option holder will exercise the option if this value is greater than 0 and let it expire if it is negative.

The value of the swap at time T^o can be written as

$$(\Delta t) \cdot \sum_{t=T^0+1}^{T^S} B(T^0, t) \cdot \max\{\upsilon - \upsilon(T^0+1), 0\}$$

where $v(T^o+1)$ is the fair value of the swap rate for a swap starting at time T^o+1.[34] Hence, the swaption can be viewed as an option on the swap rate. To price a swaption, therefore, we need to model the dynamics of the process followed by the swap rate.

32. See chapter 17.

33. See Hull (2008).

34. This can be derived with some simple algebra following the arguments in chapter 18; see also appendix C in Glasserman (2004).

Pricing a swaption becomes more complicated if the option to enter into a swap is American. As we mentioned at the end of section 19.5.2, regression-based methods for pricing American options can be very helpful in this situation. Longstaff and Schwartz (2001) describe one such application. They consider a receiver swaption such that the option holder has the right to enter into a swap in which the option holder receives fixed coupons and pays floating coupons on a semiannual cycle. The floating coupon paid at the end of the semiannual cycle is tied to the six-month rate determined at the beginning of the semiannual cycle. The time to maturity is 10 years; that is, there are 20 coupon payments. Since the underlying swap makes coupon payments at 20 different points in time, its value is sensitive to 20 points along the yield curve. Longstaff and Schwartz (2001) consider each of these points a separate but correlated factor and model the joint dynamics of the factors. These factors can be represented, for example, as the prices of zero-coupon bonds that mature at each of the 20 coupon payment dates. The simulation, then, consists of paths for which at each coupon date, the entire vector of zero-coupon bond prices is specified. The value of the underlying swap at that coupon date can be computed by discounting the remaining fixed coupon payments. The basis functions could consist of a constant, the first three powers of the value of the underlying swap, and all unmatured discount bond prices with final maturity dates up to and including the final maturity date of the swap—a total of 22 basis functions.

Summary

- Crude MC simulation methods involve the most straightforward application of simulation for pricing derivatives: generating paths for the price of the underlying asset and evaluating the average of the resulting discounted payoffs from the derivative. While not always the most efficient methods, they are intuitive and easy to apply.
- Several variance reduction methods exist to speed up the simulation and reduce the variance of the estimate. Such methods include using antithetic variables, stratified sampling, importance sampling, and control variates.
- The idea behind using antithetic variables is to generate one set of random numbers, which can then be used twice in the estimation in a smart way. A set of antithetic numbers is created from the originally generated set of random numbers, and paths for the underlying asset price are computed with both sets of random numbers. This information is then used in the calculation of the final derivative price. Since generating random numbers is computationally intensive, this method reduces both the computational time (by reusing already generated random numbers) and the variance of the estimate (by incorporating two sets of random numbers that are hopefully negatively correlated).
- Stratified sampling creates a representative sample of the entire range of outcomes by dividing the unit interval into pieces, called strata, and sampling within each stratum.
- Importance sampling changes the underlying scenario probabilities to give more weight to important outcomes in the simulation. Such outcomes are generated with greater frequency than they otherwise would. At the end, the observations' weights

are scaled back in the computation of the expression of interest so the estimation is correct.

- The control variates method uses knowledge about a function that is related somehow to the original function that we are trying to estimate by simulation. In the context of derivative pricing, the control variates method attempts to find the expected value of the discounted payoffs of a derivative for which no analytical formula is known by using knowledge about an expected value of a related variable that is known.
- Quasirandom, or quasi–MC methods can be thought of as an extreme version of stratification methods. They rely on number theory to produce sequences of numbers (called low-discrepancy sequences) that do not pretend to be random but instead cover the unit interval in a uniform way so every part of the probability distribution is represented when simulating.
- Commonly used quasirandom sequences in finance include the Van der Corput sequence, the Halton sequence, the Faure sequence, and the Sobol sequence. Some sequences work better than others for pricing specific derivatives, but there is no comprehensive way to determine that in advance without testing. For simulations in up to 15 dimensions (i.e., simulations of up to 15 random variables at the same time), the choice of a quasirandom sequence does not make a big difference.
- Simulation is a flexible technique for determining the prices of complex derivatives for which no closed-form formulas exist. It can be used, for example, for pricing exotic options such as Asian and barrier options, pricing American options and interest rate derivatives, as well as evaluating sensitivities of derivative prices with respect to a variable of interest.

20

Using Derivatives in Portfolio Management

As mentioned in chapter 18, there are many applications of financial derivatives, but the two main reasons for including them in an investor's portfolio are risk management and return enhancement. *Risk management* refers to strategies whose goal is to control risk with hedging as a special case. *Return enhancement* refers to investment strategies that seek to capitalize on the direction in which the underlying uncertainties will be resolved or take advantage of discrepancies in pricing to make a profit. This is more popularly referred to as "taking a view" on some factor that is expected to drive returns. Prior to the existence of futures, for example, an investor who wanted to take a view of the direction of future stock prices had to buy or short individual stocks to do it. Now one can buy futures on entire market indices, and the transaction costs of such strategies are a lot smaller than the transaction costs of individual stock purchases.

This chapter provides some examples of equity and fixed-income investment strategies with derivatives and explains the use of simulation for evaluating the effect of including derivatives on the portfolio risk profile. The list of investment strategies involving derivatives provided here is by no means exhaustive—there is an infinite variety of possible uses of derivatives for risk management or return enhancement purposes.

20.1 Using Derivatives in Equity Portfolio Management

Investors can use the listed options market to address a range of investment problems. In this section, we consider the use of calls, puts, and combinations in the context of the investment process, which could involve risk management or return enhancement. Recall from the discussion in chapter 18 that the distinction between options and futures is that the former have nonlinear payoffs that will fundamentally alter the risk profile of an existing portfolio. The following basic strategies can be used to establish a hedged position in an individual stock or a portfolio.

20.1.1 Risk Management Strategies

Risk management in the context of equity portfolio management focuses on price risk. Consequently, the strategies discussed in this section address the risk of a price decline or a loss due to adverse price movement in some way. Options can be used to create asymmetric risk exposures across all or part of the core equity portfolio. This allows the investor to hedge downside risk at a fixed cost, with a specific limit to losses should the market turn down. The basic risk management objective is to create the optimal amount of risk exposure and to achieve the target rate of return. Options can help accomplish this by reducing risk exposure. The various risk management strategies will also affect the expected rate of return on the position unless some form of inefficiency is involved. This may involve the current mix of risk and return or be the result of the use of options. Next, we discuss two risk management strategies: protective put and collar.

20.1.1.1 Protective Put Strategies *Protective put strategies* are valuable to portfolio managers who currently hold a long position in the underlying security or investors who desire upside exposure and downside protection by using put options. The motivation is to hedge some of or all the total risk. Index put options hedge mostly market risk, while equity put options hedge the total risk associated with a specific stock. This allows portfolio managers to use protective put strategies for separating tactical and strategic strategies. Consider, for example, a portfolio manager who is concerned about exogenous or nonfinancial events increasing the level of risk in the marketplace. Furthermore, assume that the portfolio manager is satisfied with the core portfolio holdings and the strategic mix. Put options could be employed as a tactical risk reduction strategy designed to preserve capital and still maintain strategic targets for portfolio returns. Protective put strategies may not be suitable for all portfolio managers, but the value of protective put strategies is that they provide the investor with the ability to invest in volatile stocks with a degree of desired insurance and unlimited profit potential over the life of the strategy.

The protective put involves the purchase of a put option combined with a long stock position. This is the equivalent of a position in a call option on the stock combined with the purchase of risk-free bond. In fact, the combined position yields the call option payoff pattern described in section 18.1.2. The put option is comparable to an insurance policy written against the long stock position. The option price is the cost of the insurance premium and the amount the option is out of the money is the deductible. Just as in the case of insurance, the deductible is inversely related to the insurance premium. The deductible is reduced as the strike price increases, which makes the put option more in the money or less out of the money. A higher strike price causes the put price to increase and makes the insurance policy more expensive.

The profitability of the strategy from inception to termination can be expressed as follows:

$$\text{Profit} = N_s \cdot (S_T - S_t) + N_p \cdot (\max\{K - S_T, 0\} - P)$$

where N_s is the number of stocks, N_p is the number of put options, P is the price of the put, S_t is the current stock price, S_T is the stock price at maturity, and K is the strike price.

The profitability of the protective put strategy is the sum of the profit from the long stock position and the put option. If held to expiration, the minimum payout is the strike price (K) and the maximum is the stock price (S_T). If the stock price is below the strike price of the put option at expiration, the investor exercises the option and sells the stock to the option writer for K. If we assume that the number of shares N_s is equal to N_p, the number of put options, then the loss would amount to

$$\text{Profit} = S_T - S_t + K - S_T - P = K - S_t - P$$

Notice that the price of the stock at the termination date does not enter into the profit equation.

For example, if the original stock price S_t was \$100, the strike price K was \$95, the closing stock price S_T was \$80, and the put price P was \$4, then the profit would equal

$$\text{Profit} = \$95 - \$100 - \$4 = -\$9$$

Without the protective put strategy, the manager would have realized a loss of \$20 (= \$100 − \$80).

If, on the other hand, the stock closed up \$20, then the profit would be

$$\text{Profit} = S_T - S_t - P = \$120 - \$100 - \$4 = \$16$$

The cost of the insurance is 4% in percentage terms and manifests itself as a loss of upside potential. If we add transaction costs, the shortfall is increased slightly. The maximum loss, however, is the sum of the put premium and the difference between the strike price and the original stock price, which is the amount of the deductible. The problem arises when the portfolio manager is measured against a benchmark and the cost of what amounted to an unused insurance policy causes the portfolio to underperform the benchmark. Equity managers can use stock selection, market timing, and options to reduce the cost of insurance. The break-even stock price is given by the sum of the original stock price and the put price. In this example, the break-even stock price is \$104, which is the stock price necessary to recover the premium paid for the option. The put premium is never really recovered because of the performance lag, which falls in significance as the return increases.

A graphical depiction of a protective put strategy is provided in exhibit 20.1. The graph shows the individual long stock and long put positions and the combined impact, which is essentially a long call option. The maximum loss is the put premium plus the out-of-the-money amount, which is the insurance premium plus the deductible.

20.1.1.2 Collar Strategies An alternative to a protective put is a *collar*. A collar strategy consists of a long stock, a long put, and a short call. By varying the strike prices, a range of trade-offs among downside protection, costs, and upside potential is possible.

When the long put is completely financed by the short call position (i.e., the put premium is paid for by the proceeds from shorting the call), the strategy is referred to as a *zero-cost collar*.

Collars are designed for investors who currently hold a long equity position and want to achieve a level of risk reduction. The put exercise price establishes a floor and the call exercise price a ceiling. An example of the resulting payout pattern is shown in exhibit 20.2. The graph includes the components of the strategy and the combined position. This example is a near-zero-cost collar. To pay for the put option, a call option was written with

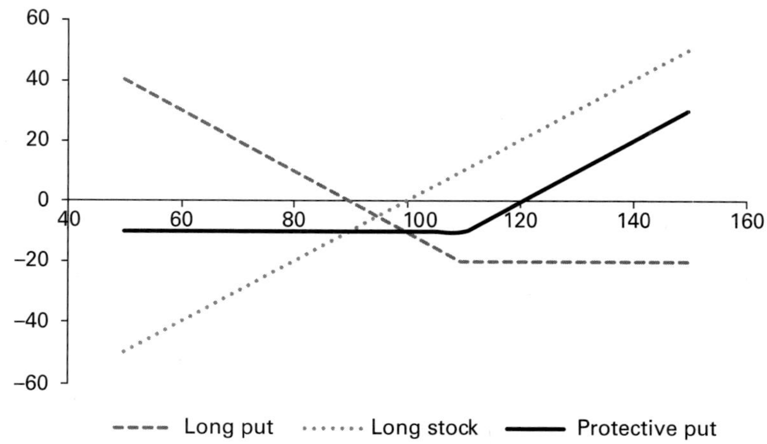

Exhibit 20.1
Example of a protective put strategy.

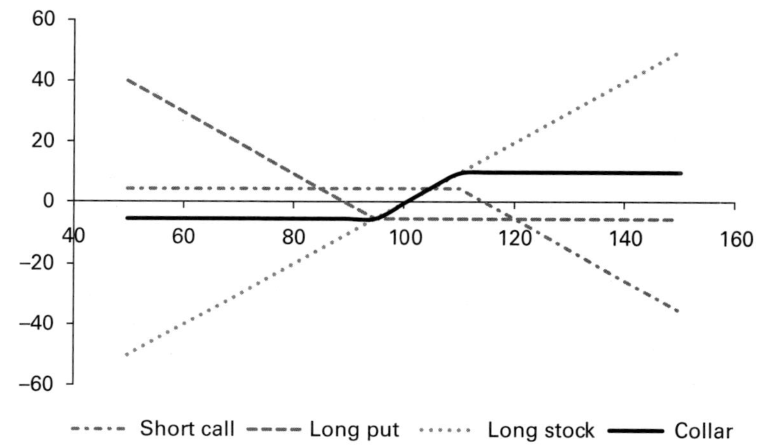

Exhibit 20.2
Example of a collar strategy.

a strike price of \$110. Selling this call option pays for the put premium but caps the upside to 10.23%. The floor completes the collar and limits downside losses to the out-of-the money amount of the put option. To provide full insurance, an at-the-money put option would cost slightly above 6%, which would be paid for by limiting upside potential returns to 5%. Portfolio managers can determine the appropriate trade-offs and protection consistent with their objectives.

The profit equation for a collar is simply the sum of a long stock position, a long put, and a short call:

$$\text{Profit} = N_s \cdot (S_T - S_t) + N_p \cdot (\max\{K_p - S_T, 0\} - P) - N_c \cdot (\max\ \{S_T - K_c, 0\} - C)$$

where K_p and K_c are the strike prices of the put and the call, respectively; N_c is the number of calls; and P and C are the put and the call premium, respectively.

20.1.2 Return Enhancement Strategies

Options can be used for return enhancement. Here, we describe the most popular return enhancement strategy: *covered call strategy*. Other return enhancement strategies include a covered combination strategy and a volatility valuation strategy.

There are many variations of covered call strategies. If the portfolio manager owns the stock and writes a call on that stock, the strategy has been referred to as an *overwrite strategy*. If the strategy is implemented all at once (i.e., buy the stock and sell the call option), it is referred to as a *buy-write strategy*. The essence of the covered call is to trade price appreciation for income. The strategy is appropriate for slightly bullish investors who don't expect much out of the stock and want to produce additional income. These are investors who are willing either to limit upside appreciation for limited downside protection or to manage the costs of selling the underlying stock. The primary motive is to generate additional income from owning the stock.

Although the call premium provides some limited downside protection, the covered call is not an insurance strategy because it has significant downside risk. Consequently, investors should proceed with caution when considering a covered call strategy.

A covered call is less risky than buying the stock because the call premium lowers the break-even recovery price. The strategy behaves like a long stock position when the stock price is below the strike price. On the other hand, the strategy is insensitive to stock prices above the strike price and is therefore capped on the upside. The maximum profit is given by the call premium and the out-the-money amount of the call option.

The payout pattern diagram is presented in exhibit 20.3. It includes the long stock, short call, and covered call positions.

20.2 Using Derivatives in Bond Portfolio Management

Derivatives are widely used in bond portfolio management for controlling different types of risk, such as interest rate and credit risk. We will describe some of these applications next.

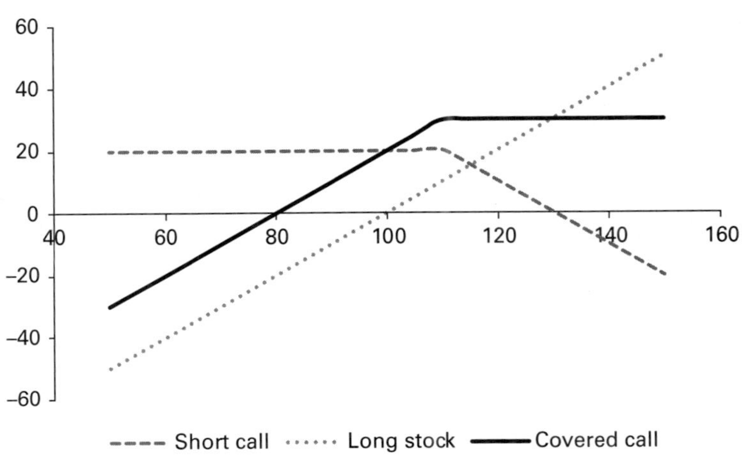

Exhibit 20.3
Example of a covered call strategy.

20.2.1 Controlling Interest Rate Risk

As explained in chapter 15, investment managers with strong expectations about the direction of the future course of interest rates will adjust the duration of their fixed-income portfolios to capitalize on their expectations. It is easy to see that a money manager who expects rates to increase will shorten duration; a money manager who expects interest rates to decrease will lengthen duration.[1] While this can be achieved by altering the portfolio composition, using derivative contracts provides a quicker and less expensive means of changing the interest rate sensitivity or duration of a portfolio (on either a temporary or permanent basis).

20.2.1.1 Using Futures A formula to approximate the number of futures contracts necessary to adjust the portfolio duration to some target duration is

$$\frac{\text{Target portfolio duration} - \text{Current portfolio duration}}{\text{Dollar duration of the futures contract}} \cdot \begin{array}{c}\text{Market value of}\\ \text{the portfolio}\end{array}$$

The dollar duration of the futures contract is the dollar price sensitivity of the futures contract to a change in interest rates.

Notice that if the asset manager wishes to increase the portfolio's current duration, the numerator of the formula is positive. This means that futures contracts will be purchased. That is, buying futures increases the duration of the portfolio. The opposite is true if the objective is to shorten the portfolio's current duration: The numerator of the formula is negative, which means that futures must be sold. Hence, selling futures contracts reduces the portfolio's duration.

Hedging is a special case of risk control where the target duration sought is zero. If cash and futures prices move together, any loss realized by the hedger from one position (whether cash or futures) will be offset by a profit on the other position. When the net profit or loss from the positions is exactly as anticipated, the hedge is referred to as a *perfect hedge*.

In bond portfolio management, typically the bond to be hedged is not identical to the bond underlying the futures contract, and therefore there is *cross hedging*. For example, a portfolio manager who wants to hedge a position in an investment-grade corporate bond using U.S. Treasury bond futures would be employing a cross hedge. This may result in substantial risk, referred to as *basis risk*.[2]

20.2.1.2 Using Options Interest rate options can be written on a fixed-income security or an interest rate futures contract. The former options are called *options on physicals*, and the latter are called *futures options*. The most liquid exchange-traded option on a fixed-income security is an option on Treasury bonds traded on the Chicago Board of Trade. Options on interest rate futures have been far more popular than options on

1. See the immunization example in chapter 15, and check this fact by using the setup in the file **Ch15-Immunization.xlsx**.

2. Specifically, *basis risk* is the risk that supposedly offsetting investments in a hedging strategy will not experience price changes in entirely opposite directions from each other. This imperfect correlation between the two investments adds risk to the position.

physicals. However, portfolio managers have made increasingly greater use of over-the-counter (OTC) options. Typically, they are purchased by investors who want to hedge the risk associated with a specific security or index. Besides options on fixed-income securities, there are OTC options on the shape of the yield curve or the yield spread between two securities.

Buying puts on Treasury futures options is one of the easiest ways to purchase protection against rising interest rates. The mechanics of this strategy involve more background in fixed income than we have given in this book.[3]

20.2.1.3 Using Swaps Hedging bonds with interest rate swaps is like hedging bonds with Treasury notes or futures contracts. To hedge a long position in a bond, an asset manager needs to establish a pay-fixed swap position since changes in the value of a swap are inversely related to changes in the value of the bond being hedged. In a pay-fixed swap position, which is analogous to a short-bond position, the asset manager pays a fixed rate to receive a floating rate. In designing a hedge using interest rate swaps, the maturity of the interest rate swap should match the maturity of the instrument that is used as the pricing reference for the security being hedged. This is analogous to hedging in the Treasury market.

For example, if a two-year corporate bond is priced relative to the two-year Treasury, the corporate bond's price changes as the yield spread changes and as the yield on the two-year Treasury changes. The appropriate swap hedge for this corporate bond is a two-year swap since it is also priced relative to the two-year Treasury. A two-year swap's value changes as the swap spread changes and as the two-year Treasury's yield changes. As a result of using a two-year swap to hedge the corporate bond, the interest rate risk of the two-year corporate bond that is attributable to movements in two-year Treasury yields can be mitigated. To the extent that the two-year corporate bond's yield spread is correlated to two-year swap spreads, spread risk also may be mitigated.

Usually, bonds are hedged in the cash market using Treasury securities or in the futures markets with Treasury futures. The Treasury market can provide effective and similar protection to interest rate swaps when hedging against interest rate risk. The advantage of the Treasury market is that it is a highly liquid market with very small bid/offer costs, especially in on-the-run maturities. It is also easy to enter and liquidate Treasury positions quickly and efficiently. In contrast, interest rate swaps, although liquid, have higher bid/offer costs (typically one basis point in yield) and are more time consuming to enter and exit. Since swaps are customized contracts between two parties and are not exchange traded, they cannot be sold and must be terminated, which is time-consuming and can be less efficient. Alternatively, a swap position can be effectively terminated by entering an opposite position in another interest rate swap; however, this strategy is not efficient. For short-term hedging purposes, Treasuries may be more desirable hedge instruments.

Often, however, hedging in the Treasury market may be expensive if a Treasury security that is on "special" or if an off-the-run Treasury needs to be utilized in the hedge. Interest rate swaps can be cheaper alternatives in these cases.

3. For more information, see Fabozzi (2009).

Swaps have other advantages over Treasury securities. Swaps are off-balance-sheet instruments, unlike Treasury securities, and therefore they should not affect the capital structure. In addition, to the extent that swap spreads are correlated with the spread of the security being hedged, an interest rate swap will provide some protection against spread risk, unlike both Treasury securities and Treasury futures contracts. Another advantage of an interest rate swap is that because it is a structured agreement, call options and amortization can be embedded into a swap. This is particularly useful when hedging amortizing and callable securities.

The use of futures in the hedging context exposes the hedged portfolio to basis risk. Thus, when hedging a security that is priced relative to an on-the-run Treasury with a futures contract, there is the risk that movements in futures prices will not fully hedge price movements in the bond. An interest rate swap does not have the basis risk that is inherent in a futures contract since on-the-run swaps are priced relative to on-the-run Treasuries. From a basis risk standpoint, interest rate swaps are better hedging instruments than futures contracts.

20.2.2 Managing Credit Risk

Credit risk can be effectively managed by the purchase of credit derivatives. Consider, for example, a credit default swap (CDS). As we explained in chapter 18, a CDS provides the buyer with insurance should a prespecified credit event, such as a default of the underlying, occur. This is in fact the most obvious way for an asset manager to use a CDS—to acquire credit protection for the holding of a credit name in the portfolio. The question is: Why doesn't the asset manager just sell the bonds? There are two reasons. First, the market for corporate bonds is not very liquid. The asset manager may find it beneficial to acquire protection rather than sell the bond when there is poor liquidity. Second, there may be a tax reason for doing so. For example, the asset manager may have to hold a corporate bond for, say, two months to benefit from favorable capital gains treatment. A CDS can be used to provide protection against credit risk during that two-month period.

If an asset manager wants to purchase the obligation of a corporate entity (i.e., gain long exposure), then the most obvious way to do so is to purchase the bond in the cash market. However, as just noted, because of the illiquidity of the corporate bond market, there may be better execution by transacting in the CDS market. More specifically, the selling of credit protection on a corporate entity provides long credit exposure to that entity. To understand why, consider what happens when an asset manager sells credit protection on a reference entity. The asset manager receives the swap premium, and if there is no credit event, the swap premium is received over the life of the CDS contract. However, this is equivalent to buying the bond of the corporate entity. Instead of receiving coupon interest payments, the asset manager receives the swap premium payments. If there is a credit event, then the asset manager under the terms of the CDS must make a payment to the credit protection buyer. However, this is equivalent to a loss that would be realized if the bond was purchased. Hence, selling credit protection via a CDS is economically equivalent to a long position in the reference entity.

Suppose that an asset manager wants to short-sell a corporate bond because it is believed that the corporation is going to experience a credit event that will cause a decline in the value of the bond. In the absence of a CDS, the asset manager would have to short the bonds in the cash market. However, it is extremely difficult to short corporate bonds. With a liquid CDS, it is easy effectively to short the bond of a corporate entity. Recall that shorting a bond involves making payments to another party and then, if the investor is correct and the bond's price declines, selling the bond at a higher price (i.e., realizing a gain). That is precisely what occurs when a CDS is purchased: the investor makes payments (the swap premium payments) and realizes a gain if a credit event occurs. Hence, buying credit protection via a CDS is equivalent to shorting.

Finally, for an asset manager seeking a leveraged position[4] in a corporate bond, this can be achieved by selling credit protection. As just noted, selling credit protection is equivalent to a long position in the reference entity. Moreover, as with other derivatives, CDS allows this to be done on a leveraged basis.

So far, we discussed the use of a single-name CDS—in other words, a CDS that involves a single bond issue. Alternatively, an investment manager can reduce or eliminate exposure to a whole index of underlying securities. Unlike a single-name CDS, the underlying asset for a credit default swap index (CDX) is a standardized basket of reference entities. There are standardized CDX compiled and managed by Dow Jones. For the corporate bond indices, there are separate indices for investment-grade corporate entities, the most actively traded being the North America Investment Grade Index (denoted by DJ.CDX.NA.IG). As the index name suggests, the reference entities in this index are those with an investment-grade rating. The index includes 125 corporate names in North America, with each corporate name having an equal weight in the index (0.8%). The index is updated semiannually by Dow Jones.

The mechanics of a CDX are different from that of a single-name CDS. For both types of CDS, there is a swap premium that is paid periodically. If a credit event occurs, the swap premium payment ceases in the case of a single-name CDS, and the contract is terminated. In contrast, for a CDX, the swap payment continues to be made by the credit protection buyer. However, the amount of the quarterly swap premium payment is reduced. This is because the notional amount is reduced as the result of a credit event for a reference entity.

A CDX allows the management of exposure to a diversified portfolio of investment-grade corporate names. Thus, an asset manager seeking credit protection for the investment-grade corporate sector of a portfolio can obtain that protection by buying a CDX. This is the same as reducing credit exposure to that sector. A corporate manager seeking to increase exposure to the investment-grade corporate sector can do so by selling a CDX.

20.3 Using Futures to Implement an Asset Allocation Decision

As explained in chapter 12, one of the major tasks in investment management is the allocation of funds among major asset classes. As the asset allocation of a client changes, it is necessary to shift funds among the asset classes. Funds can be shifted in one of two ways. The most obvious is by buying or selling the amount specified in the asset mix in

4. See section 2.3.1 for a definition of leveraged position.

the cash market; that is, purchasing or selling stocks and bonds in the portfolio. The costs associated with shifting funds in this manner are the transaction costs with respect to commissions, bid-ask spreads, and market impact. Moreover, there will be a disruption of the activities of the asset managers who manage funds for each asset class. For example, a pension sponsor typically engages certain asset managers for managing equity funds, and different ones for managing bond funds. An asset allocation decision requiring the reallocation of funds will necessitate the withdrawal of funds from some asset managers and the placement of funds with others. If the shift is temporary, there will be a subsequent revision of the asset allocation, further disrupting the activities of the asset managers.

An alternative approach is to use the futures market to change an exposure to an asset class. As explained earlier in this chapter, buying futures contracts increases exposure to the asset class underlying the futures contract, while selling futures contracts reduces it. For the major asset classes, equities and bonds, a client can use stock index futures and Treasury bond futures to alter the asset mix. The advantages of using financial futures contracts over transacting in the cash market for each asset class are (1) transaction costs are lower, (2) execution is faster in the futures market, (3) market impact costs are avoided or reduced because the asset manager has more time to buy and sell securities in the cash market, and (4) activities of the asset managers employed by the client are not disrupted. A strategy of using futures for asset allocation to avoid disrupting the activities of asset managers is sometimes referred to as an *overlay strategy*.

20.4 Measuring Portfolio Risk When the Portfolio Contains Derivatives

We have introduced some important uses of derivatives for equity and bond portfolio management. While the applications that we have described make sense at an intuitive level, one may ask for more accurate estimates of the impact of including derivative securities on a portfolio risk profile.

Simulation is essential for measuring the portfolio risk in the presence of derivatives. Closed-form measures of risk that are widely used for equity portfolios, such as variance and standard deviation, can be especially misleading when the payoffs of the financial instruments in the portfolio are not symmetric, which is the case when there are derivatives. As an example, consider the distribution of the price of the underlying stock at expiration and the distribution of a call option payoff at expiration (exhibits 20.4(A) and 20.4(B), respectively). The skewness in the distribution of the option payoffs is a lot more pronounced than the skewness in the distribution of the stock prices. In fact, the stock prices that we generated came from a geometric random walk, so the distribution in exhibit 20.4(A) is lognormal. If we worked in return space (rather than payoff space), we would have obtained a normal distribution—a perfect bell-shaped curve. Option payoffs do not follow such symmetric distributions. Using the expected value and the volatility of the probability distribution for an option payoff is not very informative (and can in fact be misleading), given how far the distribution is from normal.

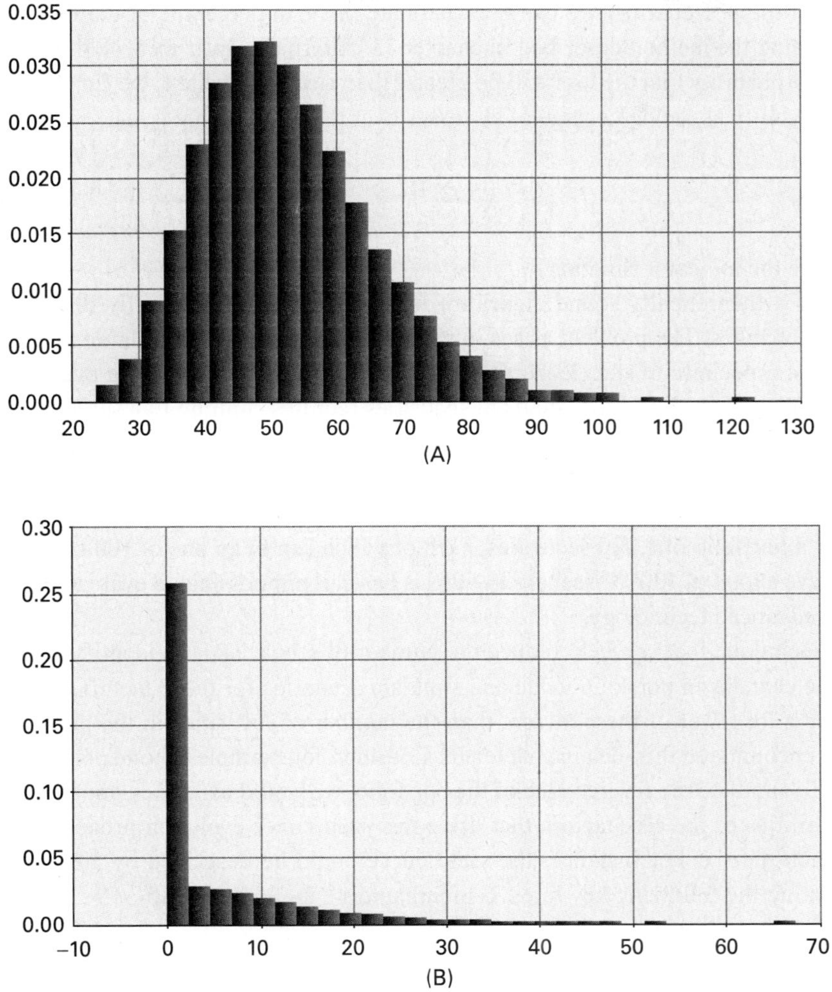

Exhibit 20.4
Probability distribution of (A) the price of a stock at expiration, and (B) the discounted payoff of a call option on the stock at expiration.

Estimating the risk of a portfolio by simulation is simple in concept. The following steps are implemented:

1. Generate N realizations of the vector whose elements are the changes in value for the M securities in the portfolio, $\mathbf{\Delta S}$.
2. For each of the N vectors (knowing the current portfolio weights), compute the resulting change in portfolio value.
3. Analyze different characteristics of the so-obtained future portfolio value probability distribution.

For example, if we would like to evaluate the value-at-risk (VaR), we can record the change in portfolio value $L = V(\mathbf{S}, t) - V(\mathbf{S} + \mathbf{\Delta S}, t + \Delta t)$, which represents the loss realized in each of the N scenarios. We can then estimate the 95th percentile of the loss distribution by using the method described in chapter 13. Alternatively, if we would like to compute the probability that the loss will be greater than a certain value x, we can compute the loss probability as the percentage of all losses over the value x; that is, as

$$\frac{1}{N} \cdot \sum_{i=1}^{N} 1\{L_i > x\}$$

where **1** is the indicator function.

This is a theoretically sound algorithm for evaluating the probability distribution of portfolio changes. The problem arises in its actual implementation for large and complex portfolios, especially in step 2, the portfolio revaluation step. Generating every scenario in step 2 for a portfolio of thousands of securities requires running thousands of numerical algorithms, including additional simulations. This can be a very time-consuming process. For example, suppose that we are trying to simulate N scenarios for each of M securities in the portfolio. The total number of scenarios for the portfolio value would be N^M. For a portfolio of 1,000 securities, each of which can be in one of 100 scenarios, we could have a total of $100^{1,000}$ scenarios—this is basically impossible to evaluate, even with today's advanced technology.

One technique that can help reduce the number of scenarios is to identify factors that drive the changes in portfolio value and simulate scenarios for those factors. (Hopefully, there are a lot fewer of these factors than the number of securities in the portfolio.) We already encountered this idea in chapter 16. Consider, for example, a bond portfolio of 100 bonds. To simulate the future value of the portfolio, we would use the current yield curve, the volatilities of the risk factors that drive the yield curve evolution process, and their correlation matrix. For instance, the yield curve could be described by 10 risk factors representing the following key rates: 6-month and 1-, 2-, 3-, 4-, 5-, 10-, 15-, 20-, and 30-year zero-coupon rates.

Jamshidian and Zhu (1997) suggested a method for further reducing the number of factors by using principal component analysis (PCA)[5] and keeping only the first two to three components. For example, suppose that the 10 key rates in this example (assume that they are the rates on zero-coupon bonds), $r_1, \ldots, r_{10}$, follow simple geometric random walks:

$$r_{t+1}^{(i)} = r_t^{(i)} + \mu^{(i)} \cdot r_t^{(i)} + \sigma \cdot r_t^{(i)} \cdot \tilde{\varepsilon}_t^{(i)}, i = 1, \cdots, 10$$

These random walks are correlated with some correlation matrix **C** (i.e., the normal random variables $\tilde{\varepsilon}_t^{(i)}$ are correlated with a 10×10 correlation matrix **C**). If we were to simulate realizations of these 10 random walks, we would generate scenarios for the standard normal random variables $\tilde{\varepsilon}_t^{(i)}$ by drawing them from a multivariate normal distribution with correlation matrix **C** and computing the values of the key rates in each of the scenarios.

5. As explained in chapter 16, PCA is a multivariate statistical technique that transforms a number of correlated variables (in this case, the factors driving the evolution of prices) into a smaller number of uncorrelated components. The first PC accounts for as much of the variability in the data as possible, and each succeeding component accounts for as much of the remaining variability as possible.

Instead, we run principal components (PCs) on the data that we would normally use to estimate the drifts $\mu^{(i)}$, the volatilities $\sigma^{(i)}$, and the correlation matrix **C**, and we obtain estimates for the loadings (i.e., the coefficients) $\beta_j^{(i)}$ in front of the PCs j.

Suppose that we keep only the first three PCs; that is, $j = 1, 2, 3$. The random walk for each key rate i becomes

$$r_{t+1}^{(i)} \approx r_t^{(i)} + \mu^{(i)} \cdot r_t^{(i)} + \sigma \cdot r_t^{(i)} \cdot \beta_1^{(i)} \cdot \tilde{z}_t^{(1)} + \sigma \cdot r_t^{(i)} \cdot \beta_2^{(i)} \cdot \tilde{z}_t^{(2)} + \sigma \cdot r_t^{(i)} \cdot \beta_3^{(i)} \cdot \tilde{z}_t^{(3)}$$

where $\tilde{z}_t^{(1)}, \tilde{z}_t^{(2)}, \tilde{z}_t^{(3)}$ are three uncorrelated standard normal random variables.

The dimension of the simulation is therefore reduced to three—we need to simulate three uncorrelated rather than ten correlated standard normal random variables. Each simulation trial will produce values for $\tilde{z}_t^{(1)}, \tilde{z}_t^{(2)}, \tilde{z}_t^{(3)}$, which we would plug into the equations for $r_{t+1}^{(i)}$ to estimate the realizations for the future values for the key rates, which will then give us estimates for possible yield curves.

Suppose that we generate 10,000 scenarios for possible yield curves. Each of these scenarios will have an equal probability of occurring. All positions in the portfolio will then be evaluated in each of the scenarios, and the distribution of the portfolio values will be stored. Still, the revaluation of the portfolio in 10,000 scenarios can be a daunting task. Furthermore, if the number of scenarios is still not enough, we may continue to difficulty obtaining a good representation of the tail of the distribution of portfolio values, which would skew the portfolio risk estimation results.

One technique used in practice is simply to run a historical simulation. Using historical scenarios allows for a compact representation of the data, and the portfolio evaluation process can be sped up significantly. Unfortunately, historical simulation suffers from many problems, as discussed in chapter 13. Forward-looking simulation is preferable, but ideally, it should be done with methods that reduce computational time. Such methods include (Glasserman 2004):

1. Reduce the time required for computing each scenario for the portfolio value by approximate portfolio revaluation.
2. Reduce the number of scenarios required to achieve a target precision by applying a variance reduction technique.[6]

We explain the intuition behind each of these approaches next.

20.4.1 Approximate Portfolio Revaluation

The approximate portfolio revaluation approach uses ideas like the ideas underlying American option pricing with regression methods, described in section 19.4.2. A fixed (relatively small) number of scenarios are generated, and the portfolio value is evaluated exactly in those scenarios. The next step is to fit a function to the portfolio values obtained in the scenarios using some kind of interpolation or nonlinear regression. If the fitted approximation is easy to evaluate, then it can be used in a simulation algorithm to generate more approximate scenarios for the portfolio value and analyze the resulting probability distribution of portfolio values. The issue in this approach is how to select the appropriate function and

6. See chapter 19 for an introduction to variance reduction techniques.

how to decide on the appropriate number of scenarios to generate for the initial valuation. While the former issue is difficult to address in a general way, the latter issue has been addressed in the literature.

Jamshidian and Zhu (1997) were among the first to propose this approach in combination with the PC decomposition to reduce the number of factors for simulation described earlier. In their model, each of the three PCs $\tilde{z}_t^{(1)}, \tilde{z}_t^{(2)}, \tilde{z}_t^{(3)}$ is allowed to take on one of a limited number of states, and the probability of being in that state is drawn from a special case of a multinomial probability distribution (a generalization of the binomial distribution in multiple dimensions). Recall that the binomial distribution assumes that there are n trials and two outcomes (success or failure) in each trial. The multinomial distribution considers n trials as well, but it assumes that there are $k+1$ possible categorical outcomes in each trial. If we assume that each of these states is equally likely, we have the following expression for the probability of the PC being in state i:

$$P(i) = \left(\frac{1}{2}\right)^k \cdot \frac{k!}{i!(k-i)!}, \quad i = 0, \cdots, k$$

In our example, we could consider five states (outcomes) for a particular PC: "no change" (middle state), "moderate up" and "moderate down" states, and "extreme up" and "extreme down" states. In this case, $k=4$. Therefore, the probabilities of the first PC being in each of these five states are

$$\frac{1}{16}, \frac{1}{4}, \frac{3}{8}, \frac{1}{4}, \frac{1}{16}$$

The middle state is more likely than the moderate states, which in turn are more likely than the extreme states. Given that the first PC is more important than the second, and the second is more important than the third, we could consider more scenarios for the first component than for the second and the third. Jamshidian and Zhu suggest using seven scenarios (states) for the first component, five for the second, and three for the third. We can then define a yield curve scenario to be a set of states for each PC, which amounts to a total of $7 \cdot 5 \cdot 3 = 105$ scenarios for the yield curve. The probability of the yield curve being in one of these 105 scenarios is given by the product of the multinomial probabilities for each state (since the states for the different PCs are independent). Moreover, we only need to do $(k_1+1) \cdot (k_2+1) \cdot (k_3+1)$ portfolio revaluations, where k_1, k_2, and k_3 are the number of states considered for PCs 1, 2, and 3, respectively.

Technically, this is not exactly Monte Carlo (MC) simulation—we do not need to draw random numbers. However, it is a scenario simulation method in the sense that it involves evaluating portfolio performance over various scenarios, and it associates probabilities with those scenarios. An attractive feature of the method is that we can generate scenarios that have very low probability of occurrence. Some of the scenarios in Jamshidian and Zhu's example of 105 scenarios for portfolio values have only 0.024% probability of occurring, which is useful in evaluating tail risk measures such as VaR.

Jamshidian and Zhu's scenario simulation method can also be extended to more complex portfolios such as multicurrency portfolios or portfolios with credit exposures. Of course, such complex situations require modeling with a greater number of risk factors, and the dimension of the problem does increase. In a special case—when different types of risks can be assumed to be independent, the number of scenarios can be reduced. For example, we may assume that credit and market risks are independent or that interest rates and exchange rates are independent. Not all these assumptions are reasonable, and risk managers need to weigh considerations for realism versus considerations for speed when implementing the model.

Given the low computational burden, Jamshidian and Zhu's scenario simulation method is expected to perform well compared to other methods for portfolio revaluation. Jamshidian and Zhu's own computational studies indicate that. However, Abken (2000) tests the method on portfolios of multicurrency interest rate derivatives, and reports mixed results.

20.4.2 Variance Reduction Techniques

Glasserman, Heidelberger, and Shahabuddin (2000) suggested and studied the performance of different variance reduction techniques for improving simulation performance in the context of estimating the VaR of a portfolio. Most generally, their idea is to use a control variate method[7] that relies on already available information. Such information can include results of simulations of the portfolio's value in recent days under similar market conditions, or approximations to the portfolio value, such as the linear delta approximation or the quadratic delta-gamma approximation, which we discuss next.

The *linear delta approximation* is basically an approximation to the portfolio value given a change of $\mathbf{\Delta S}$ in the prices of the securities in the portfolio and assuming that the change in the portfolio value is proportional to the change in the prices of the securities. If the changes $\mathbf{\Delta S}$ are multivariate normal, then the change in the value of the portfolio ΔV (and, hence the portfolio loss L) is also normally distributed. Specifically, if $\mathbf{\Delta S}$ has multivariate normal distribution with mean 0 and covariance matrix $\mathbf{\Sigma}_S$, then if we assume that the change in the portfolio value is proportional to the change ΔS, we can write

$$\Delta V = \boldsymbol{\delta}' \cdot (\mathbf{\Delta S})$$

where $\boldsymbol{\delta}$ is a vector of sensitivities. Then loss L is normally distributed with mean 0 and variance $\sigma_L^2 = \boldsymbol{\delta}' \cdot \mathbf{\Sigma}_S \cdot \boldsymbol{\delta}$, and the 95% VaR, for example, equals $\Phi^{-1}(0.95) = 1.65 \cdot \sigma_L$.[8]

The assumption that the portfolio value V is a linear function of $\mathbf{S}$ (which also implies that the change in the portfolio value is proportional to the change $\mathbf{\Delta S}$) may work if we are dealing with an equity portfolio in which S is the vector of stock prices. The change in stock prices could be evaluated using a factor model (as in chapter 16), which is also a linear function in the underlying factors. However, a portfolio that contains derivatives has a nonlinear dependence on the prices of the underlying assets, and a bond portfolio depends nonlinearly on changes in interest rates.

A better approximation in this case so that some of the nonlinearity is captured (although not a perfect solution) may be the *delta-gamma approximation*, which in effect is a second-order approximation to the value of the portfolio, based on the Taylor series expansion:

$$\Delta V = \frac{\partial V}{\partial t} \cdot \Delta t + \boldsymbol{\delta} \cdot \mathbf{\Delta S} + \frac{1}{2} \cdot (\mathbf{\Delta S})' \cdot \mathbf{\Gamma} \cdot \mathbf{\Delta S}$$

7. See the introduction to the control variate method in section 19.2.4.

8. See section 13.2.2 for calculation of the VaR for normally distributed returns.

where

$$\delta_i = \frac{\partial V}{\partial S_i}$$

and

$$\Gamma_{ij} = \frac{\partial^2 V}{\partial S_i \partial S_j}$$

are the first and second partial derivatives of V evaluated at $(\mathbf{S}_t, t)$.

Although the calculation of $\boldsymbol{\delta}$ and $\boldsymbol{\Gamma}$ can be challenging, these coefficients, which represent sensitivities,[9] are often routinely calculated by individual trading desks, In addiion, they are generally available.

We can use the delta-gamma approximation to the portfolio value as a control variate in the simulation to obtain an estimate for the actual portfolio value VaR. Glasserman, Heidelberger, and Shahabuddin (2000) report that the method reduces the variance of the estimate for the portfolio VaR obtained from the simulation by a factor of between 2 and 5.

Alternatively, improvement in the accuracy of estimation can be achieved if the delta-gamma approximation is used to guide the sampling of scenarios before computing portfolio losses, rather than to adjust the estimate after the scenarios are generated. This is done through importance sampling, another variance reduction technique introduced in section 19.2.3. Finally, stratified sampling[10] on the values for the delta-gamma approximation can be applied to reduce the variance further. In other words, we find intervals of known (and perhaps equal) probability for the portfolio loss realized according to the delta-gamma approximation.

The actual details of the implementation are technical, but the underlying ideas are intuitive. In their computational experiments, Glasserman, Heidelberger, and Shahabuddin (2000) report that the most effective variance reduction method for estimating the portfolio's VaR was realized when using a combination of importance sampling and stratified sampling methods.

Summary

- In equity portfolio management, derivatives are used for risk management and return enhancement.
- Two risk management strategies that focus on hedging downside risk at a fixed cost with a specific limit to losses are protective put and collar strategies.
- The protective put strategy involves the purchase of a put option combined with a long stock position. This is the equivalent of a position in a call option on the stock combined with the purchase of risk-free bond. Protective put strategies are valuable to portfolio managers who currently hold a long position in the underlying security or investors who desire upside exposure and downside protection.

9. See section 18.4.4.

10. See section 19.2.2 for an introduction to stratified sampling.

- A collar strategy consists of a long stock, a long put, and a short call. By varying the strike prices, a range of trade-offs among downside protection, costs, and upside potential is possible. Collars are designed for investors who currently hold a long equity position and want to achieve a level of risk reduction.
- A covered call strategy is a return enhancement strategy. It involves selling a call while holding the underlying stock. The strategy is appropriate for slightly bullish investors who don't expect much from the stock and want to produce additional income. The strategy behaves like a long stock position when the stock price is below the strike price but is capped on the upside.
- Derivatives are widely used in bond portfolio management for controlling different types of risk, such as interest rate and credit risk.
- Futures, options, and swaps can all be used for managing portfolio interest rate risk.
- Credit risk can be effectively managed using credit default swaps (CDSs).
- An investment manager can reduce credit exposure to a single bond issue by entering into a CDS, and paying a premium for protection against prespecified credit events. An investor seeking a leveraged position in a corporate bond can enter a CDS and sell credit protection.
- An investor can reduce credit exposure to an entire index of underlying securities by buying a CDS index.
- Futures can be used to change allocation of assets among classes with minimum disruption to activities of asset managers managing funds for each asset class.
- Simulation is essential for measuring the portfolio risk in the presence of derivatives. Closed-form measures of risk that are widely used in the case of equity portfolios, such as variance and standard deviation, can be very misleading when the payoffs of the securities in the portfolio are not symmetric, which is the case when there are derivatives.
- Revaluating the portfolio value for every simulation trial can be very time consuming. One technique that can help reduce the number of scenarios is to identify factors that drive the changes in portfolio value and then simulate scenarios for those factors.
- Methods to further reduce the time for revaluation include approximate portfolio revaluation and variance reduction techniques.

21

Structuring and Pricing Residential Mortgage-Backed Securities

Chapter 2 briefly introduced the various types of fixed-income securities, such as bonds, asset-backed securities (ABSs), and bank loans. This chapter deals with the valuation of specific types of ABSs, which is challenging from both a theoretical and an implementation point of view: residential mortgage-backed securities (RMBSs). As shown here, simulation and dynamic programming are valuable tools for handling the structuring and pricing of this type of ABS.

We begin with a detailed account of ABS types and important terminology. Then we proceed with defining concepts relevant for pricing these securities, such as prepayment models, including a discussion of how simulation and dynamic programming are applied in this context. We conclude the chapter with how machine learning (ML) is used in the analysis of structured products.

21.1 Types of Asset-Backed Securities

ABSs are debt instruments that are backed by a pool of loans or receivables. They are also referred to as *structured products*. The process for creating ABSs, referred to as *securitization*, is as follows. The owner of assets sells a pool of assets to a bankruptcy remote vehicle called a *special purpose entity (SPE)*. The SPE obtains the proceeds to acquire the asset pool, referred to as the *collateral*, by issuing debt instruments. The cash flow of the asset pool is used to satisfy the obligations of the debt instruments issued by the SPE. The debt instruments issued by the SPE are generically referred to as ABSs, asset-backed notes, asset-backed bonds, and asset-backed obligations.

ABSs issued in a single securitization can have different credit exposures. Based on the credit priority, securities are described as *senior notes* and *junior notes* (subordinate notes). In the prospectus for a securitization transaction, the securities are referred to as *certificates*: either pass-through certificates or pay-through certificates. The distinction between these two types is the nature of the claim that the investor has on the cash flow generated by the asset pool. If the investor has a direct claim on all the cash flows, and the certificate holder has a proportionate share of the collateral's cash flow, the term *pass-through certificate* (or *beneficial interest certificate*) is used. When there are rules to allocate the collateral's cash flow among various classes of investors, the ABSs are referred to as *pay-through certificates*.

There is a considerable variety of types of assets that have been securitized. Most generally, they can be classified as mortgage assets and nonmortgage assets. Securities backed by residential and commercial mortgage loans[1] are referred to as *residential mortgage-backed securities (RMBSs)* and *commercial mortgage-backed securities (CMBSs)*, respectively. In turn, RMBSs can be further classified as *agency RMBSs* and *private-label* (or *nonagency*) *RMBSs*. Agency RMBSs are issued by three government-related entities and constitute by far the largest sector in the investment-grade bond market (more than 35%). Private-label RMBSs are issued by any other entity. Because of the credit risk associated with private-label RMBSs, they require credit enhancement to provide some form of credit protection against default on the pool of assets backing a transaction.

Credit enhancement mechanisms are typical in ABS transactions. In the case of agency RMBSs, the credit enhancement is either a government guarantee or the guarantee of a government-sponsored enterprise. Private-label RMBSs are further classified based on the credit quality of the mortgage loans in the pool: *prime loans* and *subprime loans*. Subprime loans are loans made to borrowers with impaired credit ratings, and RMBSs backed by them are referred to as *subprime RMBSs*. The market classifies prime loans as part of the nonagency RMBS market, while those backed by subprime loans are part of the ABS market.

In addition to mortgages, other traditional assets that have been securitized include credit card loans, auto loans, bonds (corporate and sovereign), and bank loans. Some examples of nontraditional assets include future music royalties that were securitized for the recording artists David Bowie, James Brown, the Isley Brothers, and Rod Stewart.[2]

21.2 Mortgage-Backed Securities: Important Terminology

A *mortgage* is a loan secured by the collateral of some specified real estate property that obliges the borrower to make a predetermined series of payments. The mortgage gives the lender (mortgagee) the right, if the borrower (the mortgagor) defaults (i.e., fails to make the contractual payments), to foreclose on the loan and seize the property to ensure that the debt is paid. The interest rate on the mortgage loan is called the *note rate*.

The fundamental unit in a *mortgage-backed security (MBS)* is the *pool*. At its lowest common denominator, mortgage-backed pools are aggregations of large numbers of mortgage loans with similar (but not identical) characteristics. Loans with common attributes

1. *Residential mortgages* are loans to individual households. *Commercial mortgages* are loans on income-producing properties, such as multifamily properties (i.e., apartment buildings), office buildings, industrial properties (including warehouses), shopping centers, hotels, and health-care facilities (i.e., senior housing care facilities).

2. David Bowie's music rights were the first such securitization, occurring in 1997. The $55 million of securities issued were backed by the current and future revenues of Bowie's first 25 music albums (with 287 songs) recorded prior to 1990. These bonds, popularly referred to as "Bowie bonds," were purchased by Prudential Insurance Company and had a maturity of 10 years. When the bonds matured in 2007, the royalty rights reverted to Bowie.

such as note rate, term to maturity, credit quality, loan balance, and type of mortgage design are combined using a variety of legal mechanisms to create relatively fungible investment vehicles. With the creation of MBSs, mortgage loans are transformed from a heterogeneous group of disparate assets into sizeable and homogenous securities that trade in a liquid market.

The transformation of groups of mortgage loans with common attributes into MBS occurs using one of two mechanisms. Loans that meet the underwriting guidelines of three entities—Ginnie Mae, Fannie Mae, and Freddie Mac—are securitized as an agency pool. While Ginnie Mae (the Government National Mortgage Association) is an agency of the U.S. government, carrying the full faith and credit of the U.S. government, Fannie Mae and Freddie Mac are government-sponsored enterprises. Despite this distinction, MBSs issued by these three entities are referred to as *agency MBSs*. There are three types of agency MBSs: pass-through securities, stripped MBSs, and collateralized mortgage obligations.

Loans that do not qualify for agency pools are securitized in nonagency or private-label transactions. These types of securities do not have an agency guaranty and therefore must be issued under the registration entity, or "shelf," of the issuer. Private-label deals share many features and structuring techniques with agency collateralized mortgage obligations that we will describe later in this chapter. There are some important differences, however, due to the nature of the loans collateralizing the deal, as well as legal and regulatory issues associated with the various shelves. One important distinction is that such deals must have some form of credit enhancement to create large amounts of investment-grade bonds. Another is that they may include assets other than mortgages. We discuss these differences later in this chapter.

As noted in the previous section, there is a special category of mortgage-related ABSs called *subprime MBSs*. Such securities are riskier than those in prime deals, either because the loans in the pool are granted to borrowers with impaired credit (which greatly increases their expected defaults and losses), or because they are in an inferior lien position (which creates high-loss severities). As such, these loans are characterized by higher note rates than those in the prime sector, reflecting risk-based pricing on the part of the lenders.

21.2.1 Cash Flow Characteristics of a Residential Mortgage Loan

Although a mortgagor may select from many types of mortgage loans, for the sake of simplicity we use the most common mortgage design: the level payment, fixed-rate mortgage. The basic idea behind the design of the level payment, fixed-rate mortgage, or simply *level payment mortgage* is that the borrower pays interest and repays principal in equal installments over an agreed-upon period of time, called the *maturity* or *term* of the mortgage. At the end of the term, the loan is fully amortized. For a level-payment mortgage, each monthly mortgage payment is due on the first of each month and consists of the following:

- Interest of one-twelfth of the fixed annual note rate times the amount of the outstanding mortgage balance at the beginning of the previous month
- A repayment of a portion of the outstanding mortgage balance (principal)

The difference between the monthly mortgage payment and the portion of the payment that represents interest equals the amount that is applied to reduce the outstanding mortgage balance. The monthly mortgage payment is designed so that after the last scheduled monthly payment of the loan is made, the amount of the outstanding mortgage balance is zero (i.e., the mortgage is fully repaid). Thus, the portion of the monthly mortgage payment applied to interest declines each month, and the portion applied to reducing the mortgage balance increases. The reason for this is that because the mortgage balance is reduced with each monthly mortgage payment, the interest on the mortgage balance declines. Since the monthly mortgage payment is fixed, an increasingly larger portion is applied to reduce the principal in each subsequent month.

For the mortgagee, the cash flow from the mortgage loan is not the same as what the mortgagor pays. This is because of a servicing fee, which covers the collection of monthly payments and forwarding the proceeds to the owners of the loan, maintaining records, sending payment notices when payments are overdue, furnishing tax information for mortgagors, and so on. Therefore, the monthly cash flow from a mortgage loan can be divided into three parts: the servicing fee, the interest payment net of the servicing fee, and the scheduled principal payment (referred to as *amortization*).

21.2.2 Prepayments and Cash Flow Uncertainty

The most critical feature of the mortgages underlying an RMBS is that the mortgagor may pay off any portion of the mortgage balance before the scheduled due date. Payments made more than the scheduled principal repayment are called *prepayments*. Hence, the mortgagor holds a *prepayment option*.

Prepayments occur for a variety of reasons. First, borrowers prepay the entire mortgage balance when they sell their homes. Second, borrowers may be economically motivated to pay off their loans as market rates fall below a loan's note rate. This reason for prepaying a mortgage loan is referred to as *refinancing*. Third, for borrowers who cannot meet their mortgage obligations, the property is repossessed and sold. The proceeds from the sale are used to pay off the mortgage loan. Finally, if the property is destroyed by fire or if another insured catastrophe occurs, the insurance proceeds are used to pay off the mortgage loan.

The effect of prepayments is that the cash flow from a mortgage is not known with certainty—by this, we mean that the amount and the timing of the cash flow are uncertain. Consequently, ignoring defaults, the mortgagor knows that if the loan is outstanding, interest will be received, and the principal will be repaid at the scheduled date each month. By the maturity date of the mortgage loan, the investor (mortgagee) would recover the amount. However, the mortgagee does not know how long the loan will be outstanding, nor the timing of the principal payments.

The embedded prepayment option benefits the mortgagor at the expense of the lender. For example, a borrower who takes out a mortgage at a 10% interest rate may refinance if rates fall to 7%. This will lower the borrower's monthly payment; the borrower will be paying 7% interest instead of 10%. However, the lender must reinvest the returned principal at 7%, below the 10% rate previously enjoyed.

The risk of receiving principal back at an inopportune time (e.g., in a lower-rate environment) is called *prepayment risk*. The prepayment risk associated with the individual mortgages passes through to the holder of a MBS, although this risk for a pool of mortgages can be divided up unequally depending on the MBS structure.

21.2.3 Prepayments and Prepayment Conventions

In the RMBS market, several conventions have been used as a benchmark for prepayment rates. Today the benchmarks used are the conditional prepayment rate and the Public Securities Association (PSA) prepayment benchmark.

The *conditional prepayment rate (CPR)* measures the speed of prepayments by assuming that some fraction of the remaining principal in the mortgage pool is prepaid each month for the remaining term of the collateral. The CPR used for a particular deal is based on the characteristics of the collateral (including its historical prepayment experience) and the current and expected future economic environment.

CPR is an annual prepayment rate. To estimate monthly prepayments, the CPR must be converted to a monthly prepayment rate, commonly referred to as the *single-monthly mortality (SMM) rate*. The following formula is used to determine the SMM for a given CPR:

$$SMM = 1 - \left[(1 - CPR)^{1/12}\right]$$

An SMM of w percent means that approximately w percent of the remaining mortgage balance at the beginning of the month, less the scheduled principal payment, will prepay that month. That is,

$$\begin{aligned}\text{Prepayment for month } t = SMM \cdot (&\text{Beginning mortgage balance for month } t \\ &- \text{Scheduled principal payment for month } t)\end{aligned}$$

One problem with using the CPR is that it assumes a constant prepayment rate from the very outset of the origination of the loans. For example, it is not likely that prepayments will be larger in terms of the dollar amount shortly after loans are originated than later, after loans have seasoned. Yet using a constant CPR makes that assumption. For residential mortgage loans, the *PSA prepayment benchmark* deals with this problem.[3] The PSA prepayment benchmark is a monthly series of annual prepayment rates. The basic PSA benchmark model assumes that prepayment rates are low for newly originated loans, speed up as the mortgages become seasoned, and eventually reach a plateau and remain at that level. This is a phenomenon that has been observed. Usually, new mortgages tend to have lower prepayments because homeowners stay in the home for several years before moving. After several years, the expected turnover increases as people move to larger houses or new locations. The remaining homeowners will exhibit a steady pattern of prepayments for the years left.

The PSA standard benchmark assumes the following prepayment rates for 30-year residential mortgage loans:

3. The PSA and the CPR approaches are not mutually exclusive alternatives but are mostly used together—the PSA to explain the ramp-up of the expected CPR over the initial months of seasoning. Thereafter, the pool undergoes a constant CPR.

- A CPR of 0.2% for the first month, which increases by 0.2% per year per month for the next 29 months, at which point it reaches 6% per year
- A 6% CPR per annum (0.5% per month) for the remaining years

Mathematically, the monthly value for the CPR can be expressed as

$$CPR = (6\%) \cdot \left(\frac{t}{30}\right), \quad t < 30$$

and

$$CPR = \frac{(6\%)}{12}, \quad t > 30$$

where t is the number of months since the origination of the pool.

In other words, the prepayment rate is 0.2% (on an annual basis) for the first month, 0.4% for the second month, 0.6% for the third month, and so on until month 30, at which point it becomes fixed at 0.5% per month. All the months given here are counted with reference to the pool's origination.

This benchmark is referred to as 100% PSA. Slower or faster speeds are then referred to as some percentage of PSA. For example, 50% PSA means half the CPR of the PSA benchmark prepayment rate, and 165% PSA means 1.65 times the CPR of the PSA benchmark prepayment rate. A prepayment rate of 0% PSA means that no prepayments are assumed. See exhibit 21.1 for the calculated CPR and SMM for assumed 100% PSA prepayments and 165% PSA prepayments. (See also the worksheet **CPR** in the file **Ch21-Examples.xlsx** in the online appendices.)

The PSA benchmark is commonly referred to as a *prepayment model*, suggesting that it can be used to estimate prepayment. However, it is important to note that characterizing this market convention for prepayments as a prepayment model is wrong. We will discuss an actual prepayment model in section 21.4.1.

21.2.4 Prepayments and Path Dependency

A complicated aspect of prepayments is that they are a function of the entire history of interest rates during the life of the RMBS. For instance, an RMBS may experience significant refinancing when interest rates fall. Some borrowers will refinance quickly, but others may lag because they are less aware of the refinancing opportunity or do not have sufficient creditworthiness to refinance. After the first wave of refinancing, the RMBS is backed by mortgages of borrowers who are less likely to refinance. This effect is called *burnout.* So if interest rates go up and then come down again, the prepayments are expected to be much less than the first-time mortgage rates dropped. The fact that prepayments depend on the path that interest rates have taken up to a particular time is referred to as *path dependency*, and that makes pricing and structuring RMBSs much more challenging.

21.3 Types of RMBS Structures

As mentioned in the previous section, there are three basic types of agency RMBS structures: pass-through RMBSs, stripped RMBSs, and collateralized mortgage obligations.

	100% PSA		165% PSA	
Month	CPR	SMM	CPR	SMM
1	0.02%	08.0167%	0.03%	0.0023%
2	0.03%	0.0333%	0.06%	0.0552%
3	0.05%	0.0500%	0.08%	0.0829%
4	0.07%	0.0667%	0.11%	0.1107%
5	0.08%	0.0833%	0.14%	0.1386%
6	0.10%	0.1000%	0.17%	0.1665%
7	0.12%	0.1167%	0.19%	0.1946%
8	0.13%	0.1333%	0.22%	0.2227%
9	0.15%	0.1500%	0.25%	0.2509%
10	0.17%	0.1667%	0.28%	0.2792%
11	0.18%	0.1833%	0.30%	0.3077%
12	0.20%	0.2000%	0.33%	0.3361%
13	0.22%	0.2167%	0.36%	0.3647%
14	0.23%	0.2333%	0.39%	0.3934%
15	0.25%	0.2500%	0.41%	0.4222%
16	0.27%	0.2667%	0.44%	0.4510%
17	0.28%	0.2833%	0.47%	0.4800%
18	0.30%	0.3000%	0.50%	0.5090%
19	0.32%	0.3167%	0.52%	0.5381%
20	0.33%	0.3333%	0.55%	0.5674%
21	0.35%	0.3500%	0.58%	0.5967%
22	0.37%	0.3667%	0.61%	0.6261%
23	0.38%	0.3833%	0.63%	0.6556%
24	0.40%	0.4000%	0.66%	0.6852%
25	0.42%	0.4167%	0.69%	0.7150%
26	0.43%	0.4333%	0.72%	0.7448%
27	0.45%	0.4500%	0.74%	0.7747%
28	0.47%	0.4667%	0.77%	0.8047%
29	0.48%	0.4833%	0.80%	0.8348%
30	0.50%	0.5000%	0.83%	0.8650%
31	0.50%	0.5000%	0.83%	0.8650%
32	0.50%	0.5000%	0.83%	0.8650%

Exhibit 21.1
Monthly CPR and SMM at 100% PSA and 165% PSA for 32 months.

Private-label RMBSs also share many characteristics with collateralized mortgage obligations. We explain the main ideas behind these structures in this section.

21.3.1 Agency Pass-Through RMBS

In a mortgage pass-through security, or simply a *pass-through*, the monthly cash flow from the pool of mortgage loans is distributed on a pro-rata basis to the certificate holders. To illustrate the structure of a pass-through, we will look at the monthly cash flow for a hypothetical pass-through given a PSA assumption. We will assume the following for the underlying mortgages:

- Type: fixed-rate, level-payment mortgages
- Weighted average coupon (WAC) rate:[4] 6%
- Weighted average maturity (WAM):[5] 358 months
- Servicing fee: 0.5%
- Outstanding balance: $660 million

The pass-through security has a coupon rate of 5.5% (a WAC rate of 6% minus the servicing fee of 0.5%).

This first step in structuring the pass-through requires a projection of the cash flow of the mortgage pool. The cash flow is decomposed into three components:

- Interest (based on a WAC rate of 6% and a pass-through rate of 5.5%)
- Regularly scheduled principal (i.e., amortization)
- Prepayments based on some prepayment assumption

To generate the cash flow for the hypothetical pass-through security, we will assume a prepayment speed of 165% PSA. The cash flow is shown in exhibit 21.2. (See also the worksheet **Pass-Through** in the file **Ch21-Examples.xlsx.)**

Column 2 shows the outstanding mortgage balance at the beginning of the month (i.e., outstanding balance at the beginning of the previous month reduced by the total principal payment in the previous month). Column 3 gives the SMM for 165% PSA. The aggregate monthly mortgage payment is reported in column 4.[6] Notice that the total monthly mortgage payment declines over time, as prepayments reduce the mortgage balance outstanding. Column 5 shows the monthly interest that is determined by multiplying the outstanding mortgage balance at the beginning of the month by the pass-through rate of 5.5% and dividing by 12. The regularly scheduled principal repayment (amortization), shown in column 6, is the difference between the total monthly mortgage payment (column 4) and the gross coupon interest for the month (6% multiplied by the outstanding mortgage balance at the beginning of the month and then divided by 12). The prepayment for the month reported in column 7, is found by using the equation introduced in section 21.2.3. The sum of the regularly scheduled principal and the prepayment is the total principal payment, shown in column 8. The projected monthly cash flow is then the sum of the monthly interest plus the total principal payment, as shown in the last column of exhibit 21.2.

At 165% PSA, the average life for this pass-through security can be computed to be 8.54 years. The *average life* is a weighted average of the principal cash flows divided by

4. The WAC rate is obtained by weighting the mortgage rate of each mortgage loan in the pool by the amount of the mortgage balance outstanding.

5. The WAM is obtained by weighting the remaining number of months to maturity for each mortgage loan in the pool by the amount of the mortgage balance outstanding.

6. The aggregate mortgage payment is the payment that will amortize (i.e., reduce to 0) the outstanding loan after accounting for interest and principal payments. The formula for computing the mortgage payment needed to bring the balance to zero after T years is

(1)	(2)	(3)	(4)	(5)	(6)	(7)	(8)	(9)
Month	Outstanding Balance	SMM	Mortgage Payment	Net Interest	Scheduled Principal	Prepayments	Total Principal	Cash Flow
1	$660,000,000.00	0.0829%	$3,964,947.45	$3,025,000.00	$664,947.45	$546,435.32	$1,211,382.78	$4,236,382.78
2	$658,788,617.22	0.1107%	$3,961,661.43	$3,019,447.83	$667,718.35	$728,350.08	$1,396,068.43	$4,415,516.26
3	$657,392,548.80	0.1386%	$3,957,277.02	$3,013,049.18	$670,314.27	$909,894.82	$1,580,209.10	$4,593,258.28
4	$655,812,339.70	0.1665%	$3,951,794.17	$3,005,806.56	$672,732.48	$1,090,916.16	$1,763,648.64	$4,769,455.20
5	$654,048,691.06	0.1946%	$3,945,213.78	$2,997,723.17	$674,970.33	$1,271,260.68	$1,946,231.01	$4,943,954.17
6	$652,102,460.06	0.2227%	$3,937,537.63	$2,988,802.94	$677,025.33	$1,450,775.13	$2,127,800.46	$5,116,603.41
7	$649,974,659.59	0.2509%	$3,928,768.43	$2,979,050.52	$678,895.13	$1,629,306.69	$2,308,201.82	$5,287,252.34
8	$647,666,457.77	0.2792%	$3,918,909.79	$2,968,471.26	$680,577.51	$1,806,703.12	$2,487,280.62	$5,455,751.89
9	$645,179,177.15	0.3077%	$3,907,966.27	$2,957,071.23	$682,070.38	$1,982,813.03	$2,664,883.42	$5,621,954.64
10	$642,514,293.73	0.3361%	$3,895,943.30	$2,944,857.18	$683,371.83	$2,157,486.08	$2,840,857.92	$5,785,715.10
11	$639,673,435.82	0.3647%	$3,882,847.26	$2,931,836.58	$684,480.08	$2,330,573.19	$3,015,053.27	$5,946,889.86
12	$636,658,382.54	0.3934%	$3,868,685.42	$2,918,017.59	$685,393.51	$2,501,926.75	$3,187,320.26	$6,105,337.85
13	$633,471,062.28	0.4222%	$3,853,465.96	$2,903,409.04	$686,110.65	$2,671,400.85	$3,357,511.50	$6,260,920.54
14	$630,113,550.78	0.4510%	$3,837,197.95	$2,888,020.44	$686,630.19	$2,838,851.49	$3,525,481.68	$6,413,502.13
15	$626,588,069.10	0.4800%	$3,819,891.36	$2,871,861.98	$686,951.01	$3,004,136.77	$3,691,087.78	$6,562,949.76
16	$622,896,981.32	0.5090%	$3,801,557.03	$2,854,944.50	$687,072.12	$3,167,117.12	$3,854,189.24	$6,709,133.74
17	$619,042,792.08	0.5381%	$3,782,206.68	$2,837,279.46	$686,992.72	$3,327,655.50	$4,014,648.22	$6,851,927.68
18	$615,028,143.86	0.5674%	$3,761,852.90	$2,818,878.99	$686,712.18	$3,485,617.58	$4,172,329.76	$6,991,208.75
19	$610,855,814.10	0.5967%	$3,740,509.10	$2,799,755.81	$686,230.03	$3,640,871.98	$4,327,102.01	$7,126,857.83
20	$606,528,712.09	0.6261%	$3,718,189.54	$2,779,923.26	$685,545.98	$3,793,290.42	$4,478,836.40	$7,258,759.67
21	$602,049,875.68	0.6556%	$3,694,909.30	$2,759,395.26	$684,659.93	$3,942,747.93	$4,627,407.86	$7,386,803.12
22	$597,422,467.83	0.6852%	$3,670,684.27	$2,738,186.31	$683,571.93	$4,089,123.02	$4,772,694.95	$7,510,881.26
23	$592,649,772.87	0.7150%	$3,645,531.09	$2,716,311.46	$682,282.22	$4,232,297.89	$4,914,580.11	$7,630,891.57
24	$587,735,192.76	0.7448%	$3,619,467.20	$2,693,786.30	$680,791.24	$4,372,158.55	$5,052,949.78	$7,746,736.08
25	$582,682,242.98	0.7747%	$3,592,510.78	$2,670,626.95	$679,099.57	$4,508,595.02	$5,187,694.59	$7,858,321.54
26	$577,494,548.39	0.8047%	$3,564,680.73	$2,646,850.01	$677,207.99	$4,641,501.51	$5,318,709.50	$7,965,559.51

(continued)

(1)	(2)	(3)	(4)	(5)	(6)	(7)	(8)	(9)
Month	Outstanding Balance	SMM	Mortgage Payment	Net Interest	Scheduled Principal	Prepayments	Total Principal	Cash Flow
27	$572,175,838.89	0.8348%	$3,535,996.66	$2,622,472.59	$675,117.46	$4,770,776.51	$5,445,893.98	$8,068,366.57
28	$566,729,944.91	0.8650%	$3,506,478.85	$2,597,512.25	$672,829.12	$4,896,323.00	$5,569,152.12	$8,166,664.37
29	$561,160,792.79	0.8650%	$3,476,148.25	$2,571,986.97	$670,344.28	$4,848,172.03	$5,518,516.31	$8,090,503.28
30	$555,642,276.48	0.8650%	$3,446,080.00	$2,546,693.77	$667,868.62	$4,800,458.97	$5,468,327.59	$8,015,021.35
. . .								
349	$2,098,411.25	0.8650%	$215,654.93	$9,617.72	$205,162.87	$16,376.36	$221,539.23	$231,156.95
350	$1,876,872.02	0.8650%	$213,789.54	$8,602.33	$204,405.18	$14,466.63	$218,871.81	$227,474.14
351	$1,658,000.21	0.8650%	$211,940.29	$7,599.17	$203,650.28	$12,579.94	$216,230.23	$223,829.40
352	$1,441,769.98	0.8650%	$210,107.03	$6,608.11	$202,898.18	$10,716.09	$213,614.26	$220,222.38
353	$1,228,155.72	0.8650%	$208,289.63	$5,629.05	$202,148.85	$8,874.83	$211,023.68	$216,652.73
354	$1,017,132.04	0.8650%	$206,487.95	$4,661.86	$201,402.29	$7,055.96	$208,458.25	$213,120.10
355	$808,673.79	0.8650%	$204,701.85	$3,706.42	$200,658.49	$5,259.26	$205,917.74	$209,624.16
356	$602,756.05	0.8650%	$202,931.21	$2,762.63	$199,917.43	$3,484.50	$203,401.93	$206,164.56
357	$399,354.11	0.8650%	$201,175.88	$1,830.37	$199,179.11	$1,731.49	$200,910.60	$202,740.97
358	$198,443.52	0.8650%	$199,435.73	$909.53	$198,443.52	$0.00	$198,443.52	$199,353.05

Exhibit 21.2
Monthly cash flow for a $660 million pass-through security with a 5.5% pass-through rate, a WAC rate of 6.00%, and a WAM of 358 months, assuming 165% PSA. Note that rows 31–348 are hidden.

the par value, where the weight is the month when the projected principal is expected to be received.[7]

21.3.2 Agency Stripped MBS

A *stripped mortgage-backed security* (*stripped MBS*) is created by altering the principal and interest distribution from a pro-rata to an unequal distribution.

In the most common type of stripped MBS, all the interest is allocated to one class, the *interest-only* class, and all the principal to the other class, the *principal-only class*.

21.3.2.1 Principal-Only Securities A *principal-only security*, also called a *PO* or a *principal-only mortgage strip*, is purchased at a substantial discount from par value. The return that an investor realizes depends on the speed at which prepayments are made. The faster the prepayments, the higher the investor's return. For example, suppose that there is a mortgage pool consisting only of 30-year mortgages with $400 million in principal and that investors can purchase POs backed by this mortgage pool for $175 million. The dollar return on this investment will be $225 million. How quickly that dollar return is recovered by PO investors determines the actual return that will be realized. In extreme cases, if all homeowners in the underlying mortgage pool decide to prepay their mortgage loans immediately, PO investors will realize the $225 million immediately. On the other hand, if all homeowners choose to remain in their homes for 30 years and make no prepayments, the $225 million will be spread out over 30 years, which would result in a lower return for PO investors.

Let us see how the price of the PO would be expected to change as mortgage rates in the market change. When mortgage rates decline below the note rate for the loans in the mortgage pool, prepayments are expected to speed up, accelerating payments to the PO holder. Thus, the cash flow of a PO improves (in the sense that principal repayments are received earlier). The cash flow will be discounted at a lower interest rate because the mortgage rate in the market has declined. The result is that the PO price will increase when mortgage rates decline. When mortgage rates rise above the note rate for the loans in the mortgage pool, prepayments are expected to slow. The cash flow deteriorates (in the sense that it takes longer to recover principal repayments). Couple this with a higher discount rate, and the price of a PO will fall when mortgage rates rise.

$$P \cdot \frac{I}{(1-(1+I))^{T}}$$

where P is the outstanding principal and I is the interest rate (in decimal form). In our example, we are working with months (rather than years). To compute the aggregate mortgage payment for the first month, for example, we use the formula

$$660{,}000{,}000 \cdot \frac{\left(\frac{0.06}{12}\right)}{\left(1-\left(1+\left(\frac{0.06}{12}\right)\right)\right)^{358}}$$

7. In other words, the average life in years is obtained by multiplying the entries in column 8, "Total Principal," by the corresponding entries in column 1, "Month," then dividing by the collateral ($660 million) and by 12 to convert the number from months to years.

21.3.2.2 Interest-Only Securities An *interest-only security*, also called an *IO* or an *interest-only mortgage strip*, has no par value. In contrast to the PO investor, the IO investor wants prepayments to be slow because the IO investor receives interest only on the amount of the principal outstanding. When prepayments are made, less interest (in dollars) will be received as the outstanding principal declines. In fact, if prepayments are too fast, the IO investor may not recover the amount paid for the IO, even if the IO is held to maturity.

Let us look at an IO's expected price response to mortgage rate changes. If mortgage rates decline below the note rate for the loans in the mortgage pool, prepayments are expected to accelerate. This would result in a deterioration of the expected cash flow for the IO. While the cash flow will be discounted at a lower rate, the net effect typically is a decline in the price of the IO. If mortgage rates rise above the note rate for the loans in the mortgage pool, the expected cash flow improves, but the cash flow is discounted at a higher interest rate. The net effect may be either a rise or a fall for the IO's price.

Thus, we see an interesting characteristic of an IO: its price tends to move in the same direction as the change in mortgage rates when mortgage rates fall below the note rate for the loans in the mortgage pool and for some range of mortgage rates above the note rate. Both POs and IOs exhibit substantial price volatility when mortgage rates change. The greater price volatility of the IO and PO compared to the pass-through from which they were created is because the combined price volatility of the IO and PO must be equal to the price volatility of the pass-through.

21.3.3.3 Agency Collateralized Mortgage Obligations A *collateralized mortgage obligation (CMO)* is a security backed by a pool of mortgage pass-through securities. CMOs are structured such that there are several classes of bondholders—also called *tranches*—with varying average lives. The principal payments from the underlying pool of pass-through securities are used to retire the bonds on a priority basis as specified in the prospectus.

Although we will not explain the wide range of bond classes or tranches created in a CMO structure, we will provide a few to show how they are structured and how they alter the investment characteristics compared to the mortgage pass-through securities from which they were created—namely, *sequential-pay bonds*, *planned amortization class bonds*, and *support bonds*. For a more detailed description of the types of CMO bond classes, see Fabozzi, Bhattacharya, and Berliner (2007).

21.3.2.4 Sequential-Pay Structures The simplest type of CMO structure is the *sequential-pay structure*. To illustrate this structure, we will use the $660 million, 5.5% pass-through security (comprised of residential mortgage loans that conform to the underwriting standards of Ginnie Mae, Fannie Mae, and Freddie Mac) to create a simple structure. The structure is given in exhibit 21.3, and we refer to this structure as "structure 1."

In structuring an agency deal, there are only rules specified for the distribution of principal and interest. There are no rules for deals with defaults and delinquencies because the issuer guarantees the payments. In structure 1, we will use the following rules:

- *Interest.* The monthly interest is distributed to each bond class on the basis of the amount of outstanding principal at the beginning of the month.

Bond Class	Par Amount ($)	Coupon Rate (%)
A	$320,925,000.00	5.50%
B	$59,400,000.00	5.50%
C	$159,225,000.00	5.50%
D	$120,450,000.00	5.50%

Exhibit 21.3
Example of a sequential-pay structure ("structure 1").

- *Principal.* All the monthly principal (i.e., regularly scheduled principal and prepayments) is distributed first to bond class A until it is completely paid off. After bond class A has completely paid off its par amount, all the monthly principal payments are made to bond class B until it is completely paid off. After bond class B has completely paid off its par amount, all monthly principal payments are made to bond class C until it has completely paid off its par amount. Finally, after bond C is completely paid off, all monthly principal payments are made to bond class D.

Based on these rules for the distribution of interest and principal, exhibits 21.4 and 21.5 show the cash flows for each bond class, assuming one prepayment speed, 165% PSA. (See also the worksheet **Sequential-Pay** in the file **Ch21-Examples.xlsx**.) Note that bond class A is fully paid off in month 78. In the same month, principal payments begin for bond class B, which is fully paid off in month 97. Bond class C starts receiving principal payments in month 97, and bond class D in month 172.

Before explaining what has been accomplished in structure 1, a few comments are in order. First, the total par value of the four bond classes in the structure is equal to $660 million, which is equal to the par value of the collateral (the pass-through security). Second, we have simplified the illustration by assuming that all bond classes have the same coupon rate. In actual deals, the coupon rate would be determined by prevailing market conditions (i.e., the yield curve) and would not necessarily be equal to each bond class. A condition that must be satisfied is that the total interest to be paid to all the bond classes in a month may not exceed the interest from the collateral; otherwise, an interest shortfall will occur. Equivalently, the WAC rate for the bond classes in the structure may not exceed the coupon rate for the collateral (6% in our illustration). Finally, although the payment rules for the distribution of the principal payments are known, the exact amount of monthly principal is not. The monthly principal will depend on the principal cash flows generated by the collateral, which in turn depends on the actual payment rate of the collateral. Thus, to project monthly cash flows, a prepayment assumption must be made. We will discuss prepayment models in section 21.4.1.

Now let us look at structure 1. To see what has been accomplished, a summary of the average life (in years) of the collateral and the four bond classes under a range of prepayment assumptions is shown in exhibit 21.6.

Notice the substantial differences in the average life for the collateral, which depend on the speed of prepayment. Given this risk, the collateral in its original form is unappealing to institutional investors with specific liability structures, who are trying to match their liabilities with their assets. However, the average lives for the bond classes tell a different

	A			B		
Month	Beginning Balance	Principal	Interest	Beginning Balance	Principal	Interest
1	$320,925,000.00	$1,211,382.78	$1,470,906.25	$59,400,000.00	$0.00	$272,250.00
2	$319,713,617.22	$1,396,068.43	$1,465,354.08	$59,400,000.00	$0.00	$272,250.00
3	$318,317,548.80	$1,580,209.10	$1,458,955.43	$59,400,000.00	$0.00	$272,250.00
4	$316,737,339.70	$1,763,648.64	$1,451,712.81	$59,400,000.00	$0.00	$272,250.00
5	$314,973,691.06	$1,946,231.01	$1,443,629.42	$59,400,000.00	$0.00	$272,250.00
6	$313,027,460.06	$2,127,800.46	$1,434,709.19	$59,400,000.00	$0.00	$272,250.00
7	$310,899,659.59	$2,308,201.82	$1,424,956.77	$59,400,000.00	$0.00	$272,250.00
8	$308,591,457.77	$2,487,280.62	$1,414,377.51	$59,400,000.00	$0.00	$272,250.00
9	$306,104,177.15	$2,664,883.42	$1,402,977.48	$59,400,000.00	$0.00	$272,250.00
10	$303,439,293.73	$2,840,857.92	$1,390,763.43	$59,400,000.00	$0.00	$272,250.00
11	$300,598,435.82	$3,015,053.27	$1,377,742.83	$59,400,000.00	$0.00	$272,250.00
12	$297,583,382.54	$3,187,320.26	$1,363,923.84	$59,400,000.00	$0.00	$272,250.00
. . .						
74	$17,687,935.97	$3,648,575.33	$81,069.71	$59,400,000.00	$0.00	$272,250.00
75	$14,039,360.63	$3,614,937.79	$64,347.07	$59,400,000.00	$0.00	$272,250.00
76	$10,424,422.85	$3,581,598.87	$47,778.60	$59,400,000.00	$0.00	$272,250.00
77	$6,842,823.97	$3,548,555.98	$31,362.94	$59,400,000.00	$0.00	$272,250.00
78	$3,294,267.99	$3,294,267.99	$15,098.73	$59,400,000.00	$221,538.54	$272,250.00
79	$0.00	$0.00	$0.00	$59,178,461.46	$3,483,347.94	$271,234.62
80	$0.00	$0.00	$0.00	$55,695,113.52	$3,451,177.68	$255,269.27
81	$0.00	$0.00	$0.00	$52,243,935.84	$3,419,293.21	$239,451.37
82	$0.00	$0.00	$0.00	$48,824,642.63	$3,387,692.05	$223,779.61
83	$0.00	$0.00	$0.00	$45,436,950.58	$3,356,371.72	$208,252.69
84	$0.00	$0.00	$0.00	$42,080,578.86	$3,325,329.75	$192,869.32
85	$0.00	$0.00	$0.00	$38,755,249.12	$3,294,563.71	$177,628.23
95	$0.00	$0.00	$0.00	$7,149,733.68	$3,001,558.67	$32,769.61
96	$0.00	$0.00	$0.00	$4,148,175.01	$2,973,673.07	$19,012.47
97	$0.00	$0.00	$0.00	$1,174,501.93	$1,174,501.93	$5,383.13
98	$0.00	$0.00	$0.00	$0.00	$0.00	$0.00

Exhibit 21.4
Monthly cash flows for selected months for structure 1, classes A and B.

	C			D		
Month	Beginning Balance	Principal	Interest	Beginning Balance	Principal	Interest
1	$159,225,000.00	$0.00	$729,781.25	$120,450,000.00	$0.00	$552,062.50
2	$159,225,000.00	$0.00	$729,781.25	$120,450,000.00	$0.00	$552,062.50
3	$159,225,000.00	$0.00	$729,781.25	$120,450,000.00	$0.00	$552,062.50
4	$159,225,000.00	$0.00	$729,781.25	$120,450,000.00	$0.00	$552,062.50
5	$159,225,000.00	$0.00	$729,781.25	$120,450,000.00	$0.00	$552,062.50
6	$159,225,000.00	$0.00	$729,781.25	$120,450,000.00	$0.00	$552,062.50
7	$159,225,000.00	$0.00	$729,781.25	$120,450,000.00	$0.00	$552,062.50
8	$159,225,000.00	$0.00	$729,781.25	$120,450,000.00	$0.00	$552,062.50
9	$159,225,000.00	$0.00	$729,781.25	$120,450,000.00	$0.00	$552,062.50
10	$159,225,000.00	$0.00	$729,781.25	$120,450,000.00	$0.00	$552,062.50
11	$159,225,000.00	$0.00	$729,781.25	$120,450,000.00	$0.00	$552,062.50
12	$159,225,000.00	$0.00	$729,781.25	$120,450,000.00	$0.00	$552,062.50
. . .						
95	$159,225,000.00	$0.00	$729,781.25	$120,450,000.00	$0.00	$552,062.50
96	$159,225,000.00	$0.00	$729,781.25	$120,450,000.00	$0.00	$552,062.50
97	$159,225,000.00	$1,771,533.84	$729,781.25	$120,450,000.00	$0.00	$552,062.50
98	$157,453,466.16	$2,918,644.62	$721,661.72	$120,450,000.00	$0.00	$552,062.50
99	$154,534,821.54	$2,891,497.43	$708,284.60	$120,450,000.00	$0.00	$552,062.50
100	$151,643,324.11	$2,864,592.09	$695,031.90	$120,450,000.00	$0.00	$552,062.50
101	$148,778,732.01	$2,837,926.47	$681,902.52	$120,450,000.00	$0.00	$552,062.50
102	$145,940,805.54	$2,811,498.48	$668,895.36	$120,450,000.00	$0.00	$552,062.50
103	$143,129,307.06	$2,785,306.03	$656,009.32	$120,450,000.00	$0.00	$552,062.50
104	$140,344,001.04	$2,759,347.06	$643,243.34	$120,450,000.00	$0.00	$552,062.50
105	$137,584,653.98	$2,733,619.52	$630,596.33	$120,450,000.00	$0.00	$552,062.50
. . .						
171	$2,747,229.44	$1,458,601.26	$12,591.47	$120,450,000.00	$0.00	$552,062.50
172	$1,288,628.18	$1,288,628.18	$5,906.21	$120,450,000.00	$155,905.11	$552,062.50

(*continued*)

	C			D		
Month	Beginning Balance	Principal	Interest	Beginning Balance	Principal	Interest
173	$0.00	$0.00	$0.00	$120,294,094.89	$1,430,592.36	$551,347.93
174	$0.00	$0.00	$0.00	$118,863,502.53	$1,416,777.37	$544,791.05
175	$0.00	$0.00	$0.00	$117,446,725.16	$1,403,087.19	$538,297.49
176	$0.00	$0.00	$0.00	$116,043,637.98	$1,389,520.73	$531,866.67
177	$0.00	$0.00	$0.00	$114,654,117.25	$1,376,076.90	$525,498.04
178	$0.00	$0.00	$0.00	$113,278,040.36	$1,362,754.61	$519,191.02
179	$0.00	$0.00	$0.00	$111,915,285.74	$1,349,552.81	$512,945.06
180	$0.00	$0.00	$0.00	$110,565,732.93	$1,336,470.42	$506,759.61
. . .						
350	$0.00	$0.00	$0.00	$1,876,872.02	$218,871.81	$8,602.33
351	$0.00	$0.00	$0.00	$1,658,000.21	$216,230.23	$7,599.17
352	$0.00	$0.00	$0.00	$1,441,769.98	$213,614.26	$6,608.11
353	$0.00	$0.00	$0.00	$1,228,155.72	$211,023.68	$5,629.05
354	$0.00	$0.00	$0.00	$1,017,132.04	$208,458.25	$4,661.86
355	$0.00	$0.00	$0.00	$808,673.79	$205,917.74	$3,706.42
356	$0.00	$0.00	$0.00	$602,756.05	$203,401.93	$2,762.63
357	$0.00	$0.00	$0.00	$399,354.11	$200,910.60	$1,830.37
358	$0.00	$0.00	$0.00	$198,443.52	$198,443.52	$909.53

Exhibit 21.5
Monthly cash flows for selected months for structure 1, classes C and D.

Prepayment Speed	100%	125%	165%	250%	400%	500%
Collateral	11.22	10.04	8.54	6.42	4.45	3.72
Bond Class						
A	4.70	4.09	3.42	2.63	1.98	1.74
B	10.33	8.90	7.28	5.32	3.73	3.17
C	15.05	13.15	10.85	7.84	5.31	4.41
D	24.01	22.36	19.75	15.17	10.25	8.33

Exhibit 21.6
Average life for the collateral and the various bond classes of the CMO depending on the assumptions about prepayment speed as a percentage of PSA.

story. They are both shorter and longer than the collateral, thereby attracting institutional investors who prefer an average life that differs from that of the collateral. For example, a depository institution interested in the shorter-term paper would find bond class A more appealing than the collateral because, within a reasonable range of prepayment speeds, bond class A's average life will be less than 5 years under slow prepayment speeds, while the collateral's average life can extend to a little more than 11 years. At the other end of the maturity preference spectrum, consider a defined benefit pension plan that is seeking longer-term investments. That institutional investor would prefer bond class D to the collateral. While bond class D has considerable variation in its average life, the average life remains long. Notice, for example, that at the fastest prepayment speed shown in exhibit 21.6 (500%), the average life for the collateral can contract to 3.7 years, but for bond class D to only 8.3 years.

Consequently, we can see that the rules for distribution of principal among the bond classes in this structure have redistributed the prepayment risk of the collateral among the bond classes. As a result, an unattractive asset or collateral from the perspective of some investors can be used to create securities that better match the needs of those investors.

21.3.2.5 Planned Amortization Class Bonds and Support Bonds There are investors who seek securities (bond classes) that have even greater protection against prepayment risk. Planned amortization class bond structures are designed with this goal in mind. The main idea is to create a bond class, *planned amortization class bond* (popularly referred to as a *PAC*), that takes priority over all other bond classes in the structure with respect to receiving the scheduled principal repayment. The non-PAC bond classes in the structure are referred to as the *support bonds* or *companion bonds*. The support bonds accept the prepayment risk if actual prepayment speeds are faster or slower than *structuring speeds* or *structuring bands*. Hence, unlike a sequential-pay structure, in which the bond classes are given some protection against fast prepayments or slow prepayments but not both, PAC bonds offer protection against both fast and slow prepayments, thus minimizing the variability for the investor.

In practice, a typical structure may have more than one class of PAC bonds. That is, there may be a series of PAC bonds. The first PAC bond in the series has a priority over the others, the second PAC bond has a priority over the others (except the first PAC bond), and so on. Similarly, typically there are several classes of support bonds.

21.3.4 Private-Label RMBS

The private-label RMBS market encompasses a variety of product and structuring variations. Technically, any deal that is not securitized under an agency (i.e., Ginnie Mae) or a government-sponsored enterprise (GSE) shelf (i.e., Freddie Mac or Fannie Mae) can be considered private label, as the issuing entity has no connection to the U.S. government (either explicit or implicit). Private-label RMBSs are further classified based on the credit quality of the mortgage loans in the pool: prime loans (for higher-quality loans) and subprime loans (for lower-quality loans with high default risk).

As mentioned earlier, because of the lack of federal guarantee, private-label RMBS deals must have some form of credit enhancement to create large amounts of investment-grade bonds. Aside from the presence of credit enhancement, private-label deals share many features and structuring techniques with agency CMOs. There are some important differences, however, due to the nature of the loans collateralizing the deal, as well as legal and regulatory issues associated with the various shelves. First, private-label deals can be structured such that derivatives, such as interest rate swaps, can be inserted into the structures as risk mitigators. The GSEs, by contrast, do not allow the inclusion of derivatives in deals. Second, the loans collateralizing private-label deals are generally assumed to get prepaid faster than those in agency pools. The convention in the agency market is to structure deals using a base-case prepayment speed consistent with median prepayment speeds reported by Bloomberg. Private-label deals, by contrast, are structured either to a market convention (i.e., PSA speeds ranging from 250% to 300%) or a predefined ramp (i.e., 6% to 18% CPR ramping over 12 months). The ramp is defined in the prospectus, and it is typically called the *prospectus prepayment curve (PPC)*. (100% PPC is simply the base ramp defined at the time of pricing.) Finally, private-label deals typically have *cleanup calls,* which are inserted into deals to relieve the trustees from the burden of having to oversee deals with very small remaining balances. The calls are triggered when the current face of the deal and/or collateral group declines below a predetermined level.

Next, we briefly review the mechanisms involved in creating the internal credit enhancement typically utilized in private-label deals. The first step in structuring the credit enhancement for a private-label deal is to split the face value of the loans into senior and subordinated interest. The senior bonds have higher priority with respect to both the receipt of interest and principal and the allocation of realized losses, and are generally created with enough subordination to be rated AAA by the credit rating agencies. In most cases, the subordinate interests are *tranched* (subdivided) into a series of bonds that decline sequentially in priority. The subordinate classes normally range from AA in rating to an unrated first-loss piece. These securities are often referred to as the *six-pack* since there are six broad rating grades generally issued by the rating agencies. In the investment-grade category, bonds range from AA to BBB; noninvestment-grade ratings decline from BB to the unrated first-loss piece.[8] The ratings are assigned according to the amount of *credit support* (also referred to as a *buffer*) behind each bond. The structure (or *split*) of a hypothetical $400 million deal with 3.5% initial subordination is shown in exhibits 21.7 and 21.8.

8. See chapter 2 for an introduction to credit ratings.

	Face Value	Percent of Deal
AAA	$386,000,000.00	96.50%
AA	$6,000,000.00	1.50%
A	$2,600,000.00	0.65%
BBB	$1,800,000.00	0.45%
BB	$1,200,000.00	0.30%
B	$1,200,000.00	0.30%
First loss (nonrated)	$1,200,000.00	0.30%
Total subordination	$400,000,000.00	3.50%

Exhibit 21.7
Subordination by the percentage of deal size for a hypothetical $400 million deal with 3.5% initial subordination.

	Face Value	Credit Support
AAA	$386,000,000.00	3.50%
AA	$6,000,000.00	2.00%
A	$2,600,000.00	1.35%
BBB	$1,800,000.00	0.90%
BB	$1,200,000.00	0.60%
B	$1,200,000.00	0.30%
First loss (nonrated)	$1,200,000.00	0.00%

Exhibit 21.8
Tranche size measured by the percentage of subordination for each rating level (i.e., credit support). Calculated by summing the deal percentages of all the tranches that are junior in priority. For example, if cumulative losses on the deal were 0.40%, the first loss and the rated B tranche would be fully exhausted, but tranches rated BB and above would not be affected.

Internal credit enhancement requires two complementary mechanisms. Deal cash flows are allocated through a waterfall mechanism, which dictates the allocation of principal and interest payments to tranches with different degrees of seniority. The allocation of realized losses is governed by a separate prioritization schedule, with the subordinates typically being affected in reverse order of priority.

While the original subordination levels are set at the time of issuance (or, more precisely, at the time that the attributes of the deal's collateral are finalized), deals with internal credit enhancement are designed such that the amount of credit enhancement grows over time. Private-label structures generally use a so-called shifting interest mechanism, in which the subordinate classes (or *subs*) do not receive principal prepayments for a period of time after issuance, generally five years for fixed-rate deals. After the lockout period expires, the subs begin to receive prepayments on an escalating basis. It is only after 10 years that the subs receive a pro rata allocation of prepayments. Locking out the subs means that as the collateral experiences prepayments, the face value of the subs grows in proportion relative to the senior classes. The senior classes receive all the collateral prepayments during the lockout period, and for that reason they decline proportionately over time. Deals often have more than one collateral group securitized in the same transaction to minimize costs. Typically, the collateral groups have different characteristics that make them difficult to commingle. For example, a deal may have separate collateral groups comprised of 30- and 15-year loans. Depending on the collateral in question, the two groups can have separate subordination groups. Alternatively, one set of subs can serve as credit support for both groups, in a *Y-structure*. This creates larger subordinate classes, which are generally more liquid.

21.4 Pricing RMBS by Simulation

The pricing of RMBSs involves the estimation of the present value of the uncertain future cash flows, and it presents a number of challenges. There are two building blocks to RMBS pricing models: an interest rate model, which determines the discount factor, and a prepayment model, which determines the behavior of the mortgagor. However, the two models do not exist independent of one another. Historical evidence clearly indicates that interest rates affect prepayments. Furthermore, not only the current interest rate but also past interest rates matter for the amount of current prepayments. As explained in section 21.2.4, this is often referred to as the *burnout effect*: a mortgage pool that has already experienced low interest rates will prepay less quickly than a pool that has always experienced high interest rates, even if the two pools currently face the same interest rate. This means that valuation of RMBSs is path dependent; that is, it depends on the path taken by interest rates so far. Pricing models like binomial trees quickly get out of hand in this context.[9]

Simulation is, therefore, the preferred and more practical method for pricing RMBSs. Yet given the complexity of RMBS structures, simulation is often too slow for practical purposes. However, variance-reduction techniques (especially quasirandom number sequences)[10] have been successfully applied to RMBS pricing.

In this section, we explain the main ideas behind RMBS pricing by simulation. We start with a discussion of interest and prepayment models used in RMBS pricing and explain how the models are put together. We then discuss more recent developments—specifically, how quasirandom Monte Carlo (MC) methods can be applied to RMBS pricing.

21.4.1 Prepayment Models

In section 21.2.3, we introduced a prepayment function convention. Prepayment models are a very important factor for accurate pricing of RMBSs, and there is a variety of proprietary models.

Traditionally, prepayment models have been based on econometrics—they often include macroeconomic factors, such as the economy's health or the housing market activity, or identify a prepayment pattern as a function of specific characteristics of the individual mortgages in the pool. Three classical models are (1) the arctangent model, from the Office of Thrift Supervision (OTS); (2) Schwarz and Torous's proportional hazard model (1989); and (3) Richard and Roll's modified Goldman Sachs model (1989). Other models (see, e.g.,

9. See section 14.9 in Luenberger (1998) for an example of how a binomial tree for the process followed by interest rates can be applied for pricing a simple RMBS. The example points out the difficulty of using binomial lattices and the need to employ nonrecombining binomial trees. The dimension of the problem then quickly becomes computationally prohibitive.

10. See chapter 19.

Kalotay, Yang, and Fabozzi, 2004) take into consideration borrower intelligence and are based on option theory, under the assumption that the borrower acts optimally to maximize the value of the option to prepay the mortgage.

Technically, prepayment models should be based on option pricing theory. The fact that a homeowner/borrower can pay off the outstanding principal of a mortgage in full at any time and be freed from the obligations to make further payments means that he or she holds an American call option on an otherwise identical, nonprepayable mortgage. The strike of the option equals the principal amount of the outstanding loan, and it changes after every payment. Similarly, we can think of the homeowner as the issuer of a callable bond—the homeowner sells the bond, receives the proceeds, and undertakes to make a set of scheduled payments.

When pricing callable bonds issued by governments, agencies, and corporations, we may be able to assume that the driving force behind prepayments is the level of interest rates. However, individuals do not always act rationally. Furthermore, residential mortgages are often prepaid for reasons independent of the level of interest rates—homeowners move, sell their homes, and pay off the mortgage; or there are natural disasters, and the insurance policy covers the value of the home. Even if interest rates provide a strong incentive for homeowners to change the terms of their mortgages, homeowners vary greatly in financial sophistication. The cost to them to analyze the prepayment options and handle all the necessary paperwork may turn out to be too high. When they do refinance, there is still usually a noticeable delay, and valuation models from the financial markets do not reflect this properly.

As mentioned, most prepayment function models used in practice are based on statistical models. The concern with such approaches is that historical data, on which these models are based, may render the models outdated as economic conditions change. However, the theoretically superior approaches based on modeling the homeowner's decision process have not been too successful in practice and have not gained widespread industry acceptance.

It is also important to keep in mind that in the case of nonagency RMBSs, prepayments can be involuntary. In other words, prepayments can arise because of defaults by homeowners.[11] These defaults should be projected in modeling prepayments. Modeling defaults involves modeling the timing of defaults, as well as the severity of defaults (i.e., the recovery rate after the default). Both voluntary and involuntary prepayments are included in the calculation of the cash flow from the RMBS.

Next, we introduce two simple econometric prepayment models for agency RMBSs used in practice. Our goal is not to provide a comprehensive review of the subject, but rather to give the reader an idea of the kind of modeling that is involved in the pricing of RMBSs. For more details on prepayment models, see, for example, Fabozzi (2005).

21.4.1.1 Arctangent Model The arctangent model expresses the CPR at time t as a function of the WAC and the 10-year rate at time t, $r_{10}(t)$:

$$CPR(t) = 0.2406 - 0.1389 \cdot \arctan\left(5.9518 \cdot \left(1.089 - \frac{WAC}{r_{10}(t)}\right)\right)$$

11. Recall that in the case of nonagency RMBS, the mortgages do not have federal guarantees.

This kind of model is derived empirically based on the observed relationship between different factors and the prepayment rate.

21.4.1.2 Modified Goldman Sachs Model In the modified Goldman Sachs model,[12] the CPR is assumed to be a product of four factors: the refinancing incentive RI, the month multiplier MM, the seasoning factor Age, and the burnout multiplier BM:

$$CPR(t) = RI(t) \cdot MM(t) \cdot \text{Age}(t) \cdot BM(t)$$

The refinancing incentive in this model is related to the ratio or the spread between the WAC rate and the interest rate. The idea is that if the interest rate is much lower than the WAC rate, there is a higher incentive for homeowners to refinance the mortgage; that is, RI is higher. RI can be expressed as

$$RI = a + b \cdot \arctan(c + d \cdot (WAC - r))$$

or

$$RI = a + b \cdot \arctan\left(c + d \cdot \left(\frac{WAC}{r}\right)\right)$$

The relevant interest rate r can be, for example, the 10-year rate $r_{10}(t)$. The 10-year rate is often the one used as an approximation for the refinancing rate for new loans. Often a time lag is assumed to incorporate the observation that investors refinance after observing a fall in mortgage rates; that is, $r_{10}(t-1)$ is used. A specific function for RI used in practice is

$$RI(t) = 0.28 + 0.14 \cdot \arctan(-8.571 + 430 \cdot (WAC - r_{10}(\text{t})))$$

The monthly multiplier MM is associated with the specific month of the year. It has been observed that prepayments peak during the summer-fall months and bottom out in the winter. The month multipliers from the original Richard and Roll (1989) paper are as follows (starting with month i = January):

$$MM(i) = (0.94, 7.76, 0.74, 0.95, 0.98, 0.92, 0.98, 1.10, 1.18, 1.22, 1.23, 0.98)$$

The seasoning factor Age reflects the empirical observation that newer loans tend to prepay slower than old or "seasoned" loans. This factor usually follows the convention behind the standard PSA model (see section 21.2.3). A specific function used for Age is

$$Age(t) = \min\left\{1, \frac{t}{30}\right\}$$

Finally, as explained earlier, the burnout multiplier reflects the empirical observation that prepayments tend to decrease over time, even when conditions for refinancing are favorable. The reason is that not all mortgagors prepay identically. Some refinance as soon as mortgage

12. The modified Goldman Sachs model was developed by Richard and Roll (1989) and modified by the OTS. Typically, the details of prepayment models by banks are proprietary. The Goldman Sachs model formulated by Richard and Roll has probably changed dramatically over the past 20 or so years since their article appeared.

rates become lower than they are paying; others wait until rates drop further; and others never prepay. The fast prepayers leave, and only the slow ones stay behind as the pool ages. Richard and Roll (1989) use the following function for the burnout multiplier:

$$BM(t) = 0.3 + 0.7 \cdot \frac{MB(t)}{MB(0)}$$

where $MB(0)$ is the mortgage balance at the beginning, and $MB(t)$ is the mortgage balance at time t. In effect, Richard and Roll (1989) quantify the burnout by estimating how deep in the money the prepayment option is at time t. If it has been deep in the money, this suggests that all else being equal, the prepayments are smaller.

21.4.2 Interest Rate Models

There is a variety of interest rate models that can be used to generate scenarios for the term structure of interest rates. They can be most generally split into two categories: *equilibrium models*, and *no-arbitrage models*. Equilibrium models, which include the Vasicek model and the Cox-Ingersoll-Ross (CIR) model, start with assumptions about economic variables and a process for the instantaneous (short) rate r.[13] They then derive the bond prices that the process for the short-term rate imply and use those bond prices to construct the implied term structure. The disadvantage of equilibrium models is that they do not automatically fit today's term structure, so adjustments need to be made by selecting the parameters of the processes carefully to make sure that the pricing of securities using the term structure implied from these models does not create arbitrage opportunities.

The Vasicek model and the CIR model are one-factor models of the short-term interest rate because they include only one random variable. A popular two-factor model is the one proposed by Brennan and Schwartz (1979), in which the process for the short rate is assumed to revert to a long rate, which in turn follows a particular stochastic process itself. Another two-factor model assumes that the volatility in the process followed by the short-term interest rate itself follow a stochastic process.[14]

No-arbitrage models include the Ho-Lee model and the Hull-White model.[15] Those models are designed to be exactly consistent with today's term structure. Some equilibrium models can be converted to no-arbitrage models by making the assumption that the drift term in the process for the short rate depends on time. (Both the Ho-Lee and the Hull-White model do this.) This allows one to fit the parameters of the process to the shape of the term structure at time 0, and to incorporate that information for the process followed by the interest rate in the future as well.

How do we use the interest rate models for MBS pricing and risk evaluation purposes? The procedure is as follows: We use the realizations of the short-term interest rate to generate discount factors for different maturities. Usually, we need to generate long-term rates as well, such as the 10-year rate. Such long-term rates can be determined by computing

13. As we saw in section 17.4.3, the Vasicek and the CIR model assume that the short-term interest rate is mean-reverting.

14. See Longstaff and Schwartz (1992).

15. See Hull (2008).

zero-coupon bond prices. (This is easier to do for some interest rate models than for others.) Namely, from those prices, we generate a yield curve. From this yield curve, we can estimate the long-term rates or forward rates.[16]

Let us give a specific example by using the Vasicek and the CIR models for the short rate. Recall from chapter 17 that the Vasicek model assumes that the short rate r follows the random walk

$$r_{t+1} = r_t + \kappa \cdot (\mu - r_t) + \sigma \cdot \tilde{\varepsilon}_t.$$

Similarly, recall from chapter 17 that the CIR model assumes that the short rate r follows the random walk

$$r_{t+1} = r_t + \kappa \cdot (\mu - r_t) + \sigma \cdot \sqrt{r_t} \cdot \tilde{\varepsilon}_t.$$

Under these assumptions, one can generate paths for the short-term rate and use them to compute discount factors. One can also derive a closed-form expression for the price (at any time t) of a zero-coupon bond with face value of \$1 maturing at time T, $B(t, T)$, in terms of r_t. The details of the derivation are beyond the scope of this book, but the formulas turn out to be as follows:

- In the Vasicek model,

  $$B(t,T) = A(t,T) \cdot e^{-C(t,T) \cdot r_t}$$

  where

  $$C(t,T) = \frac{1 - e^{\kappa \cdot (T-t)}}{\kappa}$$

  and

  $$A(t,T) = e^{\frac{(C(t,T) - T + t) \cdot \left(\kappa^2 \mu - \frac{\sigma^2}{2}\right)}{\kappa^2} - \frac{\sigma^2 \cdot C(t,T)^2}{4 \cdot \kappa}}$$

- In the CIR model,

  $$B(t,T) = A(t,T) \cdot e^{-C(t,T) \cdot r_t}$$

  where

  $$C(t,T) = \frac{2 \cdot (e^{\gamma \cdot (T-t)} - 1)}{(\gamma + \kappa) \cdot (e^{\gamma \cdot (T-t)} - 1) + 2 \cdot \gamma} \quad A(t,T)$$

  $$= \left(\frac{2 \cdot \gamma \cdot e^{(\gamma + \kappa) \cdot \frac{(T-t)}{2}}}{(\gamma + \kappa) \cdot (e^{\gamma \cdot (T-t)} - 1) + 2 \cdot \gamma} \right)^{2 \cdot \kappa \cdot \frac{\mu}{\sigma^2}}$$

16. See chapter 2 for how to compute forward rates off the given term structure of interest rates.

and

$$\gamma = \sqrt{\kappa^2 + 2 \cdot \sigma^2}$$

Given a realization of r_t, we can plug it into these formulas, and determine $B(t, T)$. $B(t, T)$ is the price of a zero-coupon bond with a face value of 1. Thus, we can interpret the value for $B(t, T)$ as the discount factor between t and T. We also have

$$B(t,T) = e^{-r_{(t,T)} \cdot (T-t)}$$

This allows us to compute the long-term interest rate applicable for the period (t, T) as[17]

$$r_{(t,T)} = \frac{-\ln(B(t,T))}{(T-t)}$$

Thus, we can build the term structure of interest rates. Forward rates can be computed from the term structure as well. In particular, we can compute the 10-year interest rate ${}_{10}r_t$ in our notation from chapter 2, at each point in time t, to use in prepayment models.

21.4.3 Putting It All Together

As we explained in the previous two sections, the pricing of an RMBS requires a prepayment model and an interest rate model. The price of the RMBS is the expected value of the future cash flows over all generated scenarios for the interest rates and the corresponding prepayments. The procedure is as follows:

1. Generate N scenarios for interest rate paths, where a path includes the short interest rate and the corresponding discount factors for 360 months ahead. Record also the corresponding values for a required long-term rate, such as the 10-year rate.

   For each interest rate path n, $n = 1, \ldots, N$:

   A. At each point in time (360 of them), calculate the expected prepayment using a particular prepayment function. For example, if we use the modified Goldman Sachs prepayment function, we will plug in the estimated 10-year rate r_{10} at each point in time for each interest rate path.

   B. After calculating the prepayment rates, compute the cash flow $CF_n(t)$ from the mortgage pool for each time t along that interest rate path. This is a difficult step, as RMBS structures can be incredibly complex. For pass-through RMBS, we have a specific formula for $CF_n(t)$ as follows:[18]

$$CF_n(t) = MP_n(t) + PP_n(t) = TPP_n(t) + IP_n(t)$$

$$MP_n(t) = SP_n(t) + IP_n(t),$$

$$TPP_n(t) = SP_n(t) + PP_n(t)$$

17. We simply took the logarithms of both sides of the equation.

18. See chapter 19 in Fabozzi (1993).

where $MP_n(t)$ is the scheduled mortgage payment for month t, $TPP_n(t)$ is the total principal payment for month t, $IP_n(t)$ is the interest payment for month t, $SP_n(t)$ is the scheduled principal payment for month t, and $PP_n(t)$ is the principal prepayment for month t.

These quantities are calculated as follows:

$$MP_n(t) = B_n(t-1) \cdot \left(\frac{WAC/12}{1-(1+WAC/12)^{-WAM+t}} \right)$$

$$IP_n(t) = MB_n(t-1) \cdot (WAC/12);$$

$$PP_n(t) = SMM_n(t) \cdot (MB_n(t-1) - SP_n(t));$$

$$MB_n(t) = MB_n(t-1) - TPP_n(t);$$

$$SMM_n(t) = 1 - \sqrt[12]{1 - CPR_n(t)}$$

where $MP_n(t)$ is the principal mortgage balance of the RMBS at the end of month t, WAC is the WAC rate for the RMBS (weighted by the balance of each mortgage), WAM is the weighted average maturity for the RMBS (weighted by the balance of each mortgage), $SMM_n(t)$ is the single monthly mortality for month t, observed at the end of month t, and $CPR_n(t)$ is the conditional prepayment rate for month t, observed at the end of month t.

2. Calculate the total cash flow over the entire interest rate path as a sum of the cash flows at each point in time, properly discounted with the discount factor for that interest rate path at that time, plus an appropriate risk-adjusted spread K.
3. Calculate the average of the cash flows over the N interest rate paths.
   It is clear from this algorithm that once we know $CPR(t)$ for each time and each interest rate path, everything else can be calculated. $CPR(t)$ will, of course, be different depending on the prepayment model used.

This procedure is valid for pricing more complex types of RMBSs as well; we just need to be careful about estimating the cash flows $CF(t)$. For example, in a sequential-pay structure, we apply the procedure to estimate the cash flows for classes A, B, C, and so on separately. This determines the price for each class.

21.4.4 Further Analysis

In the process of evaluating the RMBS price by simulation, we obtain a variety of other information that can be useful.

21.4.4.1 Distribution of Path Values The average of the cash flows obtained along the N simulated interest rate paths gives us the price of the RMBS. However, we also obtain the distribution of cash flows; that is, N points from the probability distribution of cash flow values. This allows us to observe the variability in the cash flows and to decide how much confidence we can have in the estimate of the RMBS price obtained from the simulation.

21.4.4.2 Average Life In the process of simulating the price of an RMBS, we work with estimates of the average life of the RMBS along each interest rate path. This allows us to obtain the probability distribution of the average life, which is useful for risk management purposes.

21.4.4.3 Option-Adjusted Spread Traders like to compute a quantity called the *option-adjusted spread (OAS),* which allows them to take an estimate of the spread of the yield of the RMBS over U.S. Treasuries when the optionality has been considered. The OAS is the spread above the risk-free rate that makes the price of the RMBS equal to the observed market price. In the MC simulation, it is the spread that makes the average present value of the RMBS cash flows along all the interest rate paths equal to the observed market price.

21.4.5 Improving the Degree of Accuracy with Variance-Reduction Methods

In chapter 4, we discussed the issue of how many trials are needed in a simulation. The short answer is that this is not known. However, we can decide if the number of paths generated in the simulation resulted in an estimate of the quantity of interest with small variance (i.e., with sufficient accuracy), and increase the number of generated paths if the estimate is too variable.[19] A typical RMBS is priced using between 512 and 1,024 paths. However, this number can be brought down to as few as 128 or 64 paths by using variance reduction methods. The actual variance reduction methods used in practice are proprietary, but Akesson and Lehoczky (2000) describe the basics of how to apply quasi-MC number sequences in the context of RMBS pricing.

To price an RMBS, we need to simulate 360 monthly observations for interest rates N times. Therefore, we are dealing with generating N random points in a 360-dimensional cube; that is, a 360-dimensional problem. Quasi-MC methods (low-discrepancy sequences) are appropriate in this situation because they can generate points that can cover the space a lot better than purely random points, thus requiring fewer points to achieve the same degree of accuracy as random number generators. It is important to keep in mind, though, that not all low-discrepancy sequences outperform traditional MC simulation. The selection of the specific low-discrepancy sequence to use must be accompanied by a lot of tests. Akesson and Lehoczky (2000) use the Sobol low-discrepancy sequence, together with other simulation speed enhancements, such as PCs[20] and Brownian bridge[21] constructions for the interest rate paths. They note a substantial improvement in the speed of RMBS pricing algorithms.

21.5 Using Simulation to Estimate Sensitivity of RMBS Prices to Different Factors

Investors in RMBSs are exposed to many types of risk, such as interest rate risk, credit risk, and model risk. The sensitivity of the RMBS price to these factors is typically evaluated by simulation. This section discusses risk assessment in more detail.

19. Note that this criterion does not tell us how good the estimate is relative to the truth; only how good it is relative to the model that we are using.

20. See chapter 16.

21. A Brownian bridge construction is the generation of a sequence of values for a Brownian motion in not necessarily sequential mode after generating the end points (the first and last points in the process) first. The remaining points are then filled out in different order, depending on the variance reduction method or low-discrepancy sequence used. See chapter 17 for a definition of Brownian motion, and Glasserman (2004) for more details on Brownian bridge construction.

21.5.1 Interest Rate Risk

One of the main risks of RMBSs is interest rate risk. MBSs are fixed-income securities and, as such, are very sensitive to shifts in yields. Similar to simpler fixed-income securities, RMBS prices fall when interest rates rise and RMBS prices rise when interest rates fall. However, recall that RMBSs in effect have embedded options; that is, mortgage holders have the option to refinance if interest rates fall. This influences the life of the RMBSs. Hence, classical measures of interest sensitivity such as Macaulay duration and modified duration do not work well in the case of RMBSs.

Furthermore, in the case of plain vanilla bonds (without embedded options), duration measures underestimate price gains and overestimate price losses. In the case of a noncallable bond, this estimation error is due to positive convexity and favors the investor. However, the opposite is the case for RMBSs, which have prepayment risk. Duration overestimates price gains and underestimates price losses. This is due to negative convexity and works against the investor. The more prepayment risk a security has, the worse the estimation error will be and, in turn, the more negative its convexity will be.

That is why in the case of RMBSs, an *option-adjusted duration* is used,[22] which is computed by assuming changes of equal amounts (usually, increments of 50 basis points to 100 basis points) up or down and evaluating the new RMBS prices. The sensitivity of the RMBS price computed in this way is the option-adjusted duration.

Other measures of interest rate sensitivity that are sometimes quoted are the average life (also called *weighted average life*, or *WAL*), which is an average time to receive back principal on the underlying loans, and the WAM of the underlying loans. These can be evaluated directly, without generating scenarios. However, they are less useful as measures of sensitivity to interest rates because they do not take into consideration the inherent optionality in RMBSs.

21.5.2 Credit Risk

The credit risk associated with one type of agency RMBSs, those issued by Ginnie Mae, is minimal—Ginnie Mae MBSs can be basically treated as credit-risk-free securities because they are backed by an explicit federal guarantee. There is uncertainty as to the credit risk of securities issued by the two government-sponsored enterprises—Fannie Mae and Freddie Mac. Although both have a line of credit with the Treasury, the credit line is not sufficient to meet all obligations. There is no explicit or implicit government guarantee in the case of nonagency RMBSs. Private-label RMBSs are rated by rating agencies to incorporate information about credit risk. Considerations for their credit risk are used when pricing such RMBSs by simulating the spread over the risk-free Treasury yield curve in addition to the Treasury yield curve itself.

21.5.3 Model Risk

Virtually all security pricing models are exposed to *model risk*, the risk of using an incorrect model.[23] In the case of RMBSs, the assumptions in the prepayment model can make an enormous difference in the RMBS price estimate and risk evaluation. There is no way to fix this

22. See chapter 2 and Goldman Sachs Asset Management (2007).

23. Note that model risk is different from estimation error. The latter assumes that the model is correct, but the estimates of the inputs to the model are inaccurate.

issue, but it is important to conduct sensitivity analysis and scenario analysis that can raise a flag if the RMBS price and risk estimates are very sensitive to assumptions in the model.

21.6 Structuring RMBS Deals Using Dynamic Programming

So far, we have taken the RMBS structure as given and discussed how to price it and evaluate its sensitivity with respect to different factors. We mentioned that the procedure for determining the value of the RMBS by simulation is the same for all types of RMBSs, but that estimating the cash flow along each interest rate path is challenging. The cash flow is found according to the principal repayment and interest distributions rules of the deal. In the case of CMOs, a structuring model is needed. In any analysis of CMOs, one of the major stumbling blocks is getting a good CMO structuring deal.

Dynamic programming and integer programming (IP) methods can be used to approach the problem of optimal structuring of a CMO. From the perspective of the CMO issuer, for example, the tranches could be designed in many ways. The issuers make money on the difference between the interest collected by the mortgage holders whose mortgages are in the pool, and the interest paid to investors who buy the RMBS. While the mortgage holders pay 10- and 30-year interest rates on the principal outstanding, some tranches in a CMO pay out 2-, 4-, 6-, and 8-year rates, plus a spread. A natural question that arises is if there is a way to design a CMO so the profit to the issuer is the largest. How many tranches should there be? How large should they be? What coupon rates can the issuer afford to pay to the RMBS investors?

Cornuejols and Tutuncu (2007) describe a dynamic programming algorithm for answering these questions for a sequential-pay MBS. We provide some discussion of their approach next. The problem formulation that is described is one of the private-label CMOs, where credit quality is an issue.[24]

When structuring a CMO, several constraints need to be taken into consideration. First, we need to make sure that the payments over the life of the CMO can service the promised payments to the bond holders under different scenarios. Two extreme such scenarios include the case of full early prepayments and no early prepayments. Second, we need to estimate the average life of each tranche.[25] The price of the tranche will then be determined based on the rate of a Treasury bond with the same duration, and an appropriate spread, which depends on the tranche's credit rating. Third, we need to calculate the required credit support, or buffer, for each tranche as a function of the average life of the tranche and rating. The required buffer is computed as follows:

$$(\text{Average life of tranche}) \cdot (\text{Expected default rate}) \cdot (\text{Loss multiple})$$

and the size of the buffer determines the credit rating that will be assigned to a tranche. The larger the buffer, the more collateral is behind the tranche. If the buffer of a particular tranche is large, the CMO will have to experience a lot of defaults before payments to that tranche are stopped. The last tranche in the CMO has no buffer.[26]

24. See section 21.3.4.

25. See sections 21.3.1 and 21.3.2 for how to estimate the average life of a tranche.

26. See exhibit 21.7.

The *loss multiple* is a multiplier that is set by the rating agencies. For example, a AAA-rated tranche must have a buffer equal to six times the expected default rate, so its loss multiple is 6. Finally, the coupon paid on each tranche is estimated based on the tranche's credit rating and rates on comparable securities. Spreads on corporate bonds with similar credit ratings typically provide a benchmark.

Suppose that we would like to structure a CMO with four tranches. The objective is to maximize the profits from the issuance by choosing the size of each tranche. A dynamic programming algorithm can be developed to find the optimal sizes. As mentioned in section 6.6.3, one of the most difficult problems in dynamic programming is identifying the states and the stages. In this case, the states are t, the indices of the months, and the stages are k, the number of tranches up to month t. This enumerates all the possible tranches—there are t possible maturities for the tranches and k possible starting dates for the tranche ($k \leq t$). Tranche (k, t) starts amortizing at the beginning of month k and ends at the end of month t.

Let T_{kt} be the present value of the payments on tranche (k, t). T_{kt} can be computed exactly for every pair (k, t). Let $f(k, t)$ denote the minimum present value of total payments to bondholders in months 1 through t when the CMO has k tranches up to year t. It is easy to see that $f(1, t) = T_{1t}$. If there is only one tranche up to year t, then there is nothing to minimize—we know the present value of that tranche. For larger values of k, the dynamic programming recursion can be written as follows:

$$f(k,t) = \min_{j=k-1,\ldots t-1} \{f(k-1, j) + T_{j+1,t}\}$$

For example, if $k=2$ and $t=5$, we compute $f(1,j) + T_{j+1,5}$ for each $j = 1, 2, 3, 4$, and take the minimum. Note that for $k=4$, there is no need to compute the minimum of thousands of possible combinations of four tranches. We just need to use the value $f(3,j)$ found at the previous stage and then enumerate over the size of the fourth tranche.

In the example of an RMBS (structure 1) from section 21.3.3, we had $k=4$ and $t=358$. Suppose that we would like to find the optimal size of the four tranches. (Assume also that this is a nonagency CMO.) We would compute $f(4,358)$, giving us the minimum cost for structuring the CMO with four tranches. To determine the actual tranche sizes, we need to backtrack from the last stage and identify how the minimum was achieved at each stage.

21.7 Machine Learning and the Analysis of RMBS

Analyzing an RMBS presents significant challenges for investors. Historically, this complexity led to recruiting quantitative professionals such as mathematicians, statisticians, and physicists into the Wall Street community. These experts were first brought in during the early 1980s, specifically to address the intricate analytical needs of RMBS trading desks of banks. As pointed out by Zhang et al. (2019), the complexities associated with investing in RMBS are (1) large datasets, (2) a large set of risk factors, and (3) difficulties in model specification and estimation. Consequently, it is unsurprising that ML tools, capable of handling large databases to identify patterns in homeowner behavior regarding prepayments, have become an important tool in analyzing RMBS.

The increased availability of loan-level data, combined with advancements in computer technology, has significantly driven the adoption of ML techniques in analyzing RMBS.

Historically, the lack of detailed information on the pool of mortgage loans that serve as collateral for RMBS limited comprehensive analyses of borrower behaviors concerning prepayments for valuation and risk assessment. However, regulatory changes have markedly expanded the data available for sophisticated analysis of RMBS. Specifically, the implementation of Regulation AB by the Securities and Exchange Commission (SEC) on January 1, 2006, followed by the finalization of these rules in August 2014, mandated the disclosure of loan-level information that issuers of RMBS must provide. These regulatory enhancements have been instrumental to providing the necessary data granularity required for more sophisticated risk modeling and investment strategies using ML.[27]

As an example, the information about the mortgage pools for Freddie Mac includes (1) loan and borrower characteristics at origination (i.e., the original loan term, coupon rate, and balance); (2) the purpose of the loan (refinance or purchase); (3) the borrower's credit scores; (4) the type of documentation; (5) the type of occupancy; and (6) the lien position. Information about the borrower's payment history that details monthly loan performance, including scheduled and unscheduled payments, such as voluntary prepayments, delinquencies, and losses. Also provided are summary data, such as the total balance of all active loans, cumulative losses incurred, and aggregate performance statistics.[28]

The application of ML in the analysis of RMBSs is particularly crucial in forecasting prepayments, both voluntary prepayments and default behaviors of the underlying borrowers in the mortgage pool. Accurate prepayment models are essential because they affect the valuation of RMBSs, affecting their relative value assessment and risk analysis under varying market interest rates and economic conditions. Prepayments can significantly alter the cash flow of RMBSs, and thus, their potential yield, duration, and risk profile.

Studies have demonstrated that ML improves forecasts by analyzing large datasets to identify patterns and predictors of prepayment that might not be apparent through traditional statistical methods used for this purpose. ML models, such as regression trees, neural networks (NNs), and ensemble methods, can dynamically adjust to new data, improving their predictions over time.

Zhang et al. (2019) provided the first study to apply an ML tool, a neural network model to forecast prepayments. They report that this ML model produces forecasts that are highly accurate, in that they fit historical prepayments. Moreover, an NN model generates accurate sensitivities of prepayments in response to changing macroeconomic conditions and pool-level factors. Their findings demonstrate that an ML model can efficiently identify complex prepayment behaviors of homeowners in the mortgage pool, as well as model multiple risk factors that are nonlinear and interactive. However, the application of ML is not without its issues, which the authors describe, including model overfitting, nontransparency issues (i.e., "black box" issues), and regime shift issues.

In another study, Schultz and Fabozzi (2022a) find that one of the most powerful ML techniques to improve the performance prepayment forecasting is boosting, an ensemble

27. These rules applied to issues of all ABSs, with RMBSs being the major issuers.

28. For more information about the data provided for Freddie Mac RMBSs, see "Single Family Loan-Level Dataset," at https://www.freddiemac.com/research/datasets/sf-loanlevel-dataset.

method. They conclude that ML mortgage prepayment models are "proving competitive, if not superior, to the traditional mortgage prepayment model."

ML has also been employed to develop investment strategies when investing in the agency RMBS market. There are two types of trades in the RMBS market: to-be-announced (TBA) trades and specified pool trades. In a TBA trade, the pool number is not known, but delivery must meet certain specifications as set forth by the Security Industry and Financial Market Association. Basically, the buyer in the trade does not know what specific mortgage pool will be delivered. In contrast, in a specified pool trade, the attributes of the mortgage loans for the RMBS (e.g., loan size, age, geographical location of the properties, and type of property) are known.[29] Jagannathan and Bao (2022) introduce a systematic investment strategy for investing in specified pools of agency RMBSs, which they report outperforms a benchmark index. The strategy integrates a loan-level, gradient-boosted tree model with a pool-level, random forecast model. As with the two other studies mentioned here, they find that their ML-based prepayment model is more accurate than traditional prepayment models. They conclude that not only can ML prepayment-based models provide more accurate prepayment forecasts, but by integrating them into a systematic investment strategy, it also is possible to outperform a benchmark.

Summary

- Securitization is used to create various structured products, referred to as asset-backed securities (ABSs).
- An ABS is a debt instrument backed by a pool of loans or receivables. The cash flow from the pool of loans is used to satisfy the obligations of the debt instruments.
- Mortgage-backed securities (MBSs) are a type of ABS that is backed by pools of mortgages.
- A residential mortgage-backed security (RMBS) is an MBS backed by a pool of residential mortgage loans; a commercial mortgage-backed security (CMBS) is backed by a pool of commercial mortgage loans.
- RMBSs can be agency RMBSs or private-label RMBSs. Agency RMBSs are backed by three government-related entities (Ginnie Mae, Fannie Mae, and Freddie Mac).
- There are three types of agency RMBSs: pass-through securities, stripped MBSs, and collateralized mortgage obligations (CMOs).
- In a mortgage pass-through security, the monthly cash flow from the pool of mortgage loans is distributed on a pro rata basis to the certificate holders.
- A stripped MBS is created by altering the distribution of principal and interest from a pro rata distribution to an unequal distribution. In the most common type of stripped MBS, all the interest is allocated to one class, the interest-only class, and all the principal to the other class, the principal-only class.

29. For a description of specified pools and their appeal to sophisticated investors, see Schultz and Fabozzi (2022b).

- An agency CMO is a security backed by a pool of mortgage pass-through securities. Agency CMOs are structured so there are several classes of bonds (called tranches) with varying maturities. The principal payments from the underlying pool of pass-through securities are used to retire the bonds on a priority basis as specified in the prospectus.
- There are numerous types of agency CMO bonds, including sequential-pay bonds, PAC bonds, and support bonds.
- Private-label RMBSs are issued by any entity other than Ginnie Mae, Fannie Mae, or Freddie Mac. Because of the credit risk associated with private-label RMBSs, they require credit enhancements to provide different degrees of credit protection against defaults on the pool of assets backing a transaction.
- The uncertainty about the cash flow attributable to prepayments is called *prepayment risk* and is the major risk in agency RMBSs.
- The pricing of RMBSs involves estimating the present value of the uncertain future cash flows, and it presents several challenges. There are two building blocks to RMBS pricing models: an interest rate model, which determines the discount factor; and a prepayment model, which determines the behavior of the mortgagor.
- Prepayments depend on interest rates. Moreover, they depend on the history of interest rates, which makes RMBSs path dependent and makes their pricing challenging. Simulation is the preferred method for handling path dependency.
- Traditionally, prepayment models have been based on econometrics—they often include macroeconomic factors, such as the economy's health or the housing market activity, or identify a prepayment pattern as a function of specific characteristics of the individual mortgages in the pool. Other models are based on option theory, and they assume that the borrower acts optimally to maximize the option's value to prepay the mortgage. The latter models are more complex and less widely used in practice.
- Estimating the price of an RMBS involves simulating a particular number of interest rate paths. Along each path, the expected prepayments are simulated at each point in time (each month), and the cash flows are evaluated. The cash flows along that interest rate path are then discounted using the simulated interest rates plus an appropriate spread. The average of the total cash flows over all interest rate paths is the price of the RMBS.
- Simulation is an effective way to price the RMBS, but it can be very slow because of the problem's large dimension. Quasi–Monte Carlo (MC) methods have shown promise for reducing the necessary number of generated paths and the computational time without sacrificing accuracy.
- As a by-product of estimating the price of an RMBS by simulation, we obtain other useful information, such as the distribution of RMBS values for different interest rate scenarios, and the distribution of the average life of the RMBS.
- Simulation also is useful for estimating the sensitivity of the price of an RMBS to different factors, such as interest rates, credit events, and model risk.

- Dynamic programming can be used to structure CMOs optimally, maximizing the issuer's profit while satisfying a number of constraints.
- Machine learning (ML) methods are highly effective for analyzing RMBS due to their ability to produce more accurate prepayment forecasts for valuation and risk assessment than do traditional statistical methods.
- By integrating ML methods into the RMBS investment management process, superior strategies to outperform a benchmark can be formulated.

VI

Capital Budgeting and Real Options

22

Capital Budgeting under Uncertainty

Companies continually invest funds in assets, and these assets produce income and cash flows that the company may either reinvest in more assets or pay to the owners. The total amounts of assets that a company owns, including both tangible and intangible assets, are its *capital.* These assets include physical (tangible) assets such as land, buildings, equipment, and machinery, as well as assets that represent property rights (intangible assets), such as accounts receivable, securities, patents, and copyrights. When we say *capital investment,* we are referring to the company's investment in its assets, where the term *capital* also has come to mean the funds used to finance the company's assets and, in some contexts, refers to the sum of equity and interest-bearing debt.

Capital budgeting decisions involve the long-term commitment of a company's resources to capital investments. These decisions play a prominent role in determining whether a company will be successful. The commitment of funds to a particular capital project can be enormous and may be irreversible. Whereas some capital budgeting decisions are routine decisions that do not change the course or risk of a company, there are strategic capital budgeting decisions that either affect the company's future market position in its current product lines or permit it to expand into a new product line in the future.

The company's capital investment decision may be comprised of several distinct decisions, each referred to as a *project.* A *capital project* is a set of assets that are contingent on one another and are considered together. For example, suppose that a company is considering the production of a new product. This capital project requires the company to acquire land, build facilities, and purchase production equipment. And this project may also require the company to increase its investment in its working capital—inventory, cash, or accounts receivable. *Working capital* is the collection of assets needed for day-to-day operations that support a company's long-term investments.

There are several techniques that are used to evaluate capital budgeting proposals. These include the payback and discounted payback techniques, net present value (NPV) technique, profitability index (PI) technique, internal rate of return (IRR) technique, and modified internal rate of return (MIRR) technique. While used in practice, some of these techniques are limited in their ability to help managers identify proposed capital projects that are profitable and not necessarily consistent with maximization of shareholder wealth. Moreover, where capital rationing exists, some techniques give conflicting rankings of the relative attractiveness of capital projects.

Evaluating whether a company should invest in a capital project requires an analysis of whether the project adds value to the company. What is essential in this analysis is an assessment of the project's risk. The risk analysis of a project is challenging because most capital projects are unique, and a project's contribution to the company's risk is difficult to quantify. There are several tools available to help incorporate a project's risk into the decision. Monte Carlo (MC) simulation methods are one such tool that has grown in importance over the years.

This chapter reviews capital budgeting under uncertainty. It provides an overview of the classification of investment projects and tools for evaluating projects, such as NPV, PI, IRR, and payback period. The chapter also contains specific instructions for evaluating project risk, such as creating an investment profile, estimating market risk, and estimating project stand-alone risk using simulation. Section 22.3 presents a case study that incorporates every stage of this process.

22.1 Classifying Investment Projects

There are different ways that managers classify capital investment projects. One way of doing this is by project life, whether short term or long term. This is done because the time value of money plays an important role in evaluating long-term projects. Another way of classifying projects is by their risk. The riskier the project's future cash flows, the greater the role of the cost of capital in decision making. Still another way of classifying projects is by their dependence on other projects. The relationship between a project's cash flows and the cash flows of some other project of the company must be incorporated explicitly into the analysis since we want to analyze how a project affects the total cash flows of the company.

22.1.1 Classification According to Economic Life

An investment project generally provides benefits over a limited period of time, referred to as its *economic life*. The *economic life* or *useful life* of an asset is determined by physical deterioration, obsolescence, and degree of competition in the market for a product.

The economic life is an estimate of the length of time that the asset will benefit the company. After its useful life, the revenues generated by the asset tend to decline rapidly and its expenses tend to increase.

Typically, an investment requires an immediate expenditure and provides benefits in the form of cash flows received in the future. If benefits are received only within the current period—that is, within one year of investing—we refer to the investment as a *short-term investment.* If these benefits are received beyond the current period, we refer to the investment as a *long-term investment* and the expenditure as a *capital expenditure.*

An investment project may comprise one or more capital expenditures. For example, a new product may require investment in production equipment, a building, and transportation equipment.

Short-term investment decisions involve investments in current assets: cash, marketable securities, accounts receivable, and inventory. The objective of investing in short-term assets is the same as for long-term assets: maximizing owners' wealth. Nevertheless, we consider them separately for two practical reasons:

- Decisions about long-term assets are based on projections of cash flows far into the future and require us to consider the time value of money.
- Long-term assets do not fit the daily operating needs of the company.

Decisions regarding short-term investments or current assets are concerned with day-to-day operations. A company needs some level of current assets to act as a cushion in the case of unusually poor operating periods when cash flows from operations are less than expected.

22.1.2 Classification According to Risk

Suppose that you are faced with two investments, A and B, each promising a $10 million cash inflow 10 years from today. If A is riskier than B, what are they worth today? If you are risk averse, you would consider A less valuable than B because the chance of getting the $10 million in 10 years is less for A than for B. Therefore, valuing a project requires considering the risk associated with its future cash flows.

The investment's risk of return can be classified according to the nature of the project represented by the investment:

- *Replacement projects*. Investments in the replacement of existing equipment or facilities
- *Expansion projects*. Investments in projects that broaden existing product lines and existing markets
- *New products and markets*. Projects that involve introducing a new product or entering into a new market
- *Mandated projects*. Projects required by government laws or agency rules

Replacement projects include maintaining existing assets to continue the current level of operating activity. Projects that reduce costs, such as replacing old equipment or improving efficiency, are also considered replacement projects. Evaluating replacement projects requires us to compare the value of the company with the replacement asset to the value of the company without that same replacement asset. What we are doing in this comparison is looking at opportunity costs: what the cash flows would have been if the company had stayed with the old asset.

The cash flows from replacement projects involve little risk. The company is simply replacing equipment or buildings already operating and producing cash flows. It typically has experience managing similar new equipment.

Expansion projects, when intended to enlarge a company's established product or market, also involve little risk. However, investment projects that involve introducing new products or entering new markets are riskier because the company has little or no management experience in the new product or market.

A company is forced or coerced into its mandated projects. These government-mandated projects are typically found in "heavy" industries, such as utilities, transportation, and chemicals, all of which require a large portion of their assets to be used in production activities. Government agencies, such as the Occupational Health and Safety Agency or the Environmental Protection Agency, may impose requirements that companies install specific equipment or alter their activities (such as how they dispose of waste).

We can further classify mandated projects into two types: *contingent* and *retroactive*. Suppose that as a steel manufacturer, we are required by law to include pollution control devices on all smokestacks. If we are considering a new plant, this mandated equipment is really part of our new plant investment decision—the investment in pollution control equipment is contingent on our building the new plant. On the other hand, if a company is required by law to place pollution control devices on existing smokestacks, the law is retroactive. A company does not have a choice. It must invest in the equipment whether doing so increases the value of the company or not. In this case, the company has three choices: select from among possible equipment that satisfies the mandate, weigh the decision whether to halt production in the offending plant, or, if available, consider the purchase of pollution emissions allowances.

22.1.3 Classification According to Dependence on Other Projects

In addition to considering the future cash flows generated by a project, a company must consider how it affects the assets already in place—the results of previous project decisions—as well as other projects that may be undertaken. Projects can be classified according to the degree of dependence of other projects: independent projects, mutually exclusive projects, contingent projects, and complementary projects.

An *independent project* is one whose cash flows are not related to the cash flows of any other project. Accepting or rejecting an independent project does not affect the acceptance or rejection of other projects. Projects are *mutually exclusive* if the acceptance of one precludes the acceptance of others. For example, suppose that a manufacturer is considering whether to replace its production facilities with more modern equipment. The company may solicit bids among the different manufacturers of this equipment. The decision consists of comparing two choices, either keeping its existing production facilities or replacing the facilities with the modern equipment of one manufacturer. Because the company cannot use more than one production facility, it must evaluate each bid and choose the most attractive one. The alternative production facilities are mutually exclusive projects: the company can accept only one bid.

Contingent projects are dependent on the acceptance of another project. Suppose that a greeting card company develops a new character, Pippy, and is considering starting a line of Pippy cards. If Pippy catches on and becomes popular—but only if that happens—the company will consider producing a line of Pippy T-shirts. The T-shirt project is a contingent project.

Another form of dependence is found in *complementary projects*, where the investment in one enhances the cash flows of one or more other projects. Consider a manufacturer of personal computer equipment and software. If it develops new software that enhances the abilities of a computer mouse, the introduction of this new software may enhance its mouse sales as well.

22.2 Investment Decisions and Wealth Maximization

The value of a company today is the present value of all its future cash flows. These future cash flows come from assets that are already in place and from future investment opportunities. The value of the company today is therefore represented as

$$\sum_{t=1}^{\infty} \frac{CF_t}{(1+r)^t}$$

where CF_t is the cash flow obtained by the company in time period t and r is the required rate of return (RRR).

A company's management makes decisions about which capital projects to undertake by evaluating their value to the company. This process is referred to as *capital budgeting.* The capital budgeting decision for a project requires analysis of (1) the project's future cash flows, (2) the degree of uncertainty associated with the project's future cash flows, and (3) the value of the project's future cash flows, considering their uncertainty. The evaluation of *future cash flows* involves estimating changes in operating cash flows (changes in revenues, expenses, and taxes) and changes in investment cash flows (cash flows from the acquisition and disposition of the project's assets). The *degree of risk* associated with obtaining these cash flows is typically incorporated into the project's cost of capital. The *cost of capital* is the cost of the funds for the company's investment in the project. The value of the project's future cash flows considering the risk is computed using disciplined methods such as NPV, PI, IRR, MIRR of the return, payback period, and discounted payback period. In general, project value evaluation techniques should do the following:

- Consider all future incremental cash flows from the project.
- Consider the time value of money.
- Consider the risk associated with future cash flows.
- Have an objective criterion by which to select a project.

Not all the techniques listed here satisfy all these criteria. We will focus on the most popular methods for project value estimation: NPV, IRR, PI, and payback period.

22.2.1 Cost of Capital, Required Rate of Return, and Discount Rate

As we mentioned earlier, the future cash flows of a project are discounted to the present using an interest rate that incorporates to some extent the degree of risk associated with these cash flows. At an intuitive level, the greater the risk associated with the cash flows, the higher the *discount rate* that should be used, which is equivalent to assigning a lower present value to these future cash flows. In the case of IRR, the term used to describe this discount rate is the *hurdle rate,* and it must be exceeded by the project's return.

This rate—whether the discount or the hurdle rate—is the opportunity cost of funds. For a corporation, the opportunity cost of funds reflects the cost of capital to be paid to suppliers of capital (the creditors and owners). The term *cost of capital* is used interchangeably with the term *required rate of return (RRR).* The RRR is the rate of return that suppliers of capital demand on their investment. Cost of capital and RRR are the same concept, but from different perspectives—that of the company versus that of the investors.

The cost of capital affects almost all methods for project valuation and is therefore very important. We will review common methods for its estimation later in this chapter.

22.2.2 Net Present Value

The *net present value* (NPV) project valuation method considers the present value of all cash flows expected over the life of the project and nets the positive and the negative expected cash flows. Specifically,

$$\text{NPV} = (\text{Present value of future cash flows}) - (\text{Initial cash outlay}).$$

All cash flows are discounted by a rate involving the estimated cost of capital, which we denote by r. This is to allow for "apples-to-apples" comparison; that is, to net cash flows in today's dollars.

We can write all cash flows in the equation given here with their corresponding signs, using "plus" for inflows and "minus" for outflows. Assuming that the life of the project is N time periods, the NPV can then be computed as

$$\text{NPV} = \sum_{t=0}^{N} \frac{CF_t}{(1+r)^t}.$$

Note that the calculation involves the cash flow at time 0, and since $(1+r)^0 = 1$, the initial cash flow is not actually discounted. Typically, the initial cash flow is an outlay, and therefore it has a negative sign, but project specifications vary.

The decision rule is simple: If the NPV is greater than 0, then the value of the expected cash inflows is higher than the value of the expected cash outflows, and management should consider investing in the project. An example of an NPV calculation for project X is presented in exhibit 22.1.

Project X requires an investment of \$1.5 million today and returns \$0, \$200,000, \$500,000, \$900,000, and \$1 million in years 1, 2, 3, 4, and 5 of the project, respectively. Assuming a 10% cost of capital, the NPV is[1]

$$\begin{aligned}\text{NPV} &= -\frac{1{,}500{,}000}{(1+0.10)^0} + \frac{0}{(1+0.10)^1} + \frac{200{,}000}{(1+0.10)^2} + \frac{500{,}000}{(1+0.10)^3} \\ &\quad + \frac{900{,}000}{(1+0.10)^4} + \frac{1{,}000{,}000}{(1+0.10)^5} \\ &= \$276{,}580.09.\end{aligned}$$

Since the NPV is positive, project X is expected to contribute to the value of the company and should be considered.

It is important to study the sensitivity of the NPV estimate to the assumption made about the cost of capital. Graphing the value of the NPV for different values for the cost of capital is referred to as the *investment profile* or the *NPV profile*. Exhibit 22.2 illustrates the investment profile for project X. The NPV of project X is positive for values of the cost of capital of less than 14.84%, and negative for values of the cost of capital of more than 14.84%. As we will

1. Microsoft Excel has a command for computing NPV, which is =NPV(Discount rate, Array of cash flows). Excel assumes that the first value in Array of cash flows occurs one time period from now, and it discounts it to the present. Therefore, to obtain the correct estimate, we need to add the cash flow at time 0 to the NPV for the remaining cash flows. In this particular example, we would enter

$$-1500000 + \text{NPV}\ (0.10{,}0{,}200000{,}500000{,}900000{,}1000000).$$

Year	Cash Flow	Discounted Cash Flow
0	−$1,500,000.00	−$1,500,000.00
1	$0.00	$0.00
2	$200,000.00	$165,289.26
3	$500,000.00	$375,657.40
4	$900,000.00	$614,712.11
5	$1,000,000.00	$620,921.32
	NPV =	$276,580.09

Exhibit 22.1
Example of calculating NPV from a sequence of cash flows.

Cost of captial	NPV
10%	$276,580.09
11%	$214,229.38
12%	$154,722.03
13%	$97,901.21
14%	$43,620.18
15%	−$8,258.49
16%	−$57,863.58
18%	−$150,728.47
19%	−$194,207.88
20%	−$235,853.91

(A)

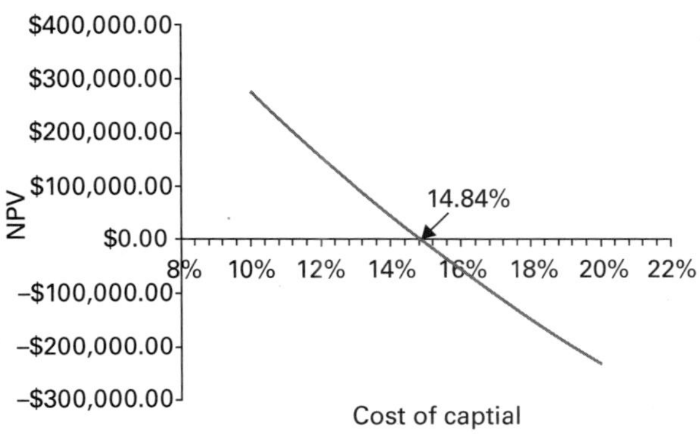

(B)

Exhibit 22.2
(A) Data table with the value of the NPV for project X for values of the cost of capital between 10% and 20%; (B) NPV profile of project X.

see in section 22.2.4, 14.84% is the IRR (discussed next); that is, the discount rate at which the NPV is equal to zero.

Creating the investment profile is useful not only because it allows us to study the sensitivity of the project NPV to the assumption about the discount rate, but also because it is a tool for comparing the NPVs of two or more projects. By plotting the investment profiles of two projects on the same graph, we can visualize what assumptions of the discount rate are preferable to the others.

22.2.3 Profitability Index

The *profitability index (PI)* uses the same information as the NPV, but it is stated in terms of an index. While the NPV is computed as

$$\text{NPV} = (\text{Present value of future cash flows}) - (\text{Initial cash outlay}),$$

the PI is computed as

$$\text{PI} = \frac{\text{Present value of future cash flows}}{\text{Initial cash outlay}}.$$

Since the PI measures performance in terms of an index and not dollar amounts, it provides a measure of the benefit per dollar investment. Therefore, the PI translates the NPV into an indexed value and has an advantage relative to NPV when ranking projects. This advantage may actually be a disadvantage, however, when the capital budget is limited (a situation referred to as *capital rationing*) and the actual dollar amounts for the different projects are of very different orders of magnitude. In this case, prioritizing projects based on their PIs rather than their NPVs will not necessarily result in the most profitable decision for the company.[2]

For project X,

$$PI = \frac{\$1,776,580.09}{1,500,000} = 1.18.$$

Since the PI is greater than 1, this means that the investment produces more benefits than costs.

22.2.4 Internal Rate of Return

The *internal rate of return (IRR)* is the discount rate that makes the present value of all cash flows (positive and negative) equal to zero. In other words, the IRR solves the equation

$$0 = \sum_{t=0}^{N} \frac{CF_t}{(1+IRR)^t}.$$

Consider the projected cash flows for project X from section 22.2.2. We want to find a value for IRR such that

$$0 = -\frac{1,500,000}{(1+IRR)^0} + \frac{0}{(1+IRR)^1} + \frac{200,000}{(1+IRR)^2} + \frac{500,000}{(1+IRR)^3} + \frac{900,000}{(1+IRR)^4} + \frac{1,000,000}{(1+IRR)^5}.$$

It turns out that

$$0 = -\frac{1,500,000}{(1+0.1484)^0} + \frac{0}{(1+0.1484)^1} + \frac{200,000}{(1+0.1484)^2} + \frac{500,000}{(1+0.1484)^3} + \frac{900,000}{(1+0.1484)^4} + \frac{1,000,000}{(1+0.1484)^5}.$$

Therefore, the IRR for project X is 14.84%.[3]

The IRR is a yield—what is earned, on average, per year. To make a decision on whether to choose an investment, we compare the IRR of the project with the cost of capital. The

2. We will see an example of this situation in section 22.2.7.

3. In Excel, the IRR can be computed with the formula =IRR(`Array of cash flows, initial guess`), where `initial guess` is an optional argument that specifies the starting point from which the numerical algorithm tries to determine the value of the IRR. It is best if `initial guess` is a point close to the actual IRR. In the case of project X, we used the investment profile to determine an approximate starting point of 14.5%.

decision rule for the IRR is to invest in a project if it provides a return that is greater than the cost of capital. The cost of capital, in the context of the IRR, is the hurdle rate—the minimum acceptable rate of return.

We need to be careful, however, when we use the IRR to distinguish among projects. The project with the highest IRR may not be the one with the best NPV.[4] The IRR and the NPV methods may suggest different decisions because of the assumption about what rate can be earned when reinvesting the cash flows. While we have not discussed this assumption, it is a property of any yield calculation, and the IRR is a yield calculation. It is assumed that the cash flows are reinvested at the computed IRR to realize the computed yield. Thus, we have the following:

- NPV assumes cash flows reinvested at the cost of capital.
- IRR assumes cash flows reinvested at the IRR.

This reinvestment assumption may cause different decisions in choosing among projects when the following is the case:

- The timing of the cash flows is different among the projects.
- There are scale differences (i.e., very different cash flow amounts).
- The projects have different useful lives.

To understand these points, note that a part of the return on a project is from the reinvestment of its future cash flows to the expected terminal date of the project. If project Y's cash flows are received sooner than project X's, there will be more return from the reinvestment of the future cash flows in the case of project Y. The question is what is done by the company with the future cash flows from a project when they are received. We generally assume that when the company receives future cash flows, they are reinvested in other assets. If the best we can do is reinvest cash flows at the cost of capital, then we should evaluate projects based on the NPV.

Another problem with the IRR becomes apparent if we note that the IRR is a percentage, not a dollar amount. Because of this, we cannot determine how to distribute the capital budget to maximize wealth because a project that produces the highest yield does not necessarily produce the greatest wealth.

Finally, the IRR suffers from a purely mathematical problem. It has to do with the uniqueness of the IRR estimate depending on the cash flow structure of the project (i.e., the pattern of positive and negative future cash flows).

Project X, the example that we have considered, was characterized by a negative cash flow at the beginning, followed by a sequence of positive future cash flows. Many projects have the same characteristics, but not all. Suppose, for example, that management is considering a project that uses environmentally sensitive chemicals. It may cost a great deal to dispose of them at the end of the project's life, and that will mean a negative cash flow at the end of the project.

4. It may, or it may not—and that is the problem. It is possible to make a value-maximizing decision by using the IRR method, but it is also possible to make a decision that is not value-maximizing by using that method.

Year	End of Year Cash Flow
0	–$1,000.00
1	$1,500.00
2	$1,500.00
3	–$2,100.00

Exhibit 22.3
Example of a project with multiple IRRs.

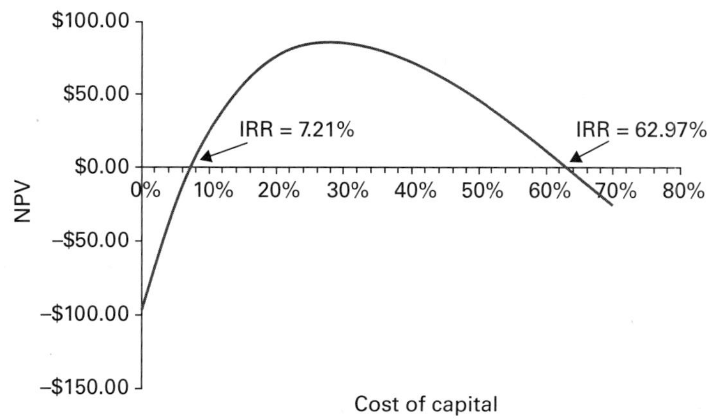

Exhibit 22.4
NPV of a project with multiple IRRs.

Projects for which there is an initial negative cash flow followed by positive future cash flows have only one IRR. However, there could be multiple IRRs for projects where negative and positive future cash flows happen in a different order. Consider, for example, a project with the cash flows shown in exhibit 22.3.

What is this project's IRR? One possible solution is IRR = 7.21%, but another possible solution is IRR = 62.97%. That is, both IRRs will make the present value of the cash flows equal zero.

The NPV of these cash flows is shown in exhibit 22.4 for discount rates from 0% to 70%. Remember that the IRR is the discount rate that causes the NPV to be zero. In exhibit 22.4, this means that the IRR is the discount rate where the NPV is zero, the point at which the NPV changes sign—from positive to negative or from negative to positive. In the case of this project, the NPV changes from negative to positive at 7.21%, and from positive to negative at 62.97%. Hence, the IRR needs to be applied with care.

22.2.5 Modified Internal Rate of Return

The NPV method assumes that future cash flows from a project are reinvested at the project's cost of capital, whereas the IRR method assumes that future cash flows are reinvested at the project's IRR. These assumptions are built into the mathematics of the methods, but they may not represent the actual opportunities of the company.

Number of Periods Earning Return	Cash Flow	Future Value of Cash Flow Reinvested at 14.84%
5	−$1,500,000.00	$0.00
4	$0.00	$0.00
3	$200,000.00	$302,889.52
2	$500,000.00	$659,385.67
1	$900,000.00	$1,033,539.93
0	$1,000,000.00	$1,000,000.00
	Terminal value =	$2,995,815.12

Exhibit 22.5
Concept of terminal value of a project.

The *modified internal rate of return (MIRR)* method is an alternative that considers a specific reinvestment rate for cash inflows from a project. MIRR is a yield on an investment considering a specific interest rate on the reinvestment of funds.

To understand this reinvestment rate assumption better, consider project X from section 22.2.2. The IRR is 14.84%. If each of the cash inflows from project X is reinvested at 14.84%, the sum of these future cash flows will be $2,995,815.12 at the end of year 5 (see exhibit 22.5). For example, year 3's cash flow of $200,000 is reinvested at 14.84% for three years (namely, years 3, 4, and 5), so its future value is $\$200{,}000 \cdot (1+0.1484)^3 = \$302{,}889.52$.

Here, $2,995,815.12 is referred to as the project's *terminal value,* which is how much the company gets from an investment at the end of the project if all proceeds are reinvested at the assumed reinvestment rate. In our illustration, we assumed that the reinvestment rate is the IRR. So, what is the return on this project? Using the terminal value as the future value and the investment outlay as the present value, we have

$$\begin{aligned} PV &= \$1{,}500{,}000 \text{ (amount invested).} \\ FV &= \$2{,}995{,}815.12 \text{ (amount at the end).} \\ N &= 5 \text{ years (investment horizon).} \\ r &= \sqrt[4]{\frac{\$2{,}995{,}815.12}{\$1{,}500{,}000}} - 1 = 14.84\%. \end{aligned}$$

This last procedure shows how to compute the MIRR for an investment in general. Given the project's initial investment, the terminal value of its future cash flows based on the assumed reinvestment rate, and the length of the investment horizon, we determine the implied return of the investment. The latter is the MIRR. The example given here was a special case. The MIRR was the same as the IRR because we assumed that all cash flows from the project are reinvested at the IRR.

Note that the pattern of the project's future cash flows makes a difference. If a project's future cash flows are received mostly at the beginning of the project, the MIRR is more sensitive to the reinvestment rate because the future cash flows are invested at the reinvestment rate for longer time periods.

The decision rule for the MIRR is to invest in a project if it provides a return (MIRR) that is greater than the cost of capital. As in the case of IRR, the cost of capital is the hurdle rate. Clearly, all else being equal, a higher reinvestment rate makes a project more attractive in terms of its MIRR.

22.2.6 Payback Period and Discounted Payback Period

The *payback period* for a project is the time from the initial cash outlay to invest in it until the time when its future cash flows add up to the initial cash outlay. In other words, how long it takes to recover the initial cash outlay. The payback period is also referred to as the *payoff period* or the *capital recovery period.* If $10 million is invested today and the investment is expected to generate $5 million one year from today and $5 million two years from today, the payback period is two years—it takes two years to recoup the $10 million investment.

Let us calculate the payback period for project X. We invest $1,500,000 at the beginning. By year 3, the entire $1,500,000 has not been paid back, but in year 4, we have not only recouped the $1,500,000, but in fact exceeded the investment amount (we have $1,600,000) (see exhibit 22.6). Therefore, the payback period for project X is 4 years.

Payback period analysis is a type of break-even measure. It tends to provide a measure of the economic life of the investment in terms of its payback period. The more likely the economic life exceeds the payback period, the more attractive the investment. The economic life beyond the payback period is referred to as the *postpayback duration.* If the postpayback duration is zero, the investment is unattractive no matter how short the payback. This is because the sum of the future cash flows is no greater than the initial investment outlay. And since these future cash flows are worth less today than in the future, a zero postpayback duration means that the present value of the future cash flows is less than the project's initial investment outlay.

A shorter payback period is better than a longer payback period, but it is not clear how short is best. The payback method should only be used as a coarse initial screen of investment projects—it can, however, be a useful indicator of some things. Because a dollar of cash flow in the early years is worth more than a dollar of cash flow in later years, the payback period method provides a crude but simple measure of the liquidity of the investment. The payback period also offers some indication of the risk of the investment. In industries where equipment becomes obsolete rapidly or where there are very competitive conditions, investments with earlier payback are more valuable. This is because cash flows farther into the future are more uncertain and therefore have lower present value. In the computer industry, for example, the fierce competition and rapidly changing technology require investment

Year	Cash Flow	Received Up to That Period
0	−$1,500,000.00	$0.00
1	$0.00	$0.00
2	$200,000.00	$200,000.00
3	$500,000.00	$700,000.00
4	$900,000.00	$1,600,000.00
5	$1,000,000.00	$2,600,000.00

Exhibit 22.6
Payback period for project X.

Year	Cash Flow	Cash Flow Discounted to Year 0	Discounted Cash Flows Up to That Period
0	−$1,500,000.00	−$1,500,000.00	−$1,500,000.00
1	$0.00	$0.00	−$1,500,000.00
2	$200,000.00	$165,289.26	−$1,334,710.74
3	$500,000.00	$375,657.40	−$959,053.34
4	$900,000.00	$614,712.11	−$344,341.23
5	$1,000,000.00	$620,921.32	$276,580.09

Exhibit 22.7
Calculation of the discounted payback period for project X.

Year	Project Bigger	Project Smaller
0	−$4,000.00	−$2,000.00
1	$1,250.00	$650.00
2	$1,250.00	$650.00
3	$1,250.00	$650.00
4	$1,250.00	$650.00

Exhibit 22.8
Cash flows for Project Bigger and Project Smaller.

in projects that have a payback of less than one year since there is no expectation of project benefits beyond one year.

The payback measure can be adjusted to account for the time value of the future cash flows. The resulting measure is called the *discounted payback period.* More precisely, the discounted payback period is the time needed to pay back the original investment in terms of discounted future cash flows. In this technique, each cash flow is discounted back to the beginning of the investment at a rate that reflects both the time value of money and the perceived riskiness of the future cash flows.

Returning to project X, suppose that the cost of capital is 10%. The first step in determining the discounted payback period is to discount each year's cash flow to the beginning of the investment (year 0) at the cost of capital. As exhibit 22.7 illustrates, the accumulated future cash flows from the investment discounted to year 0 (the last column in the table) do not become positive until year 5. Therefore, the discounted payback period of project X is 5 years.

22.2.7 Issues in Capital Budgeting

Not all discounted cash flow (DCF) methods are appropriate in all circumstances. Care must be taken when faced with mutually exclusive projects, scale differences, different and unequal project lives, and capital rationing.

22.2.7.1 Scale Differences Scale differences between projects—that is, differences in the amount of the initial investment—can lead to conflicting investment decisions among the DCF techniques. Consider two projects, Project Bigger and Project Smaller, each with

Method	Project Bigger	Project Smaller
NFV	$432.44	$304.87
IRR	9.56%	11.39%
MIRR	7.73%	8.79%
PI	1.11	1.15

Exhibit 22.9
NPV, IRR, MIRR, and PI for Project Bigger and Project Smaller.

a cost of capital of 5% per year and the cash flows in exhibit 22.8. Applying the DCF techniques to each project, we obtain the estimates in exhibit 22.9.

If there is no limit to the capital budget—that is, there is no capital rationing—then both are acceptable, value-increasing projects as indicated by all four techniques. However, if the projects are mutually exclusive projects or there is a limit to the capital budget, then the four methods provide differing accept-reject decisions.

If Project Bigger and Project Smaller are mutually exclusive projects, and if the company goes strictly by the PI, IRR, or MIRR criteria, management will choose Project Smaller. But is this the better project? Project Bigger provides more value—$432.44 versus $304.87. The techniques that ignore the scale of the investment—PI, IRR, and MIRR—may lead to an incorrect decision.

If the company is subject to capital rationing—say, a limit of $5,000—and the two projects are independent, the company can choose only one project—spend $4,000 or $2,000, but not $6,000. Applying the PI, IRR, or MIRR criteria, the company would choose Project Smaller. But is this the better project? According to the NPV criterion, the dollar contribution of Project Smaller is worse. Again, techniques that ignore the scale of the investment—PI, IRR, and MIRR—lead to an incorrect decision.

22.2.7.2 Unequal Lives If projects have unequal lives, the comparison strictly based on the techniques discussed in this chapter may lead to an incorrect decision, whether choosing among mutually exclusive projects or independent projects when there is capital rationing. Consider the projects whose cash flows are provided in exhibit 22.10. Project AA has a life of five years, project BB a life of 10 years, and project CC a life of 15 years. Projects AA and CC have a cost of capital of 4% and project BB has a cost of capital of 5%.[5]

Applying the four DCF techniques without considering their different lives suggests that project CC provides the most value added; project CC produces the higher IRR benefit per $1 invested (see exhibit 22.11).

However, comparing these projects without any adjustment for the different lives ignores the fact that at the completion of the shorter projects, reinvestment is necessary that is not reflected in the straightforward application of the techniques. In other words, this is an "apples to oranges" comparison if an adjustment is not made. One alternative is to find the

5. We will explain the concept of cost of capital and its estimation in more detail in sections 22.3.1 and 22.3.3. For now, it is important to know that different projects for the same company may have different costs of capital depending on the riskiness of the projects. A company with a large portfolio of projects has an "averaged-out" cost of capital that can be estimated from the information available from capital markets, but estimating the cost of capital for individual projects requires additional care.

Year	AA	BB	CC
0	–$1,000.00	–$1,000.00	–$1,000.00
1	$260.00	$160.00	$120.00
2	$260.00	$160.00	$120.00
3	$260.00	$160.00	$120.00
4	$260.00	$160.00	$120.00
5	$260.00	$160.00	$120.00
6		$160.00	$120.00
7		$160.00	$120.00
8		$160.00	$120.00
9		$160.00	$120.00
10		$160.00	$120.00
11			$120.00
12			$120.00
13			$120.00
14			$120.00
15			$120.00

Exhibit 22.10
Projects AA, BB, and CC.

Method	AA	BB	CC
NPV	$157.47	$235.48	$334.21
IRR	9.43%	9.61%	8.44%
MIRR	7.09%	7.24%	6.02%
PI	1.16	1.24	1.33

Exhibit 22.11
NPV, IRR, MIRR, and PI for projects AA, BB, and CC.

common denominator life for the projects. In the case of projects AA, BB, and CC, this would be 30 years. This requires then looking at project AA as being reinvested in the same project five more times, resulting in a "life" for analysis of 30 years.

The common denominator approach may be cumbersome when there are many projects. An alternative is to use the *equivalent annual annuity method,*[6] which requires two steps:

6. An annuity is an income payable in equal installments at specific intervals for a period of length N. The present value of an annuity is

$$PV = \sum_{i=1}^{N} \frac{A}{(1+r)^i},$$

where r is the interest rate per period. It can be shown that

$$PV = \frac{A}{r} - \frac{A}{r \cdot (1+r)^N} = \frac{A}{r} \cdot \left[1 - \frac{1}{(1+r)^N}\right],$$

and from there, it follows that the equal installments each period should be

	AA	BB	CC
Equivalent annual annuity	\$35.37	\$30.50	\$30.06
Value in perpetuity	\$884.32	\$609.91	\$751.47

Exhibit 22.12
Value in perpetuity for projects AA, BB, and CC, with different lives.

1. Calculate the annual annuity that is equivalent to the NPV of the project, considering the discount rate and the original life of the project. In the case of project AA, the annuity amount is \$35.37.[7]
2. Calculate the present value of this annuity if received ad infinitum. In the case of project AA, this is \$35.37/0.04 = \$884.32. This allows for comparing the projects, assuming an infinite life (which is the same for each of them, so we can compare "apples to apples").

The second step is necessary only if the comparison involves projects with different costs of capital. If the costs of capital are the same for the projects, the ranking of the projects in step 1 is identical to that of step 2. The values in perpetuity for the three projects are given in exhibit 22.12. After adjusting for the different lives, the conclusion is that project AA provides the most value added of the three projects.

22.2.8 Capital Budgeting in Practice

Among the project evaluation methods, NPV is the only one that is consistent and maximizes owner wealth under the most general circumstances. According to surveys and anecdotal evidence, it is also the most widely used in practice. Observations from recent surveys also indicate the following:

- Techniques that use DCFs are preferred over techniques that fail to take into consideration the time value of money.
- There is an increased use of the NPV method.
- Management uses more than one technique to evaluate the same projects, with a DCF techniques used as a primary method and a payback period used as a secondary method.
- The most used technique is the NPV method, although the IRR method is still widely used.

$$A = \frac{r \cdot (1+r)^N \cdot PV}{(1+r)^N - 1}.$$

If the annuity is paid for an infinite number of periods (i.e., N is infinity), its present value is

$$PV = \frac{A}{r}.$$

7. Based on the equation for calculating the annuity in note 6, we have $PV = \$157.47$, $r = 4\%$, $N = 5$, and, therefore, $A = \$35.37$.

The mechanics of calculating the measures in this chapter given the initial cash outlay, the future cash flow, and the required return (or hurdle rate) are not complicated. The most complex activity of the capital budgeting procedure in practice is estimating cash flows. How can such cash flows be estimated, especially in situations like the introduction of a new technology, which may have an impact not only on the company's future cash flows, but also on the company's domestic and global competitive positioning? Even when cash flows can be estimated reliably, they must be discounted at an assumed discount rate. Estimating this rate is a problem. Given the number of assumptions made in estimating various inputs to the model, MC simulation emerges as an even more important tool to evaluate the risk in the decisions made by using these models. We will discuss MC simulation applications in sections 22.4.3 through 22.4.5.

Finally, in addition to the possible inaccuracies associated with estimating future cash flows or the discount rate associated with investment projects, there is the potential problem of ignoring the real options that are present in projects. A *real option* associated with an investment project has a value arising from the option that the company possesses (e.g., to defer investment in the project, abandon it, or expand it). It may be the case, for example, that a new technology that provides a comparative or competitive advantage is unique, patented technology. If this is the case, the company may have a real option to defer investment, which enhances the value of the project beyond the value attributed simply to DCFs. (Real options are discussed in detail in chapter 23.)

22.3 Evaluating Project Risk

Capital budgeting decisions require analyzing a proposed project's future cash flows, the risk associated with its future cash flows, and the value of the future cash flows. When looking at the available investment opportunities, management must determine the project or set of projects that is expected to add the most value to the company. This requires evaluating how each project's benefits compare with its costs. The projects that are expected to increase owners' wealth the most are the best ones. In weighing a project's benefits and its costs, the costs include both the cash flow necessary to make the investment (the initial investment outlay) and the opportunity costs of not using the cash tied up in this investment.

The benefits are the future cash flows generated by the investment. But nothing in the future is certain, so there is risk associated with the future cash flows. Therefore, for an evaluation of any investment to be meaningful, management must represent how much risk there is that its cash flows will differ from what is expected in terms of both the amount and the timing of the cash flows.

The risk associated with the cash flow estimates arises from different sources, depending on the type of investment being considered, as well as the circumstances and the industry in which the company is operating. A project's risk may be attributable to many sources, including the following:

- *Economic conditions.* Will consumers be spending or saving? Will the economy be in a recession? Will the government stimulate spending? What will be the rate of inflation?
- *Market conditions.* Is the market competitive? How long does it take competitors to enter the market? Are there any barriers, such as patents or trademarks, that will keep

competitors away? Is there a sufficient supply of raw materials and labor? How much will raw materials and labor cost in the future?

- *Interest rates*. What will be the cost of raising capital in future years?
- *Taxes*. What will tax rates be? Will the U.S. Congress alter the tax system?
- *International conditions*. Will the exchange rate between different countries' currencies where the company transacts change? Are the governments of the countries in which the company does business stable?

Risk is typically incorporated in one of two ways: (1) discount future cash flows using a higher discount rate, the greater the cash flow's risk; and (2) require a higher hurdle rate on a project, the greater the cash flow's risk. As explained earlier in this chapter, the RRR is also called the *cost of capital*. An additional layer of risk can be incorporated by using MC simulation to generate scenarios for the factors driving the future cash flows. These approaches for incorporating risk are the focus of section 22.3.2.

It is important to realize that a company typically has a portfolio of projects, so management needs to estimate not only the stand-alone risk of the project, but also how the addition of the project to the company's portfolio of assets changes the risk of the company's portfolio. Taking this one step further, if the company's owners hold diversified investments—a safe assumption to make for all large corporations—it is the project's market risk that is relevant to the company's decision making because investors would require compensation for market risk—the risk that they cannot diversify away.

Even though market risk is generally the most important risk to analyze, stand-alone risk should not be ignored, especially when making decisions for a small, closely held company, whose owners do not hold well-diversified portfolios. Stand-alone risk is usually easier to measure than market risk and can be gauged by evaluating the project's future cash flows using statistical measures, sensitivity analysis, and simulation.

22.3.1 Measuring a Project's Market Risk

When investors are trying to evaluate the risk of an investment in a share of stock, they can look at that stock's returns and the returns of the entire market over some time period as a way of measuring the stock's market risk. While this is not a perfect measurement, it provides an estimate of the sensitivity of the stock's returns to changes in the returns of the market. Things are more complicated when one tries to evaluate the market risk of a new project. Managers can do the next best thing: they can estimate the market risk of the stock of another company whose only line of business is the same as the project's risk. If they could find such a company, they could estimate its stock's market risk and use that as a first step in estimating the project's market risk.

As explained in chapter 19, the Greek letter β (beta) is used to denote a measure of the market risk—the sensitivity of an asset's returns to changes in the returns of the market. To distinguish the beta of an asset from the beta that we used for a company's stock, the asset's beta is denoted by β_{asset} and the beta of a company's stock by β_{equity}. If a company has no debt, the market risk of its common stock is the same as the market risk of its assets. However, it is rarely the case that a company has no debt in its capital structure, so we must consider the effect of financial leverage on a company's equity beta.

Financial leverage is the use of debt obligations that require fixed contractual payments to finance a company's assets.[8] The greater the use of debt obligations, the more financial leverage there is, and the greater the risk associated with cash flows to owners. This is because creditors have seniority and receive a fixed amount (interest and principal), so a greater portion of the market risk of the equity is borne by the owners, as opposed to the creditors. In fact, the following equality holds:

$$\begin{aligned}\beta_{\text{asset}} = \beta_{\text{debt}} &\cdot (\text{Proportion of assets financed with debt}) \\ &+ \beta_{\text{equity}} \cdot (\text{Proportion of assets financed with equity}),\end{aligned}$$

or equivalently,

$$\beta_{\text{asset}} = \beta_{\text{debt}} \cdot w_{\text{debt}} + \beta_{\text{equity}} \cdot w_{\text{equity}}.$$

Since interest on debt is deducted to arrive at taxable income, the claim that creditors have on the company's assets does not cost the company the full amount, but rather the after-tax claim, so the burden of debt financing is actually less. Let D denote the market value of debt,[9] E denote the market value of equity, and τ denote the marginal tax rate. The relationship between the asset beta and the equity beta can be written as

$$\beta_{\text{asset}} = \beta_{\text{debt}} \frac{(1-\tau)D}{(1-\tau)D+E} + \beta_{\text{equity}} \frac{E}{(1-\tau)D+E}.$$

If β_{debt} is assumed equal to 0 (i.e., if debt is assumed not to be subject to market risk), we have

$$\beta_{\text{asset}} = \beta_{\text{equity}} \frac{1}{\left(1+(1-\tau)\dfrac{D}{E}\right)}.$$

This means that an asset's beta is related to the company's equity beta, with adjustments for financial leverage. If a company does not use debt, $\beta_{\text{equity}} = \beta_{\text{asset}}$, and if the company does use debt, $\beta_{\text{equity}} > \beta_{\text{asset}}$. Therefore, β_{equity} may be translated into β_{asset} by removing the influence of the company's financial risk from β_{equity}. To accomplish this, the following must be known:

- The company's marginal tax rate
- The amount of the company's debt financing in market value terms
- The amount of the company's equity financing in market value terms

The process of translating an equity beta into an asset beta is referred to as *unlevering* because the effects of financial leverage are removed from the equity beta, β_{equity}, to arrive

8. See also chapter 2.

9. It is sometimes difficult to determine the market value of debt. Generally, we would take all outstanding bond issues for the company and multiply the number of units issued by their market price. In some cases, we may substitute the book value.

at a beta for the company's assets, β_{asset}. This beta therefore is an estimate of the market risk of a company's assets.

The insights in this section can be used to compute the cost of capital and the discount rate to use in evaluating risky future cash flows. As explained in section 22.2.1, the cost of capital is the cost of funds from the providers of capital, creditors, and owners. This cost is the return required by these suppliers of capital. The greater the risk of a project, the greater the return required, and hence, the greater the cost of capital.

The project's cost of capital is comprised of two parts:

- The return if the project were risk-free, which provides compensation for the time value of money
- The compensation for risk

The compensation for the time value of money includes compensation for any anticipated inflation. The risk-free rate of interest, such as the yield on a long-term U.S. Treasury bond, is typically used to represent the time value of money. The compensation for the risk is the extra return required because the project's future cash flows are uncertain. The greater the project's market risk, the greater the return that investors should require.

22.3.1.1 Computing the Cost of Capital Based on the Capital Asset Pricing Model A commonly used method for estimating a project's cost of capital is to use the return formula from the capital asset pricing model (CAPM).[10] This requires first specifying the premium for bearing the average amount of risk for the market as a whole, and then using a measure of market risk, fine-tuning this to reflect the market risk of the project. The market risk premium for the market as a whole is the difference between the average expected market return, r_M, and the expected risk-free rate of interest, r_f.[11] If a company buys an asset whose market risk is the same as that of the market as a whole, the company expects a return of $r_M - r_f$ to compensate investors for market risk.

Adjusting the market risk premium for the market risk of the particular project requires multiplying the market risk premium by that project's asset beta, β_{asset}:

$$\text{Compensation for market risk} = \beta_{asset} \cdot (r_M - r_f).$$

This extra return is necessary to compensate for the project's market risk. The asset beta fine-tunes the risk premium for the market to reflect the market risk of the particular project. If we then add the risk-free interest rate, we arrive at the cost of capital:

$$\text{Cost of capital} = r_f + \beta_{asset} \cdot (r_M - r_f).$$

Suppose that the expected risk-free interest rate is 4% and the expected return on the market is 10%. If $\beta_{asset} = 2$, this means that if there is a 1% change in the market risk premium, a 2% change (in the same direction) in the return on the project is expected. In this case, the cost of capital is 16%:

10. See chapter 16 for an introduction to the CAPM.

11. See chapter 16.

$$\text{Cost of capital} = 0.04 + 2 \cdot (0.10 - 0.04) = 0.16.$$

If, instead, $\beta_{\text{asset}} = 0.75$, the cost of capital is 8.5%:

$$\text{Cost of capital} = 0.04 + 0.75 \cdot (0.06) = 0.085.$$

The calculation of the cost of capital takes advantage of the information in the asset beta. The application is not always straightforward, however. There are many instances in which a company invests in assets with differing risks. Using the company's asset beta would be inappropriate for evaluating the risk of a single project because the asset beta reflects the market risk of all the company's assets, and this may not be the same risk as for the project being evaluated. One approach to handle this situation is to estimate the cost of capital of a company that has a single line of business that is like the project under consideration. A company with a single line of business is referred to as a *pure-play company.* Selecting the company or companies that have a single line of business, where this line of business is like the project's, helps in estimating the market risk of a project.

One method of estimating the pure-play company's equity beta is regressing the returns on the pure-play company's stock and the returns on the market. Once the pure-play company's equity beta is calculated, management unlevers it by adjusting it for the financial leverage of the pure-play company.

Because many U.S. corporations whose stock's returns are readily available have more than one line of business, finding an appropriate pure-play company may be difficult. Care must be taken to identify those that have lines of business like the project's. Estimating a pure-play asset beta is useful in many other applications, including valuing divisions or segments of a business and valuing small businesses.

22.3.1.2 Adjusting the Company's Cost of Capital It is often the case that management is not able to estimate the project's market risk, not even the expected risk-free rate. Another way to estimate the cost of capital for a project without estimating the risk premium directly is to use the company's *weighted average cost of capital (WACC)* as a starting point. The WACC is the company's marginal cost of raising one more dollar of capital in the context of all the company's projects considered together, not just the project being evaluated.

The WACC is computed as follows:

$$r_{WACC} = \frac{(1-\tau) \cdot r_D \cdot D + r_E \cdot E}{D + E},$$

where, as before, D is the market value of debt, E is the market value of equity, and τ is the marginal tax rate. Further, r_D and r_E are the cost of debt and cost of equity, respectively, and r_D can be computed by considering the yields of the outstanding company bonds, weighted appropriately by the percentage that they represent of the total company debt. Finally, r_E is simply $r_f + \beta_{\text{equity}} \cdot (r_M - r_f)$.

The WACC of the company can be adjusted to suit the perceived risk of the project as follows:

- If a new project being considered is riskier than the average project of the company, the cost of capital of the new project is greater than the WACC.

- If the new project is less risky, its cost of capital is less than the WACC.
- If the new project is as risky as the average project of the company, the new project's cost of capital is equal to the WACC.

However, altering the company's cost of capital to reflect a project's cost of capital requires judgment. How much do we adjust it? If the project is riskier than the typical project, do we add 2%? 4%? 10%? There is no prescription here. It depends on the judgment and experience of the decision maker. But this is where the measures of a project's stand-alone risk can be used to help form that judgment.

22.3.2 Measuring a Project's Stand-Alone Risk

A project's stand-alone risk can be evaluated by performing *sensitivity analysis*. For example, we can create data tables in Excel to study the dependence of the project outcomes to slight changes in the forecasts of different variables in the model. A step further is to conduct *scenario analysis*, in which scenarios are explicitly created for the factors that affect the future cash flows. Conducting a scenario analysis is an important part of the process of assessing a project's total risk because different realizations of uncertain variables (such as sales forecasts, acquired market share, and cannibalization with other projects) can substantially change the decision of whether to undertake a project. While specific scenario analysis has many strong points, it is often useful to elevate the level of analysis to consider multiple scenarios at the same time. MC simulation is the tool for analyzing the joint effects of changes in uncertain variables.

The risk associated with the future cash flows can be expressed statistically in terms of measures such as the range, the standard deviation, and the coefficient of variation (CV).[12] Given the probability distributions of the project's future cash flows, these statistical tools can be applied to evaluate a project's risk.

The management arrives at these probability distributions based on research, judgment, and experience—for example, sensitivity analysis or simulation analysis using experience of similar projects, if available, can be used to get an idea of a project's possible future cash flows and their uncertainty. Estimates of cash flows are based on assumptions about the economy, competitors, consumer tastes and preferences, construction costs, and taxes, among a host of other possible assumptions.

22.3.3 Assessment of Project Risk in Practice

Most U.S. companies consider risk in some manner when evaluating investment projects. But considering risk is usually a subjective analysis, as opposed to the more objective results obtainable via simulation or sensitivity analysis. Surveys indicate that companies that use DCF techniques, such as NPV and IRR methods, tend to use a risk-adjusted cost of capital but generally use the company's WACC as a benchmark.[13] But a significant percentage of companies use a single cost of capital for all projects, which can be problematic. The company's cost of capital reflects its average-risk project. What happens when this cost of capital

12. See chapter 3.

13. See, for example, the survey by Graham and Harvey (2002).

is applied in DCF techniques, such as the NPV or the IRR, to all projects? This will result in the company's doing the following:

- Rejecting profitable projects (which would have increased owners' wealth) that have risk below the risk of the average risk project because the company has discounted the project's future cash flows too much
- Accepting unprofitable projects whose risk is above the risk of the average project because the company did not discount the project's future cash flows enough

Companies that use a risk-adjusted discount rate usually do so by classifying projects into risk classes by the type of project. For example, a company with a cost of capital of 10% may use a 14% cost of capital for new products and a much lower rate of 8% for replacement projects. Given a set of costs of capital, management need only figure out what class a project belongs to and then apply the rate assigned to that class.

Companies may also adjust the cost of capital for factors other than the type of project. For example, companies investing in projects in foreign countries will sometimes make an adjustment for the additional risk of the foreign project, such as exchange rate risk, inflation risk, and political risk.

There are tools available to assist the decision maker in measuring and evaluating project risk. But much of what is done in practice is subjective. Judgment, with a large dose of experience, is used more often than scientific means of incorporating risk. Is this bad? Well, the scientific approaches to measurement and evaluation of risk depend, in part, on subjective assessments of risk, the probability distributions of future cash flows, and judgments about market risk. So it is possible that bypassing the more technical analyses in favor of completely subjective assessment of risk may result in cost-of-capital estimates that better reflect the project's risk. But then again, it may not. The proof may be in the pudding, but it is difficult to assess this proof because it can never be determined how well a company may have done had it used more technical techniques.

22.4 Case Study

To illustrate the classical financial concepts behind project valuation and the richer perspective that simulation provides, let us discuss the real-life-based case study of AirMax Shoes, Inc.[14]

AirMax Shoes is considering introducing a new basketball shoe, called Rapid Bounce. The shoe would be endorsed by the most valuable player in the National Basketball Association (NBA) for the previous year. However, the company has done a poor job of anticipating consumer preferences in the basketball shoe market in recent years. Its market share has decreased from 21.6% to about 16% of the $18 billion athletic shoe industry. Moreover, the overall trend in the industry is away from basketball shoes.

14. All names and references in this case are fictional, and the situation is simplified on purpose to illustrate the main points of this chapter. This case study is based on the *Reebok International: Strategic Asset Allocation* case by Professor Mark Potter, Babson College, 1998. We thank Professor Potter for allowing us to create a version of the case for this example. We also thank Professors Kathleen Hevert and Richard Bliss, Babson College, for providing some of the data and ideas for the simulation application.

Another proposal under consideration is to launch an AirMax hiking shoe called Persistence. The hiking sector is one of the fastest-growing areas of the footwear industry—and one that AirMax has not yet entered. AirMax only has enough resources to undertake the Rapid Bounce or the Persistence project, but not both. There are several uncertainties associated with both projects. The question is which project to choose.

The project lives for both Rapid Bounce and Persistence are three years, and the federal plus state marginal tax rate for AirMax is 40%. Specific characteristics of the two projects are as follows:

Rapid Bounce

Revenues

- The athletic shoe market is projected to be $18.3 billion during year 1 and to continue growing at a rate of 3% per year. The market share projections for AirMax's Rapid Bounce shoe are year 1: 1.80%; year 2: 2.00%; and year 3: 1.70%.

Costs

- Sales of Rapid Bounce are expected to reduce the sales of other AirMax basketball sneakers. Specifically, AirMax's other sneaker sales are expected to decrease by $170 million during each year of the project. We will assume that these lost sales have the same margins as Rapid Bounce.
- To produce the shoe, AirMax will need to build a factory in New Delhi, India. This will require an immediate outlay of $100 million, which will be depreciated on a 20-year straight-line basis.[15] (In other words, the depreciation amounts for each of the three years of the project life will be $100/20 = $5 million per year.)
- AirMax must also immediately purchase equipment costing $15 million. Freight and installation of this equipment will cost $5 million. The equipment and freight/installation costs will be depreciated on a five-year straight-line basis. (In other words, the depreciation amounts for each of the three years of the project life will be $20/5 = $4 million per year.)
- Variable costs of producing the shoe are expected to be 31% of its sales.
- Selling, general, and administrative expenses are expected to be $7 million per year for the project.
- AirMax would pay its celebrity endorser $10 million annually for three years.
- Other advertising and promotion costs are expected to be $20 million per year.
- To manufacture Rapid Bounce, two of AirMax's working capital accounts (the inventory balance and the accounts payable) are expected to increase immediately. The net change in the working capital for the duration of the project will be –$45 million.

15. With the *straight-line depreciation method*, annual depreciation equals a constant proportion of the initial investment (minus the salvage value, which here we assume to be 0). In general, including salvage value in the calculations is done for financial reporting purposes. Here, we are concerned with the cash flow impact of taxes. For tax purposes, it is not necessary for firms to include salvage value.

These balances will be maintained until the final year of the project, at which time they will be recovered.

Persistence

Revenues

- The hiking and walking segment of the athletic shoe market is projected to reach \$350 million during year 1 and is growing at a rate of 15% per year. The segment market share projections for Persistence are year 1: 12%; year 2: 13%; and year 3: 16%.

Costs

- AirMax will be able to use an idle section of one of its factories to produce the hiking shoe.
- AirMax must purchase manufacturing equipment costing \$9 million. This equipment will be depreciated on a 3-year straight-line basis, with annual depreciation amounts for the three years equal to \$3 million. The cash outlay will be today, in year 0, and depreciation will start in year 1.
- Variable costs of producing the shoe are expected to be 17% of its sales.
- General and administrative expenses for Persistence will be 20% of revenues per year.
- The product will not have a celebrity endorser, and advertising and promotion costs are expected to be \$3 million per year, beginning in year 1.
- The net change in the working capital for the duration of the project will be –\$15 million. The balances will be maintained until the final year of the project, at which time they will be recovered.
- To begin immediate production of Persistence, the design technology and manufacturing specifications for a simple hiking shoe will be purchased from an outside source for \$50 million before taxes. It is assumed that this outlay takes place immediately and will be expensed immediately for tax purposes.

This information is entered into a worksheet (see exhibits 22.13 and 22.14 and the file **Ch22-AirMax.xlsx** in the online appendices), and the NPV and IRR for the two projects are computed. To do this computation, we need to estimate the cost of capital. Once the base case worksheet models for the two projects are created by using our estimate of market risk, we incorporate stand-alone risk by modeling a number of the input parameters as uncertain variables. For example, the forecasts for the market share of the two products are estimates, and so is the amount of cannibalization that Rapid Bounce will cause on other AirMax basketball shoes.

22.4.1 Computing the Cost of Capital

First, let us show how we would evaluate the cost of capital for the two projects. We will use the company's WACC as a starting point. To compute it, we need the values of the risk-free rate r_f, the company beta, the excess return on the market, the yields to maturity for AirMax's outstanding debt, and the market value weights of debt and equity for AirMax. We will assume the following:

	A	B	C	D	E	F	G	H
1	**Rapid Bounce**				**"Rapid Bounce" projected project cash flow statements ($ millions)**			
2	**Assumptions ($ millions)**				**Year 0**	**Year 1**	**Year 2**	**Year 3**
3	Length of project (years):	3		Revenues		$329.40	$376.98	$360.65
4	Athletic footwear market:	$18,300.00		Cannibalization (Erosion of existing sales)		–$170.00	–$170.00	–$170.00
5	Growth of market:	3.00%		Net revenues (after erosion)		$159.40	$206.98	$190.65
6	Market share (year 1):	1.80%		Variable costs		–$49.41	–$64.16	–$59.10
7	Market share (year 2):	2.00%		SG & A expenses		–$7.00	–$7.00	–$7.00
8	Market share (year 3):	1.70%		Endorsement		–$10.00	–$10.00	
9	Factory expansion:	$100.00		Advertising & promotion		–$20.00	–$20.00	–$20.00
10	Equipment:	$15.00		Factory depreciation		–$5.00	–$5.00	–$5.00
11	Freight and installation:	$5.00		Equipment depreciation		–$4.00	–$4.00	–$4.00
12	Variable costs as a % of sales:	31.00%		EBIT (Earnings before interest and taxes)		$63.99	$96.82	$95.55
13	Cannibalization per year:	$170.00		Taxes		–$25.59	–$38.73	–$38.22
14	SG&A expenses:	$7.00		EBIAT		$38.39	$58.09	$57.33
15	Endorsement:	$10.00		Plus depreciation of factory		$5.00	$5.00	$5.00
16	Other advertising & promotion:	$20.00		Plus depreciation of equipment		$4.00	$4.00	$4.00
17	Net change in working capital	–$45.00		Change in NWC	–$45.00	$0.00	$0.00	$45.00
18	Tax rate:	40.00%		New factory	–$100.00			
19				Equipment, freight & installation	–$20.00			
20				**Project net cash flows**	**–$165.00**	**$47.39**	**$67.09**	**$111.33**
21								
22				**Analysis of project**				
23				Assumed cost of capital:	10.51%			
24				Net Present Value:	$15.31			
25				IRR:	15.04%			

Exhibit 22.13
Rapid Bounce's NPV and IRR calculation.

	A	B	C	D	E	F	G	H
1	**Persistence**				**"Persistence" projected project cash flow statements ($ millions)**			
2	**Assumptions ($ millions)**				**Year 0**	**Year 1**	**Year 2**	**Year 3**
3	Length of project (years):	3						
4	Hiking & walking market:	$350.00		Revenues		$42.00	$52.33	$74.06
5	Growth of market:	15.00%		Variable costs		–$7.14	–$8.90	–$12.59
6	Market share (year 1):	12.00%		G & A expenses		–$8.40	–$10.47	–$14.81
7	Market share (year 2):	13.00%		Advertising & promotion		–$3.00	–$3.00	–$3.00
8	Market share (year 3):	16.00%		Equipment depreciation		–$3.00	–$3.00	–$3.00
9	Purchase of technology:	$50.00		Technology purchase	–$50.00	$0.00	$0.00	$0.00
10	Equipment:	$9.00		EBIT (Earnings before interest and taxes)	–$50.00	$20.46	$26.96	$40.66
11	Variable costs as a % of sales:	17.00%		Taxes	$20.00	–$8.18	–$10.79	–$16.26
12	Percentage increase in VC/year	0.0%		EBIAT	–$30.00	$12.28	$16.18	$24.39
13	AirMax other hiking sales:	$0.00		Plus depreciation of equipment		$3.00	$3.00	$3.00
14	Growth in other hiking sales:	0%		Change in NWC	–$15.00	$0.00	$0.00	$15.00
15	Cannibalization % of sales:	0%		Equipment, freight & installation	–$9.00			$0.00
16	SG&A Expenses (% of sales):	20%		**Project net cash flows**	**–$54.00**	**$15.28**	**$19.18**	**$42.39**
17	Other advertising & promotion:	$3.00						
18	Net change in working capital	–$15.00		**Analysis of project**				
19	Tax rate:	40.00%		Assumed cost of capital:	13.00%			
20				Net Present Value:	$3.92			
21				IRR:	16.55%			
22								

Exhibit 22.14
Persistence's NPV and IRR calculation.

1. The risk-free rate r_f is 5%. This input should be the yield on Treasury securities with approximately the same maturity as the life of the project.
2. The market risk premium $(r_M - r_f)$ is 6.2%. This is the approximate historical excess return on the market. We cannot observe the market risk premium relevant for evaluating this project, but we assume that investors will demand a premium that is consistent with historically observed values.
3. The company beta β is 1.08. This was estimated using data on past company stock returns and the returns on the Russell 3000, a broad market index (see the worksheet **Beta Data** in the file **Ch22-AirMax.xlsx**).
4. The cost of equity, therefore, is

$$r_e = r_f + \beta \cdot (r_M - r_f) = 0.05 + 1.08 \cdot 0.062 = 0.11696 = 11.70\%.$$

5. AirMax's current stock price is \$36.42, and there are 59.7 million shares outstanding. Therefore, the market value of AirMax's equity is $E = \$36.42 \cdot (59.7 \text{ million}) = \$2{,}174.27$ million.
6. Suppose that AirMax has two bond issues: short-term debt with a yield to maturity (YTM) of 2.72% and long-term debt with a YTM of 7.05%. The price per unit for the short-term debt is \$1,078.53, and there are 101,408 units in the market. The price per unit of the long-term debt is \$1,032.50, and there are 250,000 units in the market. The total market value of short-term debt, therefore, is (\$1,078.53 101,408) = \$109.37 million, and the total market value of long-term debt is (\$1,032.50 250,000) = \$258.13 million.
7. Based on step 6, the total market value for debt is $D = \$109.37 + \$258.13 = \$367.5$ million. Of those, 29.8% are short-term debt and 70.2% are long-term debt.
8. The cost of debt, therefore, is

$$r_D = (2.72\%) \cdot (29.8\%) + (7.05\%) \cdot (70.2\%) = 0.057597 = 5.76\%.$$

9. The after-tax cost of debt is

$$(1 - \tau) \cdot r_D = (1 - 0.40) \cdot 5.76\% = 3.46\%.$$

10. Based on steps 5 and 7, the total market value for debt plus equity $(D + E)$ is \$367.5 + \$2,174.27 = \$2541.77 million. The weight of debt is 14.5% of the total, and the weight of the equity is 85.5% of the total.
11. Based on steps 4, 9, and 10, the WACC is

$$\begin{aligned} r_{WACC} &= \frac{(1-\tau)\cdot r_D \cdot D + r_E \cdot E}{D+E} \\ &= (1-\tau)\cdot r_D \cdot \frac{D}{D+E} + r_E \cdot \frac{E}{D+E} \\ &= (3.46\%)\cdot(14.5\%) + (11.70\%)\cdot(85.5\%) = 10.51\%. \end{aligned}$$

Rapid Bounce is a project that is like the company's existing projects, so we will assume that it carries the same magnitude of risk, and its cash flows can be discounted using the WACC as the discount rate (i.e., we will use a discount rate of 10.51%). The Persistence

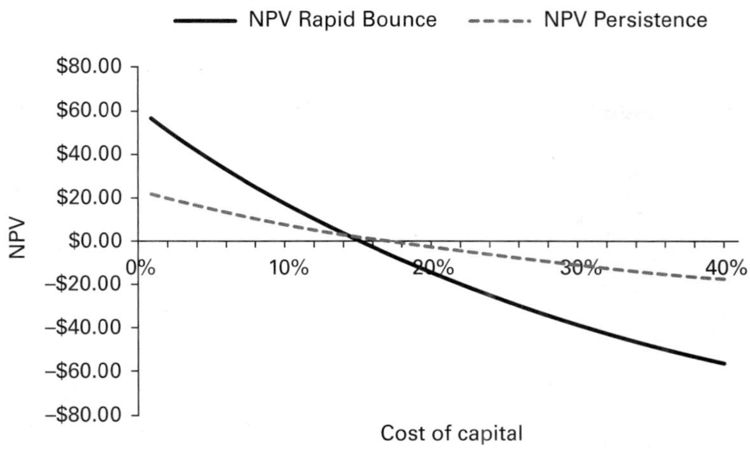

Exhibit 22.15
NPV profiles for Rapid Bounce and Persistence.

project, on the other hand, is outside AirMax's current line of business, so we may deem it riskier and use a higher discount rate than WACC (say, 13%).

With these discount rates, the NPV for Rapid Bounce is $15.31 million, and the IRR is 15.04%. The NPV for Persistence is $3.92 million, and the IRR is 16.55%.

If we use the IRR as a criterion, we will pick Persistence. But here, we have an example of capital rationing and two projects with differences of scale. NPV is the more appropriate criterion to use. Based on the NPV, we would pick Rapid Bounce.

22.4.2 Computing the NPV Profiles

The next step is to analyze how sensitive the solution is to the assumptions made about the discount rates to use in the case of each project. Exhibit 22.15 shows the NPV profiles for the two projects. We can observe that the NPV for Rapid Bounce is higher than the NPV for Persistence for low values of cost of capital, including the current assumed values. At about cost of capital of 14.5%, the two NPVs become equal, and then eventually both become negative, with the NPV for Rapid Bounce decreasing faster than the NPV for Persistence. Clearly, deciding which project to pick is very sensitive to small changes in the current estimates of the cost of capital for the two projects, so we may want additional information before we make the final decision. Note that so far, we have incorporated only considerations for market risk in the analysis of the two projects. The next step is to include the stand-alone risks as well by running a MC simulation.

22.4.3 Running a Simulation to Estimate Project Stand-Alone Risk

Let us list some sources of uncertainty for the two projects and examine how we could model them with probability distributions. See exhibits 22.16 and 22.17 for graphical representations of the different probability distributions used in the simulation. If you are using @RISK, see also the worksheet **Simulation** in the file **Ch22-AirMax.xlsx** in the online appendices.

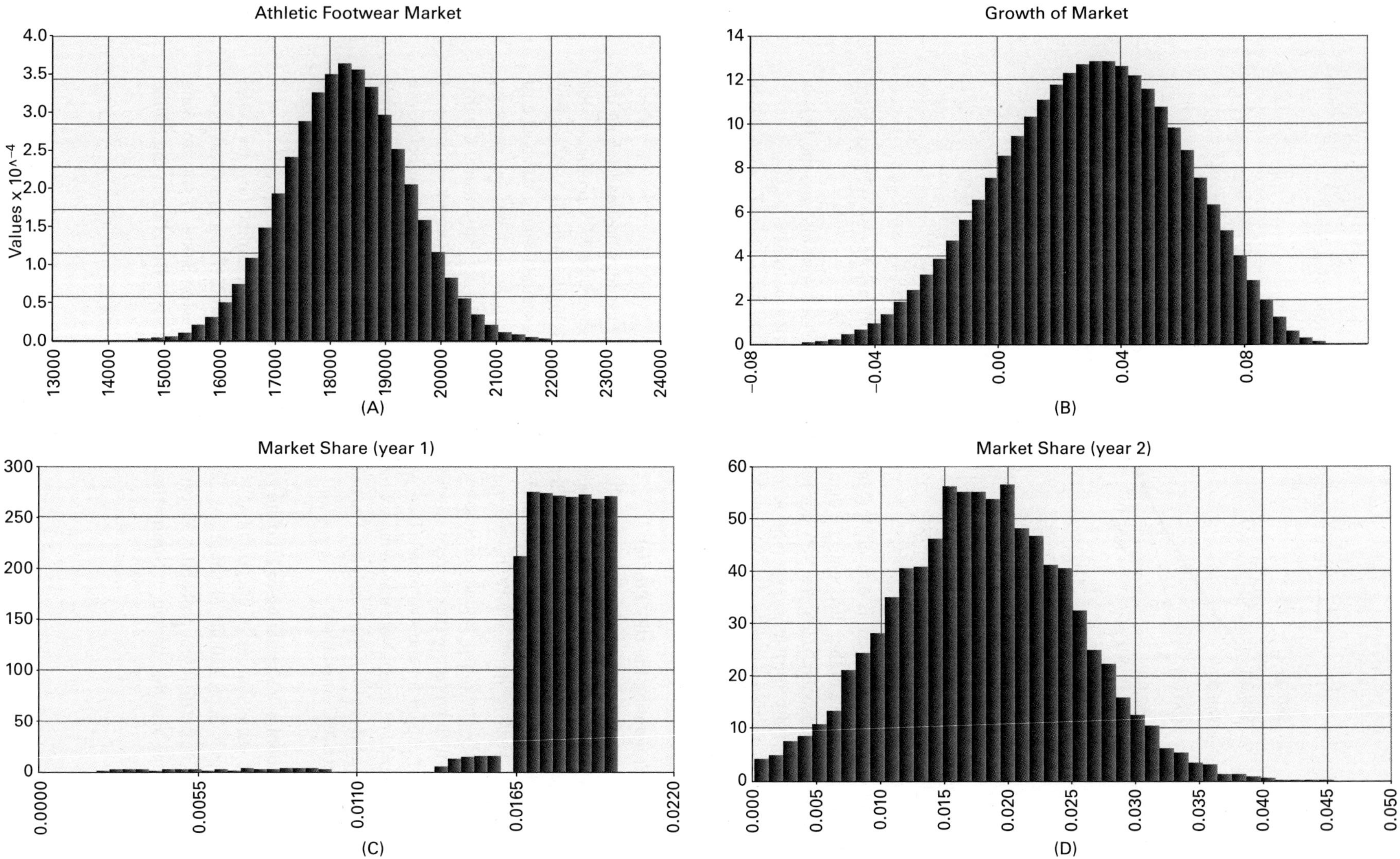

Exhibit 22.16
Probability distributions used in the simulation of the NPV of Rapid Bounce. (A) Size of athletic shoe market; (B) Growth of the athletic shoe market; (C) Market share in year 1; (D) Market share in year 2.

Rapid Bounce

1. The projected market size ($18.3 billion) for the athletic shoe market in year 1 is an estimate. We will assume that $18.3 billion is the expected value of the market size, but the actual value for the market size will follow a normal distribution that is on average $18,300 million and has a standard deviation of $1,100 million. (We will explain how we came up with these numbers later.) This distribution assumes that deviations above and below the expected market size of 18,300 are equally likely, and the average deviation from the estimate will be $1,100 million. See exhibit 22.16(A).[16]
2. The growth of the athletic footwear market was assumed to be 3% per year. Let us assume instead that it follows a general beta distribution with parameters $\alpha = 5.5, \beta = 4$, minimum = −0.08, and maximum = 0.11. This results in a mean value for growth of 3%; however, it also allows us to input an anticipated range for the market growth (between −8% and 11%), and express general optimism about the growth of the market. (The latter is because the probability distribution is left-skewed, which means that most of the mass is to the right side of the mean, and higher values for the actual market growth will be more likely to happen in the simulation.) See exhibit 22.16(B).
3. One of the important items with the Rapid Bounce project is the reliance on the celebrity endorser's reputation for advertising the new basketball shoe. His image would have a significant impact on the market share that AirMax will be able to achieve in the first year. AirMax could consider three possible scenarios: with 95% probability, there will be a very positive perception of the NBA player, and AirMax's market share in the first year will be between 1.65% and 2.00%. With 3% probability, the NBA player's name will not generate the expected buzz, and AirMax's market share in the first year will be between 1.40% and 1.60%. Finally, there is a 2% chance that the NBA player will have a negative image, and AirMax's market share in the first year will be between 0.20% and 0.40%.[17] See exhibit 22.16(C).
4. We assume that the market shares in years 2 and 3 depend on the market share established in year 1, with some probability of deviating from the previous year's market share. The market share for year 2 will follow a normal distribution, truncated at 0, with mean equal to the realized market share in year 1 and a standard deviation of 0.7%. The market share for year 3 will follow a normal distribution, truncated at 0, with

16. Note that the assumption that the market size follows a normal distribution technically does not preclude the possibility that in the process of the simulation, negative numbers for market size would be simulated. (This is because the normal distribution stretches from negative infinity to positive infinity.) In this case, we do not need to worry much about this issue because the distance between 18,300 and 0 is approximately 17 standard deviations (where the standard deviation is 1,100). Outcomes that are more than 6 standard deviations from the mean have a miniscule probability of occurring.

17. This kind of assumption—where a range for possible values needs to be selected randomly before the number within that range is selected randomly—is a little bit more difficult to model than what we have seen so far. The trick is to create a random variable that corresponds to the scenario number drawn (in this case, there are three possible scenarios—one for each range of values) and then base the random number generation on the outcome of this random variable. If we use @RISK in Excel, we can create a cell dedicated to storing the random scenario drawn (cell B31 in the worksheet **Simulation**), and then use `VLOOKUP` to reference that cell and the range of values to which the scenario corresponds when simulating market share in the first year (cell B6).

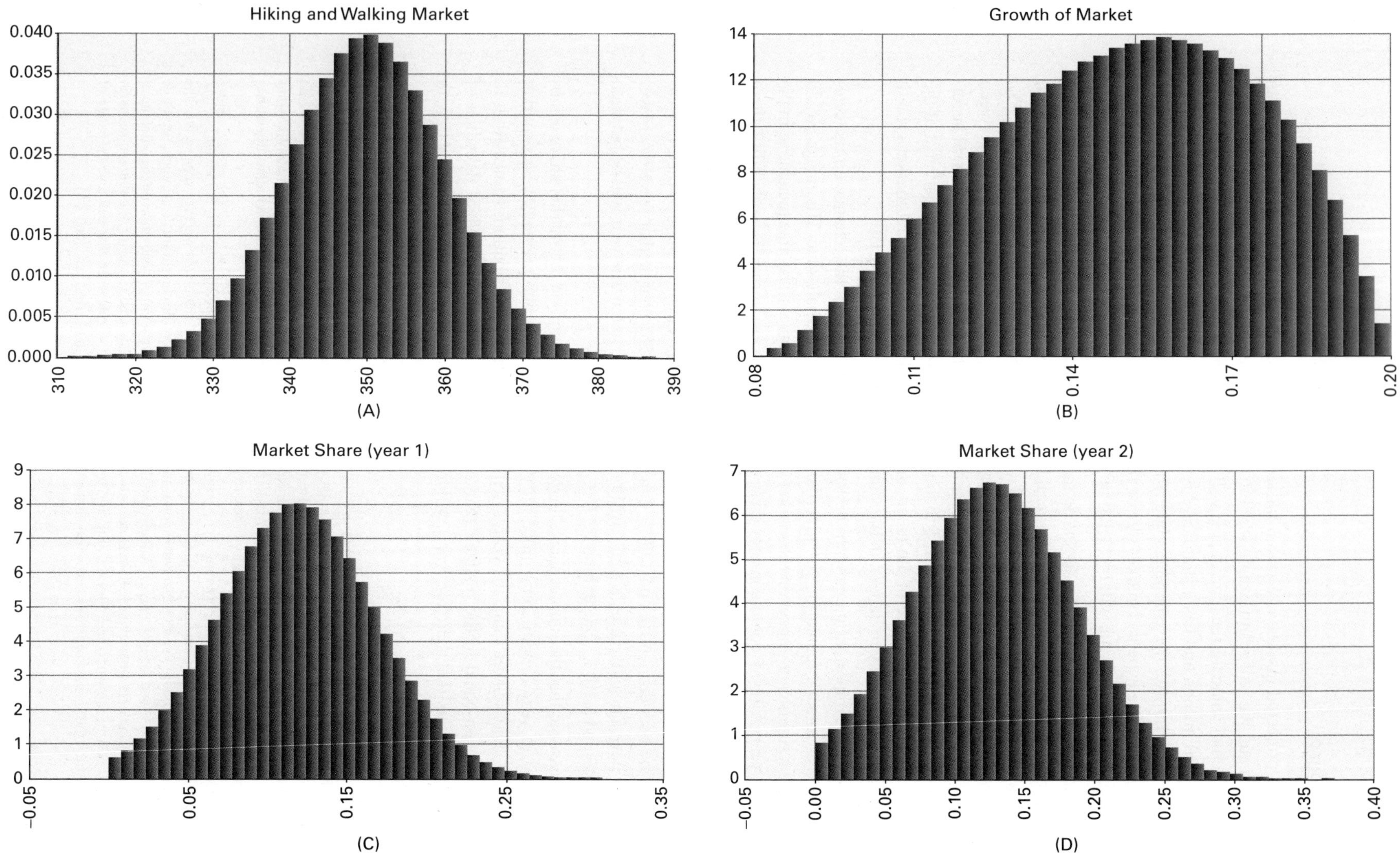

Exhibit 22.17
Probability distributions used in the simulation of the NPV of Persistence. (A) Size of hiking and walking shoe market; (B) growth of the hiking and walking shoe market; (C) market share in year 1; (D) market share in year 2.

mean equal to the realized market share in year 2 and a standard deviation of 0.7%.[18] See exhibit 22.16(D).

5. The estimate for cannibalization (erosion of sales of AirMax's current basketball shoe models) is very rough, and it makes sense to generate multiple scenarios for this assumption. We assume that the actual amount of sales erosion is normally distributed with mean equal to $170 million and a standard deviation of $20 million.

Persistence

1. The projected market size ($350 million) for the athletic shoe market in year 1 is an estimate. We assume that $350 million is the expected value of the market size, but the actual value for the market size follows a normal distribution that is on average $350 million and has a standard deviation of $10 million. See exhibit 22.17(A).[19]
2. The growth of the hiking and walking shoe market was assumed to be 15% per year. Let us assume instead that it follows a general beta distribution with parameters $\alpha = 2.6$, $\beta = 1.9$, minimum = 0.08, and maximum = 0.20. This results in a mean value for growth of approximately 15%; however, it also allows us to input an anticipated range for the market growth (between 8% and 11%), and express general optimism about the growth of the market. (As in item 2 for Rapid Bounce, the latter is because the probability distribution is left-skewed, which means that most of the mass is to the right side of the mean, and higher values for the actual market growth will be more likely to happen in the simulation.) See exhibit 22.17(B).
3. We assume that the AirMax market shares for years 1, 2, and 3 are, as forecasted, 12%, 13%, and 16% on average. The actual market share for each year will follow normal distributions with standard deviations of 5%, 6%, and 7%, respectively. We need to truncate these normal distributions at 0 because the standard deviations are large relative to the means, and there is a large probability that a negative number will be generated for market share in the simulation. When we truncate the normal distribution at 0, however, its mass shifts to the right and its mean increases. To preserve means of 12%, 13%, and 16% for the actual simulated numbers, we draw random numbers with truncated normal distributions with means of 11.88%, 12.75%, and 15.78%.
4. We also assume that the market shares in the three years are positively correlated: with correlation of 0.8 for years 1 and 2 and years 2 and 3, and with correlation of 0.4 for years 1 and 3.[20]

18. Here, we truncate the normal distribution at 0 because we have a nontrivial probability of generating a negative number for the market share during the simulation if we do not. If the standard deviation is 0.7%, then 0 is approximately two to three standard deviations from the mean of the distribution, and even though the probability of generating a negative number is still small (less than 2.5%), the event is not as unlikely to happen as it was in the case of the projected market size.

19. Similar to the projected market size for Rapid Bounce, here we are not concerned about truncating the normal distribution so that 0 is the minimum value that we can generate. The standard deviation is small relative to the mean value of the normal distribution.

20. See the worksheet **Simulation** in the file **Ch22-AirMax.xlsx** for an illustration of how to simulate correlated random variables.

We can incorporate further assumptions, of course. For example, we may assume that variable costs are uncertain with a particular probability distribution. The assumptions that we have modeled so far, however, are sufficient for illustration of the main ideas.

If we plug in the expected values for all assumed probability distributions into the worksheet, we will get NPV and IRR estimates for Rapid Bounce and Persistence that are very close to the estimates obtained in the last section. However, analyzing the probability distributions of the NPVs tells a different story. The distributions for the NPVs for Rapid Bounce and Persistence, as well as relevant statistical summaries from the simulation, are presented in exhibit 22.18.

We can observe that while the NPV for Rapid Bounce is higher on average than the NPV for Persistence ($12.68 versus $3.90 million), its variability is also higher (standard deviation of $111.04 million versus $18.42 million), with a higher standard deviation as a percentage of the mean (the CV is $8.76 million versus $4.72 million), and the lower fifth percentile of –$160.74 million versus –$26.01 million). The NPV for Rapid Bounce also has a slightly lower probability of being positive (53.11% versus 57.32% for the NPV of Persistence). Hence, in terms of risk, Persistence appears to be the more attractive project.

Additional useful information can be obtained if we compare the NPVs on a scenario-by-scenario basis. As discussed in section 4.2.3, this can be accomplished by creating an additional output variable in the worksheet that measures the difference between the two NPVs and analyzing its simulated distribution. The results are presented in exhibit 22.19. The NPV of Rapid Bounce was higher than the NPV of Persistence in about 51.5% of the generated scenarios, and by about $8.78 million on average. So on a scenario-by-scenario basis, Rapid Bounce appears to be the more attractive project.

It is difficult to decide which of the two options to choose. The answer will depend on management's priorities. However, the information obtained by running a simulation adds to the information obtained from the financial analysis at the first step of the project evaluation process, and this helps management make a more informed decision.

22.4.4 Determining the Inputs to the Simulation

In the last section, we explained how one can incorporate uncertainty about the inputs in the model and interpret the results from the simulation. How can one come up with the parameters used to construct the different probability distributions?

The first question to ask is whether the probability distribution representing an estimate should be symmetric or skewed. A symmetric distribution would assume that deviations above and below the estimated value are equally likely. A skewed distribution would enable us to impart some subjective judgment. Recall the probability distributions that we used to model the growth of the athletic footwear and the hiking and walking shoe markets. A right-skewed distribution would have more of its probability mass to the right of the mean, and most simulation trials will result in outcomes that are below the mean. On the other hand, a left-skewed distribution would have more of its probability mass to the left of the mean, and most simulation trials will generate outcomes that are above the mean.

The second question to ask is whether the actual values are clustered around the estimate or could be far from the estimate. For example, both the normal distribution and the uniform distribution are symmetric, but the uniform distribution assumes that the values can be anywhere on the specified range with the same probability, while the normal distribution

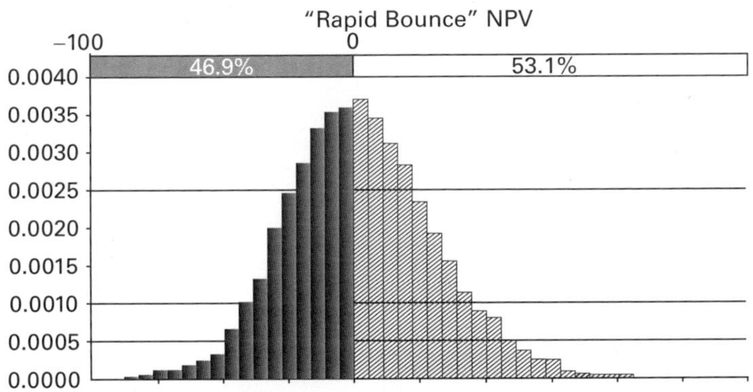

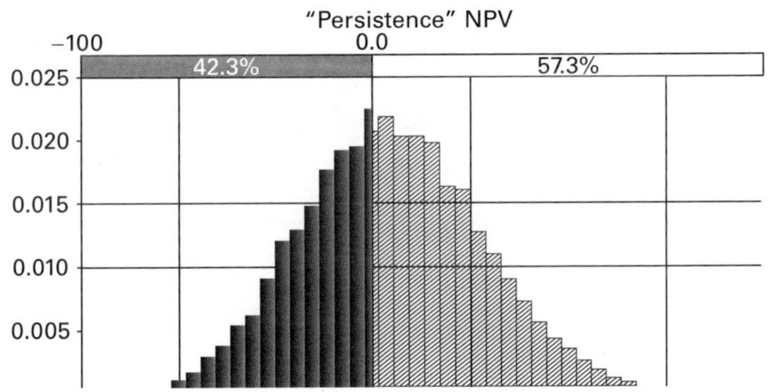

	"Rapid Bounce" NPV	"Persistence" NPV
Minimum	–$353.12	–$44.88
Maximum	$539.69	$78.75
Mean	$12.68	$3.90
Standard deviation	$111.04	$18.42
Coefficient of variation	$8.76	$4.72
Skewness	0.1840	0.1692
Kurtosis	3.1529	2.8641
Mode	$12.03	–$0.49
5% Percentile	–$160.74	–$26.01
50% Percentile	$8.33	$3.55
95% Percentile	$205.64	$35.09
Prob. NPV >=0	53.11%	57.32%

Exhibit 22.18
Simulation output: Distribution for the NPV of Rapid Bounce; distribution for the NPV of Persistence; statistical summary.

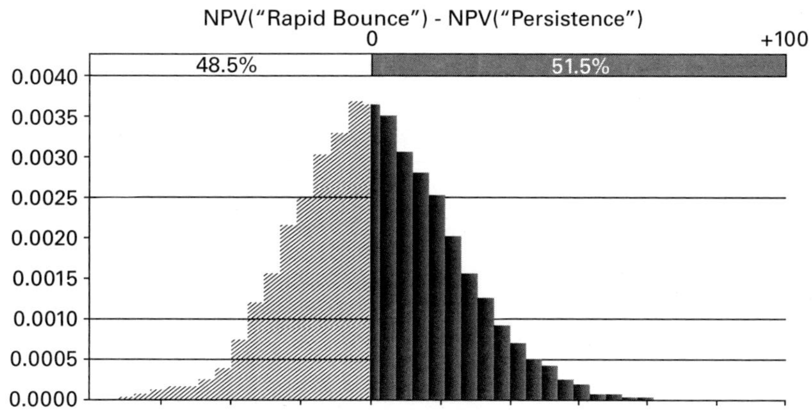

	NPV("Rapid Bounce") - NPV("Persistence")
Minimum	–$383.47
Maximum	$551.78
Mean	$8.78
Standard deviation	$112.58
Coefficient of variation	$12.83
Skewness	0.1813
Kurtosis	$3.15
Mode	–$13.50
5% Perc	–$167.18
50% Perc	–$9.42
95% Perc	$202.21

Exhibit 22.19
Simulation output for the difference between the NPV of Rapid Bounce and the NPV of Persistence.

Year	Market size ($ billions)
1	11.44
2	11.72
3	13.85
4	13.68
5	12.23
6	12.01
7	13.92
8	13.25
9	15.61
10	14.64
11	16.11
12	15.07
13	17.16
14	16.37
15	17.82
16	18.08
17	17.65
18	16.12
19	15.87
20	17.21

SUMMARY OUTPUT

Regression Statistics	
Multiple *R*	0.871153984
R-square	0.758909264
Adjusted *R*-square	0.745515334
Standard Error	1.079220811
Observations	20

ANOVA

	df	*SS*	*MS*	*F*	*Significance F*
Regression	1	65.99369721	65.9937	56.66069	5.77E-07
Residual	18	20.96491608	1.164718		
Total	19	86.95861329			

	Coefficients	Standard Error	*t*-stat	*P*-value	Lower 95%	Upper 95%
Intercept	11.68333317	0.501332015	23.30458	6.77E-15	10.63007	12.73659
Year	0.315021654	0.041850388	7.527329	5.77E-07	0.227097	0.402946

Exhibit 22.20
Data for determining the size of the athletic footwear market.

incorporates the assumption that the values are likely to be close to the mean—the closer to the mean they are, the more likely they will be generated during the simulation.

Important variables that have a big impact on the bottom line, such as sales or market share, are often forecast by analysts with a lot of experience in the industry. Simulation can be used to combine forecasts from multiple analysts by figuring out the average estimate and the variability in these estimates.

Finally, statistical techniques can be used to derive estimates from historical data. For example, our estimate of $18.3 billion for the size of the athletic footwear market was derived by recording the market size for the 20 years prior to the present time, running a regression to determine if there is a trend, and using the regression to forecast the next point, as well as the variability in the estimate. The data and the regression output can be found in the worksheet **Market Size Data** of the file **Ch22-AirMax.xlsx** and are shown in exhibit 22.20.

The response variable in the regression is the market size, and the explanatory variable is the year. The regression equation can be recovered from the regression output. We have

$$\text{Market size (\$ billions)} = 11.68 + 0.32 \cdot \text{Year}.$$

Therefore, to make a forecast for next year (year 21), we plug in 21 for Year:

$$\text{Market size forecast (\$ billions)} = \$11.68 + \$0.32 \cdot 21 = \$18.30.$$

This is the point estimate. The standard error of the regression ($1.0792 billion, or approximately $1,080 million) tells us how far the actual point will be from this estimate on average. This is why we plugged in 18,300 as the mean and $1,100 (a slightly more conservative estimate) as the standard deviation for the normal distribution that we used to model the market size for athletic footwear in year 1.

Estimating inputs to the simulation reliably adds another step to the simulation process and may require a lot of time and resources. Some software packages focused specifically on simulation, such as @RISK, contain tools that allow the modeler to decide whether achieving an additional degree of accuracy in the estimate of given simulation inputs is worth the extra

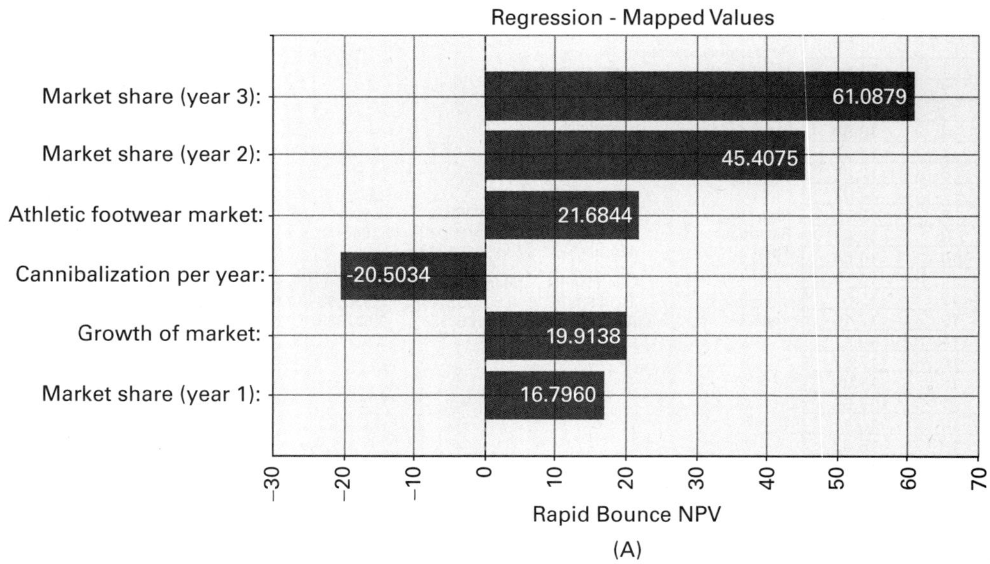

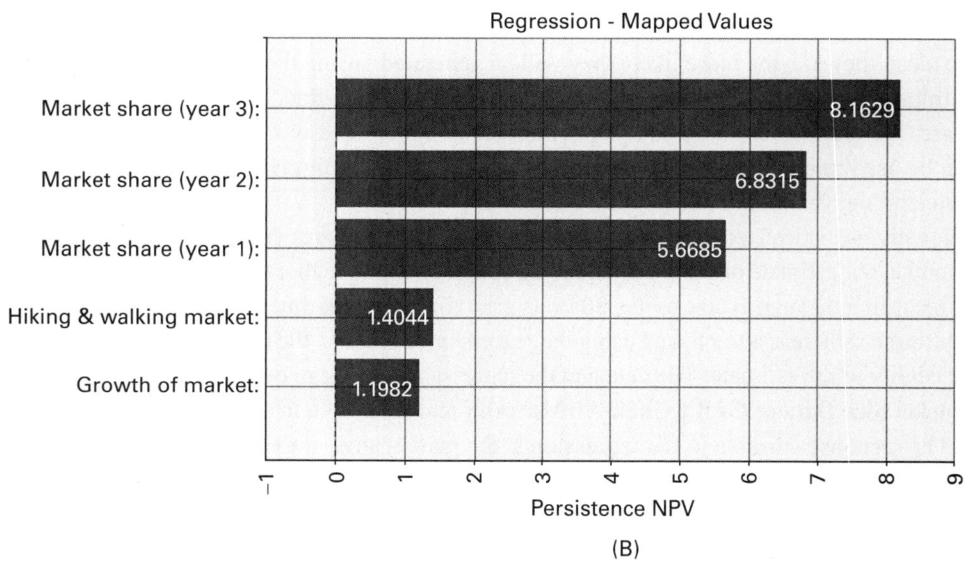

Exhibit 22.21
Sensitivity of (A) Rapid Bounce NPV and (B) Persistence NPV to various factors.

time. In particular, @RISK can create *tornado graphs*, which list the simulation input variables that affect the variability in the simulation output variable in order of importance. Exhibit 22.21 contains the tornado graphs for the NPVs of Rapid Bounce and Persistence.

There are several types of tornado graphs, including regression coefficient graphs, correlation graphs, and regression-mapped value graphs. A user of @RISK can toggle between the different types of graphs. We choose to show regression-mapped values tornado graphs in exhibit 22.21 because the interpretation is quite intuitive. The length of the bar that corresponds to a specific simulation input variable is the amount of change in the output variable that will result from a change in the input variable equal to one standard deviation change. In other words, when the input changes by 1 standard deviation, the output will change by the value on the horizontal axis associated with the length of the bar. For example, exhibit 22.21(A) tells us that the most significant variable for the variability in the NPV of Rapid Bounce is the market share in year 3. A change of 1 standard deviation in the market share from year 3 will increase the NPV of Rapid Bounce by $61.088 million. The fourth most-influential input variable is the amount of cannibalization of sales in a year. A change of 1 standard deviation in the amount of cannibalization will decrease the NPV of Rapid Bounce by $20.503 million. These estimates will vary from simulation to simulation—they are obtained by running a regression on the generated simulation inputs and outputs.

Tornado graphs showing regression coefficients and correlation coefficients contain similar information. In the regression coefficients tornado graph, the length of the bar shown for input variable shows the number of standard deviations that the NPV will change if the input variable changes by 1 standard deviation. In the correlation coefficients tornado graph, the length of the bar shows the strength of the correlation between the changes in the input variable and the NPV.

In this example, the conclusion is that it is most important to make sure that the estimates of the market shares in year 3 and year 2, as well as the size of the market, are accurate. Those input distributions are responsible for the majority of the variability in the estimate of the NPV.

22.5 Managing Portfolios of Projects

Capital budgeting shares many aspects of financial investment management. Although investment projects at companies have traditionally been evaluated on a single-project basis, there are many arguments for using tools from the management of financial investments in the corporate finance context. Projects are often linked to one another and subject to common risk factors. They can be characterized by their risk-return profiles. The theory of optimal portfolio management and operations research tools such as optimization can and should be applied in this area, although few companies actually do.

This area of research is known as *project portfolio management*. Most known methods and tools in this area are based on subjective weighted scoring methods, not quantitatively rigorous methods with their roots in modern portfolio theory or operations research. The field has traditionally been tied to information technology projects at companies and has begun to attract attention as an important area of study only recently. It is easy to understand how the problem of optimal project management can be related to the problem of optimal investment management. The important thing is to define project outcomes and risks in terms of easily quantifiable, statistically meaningful metrics.

Summary

- One of the most important functions in financial management is the evaluation of capital expenditures. Decisions involving capital expenditures are known as capital budgeting decisions.

- Unlike working capital decisions, capital budgeting decisions commit funds for a time period longer than one year and may have an impact on a company's strategic position within its industry.
- The capital budgeting process encompasses the initial investment screening and selection through the postcompletion audit of the project. Classifying capital projects along different dimensions (i.e., economic life, risk, and dependence on other projects) is necessary because these characteristics of the projects affect the analysis of the projects.
- The six most used techniques for evaluating capital budgeting proposals are net present value (NPV), profitability index (PI), internal rate of return (IRR), modified internal rate of return (MIRR), payback period, and discounted payback period.
- The NPV method and the PI are preferred because they consider all the project's cash flows, involve discounting (which considers the time value of money and risk), and are useful in cases in which projects are mutually exclusive.
- The NPV method produces an amount that is the expected value added from investing in a project. That is, the NPV is an estimate of the value added from an investment project.
- The PI translates the NPV into an indexed value and can be useful in ranking projects.
- The IRR is the yield on the investment and the discount rate that causes the NPV to be equal to zero. But the IRR is hazardous to use when selecting among mutually exclusive projects or when there is a limit on capital spending.
- The MIRR is a yield on the investment, assuming that cash inflows are reinvested at some rate other than the IRR. This method overcomes the problems associated with unrealistic reinvestment rate assumptions inherent in the IRR method. However, this method is hazardous to use when selecting among mutually exclusive projects or when there is a limit on capital spending.
- The payback period and the discounted payback period methods provide a measure of the time that it takes to recover the initial investment in a project. Both methods have limitations in that they fail to consider all cash flows from a project.
- When there are scale differences among projects, the NPV should be used.
- When evaluating projects that have different economics lives, the lives must be considered before selecting projects based on one of the six methods described in this chapter.
- Evaluating capital projects requires assessing the risk associated with the future cash flows. This risk may be measured in terms of the market risk or the stand-alone risk.
- Market risk is typically incorporated into decision making by using a cost of capital that reflects the project's risk in relation to the company's capital structure and the portfolio of projects that it holds.
- The stand-alone risk of a project can be estimated using statistics and simulation techniques.
- Simulation can be used to determine the distributions of possible outcomes for different metrics of a project's promise, as well as to compare the outcomes of different projects on a scenario-by-scenario basis.

23

Applications of Real Options to Capital Budgeting

The capital budgeting tools presented in chapter 22 are widely used and represent the fundamentals of the *discounted cash flow* (DCF) analysis framework for evaluating investment decisions. However, an explicit assumption underlying the DCF framework is that once the decision is made at the beginning, future stages of the project happen as planned. Companies are constantly reevaluating their strategies and modifying their decisions. If cash flows are better than expected, the project may be expanded. If cash flows are worse than expected, the project may be abandoned. Management may decide to postpone the project by a year, hoping for better market conditions, or change the input mix in response to changes in the prices of raw materials.

What all these situations have in common is that the company has *options*—change its course of action in the future, acquire an asset in the future, or delay the project. These options enhance a project's investment value because management has the right, but not the obligation, to take actions in the future. In each case, management can do that because it will have access to information that was unavailable at the time of the original decision.

Options in the corporate finance context are referred to as *real options*. In contrast to *financial options*, in which the underlying is a financial instrument or financial index, the underlying item in the case of real options is a physical asset. The importance of including real options in financial valuation can be appreciated by realizing that virtually no research and development (R&D) project would be undertaken according to the net present value (NPV) criterion (the overall cash flows would be negative), were it not for the option to exploit potential results from the research with follow-up investments. We will see some examples in this chapter.

Pharmaceutical companies embraced real options as a tool early on. This is not surprising because they face such situations all the time. Beginning with a small number of chemical components with the potential to induce the necessary reaction in the human body to cope with a particular illness, only about 1 in 15 eventually shows enough potential to become an actual drug. The drug then needs to undergo several stages of clinical tests to achieve U.S. Federal Drug Administration approval: preclinical testing involving animals, testing on healthy humans to evaluate side effects, and testing on human subjects with the actual illness. The life expectancy of such projects is often in the 12- to 15-year range. When the traditional NPV of such projects is evaluated at the beginning, it is often negative, given the small probability that a drug will make it through the process. However, the traditional NPV does not consider the fact that at any stage, the company can drop a project that does not appear promising. The company, therefore, does not need to incur all subsequent costs in the process. Instead of thinking of such projects as a series of cash flows, it is more correct to think of them as a series of options on options. For example, the investment in the study of the chemical components can be thought of as the purchase of an option to develop the drug, the development of the drug can be thought of as the purchase of an option to do preclinical testing, and so forth.

While real options analysis has become a standard tool for many companies' capital budgeting decisions, many have tried and abandoned the approach. A 2001 "Management Tools and Techniques" survey by Bain & Company of 451 senior executives who had tried the real options approach found that a third had given up using it in the same year (Copeland and Tufano 2004). Real option valuation is indeed a challenging undertaking. We will obtain a better intuition about this fact as we discuss examples in this chapter, but most generally, the difficulty stems from the fact that fundamental option pricing formulas from the securities markets, such as the Black-Scholes formula,[1] do not apply exactly to situations in which the underlying securities are not liquid and traded in markets in which no arbitrage can be assumed. Nevertheless, there is widespread recognition that the insights that one can obtain from real options analysis are valuable. Given that financial derivative pricing formulas do not apply easily in the real options framework, however, sensitivity analysis and simulation become even more important tools in this context.

This chapter covers some basic types of real options, such as options to expand, abandon, and wait. The variety of real option types is even wider than the variety of financial options, so we cannot easily cover even all the basic types of real options. Instead, we focus on a few fundamental applications to illustrate the advantages of simulation and dynamic programming techniques for real options valuation.

23.1 Types of Real Options

Real options can most generally be divided into the following types:

- Option to expand
- Option to abandon
- Option to delay
- Option to choose
- Option to switch
- Option for sequential investments

Let us consider some examples:

- *Option to expand or abandon.* When considering an acquisition, management thinks not only about the cash flows that are generated from the operations of the company to be acquired, but also about the strategic advantages that come with the deal. Suppose

1. See chapter 18.

that the company to be acquired owns the intellectual property of a new technology, but it needs development funding. If the new technology is highly successful, buying the company and investing capital in development will provide the acquiring company with the option to expand into further profitable areas. If the new technology is not successful, the acquiring company will have the option to abandon the project at some point in the development phase, and perhaps sell off any remaining tangible assets of the acquired company.

- *Option to delay*. Consider an American company that needs to forecast demand for equipment that it produces months in advance so it can have sufficient time to order the parts, assemble them, and ship them to its customers in Europe. Management could consider the project of building assembly plants in Europe, so it can do the assembly there and reduce the risks associated with its forecasts. While building assembly plants in Europe will incur costs, an evaluation of the overall costs and benefits of the project to the company should include the value of the option that building these plants will give the company—the option to delay making the decision on how much equipment to produce until demand is known better. In other words, the cost of acquiring an option to delay production is that of building the assembly plants in Europe, and the benefits from holding the option are the savings associated with not having to forecast demand too far in advance.
- *Option to choose*. Consider a company like Boeing that has a huge amount of development costs and many years of development for its product. The company can produce only a limited number of models at a time and cannot afford to be wrong about the type of aircraft it should be building. Such a company benefits from creating an option to choose by investing in several promising projects at the same time and running them in parallel, with the goal of eliminating all but one at the end. This way, the company can evaluate the merits and drawbacks of each version of the product as more information becomes available over time, and learn from product prototypes even if they do not become the model that it produces in the end. The cost of the option to choose is the development expenses of the parallel projects, and the benefit is the hedge that this strategy provides against choosing the wrong direction at the beginning.
- *Option to switch*. Consider a company in the oil and gas industry. The management of such a company may consider a project to invest in making its refineries more flexible with respect to output. Outputs include heating oil, diesel, or other kinds of fuel. This project will give the company the option to switch its output to one that is more profitable depending on prevailing market prices.

  Similarly, a company may vary its input mix to minimize the impact of market prices of raw materials on its operations. For example, a company may hold an inventory of excess raw materials (thus increasing inventory costs) or maintain excess contractual obligations with multiple vendors for similar materials in different parts of the world, such that it can switch vendors when a particular raw material becomes relatively expensive in that part of the world.

- *Option for sequential investments*. The pharmaceutical company that invests in a new drug's R&D is an example of a company that creates options for sequential investment. At each project stage, the company's management has the option to wait, abandon, or expand into subsequent stages. Thus, an R&D project that may appear unprofitable according to the NPV criterion could be profitable because the option to defer costs and proceed only if the current stage is promising creates additional value for the project.

23.2 Real Options and Financial Options

There are many similarities between real options and financial options. For example, the profile of a typical option to expand looks very much like the profile of a long position in a classical financial call option.[2] Specifically, it is often the case that a company pays a setup cost for the option to acquire a larger project, or expand, in the future. This setup cost is equivalent to paying the premium on a call option—the option to purchase an asset at a predetermined (strike) price in the future. The estimated current value of this future expansion project is today's stock price in the classical option pricing framework. Over time, the value of the project may change depending on market conditions and the company's strategy. In the future, management may choose to expand if the immediate cost of doing so (paying the "strike price") is lower than the value of the project at the future date. Note that the company will not have the obligation to expand, and it will expand only if the conditions are favorable. The maximum loss incurred by the company would be the value of the premium of the call option.

Similarly, the profile of a typical option to abandon looks very much like the profile of a long position in a classical financial put option.[3] Namely, a company may invest money into a project today (which is equivalent to paying the premium on a put option). If in the future the estimated benefit of continuing the project (equivalent to the future stock price) is less than the estimated cost of continuing with the project (equivalent to the strike price), then the company's management can exercise the option to abandon the project. Again, the maximum loss that the company can incur is the value of the premium for acquiring the option.

Sequential investment decisions such as R&D are best understood as compound options; that is, options on options. Other types of real options have their own interpretations, as we will see later in this chapter. The takeaway from this discussion is that, given the many parallels between real options and financial options, we should be able to tap into the large amount of research on pricing financial options to value investment projects as well. In fact, the Black-Scholes option pricing formula[4] and binomial trees are widely used for real option valuation.

However, it is important to keep in mind that there are limitations in applying financial option pricing methods for valuing real options. These limitations include the following:

- The underlying asset for a financial option is a publicly traded asset, and its market value is observable. The underlying asset for a real option is typically a physical asset, such as a plant or a resource deposit, and its value is not readily available. Real options are therefore inherently proprietary in nature, with no comparable market.

2. See chapter 18 and exhibit 18.1(C).

3. See chapter 18 and exhibit 18.1(E).

4. See chapter 18.

- Financial options typically have short maturities, whereas real options have multi-year durations.
- Financial options have clearly spelled-out exercise features. This is not the case for real options, where there is flexibility with respect to the timing and nature of exercising the option, and therefore additional assumptions must be made for the purposes of valuing the real option.
- The value of financial options cannot be manipulated by the trader because the prices of financial options are driven by the value of the underlying, which in turn is determined by exogenous market forces. In contrast, the value of strategic real options can be changed by timing, management actions, and flexibility.
- As explained in chapter 18, a fundamental principle underlying financial option pricing is the assumption that no arbitrage exists in the markets. This condition allowed us to price financial options as the expected values (under risk-neutral probabilities) of their future payoffs at the risk-free rate. Given the fact that the underlying asset is not traded in the case of real options, the no-arbitrage condition does not hold exactly, so it is not clear if the same principle can be applied. It is applied in practice for lack of a better method, but one needs to exercise caution in interpreting the results.
- Given our discussion of the previous item, there is no easy way to determine the appropriate rate for discounting the cash flows from real options. The conclusion that we should use the risk-free rate when DCFs from financial options came from the no-arbitrage assumption. This principle does not quite hold in the case of real options. We will discuss this issue further in section 23.7.1.

Some real options are directly valued by adjusting financial option pricing methods. Others require more creative modeling. Since the focus of this book is on applications of simulation and optimization in finance, we will give examples mainly of real options that allow for pricing using simulation or optimization (dynamic programming) techniques.

23.3 New View of NPV

As real options became widespread, some economists began referring to the traditional NPV as the *neoclassical net present value (NPV)*.[5] In other words, NPV is the value of a project, assuming that there is no flexibility and no optionality. If we add the present value of all options inherent in the project to NPV, we obtain NPV*—the total value of the project, including options. We may think of NPV* as a postmodern NPV. The decision rule for evaluating a project that we associate with NPV* is the same as the decision rule that we associate with NPV—if NPV* is greater than 0, we should accept the project; otherwise we should reject it. Similarly, if we are considering several projects and there is capital rationing, the project with the highest NPV* should be selected. The only difference is that NPV* reflects project potential more fully than NPV.

Is the traditional NPV bad? Not necessarily. As with any model, NPV is good if the underlying assumptions hold. And, as we will see in this chapter, the valuation of the options

5. See, for example, Dixit and Pindyck (1994).

	A	B	C	D	E	F
1	**R&D project**					
2						
3	Risk-free rate	5.00%				
4	Discount rate	14.00%				
5						
6	Time (yrs)	1	2	3	4	5
7	Costs ($m)	$1.20	$1.20	$1.20	$1.20	$10.00
8	Revenues ($m)					$21.00
9						
10	PV costs ($m)	$1.14	$1.09	$1.03	$0.98	$7.79
11	PV revenues ($m)	$0.00	$0.00	$0.00	$0.00	$10.43
12	PV cash flows ($m)	–$1.14	–$1.09	–$1.03	–$0.98	$2.64
13						
14	NPV	–$1.60				

Exhibit 23.1
Calculation of classical NPV.

embedded in projects can be challenging and not very accurate. Hence, it is valuable to have an estimate of the traditional NPV. If it is negative, we could interpret the amount that it takes to make it zero as the minimum amount at which we should value flexibility to make the project worthwhile. The NPV method still provides the framework within which to evaluate the overall profitability of the project.

Let us consider a simple example to illustrate this point. Management is evaluating the opportunity to invest in an R&D project for a new product. The life of the project is four years, and the costs are $1.2 million per year. After the end of the R&D project (in year 5), the management can spend an additional $10 million to launch the product, and the expected NPV of the cash flows from that point on is $21 million (in year 5 dollars). Assume that the risk-free rate is 5% per year and the discount rate is 14%. (For consistency, assume that both are continuously compounded.) Should the company invest in the R&D project?

Exhibit 23.1 contains a screenshot of the worksheet **Classical NPV** of the file **Ch23-ExpansionAbandonOptions.xlsx** (available from the online appendices), in which the classical NPV is computed. The costs for each year are listed in cells B7:F7. The revenue of $21 million (in year 5 dollars) is shown in cell F8. To compute the NPV, we discount the costs and the revenues to the present by multiplying each cash flow by $e^{-r \cdot t}$, where r is the applicable discount rate and t is the time period in which the cash flow happens. Since the costs are certain cash flows (which we will spend), and the revenues are uncertain cash flows, we use the risk-free interest rate of 5% to discount the costs and the discount rate of 14% to discount the revenues.[6] The discounted costs and revenues are shown in cells B10:F11. For example, the discounted value of the revenues in year 5 is $e^{-0.14 \cdot 5} \cdot (\$21) = \$10.43$ million, and the discounted value of the costs in year 5 is $e^{-0.05 \cdot 5} \cdot (\$10) = \$7.79$ million.

6. This is a commonly used method in practice. More risky cash flows are discounted at a higher discount rate.

The sum of all the DCFs results in an NPV of –\$1.6 million. Since the NPV is negative, the company should technically not invest in the R&D project. However, this valuation omits a very important detail. The NPV is computed with the information that we have currently. The revenues in year 5 are a rough estimate. That estimate can change a lot during the four years of R&D. For example, the R&D stage may not result in a viable product. If the projected value of future revenues falls, the company may decide, at the end of the R&D project, that it is not worthwhile to spend the additional \$10 million to launch the product. In addition, the company may have the option to abandon the project while it is still in development in years 1 through 4.

The NPV that takes into consideration this flexibility, NPV*, can be computed. It will be higher than the NPV. If NPV* is greater than 0, this is an argument for investing in the R&D project. We will discuss the valuation method in section 23.4.

23.4 Option to Expand

Let us consider again the example in the previous section. Suppose that after the company invests in R&D for four years, management has the option to proceed with the next stage (product launch) at a cost of \$10 million, or not proceed. How much is this option worth?

To estimate the value of this option, we need to make some assumptions on how the estimated value of future revenues from the product will change between today and year 5. Suppose that the company estimates, based on experience with similar products in the past, that there is a 10% chance that the R&D project will result in a viable product, and bring in a revenue of \$210 million (in year 5 dollars), but that there is a 90% chance that the R&D project will be a failure and not bring in any revenue. It is not difficult to see that the expected value of the future revenue is $(10\%) \cdot (\$210) + (90\%) \cdot (\$0) = \$21$ million, as in the example in the previous section.

However, note that if the R&D part of the project fails, the company does not have to spend \$10 million to launch the product. In this case, it would realize nothing in future revenues.

We can think of the \$10 million as the strike price of a European call option and the future revenue estimate in year 5 as the price of the underlying. Management will exercise the option only if the price of the underlying is higher than the strike price. There are only two possible states of the world in the future, and the discounted payoff of the option is

$$e^{-0.055} \cdot (0.10 \cdot \max\{\$210 - \$10, \$0\} + 0.90 \cdot \max\{\$0 - \$10, \$0\}) = \$15.58 \text{ million.}^{7}$$

The value of the option is very high because there the volatility of the future cash flows is high.[8]

The present value of the remaining cash flows for the project (the costs incurred in years 1–4) equals

7. Here, we used the risk-free rate to discount the cash flows from the option. The issue of what discount rate to use is complex, and we will come back to it in section 23.7.1.

8. Recall from chapter 18 that the price of a call option increases with the volatility of the process followed by the underlying asset.

$$\$1.2 \cdot e^{-0.05 \cdot 4} + \$1.2 \cdot e^{-0.05 \cdot 4} + \$1.2 \cdot e^{-0.05 \cdot 4} + \$1.2 \cdot e^{-0.05 \cdot 4} = \$4.24.$$

Therefore, the NPV that takes into consideration optionality, NPV*, equals

$$\$15.58 - \$4.24 = \$11.34 \text{ million.}$$

Since NPV* is positive, the project should be considered for funding.

The example that we gave was very simple—we assumed that the project value in the future can be either \$210 million or zero with certain probabilities. We could assume a more complex process for the random variable that is the value of the project between time 0 and time 5. For example, we can assume that it follows a geometric random walk. If this is the case, we can value the real option by using the Black-Scholes formula for European call options. Suppose that the volatility of the process is 35%. (We will talk more about estimating volatility in section 23.7.2.) The strike price is \$10 million. What about the initial price? For the initial price, we use the present value of the project discounted at the cost of capital (14%); that is, \$10.43. The risk-free rate is assumed to be 5%, as before. According to the Black-Scholes formula, the value of the real option is \$4.27 million. (See exhibit 23.2 and the worksheet **Expansion B-S Price** in the file **Ch23-ExpansionAbandon Options.xlsx**.) Based on this estimate, it is worthwhile to invest in the R&D project, but only barely—NPV* equals \$4.27 – \$4.24 (the present value of the costs in years 1–4) = \$0.03 million.

It is very important to conduct sensitivity analysis and determine how much the option price is influenced by our assumption about the volatility of the project. Exhibit 23.3 contains a data table with the price of the real option for different values for the volatility. We can see

	A	B	C
1	**R&D project with option to expand**		
2			
3	Initial price	\$10.43	
4	Strike price	\$10.00	
5	Time to expiration	5	
6	Interest rate	5.00%	
7	Volatility	35%	
8	Dividend yield	0	
9			
10	d1	0.7643	
11	d2	–0.0183	
12	Φ(d1)	0.7777	
13	Φ(d2)	0.4927	
14			
15	Call price	\$ 4.27	
16			

Exhibit 23.2
Valuation of the option to expand using the Black-Scholes formula for European call options.

Volatility	Option Price ($m)	NPV* ($m)
10%	$2.73	–$1.51
15%	$2.96	–$1.28
20%	$3.26	–$0.98
25%	$3.58	–$0.66
30%	$3.93	–$0.31
35%	$4.27	$0.03
40%	$4.62	$0.38
45%	$4.96	$0.72
50%	$5.30	$1.06
55%	$5.63	$1.39
60%	$5.94	$1.70
65%	$6.25	$2.01
70%	$6.55	$2.31
75%	$6.83	$2.59
80%	$7.11	$2.87

Exhibit 23.3
Sensitivity of the value of the expansion option to the volatility estimate.

that the option price estimates for NPV* around the current value for volatility (35%) are very unstable—they go from positive to negative with a small change in the volatility parameter. Therefore, the fact that NPV* is positive is not a reason to undertake the project.

Finally, recall from chapter 18 that we can use simulation to price the call option. The advantage of using simulation is that we can assume different processes for the price of the underlying (in this case, the value of the project). Suppose we assume that the underlying follows a geometric random walk with a volatility of 35%. In that case, we should obtain the same estimate for the option's price (or very close to it) as the estimate obtained with the Black-Scholes formula. To implement the simulation, we treat the present value of the project, $10.43 million (obtained as $21 million discounted at a rate equal to the cost of capital, 14%), as the initial price of the underlying. We then simulate the price of the underlying five years from now using the formula for the geometric random walk. We computed the drift of the geometric random walk as the risk-free rate of 5% minus half of the volatility squared, but the value of the drift may need to be adjusted. (See section 23.7.) In some situations, it may be more appropriate to assume a mean-reverting process or a specific probability distribution for the value of the project in five years.

23.5 Option to Abandon

Let us consider a slightly different example of a development project to illustrate how a real option to abandon the current course of action translates into owning a put option and increases the value of a project. Consider a pharmaceutical company (company A) that owns a patent and is trying to develop a drug based on that patent. The patent has 10 years remaining, so the life of the project is 10 years. Company A is spending $50 million in year 0 to build a new research facility for the drug development project, and $2.5 million per year in

	A	B	C	D	E	F	G	H	I	J	K	L
1	**Development project**											
2												
3	Risk-free rate	5.00%										
4	Discount rate	10.00%										
5												
6	Time (yrs)	0	1	2	3	4	5	6	7	8	9	10
7	Costs ($m)	$50.00	$2.50	$2.50	$0.00	$0.00	$0.00	$0.00	$0.00	$0.00	$0.00	$0.00
8	Revenues ($m)	$0.00	$0.00	$0.00	$8.00	$8.00	$8.00	$8.00	$8.00	$8.00	$8.00	$8.00
9												
10	PV costs ($m)	$50.00	$2.26	$2.05	$0.00	$0.00	$0.00	$0.00	$0.00	$0.00	$0.00	$0.00
11	PV revenues ($m)	$0.00	$0.00	$0.00	$5.93	$5.36	$4.85	$4.39	$3.97	$3.59	$3.25	$2.94
12	PV cash flows ($m)	–$50.00	–$2.26	–$2.05	$5.93	$5.36	$4.85	$4.39	$3.97	$3.59	$3.25	$2.94
13												
14	NPV	–$20.01										

Exhibit 23.4
Classical NPV of drug development project (the worksheet **Abandon** in the file **Ch23-ExpansionAbandon Options.xlsx**).

years 1 and 2. The development is expected to end at the end of year 2, and the drug is expected to generate $8 million per year from year 3 onward. At the end of year 2, company A has the option to reevaluate its investment. It has entered into a contract with another pharmaceutical company (company B) that lets company A sell its intellectual property and research facility to company B in year 3 for a salvage value of $70 million if the development process is not going as well as planned. What is this option worth?

Exhibit 23.4 illustrates the cash flows and the NPV of the project without considering optionality. Both costs and revenues are discounted at the cost of capital, 10%. The NPV of the project is –$20.01 million.

At the end of year 2, company A can sell the project for a salvage value of $70 million. The present value of all revenues in year 3 and onward is the sum of the values in cells E11:L11, which is $34.29 million. Thus, company A owns a put option to sell an asset with an initial value of $34.29 million for $70 million two years from now. We can use the Black-Scholes put option pricing formula to value this option (see exhibit 23.5). The value obtained from the formula is $30.21 million.

Therefore, it is worthwhile to invest in the drug development project. We can obtain a similar estimate by simulating the value of the future cash flows at the end of year 2 (if the total value follows a geometric random walk).

23.6 More Real Options Examples

The real option examples considered in sections 23.4 and 23.5 were very basic. Most real-life projects are more complicated, and the Black-Scholes formula is not as useful. In this section, to give a flavor of the variety of real option models, we discuss an example of a timing option that takes advantage of simulation to value a project, as well as examples of projects that have a multiperiod nature. Binomial trees[9] can be applied in the latter context because they allow greater flexibility in modeling the continuous nature of adjustments in investment decisions. Dynamic programming is then used to determine the optimal strategy, given some assumptions about the way the underlying process behaves.

9. See chapter 18.

	A	B
1	**Project with option to abandon**	
2		
3	Initial price	$34.29
4	Strike price	$70.00
5	Time to expiration	2
6	Interest rate	5.00%
7	Volatility	35%
8	Dividend yield	0
9		
10	d1	–0.9920
11	d2	–1.4870
12	Φ(–d1)	0.8394
13	Φ(–d2)	0.9315
14		
15	Put price	$ 30.21
16		

Exhibit 23.5
Valuation of the option to abandon the development project with the Black-Scholes put option pricing formula (the worksheet **Abandon B-S Price** in the file **Ch23-ExpansionAbandonOptions.xlsx**).

23.6.1 Project to Abandon or Expand

Let us consider a variation on the project described in section 23.4. Suppose that, as before, the company's management has the option to invest $10 million in the project in year 5, or not invest. However, suppose also that management has the additional flexibility of abandoning the project in any of years 1 through 4 if it is not satisfied with the direction of the project. We therefore have two implicit options to value: (1) a European call option with a maturity of 5 years, as before; and (2) an American put option with a maturity of 4 years. To value them together, we create a binomial tree for the process followed by the estimated value of the revenues starting in year 5.

As explained in section 23.4, the present value of the estimated cash flows of the project (discounted at the cost of capital, 14%) is $10.43 million. We assume that the volatility of the project (σ) is 35% and the risk-free rate (r) is 5%, and construct a recombining binomial tree in which the value of the project each year is expected to go up or down by certain multipliers (u and d) with certain probabilities (p and $1-p$). These parameters can be found from our assumptions about the volatility of the process and the time increment.[10] We have:

$$r = 0.05$$
$$\Delta t = 1 \text{ year}$$
$$\sigma = 0.35$$

$$\text{Discount factor for each time period } df = e^{-r \cdot \Delta t} = 0.9512$$

$$u = e^{\sigma \cdot \sqrt{\Delta t}} = e^{0.35 \cdot \sqrt{1}} = 1.42$$
$$d = e^{-\sigma \cdot \sqrt{\Delta t}} = e^{-0.35 \cdot \sqrt{1}} = 0.70$$
$$p = \frac{e^{r \cdot (\Delta t)} - d}{u - d} = 48.52\%$$

10. See chapter 18.

	A		B	C	D	E	F	G
9	Project value							
10	time period		0	1	2	3	4	5
11		0	$10.43	$14.80	$21.00	$29.80	$42.29	$60.01
12		1		$7.35	$10.43	$14.80	$21.00	$29.80
13		2			$5.18	$7.35	$10.43	$14.80
14		3				$3.65	$5.18	$7.35
15		4					$2.57	$3.65
16		5						$1.81

Exhibit 23.6
Binomial tree for the process followed by the value of future revenues (the worksheet **Expansion and Abandon** in the file **Ch23-ExpansionAbandonOptions.xlsx**).

	A		B	C	D	E	F	G
27	Value with							
28	abandonment		0	1	2	3	4	5
29		0	$1.57	$3.41	$9.28	$18.41	$31.58	$50.01
30		1		$0.00	$0.67	$4.04	$10.29	$19.80
31		2			$0.00	$0.00	$1.01	$4.80
32		3				$0.00	$0.00	$0.00
33		4					$0.00	$0.00
34		5						$0.00

Exhibit 23.7
Valuation of the real option to expand in year 5 or abandon in years 1–4 (the worksheet **Expansion and Abandon** in the file **Ch23-ExpansionAbandonOptions.xlsx**).

The binomial tree with the values of the project for years 1 through 5 is shown in exhibit 23.6.

The value of the project with the option to abandon at any time between 1 and 4 or expand at time 5 can be computed by using dynamic programming. The results are presented in exhibit 23.7.

We start at the last time period, year 5. The value at each node can be computed as the maximum of the difference between the project value at that node (exhibit 23.6) and the strike price of $10 million to expand. For example, in cell G29, we compute the maximum of ($60.01 – $10) million and 0, which is $50.01 million. In cell G32, we compute the maximum of ($7.35 – $10) million and 0, which is 0.

At the previous step (year 4), we have the option to abandon the project if the expected value of continuing is less than the value of abandoning, which carries a value of 0. The expected value of continuing is the cost of $1.2 million plus the discounted value of the expected payoffs in the next time period. For example, in cell F30, we compute

$$\max\{0, -\$1.2 + 0.9512 \cdot (0.4852 \cdot \$50.01 + (1-0.4852) \cdot \$19.80\},$$

which equals $31.58 million. At this node, it is optimal to continue. We proceed backward through the tree until we reach time 0. At that time, the value of the node is simply

	A		B	C	D	E	F	G
18	Value without							
19	abandonment		0	1	2	3	4	5
20		0	$0.13	$3.09	$9.28	$18.41	$31.58	$50.01
21		1		–$2.64	$0.02	$4.04	$10.29	$19.80
22		2			–$2.96	–$1.32	$1.01	$4.80
23		3				–$2.34	–$1.20	$0.00
24		4					–$1.20	$0.00
25		5						$0.00

Exhibit 23.8
Valuation of the real option to expand without the option to abandon (the worksheet **Expansion and Abandon** in the file **Ch23-ExpansionAbandonOptions.xlsx**).

$$0.9512 \cdot (0.4852 \cdot \$3.41 + (1 - 0.4852) \cdot \$0 = \$1.57 \text{ million.}$$

If we did not have the option to abandon the project during years 1 through 4, the value of the project would have been $0.13 million (see exhibit 23.8 and the worksheet **Expansion and Abandon** in the file **Ch23-ExpansionAbandonOptions.xlsx**). This is because instead of computing the maximum value of continuing or abandoning at each node, we would have been forced to continue. Having the option to abandon increases the value of the project.

23.6.2 Valuing an Option to Wait

There is a wide variety of situations in which real option models apply, and often there is a lot of flexibility as to how management can model its choices. In this section, we present a simulation model for estimating the value of the choice to wait or execute today. See Moore (2008) for a more general principle for valuing timing options over multiple periods that involves the profitability index (PI).[11]

We use a classic example introduced in Titman (1985).[12] Suppose that we are considering buying a parcel of land that has been zoned for multifamily housing. The size of the lot is such that we can use it either for a two-story building or for a three-story building. Each building can have three units per floor. A two-story building will therefore have six apartments, whereas a three-story building will have nine apartments. Taller buildings are more expensive because of additional foundation and elevator costs. It will cost $80,000 to build a unit in a six-unit building, and $90,000 to build a unit in a nine-unit building. The current market value of each unit is $100,000.

We also have the option to time the development. We can either construct the building this year (as soon as we buy the land), or wait until next year. The questions are: How much should we be willing to pay for the land, and what is the optimal policy?

If we build this year, the optimal strategy is easy to calculate. The six-unit building will bring in a profit of

$$6 \cdot (\$100{,}000 - \$80{,}000) = \$120{,}000.$$

11. See section 22.2.3 for a definition of the PI.

12. See also Winston (2000).

The nine-unit building will bring in a profit of

$$9 \cdot (\$100{,}000 - \$90{,}000) = \$90{,}000.$$

Therefore, we should construct the six-unit building, and we should be willing to pay up to \$120,000 for the land.

If we wait until next year, the market price of a unit is likely to change. For simplicity, however, we assume that the building costs will stay the same. To estimate whether it makes sense to wait, we need to make assumptions on the process followed by the market price of the unit. Suppose that apartment prices follow a geometric random walk. Next year, they are expected to be 5% higher on average, but the volatility in real estate prices has been about 35%. Suppose also that the risk-free rate is 3% per year.

To value the *option* to build and sell the units, we assume that the market price of the unit grows at the risk-free rate. We can compute the market price of a unit next year with the formula

$$S_1 = (\$100{,}000) \cdot e^{\left(0.03 - \frac{1}{2} \cdot 0.35^2 + 0.35 \cdot \tilde{\varepsilon}\right)},$$

where $\tilde{\varepsilon}$ is a standard normal random variable. We will build as many units as are optimal in a year; that is, the number of units that results in the maximum profit given the market price of a unit in a year. In fact, if the market price of a unit is such that we would realize a loss by building any number of units, we can choose not to build, for a profit of 0.

We also need to discount the profit in year 1 to value the real option and to make sure that we have a fair comparison with the profit in year 1. We have the following expression for the discounted profit if we wait a year:

$$e^{-0.03 \cdot 1} \cdot \max\ \{6 \cdot (S_1 - 80{,}000),\ 9 \cdot (S_1 - 90{,}000),\ 0\}.$$

After simulating 10,000 paths for the market price of a unit in a year, we obtain the output in exhibit 23.9.[13] Therefore, the value of waiting to develop for a year is approximately \$193,094.49. This number is higher than the profit that would be obtained by developing immediately (\$120,000) and is in fact the estimate that we should use to determine how much we should be willing to pay for the land. Having the flexibility to wait increases the value of the project.

23.6.3 Valuing a Multiperiod Real Estate Project

Many projects require modeling the price of a commodity or the level of an index. Such variables determine the cash flows of the project and change with market conditions. Examples include multistage oil field development (Smit 1997), in which the profitability of operations is determined by the market price of oil; and gold mine exploitation,[14] which depends on the price of gold (Luenberger 1998 and Winston 2000). Let us consider a real estate example related to the example in section 23.6.2, but over multiple years. The underlying variable is an index of property values. A real estate developer is considering investing in land that can be

13. See the file **Ch23-OptionToWait.xlsx** in the online appendices.

14. See also practice 23.1 in the ancillary materials.

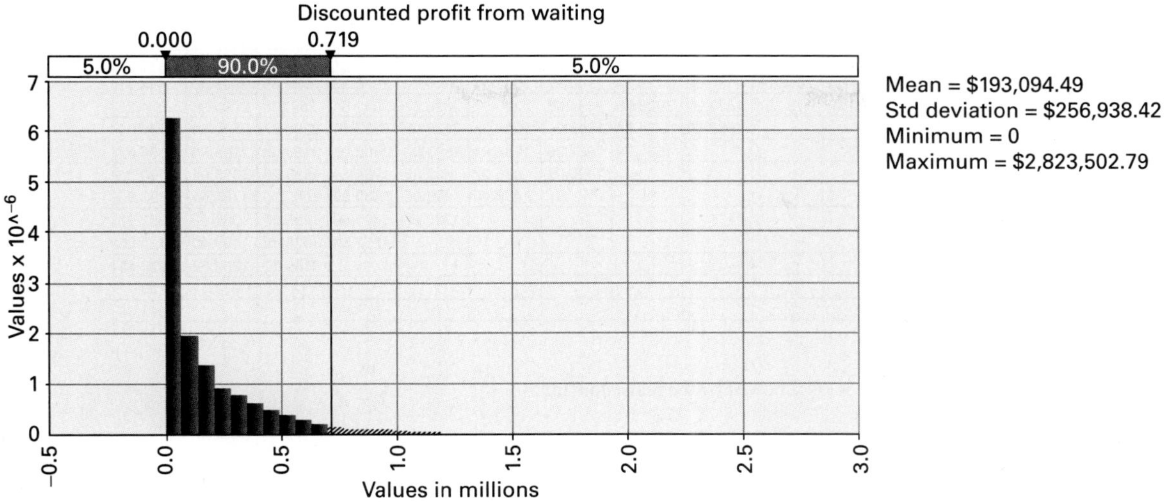

Exhibit 23.9
Simulation output for the discounted profit from waiting to develop the land for a year.

used for condominium development. The life of the project is 10 years. Every year, the developer can build and sell up to three condominiums. The cost of a single condominium is \$250,000, and the current selling price for a single condominium is \$350,000. How much should the developer be willing to pay for the land? Note that the developer has the option not to build condominiums in any particular year in which the cost of building them is greater than the market value at which they can be sold.

We have the following additional information. The value of the real estate index in year 0 is 1893, and past data indicate an annual drift of 10.3% and a volatility of 5.9%. Building costs have been increasing at a relatively constant rate of 5.53% per year. We assume that the market price for the condominiums is perfectly correlated with the price of the real estate index.

Based on this information, we can create a binomial tree for the process followed by the index level over the next 10 years:

$$r = 0.03$$
$$\Delta t = 1 \text{ year}$$
$$\sigma = 0.059$$

Discount factor for each time period $df = e^{-r \cdot \Delta t} = 0.9704$

$$u = e^{\sigma \cdot \sqrt{\Delta t}} = e^{0.059 \cdot \sqrt{1}} = 1.06$$
$$d = e^{-\sigma \cdot \sqrt{\Delta t}} = e^{-0.059 \cdot \sqrt{1}} = 0.94$$
$$p = \frac{e^{r \cdot (\Delta t)} - d}{u - d} = 74.32\%$$

The tree for the index levels is shown in exhibit 23.10. The corresponding tree for the revenues from selling three condos per year, as well as the costs of building three condos per year, are shown in exhibit 23.11.[15]

15. See chapter 18 for an explanation of how to build binomial trees, and the file **Ch23-RealEstateOption.xlsx** for an implementation of this particular binomial tree.

	A	B	C	D	E	F	G	H	I	J	K	L
9	Index value											
10	time period	0	1	2	3	4	5	6	7	8	9	10
11	0	1893.00	2008.05	2130.09	2259.54	2396.87	2542.54	2697.06	2860.98	3034.85	3219.30	3414.95
12	1		1784.54	1893.00	2008.05	2130.09	2259.54	2396.87	2542.54	2697.06	2860.98	3034.85
13	2			1682.30	1784.54	1893.00	2008.05	2130.09	2259.54	2396.87	2542.54	2697.06
14	3				1585.92	1682.30	1784.54	1893.00	2008.05	2130.09	2259.54	2396.87
15	4					1495.05	1585.92	1682.30	1784.54	1893.00	2008.05	2130.09
16	5						1409.40	1495.05	1585.92	1682.30	1784.54	1893.00
17	6							1328.65	1409.40	1495.05	1585.92	1682.30
18	7								1252.53	1328.65	1409.40	1495.05
19	8									1180.77	1252.53	1328.65
20	9										1113.12	1180.77
21	10											1049.34

Exhibit 23.10
Binomial tree for the process followed by the real estate index.

	A	B	C	D	E	F	G	H	I	J	K	L
24	Cando revenues	0	1	2	3	4	5	6	7	8	9	10
25	0	1125.00	1193.37	1265.90	1342.83	1424.45	1511.02	1602.85	1700.26	1803.60	1913.21	2029.49
26	1		1060.55	1125.00	1193.37	1265.90	1342.83	1424.45	1511.02	1602.85	1700.26	1803.60
27	2			999.78	1060.55	1125.00	1193.37	1265.90	1342.83	1424.45	1511.02	1602.85
28	3				942.50	999.78	1060.55	1125.00	1193.37	1265.90	1342.83	1424.45
29	4					888.50	942.50	999.78	1060.55	1125.00	1193.37	1265.90
30	5						837.60	888.50	942.50	999.78	1060.55	1125.00
31	6							789.61	837.60	888.50	942.50	999.78
32	7								744.37	789.61	837.60	888.50
33	8									701.72	744.37	789.61
34	9										661.52	701.72
35	10											623.62
36												
37	Costs	0	1	2	3	4	5	6	7	8	9	10
38		$0.00	$792.64	$837.71	$885.34	$935.68	$988.88	$1,045.11	$1,104.53	$1,167.33	$1,233.70	$1,303.85

Exhibit 23.11
Binomial tree for the revenues and costs associated with building and selling three condos per year.

We are now ready to compute the value of the option to develop the land (see exhibit 23.12). At every node, except at time 0, the developer will build three condos only if the price of building them exceeds the cost of building them in that particular year (based on the data in exhibit 23.11). For example, at the first node in year 10 (cell L42), the value of the project is the maximum of the revenues minus the costs, or 0:

$$\max\{\$2029.49 - \$1303.85,\ 0\} = \$725.64.$$

For the second node in year 10 (cell L43), we have

$$\max\{\$1803.60 - \$1303.85, 0\} + \$499.75.$$

Going backward through the tree, we record the reward from being at each node,[16] which is the maximum of the profit that the developer can achieve at that node and 0, as well as the discounted expected value of the profit from that node on. For example, at the first node in year 9 (cell K42), we have

$$\max\{\$1,913.21 - \$1,233.70, 0\} + 0.9704. \cdot (0.7432 \cdot \$725.64 + (1 - 0.7432) \cdot 499.75) = \$1,327.41.$$

16. See section 7.1.

	A		B	C	D	E	F	G	H	I	J	K	L
40	Value of option												
41	to develop		0	1	2	3	4	5	6	7	8	9	10
42		0	$2,652.83	$3,055.18	$3,047.77	$2,998.27	$2,898.69	$2,740.37	$2,514.13	$2,210.22	$1,818.31	$1,327.41	$725.64
43		1		$1,803.05	$1,830.98	$1,834.30	$1,806.32	$1,739.38	$1,624.98	$1,453.82	$1,216.07	$901.52	$499.75
44		2			$861.07	$885.72	$896.82	$889.20	$856.48	$790.88	$683.21	$523.02	$299.00
45		3				$241.52	$255.62	$265.55	$268.82	$261.95	$240.02	$196.12	$120.60
46		4					$0.00	$0.00	$0.00	$0.00	$0.00	$0.00	$0.00
47		5						$0.00	$0.00	$0.00	$0.00	$0.00	$0.00
48		6							$0.00	$0.00	$0.00	$0.00	$0.00
49		7								$0.00	$0.00	$0.00	$0.00
50		8									$0.00	$0.00	$0.00
51		9										$0.00	$0.00
52		10											$0.00

Exhibit 23.12
Value of the project with flexibility to develop or not develop it each year.

The value of the land with the flexibility to develop or not develop in any particular year (cell B42) is 2,652.83 thousand dollars (i.e., $2,652,830). The developer should be willing to pay up to this amount for the land.

It is useful to do some sensitivity analysis to figure out if this estimate is very sensitive to assumptions made about different input parameters. For example, a data table can be created that references the project's estimated value and computes it based on different estimates of the volatility in the process for the property value index level. Finally, additional simulation and scenario analysis can be done. For example, so far, we have assumed that costs every year are growing at a constant rate. It is possible, however, that there is some variability in our estimate. We can use simulation to determine the effect of the cost variability on the estimated value of the project. For example, suppose that our estimate of the costs in each year has a standard deviation of 3.40% of the current value. (This is consistent with historical observed volatility in the building cost index.) What is the resulting variability in the estimated project value?

Exhibit 23.13 shows the distribution of possible project values for 1,000 generated scenarios for the costs over 10 years.[17] We can see that 90% of the time, the project value can be expected to be between $2,516,000 and $2,792,000.

23.7 Estimation of Inputs for Real Option Valuation Models

An overview of real option valuation is not complete without a discussion of how important parameters, such as the discount rate and the volatility, are estimated.

23.7.1 Discount Rate

As explained in chapter 22, the discount rate commonly used for computing the classical NPV is the weighted average cost of capital (WACC). (As we mentioned earlier in this chapter, however, different cash flows in a project can be discounted using different discount rates, depending on their perceived risk.) Determining a good estimate of the WACC for

17. Note that this calculation involves recomputing the binomial tree to determine the value of the option for each scenario for the costs (i.e., in this case, computing 1,000 binomial trees).

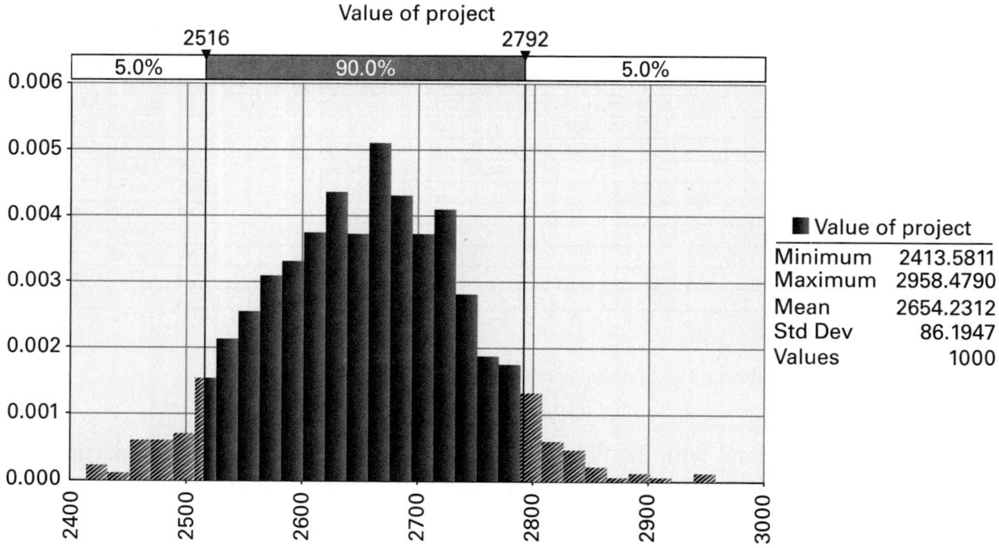

Exhibit 23.13
Variability in project value as the cost estimate varies.

calculating the pure NPV with no optionality can itself be problematic because it is based on evaluating the risk of similar projects, and many of these projects have their own options.

Finding the appropriate discount rate for the purposes of real option valuation has its own issues. As we mentioned in section 23.2, financial options are priced by discounting the cash flows from the options at the risk-free rate. This is not quite the appropriate rate to use in pricing real options, however, because the concept of no arbitrage and the idea of a risk-neutral world do not exactly apply in this context. If we use the risk-free rate to discount the cash flows relevant for the valuation for the real option, we may end up with an overly optimistic estimate of the real option value. Several adjustments are made in practice:

1. An artificially inflated discount rate is applied to cash flows affecting the real option value such that the real option value is reduced. This method can be very subjective and difficult to apply. A theoretically justified approach for inflating the discount rate is discussed next, but it can be applied only in circumstances in which we have historical data on the process followed by the underlying asset for the real option and a strongly correlated traded asset.
2. It can be shown[18] that under certain assumptions, the appropriate risk-adjusted rate to use so options are priced correctly even if we cannot talk about a risk-neutral world is

$$\mu-\lambda\cdot\sigma$$

where μ and σ are the drift and the volatility of the process followed by the underlying, respectively; and is λ the market price of risk. In other words, if we assume that the rate of growth of the underlying asset is $\mu-\lambda\cdot\sigma$ (which equals the asset's rate of

18. See Hull (2008).

growth μ adjusted downward by $\lambda \cdot \sigma$), and then discount the cash flows at the risk-free rate, we can price the real option correctly.

The *market price of risk* is related to the excess return of a traded asset over the risk-free rate r_{rf}. In other words,

$$\mu - r_{rf} = \lambda \cdot \sigma$$

If we have historical data on a traded asset and a nontraded variable (e.g., company sales), we can do the following to estimate the market price of risk for company sales:

a. Estimate the coefficient of correlation ρ between the returns on the traded asset and the percentage changes in the nontraded variable.

b. Estimate the volatility of returns of the market, σ_M. (This is usually done by estimating the volatility of a broad stock market index.)

c. Estimate the expected return on the market, r_M.

d. Find the short-term risk-free rate, r_{rf}.

e. Compute the market price of risk of the nontraded variable as

$$\lambda = \frac{\rho}{\sigma_M} \cdot (r_M - r_{rf})$$

3. Sometimes, to adjust the value of the real option downward, the price of the real option is reduced by the price of a put option. The idea is that since the underlying asset in the real option is not tradable, it cannot be sold to realize its assumed value for the purposes of valuation. This inflexibility decreases the value of the real option. The maturity of the put option is typically assumed to be lower than the maturity of the real option to reflect the time period over which tradability is an important factor, and the strike price is set at the asset value to reflect the ability to sell the asset at its estimated price at a moment's notice.

Often in practice, however, none of these approaches are taken. A simple adjustment is to use the WACC reduced by the risk-free rate as a discount rate for the purposes of valuing the real options in the project. The exact valuation does not have as much importance when comparing multiple projects, so long as we use the same methodology to value each project. In this chapter, for simplicity, we have used the risk-free rate for discounting. However, it is important to understand the underlying problems with this assumption.

23.7.2 Volatility

The volatility σ that we have been using in real option valuation is the annualized standard deviation of the continuously compounded rate of the return on the underlying asset. As discussed in chapter 18, the volatility in financial options can be estimated from observed market prices of financial derivatives. But where do we get such an estimate for the volatility of company projects? One possibility is to use data on the volatility of the company's stock prices (where the volatility is estimated either from historical returns or from market prices of options on the company's stock), but this volatility is "levered" volatility; that is, it incorporates information about the company's debt-to-equity ratio D/E. Before using it for project valuation purposes, we need to delever it. If σ_L is the implied volatility estimated from the company's stock price, we can estimate the unlevered volatility σ_U from the following relationship:

$$\sigma_L = \left(1 + \frac{D}{E}\right) \cdot \sigma_U$$

What about an estimate for the volatility of a company that is not publicly traded? We can attempt to estimate it by estimating the volatility for similar companies that are publicly traded, but this method introduces a lot of subjectivity and inaccuracy into the process.

What about the volatility of nontraded variables that determine the value of projects, such as company sales or the value of a research facility? There is not a good solution. The best approach in general is to use sensitivity analysis to evaluate whether the recommended course of action is sensitive to the current estimate of volatility. As Moore (2008) said, "real options analysis is hardly an arena for an obsession with precision. Precision can be pushed only so far."

Summary

- Evaluation of capital investment decisions is a dynamic process. Companies typically have the option to change their initial course of action. Options in the context of capital investment decisions are referred to as real options (as opposed to financial options).
- Real options enhance investment value because the company has the right, but not the obligation, to take actions in the future. The company can do that because in the future, it will have access to information that is unavailable at the time of the original decision.
- Most generally, real options fall into the following categories: option to expand, option to abandon, option to delay, option to choose, option to switch, option for sequential investments.
- There are many similarities between real options and financial options. However, it is also important to keep in mind that models for pricing financial options cannot be automatically translated into models for real option valuation because the assumptions made for pricing financial options do not hold for real options.
- A typical option to expand looks very much like a long position in a classical financial call option. The company has the right, but not the obligation, to buy an asset in the future if the future estimate of the value of that asset is more than the cost of acquiring it at that time.
- A typical option to abandon looks very much like a long position in a classical financial put option. The company has the right, but not the obligation, to abandon a project (get rid of an asset) if the estimated benefit of continuing the project in the future is less than the estimated cost of continuing with the project.
- Given the similarity between real options and financial options, the Black-Scholes formula and binomial trees are often applied for real option valuation.
- The inputs to real option valuation models, such as volatility and the correct discount rate to use, are difficult to estimate. Sensitivity analysis and simulation are even more important in the context of real options valuation.

References

Abken, P. (2000). An empirical evaluation of value at risk by scenario simulation. *Journal of Derivatives, 7*(4), 12–29.

Adcock, C., & Meade, N. (1994). A simple algorithm to incorporate transaction costs in quadratic optimization. *European Journal of Operational Research, 79*(1), 85–94.

Ahn, H., & Kim, K. -J. (2011). Corporate credit rating using multiclass classification models with order information. *International Journal of Economics and Management Engineering, 5*(12), 1783–1788.

Akesson, F., & Lehoczky, J. P. (2000). Path generation for quasi-Monte Carlo simulation of mortgage-backed securities. *Management Science, 46*(9), 1171–1187.

Almenc, N. P., Malaise, L., & Martellini, L. (2004). *Revisiting core-satellite investing—A dynamic model of relative risk management.* Working paper. EDHEC Risk and Asset Management Research Centre.

Altman, E. I. (1968). Financial ratios, discriminant analysis and the prediction of corporate bankruptcy. *Journal of Finance, 23*(4), 589–609.

Altman, E. I., Haldeman, R. G., & Narayann, P. (1977). Zeta analysis: A new model to identify bankruptcy risk of corporations. *Journal of Banking and Finance, 1*(1), 29–54.

Anderson, F., Mausser, H., Rosen, D., & Uryasev, S. (2001). Credit risk optimization with conditional value-at-risk criteria. *Mathematical Programming, 89*, 273–291.

Apelfeld, R., Fowler, G. B., & Gordon, J. P. (1996). Tax-aware equity investing. *Journal of Portfolio Management, 22*(2), 18–28.

Artzner, P., Delbaen, J. -M., Eber, J., & Heath, D. (1999). Coherent measures of risk. *Mathematical Finance, 9*(November), 203–228.

Axel, R., & Vankudre, P. (2002). Managing the yield curve with principal component analysis. In F. J. Fabozzi (Ed.), *Professional perspectives on fixed income portfolio management*: (Vol. 3, pp. 85–103). Hoboken, NJ: John Wiley & Sons.

Azar, P. D., & Lo, A. W. (2016). The wisdom of Twitter crowds: Predicting stock market reactions to FOMC meetings via Twitter feeds. *Journal of Portfolio Management, 42*(5), 123–134.

Bachar, D., & Zhao, J. (2017). Machine learning: Challenges, lessons, and opportunities in credit risk modeling. *Moody's Analytics Risk Perspectives: Managing Disruption, 9.*

Banz, R. W. (1981). The relationship between return and market value of common stocks. *Journal of Financial Economics, 9*(1), 3–18.

Barone-Adesi, G., & Whaley, R.E. (1987). Efficient analytical approximation of American option values. *Journal of Finance, 42*(2), 301–320.

Barra. (1998). *Risk model handbook United States equity: Version 3.* Berkeley, CA: Barra.

Bartram, S. M., Branke, J., De Rossi, G., & Motahari, M. (2021). Machine learning for active portfolio management. *Journal of Financial Data Science, 1*(3), 9–30.

Bartram, S. M., Branke, J., & Motahari, M. (2020). *Artificial intelligence in asset management.* Charlottesville, VA: CFA Institute Research Foundation.

Bazaraa, M., Sharali, H., & Shetty, C. (1993). *Nonlinear programming: Theory and algorithms.* New York: John Wiley & Sons.

Beasley, J. D., & Springer, S. G. (1977). The percentage points of the normal distribution. *Applied Statistics, 26*, 118–121.

Beaver, W. (1966). Financial ratios as predictors of failure. *Journal of Accounting Research, 4*(1), 77–111.

Bekkers, N., Doeswijk, R. Q., & Lam, T. W. (2009). Strategic asset allocation: Determining the optimal portfolio with ten asset classes. *Journal of Wealth Management, 12*(3), 61–77.

Bellman, R. (1957). *Dynamic programming.* Princeton, NJ: Princeton University Press.

Ben-Tal, A., Margalit, T., & Nemirovski, A. (2000). Robust modeling of multi-stage portfolio problems. In H. Frenk, K. Roos, T. Terlaky, & S. Zhang (Eds.), *High-performance optimization* (pp. 303–328). Dordrecht, Netherlands: Kluwer.

Bergstra, J., & Bengio, Y. (2012). Random search for hyper-parameter optimization. *Journal of Machine Learning Research, 13*(10), 281–305.

Berinato, S. (2016). Visualizations that really work. *Harvard Business Review*, June. Available at https://hbr.org/2016/06/visualizations-that-really-work?elqTrackId=1280ab0fc2744bb0a58aaba12e779c9a&elqaid=52857&elqat=2&source=:ow:ms:pt:

Berk Wheelock, L., & Pachamanova, D. A. (2022). Acceptable set topic modeling. *European Journal of Operational Research, 299*(2), 653–673.

Bertsekas, D. (1995). *Dynamic programming and optimal control* (Vols. 1 and 2). Belmont, MA: Athena Scientific.

Bertsimas, D., Darnell, C., & Soucy, R. (1999). Portfolio construction through mixed-integer programming at Grantham Mayo Van Otterloo and Company. *Interfaces, 29*(1), 49–66.

Bertsimas, D., & Pachamanova, D. (2008). Robust multiperiod portfolio management with transaction costs. *Computers and Operations Research, 35*(1), 3–17.

Bertsimas, D., & Tsitsiklis, J. (1997). *Introduction to linear optimization.* Belmont, MA: Athena Scientific.

Best, M. J., & Grauer, R. R. (1991). On the sensitivity of mean-variance-efficient portfolios to changes in assets means: Some analytical and computational results. *Review of Financial Studies, 4*(2), 315–342.

Best, M. J., & Grauer, R. R. (1992). The analytics of sensitivity analysis for mean-variance portfolio problems. *International Review of Financial Analysis, 1*(1), 17–37.

Birge, J. (1985). Decomposition and partitioning methods for multistage stochastic linear programs. *Operations Research, 33*(5), 989–1007.

Black, F. (1972). Capital market equilibrium with restricted borrowings. *Journal of Business, 45*(3), 444–455.

Black, F.(1976). The pricing of commodity contracts. *Journal of Financial Economics, 3*, 167–179.

Black, F., & Litterman, R. (1992). Global portfolio optimization. *Financial Analysts Journal, 48*(5), 28–43.

Black, F., & Scholes, M. (1973). The pricing of options and corporate liabilities. *Journal of Political Economy, 81*(3), 637–654.

Blei, D. M., Ng, A. Y., & Jordan, M. I. (2003). Latent Dirichlet allocation. *Journal of Machine Learning Research, 3*, 993–1022.

Bogentoft, E., Romeijn, H. E., & Uryasev, S. (2001). Asset/liability management for pension funds using CVaR constraints. *Journal of Risk Finance, 3*, 57–71.

Booth, G., Gerding, E., & McGroarty, F. (2015). Performance-weighted ensembles of random forests for predicting price impact. *Quantitative Finance, 15*(11), 1823–1835.

Borghi, R., & De Rossi, G. (2020). The artificial intelligence approach to picking stocks. In E. Jurczenko (Ed.), *Machine learning and asset management.* Hoboken, NJ: John Wiley & Sons.

Borne, K. (2014). Top 10 list—The V's of big data. Data Science Central, April 12. Available at https://www.datasciencecentral.com/profiles/blogs/top-10-list-the-v-s-of-big-data.

Box, G. E. P., & Muller, M. E. (1958). A note on the generation of random normal deviates. *Annals of Mathematical Statistics, 29*(2), 610–611.

Boyle, P. (1977). Options: A Monte Carlo approach. *Journal of Financial Economics, 4*(3), 323–338.

Boyle, P., Broadie, M., & Glasserman, P. (1997). Monte Carlo methods for security pricing. *Journal of Economic Dynamics & Control, 21*(8–9), 1267–1321.

Brandimarte, P. (2006). *Numerical methods in finance and economics* (2nd ed.). Hoboken, NJ: John Wiley & Sons.

Brennan, M. J., & Schwartz, E. S. (1979). A continuous time approach to the pricing of bonds. *Journal of Banking and Finance, 3*(July), 133–155.

Brinson, G. P., Hood, R., & Beebower, G. L. (1995). Determinants of portfolio performance. *Financial Analysts Journal, 51*(1), 133–136.

Bryzgalova, S., Pelger, M., & Zhu, J. (2020). Forest through the trees: Building cross-sections of stock returns. *SSRN Electronic Journal*. https://doi.org/10.2139/ssrn.3493458

Bukowski, P. (2011). An introduction to quantitative equity investing. In F. J. Fabozzi & H. M. Markowitz (Eds.), *Equity valuation and portfolio management* (pp. 1–24). Hoboken, NJ: John Wiley & Sons.

Campbell, J. Y., LetLettau, M. L., Malkiel, B. G., & Xu, Y. (2001). Have individual stocks become more volatile? An empirical exploration of idiosyncratic risk. *Journal of Finance, 56*(1), 1–43.

Cantelli, F. P. (1933). Sulla determinazione empirica delle leggi di probabilità. *Giornale dell'Istituto Italiano degli Attuari. 4,* 421–424.

Canuel, D., & Melchreit, C. (1998). Total return analysis in CMO portfolio management. In F. Fabozzi (Ed.), *Advances in the valuation and management of mortgage-backed securities* (pp. 41–58). Hoboken, NJ: John Wiley & Sons.

Cao, J. J., Chen, J., Hull, J., & Poulos, Z. (2022). Deep learning for exotic option valuation. *Journal of Financial Data Science, 4*(1), 41–53.

Cao, L., Guan, L. K., & Jingqing, Z. (2006). Bond rating using support vector machine. *Intelligent Data Analysis, 10*(3), 285–296.

Carhart, M. (1997). On persistence in mutual fund performance. *Journal of Finance, 52*(1), 57–82.

Carino, D., & Ziemba, W. (1998). Formulation of the Russell-Yasuda Kasai financial planning model. *Operations Research, 46*(4), 433–449.

Carr, P. (1998). Randomizing and the American put. *Review of Financial Studies, 11*(3), 597–626.

Carr, P., Jarrow, R. A., & Myneni, R. (2008). Alternative characterizations of American put options. In R. A. Jarrow (Ed.), *Financial derivatives pricing: Selected works of Robert Jarrow* (pp. 85–103). Singapore: World Scientific Press.

Ceria, S., & Stubbs, R. (2006). Incorporating estimation errors into portfolio selection: Robust portfolio construction. *Journal of Asset Management, 7*(2), 109–127.

Chapados, N., & Bengio, Y. (2001). Cost functions and model combination for VaR-based asset allocation using neural networks. *IEEE Transactions on Neural Networks, 12*(4), 890–906.

Chen, N., Roll, R., & Ross, S. A. (1986). Economic forces and the stock market. *Journal of Business, 59*(July), 383–403.

Chen, R. R., Huang, J., Huang, W., & Yu, R. (2021). An artificial intelligence approach to the valuation of American-style derivatives: A use of particle swarm optimization. *Journal of Risk and Financial Management, 14*(2), 1–22.

Chen, W. -H., & Shih, J. -Y. (2006). A study of Taiwan's issuer credit rating systems using support vector machines. *Expert Systems with Applications, 30*(3), 427–435.

Chen, X., Sim, M., & Sun, P. (2007). A robust optimization perspective on stochastic programming. *Operations Research, 55*(6), 1058–1107.

Chewlow, L., & Strickland, C. (1998). *Implementing derivatives models*. Chichester, UK: John Wiley & Sons.

Chickering, D. M., & Heckerman, D. (n.d.). Fast learning from sparse data. Microsoft Research. Available at https://arxiv.org/ftp/arxiv/papers/1301/1301.6685.pdf.

Chopra, V. K., & Ziemba, W. T. (1993). The effect of errors in means, variances, and covariances on optimal portfolio choice. *Journal of Portfolio Management, 19*(2), 6–11.

Chow, G. (1960). Tests of equality between sets of coefficients in two linear regressions. *Econometrica, 28,* 591–605.

Chryssikou, E. (1998). *Multiperiod portfolio optimization in the presence of transaction costs.* PhD. thesis, Massachusetts Institute of Technology (MIT), Cambridge, MA.

Cochrane, J. H. (2011). Presidential address: Discount rates. *Journal of Finance, 66*(4), 1047–1108.

Consigli, G., & Dempster, M. A. H. (1998). Dynamic stochastic programming for asset-liability management. *Annals of Operations Research, 81*, 131–161.

Constantinides, G. (1983). Capital market equilibrium with personal taxes. *Econometrica, 51*, 611–636.

Cont, R. (2001). Empirical properties of asset returns: Stylized facts and statistical issues. *Quantitative Finance, 1*(2), 223–236.

Copeland, T., & Tufano, P. (2004). A real world way to manage real options. *Harvard Business Review, 82*(3), 90–99.

Coqueret, G., & Guida, T. (2018). Stock returns and the cross-section of characteristics: A tree-based approach. *SSRN Electronic Journal,* http://dx.doi.org/10.2139/ssrn.3169773.

Cornuejols, G., & Tutuncu, R. (2007). *Optimization methods in finance*. Cambridge: Cambridge University Press.

Cowden, C. F., Fabozzi, F. J., & Nazemi, A. (2019). Default prediction of commercial real estate properties using machine learning. *Journal of Portfolio Management, 45*(7), 55–67.

Cox, J. C., Ingersoll, J. E., & Ross, S. A. (1985). A theory of the term structure of interest rates. *Econometrica, 53*, 385–407.

Cox, J. C., Ross, S. A., & Rubinstein, M. (1979). Option pricing: A simplified approach. *Journal of Financial Economics, 7*(3), 229–263.

Cremers, J. H. M., Kritzman, M., & Page, S. (2003). *Portfolio formation with higher moments and plausible utility.* Revere Street Working Papers, November 22.

Cremers, J. H. M., Kritzman, M., & Page, S. (2005). Optimal hedge fund allocations: Do higher moments matter? *Journal of Portfolio Management, 31*(3), 70–81.

Dammon, R. M., & Spatt, C. S. (1996). The optimal trading and pricing of securities with asymmetric capital gains taxes and transaction costs. *Review of Financial Studies, 9*(3), 921–952.

Dammon, R. M., Spatt, C. S., & Zhang, H. H. (2001). Optimal consumption and investment with capital gains taxes. *Review of Financial Studies, 14*(3), 583–617.

Dammon, R. M., Spatt, C. S., & Zhang, H. H. (2004). Optimal asset location and allocation with taxable and tax-deferred investing. *Journal of Finance, 59*(3), 999–1037.

Danielsson, J., & Zigrand, J. -P. (2001). *What happens when you regulate risk? Evidence from a simple general equilibrium model.* [Memorandum]. London School of Economics.

Decimal Point Analytics. (2020). How asset managers are leveraging natural language processing (NLP) techniques. Available at https://decimalpointanalytics.medium.com/how-asset-managers-are-leveraging-natural-language-processing-nlp-techniques-b83aa91cf9dd.

DiBartolomeo, D. (2000). *Recent advances in management of taxable portfolios*. Working paper. Northfield Information Services, Boston.

Dijkstra, T. (1995). Pyrrho's Lemma, or have it your way. *Metrika: International Journal for Theoretical and Applied Statistics*, *42*(1), 119–125.

Ding, X., Zhang, T., Liu, T., & Duan, J. (2015). Deep learning for event-driven stock prediction. In *Proceedings of the 24th International Conference on Artificial Intelligence*, 2327–2333.

Disatnik, D., & Benninga, S. (2007). Shrinking the covariance matrix—simpler is better. *Journal of Portfolio Management, 33*(4), 56–63.

Dixit, A. K., & Pindyck, R. S. (1994). *Investment under uncertainty*. Princeton, NJ: Princeton University Press.

Dowd, K. (2005). *Measuring market risk* (2nd ed.). Hoboken, NJ: John Wiley & Sons.

Drikvandi, R., & Lawal, O. (2023). Sparse principal component analysis for natural language processing. *Annals of Data Science, 10*(1), 25–41.

Duffie, D., & Garleanu, N. (2001). Risk and valuation of collateralized debt obligations. *Financial Analysts Journal, 57*(1), 41–59.

Dykes, B. (2016). Actionable insights: The missing link between data and business value. *Forbes*. Available at https://www.forbes.com/sites/brentdykes/2016/04/26/actionable-insights-the-missing-link-between-data-and-business-value/?sh=6bae62e551e5.

Ekster, G., & Kolm, P. N. (2021). Alternative data in investment management: Usage, challenges, and valuation. *Journal of Financial Data Science, 3*(4), 10–32.

Episcopos, A., Pericli, A., & Hu, J. (1998). Commercial mortgage default: A comparison of logit with radial basis function networks. *Journal of Real Estate Finance and Economics, 17*(2), 163–178.

Evans, J. L., & Archer, S. H. (1968). Diversification and the reduction of dispersion: An empirical analysis. *Journal of Finance, 23*(5), 761–767.

Evans, J., & Olson, D. (2002). *Introduction to simulation and risk analysis* (2nd ed.). Upper Saddle River, NJ: Prentice Hall.

Evans, M. N., Hastings, N., & Peacock, B. (2000). *Statistical distributions* (3rd ed.). New York: John Wiley & Sons.

Fabozzi, F. J. (1993). *Fixed income mathematics*. New York: McGraw-Hill.

Fabozzi, F. J. (Ed.). (2005). *The handbook of mortgage-backed securities* (6th ed.). New York: McGraw-Hill.

Fabozzi, F. J. (2007). *Fixed income analysis* (2nd ed.). Hoboken, NJ: John Wiley & Sons.

Fabozzi, F. J. (2009). *Institutional investment management*. Hoboken, NJ: John Wiley & Sons.

Fabozzi, F. J., Bhattacharya, A. K., & Berliner, W. S. (2007). *Mortgage-backed securities: Products, structuring, and analytical techniques*. Hoboken, NJ: John Wiley & Sons.

Fabozzi, F. J., Focardi, S., & Kolm, P. (2006). *Financial modeling of the equity market*. Hoboken, NJ: John Wiley & Sons.

Fabozzi, F. J., Kolm, P., Pachamanova, D., & Focardi, S. (2007). *Robust portfolio optimization and management*. Hoboken, NJ: John Wiley & Sons.

Fama, E. F. (1965). Portfolio analysis in a stable Paretian market. *Management Science, 11*(3), 404–419.

Fama, E. F. (1970). Efficient capital markets: A review of theory and empirical work. *Journal of Finance, 25*(2), 383–417.

Fama, E. F., & French, K. (1993). Common risk factors in the returns on stocks and bonds. *Journal of Financial Economics, 33*, 3–56.

Fama, E. F., & French, K. (1995). Size and book-to-market factors in earnings and returns. *Journal of Finance, 50*(1), 131–155.

Fama, E. F., & French, K. (1996). Multifactor explanations of asset pricing anomalies. *Journal of Finance, 51*(1), 55–84.

Fama, E. F., & French, K. (1998). Value versus growth: The international evidence. *Journal of Finance, 53*(6), 1975–1999.

Fama, E. F., & French, K. R. (1992). The cross-section of expected stock returns. *Journal of Finance, 47*(2), 427–465.

Fama, E. F., & French, K. R. (2008). Dissecting anomalies. *Journal of Finance, 63*(4), 1653–1678.

Fama, E. F., & French, K. R. (2015). A five-factor asset pricing model. *Journal of Financial Economics, 116*(1), 1–22.

Faure, H. (1982). Discrépence de suites associées à′ un systéme de numération (en dimension un). *Acta Arithmetica, 41*, 337–351.

Feng, G., Giglio, S., & Xiu, D. (2020). Taming the factor zoo. *Journal of Finance, 75*(3), 1327–1370.

Fishburn, P. (1977). Mean-risk analysis with risk associated with below-target returns. *American Economic Review, 67*(2), 116–126.

Fishman, G. (2006). *A first course in Monte Carlo*. Stamford, CT: Thomson Learning.

Fong, H. G., & Vasicek, O. A. (1984). A risk minimizing strategy for portfolio immunization. *Journal of Finance, 30*(5), 1541–1546.

Fragniere, E., & Gondzio, J. (2005). Stochastic programming from modeling languages. In S. Wallace & W. Ziemba (Eds.), *Applications of stochastic programming* (pp. 95–114). Philadelphia: MPS-SIAM Series on Optimization.

Freund, R. (2004). *Lecture notes in nonlinear optimization*. [Unpublished manuscript] MIT Open CourseWare. Available at http://ocw.mit.edu/OcwWeb/Sloan-School-of-Management/15–084JSpring2004/LectureNotes /index.htm.

Freund, Y., & Schapire, R. E. (1997). A decision-theoretic generalization of on-line learning and an application to boosting. *Journal of Computer and System Sciences, 55*(1), 119–139.

Freyberger, J., Neuhierl, A., & Weber, M. (2020). Dissecting characteristics nonparametrically. *Review of Financial Studies, 33*(5), 2326–2377.

Ganguli, S., & Dunnmon, J. (2017). Machine learning for better models for predicting bond prices. Available at https://arxiv.org/abs/1705.01142.

Gauthier, L., & Goodman, L. S. (2003). Risk/return trade-offs on fixed income asset classes. In F. J. Fabozzi (Ed.), *Professional perspectives on fixed income portfolio management* (Vol. 4, pp. 1–16). Hoboken, NJ: John Wiley & Sons.

Geitgey, A. (2023). Natural language processing is fun! Available at https://medium.com/@ageitgey/natural -language-processing-is-fun-9a0bff37854e.

Glasserman, P. (2004). *Monte Carlo methods in financial engineering*. New York: Springer.

Glasserman, P., Heidelberger, P., & Shahabuddin, P. (2000). Variance reduction techniques for estimating value-at-risk. *Management Science, 46*(10), 1349–1364.

Glivenko, V. (1933). Sulla determinazione empirica delle leggi di probabilità. *Giornale dell'Istituto Italiano degli Attuari, 4*, 92–99.

Golbayani, P., Florescu, I., & Chatterjee, R. (2020). A comparative study of forecasting corporate credit ratings using neural networks, support vector machines, and decision trees. *North American Journal of Economics and Finance, 54*, Article 101251.

Goldfarb, D., & Iyengar, G. (2003). Robust portfolio selection problems. *Mathematics of Operations Research, 28*(1), 1–38.

Gordon, M. (1962). *The investment, financing, and valuation of the corporation*. Homewood, IL: Irwin.

Graham, J., & Harvey, C. R. (2002). How do CFOs make capital budgeting and capital structure decisions? *Journal of Applied Corporate Finance, 15*(1), 8–23.

Grinold, R., & Kahn, R. N. (1994). Multiple-factor models for portfolio risk. In E. Burmeister, R. Roll, & S. A. Ross (Eds.), *A practitioner's guide to arbitrage pricing theory* (pp. 59–79). Charlottesville, VA: Research Foundation of the Institute of Chartered Financial Analysts.

Gu, S., Kelly, B., & Xiu, D. (2020). Empirical asset pricing via machine learning. *Review of Financial Studies, 33*(5), 2223–2273.

Gulpinar, N., Rustem, B., & Settergren, R. (2004). Simulation and optimization approaches to scenario tree generation. *Journal of Economic Dynamics and Control, 28*(7), 1291–1315.

Gupta, F., & Eichhorn, D. (1998). Mean-variance optimization for practitioners of asset allocation. In F. J. Fabozzi (Ed.), *Handbook of portfolio management* (pp. 191–211). Hoboken, NJ: John Wiley & Sons.

Halton, J. (1960). On the efficiency of certain quasi-random sequences of points in evaluating multi-dimensional integrals. *Numerische Mathematik, 2*, 84–90.

Hammersley, J. (1960). Monte Carlo methods for solving multivariable problems. *Annals of the New York Academy of Sciences, 86*(3), 844–874.

Hanna, A. (2016). *Corporate bond default risk: Seeing the wood through the trees?* Technical Report. Queen's University Belfast, Northern Ireland.

Harvey, C. R., Liu, Y., & Zhu, H. (2016). . . . and the cross-section of expected returns. *Review of Financial Studies, 29*, 5–68.

Haug, E. (2007). *The complete guide to option pricing formulas* (2nd ed.). New York: McGraw-Hill.

Haugh, M., & Kogan, L. (2004). Pricing American options: A duality approach. *Operations Research, 52*(2), 258–270.

Hertz, D. B. (1964). Risk analysis in capital investment. *Harvard Business Review, 42*(1), 95–106.

Hilkmah, O. (2023). NLP tutorial—Text pre-processing techniques for beginners. Retrieved July 12, 2023, from https://www.freecodecamp.org/news/natural-language-processing-techniques-for-beginners/.

Hillier, R. S., & Eckstein, J. (1993). Stochastic dedication: Designing fixed income portfolios using massively parallel Benders decomposition. *Management Science, 39*(11), 1422–1438.

Ho, T. K. (1995). Random decision forests. In *Proceedings of 3rd International Conference on Document Analysis and Recognition* (Vol. 1, pp. 278–282). IEEE.

Ho, Thomas S. Y. (1999). Key rate duration: A measure of interest rate risk exposure. In S. Nawalkha & D. R. Chambers (Eds.), *Interest rate risk measurement and management*. New York: Institutional Investors.

Hoppe, R. (1998). VaR and the unreal world. *Risk*, July, 45–50.

Huang, C., & Litzenberger, R. (1988). *Foundations for financial economics*. Englewood Cliffs, NJ: Prentice Hall.

Huang, Z. H., Chen, C. -J., Hsu, W. -H., Chen, S., & Wu, S. (2004). Credit rating analysis with support vector machines and neural networks: A market comparative study. *Decision Support Systems, 37*(4), 543–558.

Huerta, R. F., Corbacho, F., & Elkan, C. (2013). Nonlinear support vector machines can systematically identify stocks with high and low future returns. *Algorithmic Finance, 2*, 45–58.

Hull, J. (2008). *Options, futures, and other derivatives* (7th ed.). Upper Saddle River, NJ: Prentice Hall.

Hutchinson, J. M., Lo, A. W., & Poggio, T. (1994). A nonparametric approach to pricing and hedging derivative securities via learning networks. *Journal of Finance, 49*(3), 851–889.

Ibbotson, R. G., & Kaplan, P. D. (2000). Does asset allocation policy explain 40%, 90%, or 100% of performance? *Financial Analysts Journal, 56*(1), 26–33.

Ingersoll, J., Jr. (1987). *Theory of financial decision making*. Savage, MD: Rowman and Littlefield.

Ivaşcu, C.-F. (2021). Option pricing using machine learning. *Expert Systems with Applications, 163*, 113799.

Jagannathan, N. A., & Bao, Q. (2022). Machine learning–based systematic investing in agency mortgage-backed securities. *Journal of Financial Data Science, 4*(4), 95–109.

Jamshidian, F., & Zhu, Y. (1997). Scenario simulation: Theory and methodology. *Finance and Stochastics, 1*, 43–67.

Jamshidian, F., & Zhu, Y. (2006). Scenario simulation model for fixed income portfolio risk management. In F. J. Fabozzi, L. Martellini, & P. Priaulet (Eds.), *Advanced bond portfolio management* (pp. 291–310). Hoboken, NJ: John Wiley & Sons.

Jean, W. H. (1971). The extension of portfolio analysis to three or more parameters. *Journal of Financial and Quantitative Analysis, 6*(1), 505–515.

Jegadeesh, N., & Titman, S. (1993). Returns to buying winners and selling losers: Implications for stock market efficiency. *Journal of Finance, 48*(1), 65–91.

Jones, R. C. (1998). The active versus passive debate: Perspectives on an active quant. In F. J. Fabozzi (Ed.), *Active equity portfolio management*. New York: John Wiley & Sons.

Jorion, P. (1986). Bayes-stein estimator for portfolio analysis. *Journal of Financial and Quantitative Analysis, 21*(3), 279–292.

Jorion, P. (1992). Portfolio optimization in practice. *Financial Analysts Journal, 48*(1), 68–74.

Kahneman, D., & Tversky, A. (1979). Prospect theory: An analysis of decision under risk. *Econometrica, 47*(2), 263–290.

Kalotay, A., Yang, D., & Fabozzi, F. J. (2004). An option-theoretic prepayment model for mortgages and mortgage-backed securities. *International Journal of Theoretical and Applied Finance, 7*(December), 949–978.

Kalvelagen, E. (2003). *Benders decomposition for stochastic programming with GAMS.* [Paper, January 17]. Available at http://www.amsterdamoptimization.com/pdf/stochbenders.pdf.

Keynes, J. M. (1921). *Treatise on probability.* New York: Macmillan.

Khodadadi, A., Tutuncu, R., & Zangari, P. (2006). Optimization and quantitative investment management. *Journal of Asset Management, 7*(2), 83–92.

Kim, J. -M., Kim, D. H., & Jung, H. (2021). Applications of machine learning for corporate bond yield spread forecasting. *North American Journal of Economics and Finance, 58*(10), 101540.

Kim, W. C., Kim, J. H., & Fabozzi, F. J. (2016). *Robust equity portfolio management.* Hoboken, NJ: John Wiley & Sons.

Knight, F. (1921). *Risk, uncertainty, and profit.* New York: Houghton Mifflin.

Kolanovic, M., & Smith, R. (2017). Big data and AI strategies. J.P. Morgan. Available at https://cpb-us-e2.wpmucdn.com/faculty.sites.uci.edu/dist/2/51/files/2018/05/JPM-2017-MachineLearningInvestments.pdf.

Kolm, P. N., & Purushothaman, S. (2022). Systematic pricing and trading of municipal bonds. *Journal of Financial Data Science, 4*(1), 87–100.

Konno, H., & Yamazaki, H. (1991). Mean-absolute deviation portfolio optimization model and its applications to the Tokyo stock market. *Management Science, 37*(5), 519–531.

Kopcso, D., & Pachamanova, D. (2017). Case article—business value in integrating predictive and prescriptive analytics models. *INFORMS Transactions on Education.* Available at https://pubsonline.informs.org/doi/pdf/10.1287/ited.2017.0186ca.

Kuss, O. (2002). Global goodness-of-fit tests in logistic regression with sparse data. *Statistics in Medicine, 21*(24): 3789–3801.

Kwon, Y. S., & Lim, S. (1998). Performance comparison of machine learning approaches to bond rating. In *IEEE International Conference on Systems, Man, and Cybernetics.*

Ledoit, O., & Wolf, M. (2003). Improved estimation of the covariance matrix of stock returns with an application to portfolio selection. *Journal of Empirical Finance, 10*(5), 603–621.

Lee, J. -H., Stefek, D., & Zhelenyak, A. (2006). *Robust portfolio optimization—A closer look* Report. MSCI Barra Research Insights, June. New York: MSCI Barra.

Lee, Y. -C. (2007). Application of support vector machines to corporate credit rating prediction. *Expert Systems with Applications, 33*(1), 67–74.

Leung, E. H., Lohre, D., Mischlich, Y., Shea, M., & Stroh, M. (2021). The promises and pitfalls of machine learning for predicting stock returns. *Journal of Financial Data Science, 3*(2), 21–50.

Levi, Y., & Welch, I. (2014). *Long-term capital budgeting.* Working paper. University of California, Los Angeles.

Levy, H. (1992). Stochastic dominance and expected utility: Survey and analysis. *Management Science, 38*(4), 555–593.

Levy, H., & Kroll, Y. (1978). Ordering uncertain options with borrowing and lending. *Journal of Finance, 33*(2), 553–574.

Levy, H., & Markowitz, H. M. (1979). Approximating expected utility by a function of mean and variance. *American Economic Review, 69*(3), 308–317.

Liew, J., & Budavari, T. (2017). The "sixth" factor—A social media factor derived directly from tweet sentiments. *The Journal of Portfolio Management, 43*(3), 102–111.

Lintner, J. (1965). The valuation of risk assets and the selection of risky investments in stock portfolios and capital budgets. *Review of Economics and Statistics, 47*(1), 13–37.

Litterman, R., & Scheinkman, J. (1991). Common factors affecting bond returns. *Journal of Fixed Income, 1*(1), 54–61.

Liu, S., Oosterlee, C. W., & Bohte, S. M. (2019). Pricing options and computing implied volatilities using neural networks. *Risks, 7* (1), 1–22.

Ljungqvist, L., & Sargent, T. J. (2004). *Recursive macroeconomic theory.* Cambridge, MA: MIT Press.

Lo, A. W. (2004). The adaptive markets hypothesis. *Journal of Portfolio Management, 30*(5), 15–29.

Lo, A. W., & MacKinlay, A. C. (1988). Stock market prices do not follow random walks: Evidence from a simple specification test. *Review of Financial Studies, 1*(1), 41–66.

Lo, A. W., Mamaysky, H., & Wang, J. (2000). Foundations of technical analysis: Computational algorithms, statistical inference, and empirical implementation. *Journal of Finance, 55*(4), 1705–1765.

Lo, A. W., & Mueller, P. (2010). Warning: Physics envy may be hazardous to your wealth! *Journal of Investment Management, 8*(2), 13–63.

Lobo, M. S., Fazel, M., & Boyd, S. (2007). Portfolio optimization with linear and fixed transaction costs. *Annals of Operations Research, 152* (1), 376–394.

Lohre, H., Rother, C., & Theissen, E. (2014). Robustness and information content of the roll model. *Review of Derivatives Research, 17*(2), 201–228.

Longstaff, F. A., & Schwartz, E. S. (1992). Interest rate volatility and the term structure: A two-factor general equilibrium model. *Journal of Finance, 47*(4): 1259–1282.

Longstaff, F. A., & Schwartz, E. S. (2001). Valuing American options by simulation: A simple least-squares approach. *Review of Financial Studies, 14*(1), 113–147.

Lopez, H. (1999). The use of mean-variance analysis in investment decisions. *Journal of Portfolio Management, 25*(4), 85–90.

Lòpez de Prado, M. (2016). Building diversified portfolios that outperform out of sample. *Journal of Portfolio Management, 42,* 56–69.

Lowry, M., & Schwert, G. W. (2002). IPO market cycles: Bubbles or sequential learning? *Journal of Finance, 57*(3), 1173–1200.

Lucca, D. O., & Moench, E. (2015). The pre-FOMC announcement drift. *Journal of Finance, 70*(1), 329–371.

Luciano, E., & Schoutens, W. (2006). A multivariate jump-driven financial asset model. *Quantitative Finance, 6*(5), 385–402.

Luenberger, D. (1998). *Investment science.* Oxford: Oxford University Press.

Luo, X., & Yao, T. (2005). Clustering analysis in portfolio management. *Journal of Asset Management, 6*(1), 65–77.

Lütkepohl, H. (2005). *New introduction to multiple time series analysis.* Berlin: Springer-Verlag.

Lynch, A. W., & Musto, D. K. (2003). How investors interpret past fund returns. *Journal of Finance, 58*(5), 2033–2058.

Mackenzie, P., & Spears, T. G. (2002). The long-run benefits of diversification. *Journal of Financial Planning, 15*(6), 42–50.

MacKinlay, A. C. (1995). Multifactor models do not explain deviations from the CAPM. *Journal of Financial Economics, 38*(1), 3–28.

MacQueen, J., & Thorley, S. (1996). The persistence of volatility and stock market fluctuations. *American Economic Review, 86*(5), 1134–1154.

Maddala, G. S., & Kim, I-M. (1998). *Unit roots, cointegration, and structural change.* Cambridge: Cambridge University Press.

Madhavan, A. N. (2000). Market mechanisms in securities trading. *Journal of Finance, 55*(5), 2557–2589.

Maginn, J. L., & Tuttle, D. L. (eds.). (1990). *Managing investment portfolios: A dynamic process* (2nd ed.). New York: Warren, Gorham, & Lamont.

Mai, F., Tian, S., Lee, C., & Ma, L. (2019). Deep learning models for bankruptcy prediction using textual disclosures. *European Journal of Operational Research, 274*(2), 743–758.

Maio, P., & Santa-Clara, P. (2012). Multifactor models and their consistency with the ICAPM. *Journal of Financial Economics, 106*(3), 586–613.

Malhotra, N. (1987). Analyzing marketing research data with incomplete information on the dependent variable. *Journal of Marketing Research, 24*(1), 74–84.

Malz, A. M. (2011). Financial risk management: Models, history, and institutions. *Financial Analysts Journal, 67*(6), 30–55.

Mandelbrot, B. (1963). The variation of certain speculative prices. *Journal of Business, 36*(4), 394–419.

Mansuy, R. (2005). The origins of financial mathematics. *Proceedings of the American Mathematical Society, 133*(6), 2409–2418.

Marinov, S. (2019). Natural language processing in finance: Shakespeare without the monkeys. Man Institute, New York. Retrieved from https://www.man.com/maninstitute/shakespeare-without-the-monkeys.

Markowitz, H. M. (1952). Portfolio selection. *Journal of Finance, 7*(1), 77–91.

Markowitz, H. M. (1959). Portfolio selection: Efficient diversification of investments. *Journal of Finance, 7*(1), 77–91.

Maronna, R. A., Martin, R. D., Yohai, V. J., & Salibián-Barrera, M. (2019). *Robust statistics: Theory and methods (with R)*. Hoboken, NJ: John Wiley & Sons.

Marquering, W., & Verbeek, M. (2004). The economic value of fundamental and technical information in emerging currency markets. *Journal of International Money and Finance, 23*(4), 561–581.

Marshall, A. (1920). *Principles of economics* (8th ed.). London: Macmillan and Co., Ltd.

Martin, G. S., & Simin, T. T. (2003). Out-of-sample stock return predictability and the data-snooping bias. *Review of Financial Studies, 16*(1), 209–233.

Martinez, V. H., & Rosu, I. (2013). High-frequency traders, news, and volatility. *Journal of Financial and Quantitative Analysis, 48*(1), 219–244.

Mason, R., & Merton, R. C. (1985). The role of contingent claims analysis in corporate finance. In E. I. Altman & M. G. Subrahmanyam (Eds.), *Recent Advances in Corporate Finance* (pp. 7–54). Homewood, IL: Richard D. Irwin.

Massa, M., & Simonov, A. (2005). Behavioral biases and investment. *Review of Finance, 9*(4), 483–507.

Masson, R. (1998). Stock market volatility and the information content of stock index options. *Journal of Econometrics, 94*(1), 3–26.

Matsumoto, D., & Nishimura, T. (1998). Mersenne twister: A 623-dimensionally equidistributed uniform pseudo-random number generator. *ACM Transactions on Modeling and Computer Simulation, 8*(1), 3–30.

Mayer, C. J. (1990). Financial innovations in international financial markets. *Journal of International Money and Finance, 9*(1), 25–48.

Mayhew, S. (2002). The impact of derivatives on cash markets: What have we learned? *Journal of Financial Markets, 5*(3), 197–228.

McConnell, P., & Musalem, A. R. (1995). Modern portfolio theory: The principles of investment management. *Finance and Development, 32*(1), 10–12.

McCracken, P. M. (2001). Robust control of forward-looking models. *Journal of Economic Dynamics and Control, 25*(8), 1179–1195.

McDonald, R. L. (2009). *Derivatives markets* (2nd ed.). Boston: Addison Wesley.

McGrattan, E. R., & Prescott, E. C. (2005). Taxes, regulations, and asset prices. *Federal Reserve Bank of Minneapolis Quarterly Review, 29*(1), 1–14.

McLean, R. D., Pontiff, J. (2016). Does academic research destroy stock return predictability? *Journal of Finance, 71*(1), 5–32.

McLeish, D. L. (2005). *Monte Carlo simulation andfinance*. Hoboken, NJ: John Wiley & Sons.

McMillan, D. (2004). Stock return predictability and the role of monetary policy. *Journal of Finance, 59*(5), 1953–1972.

McWilliams, T., & Siegel, S. (2000). Stock performance and intermediation changes surrounding sustained increases in disclosure. *Contemporary Accounting Research, 17*(3), 485–520.

Mehra, R., & Prescott, E. C. (1985). The equity premium: A puzzle. *Journal of Monetary Economics, 15*(2), 145–161.

Meier, I., & Schaumburg, E. (2001). Do funds managers have stock-picking skills? *Journal of Finance, 56*(3), 1059–1080.

Melnikov, A. (2001). Risk analysis and assessment in network environments: A dyadic case study. *Review of Financial Studies, 14*(2), 285–307.

Menkhoff, L., & Taylor, M. P. (2007). The obstinate passion of foreign exchange professionals: Technical analysis. *Journal of Economic Literature, 45*(4), 936–972.

Merton, R. C. (1973). Theory of rational option pricing. *Bell Journal of Economics and Management Science, 4*(1), 141–183.

Merton, R. C. (1974). On the pricing of corporate debt: The risk structure of interest rates. *Journal of Finance, 29*(2), 449–470.

Merton, R. C. (1990). *Continuous-time finance.* Cambridge, MA: Blackwell.

Merton, R. C. (1995). Financial innovation and the management and regulation of financial institutions. *Journal of Banking & Finance, 19*(3–4), 461–481.

Metrick, A., & Yasuda, A. (2011). Venture capital and the finance of innovation. *Journal of Financial Economics, 111*(1), 1–21.

Meyersson Milgrom, E. M., & Roberts, J. (1992). *Economics, organization, and management.* Englewood Cliffs, NJ: Prentice Hall.

Miles, D., & Timmermann, A. (1996). Variance bounds tests and stock price valuation models. *Journal of Political Economy, 104*(6), 1079–1102.

Miller, M. H., & Modigliani, F. (1961). Dividend policy, growth, and the valuation of shares. *Journal of Business, 34*(4), 411–433.

Miller, M. H., & Rock, K. (1985). Dividend policy under asymmetric information. *Journal of Finance, 40*(4), 1031–1051.

Minsky, H. P. (1977). The financial instability hypothesis: An interpretation of Keynes and an alternative to "standard" theory. *Nebraska Journal of Economics and Business, 16*(1), 5–16.

Mishkin, F. S. (1995). Symposium on the monetary transmission mechanism. *Journal of Economic Perspectives, 9*(4), 3–10.

Mitchell, J. B., & Mulherin, J. H. (1994). The impact of public information on the stock market. *Journal of Finance, 49*(3), 923–950.

Mitchell, J. E., & Braun, S. (2004). *Rebalancing an investment portfolio in the presence of convex transaction costs.* Technical report, Department of Mathematical Sciences, Rensselaer Polytechnic Institute, Troy, NY.

Modigliani, F., & Miller, M. H. (1958). The cost of capital, corporation finance and the theory of investment. *American Economic Review, 48*(3), 261–297.

Mohanty, S. (2000). Bivariate option pricing with copulas. *Applied Mathematical Finance, 7*(1), 81–93.

Moles, P., & Terry, N. (1997). *The handbook of international financial terms.* Oxford: Oxford University Press.

Montgomery, D. C., Peck, E. A., & Vining, G. G. (2012). *Introduction to linear regression analysis* (5th ed.). Hoboken, NJ: John Wiley & Sons.

Moody's Investors Service. (2000). Historical default rates of corporate bond issuers, 1920–1999. *Moody's Investors Service Global Credit Research Report.*

Moore, M. J. (1986). Inflation illusion and stock prices. *American Economic Review, 76*(3), 326–340.

Morck, R., Shleifer, A., & Vishny, R. W. (1988). Management ownership and market valuation: An empirical analysis. *Journal of Financial Economics, 20*(1–2), 293–315.

Moreira, A., & Muir, T. (2017). Volatility-managed portfolios. *Journal of Finance, 72*(4), 1611–1644.

Morgan, J. P. (1997). *RiskMetrics—technical document.* New York: Morgan Guaranty Trust Company.

Moro, B. (1995). The full Monte risk. *Risk, 8*(2), 57–58.

Morris, S., & Shin, H. S. (2002). Social value of public information. *American Economic Review, 92*(5), 1521–1534.

Mossin, J. (1966). Equilibrium in a capital asset market. *Econometrica, 34*(4), 768–783.

Muller, P., & Watson, M. (2016). Low-frequency econometrics. *Review of Economic Studies, 83*(2), 649–667.

Mulvey, J., Vanderbei, R., & Zenios, S. (1995). Robust optimization of large-scale systems. *Operations Research*, *43*(2), 264–281.

Mundell, R. (1963). Capital mobility and stabilization policy under fixed and flexible exchange rates. *Canadian Journal of Economics and Political Science, 29*(4), 475–485.

Murphy, J. J. (1999). *Technical analysis of the financial markets: A comprehensive guide to trading methods and applications.* New York: New York Institute of Finance.

Murray, M. (1994). A drift from randomness in prices: Evidence and implications. *Journal of Finance, 49*(5), 1535–1549.

Myers, S. C., & Majluf, N. S. (1984). Corporate financing and investment decisions when firms have information that investors do not have. *Journal of Financial Economics, 13*(2), 187–221.

Nakamura, L. I., & Small, D. H. (1999). The rise and fall of bank control in the United States: 1890–1939. *American Economic Review, 89*(5), 1077–1093.

Narayanan, M. P. (1985). Challenges and opportunities in the new financial environment: A report on the fourth international conference on finance. *Journal of Banking and Finance, 28*(11), 2773–2781.

Nasir, M. A., & Redfern, R. (1999). Predicting stock returns in an emerging market: The case of Malaysia. *Journal of Financial and Quantitative Analysis, 34*(4), 159–174.

Natarajan, K., Pachamanova, D., & Sim, M. (2008). Incorporating asymmetry into portfolio optimization. *Management Science, 54*(3), 501–516.

Nazemi, A., Baumann, F., & Fabozzi, F. J. (2022). Intertemporal defaulted bond recoveries prediction via machine learning. *European Journal of Operational Research, 297*(3), 1162–1177.

Nazemi, A., Heidenreich, K., & Fabozzi, F. J. (2018). Improving corporate bond recovery rate prediction using multi-factor support vector regressions. *European Journal of Operational Research, 271*(2), 664–675.

Neely, C., & Weller, P. (2001). Technical analysis and central bank intervention. *Journal of International Money and Finance, 20*(7), 949–970.

Nelson, C. R., & Plosser, C. I. (1982). Trends and random walks in macroeconomic time series. *Journal of Monetary Economics, 10*(2), 139–162.

Newey, W. K., & West, K. D. (1987). A simple, positive semi-definite, heteroskedasticity and autocorrelation consistent covariance matrix. *Econometrica, 55*(3), 703–708.

Ng, V. K. (1991). Model specification and econometric assessment of the forward and futures foreign exchange rates. *Journal of Finance, 46*(2), 683–699.

Nguyen, N., & Cogger, K. O. (1992). Foreign exchange exposure and management practices in Australian multinationals. *Journal of International Business Studies, 23*(3), 467–489.

Nicholson, S. F., & Snyder, C. M. (2008). *Microeconomic theory: Basic principles and extensions*. South-Western Cengage Learning.

Nightingale, P. (2000). Econometric modelling of non-linear relationships: A study of growth theories. *Journal of Applied Econometrics, 15*(3), 275–292.

Nikolova, B., & Wilkens, S. (2012). Analyzing market risk and performance: Modern techniques for financial institutions. *Journal of Risk Finance, 13*(4), 321–335.

Nohel, T., & Tarhan, V. (1998). Share repurchase and firm performance: New evidence on the agency costs of free cash flow. *Journal of Financial Economics, 49*(2), 187–222.

Noronha, G., & Sarin, A. (1997). The recovery of information from multiperiod securities. *Journal of Finance, 52*(2), 507–528.

Novy-Marx, R. (2012). Is momentum really momentum? *Journal of Financial Economics, 103*, 429–453.

O'Cinneide, C., Scherer, B., & Xu, X. (2006). Pooling trades in a quantitative investment process. *Journal of Portfolio Management, 32* (4), 33–43.

Odean, T. (1998). Volume, volatility, price, and profit when all traders are above average. *Journal of Finance, 53*(6), 1887–1934.

O'Hara, M. (1995). *Market microstructure theory*. Oxford, UK: Blackwell Publishers.

O'Hara, M., & Oldfield, G. S. (1986). The microeconomics of market making. *Journal of Financial and Quantitative Analysis, 21*(4), 361–376.

Olsen, R. A., & Cox, C. C. (2001). The influence of equity valuation on the behavior of stock returns. *Journal of Financial and Quantitative Analysis, 36*(3), 357–377.

Opler, T., Pinkowitz, L., Stulz, R., & Williamson, R. (1999). The determinants and implications of corporate cash holdings. *Journal of Financial Economics, 52*(1), 3–46.

Ou, J. A., & Penman, S. H. (1989). Financial statement analysis and the prediction of stock returns. *Journal of Accounting and Economics, 11*(4), 295–329.

Pachamanova, D. A., & Fabozzi, F. J. (2016). *Portfolio management: Construction and analysis*. Hoboken, NJ: John Wiley & Sons.

Pagano, M. S., & Schwartz, R. A. (2003). A closing call's impact on market quality at Euronext Paris. *Journal of Financial Economics, 68*(3), 439–484.

Pan, Y., & Poteshman, A. M. (2006). The information in option volume for future stock prices. *Review of Financial Studies, 19*(3), 871–908.

Panda, B., & Narasimhan, V. (1997). Goals, constraints, and asset allocation. *Journal of Portfolio Management, 23*(2), 76–86.

Pantzalis, C., & Park, J. C. (2000). Stock market volatility and the information content of stock index options. *Journal of Economics and Business, 52*(5), 467–508.

Park, H., Kim, N., & Lee, J. (2014). Parametric models and non-parametric machine learning models for predicting option prices: Empirical comparison study over KOSPI 200 Index options. *Expert Systems with Applications, 41*(11), 5227–5237.

Park, J. H., & Stulz, R. M. (2000). Stock market volatility and learning. *Journal of Finance, 55*(5), 1749–1787.

Park, S., Lee, J., & Son, Y. (2016). Predicting market impact costs using nonparametric machine learning models. *PLOS One, 11*, 1–13.

Parsons, J. E., & Gotlieb, D. (2004). The science of financial market trading. *Management Science, 50*(3), 327–343.

Pascual, L., Romo, J., & Ruiz, E. (2006). Bootstrap prediction for returns and volatilities in financial markets. *Journal of Econometrics, 133*(2), 267–287.

Patell, J. M., & Wolfson, M. A. (1984). The intraday speed of adjustment of stock prices to earnings and dividend announcements. *Journal of Financial Economics, 13*(2), 223–252.

Paulson, A. S., Holcomb, J. G., & Leitch, R. A. (1997). Modeling time-varying risk premia in the market for large block transactions. *Journal of Financial and Quantitative Analysis, 32*(2), 237–255.

Pavlova, A., & Rigobon, R. (2007). Asset prices and exchange rates. *Review of Financial Studies, 20*(4), 1139–1180.

Payne, R., & Vitale, P. (2003). A transaction level study of the effects of central bank intervention on exchange rates. *Journal of International Economics, 61*(2), 331–352.

Pearson, N. D., & Sun, T. (1994). Exploiting the conditional density in estimating the term structure: An application to the Cox, Ingersoll, and Ross model. *Journal of Finance, 49*(4), 1279–1304.

Peck, A. E. (1996). *Market making and the changing structure of the securities industry.* Lexington, MA: Lexington Books.

Pedersen, L. H. (2009). When everyone runs for the exit. *International Journal of Central Banking, 5*(4), 177–199.

Peirson, G., & Bird, R. (1974). The capital asset pricing model and real-world capital market performance. *Journal of Financial and Quantitative Analysis, 9*(3), 365–381.

Peng, L., & Xion: (2003). Information in prices about future earnings: Implications for earnings response coefficients. *Journal of Accounting and Economics, 35*(1), 321–349.

Perold, A. F., & Salomon, R. S. (1991). The right amount of assets under management. *Financial Analysts Journal, 47*(3), 31–39.

Petersen, M. A. (2009). Estimating standard errors in finance panel data sets: Comparing approaches. *Review of Financial Studies, 22*(1), 435–480.

Peterson, D. R., & Peterson, P. P. (1994). Stock return adjustments to news: The case of stock splits. *Journal of Finance, 49*(3), 1023–1037.

Phillips, P. C. B., & Perron, P. (1988). Testing for a unit root in time series regression. *Biometrika, 75*(2), 335–346.

Phoa, W. (2021). Empirical yield-curve dynamics and yield-curve exposure. In F. J. Fabozzi (Ed.), *Handbook of fixed income securities* (9th ed., pp. 743–475). New York: McGraw-Hill.

Pindyck, R. S. (1988). Risk, inflation, and the stock market. *American Economic Review, 78*(3), 335–351.

Pinkowitz, L., Stulz, R., & Williamson, R. (1997). Does the stock market undervalue firms with a lot of cash? *Journal of Financial Economics, 39*(1), 297–333.

Piotroski, J. D. (2000). Value investing: The use of historical financial statement information to separate winners from losers. *Journal of Accounting Research, 38*(Suppl), 1–41.

Pogue, G. (1970). An extension of the Markowitz portfolio selection model to include variable transactions costs, short sales, leverage policies, and taxes. *Journal of Finance, 25*(5), 1005–1027.

Polk, C., & Sapienza, P. (2009). The stock market and corporate investment: A test of catering theory. *Review of Financial Studies, 22*(1), 187–217.

Poon, S. -H., & Granger, C. W. (2003). Forecasting volatility in financial markets: A review. *Journal of Economic Literature, 41*(2), 478–539.

Porter, M. E. (1985). Competitive advantage. *Journal of Business Strategy, 5*(2), 60–78.

Poteshman, A. M., & Serbin, V. (2003). Clearly irrational financial market behavior: Evidence from the early exercise of exchange-traded stock options. *Journal of Finance, 58*(1), 37–70.

Presto, C., & Schwartz, A. (1994). The long-term impacts of bank lending rates on housing markets. *Journal of Money, Credit, and Banking, 26*(3), 540–555.

Provost, F., & Fawcett. T. (2013). *Data science for business: What you need to know about data mining and data-analytic thinking.* Sebastopol, CA: O'Reilly Media.

Pulvino, T. C. (1998). Do asset fire sales exist? An empirical investigation of commercial aircraft transactions. *Journal of Finance, 53*(3), 939–978.

Pyun, C. S., & Peterson, D. R. (2000). Stock market liberalization and the information environment. *Journal of Financial Economics, 58*(3), 529–564.

Qi, M., & Zhao, X. (2011). Unobservable investment and the puzzling US boom in the 1990s. *Journal of Monetary Economics, 58*(1), 67–89.

Quinn, D. P., & Woolley, S. (2001). Democracy and national economic performance: The preference for stability. *American Journal of Political Science, 45*(3), 634–657.

Rabinovitch, R. (1989). Inflation and rent-seeking: An extension of the theory of collective action. *Journal of Political Economy, 97*(6), 1236–1252.

Radcliffe, R. C. (1994). *Diversification, cointegration, and hedge ratios: A new approach*. Greenwich, CT: JAI Press.

Rafferty, M., & Hsiao, C. (1993). Dividend yields and expected stock returns: Alternative procedures for inference and measurement. *Review of Financial Studies, 6*(3), 507–537.

Raman, N., & Leidner, J. L. (2018). Municipal bond pricing: A data driven method. *International Journal of Financial Studies, 6*(3), 80.

Ramirez, C. D. (1995). Did J. P. Morgan's men add liquidity? Corporate investment, cash flow, and financial structure at the turn of the twentieth century. *Journal of Finance, 50*(2), 661–678.

Ramsay, J. O. (2002). When the price is right: How stock prices reflect macroeconomic and firm-specific fundamentals. *Journal of Accounting and Economics, 34*(1–3), 3–31.

Rashid, A. (1998). Stock prices and exchange rates: Are they related? Evidence from emerging financial markets. *Journal of Banking and Finance, 22*(5), 781–803.

Reinhart, C. M., & Rogoff, K. S. (2008). *This time is different: Eight centuries of financial folly*. Princeton, NJ: Princeton University Press.

Rendleman, R., & Bartter, B. (1979). Two-state option pricing. *Journal of Finance, 34*, 1093–1110.

Rey, H. (2001). International trade and finance: New front the CAPM and stock selection models. *Journal of International Economics, 53*(2), 221–239.

Reyes, M. G. (1997). Capacity constraints, asymmetries, and the business cycle. *Review of Economic Studies, 64*(4), 525–542.

Rhoads, S. A. (2005). *The economist's view of the world: Governments, markets, and public policy*. Cambridge: Cambridge University Press.

Richard, S., & Roll, R. (1989). Prepayment and the valuation of mortgage-backed securities. *Journal of Portfolio Management, 15*, 73–82.

Richards, A. J. (1997). Winner-loser reversals in national stock market indices: Can they be explained? *Journal of Finance, 52*(5), 2129–2144.

Richardson, S., & Stock, J. H. (1989). Drawing conclusions from cross-country comparisons of economic aggregates. *Journal of Monetary Economics, 24*(3), 233–258.

Ritter, J. R. (1991). The long-term performance of initial public offerings. *Journal of Finance, 46*(1), 3–27.

Robbins, H., & Monro, S. (1951). A stochastic approximation method. *Annals of Mathematical Statistics, 22*(3), 400–407.

Roberts, H. V. (1967). Statistical versus clinical prediction of the stock market. *Management Science, 12*(5), 112–137.

Roberts, M. E., Stewart, B. M., Tingley, D., & Airold, E. M. (2013). The structural topic model and applied social science. In *Advances in Neural Information Processing Systems Workshop on Topic Models: Computation, application, and evaluation* (Vol. 4, pp. 1–20).

Robinson, J. (1952). The generalization of the general theory. In *The rate of interest and other essays* (pp. 67–142). London: Macmillan.

Robinson, M. (2005). Return to reason: The implications of high-frequency trading for security prices. *Review of Financial Studies, 18*(4), 1185–1216.

Rockafellar, R. T., & Uryasev. S. (2000). Optimization of conditional value-at-risk. *Journal of Risk, 3*: 21–41.

Rockafellar, R. T., & Uryasev. S. (2002). Conditional value-at-risk for general loss distributions. *Journal of Banking and Finance, 26*: 1443–1471.

Rodrik, D. (1998). Why do more open economies have bigger governments? *Journal of Political Economy, 106*(5), 997–1032.

Rogers, L. C. G. (2002). Monte Carlo valuation of American options. *Mathematical Finance, 12*, 271–286.

Rogers, L. C. G., & Satchell, S. E. (1991). Estimating variance from high, low and closing prices. *Annals of Applied Probability, 1*(4), 504–512.

Romer, P. M. (1986). Increasing returns and long-run growth. *Journal of Political Economy, 94*(5), 1002–1037.

Rosenberg, B. (1974). Extra-market components of covariance in security returns. *Journal of Financial and Quantitative Analysis*, *9*(2): 263–274.

Rosengren, E. S. (1993). Nonbank financial intermediation: Evidence from the commercial paper market. *Journal of Financial Economics, 33*(1), 195–213.

Ross, S. A. (1976). The arbitrage theory of capital asset pricing. *Journal of Economic Theory, 13*(3), 341–360.

Ross, S. A. (1989). Information and volatility: The no-arbitrage martingale approach to timing and resolution irrelevancy. *Journal of Finance, 44*(1), 1–17.

Rostek, M. (2010). Quantile maximization in decision theory. *Review of Economic Studies, 77*(1), 339–371.

Rotemberg, J. J., & Saloner, G. (1989). A supergame-theoretic model of business cycles and price wars during booms. *American Economic Review, 79*(3), 390–407.

Rouwenhorst, K. G. (1995). Asset pricing implications of equilibrium business cycle models. In *Frontiers of business cycle research* (pp. 294–330). Princeton, NJ: Princeton University Press.

Roy, A. D. (1952). Safety first and the holding of assets. *Econometrica, 20*(3), 431–449.

Rubinstein, M. (1973). A mean-variance synthesis of corporate financial theory. *Journal of Finance, 28*(1), 167–181.

Rubin, D. B. (1976). Inference and missing data. *Biometrika, 63*(3), 581–592.

Rudd, A. (1980). Optimal selection of passive portfolios. *Financial Management, 9*(1), 57–66.

Russell, S. J., & Norvig, P. (2016). *Artificial intelligence: A modern approach* (3rd. ed.). Upper Saddle River, NJ: Prentice Hall.

Russo, J. E., & Schoemaker, P. J. H. (1989). *Decision traps: Ten barriers to brilliant decision-making and how to overcome them.* New York: Simon and Schuster.

Ruszczynski, A., & Shapiro, A. (2003). *Stochastic programming.* Amsterdam: Elsevier Science.

Ryan, S. G. (1997). *Financial instruments and institutions: Accounting and disclosure rules.* Hoboken, NJ: Wiley Finance.

Sahlman, W. A. (1990). The structure and governance of venture-capital organizations. *Journal of Financial Economics, 27*(2), 473–521.

Saito, M. (2003). Smoothing the yield curve. *Journal of Financial and Quantitative Analysis, 38*(3), 887–902.

Saket, S. (2022). *Count vectorizer vs TFIDF vectorizer (sklearn)—NLP.* Retrieved from https://iamgeekydude.com/2022/12/16/count-vectorizer-vs-tfidf-vectorizer-sklearn-nlp/.

Salomon Brothers. (1989). *Salomon guide to mortgage-backed and asset-backed securities.* Hoboken, NJ: Wiley Finance.

Samuelson, P. A. (1965). Proof that properly anticipated prices fluctuate randomly. *Industrial Management Review, 6*(2), 41–49.

Sandroni, A. (2000). Do markets favor agents able to make accurate predictions? *Econometrica, 68*(6), 1303–1341.

Santos, T., & Veronesi, P. (2006). Labor income and predictable stock returns. *Review of Financial Studies, 19*(1), 1–44.

Sarin, A., & Shastri, K. (1989). The informational content of option volumes prior to takeovers. *Journal of Business, 62*(3), 369–382.

Satchell, S. E., & Timmermann, A. (1995). An assessment of the economic value of non-linear foreign exchange rate forecasts. *Journal of Forecasting, 14*(5), 477–497.

Schaefer, S. M., & Strebulaev, I. A. (2008). Structural models of credit risk are useful: Evidence from hedge ratios on corporate bonds. *Journal of Financial Economics, 90*(1), 1–19.

Scherer, B. (2002). Portfolio resampling: Review and critique. *Financial Analysts Journal, 58*(6), 98–109.

Schiller, R. J., & Schneider, R. (1998). Labor income and predictable stock returns. *Review of Financial Studies, 11*(1), 23–63.

Schinasi, G. J. (2000). *Defining financial stability.* IMF Working Paper WP/00/81. International Monetary Fund, Washington, DC.

Schleifer, A., & Summers, L. (1990). The noise trader approach to finance. *Journal of Economic Perspectives, 4*(2), 19–33.

Schmidt, L. (1992). Stockholder's returns and the cost of complexity. *Journal of Financial and Quantitative Analysis, 27*(4), 573–589.

Schreiner, J. (1980). Portfolio revision: A turnover-constrained approach. *Financial Management, 9*(1), 67–75.

Schultz, G. M., & Fabozzi, F. J. (2022a). Rise of the machines: Application of machine learning to mortgage prepayment modeling. *Journal of Fixed Income, 31*(3), 6–19.

Schultz, G. M., & Fabozzi, F. J. (2022b). Primer on agency MBS specified pools and their convexity profile. *Journal of Fixed Income*, *31*(4), 33–49.

Schwartz, E. S., & Torous, W. N. (1989). Prepayment and the valuation of mortgage-backed securities. *Journal of Finance, 44*(2), 375–392.

Schwartz, R. A., & Francioni, R. (2004). *Equity markets in action: The fundamentals of liquidity, market structure, and market design.* Hoboken, NJ: John Wiley & Sons.

Schwartz, R. A., & Shapiro, J. E. (2009). Equity market impacts of technological change and globalization. *Journal of Financial Markets, 12*(3), 288–300.

Schwert, G. W. (1981). Using financial data to measure effects of regulation. *Journal of Law and Economics, 24*(1), 121–158.

Schwert, G. W. (1990). Stock volatility and the crash of '87. *Review of Financial Studies, 3*(1), 77–102.

Seasholes, M. S., & Zhu, N. (2010). Individual investors and local bias. *Journal of Finance, 65*(5), 1987–2010.

Securities and Exchange Commission (SEC). (2011). *Report on the review of the definition of "accredited investor."* SEC Docket. Washington, DC: Securities and Exchange Commission.

Sedlacek, P. (1981). Volatility tests of financial market efficiency. *Econometrica, 49*(4), 925–954.

Sehgal, S., & Song, C. (2006). Making sense of chaos: A study of the randomness of stock prices. *Journal of Finance, 61*(2), 583–618.

Seiler, M. J., Webb, J. R., & Neil Myer, F. N. (2001). Diversification issues in real estate investment. *Journal of Real Estate Research, 22*(1–2), 75–95.

Selvin, S. (1975). A note on the statistical detection of relationships. *Biometrika, 62*(3), 635–638.

Sen, A. (1999). *Commodities and commodity derivatives: Modeling and pricing for agriculturals, metals, and energy.* Hoboken, NJ: John Wiley & Sons.

Serletis, A., & Rosenberg, A. J. (2009). Mean reversion in stock prices: Implications for long-term investors. *Journal of Investing, 18*(1), 42–52.

Shapiro, A. C. (1988). Toward a positive theory of consumer choice. *Journal of Economic Psychology, 9*(1), 39–60.

Sharpe, W. F. (1964). Capital asset prices: A theory of market equilibrium under conditions of risk. *Journal of Finance, 19*(3), 425–442.

Sharpe, W. F. (1978). *Investments.* Englewood Cliffs, NJ: Prentice-Hall.

Shiller, R. J. (1981). Do stock prices move too much to be justified by subsequent changes in dividends? *American Economic Review, 71*(3), 421–436.

Shleifer, A., & Vishny, R. W. (1997). The limits of arbitrage. *Journal of Finance, 52*(1), 35–55.

Sias, R. W., Starks, L. T., & Tinic, S. M. (2001). Volatility and the stock market: Insights from a new indicator. *Journal of Investment Management, 1*(1), 34–43.

Siegel, J. J. (1992). The equity premium: Stock and bond returns since 1802. *Financial Analysts Journal, 48*(1), 28–38.

Siegel, L. (2003). *Benchmarks and investment management.* Charlottesville, VA: Research Foundation of AIMR.

Simon, H. A. (1955). A behavioral model of rational choice. *Quarterly Journal of Economics, 69*(1), 99–118.

Simon, H. A. (1982). *Models of bounded rationality: Empirically grounded economic reason.* Cambridge, MA: MIT Press.

Simons, K. (1993). Why do banks fail? Lessons from the past. *Federal Reserve Bank of Boston Economic Review, 1993*(4), 3–31.

Sloan, R. G. (1996). Do stock prices fully reflect information in accruals and cash flows about future earnings? *Accounting Review, 71*(3), 289–315.

Smith, A. (1776). *The Wealth of Nations.* London: Strahan and Cadell.

Smith, C. W., & Warner, J. B. (1979). On financial contracting: An analysis of bond covenants. *Journal of Financial Economics, 7*(2), 117–161.

Sobel, I. M. (1967). On the distribution of points in a cube and the approximate evaluation of integrals. *USSR Computational Mathematics and Mathematical Physics*, *7*(4), 784–802.

Sobel, M. E. (1982). Asymptotic confidence intervals for indirect effects in structural equation models. *Sociological Methodology, 13*, 290–312.

Solnik, B. H. (1983). The relation between stock returns and inflation: The real and nominal sides. *Journal of Finance, 38*(3), 1045–1062.

Solow, R. M. (1956). A contribution to the theory of economic growth. *Quarterly Journal of Economics, 70*(1), 65–94.

Sorensen, E. H., Miller, E. M., & Ooi, C. T. (2000). Noise and the reality of low-frequency econometric modeling. *Journal of Econometrics, 95*(2), 291–309.

Sornette, D., & Zhou, C. (2005). Predicting the unpredictable: Critical phenomena and breakdown in financial markets. *International Journal of Modern Physics C, 16*(3), 504–509.

Spence, M. (1973). Job market signaling. *Quarterly Journal of Economics, 87*(3), 355–374.

Spiegel, M. R., & Stephens, L. J. (1999). *Statistics*. Schaumburg, IL: McGraw-Hill.

Stein, D. M. (1998). Measuring and evaluating portfolio performance after taxes. *Journal of Portfolio Management, 24*(2),117–124.

Stein, J. (2009). Presidential address: Sophisticated investors and market efficiency. *Journal of Finance, 64*(4), 1517–1548.

Stiglitz, J. E. (1981). The allocation of investment in a dynamic economy. *Quarterly Journal of Economics, 95*(4), 543–570.

Stoll, H. R., & Whaley, R. E. (1990). The dynamics of stock index and stock index futures returns. *Journal of Financial and Quantitative Analysis, 25*(4), 441–468.

Stubbs, R., & Vance, P. (2005). *Computing return estimation error matrices for robust optimization*. Report, Axioma, New York.

Stulz, R. M. (1996). Rethinking risk management. *Journal of Applied Corporate Finance, 9*(3), 8–24.

Summers, L. H. (1986). Does the stock market rationally reflect fundamental values? *Journal of Finance, 41*(3), 591–601.

Swalin, A. (2018). *CatBoost vs. Light GBM vs. XGBoost. Towards data science*. Available at https://towardsdatascience.com/catboost-vs-light-gbm-vs-xgboost-5f93620723db.

Swan, P. L. (1963). Longer-run economic growth models: Theory and empirical evidence. *Scandinavian Journal of Economics, 65*(4), 472–488.

Taleb, N. N. (2007). *The Black Swan: The impact of the highly improbable*. New York: Random House.

Tetlock, P. C. (2007). Giving content to investor sentiment: The role of media in the stock market. *Journal of Finance, 62*(3), 1139–1168.

Thaler, R. H. (1985). Mental accounting and consumer choice. *Marketing Science, 4*(3), 199–214.

Thorley, S. (1995). The time-varying risk premium in the stock market. *Journal of Business, 68*(2), 311–341.

Tirole, J. (1988). *The theory of industrial organization*. Cambridge, MA: MIT Press.

Titman, S. (1985). Urban land prices under uncertainty. *American Economic Review, 75*(3), 505–513.

Tobin, J. (1958). Liquifaction preference as behavior towards risk. *Review of Economic Studies, 25*(2), 65–86.

Tobin, J. (1969). A general equilibrium approach to monetary theory. *Journal of Money, Credit, and Banking, 1*(1), 15–29.

Toczkowska, N. (2023). Unlocking the power of singular value decomposition in natural language processing. Retrieved from https://ts2.com.pl/en/unlocking-the-power-of-singular-value-decomposition-in-natural-language-processing/.

Trichet, J. -C. (2010). State of the union: The financial crisis and the ECB's response. *Journal of Common Market Studies, 48*(Annual Review), 7–19.

Tsitsiklis, J., & Van Roy, B. (1999). Optimal stopping of Markov processes: Hilbert space theory, approximation algorithms, and an application to pricing high-dimensional financial derivatives. *IEEE Transactions on Automatic Control, 44*, 1840–1851.

Turing, A. (1950). Computing machinery and intelligence. *Mind, 59*(236), 433–460.

Turner, M. (2016). A giant hedge fund used artificial intelligence to analyze fed minutes — Here's what it found. *Business Insider*. Retrieved from https://www.businessinsider.com/two-sigma-on-fed-minutes-2016-5

Tversky, A., & Kahneman, D. (1974). Judgment under uncertainty: Heuristics and biases. *Science, 185*(4157), 1124–1131.

Vasicek, O. (1977). An equilibrium characterization of the term structure. *Journal of Financial Economics, 5*(2), 177–188.

Volpert, K. E. (2021). Introduction to bond portfolio management. In F. J. Fabozzi (Ed.), *The handbook of fixed income securities* (9th ed., pp. 1073–1093). New York: McGraw-Hill.

Wagner, W. H., & Lau, S. C. (1971). The effect of diversification on risk. *Financial Analysts Journal, 27*(6), 48–58.

Wallis, M., Kumar, K., & Gepp, A. (2019). Credit rating forecasting using machine learning techniques. In Z. Sun (Ed.), *Managerial perspectives on intelligent big data analytics* (pp. 180–198). IGI Global.

Walsh, C. E. (2010). *Monetary theory and policy*. Cambridge, MA: MIT Press.

Wang, H., Ahluwalia, H.S., Aliaga-Díaz, R.A, & Davis, J.H. (2021). The best of both worlds: Forecasting US equity market returns using a hybrid machine learning–time series approach. *Journal of Financial Data Science, 3*(2), 9–20.

Wang, J. (1994). A model of competitive stock trading volume. *Journal of Political Economy, 102*(1), 127–168.

Weber, M. (1922). *Economy and society: An outline of interpretive sociology*. Berkeley: University of California Press.

Weil, P. (1993). Precautionary savings and permanent income hypothesis. *Review of Economic Studies, 60*(2), 367–383.

Weisbach, M. S. (1988). Outside directors and CEO turnover. *Journal of Financial Economics, 20*(1–2), 431–460.

Weng, L. (2019). *Generalized language models*. Available at https://lilianweng.github.io/posts/2019-01-31-lm/

Wermers, R. (2000). Mutual fund performance: An empirical decomposition into stock-picking talent, style, transactions costs, and expenses. *Journal of Finance, 55*(4), 1655–1695.

West, K. D. (1988). Dividend innovations and stock price volatility. *Econometrica, 56*(1), 37–61.

Weston, J. F., & Brigham, E. F. (1978). *Managerial finance* (6th ed.). Hinsdale, IL: Dryden Press.

Wheelock, L. B., & Pachamanova, D. A. (2021). Acceptable set topic modeling. *European Journal of Operational Research*, *272*(2), 636–641.

White, H. (1980). A heteroskedasticity-consistent covariance matrix estimator and a direct test for heteroskedasticity. *Econometrica, 48*(4), 817–838.

Williams, J. B. (1938). *The theory of investment value*. Cambridge, MA: Harvard University Press.

Williamson, O. E. (1985). *The economic institutions of capitalism*. New York: Free Press.

Wilson, J. W., & Jones, C. P. (1993). Is cost of capital different for multinational firms? *Journal of International Business Studies, 24*(2), 357–379.

Winkler, R. L., & Barry, C. B. (1975). A Bayesian model for portfolio selection and revision. *Journal of Finance, 30*(1), 179–192.

Winston, W. (2000). *Financial models using simulation and optimization* (vols. 1 and 2). Newfield, NY: Palisade Corporation.

Winters, D. B. (1960). Forecasting sales by exponentially weighted moving averages. *Management Science, 6*(3), 324–342.

Wold, H. (1954). Causality and econometrics. *Econometrica, 22*(2), 162–177.

Wolf, A., & Ghil, M. (1991). Spectral analysis in geophysics. *Developments in Solid Earth Geophysics, 7*, 1–110.

Wolfe, J. (1977). Risk, return, and equilibrium: Empirical tests. *Journal of Political Economy, 82*(3), 607–636.

Wolff, D., & Echterling, F. (2020). Stock picking with machine learning. *SSRN Electronic Journal*. DOI:10.2139/ssrn.3607845.

Wong, M. H. F., & Wong, K. A. (2000). The impacts of knowledge of the past on the treatment of risk. *Journal of Risk and Insurance, 67*(3), 433–448.

Wood, R. A., McInish, T. H., & Ord, J. K. (1985). An investigation of transaction data for NYSE stocks. *Journal of Finance, 40*(3), 723–739.

Woodford, M. (2003). *Interest and prices: Foundations of a theory of monetary policy*. Princeton, NJ: Princeton University Press.

Wright, C., & Williams, J. (1982). The economic role of commodity speculation. *Journal of Political Economy, 90*(4), 721–740.

Wurgler, J. (2000). Financial markets and the allocation of capital. *Journal of Financial Economics, 58*(1–2), 187–214.

Xie, B., Passonneau, R. J., Wu, L., & Creamer, G. G. (2013). Semantic frames to predict stock price movement. In *Proceedings of the 51st Annual Meeting of the Association for Computational Linguistics*, 873–883.

Xiong, R., Cai, H., Diego-Guerra, I., Lu, Y., Xu, X., & Yin, Y. (2019). Forecasting credit spreads: A machine learning approach. Retrieved from https://www.iaqf.org/resources/Documents/2019%20Student%20Competition/UMich_Submartingale_Web.pdf.

Yao, J., Ma, C., & He, W. P. (2005). Dynamic capabilities and venture performance: The effects of venture capitalists. *Journal of Business Venturing, 20*(2), 161–179.

Yermack, D. (1996). Higher market valuation of companies with a small board of directors. *Journal of Financial Economics, 40*(2), 185–211.

Young, A. (1928). Increasing returns and economic progress. *Economic Journal, 38*(152), 527–542.

Yu, L., Wang, S. M., & Lai, K. K. (2008). Neural network-based mean–variance-skewness model for portfolio selection. *Computers and Operations Research, 35*, 34–46.

Zakamouline, V. (2006). European option pricing and hedging with both fixed and proportional transaction costs. *Journal of Economic Dynamics and Control, 30*(1), 1–25.

Zellner, A. (1962). An efficient method of estimating seemingly unrelated regressions and tests for aggregation bias. *Journal of the American Statistical Association, 57*(298), 348–368.

Zenios, S. A., & Kang, P. (1993). Mean-absolute deviation portfolio optimization for mortgage-backed securities. *Annals of Operations Research, 45*, 433–450.

Zhang, G., Hu, M. Y., Patuwo, B. E., & Indro, D. C. (1999). Artificial neural networks in bankruptcy prediction: General framework and cross-validation analysis. *European Journal of Operational Research, 116*(1), 16–32.

Zhang, J., Zhao, X., Zhang, F., Teng, F., Lin, S., & Li, H. (2019). Agency MBS prepayment model using neural networks. *Journal of Structured Finance, 24*(4), 17–33.

Zhang, X. (2006). Information uncertainty and stock returns. *Journal of Finance, 61*(1), 105–137.

Zheng, B., Moulines, E., & Abergel, F. (2013). Price jump prediction in a limit order book. *Journal of Mathematical Finance 3*, 242–255.

Zhou, X. Y. (1997). Stock market swings and the value of innovation, 1900–2000. *American Economic Review, 91*(4), 995–1010.

Ziemba, W., & Mulvey, J. (1998). *Worldwide asset and liability modeling*. London: Cambridge University Press.

Zimmerman, J. L. (2003). Accounting for decision making and control. *Issues and control. *Issues in Accounting Education, 18*(1), 47–64.

Zirpoli, F., & Becker, M. C. (2011). What drives the dissemination of technology for innovation in the automotive industry: A network of actors or institutional factors? *Research Policy, 40*(1), 55–66.

Zweibel, E. J. (1996). Can passive management outperform market efficiency? *Journal of Portfolio Management, 22*(2), 112–123.

Index

Exhibits are denoted by an *e* following the page number.